THE PRACTICAL
GARDENER'S
ENCYCLOPEDIA

The Practical Gardener's Encyclopedia

WHITECAP BOOKS
New York Vancouver Toronto

This edition published in Canada by
Whitecap Books Vancouver
351 Lynn Avenue
North Vancouver BC
Canada V7J 2C4
Phone (604) 980 9852 Fax (604) 980 8197
Whitecap Books Toronto
Phone (416) 444 3442 Fax (416) 444 6630

Chief Executive Officer: John Owen
President: Terry Newell
Publisher: Sheena Coupe
Managing Editor: Helen Bateman
Senior Designer: Kylie Mulquin
Editorial Coordinator: Tracey Jackson
Production Managers: Helen Creeke, Caroline Webber
Production Assistant: Kylie Lawson
Business Manager: Emily Jahn
Vice President International Sales: Stuart Laurence

Project Editor: Susan Tomnay
Designer: Melanie Feddersen, i2i design
Consultant: Geoffrey Burnie

A catalog record for this book is available from the
Library of Congress, Washington, DC.

ISBN 1 55285 076 5

Color reproduction by Bright Arts Graphics (S) Pte Ltd
Printed by Toppan Printing Co, (H.K.) Ltd
Printed in China

A Weldon Owen Production

Contents

How to Use This Book

The Practical Gardener's Encyclopedia is designed to help, encourage, and inspire gardeners, both novice and experienced. It is packed with information about buying plants, planting, propagation, soil conditions, and cultivation. The book is easy to read and each page has colorful photographs showing how beautiful your garden can be. Section Five of the book is an encyclopedia of plants to help you choose and identify them.

Each section is color-coded for easy reference.

General information about planting, propagating, and caring for your plants to get the optimum results.

The beginning of a new chapter within one of the five major sections in the book. The line above is the section heading.

Illustrations show various planting designs. There are many other helpful illustrations in the book.

Clear and simple step-by-step photographs, in this case to show you how to pot-up seedlings.

Colorful photographs give you guidance and inspiration in planning and planting your garden.

---

distribute tiny seeds more evenly, mix them with a spoonful of dry sand, and scatter the mixture over the surface of the mix with a saltshaker. Label each row of seed as you sow.

If seeds should be buried (as indicated on the seed packet), sprinkle the needed amount of dry mix over the seed. Fine seeds are usually not covered; just press them lightly into the surface of the mix with your fingers. Mist the surface lightly to moisten it. Seeds will rot if they are submerged in water.

Set the containers in a well-lit spot where you can check them daily for signs of the first sprouts. Keep the planting medium moist but not soggy. Cover the container with clear plastic wrap to keep the soil evenly moist until the seeds germinate, but make sure the plastic doesn't touch the soil. Remove the covering as soon as the seedlings appear. Ventilation is important as poor ventilation encourages the development of seedling diseases.

Temperature and Light
Most annual seeds will sprout and grow well at average indoor temperatures between 60° and 75°F (16° and 24°C); Vegetable seeds germinate best at higher temperatures—between 75° and 90°F

Get a head start on your seeds indoors heat of summer, indoors, perhaps or garage.

(24° and 32. heater or re positions f horticultu warm. Pla surface an the seedli require t 60° to with a

On impro sunn light catal pric

STEP-BY-STEP POTTING UP
1. Place moist growing medium into new containers. Make a hole large enough to accommodate the root system of the seedling

THE HE

The Herb Garden

There are so many wonderful herbs that it can be hard to decide which ones to grow. Some herbs, like oregano and peppermint, are used in cooking or for tea; others, like lavender and sage, are ideal for potpourris and other fragrant crafts. Some herbs, like bee balm, thyme,

and yarrow, are attractive in their own right as ornamentals, even if you never plan to harvest them for any purpose. Many herbs fall into more than one of these categories.

How you plan to use your herbs will affect how you'll grow them and how much attention they'll need from you. If you're just growing herbs to use fresh in cooking, you don't need much space for an herb garden, since one or two plants of each kind you like should be enough. You'll be most likely to use your culinary herbs if you plant them close to the house. If you're only growing one or two types, try growing them in large pots on the deck or patio. You'll need more space to grow quantities of herbs if you plan to harvest them for drying and crafting.

Grown in the right conditions, herbs such as chives will reward you with flowers as well as edible leaves.

Growing Your Herbs
Most herbs prefer full sun, although some (like sweet woodruff, chervil, lemon balm, and many mints) will grow in partial shade. Many herbs tolerate rocky, thin soils, but they will be more productive in average, well-drained soil. You may choose to plant your herbs in a separate garden, but they also look great mixed into flower beds and vegetable gardens.

You can grow many herbs—including such favorites as dill, sage, marjoram, and basil—from seed sown directly in the garden. Other herbs are easier to grow from transplants than seeds; these include rosemary, lavender, peppermint, and tarragon, among others.

When planning your herb garden, don't forget to take into consideration your climate, topography, and soil conditions. Ask your neighbors what grows well in their garden—and what doesn't!

Herb Garden Style
Regardless of the size, shape, or location of your garden, its style is a reflection of your own tastes. At one extreme are the formal herb gardens with their angular knots and pruned hedges, and at the other are random groupings of whatever suits the season. The number of possible herb-garden styles is limited only by your imagination and creativity. You can plan one or more theme gardens to concentrate on a particular aspect.

These diagrams show four practical approaches to designing an herb garden. Avoid circles and curves if space is limited.

them to accent the shape of a building. If you want to be especially creative, garden within unusual boundaries like circles or ovals. You can make a garden in the shape of a spiral with one continuous bed beginning in the center and spiraling out in circles. A book or magazine on garden landscaping will offer you examples to follow in shaping your garden beds.

If you choose to garden in several small patches, position plants that need daily attention or frequent picking close to the

As you choose herb plants, consider how they are going to look when grouped together.

Garden Shape
The simplest gardens to set out and manage are square or rectangular. If you must take advantage of every square inch of space, it makes sense that you will follow the general outline of your property, and land is most often sold in boxlike shapes. Laying out your herb garden with square or rectangular beds may be not only the most practical way, but can give the garden a formal look that appeals to many gardeners.

Of course, squares and rectangles aren't the only shapes. You may choose to lay your garden beds following the curve of a hill, stream, fence, or stone wall, or design

house. If space is limited, take advantage of borders along paths and fences. At the least, you can dress your windows close at hand.

Garden Design
Whatever design you choose, try it out on paper first. If you're planting in beds, keep them under 5 feet (1.5 m) wide, not more than twice the distance you are able to reach from the side. You'll want to avoid walking on beds as you work. Make garden paths 4 to 5 feet (1.2 to 1.5 m) wide. Once you've located your paths, beds, or rows, begin selecting and

Working with the natural landscape, simple terracing is used to create a level herb garden on a slope.

Chapter heading indicates the subject being discussed within a main section.

Detailed information about problems with plants and how they can be dealt with.

Photograph of individual plants, showing what they look like when grown in the right conditions.

Botanical name

Family name

Common name

Information about plant

---

lights sold in home centers also provide excellent results, and they're generally much less expensive than grow lights. The young plants will need between 10 and 16 hours of light each day. They will tolerate low-light conditions best if you keep temperatures on the low side.

Thinning and Transplanting
The first leaves to appear on the plant are actually specialized food-storage organs. These drop away quickly, and the leaves that follow are the first "true leaves." When seedlings develop their first set of true leaves, they'll need special attention.

If seedlings are in separate pots or cells, thin away the extra seedlings by clipping them off at soil level with sharp scissors. One healthy specimen should remain in each pot or cell. If your seedlings are crowded together in a flat, you'll need to transfer them to their own containers. Fill pots or cells with a nutrient-rich medium. Scoop one or more seedlings from the flat (a teaspoon works well), separating their root systems as gently as possible with your fingers. Poke a hole in the potting soil deep enough to accommodate the new seedling and its root system, then transfer it and firm the soil. Water as often as necessary to keep the soil moist and to prevent wilting. When you water,

3. Holding the seedling by its leaves, place it into its new container and gently firm the soil around it. Thin seedlings by clipping them off at soil level with a pair of scissors.

set the container of seedlings in a tray of water so the growing medium can soak up moisture without disrupting the seedlings. If you water from overhead, you may wash the seedlings away. Place pots away from the direct light and wind for a day until the shock of transplanting is over. Feed the young plants lightly with compost tea or liquid seaweed.

Hardening Off
Hardening off allows young plants to adjust slowly to the extremes of wind, temperature, and light. At least two weeks before transplanting time, begin watering less frequently and withhold fertilizer. One week before you transplant, move the plants outdoors to a spot protected from strong light and wind. Starting with one or several hours, gradually increase their time spent outdoors. Within a week, they should be outdoors permanently. They'll need more water at this time, since sun and wind quickly dry the soil. Be prepared to bring them back indoors if a cold snap or storm threatens.

Sowing Seed in the Garden
Some plants like morning glories (Ipomoea spp.), beans, peas, and root crops, grow better from direct-sown seed because they prefer cool outdoor temperatures or because they don't respond well to transplanting. Planting seeds outdoors is not a good idea for seeds that are hard to germinate, or for plants that need a long, warm growing season.

Before the season begins, check your seed packages or catalog for the best time to plant outdoors. You'll need to know the expected date of the last frost for your area; ask local gardeners, or contact your local Cooperative Extension Service.

Get the soil ready for planting (see page 50) and if you're planting in rows, as with vegetables, mark them before planting with wooden stakes at both ends. Stretch a section of lightweight string down the row, and use it as a guide to keep your rows straight while you plant.

Dealing with Damping-Off

Damping-off is a disease that can strike young seedlings, killing them just before or after they emerge. Affected seedlings tend to topple over, since their stems are damaged at the soil level. Once a few seedlings are affected, the disease can quickly spread to other seedlings in the same pot or tray.

Since there's no real cure, the best way to handle damping-off is prevention. Here are some tips that might help.

- Always use fresh, "sterile" seed-starting mix.
- If you're reusing old pots or trays, knock out the old soil, dip the containers in a 10 percent bleach solution (1 part household bleach to 9 parts water), and let the containers dry before using them.
- Sprinkle a thin layer of milled sphagnum moss on top of newly planted seeds.
- Improve air circulation with a small fan set to blow lightly just over the tops of the seedlings.
- If damping-off strikes outdoor-sown seeds, discard them, wait until the weather warms up (maybe two to three weeks), then try sowing again.

Lupine seed, like others of the pea and bean family, can be sown directly into the soil in fall.

with a layer of floating row cover helps to keep the soil moist and protects the seed from drying winds, heavy rain, and birds. (Remove the cover once the seedlings start to emerge.)

If seedlings are crowded, you'll need to thin them out for good growth. Dig up and carefully transplant extra seedlings, or use scissors to cut off the stems of unwanted seedlings at ground level.

If you're planting annuals and large perennials, sow medium-sized and large seeds individually, or scatter them evenly over the surface. Try to space them ½ to 1 inch (12 to 25 mm) apart. If you have very small seeds, mix them with a handful of dry sand and scatter over the surface.

Cover most seeds with a thin layer of fine soil or sand. After sowing, make sure the seedbed stays moist until the seedlings are visible. If rainfall is lacking, water gently with a watering can, sprinkler, or fine hose spray. Covering the seedbed

Planting Container-Grown Plants
If you are planting a potted plant, you can easily see how deeply to plant it. Dig deeply enough so the surface of the container soil will be at the top of the hole (adjusting accordingly for new beds).

Centaurea cyanus
COMPOSITAE

CORNFLOWER

Stick brushy prunings into the ground around young cornflower plants to support the stems as they grow. Pinching off spent blooms can prolong the flowering season.

Other common names Bachelor's buttons.
Description This is a dependable, easy-care, hardy annual. The bushy plants have narrow, lance-shaped, silvery green leaves and thin stems topped with fluffy flower heads. The 1–2-inch (2.5–5-cm) flowers bloom through the summer in white or shades of blue, purple, pink, or red.
Height and spread Height 12–30 inches (30–75 cm); spread to 12 inches (30 cm).
Best site Full sun, but tolerates partial shade; average, well-drained soil.
Growing guidelines Grows easily from seed sown directly into the garden in early fall (in mild-winter areas) or early spring. Plant seed ⅛ inch (3 mm) deep. To extend the flowering season from an early-spring planting, sow again every two to four weeks until midsummer. Other ways to establish cornflowers include buying transplants in spring or starting the seed indoors about eight weeks before your last frost date. Set plants outdoors about two weeks before the last frost date. Cornflowers will self-sow if you leave a few flowers to set seed.
Landscape uses Cornflowers are charming in meadow gardens and flower beds. They are also excellent cut flowers.

Cheiranthus cheiri
CRUCIFERAE

WALLFLOWER

The fragrant blooms of wallflowers are normally orange or yellow, but they also bloom in shades of red, pink, or creamy white. The flowers are ideal for spring arrangements.

Description This perennial is commonly grown as a half-hardy annual or biennial. The bushy clumps of slender green leaves are topped with clusters of 1-inch (2.5-cm) wide four-petaled flowers from midspring to early summer.
Height and spread Height 12–24 inches (30–60 cm), spread to 12 inches (30 cm).
Best site Full sun to partial shade; average to moist, well-drained soil, ideally with a neutral to slightly alkaline pH.
Growing guidelines Sow outdoors in early spring or indoors about eight weeks before your last frost date. Plant seed ⅛ inch (6 mm) deep. Set plants out 8–12 inches (20–30 cm) apart around the last frost date. In frost-free areas, grow wallflowers as biennials. Sow seed in pots or in a nursery bed in early summer; move plants to their flowering position in early fall. Water during dry spells to keep the soil evenly moist. Pull out and compost plants when they have finished blooming.
Landscape uses Grow in masses or in flower beds for spots of early color. One classic combination is orange wallflowers underplanted with blue forget-me-nots (Myosotis sylvatica). Wallflowers also combine beautifully with tulips.

Cleome hasslerana
CAPPARACEAE

CLEOME

Cleome is a must for butterfly-attracting gardens; it's also popular with bees. Plant it in large groupings to show off the spidery white, pink, or rosy lavender flowers.

Other common names Spider flower.
Description Cleome is a fast-growing half-hardy annual. Its tall, sturdy stems and palmlike leaves are slightly sticky and have a musky (some say skunk-like) odor. Small spines form on the stems and on the undersides of the leaves. From midsummer until midfall, the stems are topped with globes of four-petaled flowers. Long stamens protrude from the flowers, giving them a spidery look. The blooms are followed by long, narrow seedpods.
Height and spread Height 3–4 feet (90–120 cm); spread 18 inches (45 cm).
Best site Full sun to light shade; average, well-drained soil with added compost.
Growing guidelines Easy to grow from seed sown directly in the garden in mid- to late-spring. For earlier bloom, buy transplants or start your own by sowing seed indoors about four weeks before your last frost date. Lightly press the seed into the surface, then enclose the pot in a plastic bag until seedlings appear. Set plants out around the last frost date.
Landscape uses Try cleome in the back of beds and borders. Its pretty, delicate blooms look particularly nice in cottage gardens.

Coleus x hybridus
LABIATAE

COLEUS

Keep favorite coleus plants from year to year by taking cuttings in summer; they'll root quickly in water. Pot up the cuttings for winter; then put them outdoors in spring.

Description These tender perennials are grown as a bushy, tender annuals. Their sturdy, square stems carry showy, patterned leaves with scalloped or ruffled edges. Each leaf can have several different colors, with zones, edges, or splashes in shades of red, pink, orange, yellow, and cream.
Height and spread Height 6–24 inches (15–60 cm); spread 8–12 inches (20–30 cm).
Best site Partial shade; average to moist, well-drained soil with added well-rotted organic matter.
Growing guidelines Buy transplants in spring, or start your own by sowing seed indoors eight to ten weeks before your last frost date. Don't cover the seed; just press it lightly into the soil and enclose the pot in a plastic bag until seedlings appear. Set plants out 8–12 inches (20–30 cm) apart after the last frost. Water during dry spells. Pinch off the spikes of the pale blue flowers to promote more leafy growth.
Landscape uses Coleus are great for adding all-season color to beds, borders, and container plantings. Groups of mixed leaf patterns can look too busy when combined with flowering plants, so grow them alone in masses.

Coreopsis tinctoria
COMPOSITAE

CALLIOPSIS

Calliopsis grows easily from direct-sown seed and needs little fussing. Shearing the plants back by one-third in mid- to late-summer can prolong the bloom season.

Description Calliopsis is a colorful, fast-growing, hardy annual. Its wiry stems carry narrow, green leaves and 1–2-inch (2.5–5-cm)-wide, single or double, daisy-like flowers. The flowers are usually golden yellow with maroon centers but may also be all yellow or all orange. Plants can bloom from midsummer until frost.
Height and spread Height 24–36 inches (30–90 cm), depending on the cultivar; spread to 12 inches (30 cm).
Best site Full sun; average to moist, well-drained soil. Adapts well to poor soil.
Growing guidelines Grows quickly from seed sown directly into the garden in early- to mid-spring. Plant seed ⅛ inch (3 mm) deep indoors about six weeks before your last frost date. Set plants out around the last frost date. Space transplants or thin seedlings to stand about 8 inches (20 cm) apart. Push twiggy brush into the soil around young plants of tall-growing cultivars to support the stems as they grow.
Landscape uses Depend on calliopsis for adding fast, easy-care color to beds and borders. It also looks wonderful in meadow gardens. Grow some in the cutting garden for fresh arrangements.

Cosmos bipinnatus
COMPOSITAE

COSMOS

Use fast-growing cosmos to fill spaces left by early-blooming annuals and perennials. Pinch off spent flowers to encourage more bloom; leave a few to self-sow.

Description These popular half-hardy annuals are grown for their colorful blooms. The bushy plants bear many finely cut, green leaves. In late summer and fall, the stems are topped with white, pink, or rosy red flowers. The single or semidouble, daisy-like blooms can grow up to 4 inches (10 cm) across.
Height and spread Height 3–4 feet (90–120 cm); spread to 18 inches (45 cm).
Best site Full sun is best, although plants can take partial shade; average to moist, well-drained soil.
Growing guidelines For earliest blooms, buy transplants in spring or start seed indoors three to four weeks before your last frost date. Plant seed ¼ inch (6 mm) deep. Set plants out 12 weeks after the last frost date. You can also sow seed directly into the garden around the last frost date. Pinch off stem tips in early summer to promote branching and more flowers. Stake individual stems as needed, or just let the plants sprawl; they'll send up more flowering stems.
Landscape uses Cosmos adds height and color to flower beds, borders, and meadows. They look great in cottage gardens. Grow a few in the cutting garden for arrangements.

Gardening Basics

*You need the right growing conditions, the right tools,
the right plants and, most important of all,
energy and enthusiasm. These are
the basics of good gardening.*

Understanding Your Garden

You may have some idea of what you want from your garden but do you know what kind of growing conditions you have to give the plants? A new garden will get off to a successful start if you take stock of your growing conditions, including your climate and your garden's soil, topography, and exposure. These factors will have a great effect in determining which plants will grow well in your garden, as well as how and where you plant them.

Basic Botany

What's in a Name?

One of the tricks to growing plants successfully is to learn their names. Members of your neighborhood plant society may understand common names, like bee balm for instance. But if you go to an out-of-town nursery and ask for bee balm, you may only get puzzled stares. Perhaps they call the plant Oswego tea, based on the fact that American pioneers used it as herbal tea. Or if you are looking for bee balm in a catalog, you may only find it listed under its botanical name, *Monarda didyma*.

You can see from this example that one plant can have several common names. Likewise, one common name can apply to several different plants. For instance the common name loosestrife can refer to a creeping perennial with golden flowers known by the botanical name *Lysimachia nummularia*; to a tall perennial with white flowers in a swan-necked spike, *Lysimachia clethroides*; to its less invasive counterpart, *L. ephemerum*; or to a spreading, long-blooming purple-flowered plant, *Lythrum salicaria*. If you order "loosestrife" by mail without using a botanical name, you have a good chance of receiving the wrong plant.

Get to know botanical names so you know exactly which plant you are talking about, planting, or ordering. Most botanical names are based on Latin, so they can be a mouthful. However, they will be the same in America, Japan, and Europe, despite differences in the native language. Botanical names change rarely, usually only when scientists update the name to better reflect what they have discovered about the plant's heritage. If you have learned an older name, you will usually find it listed beside the newer names in nursery catalogs. For instance, hollyhock has changed from *Althaea rosea* to *Alcea rosea*. Both may be listed for the same plant.

As you've probably noticed by now, botanical names are usually given as two words. The first word, the name of the genus, refers to a group of closely related plants. The second word indicates the species, a particular kind of plant in that genus. You may end up growing several different species from the same genus. *Achillea millefolium* and *Achillea tomentosa*, for example, both belong to the genus Achillea, commonly known as yarrow.

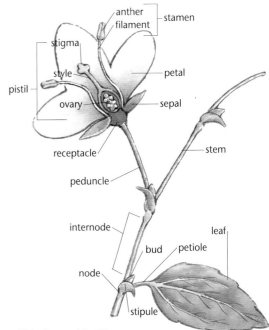

This diagram identifies some of the most common plant parts. Knowing a bit of botanical jargon will help you understand the plant descriptions you read in books and catalogs.

But *Achillea millefolium* refers to a species with finely cut leaves, while *Achillea tomentosa* refers to one with particularly fuzzy leaves.

Botanical names can be easier to remember if you determine what they tell about the plant. Some refer to the person who discovered the plant or to what part

LEFT: Bearded irises are among the most lovely of the *Iris* spp. They flower in early summer.
RIGHT: As its name suggests, sweet violet (*Viola odorata*) bears charming spring flowers that are delightfully fragrant.

of the world it was discovered in. For instance, *Sanguisorba canadensis* is Canadian burnett, native to Canada and the Eastern United States. Other botanical names are descriptive. *Viola odorata* is sweet violet, which bears an especially fragrant flower.

Horticulturists and botanists recognize two other classifications of plants that you will often encounter: varieties and cultivars. Although the names are sometimes used interchangeably, plants that develop a natural variation in the wild are called varieties, and the varietal name is included as part of the botanical name after the abbreviation "var." This is the case, for example, with the white-flowered, peach-leaved bell-flower (*Campanula persicifolia* var. *alba*). In this case the species, which normally has blue flowers, produced plants with white ones. Cultivars, whose names are set in single quotes after the botanical name, are plants that gardeners or horticulturists have selected and propagated as part of a breeding program or from a chance mutation in a garden. For example, *Aster novi-belgii* 'Professor Kippenburg' is a dwarf type of lavender-blue Michaelmas daisy.

You may also come across hybrids, blends of two species or, more rarely, two genera. One example is *Anemone* x *hybrida*—the "x" indicates that this plant is a hybrid. A few hybrids come from two different but related genera, such as x *Heucherella tiarelloides*.

In this book, you will find plants listed by the most widely used common name. But to avoid confusion, we will also include the botanical name. When we use "spp." we are discussing several related species in the same genus. For *Iris* spp., this could include bearded, Siberian, and Japanese irises. Take note of both common and botanical names for your garden planning.

Parts of Plants

You can choose plants for your garden for their attractive leaves, useful fruits, fragrant flowers, or perhaps deep taproots

The Logic of Botanical Names

Learning botanical names may seem intimidating at first, but you'll be surprised at how easily you pick them up as you read. Besides being a tool for accurately communicating about plants, a botanical name can often tell you something about the plant it identifies, such as its flower color or growth habit. Listed below are some words that commonly appear in botanical names, along with their definitions.

Albus: white
Argenteus: silver
Aureus: golden yellow
Caeruleus: blue
Luteus: yellow
Nanus: dwarf
Niger: black
Palustris: swampy, marshy
Perennis: perennial
Prostratus: trailing
Punctatus: dotted
Purpureus: purple
Reptans: creeping
Roseus: rosy
Ruber: red
Sempervirens: evergreen
Speciosus: showy
Spinosus: spiny
Stoloniferus: with stolons
Tomentosus: with thick, short hair
Variegatus: variegated
Viridis: green
Vulgaris: common

that cope better with poor water supply. Knowing about the functions and characteristics of the various plant parts will help you identify, select, and maintain your plants most effectively.

Foliage Leaves come in a tremendous variety of shape and color. It's true that most leaves are green, but there are many shades of green! Leaves that are striped, edged, or blotched with different colors, like those of some types of geranium, are called variegated.

Plant Stems The stems of plants not only support the leaves, but also serve as pathways for movement of nutrients and water between roots and leaves. Like roots, stems are storage organs, too. Bulbs, like garlic, are actually specialized storage stems. Some plants have stems that are specially adapted for vegetative reproduction. Stolons (also called rhizomes) are stems that travel horizontally along the soil surface. At certain intervals along the stolon, new shoots and roots will form, giving rise to new plants. Sweet woodruff and sweet violets are examples of plants that produce stolons.

Plants like mint form new plants from underground stems, called rhizomes. The creeping stems of mint spread quickly, traveling just below the surface of the soil

rhizome

fibrous root

bulb   corm   tuberous root

Although they grow in the ground, bulbs, corms, and rhizomes are not true roots, they are underground stems.

and rooting as they go. For this reason you may want to grow them in containers, preferably large bottomless tubs or plastic pots. Otherwise build a wooden barrier about 12 to 14 inches (30 to 35 cm) deep around the mint patch to keep the plants under control.

Many plants can be easily propagated by taking stem cuttings. Swollen buds, or nodes, located along the stems are the sites for new growth. When you take stem cuttings to make new plants, the new root systems form underground at active nodes on the cutting.

Root Systems Roots help to hold the plant firm in the soil and provide it with a system for absorbing water and nutrients. They may also act as storage organs, as in the carrot family, holding nutrients to be used later, during times of vigorous growth or flowering.

Many plants have a fibrous root system, made up of many fine and branching roots. Annual herbs, for example, have fibrous roots which do not penetrate particularly deeply, so you'll need to pay special attention to the water requirements of such plants when rain is scarce.

Some plants have strong central roots, called taproots, that travel straight down in search of water and nutrients. The taproot is a single, thick, and tapering organ (a carrot is actually an enlarged taproot) with thin side branch

Grasses and annual plants tend to form spreading, branching root systems. Biennials (like carrots) and many perennials produce deeper taproot systems.

roots. Taprooted plants can more easily withstand fluctuating soil moisture conditions, but many, like parsley, are more difficult to transplant because their roots are so sensitive.

About Plant Growth
Throughout the life of your plants, the soil provides many of the things they need to germinate, grow, and thrive. Understanding how your plants interact with the soil will help you manage your garden to provide the best possible growing conditions.

Start with the Seed
The first two things a seed needs are warmth and water. If the soil is too cold or too dry, the seed remains dormant. This makes sense; it would do a seed little good to germinate if it's still winter or if there isn't enough water around to support growth.

TOP: Orange coneflowers (*Rudbeckia* spp.) may reseed prolifically if you don't cut off the spent flowers in fall.
BOTTOM: Annual roots don't grow very deep, but they do spread wide to get the nutrients the plants need for fast growth.

Warmth is usually more reliable than water. Soil temperatures don't change as rapidly as air temperatures, so once the soil is warm enough for growth to begin—and that temperature varies, depending on the plant species—it usually stays warm enough for growth to continue. If you want to warm the soil more quickly in spring, there are a few things you can do: Remove heavy mulches, cover the soil with black plastic, or plant in raised beds.

Water is less dependable than warmth. If the soil dries out after germination begins, the young seedling soon dies. Soils with good structure increase the odds that the seed will germinate; the soil particles in rich, loamy soil are fine enough to closely surround the seed, holding moisture against it. Clayey soils hold too much moisture, while loose, sandy soils may dry out too quickly. Improving your soil by digging and adding organic matter can help keep moisture at the ideal level for seedling growth.

Shoots and Roots
When the seed germinates, it puts out a temporary root, called the primary root or radicle. The radicle stores some of the food that provides the energy that the first aboveground shoot needs to push up through the soil (the rest is in the seed leaves, which are the leaf-like parts attached to the shoot). The radicle also anchors the plant, so the shoot won't blow or wash away.

About the time the first shoot reaches the soil surface, lateral roots begin to grow from the radicle. Like the radicle, the lateral roots anchor the plant in the soil. Throughout most of the plant's life, the roots expand to counterbalance the aboveground parts of the plant. In many cases, the root mass is larger than that of the stems and leaves.

As roots grow, they produce chemical compounds that help make nutrients more soluble and therefore more available to the plant. Throughout their life, roots absorb water and dissolved nutrients from the soil. When they die, the roots add organic matter to the soil.

The chemicals roots produce and the dead cells they shed create an environment that soil microorganisms find attractive. They multiply more rapidly in the root zone than they do in the surrounding soil. As a result, organic matter breaks down faster, making nutrients more available in the soil the roots touch.

All the things you do to encourage soil organisms—providing air, moisture, and ample amounts of organic matter—will help ensure a steady supply of nutrients when and where plants need them. Plus, the moist, well-aerated, fertile conditions that promote a healthy soil community also provide ideal conditions for root growth. More roots encourage more organisms, which release more nutrients that promote more roots—a productive natural cycle.

Growth and Flowering

As plants grow, the water and nutrients the roots absorb flow up through the plant to the leaves and stems. During photosynthesis, the leaves and stems convert the water and nutrients to sugars; the sugars then flow down to the roots to be stored as carbohydrates—food energy.

Before it flowers and sets seed, the plant uses that energy for growth. While the stems and leaves are growing, the roots rapidly expand both out and down through the soil to reach water and nutrients. Root growth slows once the plant flowers and the seed ripens.

If the plant is an annual, it grows old and dies after the seed ripens. Its decaying roots, leaves, and stems return nutrients

Hardiness Zones

It's important that you know what hardiness zone you live in so you can choose appropriate plants. The most commonly used hardiness zone reference is the United States Department of Agriculture Plant Hardiness Zone Map (see page 310). It divides the continental United States and Canada into several numbered zones, from 10 in the South to 1 in the North. Many common plants grow well in the middle range of hardiness zones. If you live in the very warm and cold climates at either end of the zone scales, it is still possible to have a lovely garden, but you'll need to take a bit more care in selecting plants that can tolerate your extreme conditions. If you want to know if a plant may be hardy in your zone, look in the Encyclopedia of Popular Garden Plants, starting on page 170. Nursery catalogs also often list hardiness zones for their plants.

to the soil. If the plant is a perennial, it stores carbohydrates in its roots to use to start growing in the spring. Its leaves and stems die back, adding nutrients to the soil to start the cycle over.

What Are Annuals, Biennials and Perennials?

Annuals

True annuals germinate, grow, flower, set seed, and die all in one season. Their single goal is to reproduce themselves. This is good news for the gardener, since it means that most annual plants will flower like mad to achieve this goal. Some of the best known annuals—including petunias and marigolds—have achieved their popularity because of their free-flowering nature. If you use tricks such as

deadheading (removing spent flowers) to prevent seed formation, many annuals will step up flower production and bloom well over an extended period until cold weather arrives. The first hard frost usually kills the plants and signals the end of the bloom season for that year. Although you'll need to replant most annuals the following spring to get another show, some will sprout from seed dropped by last year's plants. Besides these true annuals, there are a number of perennial plants that are often thought of as annuals. These include tropical perennials, such as zonal geraniums, or perennials that will flower the first season from seed, such as four-o'clocks (*Mirabilis jalapa*). These plants can live for years in frost-free climates and flower season after season, but, like true

TOP: Shirley poppies (*Papaver rhoeas*) are hardy annuals. You can sow them in early spring, or even in fall in mild areas.
BOTTOM: Evergreen perennials, such as bergenias, offer winter interest in climates that don't have heavy snow cover.

annuals, they meet their death at the hands of freezing temperatures in cold-winter climates.

Kinds of Annuals

Annuals are sometimes further separated into three groups—hardy, half-hardy, and tender—based on their cold tolerance. It's useful to know which kind of annuals you're growing so you'll know how soon you can get away with planting the annuals in the spring. The catalog, seed packet, or plant tag should tell you whether your plant is hardy, half-hardy, or tender.

Hardy Annuals Hardy annuals include forget-me-nots (*Myosotis* spp.), pansies, snapdragons, and other plants that withstand several degrees of freezing temperatures. Most of these plants perform best during cool weather. They are often planted in early spring by gardeners in cold-winter areas or in winter by gardeners in the South and West. Some hardy annuals, such as ornamental kale, are also associated with cool fall weather.

Half-Hardy Annuals Half-hardy annuals fit somewhere in the middle of hardy and tender. They will often withstand a touch of frost near the beginning or end of the gardening season. Many of the most commonly grown annuals fit in this middle category.

Tender Annuals Tender annuals, originally from tropical or subtropical climates, can't stand a degree of frost. More than that, they often grow poorly during cold weather and may be stunted by prolonged exposure to temperatures below 50°F (10°C). For best results, wait until late spring to plant tender annuals, such as celosia (*Celosia* spp.) and Joseph's-coat (*Amaranthus tricolor*).

Biennials

Biennials have much in common with annuals, but they differ in one major respect: They take two years to complete their life cycle. The first year after sowing, they produce a leaf structure, building energy for the next year. The second year they flower, set seed, and die. Common garden biennials include honesty (*Lunaria annua*), foxglove (*Digitalis purpurea*), and sweet William (*Dianthus barbatus*).

Perennials

Perennial plants live and bloom for more than two growing seasons. Many will survive a decade or longer if planted in the right location. But even the shorter-lived plants are worth growing. For instance, blanket flowers (*Gaillardia* x *grandiflora*) bloom vigorously for a long portion of the summer, although they seldom return more than two years. Other perennials, such as columbines (*Aquilegia* spp.) and hollyhocks (*Alcea rosea*), have a short natural life span but set seed that replaces the parent plant. Occasionally, a biennial plant like foxglove (*Digitalis grandiflora*) or sweet William (*Dianthus barbatus*), which normally grows foliage the first year and flowers the second, will live on for the third year. Despite their differences in life span, you can call all of these perennials. In most cases, the foliage of perennials dies back to the underground roots each dormant season. A few perennials, like coral bells (*Heuchera* spp.) and rock cresses (*Arabis* spp.), have evergreen foliage that persists through the winter.

How to Create a Healthy Garden

Creating and maintaining a naturally healthy garden isn't a simple one- or two-step process. Every decision you make (or don't make) plays a part in the results you get throughout the season. And every year you're faced with new conditions, new questions, and different results. That's what makes gardening such a challenging but rewarding hobby.

Fortunately, there are some simple but effective steps you can follow each year to help promote the health of your garden.

The basic thing to remember is this: Vigorous plants grown in fertile soil attract fewer pests and are less susceptible to infection by plant pathogens than plants grown in poor soil. Start with a variety of healthy plants suitable for your climate, give them the right growing conditions, and keep an eye out for potential problems. These simple steps will go a long way toward producing a successful garden.

TOP: Mixing annuals, bulbs, and grasses with your perennial plantings adds height, color, and season-long interest.

BOTTOM: Including a diversity of flowering plants helps attract beneficial insects and makes your garden beautiful as well.

Create Diversity

Diversity is a key part of growing a healthy garden. Nature creates diversity by mixing many kinds of plants together. Think of a forest, with a mixture of trees, shrubs, vines, and wildflowers, or maybe a meadow, with a variety of flowers and grasses. These ecosystems provide habitats for a wide range of insects and animals. Predators and parasites help to keep pest populations at a relatively constant level.

In your garden, you can promote this natural system of checks and balances by growing lots of different kinds and cultivars of vegetables, flowering plants, and fruits. Diverse plantings attract beneficial insects and may deter some garden pests. You can take this diversity a step further by practicing crop rotation and changing the location of annual plants each year. This will help to discourage the buildup of some soilborne pest insects like beetle grubs, and diseases like potato scab.

Provide Good Growing Conditions

Many good garden plants are adaptable to a wide range of growing conditions. But if you want your plants to thrive, not just survive, it's worth your time to investigate their particular needs. Vegetables, for example, generally grow best on a site that has lots of air circulation and good water drainage, with 8 to 12 hours of full sunlight each day and at least 1 inch (2.5 cm) of water each week. Fruits also tend to need lots of sun and fertile soil, while ornamental plants vary widely in their sun and soil needs. Before buying new plants, make sure you can supply the conditions they prefer. If you already have a plant that is struggling to survive in less than ideal conditions, consider moving or replacing it before problems strike.

Build Soil Fertility

Healthy soil produces healthy plants. Adding lots of organic matter will improve the physical characteristics of your soil and encourage the beneficial soil microorganisms that help make nutrients available to your plants.

Scout for Problems

Giving all of your plants a close look at least once a week can help you spot potential problems before they get out of hand. Become familiar with both pests and beneficials so you'll know which to control and which to leave alone. If you do spot pests, don't immediately grab a bottle of insecticide. Check again each day over the next few days to see if the beneficial insects step in to help. If the pests are multiplying rapidly, then consider taking control measures. With a little experience, you'll learn how much damage your plants can tolerate before you have to take action.

Before spraying for pests, look around for beneficial insects, like lady beetles.

You'll also want to keep an eye out for signs and symptoms of plant diseases. Snipping off the infected part is often enough to stop a disease before it spreads. If you're growing disease-susceptible plants like fruit trees, you should also keep track of the environmental conditions that favor disease development—like wet, warm spells—and be prepared to apply preventive measures like sulfur or copper sprays.

Know Your Options

Become familiar with the types of controls available to you before you need them so you will know when and how to use them. The best pest control strategies usually include a combination of control methods.

Monitoring soil fertility will help ensure strong, healthy stems and leaves, vigorous roots, and beautiful flowers.

Keep Good Records

Good garden records can be one of your most valuable control tools. As you scout for and deal with problems, keep track of when and where they occurred and what you did to control them. Write down what worked and what didn't work. If you tried new cultivars for their insect or disease resistance, jot down a few sentences on how they performed during the season. In future years, you can review your notes and be prepared for problems before they happen.

Ask about Organics

If you want your garden to be completely organic, don't forget to ask your plant suppliers how they raise their stock. Many conventional growers use synthetic fertilizers and pesticides. Organic growers use starting and growing mediums that are high in organic matter and free of pesticides or synthetic nutrients. If you can't find a supplier of organically grown plants, you may decide to start them yourself.

Petunias

Companion Planting

In the simplest terms, companion planting is the technique of combining two plants for a particular purpose (usually pest control). In practice, though, you'll find that there are many different factors that influence how plants work together as companions. For instance, if your plants are regularly attacked by insects, you can use companions to hide, repel, or trap pests. Other companions provide food and shelter to attract and protect beneficial insects. And some plants grow well together just because they don't compete for light or rooting space.

Cabbage, lobelia, and yellow calendulas make colorful companions. Calendulas also attract beneficial insects, like hoverflies.

Repelling with Smells

One way to use companion planting to protect your plants is to mask their odors with other powerful smells. Plants like garlic, for instance, release deterrent aromas into the air that may chase away insects such as bean beetles and potato bugs. Try pungent plants as an edging around garden beds or mix them in among your other plants. Or, try spreading clippings of the scented plants over garden beds for the same effect.

Luring Pests from Your Garden

Some plants have an almost irresistible appeal for certain pests. Nasturtiums, for instance, are an excellent attractant plant because they're a favorite of aphids. Attractant plants can protect your plants in two ways. First, they act as decoys to lure pests away from your desirable plants. Second, they make it easier to control the pests since the insects are concentrated on a few plants. Once pests are "trapped," you can either pull out the attractant plants and destroy them along with the pests, or apply some other type of control measure to the infested plants.

The aroma of garlic is a powerful deterrent to many pests.

Sheltering Beneficial Insects

Not all insects are garden enemies. Many actually help your garden grow by eating or parasitizing plant pests. You can encourage these beneficial creatures to make a home in your garden by planting their favorite flowering plants. Growing dill, for example, can attract pest-eating spiders, lacewings, and parasitic wasps, which will help control caterpillars on cabbage, beetles on cucumbers, and aphids on lettuce.

Combining Complementary Plants

Some plants make ideal garden companions simply because they don't compete, even when planted close together in small spaces. Plants like deep-rooted squash and shallow-rooted onions occupy different soil zones, so their roots can draw on different nutrient

Nasturtiums entice aphids away from the vegetables and deter whiteflies and squash bugs.

Lettuce and sunflowers can be good garden companions. The low-growing lettuce acts as a living mulch to keep the soil moist, while tall sunflowers to the south or west provide light shade for this heat-sensitive salad crop.

LEFT: Besides producing pretty (and edible) flowers, nasturtiums may lure aphids from your crops.
RIGHT: A fence can reduce the force of winds, so your plants are less likely to be blown over.

sources. Plants that need lots of nutrients (heavy feeders, like cabbage, corn, eggplant, and squash) combine well with light feeders, like garlic and beans. Taller plants like corn, trellised beans, and sunflowers can provide welcome light shade for ground-hugging cucumbers and lettuce. Besides making more efficient use of space, mixing plants with compatible growth habits also increases the diversity in your garden. This, in turn, makes it harder for some pests to find and move between your plants.

Climate

Climate—the seasonal cycles of rainfall, temperatures, humidity, and other factors—has a major influence on which plants will thrive in your landscape. Some tough plants, like daylilies (*Hemerocallis* spp.) and hostas (*Hosta* spp.), can grow in a wide range of temperature and moisture conditions. Other plants can take varying temperatures but absolutely must have a certain amount of rainfall (or irrigation if the rains don't come).

All plants have a certain range of temperatures and moisture levels that they will grow best in. If you know what your garden has to offer, you can look for plants that are naturally adapted to those conditions and be fairly confident that they will grow well with a minimum of fuss on your part.

Think about Temperature

If you want to grow plants that will live for more than one year—including trees, shrubs, grasses, and perennials—you have to consider your area's average low and high temperatures. Plants that are naturally adapted to this temperature range will tend to survive and thrive in your landscape.

Most plant recommendations are based on an area's low temperatures. Refer to USDA Plant Hardiness Zone Map on page 310 to find the zone you live in, and limit your selections to plants that are reliably cold-hardy for your area. Marginally hardy plants may survive for several years, but it's likely that they won't thrive, and an unusually cold spell can kill them off.

Summer high temperatures also limit which woody plants, flowers, and turf grasses you can grow. Even if a plant can

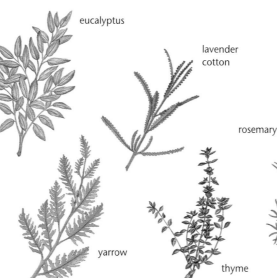

eucalyptus

lavender cotton

rosemary

yarrow

thyme

Plants with small or silvery leaves are often well adapted to low-water conditions.

tolerate the heat, it may demand frequent watering in return, and it probably won't look great. Many delphiniums, for instance, will limp along in hot Southern summers and die out after one or two years, while the same plants grown in the North will probably bloom and thrive for several years.

Plants that can't take the heat are a bad choice if you want a good-looking, easy-care garden. Unfortunately, it's difficult to put a number on a plant's heat tolerance. Plant descriptions in books and catalogs often suggest both lower and upper hardiness zone ranges (as in "Zones 5 to 8"). Use these recommendations as guidelines, but also check around local neighborhoods and botanical gardens to see how the plant actually performs in your area before you decide to include it in your landscape.

Rainfall

Rainfall, like temperature, has a great impact on determining which plants will grow in an area without supplemental water. If you don't mind lugging hoses around for frequent watering or if you plan to have an automatic irrigation system, you may choose to grow plants that need extra water. If you want to grow just a few moisture-loving plants, site them close to the house where you can give them special attention more easily. But if

The Effect of Water

Large bodies of water like oceans and lakes influence the climate of the land nearby. The larger the body of water, the greater its effect. Since water temperatures rise and fall more slowly than land temperatures, they modify the air temperatures of the surrounding land. Coastal gardens, for example, do not experience the same extreme temperatures as inland gardens. Similarly, a garden near a lake will experience less extreme air temperatures than one farther away. The effect of the water on temperatures may be enough to hold late and early frosts at bay, giving you a longer growing season, and temper the summer heat, making it possible for you to grow a wider range of plants.

your goal is to save time, money, and natural resources, you'll definitely want to include naturally adapted plants in your landscape. Small, fuzzy, or silvery leaves—such as those on many herbs—are fairly reliable clues that a particular plant is

Columbines provide colorful late-spring flowers for shady gardens.

adapted to low-water conditions. One of the best ways to get ideas on other plants that grow well in your region without extra water is to investigate what's growing in local natural areas that have similar conditions to your yard.

Microclimates

Microclimates are small areas where the growing conditions differ from the norm. As an example, an L-shaped corner next to your house might be sheltered enough from the winter wind and hold enough of the heat radiating from the house to let you grow a special marginally hardy plant that would struggle along in an open area. Tomatoes planted in the warm soil on the south side of your house can get a head start on more exposed plants in the middle of the yard.

Topography

Topography means the lie of the land. As hills and valleys dip and rise, small changes in altitude and slope and wind

shelter create microclimates in particular areas. If your garden is on a hill or in a valley, you'll probably be faced with slightly different conditions from the average climate of your region.

Gardening on a Flat Area

If you live in a relatively flat, exposed area, you may need to deal with soil erosion—not by water, but by wind, which blows strongly across level open areas. You may also find you have drainage problems after heavy rains, when the level land fails to channel away excess water. If you're near a body of water, the land may flood.

Gardening in a Valley

Valleys tend to be cooler than the higher land around them. This happens because cool air is heavier than warm air. Cool air tends to drain toward lower ground. For this reason, gardens located at the bottoms of valleys suffer the latest frosts in the spring, the earliest frosts in autumn, and the severest frosts in winter. The absence of wind in valleys increases susceptibility to frost.

Soil tends to be wetter in a valley, and where drainage is poor, water will puddle, creating spongy, wet areas so fungal diseases of plants are more likely to occur.

Moisture-loving plants like primulas and astilbes thrive in cool, humid climates with high rainfall.

Cool-loving English primroses will thrive and spread in a shady microclimate.

Sunny walls can provide a warm, protected microclimate that is ideal for heat-loving plants.

On poorly drained flat sites, a raised bed can provide ideal conditions for a wide range of colorful plants.

One of the great advantages of gardening in a valley is that you are likely to find the best topsoil there. As water flows downhill, it washes away the slopes above and carries topsoil and organic matter away, depositing it lower down.

Gardening on a Hilltop

Air temperatures on hills tend to be lower than on flat land. You'll have greater protection from frost and plant disease on a hill, compared with a valley, since air movement is greater. Excessive winds, however, can damage plants, increase soil erosion, and speed the loss of moisture from the soil. The soil will generally be thinner and more easily lose its nutrients.

Many colorful plants, including irises and primroses, thrive in shade.

Gardening on a Slope

Slopes are often cooled by breezes in the afternoon or evening, while warm air rising over them in the morning keeps away frost. In cool Northern climates, a slope with a southern exposure warms more quickly in the spring, and remains warm for a longer period at the end of the growing season.

Slopes, however, are subject to erosion from water drainage and wind.

Exposure

Exposure refers to the amount of sun and shade your yard receives throughout the day. The exposure of different places on your property can vary widely, depending on where each garden is in relation to the house and to other shade-casting features such as trees and fences.

South-Facing Sites

Locating a garden on the south side of your house (or a wall or fence) provides the maximum amount of light in the Northern Hemisphere.

Eastern Exposures

Many plants thrive with an eastern exposure. Plants on these sites receive up to a half day of direct light, and they're sheltered from the hot afternoon sun, prolonging bloom time in hot summers.

Reduce maintenance on tough-to-mow slopes by replacing turf with a mixture of wildflowers.

The amount of sun your yard receives can vary through the day. Consider this factor as you plan your plantings.

West-Facing Sites

Western exposures are a challenge for plants. The site is generally cool and shady in the morning, but the temperature can change dramatically when strong sun hits it during the warmest part of the day.

Northern Exposures

A north-facing garden receives much less light and remains cool throughout the day. If the site is open (without large trees or buildings to the east or west), it will probably still be bright. A bright, evenly cool spot is ideal for most shade-loving plants; even those preferring full shade should grow well here.

Sunny sites can provide ideal conditions for lush borders packed with light-loving, flowering plants.

All about Soil

Study Your Soil

Before you start planning and planting, invest a little time in learning about your soil. Once you know what soil conditions your yard has to offer, you can choose plants that will grow and thrive there for years to come. Your hands, a trowel to dig up a little soil, and a simple soil test kit are all you need to get a basic picture of what's going on in the earth beneath your feet.

Clay soil is nutrient-rich but drains poorly.

Sandy soil drains quickly and is usually dry and infertile.

Loamy soil tends to be moist and fertile.

Structure below the Surface

While it's relatively easy to develop good soil structure at the surface, you have much less influence over the subsoil. There, the parent material plays a greater role in determining how the particles group themselves.

Next time you dig a deep hole, take a look at the structure of the deepest soil you can see. Observe the soil in place on the side of the hole, break off a hand-sized piece. Loose, structureless subsoil may allow water and nutrients to drain away from roots too quickly, leading to droughty conditions at the surface. A tight, massive subsoil will interfere with the drainage of excess water, usually leading to waterlogged conditions.

While granules are fairly uncommon in the subsoil, you may see other kinds of structures there. In uncultivated soils, or those laid down by water or ice (along rivers and streams or in glacial areas), particles often arrange themselves in flat sheets, called plates. In dry regions, you're likely to see vertical columns that may be 6 inches (15 cm) or more in diameter and of varying lengths.

In humid regions the subsoil is usually made up of angular or slightly rounded cubes that range in size from less than 1 inch (2.5 cm) wide to 2 inches (5 cm) wide or more.

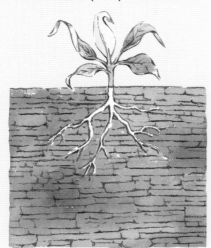
Tight, platy soil can discourage growth.

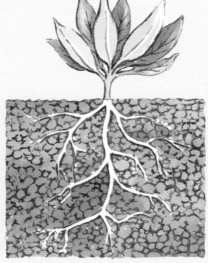
Roots grow easily in granular soil.

Soil Structure Helpers

You have allies in your battle for good soil structure—the small creatures that crawl through your soil. Earthworms are perhaps the most famous soil builders. Their tunneling loosens and aerates tight soil, and the organic matter they drag down encourages stable soil granules. Rodents churn the soil as they dig and mix organic matter into the subsoil. Plant roots also improve soil structure by adding organic matter below the surface as they break down. Plus, the tiny passages left by the decayed roots allow water and air easier access to lower soil layers, in turn encouraging even better micoorganism and plant growth.

RIGHT: Healthy soil builds healthy plants. Your role in the cycle is keeping the soil stocked with organic matter to provide ideal conditions for beneficial soil organisms and good root growth.

Soil Texture

Almost all soils are made up of three basic mineral components: sand grains, somewhat smaller silt particles, and extremely fine clay particles. The relative amounts of these three mineral particles determine the texture of your soil.

You can get a very basic idea of your soil's texture by doing a simple test: Just take a handful of moist soil, squeeze it, and match the results you get with one of the points below.

- If the soil won't stay in a clump in your open hand, it's on the sandy side.
- If the soil forms a loose clump that breaks apart when you tap it lightly with your finger, it's a loam—a balanced mixture of sand, silt, and clay that's ideal for many garden plants.
- If the soil forms a sticky lump that you can mold into various shapes, it's high in clay.

Soils that have lots of sand are said to be light or sandy. Light soils lose water and dissolved nutrients quickly, so they tend to be dry and infertile. Loamy soils usually drain well but hold enough water and nutrients for good plant growth. Heavy (clayey) soils tend to hold a lot of water and nutrients, but they can be waterlogged when wet and hard when dry.

There isn't any practical way to change the texture of your soil. You can, however, improve the soil's structure to make it more suitable for the plants you want to grow in your garden.

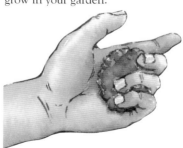

Puzzling Out pH

Plant nutrients tend to be most available to roots when the soil pH is near neutral (around 6.5 to 7.0). When the soil is either very acid (with a lower pH) or alkaline (with a higher pH), some nutrients form chemical compounds that make them unavailable to your plants. A home test kit (which you can buy at a garden center) or a professional soil test can tell you what pH your soil has. Balance acid soils by adding lime and alkaline soils by adding sulfur. Your test kit or results sheet should tell you how much to apply.

To have your soil analyzed by a professional soil laboratory, contact your local Cooperative Extension agent, land-grant university, or professional soil-analysis laboratory for information or directions.

Plants for Acid Soil

Here are just a few plants that appreciate or tolerate soil with a pH below 6.5.

Shrubs
    Camellias (*Camellia* spp.)
    Heaths (*Erica* spp.)
    Bayberries (*Myrica* spp.)
    Pieris (*Pieris* spp.)
    Yews (*Taxus* spp.)
    Mountain laurel (*Kalmia latifolia*)
    Azaleas and rhododendrons (*Rhododendron* spp.)
    Blueberries (*Vaccinium* spp.)

Flowers
    Chrysanthemums (*Chrysanthemum* spp.)
    Lily-of-the-valley (*Convallaria majalis*)
    Lilies (*Lilium* spp.)
    Marigolds (*Tagetes* spp.)

Trees
    Firs (*Abies* spp.)
    Cedars (*Cedrus* spp.)
    Spruces (*Picea* spp.)
    Pines (*Pinus* spp.)
    Oaks (*Quercus* spp.)

Soil Structure

Structure refers to how the sand, silt, and clay particles in your soil stick together. Many small, crumb-like clumps create ample space for the air and water that roots need to grow well. Tight, compacted soils have little or no structure, making them hard for you to dig and hard for the roots of your plants to grow through. Loose, sandy soils with little structure lose water and nutrients quickly.

Organic matter provides the basic materials that help to clump the soil particles together. To improve and maintain good soil structure, work in generous amounts of decomposed garden compost before planting, and use organic mulches like chopped leaves and grass clippings, or, for the vegetable garden, hay and straw, to keep the soil well stocked with organic matter.

Understanding Organic Matter

Organic matter and humus are essential parts of healthy soil. Organic matter is the "fresh" dead material that gets added to the soil, such as fallen leaves and grass clippings. As soil organisms feed on the organic matter, they break it down into nutrients, which your plants can use, and humus. Humus forms loose connections between soil particles and gives the soil a good crumbly structure. It acts like a sponge to hold water and nutrients where roots can absorb them. Adding ample quantities of organic matter—in the form of aged compost, chopped leaves, grass clippings, mushroom compost, or similar materials—will help to improve just about any kind of soil.

Knowing about Nutrients

Soil with lots of organic matter is called "rich" because it holds ample reservoirs of nutrients. The big three plant nutrients are nitrogen (N), phosphorus (P), and potassium (K). (The 5-10-5 or 5-10-10 listed on bags of fertilizer is the percentage of these three elements [N-P-K].)

Plants need nitrogen to grow healthy green leaves and to regulate the use of other nutrients. Phosphorus helps form healthy roots and flowers; it also strengthens resistance to pests. Potassium also promotes strong roots and general resistance, but it's important in photosynthesis as well.

Plants need several other nutrients, such as iron and calcium, in smaller quantities. Soils with ample amounts of organic matter usually contain enough nutrients to keep many kinds of plants thriving. But you'll also need to make sure your soil is at the right pH so those nutrients will be available to your plants. A soil test can tell you whether your soil is acid or alkaline and if the supply of different nutrients is adequate for your needs.

While most plants grow best when the soil contains an ample supply of balanced nutrients, some actually grow better if soil nutrients are low. Nitrogen-rich soils, for instance, will cause plants like yarrow and coreopsis to form lush, floppy growth that requires staking. In less fertile soil the same plants will grow stronger. Knowing the nutrient content of your soil will help you select the most appropriate plants for your conditions.

As these leaves break down, they'll return nutrients to the soil; the tree's roots will take in the nutrients to help boost next year's growth.

Plants for Alkaline Soil

If you soil's pH is on the high side (7.0 or higher), consider some of these plants; they're naturally adapted to alkaline soil.

Trees
  Catalpas (*Catalpa* spp.)
  Redbuds (*Cercis* spp.)
  Green ash (*Fraxinus pennsylvanica*)
  Bur oak (*Quercus macrocarpa*)
  Lilacs (*Syringa* spp.)

Flowers
  Ageratum (*Ageratum houstonianum*)
  Japanese anemone (*Anemone* x *hybrida*)
  Snapdragon (*Antirrhinum majus*)
  Cosmos (*Cosmos* spp.)
  Pinks (*Dianthus* spp.)
  Baby's-breath (*Gypsophila paniculata*)
  Peonies (*Paeonia* spp.)
  Zinnias (*Zinnia* spp.)

Vines
  Clematis (*Clematis* spp.)
  Virginia creeper (*Parthenocissus quinquefolia*)
  Boston ivy (*Parthenocissus tricuspidata*)

Shrubs
  Barberries (*Berbis* spp.)
  Boxwoods (*Buxus* spp.)
  Cotoneasters (*Cotoneaster* spp.)
  Forsythias (*Forsythia* spp.)

Snapdragon

Taking Care of Your Soil

- Keep the soil covered. Use organic mulches like compost, shredded leaves, and grass clippings around plants to help prevent soil erosion, retain soil moisture, keep the soil cool, add organic matter and nutrients, and provide safe hiding places for beneficial insects like ground beetles. Mulches also serve as a barrier between plants and pathogens.

- Grow a flowering, living mulch. Sow cover crops like buckwheat or clover in any vacant garden spot. The living mulch will protect the soil as it provides nectar and shelter for beneficial insects.

- Keep tillage to a minimum, especially when soil is wet or dusty dry. Soil is too wet to work if it sticks to your shoes or easily holds its shape when formed into a ball. Working wet soil can ruin the soil's structure. Tillage destroys some insect pests, but kills beneficial insects and animals as well.

Tools and Equipment

Choosing the Right Tool

Using the right tool really does make any job easier, as you know if you've ever used a butter knife when you couldn't find the screwdriver or the heel of a shoe as a substitute for a hammer. But a shopping trip for garden tools can be so baffling that you may well decide to stick with the butter knife and shoe. When faced with a wall-long display of shovels, spades, forks, rakes, trowels, and cultivators, it can be hard to decide what tools, and what version of them, you need.

A Basic Tool Collection

Fortunately, most gardeners can get away with a half-dozen basic tools. You'll need a spade to turn the soil and a shovel for digging holes and for moving soil, sand, and amendments around. A spading fork is useful for turning the soil, working in amendments and green manures, turning compost, and dividing perennials. You'll also need a metal rake for smoothing the soil, a hoe for weeding, and a trowel for planting and transplanting. If you have a huge vegetable garden, you may want to get a rotary tiller, wheel hoe, or even a garden tractor to which you can attach various implements. If you garden in containers, a trowel and hand cultivator will suffice.

Buying Good Tools

There's nothing quite like the feel of working your soil with a good-quality, well-constructed tool. Here are some things to consider as you shop for garden equipment, so you'll get the best tools for your money.

Cost How much you spend on your tools depends on how long you want them to last. If you want to keep the tools for decades, get the best you can afford. If you're on a tight budget, if you plan to move in a few years and don't want the extra baggage, or if you leave your tools outside all the time, buy the bargain basement kind. Be warned, though, that cost-cutting materials and designs make cheap tools more difficult to use than their more expensive counterparts. And cheap tools might not even make it through a season without bending or breaking.

Construction When you go tool shopping, read the label to see whether the metal part of the tool is stamped steel or forged steel. Forged steel is much stronger, but makes the tool cost 20 to 30 percent more than a tubular steel tool. If you want the item to last, go for a forged steel product; if budget is a limitation, consider stamped steel.

Whether you have a whole collection of garden tools or just a few basic ones, you need to know when and how to use them properly.

Also investigate how the handle attaches to the metal part. Don't buy the tool if the metal wraps only partway around the handle; this construction, called open socket, leaves the wood exposed to water and mud, which can lead to rot. Also avoid tools where the handle is poked onto a spike at the top of the metal portion of the tool, then surrounded with a metal collar to keep the handle from splitting. Neither this type of construction, called tang and ferrule, nor open socket is durable and may only last a season or two.

Instead, choose tools with metal that wraps all the way around the handle (called solid-socket construction) or has strips of metal bolted to the handle (known as solid-strap construction).

Handles If you want a wooden handle, look for one made of white ash. Handles of spades and forks are sometimes made from hickory, but it's heavier and less flexible. The grain should run the length of the handle, without knots. Painted handles often hide low-quality wood;

Good-quality tools can be expensive, but they are a pleasure to use and can last for many years with good care.

don't buy them. Alternatives to wood are fiberglass or solid-core fiberglass. Both are stronger than wood; solid-core fiberglass is nearly unbreakable. They cost more than wood, but it's worth it if you want a tool that will last for many years.

Grips If the end of the handle has a grip for you to hang on to, check how the grip is designed. Make sure it is fastened to the handle and not just slipped over it. Beyond that, the style you choose is a matter of preference (and availability). Try out a few to see which feels best.

Size If you have a choice, pick the handle length that feels most comfortable. Shovels should be at least shoulder height; rakes can be even longer to give you a better reach. A hoe's handle should

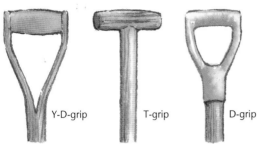

Y-D-grip   T-grip   D-grip

Tool handles come with several types of grips; choose the one that feels most comfortable to you.

be long enough to let you stand upright when the blade is about 2 feet (60 cm) from your feet and just about flat on the ground. Short-handled tools, such as spades and spading forks, usually have 28-inch (70-cm) handles, but tall gardeners should look for ones with 32-inch (80-cm) handles. For hand tools such as trowels, choose the length that

Neater Weeders

Ordinary hoes are traditional favorites for weeding vegetable gardens, but they aren't the last word in weeding tools. If you need a special tool for weeding in tight spots or if you just enjoy trying out handy garden gadgets, give some of the implements discussed below a try.

Pavement weeders are short-handled, with an angled, pointed blade used to scrape weeds growing between bricks or sections of sidewalk or in driveway cracks.

Dandelion weeders, also called asparagus knives or fishtail weeders, have a blade that resembles a forked tongue; the handle may be long or short. Use this tool to dig out grasses, small tree seedlings, or weeds with long taproots (such as curly dock [*Rumex crispus*]).

Cape Cod weeders and hot-bed weeders are short-handled, angled blades for cutting small weeds in tight places.

Hand cultivators have three clawlike tines for raking weeds from the soil; they may have short or long handles.

String trimmers can be powered by gas or electricity; high-powered models may have a blade attachment that can handle tough-stemmed weeds. Power trimmers are useful for quickly cutting weeds along fences and walls and for mowing small meadow areas. The drawbacks are their noise and the safety hazards they present.

Clippers, shears, and pruners are handy for cutting back vines and clump-forming weeds.

Mattocks and pick axes give the "umph" you need to dig out the roots of weedywoodies, such as shrubs and some vines.

feels comfortable in your hand. When buying a mattock or pick, choose a weight that you can lift and swing without strain.

Caring for Tools

Once you've gone to the trouble of buying good tools, it's worth a little extra effort to keep them in shape. Without proper care, even the best built and most expensive tool can get corroded and dull after a season or two, making it as unpleasant to use as the cheapest department-store tool. When you are ready to dig, you'll be glad of the few minutes you put into keeping your tools clean and sharp.

Keep Them Clean

It's pretty easy at the end of a hot and grimy day in the garden to justify putting the tools away dirty. And you can even get away with it a few times. But eventually the moist soil clinging to your tools will make them rust. And once you finally do get around to cleaning them, the dry soil is harder to get off than the moist soil would have been.

For that reason, it's a virtue to force yourself into the habit of cleaning your tools when you're done with them. This doesn't mean just scraping the shovel off with the trowel. For one thing, then you have to scrape the trowel off with the shovel, then the shovel off with the trowel again, and so on. Also, all that scraping of metal against metal damages tools.

Better alternatives include using a stick, wooden spoon, or paint stirrer to scrape off the clinging soil. Or use a long-handled scrub brush that you keep in a convenient spot. Another trick is to keep a tub of sharp sand around and dip the tool up and down in it until the soil comes off.

It's especially worthwhile to clean tools before you store them for the winter. Clean off the soil, then use steel wool or a wire brush to remove any rust. Coat the metal with a light oil and hang the tools someplace where you can see and admire them all winter long.

Since your skin touches the handle the most, you may want to keep wooden

handles smooth by sanding any rough spots. If you wish, apply varnish or another sealer (like tung oil) to protect the wood. If a handle breaks, pick up a replacement during your next trip to the hardware store; don't just try to tape the old one.

Keep Them Sharp

Your spade and hoe will do a better job for you if you keep them sharpened. You'll get the best results if you sharpen them briefly and often rather than making it a big job for the end of the year. For most gardeners, a metal file is an adequate

Spare Your Back

If Monday mornings often find you aching from a weekend of digging, don't give up on the garden; learn how to dig the right way! Here are some tips that can help save your muscles next time you turn the soil.

First, insert the tool into the soil so the blade is straight up and down. Now follow these steps:

1. Keeping your back straight and your foot on the upper edge of the spade, use your weight to push the spade into the soil.
2. Bend both your waist and knees as you slide the spade under the soil, then straighten both to lift the load.
3. Turn your whole body before depositing the dirt—don't just twist your torso as you fling the soil off to the side.

It's easy, in your rush to finish up, to ignore pain. But pain has a purpose, and that purpose is to tell you to knock it off and go in the house for some lemonade. You'll get more done and feel better if you take regular breaks, preferably before you start to feel pain!

sharpening tool. Use a file that matches the contour of the tool's surface—a flat file for a flat-bladed hoe or spade and a half-round file for a curved shovel blade. If you have many tools, a whetstone or grindstone will take care of them more quickly. If you don't want to sharpen them yourself, you can take your tools to someone who does it professionally (some hardware stores offer this service). The best time to do this is in late fall, as you are preparing your tools for storage. Professional sharpeners are often swamped with work in spring, and they may not have time to do your tools as soon as you need them if you wait until the last minute.

To Sharpen a Hoe

Hold the hoe where the metal and handle meet, with the cutting edge face down and the handle pointing away from you. Holding the metal file flat against the beveled edge, stroke downward toward the edge of the blade, at a 30 to 40 degree angle to the length of the blade. Use medium pressure and make quick strokes. Go in one direction only—don't saw the file back and forth across the blade.

Maintaining a Tiller

If you own a rotary tiller, it's important to clean off the soil after each use. Wash both the tines and the body with a soft cloth. If you keep the painted parts waxed, you'll find the soil will dislodge much more easily.

Look for any loose or missing screws, nuts, or bolts; replace as necessary. Once a year, or every 25 hours of use (whichever comes first), clean the air cleaner by tapping it against something; if it's really filthy, wash it. You'll need to clean it more often if your soils are powdery. Use the same timetable for changing the oil. Change the spark plug every year, too, or every 50 hours of use.

Before storing the machine for winter, clean out the fuel line by draining out all the gasoline and then running the machine until it stops. Remove, clean, and replace the spark plug, leaving the spark plug wire disconnected. If the machine has a four-cycle engine, change the oil. Check the blades or tines, and sharpen them if needed. Check with your owner's manual for other suggested maintenance tips.

The Trouble with Tillers

Their speed and power makes rotary tillers very useful, but they do have several drawbacks. For one thing, they're a big investment. Unless you have a huge garden, you may not want to spend the money for a machine that you'll only use for a few hours each season. (Of course, if you can't afford to buy your own tiller, you can usually rent one for a day or weekend for a reasonable fee.) Tillers also use gasoline, which bothers gardeners trying to cut back on the use of fossil fuels. And some people just don't like the noise.

But perhaps the biggest drawback is that they are tempting to use, and their overuse can damage the soil. The spinning metal blades can break crumbly granular soil into fine powder, ruining soil structure. If you repeatedly till to the same depth, you can create a layer of hardpan right below the blade depth. Finally, tillers work in large quantities of air, which can cause a population boom of soil microorganisms. While this is good to some extent, the stimulated microorganisms can rapidly deplete your soil's supply of organic matter unless you add enough material to make up for it.

Scrape any clinging soil off the blade of spades, shovels, forks, and hoes to prevent rusting.

Brush your tools off after each use, and give them a thorough cleaning and oiling before storage.

Planning Your Garden

Starting from Scratch

If you've just moved into a new development, built a new house, or inherited a particularly uninspired all-lawn landscape, you may be staring at bare soil or an expanse of grass where you want a garden to be located.

Live with It

The best way to start a new landscape may be not to start it—at least for a year or so. If you can stand it, live with the landscape through one year. See where water puddles after storms or where it runs off quickly, taking valuable topsoil with it. Note where structures and trees cast shadows on your property throughout the seasons. See how traffic patterns develop: Where do you always walk to reach the car? Where do visitors and utility people tend to tread on their way to the door? Take note of these patterns and problems, and incorporate them into your landscape plan.

Look at Your Landscape

Before you start digging, walk around your yard and look at it from all angles—from the street, from the back door, from the side yard. Think about where a garden would look good and enhance your yard. You might decide on a perennial planting

in front of a shrub border, and a herb and vegetable garden just outside the back door. In short, you want to give the garden a reason for being wherever it is.

Garden Styles

You'll also need to decide whether it is to be a formal or informal garden, or a mixture of both.

Formal Gardens

Formal landscaping uses straight lines, sharp angles, and symmetrical plantings with a limited number of different plants. They are usually laid out in squares or rectangles with low hedges of clipped boxwood, hollies, or other evergreens to define different spaces in the garden. Often the beds on either side of a straight central path are planted with the same sequence of plants, forming a mirror image of each other. Formal designs tend to have a restful feel. But they may not be as restful for the gardener since you'll need to clip, stake, and weed on a regular basis to keep the plants looking perfect.

For a formal look, include elements like straight paths, symmetrical plantings, and tightly-clipped, closely-planted low edgings.

Informal designs include mixed plantings, curved edges, and winding paths.

Informal Gardens

Informal landscapes use curving lines to create a more natural feeling. They tend to have few permanent features such as walls, although elements such as rustic split-rail fences and wood-chip paths add greatly to the informal feel. These kinds of gardens generally include many different kinds of plants—trees, shrubs, annuals, herbs, vines, and perennials. Informal designs are relaxed and lively. Since the plants are free to spread, sprawl, and lean on each other, they tend to need less regular maintenance to still look well tended. You won't need to keep sharp edges on the beds, and the few weeds that pop up won't be immediately obvious and ruin the look of the garden.

Beautiful gardens such as this don't happen by accident—they start with careful planning.

For a formal look, try a classic single border. A hedge or fence provides a good background; a solid edging strip makes for easy maintenance.

Mixed Gardens

It's difficult to mix informal and formal areas effectively, but sometimes the classic formal garden seems too rigid. The modern approach is to plant sections of a formal garden with a touch of informality by maintaining the basic geometric shapes but softening the angles with creeping and trailing edgers.

Put Your Ideas on Paper

Once you've chosen a site and style for your garden, you can start putting your plans down on paper. Measure the length and width of the area you have targeted for your garden. Determine an appropriate outline and draw it to scale on a piece of graph paper. Draw in the major existing features, such as buildings, trees, shrubs, and paths. This is also a good place to jot down notes about the soil conditions in

Design Rules for Your Garden

While designing a garden is a very personal and creative activity, following some basic design rules will give your finished garden a very polished or natural look. The key rules are to create balance and rhythm and to add a dominant feature to tie the garden together.

First, keep the garden in balance. Include plants with a mix of heights and sizes throughout your plantings. Don't plant all of the tall or massive flowers on one side, with a group of low, delicate plants at the other end. In formal gardens, you may balance one side of the garden by planting the same design on the other, making a mirror image. For an informal garden, you can vary the plantings, perhaps matching a large blue-flowered perennial on one side with a lower-growing plant that has bright red flowers. In this case, you are balancing brighter color with larger size.

Second, create a rhythm, or a sense of continuity, throughout the entire garden. You can repeat groupings of the same plant or use other plants with identical colors or similar flower shapes. Let a middle-of-the-border plant drift from the foreground to the background, giving a sense of movement and uniting the different layers of the garden.

Third, establish a dominant feature. This focal point can be a path, sculpture, birdbath, or tree with the garden built around it.

the various planting areas (is it frequently wet, often dry, or evenly moist?), as well as the amount and type of sunshine available (does it get full sun, just a few

This charming cottage garden combines perennials with annuals, shrubs, and trees for season-long interest.

hours of morning or afternoon sun, or no direct sun at all?). Make a couple of photocopies of your base plan, or lay sheets of tracing paper over the original sketch. On one copy or overlay, circle or otherwise mark the problem areas you identified on your stroll around the yard. On the other copies, try sketching in possible solutions. Maybe you could plant groundcovers on that grassy slope to eliminate mowing; or link that group of shrubs with mulch and groundcovers, so you don't have to mow around the individual plants. Experiment with different arrangements until you're happy with the results on paper. Then go out into the yard and try to visualize how the landscape will look with the solutions you've come up with. Make sure you've planned for access by equipment (like mowers and wheelbarrows).

For a charmingly informal look, interplant your vegetables with other flowering plants and herbs to add color, and also to save space.

Pick Your Plants

Now you can start identifying the plants you want to grow. A fun way to do this is to keep a wish list of plants that you've admired in catalogs, read about in books, or seen in neighbors' gardens. For each species or cultivar, write down growth rates and mature sizes, flower color, shape, height, season of bloom, foliage appearance, and cultural requirements. Then you can start matching up the plants you want with the growing conditions you have available.

Putting Plants into Your Plan

As you finalize your plant list, start thinking about how to organize the different plants in the garden. To visualize possible color combinations, cut circles representing each group of flowers out of colored paper, matching the paper color to the flower color. Juggle these around until you find combinations that you like.

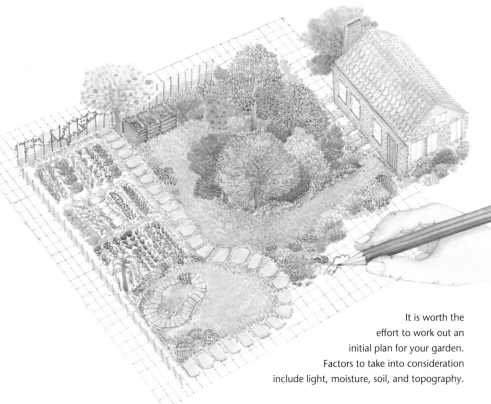

It is worth the effort to work out an initial plan for your garden. Factors to take into consideration include light, moisture, soil, and topography.

Set Priorities

As you install your new landscape, it's wise to start on the "hard" elements—like walls, fences, and paths—first. This is also a good time to plan and install an automatic irrigation system if you need one. Once the permanent elements are in place, then you can start planting. Whenever possible, begin with slow growers like trees and shrubs, then the groundcovers. You may choose to plant a few beds of annuals for quick color during the first few seasons or to just wait for the perennial garden to develop. Don't forget that annuals are also great for filling in gaps in young perennial gardens.

Regrading

Sometimes terracing or regrading is necessary to make land usable. Consult professionals such as landscape architects, engineers, or surveyors if extensive grading is necessary. If you do have regrading done on your property, make sure you keep the topsoil separate from

the subsoil. When you're ready to finish the job, use the reserved topsoil as the top layer—it's much better and richer soil for your plants.

Protecting Trees During Regrading

If you plan to have regrading done on your property, keep in mind that changing the soil level around a tree can severely damage it. If you add soil over its roots, they may die due to reduced soil oxygen or due to excess water held against them. If you remove soil, you'll actually remove much of your tree's roots, because most of the small feeder roots are within the top foot of soil. Removing roots prevents your tree from absorbing enough water and nurients for growth and may hinder its ability to hold itself upright. One strong windstorm can easily topple a tree with damaged roots.

If you must grade around trees, build "wells" around your trees large enough to protect their roots. Use brightly colored construction tape to mark off a protected

area around your trees, at least as far away from the trunks as the drip line, further if it is possible, to keep heavy equipment from compacting or damaging the roots and soil.

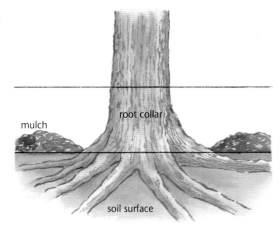

During regrading, avoid piling soil around the root collar of your tree. Keep mulch a few inches away, too.

Liven up mass plantings with a focal point. A birdbath, for example, adds interest to this bed of mums.

A flagstone path admits visitors to the heart of a cottage garden. Low-growing plants between the paving soften the edges.

Adapting an Existing Landscape

In some ways, adapting an existing landscape is more challenging than starting from scratch. Although your yard may have nice features like large trees or an established lawn to work with, you also have someone else's mistakes to undo (or maybe your own, which are even harder to face).

If you've lived with the yard for at least a year, you are probably acutely aware of its troublesome or high-maintenance points. Don't try to change the whole yard at once, or you may create more headaches than you solve. Identify the elements you want to change, and choose a few (or one major one) to work on each year.

Trees and Shrubs

Whenever possible, try to keep existing trees and shrubs. If the shrubs are overgrown, you might be able to give them a face-lift with drastic pruning. If you do decide to remove a tree or shrub, make sure you dig out the stump, too—it's a lot of work, but it will make replanting

much easier, and you won't have to deal with suckers sprouting from the roots. If you are tired of pruning hedges, consider replacing these high-maintenance elements with informal shrub borders.

Flowers

If your existing perennial plants are overgrown, dig them out, divide them, and replant the vigorous outer parts into enriched soil. If they are in the wrong spot, dig and move them in the spring.

If you don't mind replanting them each year, annuals are great for season-long color. For lots of color without the hassle of digging flower beds, consider a few container plantings (if you're willing to do some extra watering).

Lawns

Reduce mowing chores by replacing some of the lawn with shrubs, trees, or groundcovers. Install mowing strips to cut down on edging chores. Make maintenance easier by eliminating grass growing under or along fences and walls, on steep slopes, and under any trees with

low branches or shallow roots, or anywhere where the grass is not green, lush, and thriving.

Paths and Walkways

If your existing paths are in the wrong spot, or made from the wrong material, it's simplest in the long run to rip them up and start again. The paving material you choose should match or complement the style or color of your existing landscape or home. For example, a brick path looks good with a brick home. A stone walk complements a country cottage. The paving material should also be easy to maintain. Although they are expensive to buy, paving block, stone, and brick require little additional maintenance after they are installed.

Make sure your path is wide enough so that it is easy to use. A walk to your door should be 4 feet (1.2 m) wide, spacious enough to accommodate two people walking side by side. It's important too that the path is well drained so you can use it during wet weather and so it won't shift as the soil freezes and thaws.

Designing Your Garden

Creating a Color-Theme Garden

You can design beautiful gardens around a theme as simple as a single color. This may sound plain, but it's anything but that—color-theme gardens are attractive and dramatic additions to any landscape. Even gardens that are based on green leaves contain varying tints and shades, as well as textures and patterns, from the frosty blue-greens of some hostas to the deep glossy green of European wild ginger (*Asarum europaeum*). When you start including flower colors against the greens, you add an extra level of interest. Even if the flowers you choose are all in the same color group, the many different shades and tints create a mosaic of changing colors throughout the season.

Planning a color-theme garden starts by picking the color you want to work with. Try a monochrome (based on one flower color) border if you have a favorite color or love collecting flowers of a particular color. Or make a small monochromatic section part of a long mixed-color border, perhaps using silver foliage to separate it from flowers of other colors.

If you have a couple of unconnected small beds, you might want to try a different color in each. Or choose a single color for the whole garden in each season: perhaps pink for spring, white for summer, and yellow for fall, or whatever colors appeal to you.

Another option to consider is a two-color border. Blue and white make a classic combination. Or perhaps pinks and yellows are more to your liking. Yellow or chartreuse with maroon or burgundy is another popular color combination.

The key to creating a beautiful and effective color-theme garden is to pick the colors that you like and those that blend well with your house. White flowers, for instance, can look dirty

against cream-colored siding, while bright pinks can clash unmercifully with rusty orange brick. Try growing the plants there in a container for a year. If the colors look good to you, go ahead and plan a full-scale garden; if they don't fit the bill, move the pot elsewhere, and try a different combination in that spot next year. If you're not sure exactly which color to choose, think about the time of day you'll usually view the garden and what kind of weather prevails in your area. If your climate tends to be cloudy and misty, whites, yellows, and pastels can be useful for adding a bright touch to your yard. White flowers also tend to glow luminously in twilight or moonlit gardens. If sun shines down on your garden for most of the season, consider bright colors for your theme.

Themes to Try

Hot-Color Borders If knock-your-socks-off color is what you want, consider planning a garden around the hot colors: reds, oranges, and yellows. These colors are ideal for accenting outlying areas of your yard, since they tend to catch your eye from a distance.

Hot-color borders are exciting and vibrant. Yellow gardens have a sunny, cheerful look and are fairly easy to arrange without fear of clashing colors. Reds and oranges make the loudest statements of the various color themes, but red flowers also have the greatest potential to clash with each other. Before planting a whole border of these bright colors, consider trying a small bed or part of a border first to see if you like the effect.

TOP LEFT: Add sparkle to beds and borders by pairing spring bulbs with early annuals.
MIDDLE LEFT: Red flowers look marvelous against green leaves. The contrast of these colors is dynamic and exciting.
BOTTOM LEFT: Bluebells (*Hyacinthoides* spp.) and other early bulbs blend beautifully with spring-flowering shrubs.

Cool Color Borders If you're not especially adventurous in your color choices, a planting of cool colors may be more to your liking. Blue-theme gardens have a cool, restrained look, but they're tricky to pull off successfully. Blue and green are such similar colors that blue flowers tend to blend into the background sea of green leaves. Blues, violets, and greens are best planted where you can see them up close—perhaps along a path or near a deck.

Annuals for an All-Blue Garden

Varying the different kinds of blue—from soft lavender-blue to bright sky blue and deep cobalt blue—is one way to add extra interest to a cool-color planting. Companion plants with silver or chartreuse leaves, such as dusty miller or golden feverfew (*Chrysanthemum parthenium* 'Aureum'), are also excellent additions for contrast.

The following list contains a few blue-flowered annuals you might want to include in your cool-color garden.
Ageratum houstonianum (ageratum)
Brachycome iberidifolia (Swan River daisy)
Browallia speciosa (browallia)
Centaurea cyanus (cornflower)
Consolida ambigua (rocket larkspur)
Convolvulus tricolor (dwarf morning glory)
Ipomoea tricolor (morning glory)
Lobelia erinus (edging lobelia)
Myosotis sylvatica (forget-me-not)
Nemophila menziesii (baby-blue-eyes)
Nigella damascena (love-in-a-mist)
Salvia farinacea (mealy-cup sage)

Perennials for an All-Blue Garden

Blue is also a popular color theme for perennial plantings. Many beloved summer-blooming perennials have blue flowers, including delphiniums, Siberian iris (*Iris sibirica*), bellflowers (*Campanula* spp.), and pincushion flower (*Scabiosa caucasica*).

To extend the season, add blue-flowered shrubs, such as caryopteris (*Caryopteris* x *clandonensis*), and annuals, such as ageratum and lobelia. For spring

Baby-blue-eyes

A silver-and-white garden looks crisp and clean during the day. The light colors stand out at night, too.

color, plant bulbs such as Spanish bluebells (*Hyacinthoides hispanicus*) and Siberian squills (*Scilla sibirica*). For even more choices, expand your list to include the many flowers in the blue-violet range.

Several plants offer bluish foliage; amethyst sea holly (*Eryngium amethystinum*) and blue false indigo (*Baptisia australis*) offer blue flowers as well. Many of the finest hosta cultivars—including 'Krossa Regal', 'Blue Giant', and 'Hadspen Blue'—have cool blue leaves that look super in shady gardens. Rue (*Ruta graveolens*) and blue fescue (*Festuca cinerea*) produce their best blues in full sun. Also include silver foliage, which is stunning in blue borders.

Wonderful White Gardens

All-white designs are sometimes called "moon gardens" because the flowers almost glow under the light of a full moon. This effect can also be achieved under street lights in urban gardens or at the edge of a well-lit patio. Moon gardens include many plants with silver or gray foliage; they may also include flowers in the palest pastels, as these reflect moonlight almost as well as white. For gardens near the house, include fragrant types of white roses, and peonies, along with fragrant annuals such as sweet alyssum and flowering tobacco (*Nicotiana alata*).

Madagascar periwinkle, mealy-cup sage, and yellow cosmos

Pretty Pastel Plantings

Like cool color plantings, soft pinks, yellows, and baby blues planted together tend to have a calm, soothing look. To keep the garden from looking too washed out, consider adding a little spark with some bright whites or a deeper hue of one of the colors—perhaps pure yellow marigolds or bright pink verbena (*Verbena* x *hybrida*). Pink is an easy choice for a color theme, since so many perennials, hardy bulbs, and flowering shrubs come in this color.

Don't Forget Foliage

As you experiment with different color combinations, remember that flowers aren't the only source of color; leaves have lots to offer, too. They come in a surprising array of different greens, from the blue-green of California poppy (*Eschscholzia californica*) to the yellow-green of summer cypress (*Kochia scoparia*) or the deep green of geraniums. Nearly all greens go well together.

Besides the various greens, leaves can come in other colors, too. Silver-leaved plants such as dusty miller look great in almost any kind of garden. Yellowish leaves, such as those of golden feverfew or some coleus, can be pleasing with pinks and blues. You can add a bold spire of color with the blazing red leaves of Joseph's coat (*Amaranthus tricolor*) or a subtle accent with the bronzy leaves of wax begonias.

Creating a Cottage Garden

The ultimate in informality, cottage gardens display a glorious riot of colors, textures, heights, and fragrances. Cottage gardens defy many gardening "rules": Plants are packed closely together, ignoring standard spacing; colors aren't organized into large drifts; tall plants pop up in front of shorter ones; flowers are allowed to flop over and grow through

The bright flowers and ferny foliage of cosmos are excellent additions to a cottage garden. They bloom in late summer.

Sweet pea

each other to create a delightful, casual mixture. While cottage gardens may appear effortless and unorganized, they need to be planned, planted, and maintained just like any other garden.

The classic cottage garden is an eclectic collection of plants, including perennials, annuals, herbs, and roses, allowed to ramble and intertwine. Cottage gardens usually are at least partially enclosed within walls, hedges or fences, making them a natural choice for a small suburban house or a contemporary townhouse with an enclosed yard. You might allow the plants to spread unchecked or to self-sow, letting the seedlings arise where they may. For this to work well, though, you must be willing to do some rearranging if the plants pop up where they're not wanted. Unify the scene with a permanent focal point, such as a path that marches through the garden's center to a door, patio, or bench.

Choosing a Site

Locate cottage gardens next to the house, especially by a door. A rambling rose or flowering vine draped around a door is one of the classic features of a cottage garden. If your front or side yard is small, you may want to devote the whole space to the garden. In this case, a gravel, brick, stone, or even cement path is essential; make it wide (at least 3 feet [90 cm]) to allow room for plants to spill out onto it, softening the edges and creating an attractive, inviting walkway. A wide path tends to make you walk more slowly.

Cottage gardens work best when they're close to the house. A mix of rounded and spiky blooms add interest. Fragrant leaves and flowers are nice too.

Picking the Plants

To create a pleasing jumble rather than a chaotic mess, combine a variety of different flower shapes and sizes. Thinking of flowers in terms of their visual impact will help you get the right balance.

"Feature" flowers are the ones that first catch your eye; they have strong shapes—like spiky lupines (*Lupinus polyphyllus*) and massive peonies—or bright colors.

"Filler" flowers tend to be smaller and less obvious than the feature plants. Baby's-breath is a classic filler flower.

"Edgers" are low plants used in the fronts of beds or spilling over onto paths; think of thymes, edging lobelia, and catmint (*Nepeta* x *faassenii*).

These categories aren't rigid: Lavender and the flowers of lady's mantle (*Alchemilla mollis*) make nice fillers, but both are often used to edge paths as well. Rose campion (*Lychnis coronaria*) works as a filler, but if set among flowers with contrasting colors, its bright magenta flowers may stand out as a feature. The key is to use some flowers that serve each purpose, so you don't have all bright (and probably clashing) feature flowers, all small, modest filler flowers, or all low edging plants.

As you choose plants for the garden, include some that have scented foliage or flowers; fragrance is a traditional part of the cottage garden feeling. It's also important to choose flowers that bloom at different times for a continuous display.

Perennials aren't the only plants you can grow in your cottage garden: Annuals, herbs, shrubs, vines, and bulbs all can have a place in your cottage garden, too. Old-fashioned roses, either shrub types or climbers, are a classic ingredient and an important source of fragrant flowers. Climbing roses or honeysuckles look great trained over a door or archway; let clematis climb up lampposts or railings.

Including unusual and unlikely plants is a long-standing cottage tradition. Accent your cottage garden with dwarf fruit trees, and tuck in some other edibles for surprise: Try colorful lettuces, curly parsley, red-stemmed 'Ruby' chard, and maroon-podded 'Burgundy' okra.

These great cottage garden flowers have been favorites for years. Use feature flowers for bold colors and textures, edging plants to line the front, sides, and edges of paths, and filler flowers to tie the whole design together.

Feature Flowers

Alcea rosea (hollyhock)
Campanula persicifolia (peach-leaved bellflower)
Delphinium x *belladonna* (Belladonna delphinium)
Dictamnus albus (gas plant)
Iris, bearded hybrids (bearded iris)
Iris sibirica (Siberian iris)
Lilium hybrids (lilies)
Lupinus polyphyllus (garden lupine)
Paeonia lactiflora (common garden peony)
Papaver orientale (oriental poppy)
Phlox paniculata (garden phlox)
Verbascum chaixii (nettle-leaved mullein)

Edging Plants

Aubrieta deltoidea (purple rock cress)
Aurinia saxatilis (basket-of-gold)
Campanula portenschlagiana (Dalmatian bellflower)
Cerastium tomentosum (snow-in-summer)
Dianthus gratianpolitanus (cheddar pinks)
Euphorbia epithymoides (cushion spurge)
Heuchera sanguinea (coral bells)
Lobelia erinus (edging lobelia)
Nepeta x *faassenii* (catmint)
Primula vulgaris (English primrose)
Pulmonaria saccharata (Bethlehem sage)

Filler Flowers

Alchemilla mollis (lady's mantle)
Aquilegia x *hybrida* (hybrid columbine)
Aster novae-angliae (New England aster)
Astrantia major (masterwort)
Centaurea hypoleuca (knapweed)
Centranthus ruber (red valerian)
Chrysanthemum x *superbum* (shasta daisy)
Coreopsis verticillata (thread-leaved coreopsis)
Geranium sanguineum (blood-red cranesbill)
Gypsophila paniculata (baby's-breath)
Lychnis coronaria (rose campion)

Creating a Cutting Garden

If you enjoy having armloads of flowers to bring indoors for fresh arrangements, consider adding a cutting garden to your landscape. A cutting garden is simply one or more beds where you grow flowers just for arrangements. You can collect beautiful blooms from your cutting garden without raiding your carefully planned displays in the rest of the yard.

Cutting Garden Basics

Few people have enough space to put a cutting garden truly out of sight, but the more removed it is, the less you'll worry about making it look nice. Some gardeners turn over a corner of their vegetable garden to cut flowers; others create separate cutting beds along a garage, in a sunny side yard, or in a sheltered corner of the backyard.

Wherever you put your cutting beds, you want them to be easy to reach and maintain. Prepare the soil well, sow seeds or set out transplants just as you would for any garden, but don't worry about grouping specific heights and colors; just plant them in rows. Mulch between the rows with a loose organic material (such as straw) to discourage weeds, keep the soil moist, and prevent soil from splashing up on the flowers. Stake floppy or long-stemmed flowers—including peonies, baby's-breath, and delphiniums—to keep the stems upright and the flowers clean.

If you don't want to set aside an area just for cut flowers, you can snip blooms from beds and borders as needed.

The daisy-like blooms of asters and orange coneflowers add bright color and dramatic form to any arrangement.

Choosing Plants for Cutting

Choose plants that will thrive in your growing conditions; if they aren't growing well, they won't produce many flowers. Here are some other things you'll want to consider when you're deciding what plants to include:

- If space is limited, concentrate on growing plants in your favorite flower colors; if you have lots of room, plant a variety of colors to have lots of options.
- Grow plants that have different shapes to keep your arrangements from looking monotonous. Include spiky flowers and foliage for height, flat or round flowers and leaves for mass, and small, airy flowers and leaves for fillers.
- Look for flowers with long stems. Cultivars described as dwarf or compact are great for ornamental plantings, but their stems are usually too short for easy arranging, unless you have small vases.
- For extra special arrangements, include some fragrant flowers.
- Don't forget to include foliage—it adds body and filler to arrangements. Use subtle greens and silvers to emphasize individual flowers or colors; variegated leaves make striking accents.

To add extra excitement to your arrangements, include perennials, annuals, grasses, and hardy bulbs in your cutting garden. Cosmos, snapdragon, larkspur (*Consolida ambigua*), and calendula (*Calendula officinalis*) are a few of the easy-to-grow annuals that are wonderful for fresh arrangements. Ornamental grasses are great for both flowers and foliage. Spray their delicate flowers with lacquer or cheap hairspray to make them last longer.

Collecting Cut Flowers

Taking a little extra care when you collect your flowers and foliage will help them look great over a longer period. In the cool of the morning, harvest flowers that haven't fully opened using sharp clippers or a knife; immediately plunge the stems into a bucket of warm water. As you arrange the flowers, cut the stems to their final lengths under water so no air bubbles enter. Remove leaves that will be below the waterline in the finished arrangement.

After arranging your flowers, fill the vase to the top with water; refill as soon as the level drops. Add a shot of lemon-lime soda or a commercial floral preservative to keep the water fresh. Flowers will last longest in a cool room out of direct light.

Annuals for Cutting

As you decide which annuals you'll grow for cutting, keep in mind that some thrive in the heat of summer while others prefer cooler temperatures. Plan to sow some each of early-, mid-, and late-summer flowers to have a steady supply of blooms.

Following is a list of some suitable annuals and perennials for cutting, along with their normal peak bloom season.

Annuals

Antirrhinum majus (snapdragon; midsummer)
Calendula officinalis (pot marigold; early summer)

Callistephus chinensis (China aster; midsummer)
Celosia cristata (celosia; late summer)
Centaurea cyanus (cornflower; midsummer)
Consolida ambigua (rocket larkspur; midsummer)
Cosmos bipinnatus (cosmos; late summer)
Cosmos sulphureus (yellow cosmos; midsummer)
Dianthus barbatus (sweet William; early summer)
Gaillardia pulchella (blanket flower; midsummer)
Gypsophila elegans (annual baby's-breath; early summer)
Helianthus annuus (common sunflower; late summer)
Iberis umbellata (annual candytuft; early summer)
Lathyrus odoratus (sweet pea; early summer)
Matthiola incana (stock; early summer)
Rudbeckia hirta (black-eyed Susan; midsummer)
Tithonia rotundifolia (Mexican sunflower; late summer)
Viola x wittrockiana (pansy; early summer)
Zinnia elegans (zinnia; midsummer)

Perennials
Achillea filipendulina (fern-leaved yarrow; summer)
Alchemilla mollis (lady's-mantle; early summer)
Aster novae-angliae (New England aster; late summer)
Astrantia major (masterwort; midsummer)
Baptisia australis (blue false indigo; early summer)
Boltonia asteroides (boltonia; late summer)
Chrysanthemum x superbum (shasta daisy; summer)
Delphinium x belladonna (belladonna delphinium; summer)
Dictamnus albus (gas plant; early summer)
Echinacea purpurea (purple coneflower; midsummer)
Helenium autumnale (common sneezeweed; late summer)
Heuchera sanguinea (coral bells; summer)

Iris spp. (irises; early summer)
Liatris spicata (spike gayfeather; midsummer)
Lilium hybrids (lilies; summer)
Monarda didyma (bee balm; summer)
Narcissus hybrids (daffodils; spring)
Nepeta x faassenii (catmint; early summer)
Phlox paniculata (garden phlox; midsummer)
Physostegia virginiana (obedient plant; late summer)
Platycodon grandiflorus (balloon flower; summer)
Rudbeckia fulgida (orange coneflower; midsummer)
Salvia x superba (violet sage; midsummer)
Scabiosa caucasica (pincushion flower; summer)
Thermopsis caroliniana (Carolina lupine; early summer)

Easy Everlasting Flowers
"Everlasting" annuals, which include strawflowers and statice, produce papery flowers or showy seedpods that hold their color when they dry. They can be used in either fresh or dried arrangements, although most people grow them specifically with drying in mind.

For best results, pick flowers for drying in the morning, before they are fully open and when the dew has dried. To keep the stems straight and stiff for easy arranging, separate them into groups of six to eight stems, secure the stems with a rubber band, and hang them upside down. A dark, dry place is best for drying, since those conditions help to preserve the colors. Many gardeners use a garage, barn, or attic. Hang the bunches from a clothes-drying rack, or suspend them from lines strung between the rafters.

Best Annuals for Drying
Ammobium alatum (winged everlasting)
Carthamus tinctorius (safflower)
Celosia cristata (cockscomb)
Gomphrena globosa (globe amaranth)
Helichrysum bracteatum (strawflower)
Helipterum mangelsii (Swan River everlasting)
Limonium sinuatum (annual statice)
Lunaria annua (honesty)
Molucella laevis (bells-of-Ireland)
Nigella damascena (love-in-a-mist)
Scabiosa stellata (drumstick flower)
Xeranthemum annuum (immortelle)

Gardening with Fragrance
Plants with fragrant leaves and flowers have a place in any landscape. There's nothing like the fresh scent of mint to perk you up after a long day at the office. And who could resist resting on a cozy garden bench near a patch of peonies in full, fragrant bloom? A pot or window box of basil in the kitchen not only scents the

Strawflowers are great for cutting gardens, since you can use them in either fresh or dried arrangements.

Heady-scented roses are a classic part of a fragrance garden. Combine them with perennials for extra color.

air, but keeps insects away as well. In beds, borders, cottage gardens, container gardens, and foundation plantings, mixing in some scented plants will add an extra special touch to your yard.

Fragrance in Flowers

When you mention fragrance in the garden, most people automatically think of flowers. Peonies and lilies are probably the most well known, but many other plants have pleasing scents as well.

Traditionally, scented flowers were grown close to the house so their fragrance could be appreciated through open doors and windows. They're equally nice near outdoor eating areas, patios, and porches—any place where people linger. Raised planters are great for short, fragrant flowers so you don't have to get down on your hands and knees to enjoy the scents.

Many fragrant flowers are also beautiful, so you can enjoy looking at them and sniffing them as you walk around or work in the yard. Cutting these flowers for arrangements brings this pleasure indoors.

Fragrance in Foliage

A number of plants have fragrant foliage, but you need to touch these to smell them. Plant lavender and bee balm (*Monarda didyma*) at the edge of paths where you'll brush against them as you walk by. Grow lemon balm (*Melissa officinalis*) near a garden seat or in a raised container so you can easily rub the leaves to release their delicious lemony odor. Some plants, like wormwood (*Artemisia absinthium*) and rue (*Ruta graveolens*) have leaves with a pungent scent that some people find pleasing and others find disagreeable; try sniffing these plants before you buy.

Buying and Growing Fragrant Plants

The real key to having a scented garden that you enjoy is smelling plants before you buy them. The fragrance that a friend raves about may be undetectable or even unpleasant to you. Visit nurseries or public gardens when the plants you want are blooming, and sniff the flowers or foliage to see what you think. Different cultivars of the same plant may vary widely in their scents, so smell them all before you choose.

Just as a bed of many different flower colors can look jumbled, a mixture of many strong fragrances can be distracting or even downright repulsive. As you plan your garden, try to arrange it with just one or two scented plants in bloom at any given time. That way, you can enjoy different fragrances all through the season without being overwhelmed by too many at once. Some plants release their scent only at night and they can be overpowering, particularly on hot summer nights, so try to sniff them several times at night before you decide to buy them for your garden.

Favorite Fragrant Annuals

Cheiranthus cheiri (wallflower)
Dianthus barbatus (sweet William)
Dianthus chinensis (China pink)
Heliotropium arborescens (common heliotrope)
Ipomoea alba (moonflower)
Lathyrus odoratus (sweet pea)
Lobularia maritima (sweet alyssum)
Matthiola incana (stock)
Mirabilis jalapa (four-o'clock)
Nicotiana alata (flowering tobacco)
Petunia x *hybrida* (petunia)
Tagetes hybrids (marigolds)

Perennials for Fragrance

There are perennials with fragrant and unfragrant cultivars. This list includes the names of a few of the fragrant ones.
Convallaria majalis (lily-of-the-valley): flowers
Dianthus gratianopolitanus (cheddar pinks): flowers
Hemerocallis hybrids (daylilies): flowers of a few (mainly yellow) types
Lavandula angustifolia (lavender): leaves and flowers
Lilium hybrids (lilies): flowers of some types, including regal lilies, trumpet hybrids, and oriental hybrids (such as 'Casa Blanca'), and *L. speciosum* 'Rubrum'
Narcissus hybrids (daffodils): flowers of some cultivars, including 'Geranium', 'Cragford', 'Actaea', 'Minnow', 'Baby Moon', 'Pipit', and 'Cheerfulness'
Nepeta x *faassenii* (catmint): leaves
Paeonia lactiflora (common garden peony): flowers of some cultivars, including 'Festiva Maxima', 'Pink Parfait', 'Sara Bernhardt', 'Edulis Superba', and 'Big Ben'

Lily-of-the-valley

A mixture of bulbs, perennials, annuals, and grasses creates a cheerful meadow garden scene with little maintenance.

Making a Meadow

Natural gardens combine the beauty of local wildflowers with an informal, often low-maintenance, design. The most popular of these are meadow gardens—informal blends of flowers and grasses growing in a sunny, open spot. They provide food and shelter for birds, beneficial insects, and butterflies. They also add a casual, country touch to any yard. Best of all, established meadows require little upkeep.

If you don't have room for a whole meadow, you can create a meadow look in a smaller garden by using plenty of reliable cultivated perennials and mixing in meadow flowers and grasses among them. Common perennials that are natural choices for most meadow gardens include butterfly weed (*Asclepias tuberosa*), New England aster (*Aster novae-angliae*), purple coneflower (*Echinacea purpurea*), and bee balm (*Monarda didyma*). Look in wildflower gardening books or check with local wildflower societies to find out which plants grow best in your area.

If lawn mowing is a chore you dread, consider replacing at least part of the grass with wildflowers. Once you get them established, a few hours weeding every year and an annual mowing will keep them looking good.

Steps to a Great-Looking Meadow

Once you've chosen the plants that will be in your meadow, you'll need to help them gain a roothold by preparing a good seedbed. You can't just scatter seed in a lawn or open piece of ground and expect good results.

1. Pick a site with well-drained soil and at least six hours of sun a day.
2. In spring, summer, or fall, remove existing grasses and aggressive weeds; lawn grasses can spread vigorously and smother small, new plants. Skim off slices of turf with a spade. Compost the

pieces of sod you remove or use them to fill holes in the remaining lawn.

3. Spread 1 to 2 inches (2.5 to 5 cm) of compost over the area, and dig or till it into the top 4 to 6 inches (10 to 15 cm) of soil. Use a rake to remove any rocks and smooth the soil.

4. To reduce the bank of weed seeds in the soil, water the area thoroughly to encourage surface weed seeds to sprout; then rake or hoe shallowly to kill the seedlings. Repeat the process several times before planting. Or use mulch instead of watering and hoeing; cover the area with black plastic or at least 12 layers of newspaper.

5. In fall, set out your meadow perennials, grasses, and bulbs, and mulch them well. By spring, the roots will be well established, and your plants will be ready to put on great growth.

6. In spring, if you wish, rake away some mulch to sow annual wildflower seeds between the perennial meadow plants. Annuals will provide quick color the first year while the perennials are getting established.

7. Through the first growing season, water your meadow when the top 1 to 2 inches (2.5 to 5 cm) of soil is dry to help the growing young plants get established.

Routine Meadow Maintenance

Mow your meadow once a year to keep it looking good and to keep weeds, shrubs, and trees from invading. Late fall to early winter, after plants have formed seeds, is the best time. If you want to feed the birds, leave seed heads standing until late winter or early spring; just be aware that they'll be harder to mow after winter rain and snow have beaten them down.

Cut the whole meadow to a height of about 6 inches (15 cm). Use a sickle-bar mower for large areas; a string trimmer or hand clippers can handle small patches. A regular lawn mower won't work; it cuts too low. Leave trimmings in place so plants can self-sow, or collect them for your compost pile.

Aside from the yearly trim, your only maintenance is to dig out tree seedlings and aggressive weeds such as quack grass, poison ivy, bindweed, and burdock as soon as they appear. Established meadows don't require water, fertilizer, or mulch. As the plants get established, your meadow garden will look different each year, but it will always be beautiful.

Marvelous Meadow Perennials

The recipe for a magnificent meadow includes a blend of tough perennial flowers and noninvasive perennial grasses, with a dash of daffodils and other naturalized spring bulbs for early color. Below you'll find some suggested flowers you can consider for your moist or dry site, along with some great meadow grasses.

Perennials for Dry Meadows

Achillea filipendulina (fern-leaved yarrow)
Asclepias tuberosa (butterfly weed)
Baptisia australis (blue false indigo)
Echinacea purpurea (purple coneflower)
Gaillardia x *grandiflora* (blanket flower)
Helianthus x *multiflorus* (perennial sunflower)
Liatris spicata (spike gayfeather)
Oenothera tetragona (common sundrops)
Rudbeckia fulgida (orange coneflower)
Solidago rigida (stiff goldenrod)

Perennials for Moist Meadows

Aster novae-angliae (New England aster)
Chelone glabra (white turtlehead)
Eupatorium maculatum (spotted Joe-Pye weed)
Eupatorium rugosum (white snakeroot)
Filipendula rubra (queen-of-the-prairie)
Helenium autumnale (common sneezeweed)
Lobelia cardinalis (cardinal flower)

Meadow and woodland gardens are excellent options for brightening up out-of-the-way corners.

Physostegia virginiana (obedient plant)
Thermopsis caroliniana (Carolina lupine)

Great Grasses for Meadows

Andropogon virginicus (broomsedge)
Bouteloua curtipendula (sideoats grama grass)
Festuca spp. (fescues)
Schizachyrium scoparium (little bluestem)
Sporobolus heterolepis (prairie dropseed)

Woodland Gardens

If you have a wooded lot, take advantage of the shade to create a woodland garden. To brighten the area in early spring (before the trees leaf out and shade the area), try early blooming woodland wildflowers like wood anemone (*Anemone nemorosa*), wild columbine (*Aquilegia canadensis*), Virginia bluebell (*Mertensia virginica*), and common bleeding heart (*Dicentra spectabilis*). To extend the season of interest, add ferns and shade-tolerant perennials that retain their handsome foliage all season. These include hostas, lungwort (*Pulmonaria saccharata*), Lenten rose (*Helleborus orientalis*), Siberian bugloss (*Brunnera macrophylla*), and Solomon's seal (*Polygonatum odoratum*).

Plant your rock garden with flowers and foliage plants to add year-round interest and splashes of seasonal color.

A bog garden is a great site for many kinds of irises. The flowers are beautiful in early summer, and the spiky leaves look great all season.

Rock Gardens

Some plants are particularly attractive grouped among rocks in a wall or rock garden. They grow best in full sun and soils that have exceptionally good drainage and low fertility. Some, such as perennial candytuft (*Iberis sempervirens*), wall rock cress (*Arabis caucasica*), and basket-of-gold (*Aurinia saxatilis*), cascade gracefully over the rock surface. Others, like the more petite Labrador violets (*Viola labradorica*) and primroses (*Primula* spp.), as well as a host of unusual alpine plants, nestle between the rocks. All of these plants are delightful choices for planting on rocky slopes, in raised beds, or in dry stone retaining walls.

Bog Gardens

Some plants have an affinity for wet ground and will thrive at the edge of a pond or in boggy or marshy areas. Plants for low, moist areas include Japanese iris (*Iris ensata*), goat's beard (*Aruncus dioicus*), marsh marigold (*Caltha palustris*), and cardinal flower (*Lobelia cardinalis*).

If you do not have a naturally wet area but enjoy the beauty of bog plants, you can create your own bog. Dig a trench at least 12 inches (30 cm) deep and line it with a heavy plastic pond liner. Put a soaker hose on the top of the plastic and refill the trench with humus-rich soil. The open end of the hose should protrude slightly so that you can attach it to your garden hose and fill the "bog" with water. Repeat as necessary to keep the soil moist.

Container Gardens

If you live in a high-rise apartment building or condo where you have no ground for a garden, you can create a lush green oasis with container-grown plants on a tiny balcony or outdoor stairway. City dwellers can grow large gardens entirely in containers on building rooftops. Even if you have nothing but a wall and windows to call your own, you can fill hanging baskets with trailing plants and pack window boxes full of flowers, herbs, and vegetables.

Annuals make perfect container plants. They grow quickly, flower profusely, and provide a long season of

A large container can support a pleasing mixture of bushy and trailing plants.

good looks. Some also offer distinctive foliage, while others perfume the air with their sweet scents. Groups of small- and medium-sized containers create charming spots of movable color; large planters can showcase a stunning mix of colorful flowers in a relatively small space. Window boxes and hanging baskets are other options for displaying a wide range of flowering and foliage annuals.

Wonderful Window Boxes

Nothing adds country charm to a house like lush window boxes dripping with cascades of colorful flowers and foliage. While the general principles of container planting apply here, there are a few special tips to keep in mind to plan and maintain great-looking window boxes.

Treasure flower

- Consider the site. Before you put up any window boxes, make sure you'll be able to reach them easily for watering and maintenance. Also check that the ledges or brackets that hold the window box are strong enough for the purpose. Because window boxes are so visible, it's especially important to keep them well groomed; that means regularly removing spent flowers.
- Stick with short plants. Window boxes are usually planted to be seen from the outside, but you also need to consider the view from the inside. It's generally best to stick with plants no taller than about 8 inches (20 cm); those much taller than that can block your view.
- Choose compatible colors. Look for flower and foliage colors that complement those of the house and trim. Silvers and whites look crisp and cool against warm-toned brick, for instance, while blues and purples look pretty against cream colors, and pinks and yellows add life to somber gray siding.

Creating Your Garden

This is the hands-in-the-soil part of gardening, the ongoing, regular garden maintenance that separates the gardening dilettante from the gardener-for-life. It is the essence of good gardening.

Buying and Selecting Plants

For many people, choosing and buying plants is one of the most pleasurable aspects of creating a new garden. In the frenzy of shopping, it's easy to get carried away and go home with lots of plants you don't really need. But with a little preparation, you can take your time and get the right plant at the right price.

Begin your search in the depths of winter by browsing through the colorful and informative mail-order catalogs. Make a list of plants that appeal to you and that will suit your growing conditions. When the planting season comes, go shopping at plant sales, nurseries, garden centers, and greenhouses.

There are a few common temptations to avoid. First of all, don't fall for every pretty flower. A plant blooming in the protected environment of a greenhouse may be lovely, but its beauty does not tell you whether it is prone to problems or whether it will be suited to your garden conditions. If you see a plant you love but know little about, take a 24-hour cooling-off period. Do a little research on its preferred growing conditions, seasonal appearance, and potential problems. If you find it will grow well in the conditions your garden has to offer, determine if you have a place for it.

Second, use the same frame of mind to shop for plants as you would to expand your wardrobe. When you need a new shirt or skirt, you look for one that fits with the rest of your clothes. Likewise, buy only those plants that will work into your garden plans. If you like a little garden spontaneity, leave openings here and there for trial plants.

Finally, if you simply cannot resist buying or saving every plant that catches your eye, perhaps you are a candidate for a casual cottage garden rather than a more formal perennial bed or border.

Buying Healthy Plants

One of the most basic steps in preventing pest and disease problems is starting with healthy, pest-free plants. They'll become established in their new home quickly, and

When you combine plants that have similar needs, it's easy to provide the right care to keep them in top condition.

you'll avoid importing pests and plant pathogens that could spread to other plants in your garden.

Start with a Strategy

Problem prevention begins long before the growing season starts. When you're making up your list of possible plants from seed catalogs and garden books, look for plants with resistance to the pests and diseases that occur locally.

Consider the Container

Some vegetable seedlings, like zucchini and cucumbers, and herbs, like dill and parsley, don't transplant well. Look for seedlings growing in peat pots. At planting time, you can plant the whole seedling, pot and all; that way, you'll avoid disturbing the root system. Otherwise, the shock of transplanting can weaken these plants and make them more susceptible to disease and pest attack.

TOP: Gently slide a plant from its pot to check the roots before buying. Avoid plants with massed or circling roots.
BOTTOM: Good-quality plants will have healthy white roots that are still growing through the soil ball.

Inspect the Root System

Strong, healthy roots are a vital part of determining plant health. If a plant is growing in a plastic or clay container, gently remove the container and look at the roots. Roots should penetrate the soil without circling the outside of the root ball. They should be uniformly white, moist, and without breaks, bumps, or brown spots. Several exposed roots don't indicate stress, but avoid plants with lots of matted roots or plants that are tightly rooted to their neighbors. These plants have been sitting around for a long time in a small pot, and separating closely rooted plants can severely damage the individual root systems. It shocks the young plants and can set them back by several weeks as they grow new roots.

Check the soil, too. It should be evenly moist, or at least moist just below the surface. Plants that are allowed to dry out frequently become stressed and weakened, and their growth may be stunted.

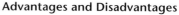

Check Plant Color

Healthy seedlings are usually deep green, although you can expect color to vary among plants and cultivars. An overall pale, washed-out appearance often indicates that a nutrient is lacking. If you're not sure what a particular plant is supposed to look like, compare it with a photo from a book or catalog. This will help you determine if those stripes, spots, or colors are normal or if they indicate a deficiency of some kind.

Probe for Problems

Examine plants carefully before you buy them and reject any with signs of pests or their damage. As you inspect the foliage, make sure you turn the leaves over and check their undersides as well as the tops; lower leaf surfaces are favorite pest hideouts. Common signs of insect and other pest damage include:

- Leaves with chewed holes or edges
- Shiny slime trails
- Webs on leaves or stems
- Tiny eggs on leaves or stems
- Brown or greenish droppings
- Wilted, curled, or discolored leaves.

Don't forget to look for signs of diseases during your inspection. Also look at other plants growing in the same area—if they are showing signs of disease, another plant that looks healthy may already be infected. Common symptoms of

disease, nutrient deficiency or environmental damage include:

- Spotty, discolored, or wilted leaves
- Dead areas in leaves or stems
- Fuzzy patches of fungal spores
- Leaves, roots, or stems with a soggy appearance.

How to Buy Plants

A good local nursery or garden center—one that offers a variety of plants and takes good care of them—is a real treasure. Usually its staff members are good sources of information specific to your area, such as which plants grow well there. The nursery may even have a demonstration garden where you can see how plants look when full grown and compare different cultivars.

If you begin with healthy plants your garden has a better chance of being pest- and disease-resistant.

Advantages and Disadvantages

One advantage of buying locally is that you can inspect plants before buying them. Also, your plants won't have to suffer through shipping. Most nurseries and garden centers offer container-grown plants, which are easiest to handle. On the down side, your selection may be limited in color and variety, and the plants may be more expensive.

Buying Tips

When you have a choice, select small, vigorous-looking plants; they'll grow faster and soon outpace larger, already-blooming plants. While it's fun to see what flowers you're getting (and sometimes you'll want to make sure you get just the right color), it's generally better to buy and plant perennials before they bloom. That way, they can settle into the garden and establish new roots before they use their energy for flowering.

With bulbs, purchase the largest size you can afford for flower beds and borders. Smaller-sized bulbs are great for naturalizing in lawns and low-maintenance areas, and you can sometimes buy quantities of 50 or 100 at a reduced price. Choose bulbs that are plump and firm with no soft spots or moldy areas.

Buying by Mail

If you want unusual plants, don't have access to a local nursery, or want to get the best possible prices, mail-order sources provide limitless possibilities. Write for catalogs several months before you want to plant so you'll have time to compare selections and prices. Some catalogs are great sources of information on the virtues of specific plants and cultivars; a few even have color photos and useful planting and growing information.

Advantages and Disadvantages

Catalog shopping is a fun way to while away dreary winter evenings, and it's convenient, too. You can learn about exciting new plants and often find good prices when you compare several catalogs. On the down side, you don't really know what you're paying for until you get it. Shipping stress can weaken even the strongest plants. If you get bareroot perennials (with roots that are wrapped in packing material), they'll need to be planted or potted up immediately.

Buying Tips

The best approach to ordering by mail is to ask gardening friends which catalogs they've ordered from and which they would buy from again. If you don't know anyone who orders by catalog, visit a library and get addresses and phone numbers from advertisements in recent gardening magazines.

When you order from a source for the first time, just buy a few plants and see how they look. If you're happy with the quality for the price, order more; otherwise, shop elsewhere. Remember, if an offer sounds too good to be true, it probably is!

Inspect mail-order plants as soon as they arrive. If they are damaged, you should return them; contact the source right away to find out how to do so. Mail-order perennials are often shipped when they are dormant (not actively growing) and may look dead. Plant them anyway and water them well. If they don't produce any buds or new growth in a few weeks, contact the source.

If your plants were shipped in pots, water as needed and keep them out of bright sunlight for the first few days. Mail-order plants may also arrive bareroot—without any pot or soil. If they're bulbs, they're happy that way; keep them cool and in the dark until you're ready to plant. Other bareroot plants need more attention; for best results, plant them within a day or two after they arrive. If you can't plant right away, keep the packing material moist—not soggy—and store the plants in a cool, shaded place. If there isn't any packing material, soak the roots in room-temperature water for an hour or two, then wrap with damp paper towels or cover with compost.

Different Ways to Buy Plants

There are several ways to buy plants— container-grown, containerized, bareroot, field-dug, and balled-and-burlapped. Each method has advantages and disadvantages. The planting techniques you use will depend on the way the plants were grown and sold. Whatever type you buy, keep plants protected from wind and sun when you transport them home.

Container-Grown Plants

Perennials, shrubs, and vines are most commonly sold in containers. Container-grown plants are convenient and easy to handle. Keep the pots in a well-lit location until you are ready to plant. Then you can slide the root ball out and plant it in the garden. The transition will cause minimal disturbance.

However, there is a catch. Horticultural researchers are finding that roots tend to stay in the light, fluffy "soil" of synthetic mixes, rather than branching out into the surrounding garden soil. But you can prevent this from happening by loosening the roots on the outside of the ball and spreading them out into the soil as you plant.

Container-grown plants come in different sizes, so their prices vary widely. Larger-sized pots, usually 1- and 2-gallon (4.5- to 9-L) containers, are generally more expensive. The cost may be worthwhile if you need immediate garden impact. On the other hand, you can buy younger plants inexpensively in multicell packs or small pots. You'll have to wait a year or more for them to fill out and bloom, but young plants tend to become established in the garden faster than older ones, catching up to the bigger plants in a short time. Often, too, they grow into healthier, more vigorous specimens than larger transplants.

Your local garden center will sell a wide variety of colorful plants, but mail-order sources will have even more uncommon kinds.

Bareroot Plants

You will come across many species of dormant bareroot plants for sale early in the growing season. Bareroot trees should be bought and planted from late fall to early spring. In late summer or early fall, you can also find bareroot items such as bearded irises, common bleeding heart (*Dicentra spectabilis*), peonies, and oriental poppies. You may choose to buy bareroot plants to save money—they are usually less expensive than large container-grown plants—or you may receive them unexpectedly. Mail-order companies often send plants bareroot to save on space and shipping. You open the box to find long spidery roots and—at best—a small tuft of foliage. These plants look more dead than alive, but fortunately, in this case looks are deceiving. If you keep the roots moist and cool and plant them quickly and properly, most plants will recover and thrive. The roots will easily adjust to your garden's soil, whereas the roots of container-grown plants have to make the transition from the nursery soil to yours.

Most deciduous trees, shrubs, and vines can be successfully grown from bareroot stock. Don't buy large trees or any evergreens bareroot; their roots can dry out easily, causing damage that's very hard to overcome.

When the plants arrive, tend to them promptly. Open the box to let some air in. Your plants' roots should be wrapped in a protective medium like shredded newspaper, excelsior, or sphagnum moss. Keep this medium moist but not soggy. When it's time to plant, soak the roots in a bucket of lukewarm water for a few hours, then plant. If you can't plant right away, keep the roots moist and store them, in their original package, in a cool location for a day or two. If you need to wait longer than that to plant, pot up the roots or set them into a nursery bed until you are ready. Trees should be temporarily "heeled in" by laying them along a shallow trench in a shady, protected area and covering their roots with soil.

Containerized Plants

Not to be confused with container-grown plants, containerized or processed-balled plants are initially dug bareroot. Their roots are then packed or potted in organic matter or potting medium, not field soil. As with bareroot stock, most of the roots are left behind in the field. When you buy, check inside the packing or slip the pot off and look for new roots. If all you find are a few large, cut roots but no fine, small roots, don't buy the plant. The nursery didn't hold it long enough for new roots to grow, and the plant will be slow to establish.

Big or Little?

In general, the smaller the plant, the less transplant shock it will undergo. It will begin putting out new roots and leaves sooner than larger plants and may quickly catch up in size. But what if you want to establish a garden quickly? Buy the largest plants you can afford and properly handle, or, in the case of large trees and shrubs, have the nursery plant them. Many nurseries offer warranties on plants that they install.

Container-grown plants should have healthy top growth that is in proportion to the container. You can plant them anytime during the growing season.

Field-Dug Plants

You may be able to find a farmer, hobbyist plant breeder, plant collector, or nursery owner who will sell you mature plants dug from the field. If you handle the root ball carefully, you can move field-dug plants much later into the summer than bareroot plants because the roots are protected by soil. To transport it, set the root ball, surrounded by soil, in a firm wooden flat or sturdy bucket. Cover it with a moist towel, damp peat moss, or compost to keep the roots and soil moist. Replant it as soon as you get home.

Balled-and-Burlapped Plants

These are field-dug plants, usually larger trees and shrubs, with a ball of soil around the roots. The soil ball is wrapped in natural burlap or synthetic material. They are wrapped in this way either because they resent being transplanted bareroot, or so that you can plant them even when they are not dormant. B&B plants are often the most expensive, and the soil ball makes them heavier to handle. Be sure the root ball is large enough to support and anchor your plant. Properly handled root balls should be well wrapped, firm, and moist. Avoid lifting B&B plants by the trunk, and handle them carefully or the root ball might break apart and damage the roots. Keep them in the shade, covered thickly with mulch, and water often until you can plant them.

Since B&B stock comes with soil, plants have to make the transition from the nursery soil to yours. The difference in soil type can cause uneven water distribution, so water deeply and check the soil moisture regularly. There is no need to remove the burlap wrapping when planting.

Preparing for Planting

When to Start

If you can, prepare planting areas at least a month before you plant to give soil time to settle. Ideally, start in the fall for spring planting, or in spring for fall planting.

Start digging when the soil is moist, but not wet. Digging moist soil is relatively easy, but dry soil requires extra effort, and working soil that's soggy can turn it into rock-like lumps. After two or three days without rain, dig up a shovelful in a couple of different spots and test for moisture by squeezing a handful of soil. If the soil oozes through your fingers or forms a sticky lump, it's too wet; wait a few days and repeat the test before digging. If the soil is dry and powdery or hard, water the area thoroughly and wait a day or two to dig.

Time your planting efforts so your new plants will start growing in a period of abundant rainfall and moderate temperatures—usually spring or fall. Check planting instructions on the plant label and refer to the USDA Hardiness Zone Map on page 310 to find out what climate zone you live in.

Preparing the Planting Bed

Along with proper plant selection, preparing a good planting bed is critical to the success of your garden. If you do a thorough job here, you will be rewarded by quicker plant establishment and less weeding.

Making New Beds

First lay out the area you want to dig, as you determined when you drew up your garden plan. Use stakes and string for marking the straight sides; lay out curves with a rope or garden hose. Step back and double-check your layout from several viewpoints, including indoors.

Next, remove existing grass and weeds. Slice off manageable pieces of sod by cutting small squares, then sliding your spade just under the roots. Toss the sod into the compost pile or use it to repair bare spots in your lawn. As an alternative, you can kill the grass by covering it with black plastic. It's unattractive, but effective. However, it can take several weeks or more than a month depending on the weather—the hotter it is outside the faster the plastic works. Till in the turf when it has decayed. Pull out as many weed roots as you can. You may have to follow those like docks (*Rumex* spp.) and bindweeds (*Convolvulus* spp.) for quite some distance to get the entire root

1. To prepare a new bed, start by outlining the edge with rope or string.
2. Use a spade to strip off the sod and expose the soil.
3. If a soil test indicates the site is too acid, apply an even layer of lime to the soil.
4. Spread a layer of compost over the surface and work it into the bed.

system. If you merely snap off the top, the root will probably resprout.

Once you've cleared the beds, it's time to break up the soil. Consider your choice of tools carefully. Decades ago, gardeners turned the soil with shovels, garden spades, forks, and other hand tools. In recent years, many have turned to rotary tillers. These machines can churn the top 5 to 6 inches (12.5 to 15 cm) of soil with much less effort on your part. However, tillers aren't always the best choice. Excessive tilling, or tilling when the soil is too wet or too dry, will break up the granular soil structure into tiny particles and lead to soil compaction. If you choose to use a rotary tiller, make sure you work the soil when it's evenly moist.

If you're using a spade or shovel, dig down as far as your spade will reach and turn over this top layer of the soil. For even better results, double dig the bed. Double-digging loosens the soil to twice the depth of single digging, providing ideal conditions for great root growth and helping to correct heavy or poorly drained soil.

Once your soil is loose, mix in fertilizer to feed the plants, and organic matter to condition the soil. Any balanced organic fertilizer will do. Scatter the fertilizer over the planting area at the application rate listed on the label.

Now spread a very thick layer of organic matter over the entire area. It should be at least 4 inches (10 cm) deep to be effective. If your soil feels as loose as a kid's sandbox (indicating drainage that's too fast) or if puddles always remain after a rain (indicating poor drainage), add even more organic matter. Use less if you want to grow yarrows, artemisias, and other plants that grow best in dry, sunny sites.

Dealing with Problem Soils

Planting naturally well-adapted species is the best way to handle problem soils, particularly those with slow drainage. Building raised beds and filling them with improved soil is an option for shallow-rooted plants. But the roots of trees and many shrubs will soon outgrow the beds. If your soil is extremely sandy or clayey, save your raised beds for flowers and vegetables, and choose species of trees, shrubs, and vines that are compatible with your soil conditions.

Compost is the best source of organic matter; if you don't have enough, you may be able to buy more at your local garden center. Leaves are excellent, too; run the lawn mower over piles to chop them first or mix them with grass clippings. Sawdust and straw are good if you also add a source of nitrogen (in the form of manure or bloodmeal) to help them decompose. Manure alone is fine but can contain many weed seeds. Whichever material you choose, mix it well into the top 8 inches (20 cm) of soil.

After digging in the fertilizer and organic matter, water the area thoroughly. Remember to let the soil sit for a month before planting to give the organic matter time to break down (unless you used well-decomposed compost, in which case you could plant right away). Rake just before planting to level the bed.

Double-Digging for Great Plant Growth

Digging the top 8 inches (20 cm) or so of your soil will provide good growing conditions for most plants. But in many cases, digging twice as deep can give you twice the benefits. Double-digging is a useful technique for breaking up compacted soil below the surface, improving drainage. It also provides twice the rooting room for deeper-rooted plants, like perennials. There's no doubt about it—double-digging is a lot of work. Fortunately, the beneficial effects can last for years. And the strong, vigorous growth of your plants will more than repay the few hours of sweat you invested before planting.

Before digging, make sure the soil is at the right moisture level, or you may end

up doing more harm than good. If the soil is too dry, soak the area and then wait a few days before digging. If you are preparing a new area, strip off the sod before double-digging.

Start at one edge of the area by digging a 1-foot (30-cm) wide, 8- to 12-inch (20- to 30-cm) deep trench. Put the soil you are digging in a wheelbarrow. Spread a 1- to 2-inch (2.5- to 5-cm) layer of finely textured organic matter such as compost or aged manure over the newly exposed soil in the trench, and add any fertilizers or amendments the soil needs—perhaps lime or sulfur to adjust the pH, or maybe a source of phosphorus. Use a spading fork to loosen the subsoil by sticking the tines through the amendments and wiggling them in the soil.

Then step backward to dig the second trench. Slide the soil from this 1-foot (30-cm) strip into the first trench, then work organic matter and amendments into the newly exposed bottom layer of soil. Repeat the process of moving a top layer and loosening the bottom layer until you get to the last strip. Cover the last bottom layer with the soil from the first trench in the wheelbarrow.

All that loosening and amending will raise the soil level a few inches. Give it a few weeks to settle before you plant, keeping it moistened in dry weather. Never walk directly on the loosened soil, or you'll undo all your hard work by compacting the soil. If you must step into the bed, lay broad boards over the bed, and walk on those instead; lift the boards when you're done.

TOP: In poor soil, double-digging can help give your plants the best possible start in life.

BOTTOM: Compost bins can be attractive as well as functional—use locally available materials to make your own.

Making and Using Compost

Compost is the key to success in any kind of gardening. It is a balanced blend of recycled garden, yard, and household

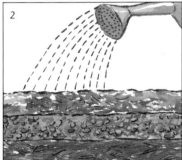

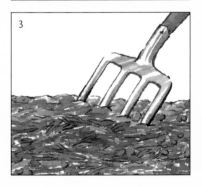

MAKING HOT, FAST COMPOST

1. Build your compost heap with equal amounts of high-carbon and high-nitrogen materials; add in layers or mix them up.

2. As you add new materials, sprinkle them with a watering can to keep them moist and to encourage decomposition.

3. Aerate the compost pile by turning it once every couple of days using a garden fork. This hastens the microbial activity.

wastes that have broken down into dark, crumbly organic matter. The time you spend making compost and applying it to your garden will be more than returned by improved soil and plant health.

Composting is the best way to dispose of garden and kitchen wastes, and it provides you with a free supply of organic fertilizer and soil conditioner at the same time. In addition, beneficial organisms present in finished compost may help to prevent some plant pathogens from infecting your plants in the garden.

Making compost is a lot like cooking—you mix together ingredients, stir them up, and let them "cook." But with a compost pile, the source of heat isn't electricity or gas—it's decomposer organisms like bacteria and fungi that live in soil and break down dead plant and animal tissues. These organisms work best when given warmth, moisture, plenty of oxygen, and the correct balance of carbon and nitrogen.

Composting can be fast and labor-intensive or slow and simple, depending on your needs and energy. You don't need any fancy materials to start composting—just a level, well-drained site. If you have lots of room and don't mind the appearance, you can have an uncontained heap. If you like things to be tidy, you can build a bin or pen out of wood, cement blocks, or woven wire fencing, or you can buy an already-made bin. Besides keeping the compost materials in one neat pile, a container will help keep pets and wildlife out. Choose a shady, well-drained spot for your compost pile. For your convenience, put it as close to your garden as possible.

Ingredients

You can add a wide variety of materials to your compost. Vegetable scraps from the kitchen, grass clippings, fallen leaves, and soft plant trimmings are all appropriate choices. If you have access to manure from animals like chickens, rabbits, cows, or horses, you can add that also. There are some things you should avoid, including fats, bones, and meat scraps, which can

attract scavengers to your pile. Also avoid composting manure from humans, dogs, and cats—this material can carry disease organisms. Don't add infested or diseased plant material to your compost unless you are making a hot compost pile. Even then, the temperatures will not get high enough to kill some plant viruses. If you have virus-infected plants, bury them or place them in sealed containers for disposal with household trash.

Any kind of organic material will break down more quickly when it's already in small pieces. Use a leaf shredder or lawn mower to chop materials like leaves, hard stems, bark, and twigs.

Hot, Fast Compost

Hot composting takes some work, but you'll get results quickly—sometimes as fast as two weeks. Plus, composting at high temperatures can kill pests, some plant pathogens, and weed seeds that find their way into the pile.

The key to hot composting is getting a balance between high-carbon and high-nitrogen ingredients. High-nitrogen ingredients are green, sloppy materials like fresh grass clippings, kitchen scraps, and manure. High-carbon ingredients include brown, woody materials like fallen leaves, straw, and newspaper.

Build the pile by alternating layers of high-nitrogen materials with high-carbon materials. Use approximately equal volumes of each. If you are adding plants infested with pests or pathogens, place them in the middle where temperatures will get the hottest.

If your ingredients are fairly dry, sprinkle each layer with water as you work. The materials should be spongy moist, but not soggy. Make sure the finished pile is at least 3 feet (1 m) on each side—a smaller pile won't heat up as well and will take longer to break down.

A properly built hot compost pile will be warm to the touch in a day or two. Use a compost thermometer to monitor your pile's progress. The temperature inside the

Brew a Bucket of Compost Tea

Compost tea is a liquid fertilizer made by soaking compost in water. Put a shovelful of compost into a bag made of cheesecloth or burlap. Tie the bag closed and suspend it in a garbage can, bucket, or watering can filled with water. Keep it covered for a few days. Once it has steeped, use the liquid to drench the soil at the base of plants you want to fertilize. It's a particularly good way to fertilize container-grown plants. Or dilute the liquid with water until it is the color of weak tea, then spray it on plant leaves. Because the nutrients are dissolved in water, the plants can take them up immediately for a quick burst of energy. (Reuse the "tea bag" several times, then add the soaked compost to the garden.)

pile should stay near but below 160°F (71°C), since higher temperatures kill important decomposer organisms. When the pile cools off (in a few days), turning it should raise the temperature. Using a garden fork, invert the pile one forkful at a time just next to the original pile, fluffing it as you work. The more frequently you turn the pile, the more quickly it will break down. If the pile gets too hot, let it sit for a few days or add water to it.

Using this technique, you can have finished hot compost within two to six weeks. You'll know it's finished when the temperature stabilizes and the individual materials are no longer recognizable.

Cold, Slow Compost

If you aren't in a hurry for finished compost, cold composting may be a good option for you. The most basic method is to simply pile together all the materials you have and let them sit for a year or more. Eventually, the pile will break down into usable compost.

For a slightly quicker version, build the pile following the directions for hot compost, then leave it for 6 to 12 months without turning.

A cold compost pile won't actually feel cold—it just won't get as warm as a hot pile. The temperatures in a cold pile won't be high enough to kill pests, pathogens, or weed seeds, so don't add these materials to a cold pile.

Using Compost

Compost makes an excellent, disease-free medium for starting your own plants. Begin with compost from a hot pile, then let it rest for an additional 6 to 12 months. Shake the finished compost through ½-inch (12-mm) wire mesh to screen out large particles. Use the screened compost alone or mix it with potting ingredients like vermiculite. In the garden, compost helps to improve soil structure and increases the soil's water-holding capacity. Spread 1 to 2 inches (2.5 to 5 cm) of finished compost over the surface of your garden each year. You can work the compost in or leave it on top as a mulch. Mixing compost into the soil distributes beneficial microorganisms that help to control soilborne pests and diseases. As a fertilizer, homemade compost contains between 1 and 2 percent each of nitrogen, phosphate, and potash, plus small quantities of trace elements.

Enclosing Your Compost

It's not essential to enclose composting areas. You can simply heap garden leftovers up in a pile or spread them over empty garden beds to rot in place. But if you want to keep your compost neatly contained, you can enclose your pile in a bin. Commercially available barrels and bins look nice—some specially designed units may even help speed up the composting process—but they can be expensive to

buy. You can build your own three-sectioned bin with chicken wire tacked to lumber framing. Make sure each section is about 3 to 4 feet (90 to 120 cm) high, wide, and deep. Devote one bin to aged compost that is ready to use, another to half-cooked compost, and the last to accumulating fresh scraps. Or use two or three plastic trash cans with the bottom cut out and airholes cut in the sides.

Compost Troubleshooting

If your compost pile isn't looking like it should, check the list below to see what the problem is.

- Pile doesn't heat up. Add more high-nitrogen material. If the pile is dry, add water. Try turning the pile to add more air.
- Pile smells bad. Add more high-carbon material. If the pile is too wet, turning may help to add more air.
- Finished compost is covered with seedlings. If your compost doesn't heat up enough, seeds of weeds and other plants may survive. Either avoid adding materials with seeds or put them in the center of a hot compost pile.
- Material doesn't break down. Woody stems, prunings, and dry leaves are often slow to break down; try shredding or chopping them into smaller pieces. Add more high-nitrogen ingredients to balance these high-carbon materials.

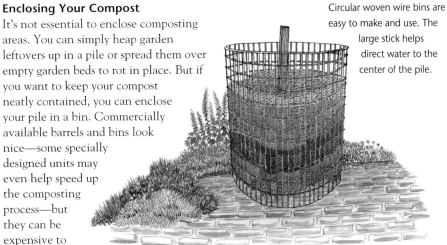

Circular woven wire bins are easy to make and use. The large stick helps direct water to the center of the pile.

Basic Planting Techniques

Timing

For most of us, the garden year begins in spring. A sudden spell of warm weather may have your fingers itching to dig and plant, but don't be too hasty—even cool-season crops will not grow in ice-encrusted soil. But if you wait for the right planting conditions and choose the right crops, you can start harvesting weeks before your neighbors.

How Soon Can You Plant?

There are two ways you can determine the right planting time for your area: By soil temperature or by the last frost date. Monitor the soil warmth with a soil thermometer, and plant when the temperature is consistently at least 55°F (13°C) but less than 70°F (21°C). Alternatively, contact your county's Cooperative Extension Service, farm bureau, or local botanical garden to find out the average date of the last spring frost in your area. Then count back two to eight weeks, depending on what you're going to plant.

You can plant the hardiest of the cool-weather plants as soon as the soil is thawed and dry enough to work in spring.

Less hardy plants should wait until two to four weeks before the last frost. If the weather seems exceptionally cold, wait a few days or a week to plant—most plants will grow much faster in a cool, rather than cold, soil.

Seeds or Seedlings?

Seeds are much cheaper than seedlings. A single packet of seeds can produce dozens or even hundreds of plants for a fraction of the cost of buying transplants. Starting from seed also gives you a much greater variety of plants to choose from, since most retail sources only grow a few cultivars of the most popular plants. The disadvantage is, of course, that you have to wait for the seeds to germinate, so if you want a head start on your flowers, vegetable and herbs, it's best to buy them as seedlings.

Always use high-quality seed, packed for the current year. Buy from a reputable seed company that offers high germination rates. You can find out the rates from the percentage of viable (live) seeds listed on the package. If you have any seed left over from last year or home-collected seed, try sprouting a few before

you sow a whole packet. Roll the seeds in a moist paper towel and enclose the rolled towel in a plastic bag. Keep the bag warm and watch for germination in the next several weeks. If only half of the seeds sprout, you will know you need to sow twice as much seed to get the number of plants you want.

Starting Seeds Indoors

Starting seeds indoors enables you to begin the new season earlier than if you plant outdoors. You'll have more control over the environment, so seeds will germinate faster and the seedlings will grow vigorously.

When to Sow

Check seed catalog descriptions or seed packets for sowing timetables. You can sow most seeds indoors in early spring, about six to ten weeks before your last frost date, although some need to be started earlier or later.

Containers

You can start seedlings in just about any container that has holes for drainage. Seedlings started in their own pots won't require potting-up later. You can even purchase ready-to-use flats with cells for sowing single seeds. If you use containers such as peat pots or pellets, you can plant the pot along with the plant. They are a good choice for plants that transplant poorly, like cucumbers and rocket larkspur (*Consolida ambigua*).

If you're reusing last year's flats and pots, either dip them in boiling water for several minutes or rinse them in a 10 percent bleach solution (one part household bleach to nine parts water) to kill disease organisms.

Growing Medium

New seedlings need a light, moist medium for a quick start. Fill containers with a special seedling mix or moistened vermiculite, milled sphagnum moss, perlite, or sifted compost. Materials like perlite and vermiculite don't provide any

It's easy to grow annual, biennial, and perennial herbs all together in one garden. Just start the annuals and biennials from seed and use them to fill in between the longer-lived perennials.

nutrients to your seedlings. Once true leaves have developed, the young plants will require extra nutrients. Water them with a liquid organic fertilizer like fish emulsion, at half strength. Gradually increase the dose to full strength. Alternatively, you can transfer seedlings to a potting blend with extra compost, or prepare a nourishing substitute by adding ½ cup (4 fl oz/125 ml) or less of dry, organic fertilizer to each 5-gallon (22.5-L) batch of homemade potting medium. Remember, the longer the seedlings remain in pots, the more nutrients they'll need.

Getting Ready

When you're ready to sow (or, even better, the night before), dump your seed-starting mix in a large bucket or tub and add some warm water to moisten it. Start with a few cups of water, and work the mix with your hands to help it absorb the moisture. Keep adding several cups of water at a time and working it into the mix until the mix feels evenly moist but not soggy. (If you squeeze a handful of mix and water runs out, it's too wet; add some more dry mix to get the balance right.)

Once the mix is moist, you can fill your chosen containers. Scoop the mix into each container and level it out to about ¼ inch (6 mm) below the upper edge of the container. Don't pack down the mix; just tap the filled container once or twice on your work surface to settle the mix and eliminate air pockets.

Prepare markers for each of the plants that you plan to sow, for easy identification when transplanting.

Sowing the Seed

When you're sowing large seeds, such as four-o'clocks (*Mirabilis jalapa*), use a pencil to make individual holes ½ to 1 inch (12 to 25 mm) apart. Sow more thickly if you expect poor germination. For small seeds, use a pencil to make shallow furrows, and sow as evenly as possible into the furrows. Fine seeds, such as those of petunias and begonias, can be hard to sow directly from the packet. To

Sowing Seed

1. Fill the container with a seed-raising mix.

2. Press the mix into the corners.

3. Level to ¼ inch (6 mm) from the top.

4. Scatter seeds and gently press in.

5. Cover with a fine layer of mix.

6. Water them with a fine mist spray.

7. Label the container.

8. Cover with plastic, glass, or damp newspaper.

distribute tiny seeds more evenly, mix them with a spoonful of dry sand, and scatter the mixture over the surface of the mix with a saltshaker. Label each row of seed as you sow.

If the seeds should be buried (as indicated on the seed packet), sprinkle the needed amount of dry mix over the seed. Fine seeds are usually not covered; just press them lightly into the surface of the mix with your fingers. Mist the surface lightly to moisten it. Seeds will rot if they are submerged in water.

Set the containers in a well-lit spot where you can check them daily for signs of the first sprouts. Keep the planting medium moist but not soggy. Cover the container with clear plastic wrap to keep the soil evenly moist until the seeds germinate, but make sure the plastic doesn't touch the soil. Remove the covering as soon as the seedlings appear. Ventilation is important as poor ventilation encourages the development of seedling diseases.

Temperature and Light

Most annual seeds will sprout and grow well at average indoor temperatures between 60° and 75°F (16° and 24°C). Vegetable seeds germinate best at higher temperatures—between 75° and 90°F

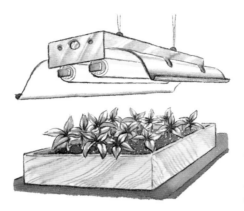

Get a head start on spring plants by germinating your seeds indoors under lights. Or, during the heat of summer, start seeds of cool-season plants indoors, perhaps under lights in a cool basement or garage.

(24° and 32°C). On top of the water heater or refrigerator are both good positions for these. You can even buy horticultural heating mats to keep the soil warm. Place the mats on a heatproof surface and set flats or pots on top. Once the seedlings are up and growing, they will require less warmth and will do best at 60° to 70°F (16° to 21°C) during the day, with a 10°F (5°C) drop each night.

Once your seeds have germinated, it is important that you keep them near a sunny window or under fluorescent plant lights. Garden centers and garden-supply catalogs sell lights in a variety of sizes and prices. Four-foot (1.2-m) fluorescent shop

lights sold in home centers also provide excellent results, and they're generally much less expensive than grow lights. The young plants will need between 10 and 16 hours of light each day. They will tolerate low-light conditions best if you keep temperatures on the low side.

Thinning and Transplanting

The first leaves to appear on the plant are actually specialized food-storage organs. These drop away quickly, and the leaves that follow are the first "true leaves." When seedlings develop their first set of true leaves, they'll need special attention.

If seedlings are in separate pots or cells, thin away the extra seedlings by clipping them off at soil level with sharp scissors. One healthy specimen should remain in each pot or cell. If your seedlings are crowded together in a flat, you'll need to transfer them to their own containers. Fill pots or cells with a nutrient-rich medium. Scoop one or more seedlings from the flat (a teaspoon works well), separating their root systems as gently as possible with your fingers. Poke a hole in the potting soil deep enough to accommodate the new seedling and its root system, then transfer it and firm the soil. Water as often as necessary to keep the soil moist and to prevent wilting. When you water,

STEP-BY-STEP POTTING UP

1. Place moist growing medium into new containers. Make a hole large enough to accommodate the root system of the seedling.

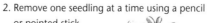

2. Remove one seedling at a time using a pencil or pointed stick.

3. Holding the seedling by its leaves, place it into its new container and gently firm the soil around it. Thin seedlings by clipping them off at soil level with a pair of scissors.

set the container of seedlings in a tray of water so the growing medium can soak up moisture without disrupting the seedlings. If you water from overhead, you may wash the seedlings away. Place pots away from direct light and wind for a day until the shock of transplanting is over. Feed the young plants lightly with compost tea or liquid seaweed.

Hardening Off

Hardening off allows young plants to adjust slowly to the extremes of wind, temperature, and light. At least two weeks before transplanting time, begin watering less frequently and withhold fertilizer. One week before you transplant, move the plants outdoors to a spot protected from strong light and wind. Starting with one or several hours, gradually increase their time spent outdoors. Within a week, they should be outdoors permanently. They'll need more water at this time, since sun and wind quickly dry the soil. Be prepared to bring them back indoors if a cold snap or storm threatens.

Sowing Seed in the Garden

Some plants like morning glories (*Ipomoea* spp.), beans, peas, and root crops, grow better from direct-sown seed because they prefer cool outdoor temperatures or because they don't respond well to transplanting. Planting seeds outdoors is not a good idea for seeds that are hard to germinate, or for plants that need a long, warm growing season.

Before the season begins, check your seed packages or catalog for the best time to plant outdoors. You'll need to know the expected date of the last frost for your area; ask local gardeners, or contact your local Cooperative Extension Service.

Get the soil ready for planting (see page 50) and if you're planting in rows, as with vegetables, mark them before planting with wooden stakes at both ends. Stretch a section of lightweight string down the row, and use it as a guide to keep your rows straight while you plant.

Dealing with Damping-Off

Damping-off is a disease that can strike young seedlings, killing them just before or after they emerge. Affected seedlings tend to topple over, since their stems are damaged at the soil level. Once a few seedlings are affected, the disease can quickly spread to other seedlings in the same pot or tray.

Since there's no real cure, the best way to handle damping-off is prevention. Here are some tips that might help.

- Always use fresh, "sterile" seed-starting mix.
- If you're reusing old pots or trays, knock out the old soil, dip the containers in a 10 percent bleach solution (1 part household bleach to 9 parts water), and let the containers dry before using them.
- Sprinkle a thin layer of milled sphagnum moss on top of newly planted seeds.
- Improve air circulation with a small fan set to blow lightly just over the tops of the seedlings.
- If damping-off strikes outdoor-sown seeds, discard them, wait until the weather warms up (maybe two to three weeks), then try sowing again.

If you're planting annuals or perennials, sow medium-sized and large seeds individually, or scatter them evenly over the surace. Try to space them ½ to 1 inch (12 to 25 mm) apart. If you have very small seeds, mix them with a handful of dry sand and scatter over the surface.

Cover most seeds with a thin layer of fine soil or sand. After sowing, make sure the seedbed stays moist until the seedlings are visible. If rainfall is lacking, water gently with a watering can, sprinkler, or fine hose spray. Covering the seedbed

Lupine seed, like others of the pea and bean family, can be sown directly into the soil in fall.

with a layer of floating row cover helps to keep the soil moist and protects the seed from drying winds, heavy rain, and birds. (Remove the cover once the seedlings start to emerge.)

If seedlings are crowded, you'll need to thin them out for good growth. Dig up and carefully transplant extra seedlings, or use scissors to cut off the stems of unwanted seedlings at ground level.

Planting Container-Grown Plants

If you are planting a potted plant, you can easily see how deeply to plant it. Dig deeply enough so the surface of the container soil will be at the top of the hole (adjusting accordingly for new beds).

Nursery Beds for Biennials

If you decide to grow biennial plants, such as foxgloves (*Digitalis purpurea*) and forget-me-nots (*Myosotis sylvatica*), you need a slightly different growing approach. Most biennials will sprout well when sown outdoors, so that part is easy. But if you sow them directly into the garden, their leafy, first-year growth will take up room without adding much interest to your flower display.

The easiest approach is to set aside a temporary growing area (called a nursery bed) where your biennials can grow through the summer. Prepare your nursery bed just as you would any garden area, but site it in an out-of-the-way spot. Sow the biennial seeds into the bed in spring or summer, and thin them as needed. Dig the plants and move them to their final garden spots in late summer or early fall for bloom the following year.

Forget-me-not

Fill the hole with water to moisten the soil, and let it drain away before you begin to plant. Slip the roots out of the pot. Most larger plants are root-bound enough to slide out easily. If not, you can gently squeeze the base of a plastic pot to loosen the root ball. Break up the edges of the root ball so the roots will have more contact with the surrounding soil. If the roots are wrapped around themselves, they may not break free and root into the soil. You will have to work them loose.

You can quarter the roots of fibrous-rooted perennials like chrysanthemums. Although the process may seem harsh, it will encourage new root growth. Make four deep slices, one on each side of the root ball, or make a single cut two-thirds up the center to divide the ball in half. Mound some soil in the center of the planting hole. Open the root quarters out from the cuts and spread them out over the mound. Cover the rest of the roots up to the crown. Don't try this technique on plants with taproots like monks-hoods.

After planting, firm the soil gently around the plant, water it well, and mulch. Mulching your bed with organic materials like compost, straw, or shredded leaves will conserve moisture and reduce weed competition. (New beds are especially weed-prone, since turning the soil exposes weed seeds.)

Planting Field-Dug Plants

Plant field-dug plants that have a large amount of soil still around the roots in a hole the same size as the root ball. If much of the soil has fallen off the roots, make the hole slightly larger so you can move the roots into the best position. Drench the hole with water and set in the plant at the same depth it was originally growing. Work any exposed roots into the surrounding soil as you refill, then firm the soil gently.

Planting Bareroot Perennials

When you start with bareroot plants, you will have to take more time settling the plants into the ground. This process can be tricky the first few times, but be patient and don't be afraid to work with the roots. You'll soon get it right.

First, soak the roots in a bucket of lukewarm water for a few hours to prepare them for planting. When you are ready to plant, identify how deeply the plants had been growing in the nursery. The above-ground portions—green foliage tufts, leaf buds, or dormant stems—usually emerge from the root system above the former soil line. Plant so that these structures will stay slightly above the soil in your garden. (Peonies are an exception, since their shoots will emerge through the soil from about 1 inch [2.5 cm] underground.)

Next, make a hole that is deep and wide enough to set the plant crown at the

1. Dig a planting hole that is larger than the root ball of the transplant.
2. If desired, add a handful or two of compost to the hole.
3. Add water to moisten the soil before planting.
4. Gently slide the plant out of its container.
5. Use your fingers to loosen the soil mix around the roots.
6. Set the plant in the hole. Backfill with soil; firm lightly with your hands.

soil surface and stretch out the roots. Form a small mound of soil in the bottom of the hole. Set the root clump on it with the crown resting on top of the mound. Spread the roots gently in every direction and fill in around them with soil. Then firm the soil gently, water, and mulch. Keep the soil evenly moist for the next few weeks.

Planting Trees and Shrubs

You can plant anytime the ground isn't frozen. Plant bareroot stock when it's dormant, from late fall to as early in spring as possible. Balled-and-burlapped (B&B) stock does best when planted in the cooler months of spring or fall. You can plant container-grown stock anytime during the growing season, but if you

Quartering

1. To loosen a tight root ball, use a knife to make four deep cuts.
2. Spread the quartered root ball over a mound of soil and backfill.

plant during summer, make sure you give the plants plenty of water and watch carefully that they don't dry out.

In most cases you'll set new plants in the ground at the same depth at which they are growing presently. Replanting at the same depth keeps the crown—the point from which shoots emerge—from being buried in damp soil, where it is likely to rot. However, if you have just prepared the soil, it will settle 1 to 2 inches (2.5 to 5 cm) over the coming months. In a new bed, plant slightly deeper so the plant's roots and crowns do not stick out of the soil when it has settled. Exactly how you plant depends on whether you are using bareroot, container-grown, or field-dug stock.

How to Plant

Keep a firm, level area of soil in the bottom of the hole on which to set the plant, and dig a few inches deeper around it so that extra water can drain away from the roots easily. Now set the plant into the hole. (If you're planting bareroot stock, build a cone of soil in the hole to support the roots. Firm the soil well and settle the plant on top of the cone, spreading the roots over it.) Stand back and make sure the plant is straight.

Now start refilling, or backfilling, with the soil you removed when you dug the hole. Backfill half the hole, then water the soil to remove large air pockets. Once the water drains away, finish backfilling and water again. With the leftover soil, build a well around the planting hole to trap and hold water over the plant's roots.

Planting in Containers

Container plants share closer quarters than garden plants, so they need some special care to stay lush and lovely. The first step to successful container growing is choosing a good container. Large pots tend to provide the best conditions for growth, since they hold more soil, nutrients, and water, but they are also quite heavy if you need to move or hang them. Pots or baskets that are about 8 inches (20 cm) deep can usually hold enough soil for good growth without getting too heavy. If you don't plan to move the planter, it can be as big as you want; containers as large as half-barrels will give you ample planting space for a wide variety of plants.

Fill your container with a general potting mix that you buy at your local nursery or garden center. Straight garden soil is generally not suitable for containers, since it will pack down with repeated watering. Add some compost to the mix to promote root growth.

Set your plants into the container soil, firm them in, and water to keep the soil moist through the season.

Planting Hanging Baskets

Most hanging basket containers look like regular pots, and you plant them in basically the same way. Baskets dry out even faster than other container plants, however, so it's a good idea to use a potting mix that holds plenty of water. Adding extra vermiculite will help. It also helps to use larger baskets—at least

To keep hanging baskets looking lush through the season, water them regularly, fertilize often, and pinch off spent flowers.

12 inches (30 cm) in diameter, which will dry out more slowly. During hot summers, hanging baskets may have to be watered twice a day.

Great Balls of Flowers

If you want your hanging baskets to be a solid ball of color, plant the sides of the containers as well as the tops. You can buy special baskets that have holes around the sides, or use wire baskets with fiber or moss liners, which allow you to cut holes for planting all around the sides.

To plant into the holes in the sides of a hanging basket, first fill the basket with potting mix to just below where the holes begin. Then remove a plant from its cell pack, and wrap it loosely inside a little cylinder of newspaper. From the inside of the basket, slip the top part of the cylinder out through a hole, so the leafy top of the plant is on the outside and the roots are on the inside. Slip off the newspaper, then settle the roots in the soil. When you have all the holes filled, add more soil to within 1 inch (2.5 cm) of the rim, then set in more plants on top. Water thoroughly to allow the soil to settle around the roots.

Propagation Techniques

Depending on which propagation method you choose, you can end up with a few to a few hundred new plants, taken from a single specimen. Vegetative methods of propagation, such as division, layering, and cuttings, will produce an exact clone of the parent plant in nearly every case. These are the best methods to use if you want to propagate cultivars or hybrids, which usually produce variable offspring when grown from seed.

Reproduction by Division

Many perennials flower best when they're young, and their flower production drops as they mature. To keep them flowering well, you must divide them—dig them up and split the root mass into pieces. In addition to reviving older plants, division is the easiest and fastest technique for propagating perennials. It's also a good way to keep fast-spreading perennials under control. Plus, it will give you lots of extra plants to share with family, friends, and neighbors.

Division is a reliable way to propagate many clump-forming perennials, including daylilies, chrysanthemums, and irises. It may not work as well with the more sensitive perennials like sea hollies (*Eryngium* spp.) and gas plant (*Dictamnus albus*).

How to Divide

Early spring and autumn are good times to divide plants, when the air temperature is low and soil moisture is usually high. Begin dividing by digging up the root system. Shake off as much loose soil as possible and remove any dead leaves and stems. You may also want to wash most of the soil off the roots and crown so you can see the roots and buds clearly.

Plants with fibrous roots, such as chrysanthemums and asters, are the easiest to dig and divide. You can pull them apart with your hands or cut them with a spade. Others, like daylilies and astilbe, can grow woody with age. You may have to pry these roots apart with a crowbar or two garden forks held back to back, or cut them with a saw or ax. Discard the woody parts, which will not reroot well.

Divide the plants into small pieces, making sure you keep several buds or growing shoots on the sections you will replant. Look for the buds growing along the length of the roots or clustered together in a central crown.

Work compost and other soil amendments into the soil before replanting. Reset divisions at the same level as they were growing originally.

Plants that send out underground rhizomes, like mint, are just as easily divided without digging up the whole plant. If you follow the underground stems that sprout new plants, you can simply lift out each new plant with a spade.

Layering

Some plants are easy to root while still attached to the mother plant, a technique called layering. Burying a section of the stem encourages roots to form at each buried leaf node (the place where a leaf joins the stem). Layering does take up some space since you need to bury the attached stem close to the parent plant. You won't get many new plants from this method (usually only one per stem), and it can take weeks or months for the stem to root. But layering is easy to do, and the resulting plants will be exact duplicates of the parent plant.

You can use this technique with plants that have flexible stems or a creeping habit and the ability to root at the leaf axils. Good candidates for layering include pinks (*Dianthus* spp.), cranesbills (*Geranium* spp.), wall rock

STEP-BY-STEP DIVISION

1. Dig around the clump.
2. Shake off as much soil as possible. Separate good shoots with roots from the parent plant.
3. Cut back ragged tops and shorten the stems.
4. Place some well-rotted compost into the planting hole and position the plant at the same depth as it was growing before.
5. Water the plant with a soluble organic fertilizer to minimize transplanting shock.

STEP-BY-STEP LAYERING

Layering is a slow but reliable method for propagating many kinds of plants, especially trees, shrubs, and vines.

1. Select a young, flexible, healthy branch about as thick as a pencil.
2. Cut off any leaves and side shoots from the section to be buried.
3. Make a slit on the underside, and insert a toothpick to keep it open (this is not necessary with thin stems).
4. Bend the stem into the hole and anchor it with bent wire.
5. Fill the hole with enriched soil mixture and water thoroughly.
6. After a couple of months, cut off and transplant the new plant.

cress (*Arabis caucasica*), snow-in-summer (*Cerastium tomentosum*), and bellflowers (*Campanula* spp.). Layering will not work on daylilies, ornamental grasses, hostas, irises, peonies, or other bushy perennials. Spring is a good time to start a layer, although it can work anytime during the growing season.

How It Works

The first step to successful layering is finding a suitable stem. If the plant is upright, look for one or several long stems that bend easily to the ground; if the plant has a creeping habit, any stem is suitable. Leave the top three sets of leaves on the stem to nourish the plant, but remove the leaves from the stem for 2 to 7 inches (5 to 17.5 cm) below the top greenery. Strip the leaves from at least two nodes (leaf joints), carefully leaving the dormant buds undamaged. Bend the stem down

and see where the stripped area will contact the soil. Loosen the soil in that area about 4 inches (10 cm) deep and water it. Bury the stem in the loosened soil, holding it in place with a bent wire pin, and firm the soil over the stem. The stem should be buried 2 to 3 inches (5 to 7.5 cm) deep with the leafy tip still exposed. If you are layering an upright shoot, encourage the tip to return to its upright position by tying it to a small stake if necessary.

Keep the area moist and mulched while the buried stem roots. Depending on the temperature and species, it will take several weeks to several months. The easiest way to layer is to leave the plant in place until the following season. If you want faster results, check its progress by gently uncovering the stem and looking for roots, or tugging lightly to see if the shoot has become more secure in the

ground. Once the roots reach about 1 inch (2.5 cm) long you can cut the shoot free from the mother plant. Wait several weeks for more rooting, then dig and transplant the new plant.

Cuttings

Cuttings—small pieces of stem or root—are another way to propagate many plants. Cuttings take more care than other methods, like layering and division. But if you like a challenge, you can use cuttings to create many new plants from your existing perennials. Cuttings are a good way to propagate perennials that are difficult to divide and cultivars that don't come true from seed.

Stem Cuttings

Stem cuttings are effective for many kinds of plants. Try perennial flowers such as wall rock cress (*Arabis caucasica*), chrysanthemums, common sneezeweed (*Helenium autumnale*), garden phlox (*Phlox paniculata*), and pinks (*Dianthus* spp.), and herbs like scented geranium, bay, lavender, and oregano.

You should take stem cuttings when perennials are in vegetative growth: Either in spring before blooming or after flowering is finished for the season. You should select a healthy medium-soft stem—one that is not soft, new growth or hard, old growth—from the lower portion of the plant, where shoots are more likely to root quickly. Cut the stems free with a sharp, clean knife or pair of shears.

Preparing the Cuttings

Slice the stem into sections between 2 and 4 inches (5 to 10 cm) long, so that each cutting has two or three sets of leaves on the top and a couple of nodes (leaf joints) stripped of leaves on the bottom. These nodes will produce roots when you insert them into a pot of moist, sterile, peat-based growing mix. Don't be tempted to use garden soil—it's too heavy for cuttings.

Some stem cuttings, like those from blue false indigo (*Baptisia australis*), will

1   2

3

4   5

STEP-BY-STEP CUTTINGS
1. Select healthy green growth.
2. Cut stem below the leaf node.
3. Remove the lower leaves.
4. Insert cutting firmly into mix.
5. Cover the cutting with a glass jar to maintain humidity. Keep out of direct sun.

root more easily if you dip their lower ends in a commercially available rooting hormone powder. However, if you find the right moisture, light, and warmth levels, most plants will root without this treatment. Make a hole in the mix with a clean pencil and slide the cutting in. Firm the mix around it gently with your hands, and water with a fine spray to settle the cutting into the soil.

Caring for Cuttings

Cover the container with a clear plastic-wrap tent. Prop the plastic above the plant foliage to avoid rot. Keep the cuttings in a warm place and in indirect light until they root, about two to four weeks. When they begin to grow, remove the plastic and move the plants into brighter light.

To determine if the cuttings have rooted, look to see if roots are emerging from the pot's drainage hole. You can also tug gently on the stem—if you meet resistance, the cuttings have rooted. Transplant the rooted cuttings into larger containers or a nursery bed to grow them to garden size.

Root Cuttings

Less common than stem cuttings, root cuttings are another way to produce new plants that are usually identical to the parent plant. Root cuttings are suitable for several kinds of perennials, including Siberian bugloss (*Anchusa azurea*), oriental poppies (*Papaver orientale*), and garden phlox (*Phlox paniculata*).

Take root cuttings from fall to early spring, while the parent plant is dormant. Carefully lift the plant from the garden and wash the soil from the roots. Using a sharp, clean knife, cut off a few pencil-thick roots close to the crown. Cut each root into 2- to 4-inch (5- to 10-cm) pieces, making a straight cut at the top (the end that was closest to the crown) and a slanted cut at the bottom. Insert the cuttings into a

pot filled with moist, sterile potting mix, so that the flat top of each cutting is level with or slightly below the surface of the mix. Place the cuttings in a cold frame until they root and then pot them individually. Once the plants reach the desired size, move them into the garden.

Saving Seed

Although most perennial flowers and herbs are easy to propagate vegetatively— by division, layering, or cuttings—you can grow many plants from seed if you have the patience.

Annuals and biennials will seed themselves before the season ends. All that's required next season is patience while you leave the soil undisturbed to see which seedlings volunteer. Resist the temptation to dig or hoe in areas that were heavily seeded naturally the previous season.

When the new plants are established, dig them up while the weather is cool and move them as needed. Leave them in clumps or divide them up into individual plants as required in your garden.

To save seed for planting next spring, wait until they've matured on the plant before collecting them. Hold the seed heads over a container and gently tap to release the seeds. Alternatively, you can harvest the seed heads and then hang them upside down in paper bags to dry. The seeds should be thoroughly dried before being stored in airtight containers.

Creating the Right Environment

It is vital to prevent most cuttings from drying out while roots develop. If you have just a few cuttings, you can enclose them, pot and all, in a plastic bag; for large numbers, a cold frame may be more practical. Set your pots in a bright place out of direct sunlight, or cover your cold frame with wooden lattice to shield the cuttings from the full brunt of the sun.

Propagating Garlic

Growing your own garlic is easy and rewarding. Mid-autumn is the best time for planting. The bulbs will produce roots and small shoots before the ground freezes. When the weather warms in spring, the shoots will start growing actively.

1. Harvest the bulbs as usual, allowing them to dry. Save the largest bulbs with the largest cloves for replanting and use the rest in the kitchen. There's no need to clean the bulbs you plan to replant. The more they're handled and peeled, the more likely they'll rot in storage. Store them in a dark, cool location until you're ready to plant.

2. To plant, divide the bulbs into individual cloves. Plant only the outer, large cloves; small, inner cloves will yield smaller bulbs. Keep the small cloves in the kitchen to use soon—once separated from the bulb, they won't store well.

3. Plant the individual cloves root-side down, approximately 1 inch (2.5 cm) deep and 6 inches (15 cm) apart in a deep bed with loosened soil. Work in plenty of organic materials like compost, but go easy on fertilizer. Dig up when the tops die down.

WHIP-AND-TONGUE GRAFTING

1. Make a long sloping cut at the top of the rootstock.
2. Make a shallow cut down through the middle of the rootstock stem.
3. Prepare the scion with a matching sloping cut at the base.
4. Cut shallowly into the middle of the scion's base.
5. Slip the stock and scion together so the "tongues" interlock.
6. Wrap the graft with tape to provide support and hold in moisture.

Grafting Trees and Shrubs

Grafting is the process of uniting two related plants using the root system of one to nourish the top of the other. An alternative to propagating by layering, cuttings, or seed, grafting produces large plants quickly because the roots are already well established. The technique is used to propagate species and cultivars of flowering cherries (*Prunus* spp.) and pears (*Pyrus* spp.), dwarf conifers, and Japanese maples (*Acer palmatum*) that won't come true from seed and don't root easily from cuttings or layering.

The key to grafting is to match the cambium layers—the actively growing green tissue under the bark—of the rooted

1. Save large, healthy garlic bulbs for replanting. Store in a dark, cool place.

2. Divide the bulbs into individual cloves, keeping the smaller ones for cooking.

3. Plant the cloves root-side down. Cover with soil rich in organic matter.

plant (called the rootstock) and the new top (called the scion). Once these two cambium layers unite, the graft grows as one plant.

Choosing a Rootstock

Grafting joins two or more pieces of different plants together to form a new plant. Compatibility between rootstock and scion is a must. Select closely related plants of the same genus or cultivars within the same species or, sometimes, species within the same family. You can grow your own rootstocks from seeds or cuttings or graft onto a mature tree. The multiflora rose (*Rosa multiflora*), for example, is a hardy, pest-resistant species that is grown easily from seed. Because of its vigor, it makes a good rootstock for a hybrid tea or an heirloom rose.

Tools and Supplies

For most home gardeners, a very sharp knife, a pair of pruners that makes clean cuts, and materials to tie and seal off the graft are all that's needed. Tying and wrapping materials hold the rootstock and scion together and keep the cambium layers from drying out. Wide rubber bands or waxed string are good for tying. Sealing materials, such as grafting wax or rubber tape, are widely available at garden centers, or you can improvise with plastic tape or petroleum jelly.

Grafting Techniques

Learning to make successful grafts requires practice. Several grafting techniques are available for you to try, including whip-and-tongue, side veneer, and cleft grafts, and T and chip buds. Consult a propagation reference and choose the best method depending on the amount of scion wood you have, the size of the rootstock, the time of year, and the effect you want to obtain. Grafting is usually done from late winter to early spring depending on the method used. Most grafts, properly done, will unite within one to two months.

Taking Tree and Shrub Cuttings

Depending on the species you're propagating and the time of year, you can take cuttings from plants with softwood, semihardwood, or hardwood stems.

Getting Started

A sharp knife, a plastic bag, clean pots, and a well-drained soilless growing medium are all you need. Be sure your knife (or pruning shears) is sharp; a dull blade will crush plant tissue and invite disease. Scrub your pots—clay and plastic are both suitable—and rinse with a solution of one part bleach to nine parts water.

Use a lightweight, moisture-retentive propagation medium, free of insects, diseases, and weed seeds. Garden soil is not a good choice. Use a 50-50 mix of peat moss and perlite, peat and vermiculite, or peat and sand.

Softwood Cuttings

Take softwood cuttings from the succulent new growth that occurs in the spring. Softwood stems snap easily when bent. Some plants have spurts of new growth later in the year that can also be used for softwood cuttings. Many species of shrubs and vines, and some trees, root well from softwood cuttings, including crab apples (*Malus* spp.) and crape myrtle (*Lagerstroemia indica*).

Take softwood cuttings from April to June, when stems are soft and new leaves are fully open. Have ready a container of moist propagation medium. Snip 3- to 6-inch (7.5- to 15-cm) cuttings, including the branch tip, on a cool overcast morning, cutting just below a node (the swollen area on the stem where a leaf emerges). Remove leaves from the bottom half of the stem with pruning shears. Carefully insert the

Hydrangea (*Hydrangea macrophylla*) responds well to pruning and will root from softwood, semihardwood, or hardwood cuttings.

cutting into the medium to about one-third of its length and tamp it into place.

When the tray or pot is full, gently water the cuttings to settle the medium, then enclose the container in plastic or in a cold frame. Roots will usually form in two to five weeks. If the cuttings resist when you gently tug on them, they have rooted. Harden off rooted cuttings, gradually increasing the light intensity and decreasing the humidity to adjust them to normal growing conditions. Transplant the cuttings to a nursery bed or to individual containers.

Semihardwood Cuttings

Once the flush of spring growth is over, stem wood becomes firmer and leaves become fully expanded or mature. Pieces taken from this maturing wood are called semihardwood cuttings. Use semihardwood cuttings to propagate broad-leaved evergreens, such as hollies (*Ilex* spp.) and rhododendrons (*Rhododendron* spp.), or deciduous shrubs that don't root very well from softwood cuttings, such as winged euonymus (*Euonymus alata*).

SEMIHARDWOOD CUTTINGS

Semihardwood cuttings are a good way to propagate broad-leaved evergreen trees and shrubs, like hollies, rhododendrons, and camellias. Take cuttings from partially hardened wood in later summer. Keep the finished cuttings in a humid environment to promote rooting.

1. Take cuttings from healthy, vigorous growth and remove the leaves from the bottom half.

2. Cut large leaves in half to reduce evaporation and to save space in the container.

3. Insert cuttings halfway into moist potting mix and place them in a shady position.

Take 3- to 6-inch (7.5- to 15-cm) cuttings of semihardwood in late summer and remove the leaves from the bottom half. Cut the foliage of broad-leaved evergreens in half to save space and to reduce water loss. Some cuttings, like hollies and rhododendrons, benefit from having a small sliver of bark sliced off the side of the base. This wounding encourages new roots to form.

Insert the cuttings into a tray or pot of moist propagation medium, spacing them far enough apart so the leaves don't touch. Keep the air around the cuttings moist by misting them frequently, or enclose the whole container in clear plastic. (Use bent wire hangers to keep the plastic from resting on the cuttings and encouraging rot.) Set the cuttings where they will get bright light but no direct sun.

Semihardwood cuttings usually root in one to three months. Transplant rooted cuttings into individual pots or a nursery bed until they're ready for their final position in the garden.

Hardwood Cuttings

Take hardwood cuttings from mature wood in mid- to late fall or in winter.

Deciduous shade trees and needled evergreen shrubs, such as arborvitae (*Thuja* spp.), junipers (*Juniperus* spp.), and yews (*Taxus* spp.), can be propagated successfully from hardwood cuttings.

Look for mature, one-year-old wood with bark that has turned from green to (usually) brown or gray. For deciduous plants, take stem pieces 4 to 8 inches (10 to 20 cm) long starting a few inches below the terminal bud. Make a straight cut at the top of each piece just above a node or bud and a sloping cut at the base just below a node or bud. For evergreens, take 4- to 6-inch (10- to 15-cm) tip cuttings and clip off the bottom leaves.

Stick the cuttings right-side up (with the straight-cut end up) in your propagation medium. The top bud should be about 1 inch (2.5 cm) above the soil surface. Set the pots outdoors or in a cold frame. Keep the propagation medium evenly moist, but don't worry about misting the cuttings or enclosing them in plastic; since they're not actively growing, the cuttings won't lose much water. After the ground freezes, cover your cuttings with a 6- to 8-inch (15- to 20-cm) deep layer of loose mulch, like straw. Remove the mulch in spring.

Hardwood cuttings often take several months to root. Tug gently on them to check for roots the summer or fall after planting. Transplant rooted cuttings to individual pots or to a nursery bed for a few years. When the rooted cuttings have reached the size you need, move them to their final place in the garden.

Juniper

Caring for Your Garden

If you have chosen plants that match your site, prepared the soil thoroughly, and planted carefully, you will probably find your garden demands less maintenance than your lawn. However, low maintenance isn't no maintenance. Even the toughest plants will need a little watering, fertilizing, staking, and weeding.

Watering

Water stress, a result of both too little or too much water, is one of the major causes of poor plant growth or even death. Selecting plants that are adapted to your site and climate is the best thing you can do to avoid problems with water stress—and to reduce watering chores. A deep layer of mulch will also help reduce water-stress problems because it helps soil retain water and controls competition from grass and weeds.

Water makes up from 85 to 95 percent of the weight of living plants. It's not surprising that when water is lacking, a plant stops growing and wilts. After wilting comes collapse of the cell structure in the wilted leaves and stems. After that, if much of the plant is affected, comes the death of young or delicate plants! Your goal is to water before wilting occurs.

Garden plants require about the equivalent of 1 inch (25 mm) of rainfall each week under average soil and climate conditions. Gardens in hot, dry climates will lose moisture faster and may need the equivalent of up to 2 inches (50 mm) each week. In cool and wet climates, plants lose less moisture and less water evaporates from the soil, so you may not have to water at all.

To monitor rainfall, purchase a rain gauge (available at most hardware stores) and set it in or near your garden. Check it immediately after rain, before water in the gauge is lost to evaporation. If natural rainfall is inadequate, you should plan to water regularly to maintain plant health and growth. Checking your soil for moisture is also a good idea.

There are several methods of checking soil moisture. Move the surface soil or

Hand-watering with a hose is fine for small gardens, but for a larger area you'll probably need soaker hoses or a drip system.

mulch and look at the soil in the root zone. Most plant roots are in the top 12 inches (30 cm) of soil. If the soil is cool and moist and there are no signs of stress—wilting—you can probably hold off on the hose. A daily check is a good idea in dry weather, particularly if it is also hot.

Or take a soil sample from the root zone and examine it. Dry, sandy soils will flow freely through your fingers but will stick together slightly with adequate moisture. Heavier clay soils will appear hard and crumbly when dry, and feel slick when adequately moist.

Water Wisely

The key to wise watering is to water slowly and deeply. You should water sufficiently to keep your plants growing, but not so much that the roots become oxygen-starved. Watering slowly ensures that all the water soaks into the soil—you don't want any water to run off or cause soil erosion. In most soils, one good

soaking is better than several shallow waterings because it encourages roots to spread deeper and wider in search of water that is farther away.

Deep watering encourages deep rooting, which makes plants more drought-tolerant. Water early or late in the day when temperatures and winds are generally lower, decreasing evaporation.

If your soil has a crust that reduces water penetration, cultivate shallowly with a trowel or hand fork. Then apply a layer of organic mulch around your plants to conserve soil moisture and to prevent future crusting.

Hand Watering

Rain-water tubs, watering cans, and hand-held hoses work well if you have a small garden and plenty of time. You'll know just how much water you are actually applying and where it is going. If you're tending a large garden, though, you'll probably choose overhead sprinklers or trickle irrigation.

Overhead Sprinklers

Although popular and inexpensive, overhead watering systems have two main disadvantages. First, they assume a plentiful, even extravagant, water supply. In the time it takes water to reach the soil, 30 to 50 percent of the water used may be lost to evaporation on a hot, windy day. Secondly, sprinklers take longer to wet the soil, especially if the water must first penetrate a mulch. Fungal diseases that thrive in moist conditions spread easily and quickly when the foliage is wet. Most pathogens can remain dormant in the soil for several years, then become activated when water films form on plant surfaces. That's why you'll find more symptoms of plant disease after periods of high humidity or rainfall.

The advantage of an overhead watering system is that it requires only an inexpensive sprinkler unit and enough hose to reach the garden.

While watering, monitor the rate of application by placing one or several rain gauges in your garden under the overhead sprinkler. Water for 20 to 40 minutes and check the soil again. You'll want to water until the roots receive some relief.

Hand-watering with a watering can is often a more realistic option for irrigating small gardens, potted plants, and for spot-watering thirsty plants.

Water hellebores (*Helleborus* spp.) regularly for the first few years; after that, they'll tolerate dry shade.

The time required to water sufficiently will depend on your water pressure, the size of the nozzles, the distance from the pump, the diameter of your hose, your soil type, and the drying effect of wind and sun. You may need to water two or three times each week or even daily in hot, dry periods. Check the soil at root depth soon after watering to be sure you're watering enough.

Drip Systems

Drip irrigation uses less water, since it is applied directly to the soil, where plants need it. You can water more efficiently in less time since almost no water runs off or evaporates. The water stays cool and helps keep the soil temperature low, especially if you mulch. And since foliage remains dry, fungal diseases are less threatening.

The disadvantage is that drip systems, using water emitters, pressure regulators, and timers, are more expensive and require installation. Once they're installed, however, you'll only need to turn on the faucet to water your garden.

If you're considering purchasing a drip-irrigation system, start out small and add as you grow. Use a map of your garden to help during the planning stages. Most companies that sell drip-irrigation equipment have starter kits and will design a system to fit your needs and estimate the amount of water it will deliver.

Soaker Hoses

You can design your own much simpler drip system by using soaker hoses. Also known as dew hoses, these are much less expensive than emitter drip systems but provide many of the same benefits. Some soaker hoses release water over their entire length, while others spurt water

How to Conserve Water

- Designate separate parts of the garden for plants with low, medium, or high water requirements and water them individually. Annuals will need more water than the deep-rooted, established perennials.
- Insulate the soil surface with a thick layer of organic mulch.
- Maintain your soil's organic matter by working in plenty of compost. Organic matter holds water in the soil like a sponge.
- Eliminate weeds as they appear.
- In dry climates, select plants that are drought-tolerant.
- If paths are included in your garden design, use gravel or pulverized bark to pave them. A living cover like grass will compete with your plants for moisture.

Working compost or organic fertilizer into the soil at planting time will supply the nutrient needs of many different annuals.

Caring for Container Gardens

Container gardens dry out quickly, so you may need to water every day during hot weather. Very small pots, small- and medium-sized clay containers, and hanging baskets dry out especially quickly; you may have to water these as often as twice a day.

If a pot or basket dries out completely, you still may be able to save the plants. Set the pot or basket in a larger container filled with water, let it sit there for an hour or two, and then set the pot or basket in a shady spot for a few hours until the plants perk up again. Then move the pot or basket back to its original spot, but be extra careful to keep those container plants well watered from then on.

Besides regular watering, the other key to lush-looking containers is regular fertilizing. Give them a boost by watering them with diluted fish emulsion or compost tea (made by soaking a shovelful of finished compost in a bucket of water for about a week, then straining out the soaked compost). Start in late spring by feeding once every two weeks, then judge the containers in midsummer. If plants look lush but aren't flowering well, change to fertilizing once every three weeks. If the plants look somewhat spindly, start fertilizing every week. If the plants seem to be growing and flowering well, stick with the two-week schedule.

through tiny holes. Make sure the holes face down into the soil when using this type of hose. A soaker-hose system needs no assembly—simply lay the hoses between plants where you need them. The hoses can be made of various kinds of plastic, rubber, or canvas.

Different Plants Have Different Needs

Some plants thrive in moist soils. Others will grow weakly or rot where water is abundant. Water more often if you grow plants that need evenly moist soil. These include delphiniums, astilbes, and moisture-loving bog plants like Japanese primroses (*Primula japonica*) and marsh marigolds (*Caltha palustris*).

Let the soil dry more between waterings for drought-tolerant plants, such as lavender, perennial candytuft (*Iberis sempervirens*), Cupid's dart (*Catananche caerulea*), and torch lilies (*Kniphofia hybrids*). These plants probably need no more than ½ inch (12 mm) of water per week.

Expect to coddle new plants until their roots spread far enough to support them. If the weather is warm and dry, you may

have to water daily until a drenching rain comes. If the season is cool and rainy, you can let nature handle the irrigation.

Newly planted trees, shrubs, and vines will need special watering attention for at least the first full year of growth after planting—or better yet, two years. After that—provided you've selected plants adapted to your site, prepared the planting area properly, and kept the plants well mulched—their roots should be far-reaching enough to collect adequate moisture during times of drought.

Fertilizing

Supplying your plants with the nutrients they need is a critical part of keeping them healthy and vigorous. How much fertilizer you should add to your garden will depend on how fertile the soil is and which plants you're growing. Small garden plants like vegetable and annuals need more fertilizer than large, established trees and shrubs. However, in the first few years after planting trees and shrubs, their young root system may not yet be able to reach all the necessary nutrients in the soil and they will need supplemental feeding.

How Soil Affects Fertilizing

The texture and natural fertility of your soil will have a great impact on how much and how often you need to add supplemental nutrients. A sandy soil will hold fewer nutrients than a clayey soil or a soil that's high in organic matter, so you'll need to fertilize a sandy soil more frequently. If you prepared the soil thoroughly before planting and corrected nutrient shortages, you may not have to fertilize a new garden for a year or more.

Nutrient Needs Vary among Plants

Fertilizer requirements vary widely among different plants. Some are light feeders, including common sneezeweed (*Helenium autumnale*), oxeye (*Heliopsis helianthoides*), and daisy fleabane (*Erigeron speciosus*). A light layer of compost applied once or twice a year should meet their nutrient needs. Other perennials are heavy feeders; these include delphiniums, astilbes, and garden phlox (*Phlox paniculata*). They need more frequent fertilizing to stay in top form.

You may want to give your plants a little fertility boost to encourage new growth or rejuvenation. Fertilize in spring

Identifying Nutrient Deficiencies

Your plants will tell you if they are suffering from nutrient imbalances or deficiencies. Look for leaves that show signs of yellowing (chlorosis). An overall yellow color may indicate severe nitrogen deficiency; yellow at the tips or edges points to a lack of potassium; yellow between the veins may result from too little iron, molybdenum, manganese, magnesium, or zinc. A phosphorus deficiency may cause red or purple leaf coloration or premature fall color.

If your plants exhibit signs of nutrient imbalances or deficiencies, try a foliar spray of seaweed extract for fast relief. For the long-term health of your plants, have your soil tested for minor nutrient recommendations and apply the appropriate dry material, such as compost or kelp meal, to the soil.

as plants begin growing, also after planting or dividing, and after cutting back or deadheading.

Types of Fertilizers

When you fertilize, you can eliminate deficiencies by applying either liquid or dry fertilizer or both. If you decide to use a combination of fertilizers, make sure you don't apply more total nutrients than your plants need. Remember that too much fertilizer can be as bad as not enough, leading to weak stems, rampant sprawling growth, and disease problems.

Liquid Fertilizers Commonly used liquid fertilizers include fish emulsion, liquid seaweed, and compost tea (see page 53). Use a single dose of liquid fertilizer for a quick but temporary fix of a nutrient shortage, or apply it every two weeks for a general plant boost. You can spray these materials directly on the plants, which will absorb the nutrients through their foliage.

see page 53

Applying Fertilizer

Whichever fertilizing method you use, make sure you always follow the application rates given on the package. Adding too much fertilizer can actually harm your plants.

You can punch holes in the soil and fill them with dry fertilizer.

Or sprinkle dry fertilizer around the base of the plant.

Liquid fertilizers are easy to mist right onto plant leaves.

Dry Fertilizers Dry fertilizers are released to plants more slowly than liquid fertilizers. Scratch them into the surface of the soil in a circle around the perimeter of the plant's foliage, so the nutrients are released gradually as they dissolve in soil moisture. This encourages roots to extend outward.

Applying Fertilizers

How you physically apply the nutrients—broadcasting, drill-hole application, irrigation, or foliar feeding—depends on the type of fertilizer you choose.

Broadcasting Broadcasting involves spreading the fertilizer material evenly onto the soil over the roots. Before you apply fertilizer, pull back the layer of mulch around your plants; then scatter the material over the soil and replace the mulch.

Drill-Hole Application If the soil around your plants is compacted or clayey, broadcasting may not be effective in getting the nutrients where they're needed. In this situation, use an auger or steel pipe to punch holes into the ground around the plant. Make the holes 4 to 6 inches (10 to 15 cm) deep and fill them with fertilizer or compost. The holes help break up the compaction, get needed oxygen to the roots, and place the fertilizer directly into the root zone.

Fertilizing Guidelines for Trees and Shrubs

Roots absorb nutrients from the soil when it is adequately moist and when its temperature is between 40° and 80°F (4° and 27°C). In temperate regions, apply fertilizers in spring or in mid- to late fall. In warmer areas where plants grow year-round, apply fertilizers when plants are most actively growing.

Established Plants

Once trees, shrubs, and vines are established, your fertilizing chores will be minimal. Regular applications of organic mulch are all that most of these plants need. If you have extra compost on hand, you can apply an even layer of it underneath the mulch.

New Plants

Apply an even layer of compost around the base of a new plant in a circle extending 2 to 3 feet (60 to 90 cm) past the drip line. Then cover the compost with a 2- to 3-inch (5- to 7.5-cm) deep layer of mulch. Keep both the compost and the mulch a few inches away from the stem to prevent rodent damage and to allow the air to circulate freely.

Irrigation If you have a drip or soaker-hose irrigation system, you can use it to apply liquid fertilizer. Be sure to use a product such as kelp that dissolves thoroughly to avoid clogging your emitters or pipes.

Foliar Feeding You can apply liquid fertilizers with a hand-held sprayer or mister or with a knapsack sprayer. Set the

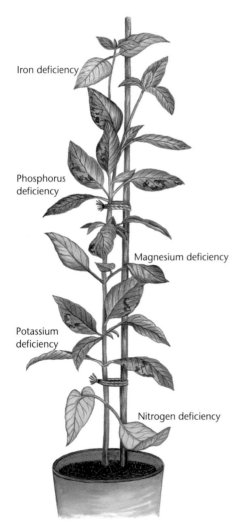

Iron deficiency

Phosphorus deficiency

Magnesium deficiency

Potassium deficiency

Nitrogen deficiency

Thankfully, plants rarely show all of these nutrient deficiencies at once. If one of your plants shows any of these symptoms, try seaweed spray for a quick fix. Then amend the soil with compost for a long-term solution.

nozzle to release the finest spray possible. A surfactant such as ¼ teaspoon of mild soap per gallon (3.8 L) of spray will improve coverage, preventing the spray from beading up on the leaves. Spray in early morning or late afternoon to avoid leaf burn. Be sure to follow the instructions and suggested application rates on the labels of commercial foliar sprays.

Mulching

Mulching is what is known in scientific lingo as an "elegant solution"—it's simple, but it works. All you do, in essence, is put something on top of the soil that covers up weed seeds and gets in the way of emerging weed plants. Either the seeds don't sprout at all, or the seedlings use up all of their energy and die before they reach the sunlight.

Even if it just helped to control weeds, mulch would be an important part of any garden. Happily, mulch offers many other benefits as well. It holds moisture in the soil, so you water less. It keeps soil cooler in the summer, so plant roots face less heat stress. In the winter, it keeps the ground frozen; this way, soils don't freeze and thaw repeatedly, heaving shallow-rooted plants out of the ground and leaving them on the soil surface to die. Mulch also helps reduce soil erosion, and it keeps soil from splashing up on your house or plants when rain falls. If you use a mulch that comes from a plant or animal, such as grass clippings or manure, it will also improve your soil by adding organic matter.

Unfortunately, mulch can have a few drawbacks. Slugs, cutworms, mice, and some other garden pests like to hide in it. And unless you keep it a few inches away from plant stems, mulches can promote crown and stem rot. But if you select the right mulch for your conditions and manage it properly, you'll find that mulch is a valuable and easy part of your weed control program.

Finally, a wide ring of mulch around plants is good protection against accidental nicks and bangs from string trimmers and lawn mowers.

Bark chips are a good-looking and long-lasting mulch for permanent plants, like perennials.

Selecting a Mulch

There are two general types of mulch—organic and inorganic. Both help control weeds and hold moisture in soil, but organic mulches also add all-important organic matter to soil. Inorganic mulches don't improve soil, but they last longer than organic types. Another factor you may want to consider when choosing a mulch is its appearance. Coarse mulches like bark chunks may look fine around large trees but are overwhelming in delicate flower beds; straw is fine for the vegetable garden but too rough-looking for ornamental plantings.

Organic Mulches

Shredded leaves, grass clippings, and bark chips are all examples of organic mulches. In addition to keeping soil cool and moist, organic mulches help improve soil structure by encouraging the activity of earthworms and other soil organisms. They also add nutrients and organic matter to soil as they decompose. Good organic mulches are wood and bark chips, shredded bark, pine needles, and chopped leaves. Hay, straw, and grass clippings are also good mulches, and you can top them

CARING FOR YOUR GARDEN 71

Fallen leaves make an attractive, natural-looking mulch. However, they break down quickly, so must be replaced often.

These bark nuggets are rather coarse-looking, but they are long-lasting and useful in low-maintenance areas.

Inorganic Mulches

Inorganic mulches include stones, marble chips, and lava rock, as well as black plastic and various landscape fabrics. Inorganic mulches don't decompose, so they won't need renewing like organic mulches. But they also don't improve soil as organic mulches do.

Since you won't be disturbing stone or gravel mulches with fresh applications, weeds can become a problem. You will have to hand pull weeds that sprout in these materials. These mulches are often used in combination with a weed barrier such as landscape fabric to greatly reduce the chance of weed problems.

Dark-colored inorganic mulches heat soil, sometimes too much. A plant that prefers cool roots (such as clematis) or one that is growing in full sun may suffer stress from the heat retained by the dark stones. On the other hand, light-colored inorganic mulches, such as marble or quartz chips, reflect sunlight and heat, which can cause leaf damage.

Mulches at a Glance

Bark Pieces Chunks, chips, and shreddings of bark are attractive, long-lasting mulches. The big chunks, sometimes called nuggets, are better than bark chips and shredded bark at discouraging weeds. Weed control is best when the bark is about 6 inches (15 cm) deep. If you're using it in garden beds, however, it's better to apply it only 3 to 4 inches (7.5 to 10 cm) deep; otherwise, you might also smother your desirable plants. Bark mulch is a little expensive, but you'll pay less if you can find a source that sells it unbagged.

There are a few cautions you should keep in mind when considering and using bark mulches:
- Bags labeled "wood chips" can contain wood other than bark, including leftovers from the timber industry that might have been treated with chemicals that could harm plants.
- If you chip your own bark, let it sit outside for a few months before you use

it to leach out any natural substances harmful to young plants. Turn the pile every few weeks to keep the chips from turning "sour."
- Cypress bark can be toxic to young, tender plants.
- Small chips and shredded bark can wash onto nearby sidewalks during a downpour, leading to more work keeping paths near mulched beds clean.

Newspaper and Cardboard Mulches of cardboard or a thick layer of newspaper aren't especially attractive, but they are effective for smothering weeds. They create a barrier that even aggressive perennial weeds have a tough time breaking, while at the same time still allowing water to pass through.

Newspaper and cardboard are inexpensive and readily available. How thick the layer is and how rainy the season is affect how long these mulches last, but you can usually count on them to last one season. It's a good idea to cover them with another mulch to make them more attractive and to anchor them; at the very least, cover the edges with soil or a few rocks to keep them from blowing away.

Leaves Leaves make a good weed-suppressing mulch. You can shred them if you want a good-looking, fine-textured

with a layer of wood chips or shredded bark to improve their appearance.

The larger the particle size, the more slowly the mulch will decompose and need to be replenished. Grass clippings decompose quickly and need frequent renewal, while large bark chips will last several seasons. Flat, leathery tree leaves such as oak and sycamore will last a long time but can mat and shed water: Chop these leaves in a chipper or with your lawn mower before using them as mulch.

Some organic materials are unsuitable for use as mulch because they are too attractive to weeds. Compost, aged manure, or other finely shredded organic materials act like potting soil to weed seeds. In a frequently tended vegetable or flower garden, these mulches are fine. But select a less-hospitable mulch for your low-maintenance permanent plantings, or use these mulches as a base and top them with a thick layer of wood chips or other weed-resistant mulches.

You can collect materials like leaves and pine needles for mulches from your own and your friends' gardens. Wood chips and bark are widely available in bags at garden or home centers. Composted yard waste and wood chips are sometimes available for little or no cost from municipal composting facilities or tree-care companies.

mulch or use them whole to form a dense mat. Apply either shredded or whole leaves in a 4- to 6-inch (10- to 15-cm) layer. If you're using leaves as a long-term mulch around perennials, trees, or shrubs, rake them off for a few weeks in the spring to let the soil warm up.

Landscape Fabric Good landscape fabric—also known as a weed barrier—can keep the areas under and around trees and shrubs nearly weed-free. For new plantings, spread these water-permeable sheets of spun or pressed plastic (now they also are made from wool!) on top of the soil; then cut holes or Xs to make room for the plants. In existing plantings, do your best to fit the fabrics around the base of the plants. Landscape fabrics can also be useful under decks, paths, and walkways; lay them before you build the deck or set the paving to prevent weeds from sprouting.

The barriers do have a few drawbacks. First, they're more expensive than most organic mulches. Also, they will eventually break down, so they have to be replaced every few years; exactly how long they last varies with the brand. Some fabrics are so loosely woven that they let weeds through. And in some cases, the roots of trees and shrubs grow through the fabric, making it tough to move or remove the mulch. You'll also need to cover the fabric with a layer of other mulch to make it look more attractive and to block sunlight, which breaks it down.

Plastic Sheeting Plastic, like landscape fabric, cardboard, and newspaper, is a tough barrier. Unlike those materials, however, plastic doesn't let water through. If you use it around plants, either punch little holes in it or run a soaker hose underneath so your plants will get the water they need. Or use plastic mulch where you want nothing to grow, such as under fences and along walks. When exposed to light, plastic becomes brittle and can rip; cover it with another mulch to reduce these problems.

Compost Compost is partially or completely decomposed yard waste and nonmeat kitchen scraps. While it makes a great soil amendment, it's only so-so at smothering weeds because it's usually fine-textured enough for weed seeds to grow in. And it's so rich in nutrients that weeds will thrive. For best results, apply a layer of compost under another mulch, like bark chips or shredded leaves.

Keep in mind that if you've thrown seedy plants (weeds, flowers—even rotting tomatoes) into the pile, you may end up spreading the seeds around your garden and creating a worse weed problem than before! Avoid throwing seeds into any pile, or save that compost for use as a soil amendment instead of as a mulch.

Hay and Straw Both hay and straw are loose mulches, so you have to apply a thick layer—6 to 10 inches (15 to 25 cm)—to get much weed control from them. Even then, tough perennial weeds that you missed before mulching can pop through, although they'll be weaker than normal. Straw is usually free of weed seeds, but hay might not be and can add to your weed problems.

Grass Clippings Grass clippings add organic matter to the soil, but you need to apply them deeply—about 6 inches (15 cm) of dry clippings or 1 inch (2.5 cm) of fresh clippings—to control annual weeds. Because clippings are lightweight and break down quickly, they aren't effective against most perennial weeds. Fresh grass clippings can mold and smell if you apply them too thickly; try mixing them with a dry mulch such as sawdust, shredded leaves, or bark chips. Avoid using clippings from lawns where the grass or weeds have gone to seed and also from lawns that have been treated with pesticides or herbicides.

Straw mulches are too coarse for flower gardens, but they are great for protecting vegetable and fruit plantings.

Pine Needles Pine needles, also called pine straw, are used widely in the southern United States. They last for a long time (up to several seasons) and increase soil acidity (a real plus for acid-loving plants like blueberries, azaleas, and camellias). Another advantage is their fresh piney smell. But, like grass clippings, pine needles are too loose to keep down perennial weeds. And the needles are a fire hazard during droughts. Don't collect them from the forest; leave that organic matter to fertilize the trees. Apply a 6-inch (15-cm) layer, especially around acid-loving plants.

Mulch to Deter Pests

Mulching is a routine part of conserving soil moisture and preventing weeds, but it's also effective in controlling some pests and diseases. Materials like newspaper, biodegradable paper mulch, and black plastic mulch help to control thrips, leafminers, and other pests that must reach the soil to complete their life cycle. Strips of aluminum foil repel aphids, leafhoppers, and thrips on garden and greenhouse crops. (Leave the foil in place only as long as pests are a threat to avoid leaf damage from reflected heat.) Mulches also prevent raindrops from splashing soilborne disease spores onto plant leaves.

Applying Mulch

You'll get the best results if you mulch bare soil—that means before the weeds start growing or right after you hoe, cut, or pull weeds that have already come up. Also make sure the soil is moist (but not soggy) before you mulch. Then spread a layer of mulch that is thick enough to discourage new weeds from sprouting. If your mulch has large particles, such as large wood or bark chips, use a 3- to 5-inch (7.5- to 12.5-cm) thick layer. Mulches with smaller-sized particles, such as grass clippings or shredded bark, allow less space for sprouting weeds, so you can apply them in a thinner layer of 2 to 3 inches (5 to 7.5 cm).

Cover the soil with a uniformly thick layer, but taper the depth of the layer near the trunks or stems of plants. Never pile mulch against your plants' trunks or stems. Mulch can hold excessive moisture around them and also reduce the amount of oxygen that reaches the crowns of the plants. To prevent this problem and to keep rodents from nesting nearby and feeding on the bark, leave about 6 to 12 inches (15 to 30 cm) between the mulch and tree and shrub trunks, and 4 to 6 inches (10 to 15 cm) between mulch and vines.

Also be aware that mulch can thwart desirable seedlings as well as weed seedlings. If you're growing plants from direct-sown seed or if you're depending on self-sown seedlings from last year's plants, wait until the seedlings are about 4 to 6 inches (10 to 15 cm) tall before mulching. An added benefit of waiting is that bare soil warms up more quickly in the spring than mulched soil.

How frequently you need to renew the mulches depends on which kind you use. Long-lasting materials like wood chips may need refreshing only every two to three years. Finer materials, like compost or grass clippings, should be renewed once or twice a year. Top these materials with coarse mulches to help them last longer.

The Latest News in Mulching

To control severe weed problems, you can get extra protection by laying sheets of newspaper beneath an organic mulch. Wet the papers lightly to keep them from blowing around and overlap neighboring sheets to cover the soil surface. Then cover the paper with several inches of an organic mulch. In a month or two, the newspaper will gradually break down with the mulch, adding extra organic matter to the soil.

Staking and Supporting Your Plants

Staking Trees and Shrubs

Staking holds trees and shrubs in place while their roots grow out from the root ball into the surrounding soil. Trees taller than 8 feet (2.4 m) or top-heavy trees with a large crown in relation to the size of the root ball benefit from the support of stakes to prevent them from falling over. Trees with straight, strong trunks that are less than 8 feet (2.4 m) tall and have small crowns usually need no staking unless they are planted in a windy location. Unstaked trees, or those staked with some slack, develop thicker, stronger trunks faster than staked trees.

If staking is necessary, use one or two stakes for small trees, two or three for large trees. Select stakes that are tall and strong enough to support your trees.

Locate the first stake facing the prevailing wind and space the others equally around the trees.

Drive the stakes several inches into firm soil on the outside of the root ball before you finish backfilling the planting hole. Attach the stakes to your trees with materials that won't cut, rub, or damage the trees' bark. Plastic bands, nylon webbing, and strips of manufactured fabric are good choices. Allow a few inches of slack when you attach these materials so that your trees can move slightly in the wind. This movement promotes the development of strong wood, so the tree will be able to support itself when you remove the stakes.

Unstake your trees one year after planting. By that time, a healthy tree will be well anchored into the ground with its own roots.

Staking Flowers

If you grow only short-stemmed plants, or you don't mind your flowers sprawling or leaning on each other, you won't have to worry about staking. But anyone who has seen peonies flattened by rain or has watched a perfect giant delphinium toppled in a strong wind knows that a few minutes spent placing a few stakes is time well spent.

Stake delphiniums, foxgloves, and other tall perennials to keep them upright.

Weeding

Plan a Weed Control Strategy

To control your lawn and garden weeds effectively and efficiently, you need to use the right technique at the right time. This requires an essential piece of knowledge: How long do your particular weeds live? All plants have one of three life cycles—they can be annuals, biennials, or perennials. Knowing the life cycles of your weeds is your key to determining how they spread and how you can stop them.

Annual Weeds Spread by Seed

Annual weeds, such as lamb's-quarters (*Chenopodium album*), live an entire life within one year; they sprout from seed, grow, flower, set seed, and die.

One part of controlling annuals is never letting them set seed. If the original plants die without making more seed, they won't come back the following year.

Biennials Take Two Years

For biennial weeds, such as Queen-Anne's-lace (*Daucus carota* var. *carota*), the seed-to-seed cycle spreads over two years. These weeds sprout from seed in the spring or summer, then usually grow into a ground-hugging circle of leaves called a rosette. The leaves produce sugars that move down to the roots and are stored as starch. The next spring, the plant uses the stored food energy to send up a flowering stalk, which may or may not have leaves. The plant flowers, sets seed, then dies.

You have two main options for controlling biennial weeds. You could dig out the rosette—root and all—the first year. Or you could wait until the second year and cut the plant down to the ground. If you wait until the weed is just about to flower, the plant will have used up most of its stored energy and will likely not return.

Perennials Are Persistent

Wild garlic (*Allium vineale*), kudzu (*Pueraria lobata*), and other perennial weeds live for three years or more. Perennials, like biennials, store carbohydrates to fuel early growth the next spring. That food energy may be stored in a taproot, in spreading underground stems called rhizomes, or in spreading aboveground stems called runners or stolons. Or it may be in a tuber (like a potato) or a bulb (like an onion).

Perennials are generally the most difficult weeds to control. The stored carbohydrates give them a strong start each spring, as well as the power to grow again if their leaves are lost or damaged. Just preventing seed formation on perennials is not enough to get rid of them; you need to either dig up all of the underground structures or force them to use up their food reserves by repeatedly removing their aboveground growth.

How to Weed

The particular weeding technique you'll use depends on how many weeds you have to control, how large an area they cover, and how much time you want to spend on them.

Take a Physical Approach Weed control methods that involve pulling, cutting, or directly injuring weeds are called physical or mechanical controls. These methods are the most common because they are convenient and they work.

Pulling and Digging These techniques are simple and effective for getting rid of a few weeds but are pretty tiring when you're weeding large areas.

Pulling gets rid of annual weeds well, especially if the soil is damp enough that the roots come up. Just be sure not to toss weeds that reroot easily, such as purslane (*Portulaca oleracea*), on the ground. If you pull annual grasses, get as much of the roots as possible; the growing point of grasses is below the ground, and the plant might resprout if you just remove the aboveground portion.

Always try to pull annuals before they begin to flower and set seed. If they have already started flowering, collect the pulled weeds in a bucket; don't leave

When you've put time and effort into planning and planting the perfect flower garden, you don't want weeds popping up to spoil the effect.

them on the ground, since their seeds could still ripen and drop onto the soil.

Digging is a slightly better choice for perennials, assuming you get all of the buried portions. If you don't, these buried portions can produce new plants. Use hand tools to dig out small or shallow-rooted perennials. You may need a spading fork, spade, or shovel for tough, deep roots, like those of pokeweed (*Phytolacca americana*).

Thorough hand-weeding before planting will help get new gardens off to a weed-free start.

Hoeing and Tilling When the weeds are too numerous to pull, a sharp hoe is a good solution. In most cases, hoes are best for young or annual weeds. But you can also deal a damaging blow to some established perennials—primarily those with thin or soft stems—by forcing them to use food reserves to replace the decapitated top growth.

If you're trying to control perennial weeds, it's most important to hoe every 7 to 14 days to cut off the top growth before it starts sending food back down to the roots.

If you have a large vegetable garden, with crops planted in rows, cultivating with a wheel hoe or rotary tiller may be more practical than with a handheld hoe. Shallow tilling—about 1 inch (2.5 cm) deep—can uproot young weeds without bringing up too many buried seeds.

In almost all cases, it's best to avoid tilling perennial weeds with spreading roots, such as quack grass (*Agropyron repens*) and Canada thistle (*Cirsium arvense*). Even small pieces of chopped-up roots can sprout, multiplying your perennial weed problems. If you must rid an area of these weeds and can leave the spot unplanted for a growing season, you could try tilling the area shallowly every week or two until the root pieces stop sprouting new plants.

Mowing Mowing doesn't get the roots, but it can keep all but the lowest-growing weeds from setting seed. And if you mow often enough (every week or two), it can weaken perennial weeds by making them use up their food reserves to replace the top growth you removed.

Mowing works on woody shrubs and vines as long as the stems aren't too thick for the machine. For tall, tough weeds and tree seedlings no more than ¼ inch (18 mm) in diameter, use a heavy-duty string trimmer with a blade attachment. If you must control brush over a large area, consider

Canada thistle

renting a walk-behind tractor with a sickle bar attachment.

Try Organic Herbicides

Organic herbicides won't solve all of your weed woes, but they can be a useful alternative in certain situations. The herbicides that are acceptable to organic gardeners—basically soap, vinegar, and salt—all have one thing in common: They can kill any plant they touch (assuming you get enough of the material on the plant). In gardening lingo, these are called non-selective herbicides. You must use them with caution to avoid damaging the plants you want to keep.

Soap-Based Herbicides

If you've ever used soap sprays to control insect pests, you may have noticed the warnings that these sprays can injure some plants; you may have even seen the damage yourself. Herbicidal soap sprays take this damage one step further. They are formulated to break up the protective waxy covering on the leaves, causing the weeds to slowly dry up and die.

The soap works on contact—it isn't absorbed and moved through the plant—so you need to spray the entire plant thoroughly. It takes at least a few hours for the damage to show; the plant gradually turns brown.

Herbicidal soaps work best on young weeds that haven't had time to establish a good root system. Older annuals often grow back and usually require more than one application. Perennials with well-established food reserves can grow back so many times that, unless you want to run for the herbicide every week, it's probably easier to cut off the top growth until the food stores are depleted.

Vinegar and Salt

These two controls need to be used with even more caution than herbicidal soap because they can sterilize the soil for months. The first approach is to

Whatever control you choose, use it before weeds set seed; otherwise, you'll have to deal with seedlings too.

pour vinegar in the soil, making it too acid for plants to grow. The other is to pour salt on the soil and water it in, which kills the roots. For best results in either case, cut off or pull as much of the weed as you can before applying the control.

Because both of these substances have such a drastic effect on the soil, they are only appropriate where you want nothing else to grow, such as between the cracks in a sidewalk. Otherwise, consider less-toxic controls like dousing with boiling water, or pulling by hand.

When not maintained, fence lines and pathways can become an ideal site for weeds to take over.

Pests and Diseases

If pests stood up to be counted, gardeners would find pest identification and control an easier task. Unfortunately, pests often remain undetected until the harm is done. Even if you do spot damage on your plants, you may have difficulty identifying the culprit. Nutrient deficiencies or even air pollution can cause similar symptoms. But getting an accurate diagnosis is the only way to choose an appropriate and effective pest control measure.

Diagnosing Insect Damage

Fortunately, there are clues you can look for to help pin down plant problems. Follow the steps below to spot developing damage and to identify the causes.

1. Give plants a thorough inspection at least once a week. Look at both sides of the leaves, around buds and flowers, and along the stems.
2. If you find damage, jot down a few notes: The identity of the affected plant, the plant parts that are affected, and the kind of damage (such as "large holes in leaves" or "distorted fruit").
3. Check the undersides of plant leaves, and shallowly scratch the soil or mulch, looking for likely culprits. Also search for clusters of eggs, webs, or pellet- or sawdust-like insect droppings. See if neighboring plants show similar symptoms.
4. If you actually find insects, examine them with a 10x magnifying lens (available through garden suppliers or at college bookstores). Look through the photos in insect field guides to try to identify them. Don't assume that the insects must be pests—they could just as easily be beneficials that stopped by to help.
5. If you can't find any suspects, or can't identify the ones you have, try matching the damage symptoms with those in "Signs of Damage," opposite. This approach may help you close in on a possible cause.
6. If you still aren't sure of the cause, consider other possible sources, like

wind damage, nutrient deficiency, or animal pests.
7. If all else fails, you may want to take the notes you've made, and perhaps a piece of the affected plant to your local Cooperative Extension Service or garden center for help in making an accurate diagnosis.

Pyrethrum daisies are the source of pyrethrin, a potent botanical insecticide.

Diseases

What Is a Disease?

Before you can cope with diseases, you need to understand what they actually are. Unfortunately, diseases are more difficult to define than insects. After all, insects are actual organisms with specific traits and characteristics. Plant diseases, on the other hand, can be anything that interferes with normal growth functions (like water uptake and photosynthesis).

To make this definition a little more useful, it's helpful to divide plant disease

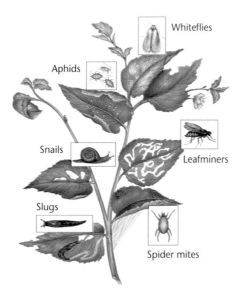

As you scout for damage, inspect plants thoroughly. If you see signs of damage, look closely to check for the pests.

into two categories. Infectious diseases can spread from one plant to another. They're the problems we usually think of as plant diseases—like rust, fire blight, powdery mildew. Noninfectious diseases cannot be transmitted from one plant to another. Nutrient imbalances, air pollution, and waterlogged soil are a few causes of noninfectious diseases.

Infectious Diseases

Infectious plant diseases are caused by microscopic living organisms called pathogens. Pathogens are commonly broken down into four groups: fungi, bacteria, viruses, and nematodes.

Fungi Many kinds of molds, mildews, and mushrooms play an important part in breaking down organic matter in soil and compost. There are, however, a number of fungi that also attack living plants. These plant pathogenic fungi are the most common causes of garden diseases. Powdery mildew, damping-off, anthracnose, apple scab, club root, late blight, and black spot are all fungal.

Some pathogenic fungi are host-specific, but most will attack a variety of garden plants. Fungi produce spores that move with wind, soil, water, and animals to plant surfaces. Given the right environmental conditions and the right host plant, spores of plant pathogenic fungi will germinate and infect plants.

Bacteria Like fungi, bacteria are specialized organisms with both beneficial and pathogenic species. Beneficial bacteria recycle soil organic matter and nutrients, and they can even help control insect pests, like caterpillars and beetles. Plant pathogenic bacteria, however, can infect plants and cause diseases like crown gall, bacterial wilt, and fire blight.

Bacterial cells travel to plants the same way as fungal spores. Once they reach a susceptible plant, bacteria move into and infect plants through wounds and natural openings in leaves, stems, and roots.

Viruses Viruses are the smallest disease agents. Once inside a living cell, they multiply by making their host plant produce even more virus particles, upsetting the plant's normal metabolism and causing disease symptoms. Virus particles are carried to healthy plants by pests like insects, mites, and nematodes. They're also spread by taking cuttings, grafts, layers, or divisions from infected plants. Compost that contains infected plants and is not properly decomposed can also spread viruses.

Viral diseases can be the most difficult to diagnose. Some common indications of viral attack include mottled or discolored leaves. Symptoms can vary from one plant to the next; infected plants may not even show symptoms. If your plants have suffered from viral infection in the past, your best course is to become familiar with the common viruses in your area and the symptoms they cause so that you'll know when to take control measures.

Nematodes Nematodes are microscopic roundworms, which are found free-living in soil and as parasites on plants and animals. Beneficial nematodes are important members of the soil community, since they feed on decaying material and pests like cut-worms and grubs. Pest nematodes damage plants by puncturing cell walls with their needlelike mouthparts and drawing out the cell contents. This causes disease-like symptoms—including yellowing, wilting, stunting, and reduced yields—that are difficult to distinguish from other causes.

Plant parasitic nematodes travel to healthy plants in water and in infested soil carried on tools, boots, and animals. If you suspect your plants suffer from nematode damage, you can submit root and soil samples to a diagnostic laboratory or your Cooperative Extension Service for positive identification.

Signs of Damage

Damage	Possible Causes
Leaves with large, ragged holes	Adult or larval stages of beetles like Japanese beetles, Mexican bean beetles, and others; grasshoppers; moth larvae like armyworms or hornworms; slugs or snails; animal pests
Leaves curled, twisted, puckered, or distorted	Aphids; leafhoppers; tarnished plant bugs; nutrient deficiency
Leaves curled, webs present	Webworms; obliquebanded leafrollers
Leaves with numerous, small holes	Adult flea beetles; plant diseases
Leaves spotted	Tarnished plant bugs; spider mites; thrips; lace bugs; plant diseases
Leaves or stems speckled or silvery	Thrips
Leaves and stems with hardened bumps, scales, or cottony growths	Scales; mealybugs; plant diseases
Leaves with shallow tunnels under leaf surface	Larval leafminers; sawflies
Leaves with shiny, slimy, frothy, or sticky coating	Aphids; mealybugs; slugs and snails; pear psyllas; scales; spittlebugs; whiteflies; plant diseases
Fruit with tunnels throughout	Apple maggots; moth larvae like codling moths or European corn borers
Fruit distorted, twisted	European corn borers; tarnished plant bugs
Fruit spotted, sticky	Aphids; leafhoppers; spittlebugs; plant diseases
Roots or bulbs with signs of feeding or dead spots	Wireworms; many kinds of beetle grubs; weevils (black vine, carrot, or strawberry root weevils)
Roots or stems with galls, swellings	Gall wasps; nematodes; plant diseases
Roots or stems with excessive branching	Nematodes
Stems hollowed, with larvae inside and leaves wilted	Borers (European corn, flatheaded appletree, fruit, peachtree, roundheaded appletree, and squash vine borers)
Flowers eaten	Japanese beetles; rose chafers
Flowers fall before opening	Tarnished plant bugs
Seedlings chewed off at soil level	Cutworms; animal pests

Noninfectious Diseases

Changes in the environment and in your gardening techniques can also interfere with normal plant functions, so technically they are considered diseases. Unlike infectious diseases, though, noninfectious diseases (also called disorders) cannot be transmitted from plant to plant. Disorders can still be very serious once they occur, but they're often easy to prevent and remedy with good gardening practices, like regular soil improvement.

Symptoms of disorders vary widely, depending on the cause and the plant. You'll find more about identifying disorders under "Disease Look-Alikes" on page 79.

Keeping your garden neat and free of debris helps remove sites for pests and disease spores.

Diagnosing Disease Problems

Like most garden problems, plant diseases are easiest to control if you catch them early. But unlike insect pests, pathogens are generally too small to see without magnification. In most cases, you won't know they've struck until your plants begin to suffer and display symptoms. Environmental and cultural problems, like frost injury, air pollution, or nutrient imbalances, can also be tricky to diagnose, since the conditions that cause them are seldom visible.

Step-By-Step Disease Diagnosis

1. Identify the plant. Although it sounds obvious, this one simple step can put you surprisingly close to an accurate diagnosis in just a few minutes. Many popular garden plants are commonly attacked by easy-to-identify diseases and disorders, like black spot on roses, powdery mildew on lilacs, smut on corn, or blossom end rot on tomatoes.

   If you're not sure what the plant is, ask a fellow gardener, a local nursery or botanical garden, or your local Cooperative Extension Service for help. Even if identifying the plant doesn't help you diagnose the disease, it can be important later on when you are deciding on a control measure. Some plants, for instance, are sensitive to soap- or oil-based sprays, so you'd want to use a different type of control on these plants to avoid causing even more damage.

2. Take a good look. Jot down anything that you notice about the affected plant. What parts seem to be most affected: The leaves, stems, flowers, or fruits? If the plant parts are spotted or discolored, note the color, size, and general shape of the patches. If leaves are affected, is it the old or new leaves? Is the plant shorter than similar plants around it? Was it recently planted, or has it been in your landscape for many years? Anything you know or notice about the affected plant—no matter how minor—may help you or your consultant make or confirm a diagnosis of the problem.

3. Consider the environment. Extreme weather conditions, like strong wind, hail, and waterlogged or dry soils, can give plants an unhealthy appearance that resembles symptoms of plant disease. Make a note of any unusual weather conditions that you can remember. (Actually, it's smart to jot down weather occurrences, like frosts, heavy rains, or dry spells, as they happen so you'll have those notes to refer back to when a problem strikes.)

Also consider whether your plants have been exposed to pollutants like acid rain, herbicide drift, or road salt.

4. Rule out insect pests. Some insects cause damage that resembles plant disease symptoms. When in doubt, use a magnifying lens to check for insect signs like webbing or droppings. Symptoms that are particularly unusual might mean that damage is the result of two or more pathogens or pests; open wounds from insects or other damage make convenient entrances for plant pathogens.

5. Do some research. Discuss the problem with neighbors who have similar plants and check reference books in your local library.

6. Consult the experts. If a particular problem has you stumped, submit samples to your local or state plant disease diagnostic laboratory. Personnel at Cooperative Extension Service offices can provide you with the right forms, mailing supplies, and instructions for sending plant samples by mail. Local botanical gardens and arboreta may also be willing to help you identify plant problems.

Common Signs and Symptoms

Unhealthy plants have special distress signals that let you know when pathogens have attacked. Plants will respond to the stress of infection with a wide range of symptoms, from leaf spots and damaged fruit to wilting and even death. To help narrow down your diagnosis, see if any of the descriptions below match the affected parts of your plant.

Blights Leaves, flowers, stems, and branches that suddenly wilt, wither, and die are common indications of blight. Common garden blights include Botrytis, early and late blight (caused by fungi), and fire blight (produced by bacteria).

Cankers Affected woody plants produce dead, and often sunken, patches in stems and branches. These cankers may ooze a

Late blight on celery causes spots on leaves and may spread to stems.

sticky or foul-smelling material and can spread to kill whole trunks or shoots. The fungal Cytospora canker is a common orchard problem; bacterial fire blight is another canker-causer.

Galls Swellings or overgrown patches of leaf or stem tissue are commonly known as galls. They may be caused by fungi (like leaf gall), bacteria (such as crown gall), or even insects (such as gall wasps).

Leaf Curl Deformed and discolored leaves suffer from leaf curl. Peach leaf curl is caused by a fungus; viruses may also produce these symptoms.

Leaf Spots Rounded or irregular areas in various colors are common leaf symptoms. They are produced by many pathogens.

Mildews Dusty white, gray, or purplish patches on the surfaces or undersides of leaves are an easy clue to the fungal powdery and downy mildews.

Rots Soft or discolored and dying plant tissue generally indicate some kind of rot. Fungi and bacteria can cause rot on fruit, stems, flowers, or roots.

Rusts Orange or yellowish spots, galls, or coatings are caused by rust fungi. Rusts may affect leaves, stems, flowers, or fruits.

Wilts Drooping leaves and stems indicate that the plant isn't getting enough water.

Removing and destroying rust-infected leaves can be an effective control for this fungal disease.

This may be caused by improper watering or by fungi and bacteria that can clog the plant's water conducting system. Fungi cause Fusarium and Verticillium wilt; bacterial wilt is a problem in cucumbers and related crops.

Disease Look-Alikes

Although plants can adapt to many different environments, they all have certain conditions that they need to grow their best. Factors like air pollution or widely fluctuating temperatures can upset a plant's normal functions, causing symptoms that resemble plant disease. Since such problems aren't transmitted from plant to plant, they are called noninfectious diseases or plant disorders.

It's a good idea to be aware of the symptoms produced by common disorders so you can deal with them effectively when they do occur instead of mistaking them for an infectious disease.

Excessive Water Too much water means that most or all of the tiny soil pores, which normally hold some oxygen, are filled with water. When roots don't get the oxygen they need, they can't function properly and are more prone to infectious diseases, like root rot. Affected plants lack vigor and may wilt; leaves become yellow. Raised beds can help improve drainage.

Drought A shortage of soil water can stunt plant growth and slow flower and fruit production. Leaves either turn pale and wilt or develop brown, scorched areas. Shallow-rooted annual plants are often most affected. Regular deep irrigation can help mildly affected plants recover and prevent future problems. Soaker hoses are an efficient and economical way to give your plants the water they need.

Cold Stress Sudden cold snaps can kill tender buds, growing tips, and other woody plant parts. Leaves turn yellow or drop, buds may drop, stems can crack, and bark may split. Unseasonably low temperatures during the growing season can damage warm-weather vegetables like corn, beans, and tomatoes. Protect actively growing plants with floating row covers or other frost shields. Avoid fertilizing after midsummer; later fertilizing promotes soft growth that is more frost-prone.

When the ground is frozen, dry winter winds can pull moisture out of buds and evergreen leaves, causing browning and tip dieback. Protect dormant plants with windbreaks or spray with an anti-transpirant to block moisture loss.

Heat Stress Young plants exposed to high temperatures often wilt and may die. Cold-weather vegetables like lettuce and spinach stop producing new leaves and will bolt (go to seed). Shade and water may help plants recover; shade can also help prevent damage. Water well in the early morning and again in the evening if necessary. Avoid planting cool-weather crops that will mature in midsummer. Pull out and compost plants that bolt.

Insufficient Light Plants become spindly and are more susceptible to lodging (falling over) when light is inadequate. Green leaves become pale, and variegated or colored leaves may turn evenly green if they don't get enough light. If plants show these symptoms, try moving them to a sunnier spot.

Plant Disease Symptoms and Causes

What You See	Possible Causes
Leaves mottled or discolored	Mosaic; nutrient deficiency; ozone, or sulfur dioxide injury; sooty mold; sunscald; yellows; insect pests
Leaves with yellow or brown spots	Anthracnose; apple scab; bacterial spot; Botrytis blight; cedar-apple rust; downy mildew; Septoria leaf spot
Leaves with black or brown spots surrounded by yellow	Bacterial spot; black spot; cherry leaf spot; late blight
Leaves curled, cupped, or blistered	Leaf gall; mosaic or other viral diseases; peach leaf curl; herbicide drift; insect pests
Leaves, shoots, or fruit with white spots or patches	Downy mildew; powdery mildew; salt injury
Leaves and stems wilted and dying	Bacterial wilt; Dutch elm disease; Fusarium wilt; oak wilt; Verticillium wilt; waterlogged soil; lack of water
Leaves or stems with orange spots	Rust
Stems with irregular swellings	Black knot; cedar-apple rust; crown gall
Stems with oozing slimy or gummy substance	Cytospora canker; slime flux
Stems condensed into short, bushy "rosettes;" plant stunted	Peach rosette; nematodes
Stems of seedlings rotted at the soil line; infected seedlings collapsed	Damping-off
Flowers or fruit with brown spots	Brown rot; Botrytis blight or fruit rot; fire blight; frost damage
Fruit with small, dark sunken spots	Anthracnose
Apple fruit with green or velvety brown spots that turn into raised, dark, corky areas	Apple scab
Fruit with water-soaked spots that turn brown and leathery at the blossom end	Blossom end rot
Roots of young and old plants rotted; plants stunted or wilted	Root rot
Roots with irregular swellings	Club root; crown gall; nematodes

Strong Wind Leaves develop a silvery discoloration and tattered leaf edges when exposed to prolonged high winds. Windblown plants may lose large amounts of water through their foliage, causing leaves to appear wilted. Walls and windbreaks may be the solution.

Deficient Nutrients When nutrients are lacking, plants are less vigorous and yield poorly. Common deficiency symptoms are abnormal leaf color, curled or stunted leaves, and dead growing tips. Regular soil tests can alert you to developing deficiency problems.

Excessive Nutrients High concentrations of nutrients may cause the same symptoms as nutrient deficiencies. In some cases, the effects of excess nutrients are indirect. Too much nitrogen, for example, often produces lush plants with few flowers or fruit. Soil tests can show you if an imbalance is developing. Follow package directions for fertilizer application rates.

Ozone Pollution Ozone pollution, from automobile exhaust and other internal combustion engines, causes stippling or yellowing of leaves. Damage is especially severe on the upper leaf surfaces and on leaves that have just matured.

Herbicide Drift Under windy conditions, herbicides applied along roadways, in farm fields, or in neighboring yards may drift over to your property and injure your plants. Depending on the product used, leaves may appear burned, bronzed, distorted, or discolored, or plants may die. Protect your plantings with walls, windbreaks, or other barriers.

Excessive Light When exposed to direct sunlight, some fruits and leaves develop sunscald, discoloration, or blisters. Too much light can burn the foliage of shade-loving plants, causing brown patches or dead leaves. Plants with purple or yellow leaves often fade or burn in direct sunlight. If you're not sure how much light a plant needs, see how it grows in partial shade; if it turns pale or spindly, gradually move it into more sunlight. Always place seedlings or young plants in the shade, slowly introducing them to more light as they grow.

Late cold snaps can injure flowers and reduce crop yields.

Beneficial Insects

Almost none of the insects that you'll come across in the garden are harmful to you or your plants. Some insects feed primarily on wild plants and leave your garden plants alone. Other insect species directly benefit the garden. Wild and domestic bees, for example, perform vital functions like pollination. And some species survive by preying (feeding) on or parasitizing (living within) other insects. The species that attack other insects are especially significant to the gardener, since they're one of the tools you can rely on for pest control.

Predators Predators eat other organisms. Most insect predators, like ground beetles or rove beetles, aren't fussy eaters. They're called generalists, and they'll eat pest insects as well as fellow predators that are small enough to catch. Other predaceous insects are prey-specific. For example, some lady beetle species prefer spider mites, some consume only mealybugs, and others restrict their diet to aphids. Not all predators are insects. Insect predators like spiders, centipedes, and several species of mites are also important pest controllers.

Parasites Parasites are among the most important biological pest controls. They live on or in other organisms. Parasites steal nutrients from their host but they usually don't kill it.

Parasitoids are a special kind of parasite. They make ideal biological pest controllers because they kill their host. Most parasitoids are tiny, aggressive wasps or bees that lay their eggs within the living host. Parasitoid larvae hatch and consume their host, then form a cocoon before emerging as adults that are eager to find more pests. Most parasitoids are species- and host-specific. One kind may attack only a pest's larval stage, for example, while another kind will parasitize the adult form of the same pest.

Adult lacewings feed mostly on nectar and honeydew, but their larvae are voracious predators of many pest insects.

Attracting Beneficials

You can entice beneficials to frequent your yard and garden by providing them with the three basic necessities: water, food, and shelter.

Water A water source will attract most kinds of beneficials (as well as insect-eating birds and toads), especially during dry spells. Fill shallow pans with water and set them in protected nooks and corners of your garden. Set rocks in the pans to serve as insect perches.

Food Access to suitable food is vital for beneficials. During various stages of their life, beneficials may need different types of food. Larvae, for instance, often prey on pests, while adults feed on pollen and nectar. Small-flowered plants are ideal food sources for beneficials. Particularly good choices include members of the plant families Umbelliferae (such as dill, lovage, parsley, and fennel) and Labiatae (including mint, hyssop, catnip, and lemon balm). Plant these herbs among your flowers and vegetables to attract beneficials in areas where pests are a problem. Clover and buckwheat are also good food sources.

Spotted cucumber beetle

Some species of lady beetles feed only on aphids.

Shelter Once they have food and water, beneficials will look for a safe place to live and to lay their eggs. Provide shelter by adding organic mulches like straw, leaves, or compost to the soil surface around plants and along paths. Beneficials also appreciate the protection of trees, perennial plantings, and cover crops that aren't frequently disturbed by harvest and tillage.

You can maintain a friendly environment for beneficials by avoiding broad-spectrum pesticides (those that kill a wide range of insects). Even organically acceptable chemicals like rotenone will wipe out beneficials as readily as pests. Often, pest populations recover more quickly than the beneficials and multiply unchecked. This leads to a vicious circle—you'll need to apply stronger control measures and the beneficials will not get a chance to recover.

Other Beneficial Critters

Insects aren't the only beneficial creatures in your garden. Lizards and toads consume their share of pest insects, and snakes help to keep rodent populations in control. Bats consume thousands of mosquitoes each night, while barn swallow, purple martins, and woodpeckers control flying insects by day.

Pruning and Training

Proper pruning can promote healthy growth on ailing plants, improve the form of poorly shaped ones, show off the natural beauty of good-looking plants, and encourage the production of more or better fruits or flowers.

Why Should You Prune?

There are many reasons you may want or need to prune. Judicious pruning at planting time defines the shape of your new trees, shrubs, and vines. As your new plants grow, they will need pruning to keep them in shape. Also, they will occasionally need pruning to correct structural problems that develop, such as branches that rub or grow at tight angles. Maintenance pruning is also necessary to remove damage caused by weather, animals, people, or insects and diseases. You may need to direct growth, especially of fast-growing vines, or control the height or spread of your plants. Some vines, especially vigorous growers like trumpet creeper (*Campsis radicans*) and wisteria (*Wisteria* spp.), need heavy pruning to keep them a manageable size and to increase the number of flowers.

When to Prune

Timing is critical to successful pruning. Adapt your pruning schedule depending on what you want to accomplish. Here are the benefits and drawbacks of pruning in each season:

- Spring pruning stimulates a flush of vigorous growth. It's a good time for heavy pruning because plants will recover fast.
- Summer pruning is a good time for tidying up, but avoid heavy pruning, which can stress plants in hot weather.
- Fall is a good time to make thinning cuts, removing branches back to a main stem. Don't prune back branch tips in fall because the tender new growth that results can be easily damaged by freezes.
- In winter, dormant plants are particularly easy to prune to shape, since the lack of leaves makes it easy to see the plant's structure.

There are times, however, when you need to ignore the season and pick up the pruners. If damage from storms, equipment, or disease occurs, you should prune immediately, removing all damaged wood.

Pruning Tools

The pruning tools you'll need depend on what you will be trimming. Hedge clippers are the traditional choice for formal hedges. Pruning shears are best for stems and twigs. As the diameter of the branches increases, switch to loppers, which work well on branches that are finger-sized or larger. When loppers aren't large enough, use a pruning saw.

Pruners and loppers are available in two types. Bypass pruners cut with a scissor action; anvil pruners cut with a sharp blade that closes against a metal plate. Lopping shears have long handles to give you leverage and a longer reach. Test pruning tools before buying them to make sure the grip is comfortable and the mechanism is easy to work.

Pruning Techniques

Start any pruning job by removing dead wood. Dead wood is easy to spot during the growing season because it bears no leaves. It snaps easily, revealing no green under the bark.

After removing the dead wood, prune your trees and shrubs to improve their structure, making them more attractive and stronger. Remove any branches that are badly crossed or rubbing, leaving the best of the pair. Thin out or head back misplaced branches that crowd walkways or other plants.

Pruning Cuts

Pruning basically comes down to two types of cuts: thinning and heading. A thinning cut removes branches where

Thinning cuts help to retain a plant's natural branching structure and open up dense, crowded growth.

they join the stem. Be sure to cut just outside the branch collar—the raised or otherwise distinct area at the branch base. Cuts that are flush to the stem, removing the collar area, don't heal (close) well. Use thinning cuts to open the interior of a shrub or tree or to remove misplaced or crossed branches.

Heading cuts stimulate regrowth. Save them until the end of the pruning job. A nonselective heading cut slices off branch tips in midstem, bringing on a thick flush of uniform growth. Selective heading snips off the tip of a branch back to a bud or side branch. Cut slightly above a bud pointed in the direction in which you want new stems to grow. In general, prune above buds that face outward, not inward.

Pruning Terms

Just like any skill, pruning has its own terminology. We've tried to keep the jargon to a minimum, but there are some terms that you really need to understand to be an effective pruner. Here are definitions for some common pruning terms.

Apical dominance The condition in most plants where the tip bud grows more strongly than the buds lower on the stem. If you cut off the top bud, apical dominance is lost and the remaining buds grow more quickly.

Branch collar The zone where a branch meets a stem. The collar is usually easiest to see as a bulge at the base of a large branch, but even small branches have collars. When you make a pruning cut, always leave the collar; this is a site of rapid cell division and wound closure.

Callus The scar tissue that naturally forms around wounds, such as pruning cuts, on woody plants.

Candle The compact, expanding new growth that appears on pines, spruces, and firs in the spring.

Cane A long, slender branch that originates directly from the roots.

Crotch The angle formed between two branches or between a branch and the trunk.

Deadheading The removal of spent flowers or unripe seedpods.

Lateral branch Any branch growing from a larger branch.

Leader The main, primary, or tallest vertical branch originating from the trunk of a tree.

Scaffold branches The primary limbs that originate from the main trunk of a tree and form its structure.

Spur A short, often thornlike shoot that produces flowers, fruit, and leaves. Some spurs are permanent; some only live a few years. Landscape plants that have spurs include ginkgo, larch, some apples, and kiwi fruit.

Stub An unsightly and soon-to-be-dead branch piece left when a cut was not made to a bud or originating branch.

Sucker shoot An upright shoot growing from a root or graft union.

Watersprout A vigorous upright branch that originates along another branch.

Pruning Large Limbs

To prune a large limb, first cut halfway through the branch from underneath, about 1 foot (30 cm) out from the trunk. Move your saw a few inches in toward the trunk from the first cut and saw down from the top until the branch drops. Finish the cut by sawing just outside the

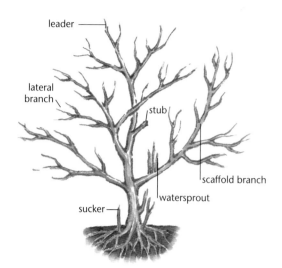

branch collar. If the crotch is too tight for easy maneuvering, saw from the bottom up. Pruning cuts, even on large branches, need no paint or other wound dressings. They will heal fastest on their own.

Renewal Pruning

If your plants grow too large or if they contain many old or dead stems, drastic measures are often effective. Many vigorous vines, including autumn clematis (*Clematis maximowicziana*) and perennial sweet pea (*Lathyrus latifolius*), can be pruned to within a few inches of the ground in late winter if they have grown much too large. In spring, the vines will regrow at a manageable size.

Multistemmed deciduous shrubs, such as forsythia (*Forsythia* x *intermedia*) and lilacs (*Syringa* spp.), which have grown old and woody with limited bloom, can also be given this drastic treatment to

stimulate new growth. However, it will take several years after such a severe pruning for the shrub to recover completely and flower again. A less-stressful renewal method for reclaiming overgrown deciduous flowering shrubs is to prune one-third of the plant each year over a period of three years. Selectively cut a few of the old stems to the ground each year until you finally have an entirely new plant with new growth, an attractive shape, and a new lease of life.

When pruning, make a sloped cut just above a bud (left). Avoid cutting too close (center) or leaving a stub (right).

Neglected young trees can develop serious flaws as they mature. Pruning a young tree carefully will give you a safe, handsome mature tree.

1. Start with a cut from underneath the branch, out from the trunk.

2. Make another cut a few inches in from the first; saw off the branch.

3. Remove the stub by carefully sawing it off just outside the branch collar.

Topping

Topping is a favorite technique of utility crews and, sometimes, of desperate homeowners: Large trees that interfere with wires or grow too tall for their site are simply sliced off across the top. Large branches are sawed off in midlimb instead of being pruned at main stems.

Topping disfigures and weakens trees, stimulating undesirable water sprouts that actually accelerate the rate of top regrowth. The slow-to-heal wounds of topping are open invitations to insects and diseases, and limbs that die from these causes will soon fall in a storm, creating a danger to people and property. If your trees are so badly out of place that you would consider topping, remove them entirely and plant a better-suited species.

Pruning Hedges

How you prune your hedges depends on the effect you're looking for. If you want a natural-looking screen, a bit of selective pruning is all your hedge really needs. Prune flowering shrubs after they bloom. To keep the hedge vigorous, cut two or three of the oldest stems down to the ground each year.

Many gardeners appreciate the formal look of neatly trimmed hedges. But before you decide to go this route, consider whether you'll be eager to do the frequent pruning that is necessary to maintain them. After planting, the new shoots of broad-leaved plants should be trimmed back by one-third or more each year until the plants reach the desired size. After that, shear often during the growing season to keep the hedge neat.

Pruning Vines

Most vines require little special care other than pruning to train them, limit their growth, or encourage flower or fruit production. Prune away dead wood at any time during the year. To control growth or to shape a vine grown for foliage, such as Virginia creeper (*Parthenocissus quinquefolia*) or Boston ivy (*P. tricuspidata*), prune in late winter or

A stake-and-string guide is handy to direct your cuts; this is critical for good results on formal clipped hedges.

early spring. Cut back flowering vines shortly after bloom. Trim spring-blooming vines, such as wisteria and Carolina jasmine (*Gelsemium sempervirens*), by early summer—before the next year's flower buds develop. Summer bloomers, such as honeysuckles and climbing hydrangeas, produce flowers on new stems that grow during the spring. Prune summer-blooming vines from late fall until late winter.

Pruning an Overgrown Vine

Every now and then you'll be faced with a long-neglected vine that's a hopeless tangle of big, woody stems. While you might be able to pick your way through the mess and remove the dead growth, the remaining stems often end up much worse for the wear.

Fear not. One of the finer qualities of vines is their ability to respond to rejuvenation pruning—the kind where you cut the entire overgrown mess to the ground and start again. Remember that the root system has been growing for years and—especially during the dormant season—stores much in the way of energy reserves. Take advantage of this stored energy by cutting the vine down in late

Caring for mature vines can be a maintenance hassle. Be sure to consider how big the vine will grow before you plant.

winter. Leave a few of the newer stalks—if there are any—at the base of the vine. When growth begins in the spring and the vine sends up vigorous new shoots, remove all but the few that you'll need to train up the supports. Train them as you would any new vine.

Can Vines and Walls Coexist?

Think very carefully before deciding to train clinging vines to the walls of your house. While the vines aren't inherently destructive, the aerial roots or adhesive disks can infiltrate already-soft mortar. If you remove a clinging vine that's been growing for many years, the exposed disintegrating mortar will be subject to further damage from wind and rain. At the very least, you'll be left with a mess of tiny rootlets stuck tight to the wall. These tenacious vines can also damage aluminum siding, leaving a spotting pattern when you pull them off the metal.

Aggressive climbers like wisteria are notorious for taking over anything in their path. Proper pruning can help to keep these ramblers in line, but it's laborious and time-consuming work.

When planting a vine next to a wall, it's important to choose the vine carefully and, in some cases, to consider a support system that holds the vine away from the wall. Also be vigilant in training vines away from roofs, gutters, and downspouts to prevent damage.

Cutting Back and Thinning Flowering Plants

Like giving your plants a haircut, you can cut back long or straggly stems to make a plant tidier and to encourage it to produce healthy new growth. Cutting back (also known as shearing) differs from pinching because it is done after flowering, and from deadheading because it can be more radical. Thinning involves removing whole stems, giving the remaining stems more room to expand and improving air circulation around the plant.

Cutting Back Perennials

If you have a small number of plants, use hand clippers to cut back each stem to just above a leaf or bud. You should remove one-third to one-half of the stem length, encouraging a neater shape and rebranching, while deadheading at the same time. For large gardens, some landscape contractors use a string trimmer. This method is certainly fast, although it might be too rough for more delicate or disease-prone perennials like pinks (*Dianthus* spp.).

Besides making them look neater, cutting plants back can also help control insect and disease outbreaks. Simply cut back diseased or insect-infested plants to the ground and dispose of the trimmings with household trash. The shoots may reemerge with clean and healthy foliage. This technique works well for controlling powdery mildew on bee balm (*Monarda didyma*), leafminers on columbines (*Aquilegia* spp.), and galls on goldenrods (*Solidago* spp.). It is unlikely that plants will reflower during the year in which they have been subjected to this drastic treatment, but their foliage will look much more appealing for the rest of the season.

Thinning

Some mature clump-forming plants send up such a thick crop of stems that they crowd and shade each other out. As a result, they flower sparsely, and the poor circulation within the clump makes them more susceptible to diseases. Thinning—removing about half of the crowded stems—can help such mildew-prone perennials as garden phlox (*Phlox paniculata*), bee balm (*Monarda didyma*), and common sneezeweed (*Helenium autumnale*).

If your phlox has been mildewed in previous seasons, try radical thinning, leaving only four or five of the strongest stems. Prune the weaker shoots back to the ground when you can see how dense the clump will be but before it expends much energy in growth.

The remaining strong stems should be more vigorous and often are less disease-prone as a result. Dividing large clumps is another way to encourage strong new growth.

Columbines (*Aquilegia* spp.) are beautiful in bloom but decline after flowering. Cut them back to get new leaves.

Deadheading

Deadheading—removing spent flowers—is an essential part of gardening. When you deadhead, you can enjoy a garden unmarred by brown or drooping petals. Your plants will be free from rots and other diseases that invade the decaying blossoms. And since deadheaded plants don't waste energy on seed production, they have more strength for flower production and plant growth.

When Not to Deadhead

Despite the advantages of deadheading, you may have good cause to skip it on occasion. Spare the seedpods of perennials that you want to self-sow, like wild columbines (*Aquilegia canadensis*) and foxgloves (*Digitalis* spp.). You may also want to leave attractive seedpods or cones, which can extend the beauty of certain perennials through the dormant season. Try this with the velvety black or orange-brown cones of coneflowers (*Rudbeckia* and *Echinacea* spp.), the glossy, dark seed clusters of blackberry lilies (*Belamcanda chinensis*), the dry, feathery plumes of astilbes, the russet pods of 'Autumn Joy' sedum (*Sedum* 'Autumn Joy'), and the papery "flowers" of Lenten roses (*Helleborus* x *orientalis*). You also may want to spare the plume-like seed heads of ornamental grasses that you grow with your perennials.

Pruning shears are handy for snipping off spent flowers that have thick or wiry stems.

What to Cut Back

Certain perennials are sure to benefit from cutting back. Give spring bloomers a trim after they flower to make them look neater for the rest of the season. Cut back summer bloomers after their first flush of bloom; some may bloom again later in the season. Listed below are some of the most common perennials that benefit from being cut back.

Spring bloomers: Rock cress (*Arabis caucasica*), creeping phlox (*Phlox stolonifera*), goat's beard (*Aruncus dioicus*).

Summer bloomers: Frikart's aster (*Aster x frikartii*), catmint (*Nepeta x faassenii*), Persian cornflower (*Centaurea dealbata*), common spiderwort (*Tradescantia x andersoniana*), common thrift (*Ameria maritima*), bellflowers (*Campanula* spp.), blanket flower (*Gaillardia x grandiflora*), sages (*Salvia* spp.), lavender cotton (*Santolina chamaecyparissus*), spotted lamium (*Lamium maculatum*), pincushion flower (*Scabiosa caucasica*), soapworts (*Saponaria* spp.).

Encourage evergreens to grow thicker by pinching new growth.

season's bloom. For asters and chrysanthemums, you may need to pinch twice. Make the first pinch when shoots are about 6 inches (15 cm) tall. Repeat the pinching at 8 inches (20 cm), but not later than the end of June.

Pinching

Pinching is underrated as a pruning technique, perhaps because it requires no fancy tools—only your hands! A pinch is a heading cut, used only on very soft tissue. By removing the growing tip of the stem, you cut off the source of hormones that make that branch elongate; this frees buds lower on the stem to develop into side branches. It will make leggy plants more bushy and compact, with better branching and more (although often smaller) blooms. Perennials like common sneezeweed (*Helenium autumnale*), boltonia (*Boltonia asteroides*), or 'Autumn Joy' sedum (*Sedum* 'Autumn Joy') that otherwise need staking will be able to stand on their own if you pinch them back.

Pinch the plant when it is young enough to develop a full shape but not so early that later growth becomes scrawny over the shapely base. Also, pinch before flower buds develop. Otherwise, you could remove them all and lose the

Pruning Roses

Well-timed, careful pruning helps to keep roses healthy, vigorous, and free-blooming. Although the specific recommendations for different types of roses vary, there are some basic techniques that apply to all. For instance, you'll always start pruning any rose by removing dead, damaged, diseased, thin, weak, or crossing branches. Deadheading and

Pruning Tools and Power Lines

When using pole pruners or any other extension tool, check carefully to make sure that there are no power lines running through or by the tree. Also remember that high-voltage electricity can arc over several feet outside the wires. Since you and your pole pruners do not want to be the ground for this electricity, stay far away from power lines. If tree limbs need to be pruned away from lines, call your electric company or a qualified arborist to do the work.

removing blind shoots (those with no flower buds) are also common pruning tasks on certain types of roses. Of course, you'll want to harvest some of those roses to bring into the house to scent and liven up your rooms; that's pruning, too!

Tools and Supplies

A good pair of bypass (scissor-style) pruners and loppers are all you need to do most rose pruning. For renovation, or for large bush roses, you may also need a pruning saw. If you know that your plants are infected with a disease like canker or crown gall, plan to disinfect your tools by dipping or wiping the blades with isopropyl alcohol between cuts or at least between plants. Painting pruning cuts with wood glue can help prevent borers

The thorns on roses make pruning them difficult and sometimes painful. Long pants, long sleeves, and a sturdy pair of gloves can help.

from entering the stems. For small jobs, apply the glue right out of the bottle or tube; for large jobs, dab on the glue—from a can—with a small, cheap, and disposable brush.

Finally, protect your hands and arms from thorns (and from your pruners!) with a good pair of thick gloves. Long gauntlet-style gloves are especially useful for rose pruning, since they shield both your hands and your forearms. A long-sleeved shirt and long pants can also help prevent nicks and scratches from thorny canes.

This is the delightful rugosa rose (*Rosa rugosa*) shown with its fleshy red "hips." Its many thorns make it difficult to prune.

When to Prune

Good pruning starts at planting time. If you're planting a rose from bareroot stock, first look carefully at the roots. Healthy roots are normally light-colored, firm, and fibrous. Prune away any roots that are broken, dried, dead, or rotten. Trim healthy roots only if you must. Try not to prune healthy roots just because they won't fit into the hole that you've dug; first consider enlarging the hole. Spread the roots out over a cone of soil in the hole, then fill the rest of the hole with soil, and water well.

On container-grown stock, remove the pot and loosen any circling roots. Put the

Pruning off developing fruits can encourage your rose plant to produce more flowers.

root ball in the hole, backfill with soil, and water the plant well.

Once your bareroot or container-grown rose is in the ground, remove any dead, damaged, or weak twigs. Be sure to cut back into good wood and to buds pointing in directions where you want the new growth to go.

On established roses, late winter or early spring is generally the best time for major pruning. Swelling growth buds on the canes is a good sign that the time is right. During the season, remove any dead or dying stems as you see them. If you are not growing a rose for its showy fruit (hips), cut off the flowers as they fade. This kind of pruning will encourage new growth, though, so stop deadheading by late summer. Otherwise, the new growth may not have time to harden before cold weather sets in, and it may get killed or damaged by the first winter freezes.

How to Prune

Start any rose pruning session by removing any dead or diseased stems. If you need to remove a whole stem, cut it to the ground or graft union; otherwise, just trim back into good wood at least 1 inch (2.5 cm) below where any damage is evident.

If the center, or pith, of the stem is still dark or discolored at that point, cut the cane back farther until the pith is white. Look for and remove any weak or spindly stems that are much thinner than the others. If you see any canes that cross or rub, remove one of the two. Make each cut about ¼ inch (6 mm) above a bud, at a 45 degree angle away from the bud. In most cases, you'll want to cut to a bud that faces away from the center of the plant to encourage outward growth and good air circulation.

Sucker Removal

Most modern roses are budded onto more vigorous species-rose rootstocks, so you'll want to control any sucker growth that you see coming from the roots. Growth from these suckers is often stronger than

the top growth (what you actually bought the rose for). If left unchecked, suckers can crowd out the more desirable growth.

To properly remove a sucker, scrape the soil away from its base, and snap it off where it joins the rootstock. This technique removes any dormant buds that might be present at the point where the sucker joins the root. Don't simply cut the sucker off at ground level, because more sucker shoots will probably arise for you to deal with later.

Basic Bonsai

Bonsai is an art that attempts to replicate, in a container, the look of an old tree that has been shaped by time and the elements. The process of training beautiful bonsai requires time and patience, but the results can be stunning and gratifying.

Caring for Bonsai

Before you buy or begin a bonsai project, be aware that these plants will need some special care. Hardy bonsai normally prefer to be outdoors during the growing season. They enjoy the shelter of a lath house or some other shade-producing structure, where they will receive bright indirect light and protection from the elements. One big gust of wind can easily knock over small plants and undo months, or years, of care!

Bonsai generally grow in shallow pots, so you'll have to water them frequently—possibly as often as twice a day in hot dry weather—to keep the soil evenly damp. During the winter months, you'll need to protect bonsai from excessively cold temperatures. Many overwinter best in a cool greenhouse, where they will get a dormant, or rest, period. Without this cold period, many hardy plants will not bloom, and they'll gradually become weak and spindly. Bonsai created from houseplants such as weeping fig (*Ficus benjamina*) are somewhat easier to care for: They can adapt easily to indoor culture on sunny windowsills or under lights year-round.

When choosing plants for bonsai, consider those that produce showy flowers and fruit as well as attractive foliage.

Picking a Plant

Generally speaking, the species that adapt best to bonsai training have small leaves, woody trunks, stout limbs, and flowers, fruit, or good fall color. Deciduous plants that make great bonsai subjects include azaleas, beeches (*Fagus* spp.), flowering quinces (*Chaenomeles* spp.), hawthorns (*Crataegus* spp.), ginkgo (*Ginkgo biloba*), Japanese maple (*Acer palmatum*), hornbeams (*Carpinus* spp.), hardy orange (*Poncirus trifoliata*), and zelkova (*Zelkova serrata*). Good choices for evergreens include arborvitaes (*Thuja* spp.), cryptomeria (*Cryptomeria japonica*), boxwoods (*Buxus* spp.), junipers (*Juniperus* spp.), false cypress (*Chamaecyparis* spp.), pines (*P. mugo* and *P. parvifolia*), spruces (*Picea* spp.), and yews (*Taxus* spp.). If you want a bonsai that can grow indoors year-round, consider woody houseplants like serissa (*Serissa foetida*) or weeping fig (*Ficus benjamina*).

When choosing a young plant for bonsai, you don't necessarily want a symmetrical, well-balanced specimen. Stems with bends, twists, scars, or stumps can give a bonsai real character; even some dead wood can be desirable! Ask the staff at your local nursery to find out if they have any mangled, misshapen plants that are otherwise destined for the compost pile; with some trimming, these can have immediate impact as bonsai. Of course, potential bonsai specimens should otherwise be healthy and free of insects and disease. Whatever you pick, just try to start small, with a plant growing in a 1-gallon (4.5-L) or smaller container.

Training Bonsai

Choose a shallow pot that looks in scale with the young plant. Cover the drainage holes with a piece of wire screen for good drainage. Use two parts potting soil mixed with one part leaf mold (screened through a ¼-inch [6 mm] sieve).

After planting, the next step is to decide what shape you want the plant to grow in. You may allow it to grow upright or encourage a leaning or cascading form. Part of choosing an appropriate style is knowing how a plant grows in its natural setting; books with photographs of the plant in the wild may help inspire you. Also consider how your particular plant is growing; it may naturally have a form that suggests a certain shape for easier training.

Pruning, pinching, wiring, and root pruning are standard training techniques you'll use to work with your bonsai. On deciduous plants, do most of your pruning during the dormant season, but don't hesitate to remove undesirable growth as soon as it appears. It's common to remove crossing or rubbing limbs, but you may choose to leave poorly placed branches, depending on the effect you're trying to create. On pines, spruces, and firs, pinch the "candles" (new shoots) back by about half in spring. Carefully trim other evergreens in summer. Pinch any plant through the growing season to direct its growth and to keep it compact.

To shape individual stems, use annealed (softened) #14- to #26-gauge copper wire. Coil the wire gently but firmly over the length of the stem or branch to shape and direct the growth. Check the wire frequently to make sure it isn't cutting into the stem. Take the wire off after several months. To bring upward-pointing branches down to a more horizontal position, use twine or soft string to tie on small weights. Remove these after a month or two.

Root pruning is a scary but very necessary aspect of bonsai. It is a key part of keeping the plants in their smaller scale. Do this every four to five years, in late winter before growth begins for the season, or when you need to repot the plant. Allow the soil to dry slightly more than usual and remove the plant from its pot. Loosen the roots and tease away the soil in the outer third of the root ball. Using thinning cuts, trim away the roots in this outer third. Repot the plant and resume normal maintenance.

Shaping Espalier

Espalier is a training technique that turns a normally bushy plant into a flat, almost two-dimensional form. Although the technique requires persistent attention and fearless pruning, the results are tremendously rewarding. Use espalier training to cover a blank or nondescript wall, to create a leafy screen that gives privacy to a doorway, deck, patio, or porch or to grow faster-yielding fruit in a small space.

Plants to Consider

Dwarf fruit trees are popular subjects for this technique. When choosing one, consider that spur-bearing selections—such as pears and many apples—lend themselves well to this method of training because the spurs are long-lived. Tip-bearers such as peaches and plums pose more challenges because you must balance the need for vigorous new growth with the need to control size. On tip-bearers, your annual routine will include the removal of older branches to let new ones take their place—a pretty labor-intensive arrangement. For many fruit trees, you will also need to plant at least two different cultivars to get cross-pollination.

Other plants worth considering include atlas cedar (*Cedrus atlantica*), sweet bay (*Laurus nobilis*), camellias (*Camellia* spp.), citrus fruits (*Citrus* spp.), cotoneasters (*Cotoneaster* spp.), crabapples (*Malus* spp.), figs (*Ficus* spp.), forsythias (*Forsythia* spp.), ginkgo (*Ginkgo biloba*),

Espalier training takes patience and careful pruning, but the result is a unique and beautiful addition to any yard.

hawthorns (*Crataegus* spp.), evergreen magnolias (*Magnolia* spp.), pyracanthas (*Pyracantha* spp.), and flowering quince (*Chaenomeles speciosa*).

If you plan to create a formal espalier, you'll get the best results if you start with a young single-stem tree (commonly known in the nursery trade as a maiden or whip). If you can't find an unbranched tree, at least look for a young plant with an uncut main stem, then trim back the side branches to the main stem. For informal designs, look for a small- to medium-sized plant that already has a pleasing shape; if it already has a somewhat flat habit, so much the better!

Training Outdoor Topiary

Training shrubs, trees, herbs, and vines into fanciful shapes is another practice that carries pruning into the realm of sculpture. A single topiary creation can be a graceful or stunning focal point or conversation piece in a small garden; multiple figures can transform a larger space into a magical land peopled with strange and wonderful creatures.

Picking a Plant

Evergreen, small-leaved plants are usually the plants of choice for garden topiary projects. Yews (*Taxus* spp.) and boxwoods (*Buxus* spp.) are traditional favorites. For best results, start with a young or newly planted shrub; older shrubs may require more drastic pruning to get them in the shape you want. If you are buying a shrub for a topiary project from a local nursery, you may want to ask to see any misshapen plants that they can't sell for normal landscaping purposes. A plant with a naturally interesting shape can give your topiary almost immediate interest.

Picking a Pattern

Topiaries are generally trained in either geometric or representational forms. Geometric shapes such as boxes and spheres take less time, thought, and planning, as evidenced by the abundance of such unwitting "topiaries" in residential landscapes.

For a more whimsical look, you may shape your topiary into a more unusual form, such as a boat, bird, giraffe, dog, chair, or wishing well. If you plan to try a complicated figure, it's helpful to sketch out the final shape you want; then you can refer to the sketch as you prune. Try to keep the figure fairly simple; it can be hard to maintain fine details.

Shaping and Training

Pruning a topiary involves the same kinds of cuts you use on other landscape plants. Make thinning cuts to remove unwanted growth; use heading cuts to encourage areas to fill in. If you start with small plants, you can train your topiary gradually into its intended form. You may even want to use stakes or bent rods to train key stems into position. (Be sure to attach the stems with twine or some other material that will eventually rot away; it's easy to forget plastic or wire ties until they girdle a stem and part of your topiary dies!) As with other intensively managed

Tips for Espalier-Trained Fruit Trees

Besides routine pruning and training, fruit trees need a little special attention to give good yields. You'll probably need to do some thinning to get a high-quality harvest of full-sized, well-colored fruit. While fruits are still small, remove any that are damaged or deformed. On plants that will produce large fruit, like apples and peaches, thin the remaining fruits to 6 to 8 inches (15 to 20 cm) apart. Thin smaller fruits, like plums and apricots, to 3 to 5 inches (7.5 to 12.5 cm) apart. If you have to do a lot of thinning, your plant probably has too many fruiting spurs. Remove some, leaving 6 to 8 inches (15 to 20 cm) between spurs.

Some growers root prune their espalier-trained fruit trees to keep them growing compactly and to get them to bear earlier. During the dormant season, use a spade to slice a circle (or half-circle for wall-trained trees) in the soil around the base of the trunk. Make the circle 1 foot (30 cm) in diameter for every inch (2.5 cm) of stem diameter.

evergreens, trim topiaries as needed throughout the growing season. Stop after midsummer to allow new growth to harden off before cold weather comes.

This whimsical piece of living sculpture is a peacock. It takes commitment to indulge in topiary. It must be constantly trimmed to keep it looking good.

Protecting Your Plants

Extending the Season

To extend the growing season of your vegetable garden, you must select the right plants for the conditions, plant them at the right time, and shield them from the cold spring or fall temperatures.

Picking the Right Plants

Look for cultivars that are suited to extra-cold conditions. For late-summer and fall crops, check out the array of winter-keeping cultivars of cabbage, lettuce, and beets. 'Springtide' Chinese cabbage, corn salad, 'Easter Egg' radishes, and 'Tyee' hybrid spinach are good choices for early spring. Traditional cool-season crops, like spinach, endive, escarole, broccoli, carrots, chives, and kale, are natural choices for early-spring or fall growing.

Planting at the Right Time

To start extra early in spring, prepare the soil on a well-drained site in fall. Two weeks before you plant, heat the soil by covering it with green or black plastic. Plant thoroughly hardened-off seedlings or presprouted seeds through slits or holes cut in the plastic.

To harvest in late fall or winter, plant crops in midsummer to late summer. You can sow fast-growing crops like lettuce, spinach, and radishes every two weeks, up to two weeks before your first fall frost date if you protect the young plants. Plant beets and carrots about 65 days before the first fall frost.

Using Frost Protectors

If cool-season crops will be growing in weather colder than about 40°F (4°C), they'll do better with some form of protection. Protective devices will also prevent frost-tender peppers, pumpkins, and other long-yielding summer crops from being damaged by an early frost or two. Surround the plants with hay bales or trellising and drape burlap over them at night or during short cold spells. When Indian summer returns, these tender plants may be able to finish maturing their fruits.

Protect your tender plants from frost with a plastic row cover.

Use smaller enclosures to protect young plants in early spring or late fall. Cover them with a floating row cover, which will help keep the air around the plants a few degrees warmer than the surrounding environment.

You also can cover plants with plastic jugs that have the bottom removed, plastic umbrellas, or plastic tunnels stretched over wire hoops. These "minigreenhouses" can hold in too much heat during a warm sunny day, so be prepared to provide some ventilation.

Cold Frames

Use a growing frame for hardening off tender transplants and for growing cold-tolerant vegetables when garden temperatures are too low. The most simple growing structures are wooden, bottomless, boxlike frames topped with a window sash roof. They're usually called cold frames, since they're unheated.

Hot Beds

Hot beds are simply growing frames with a heat source; they are useful if you live in an area where it snows. Most gardeners rely on electric heating cables to keep their seedlings warm. First, dig a pit 12 inches (30 cm) deep to fit your frame. Follow the manufacturer's instructions for placing the cables correctly so they don't cross. Sandwich the cables at the bottom between layers of sand for drainage. Cover with a screen for protection. Top with 4 to 6 inches (10 to 15 cm) of sand. Push pots into the sand to secure them.

FOUR SEASONS IN A COLD FRAME

Spring: Harden off seedlings in your cold frame before transplanting to the garden.

Summer: Sow salad crops like spinach for fall harvest. Lath shade keeps plants cool.

Fall: A cold frame ensures survival of late-fall leaf crops like lettuce well after the first frost.

Winter: Use your cold frame to give spring bulbs their cold treatment before forcing.

Overwintering

Some tender perennials won't survive when exposed to cold-climate winters. Cuttings that you take in early autumn will be ready to move to the garden in spring if you nurture them indoors all winter. You can also pot up annuals and bring them indoors for winter use, or start fresh ones from seed.

Bringing Perennials Indoors

Perennials can be grown in the garden soil in summer, then potted up for winter indoors. At the beginning and end of the season, leave the plants in their pots in a shady spot outdoors for at least a week before moving them to their new home.

You can also start new plants for the winter from cuttings. You can take cuttings from established plants outdoors well into autumn, as long as there is new growth to choose from and the plants have not become dormant.

Bringing Annuals Indoors

The first frost of fall doesn't have to signal the end of your annuals' bloom season. With just a little effort, you can enjoy their colorful flowers on your windowsills all winter.

Tender perennials that are commonly grown as annuals usually adapt best to life indoors. These include wax begonias, geraniums (both flowering and scented-leaf types), coleus, impatiens (including New Guinea types), and heliotrope (*Heliotropium arborescens*).

To overwinter annuals indoors, dig up whole plants before the first fall frost, cut them back by about one-third, and plant them in pots. Or take 3- to 5-inch (7.5- to 12.5-cm) cuttings from healthy, vigorous stems in mid- to late-summer and insert the bottom one-third of the stem into a pot of moist potting soil. Enclose the pot in a plastic bag and set it in a bright place out of direct sun. When cuttings are well rooted—usually in three to four weeks—remove the bag and move the pot to a sunny windowsill. In spring, move them outside to a shady spot to adjust.

Overwintering Outdoors

The success of overwintering your perennials outdoors in the garden depends on your climate. Hardy perennials will survive a cold winter in perfect condition, ready to grow again when temperatures rise in spring. Some of the less hardy plants may need help getting through a cold winter.

The best protection is a blanket of snow. If snowfall is minimal or absent, protect perennials from the drying effects of winter winds by covering them with evergreen boughs or surrounding them with sacking or plastic sheeting (especially bubble glaze). To overwinter small perennials, wait until the soil has frozen, then mulch heavily with straw or leaves. Remove the mulch in spring.

Putting the Garden to Bed

When all your plants are through producing for the season—except perhaps a few late crops snuggled in a cold frame or under row covers—it's time to clean up. Spring may inspire you to clean indoors, but fall is the best time to clean up out in the garden. Pests and diseases often linger on old plant debris or dig in near plant roots to spend the winter close to their preferred food source. When the plants go dormant, pests are trapped there, so it's the perfect opportunity for you to destroy them as you tidy up. If you get rid of old debris and weeds now, you will eliminate many pest and disease problems for the following growing season.

Dispose of Debris

Cut off old stems and put any that are disease- and seed-free in your compost pile. (Bury the rest or dispose of them with household trash.) You want to clear out all the brown vegetation, with a few exceptions. You can leave fallen asparagus stems (if they are not bothered by asparagus beetles) to act as a mulch. And spare the dried seed heads of companion coneflowers (*Rudbeckia* and *Echinacea* spp.)—they can look attractive in winter and provide bird-luring seeds.

Blanket the Soil

As garden space becomes vacant in late summer and fall, turn the soil with a spade or rotary tiller to expose hibernating pests, larvae, or eggs near the soil surface. This also kills many weeds. But to be doubly thorough, pull out any roots of perennial weeds that you turn up—otherwise they could resprout. If there are several weeks before the first hard frost, plant a cover crop, such as clover or winter rye, to protect the soil from erosion and compaction. Work the crop into the soil about two weeks before planting the following spring.

If you are planting a late vegetable crop but still want a cover crop for winter, try interplanting them. Plant the vegetables as usual for fall, and let them grow for about a month, keeping the space between plants weed-free. Then broadcast the seed of the cover crop over the growing area. By the time your late vegetables are ready for harvest, the cover crop will be large enough to walk on without damaging it.

A thick layer of mulch will provide ample protection for hardy root crops like parsnips, carrots, and beets that you leave in the ground. You can also mulch some perennials once the soil freezes in late fall. Mulch prevents the soil from heaving (shifting as it freezes and thaws), which can damage shallow-rooted perennials. Cover them with a loose, airy material such as straw or pine boughs.

Planting a clover crop is a great way to protect the soil from erosion or compaction over winter.

The Ornamental Garden

A windowbox full of annuals on a sunny windowsill, a formal garden of neatly clipped trees and shrubs, a wild meadow in which naturalized bulbs come up year after year, a classic flower border. Whether you have lots of time, or none at all, you can have a beautiful ornamental garden.

Perennials

Aster

With so many wonderful perennials to choose from, it's hard to resist planting one of each. But if you buy them one by one and plop them in the ground wherever there's room, your garden will look like a plant collection—interesting, perhaps, but not beautiful.

Before you dig your garden, buy plants, or start rearranging an existing planting, you need to figure out what you want to grow and where you want to grow it. Garden design is basically the process of refining your plant choices, placement, and combinations to get the best effect. It's what transforms a bunch of individual plants into a pleasing composition.

Part of the fun of landscaping with perennials is creating an ever-changing display. Working with living material that changes from week to week and season to season makes designing a garden different from redecorating a room, even though it builds on the same principles of contrast, balance, texture, and color.

For a garden design to be effective, it has to match your site conditions, your style, the amount of time you have for gardening, and the results you want from the garden. Ideally it should also blend in with the topography and complement your house so everything looks like it belongs right where it is.

Why Grow Perennials?

Take a few minutes to jot down why you want to add perennials to your yard. Do you want a parade of flowers all season long or just a bit of color to liven up a drab, shady spot? Do you want to attract butterflies, or do you want a wide selection of fresh flowers for arrangements? Do you want to plant perennials to fix an eroding hillside or camouflage the compost bin?

Identifying what you want your perennials to do will help you narrow down your planting options. If you're trying to grow perennials to solve a landscaping problem, you'll need to stick with plants that can adapt to those conditions. If you want perennials for cutting or for attracting butterflies, you'll want to choose plants that have proven themselves to be good for those purposes.

Where Can You Plant?

If you have a fairly flat site with moist but well-drained soil, you can plant a wide variety of perennials almost anywhere. But chances are good that you'll have at least one area in the yard with more challenging conditions, such as slopes or wet spots.

If you have a difficult spot, you might decide to ignore it and limit your perennial plantings to the most hospitable areas of the yard. Or you may choose to take up the challenge and plan a garden of perennials that are naturally adapted to those tough conditions. You may be pleasantly surprised to see how well-chosen perennial plantings can turn a problem site into a pleasing garden spot.

How Big Should Your Garden Be?

A key part of planning a great-looking landscape is being realistic about how much time you have to spend on it. Digging up and planting the area is the most obvious chunk of time you'll spend on the garden. But you'll also need to allow for the aftercare—the mulching, weeding, watering, fertilizing, staking, and pest control that your chosen plants will need to look their best.

Foxgloves are one of the most popular choices for a perennial border or cottage garden.

For example, you'll probably need to spend a few hours each month to maintain a 200-square-foot (18.6-sq-m) flower garden once it's established. That doesn't include any planning or preparation time. It also assumes you keep it mulched to discourage weeds and reduce the need for watering.

Your own garden may take more or less time, depending on the plants you choose, how perfect you want them to look, and how carefully you've planned it. It's always safe to start small, so plan your first garden a bit smaller than you think you want. Live with your first garden for a few years, and see how comfortable you are with the time you spend on it. As the plants become established, you'll have less watering and weeding to do, and you'll get a good idea of how much maintenance your garden really needs. Then, if you want to expand, you'll have a more realistic feel for how much garden you can actually handle.

Buying Healthy Perennials

Before you pull out your wallet to buy a new perennial, follow this checklist to help you verify the plant's quality:

1. Look to see if the plant is tagged with its botanical and cultivar name. If not, or if it's labeled only by common name or color, chances are that it's not an improved type and you may not want it.
2. Test for root-bound plants, which may have been sitting around for a long time in a small pot. Give the plant a soft tug from the top and see if the root ball pops out of the pot readily. If the roots are packed into a solid mass or are circling around the inside of the pot, the plants are root-bound and may be slow to adapt to garden conditions.
3. Look at the roots. Firm, white roots are a sign of good health. If you can't pull the plant out of its pot to see the roots, check where the shoots emerge from the soil.

The trick to perennial gardening is finding and combining plants that will thrive in your particular conditions.

Perennials in Pots

Some perennials work very well in containers. Top choices include those with a long season of bloom, such as compact, golden orange 'Stella d'Oro' daylily. Other perennials that look especially nice in containers are those with interesting foliage, such as hostas, ornamental grasses, and lady's mantle (*Alchemilla mollis*). Try using some of these plants in large containers, mixed with annual flowers to provide constant color.

Perennials need a little more care than annuals, since you don't just pull them out at the end of the season. Because they are growing in containers, they are much more susceptible to winter damage than plants growing in the ground. In the North, you'll want to move container perennials to an unheated garage or cold basement to protect them from the alternate freezing and thawing cycles, which can damage or kill them. You'll need to water the pots lightly during the winter months.

Crocus and primrose

Emerging stems should not be brown, soft, blemished, or wilted— these are symptoms of rots and other diseases.

4. Give the same thorough inspection to the stems and foliage. Look for signs of diseases such as brown or black leaf spots, white powdery mildew, or tiny orange spots of rust. You don't want to bring these problems home with you to infect the plants in your garden.
5. Check the color of the foliage. If it is a deep and uniform color, the plant is most likely to be healthy and well fed.
6. Be on the lookout for weed shoots emerging through or near the crown (base) of the perennial. Although the weed leaves may have been clipped off in a presale grooming, grasses and perennial weeds will reemerge and can invade your newly planted garden.
7. Last, check for insect pests. Look beneath the leaves, along the stems, in shoot tips, and on flower buds for soft-bodied aphids, cottony mealybugs, and hard-shelled scale insects. Spider mites, another common pest, will make leaves stippled or turn them yellow or bronze. If pests are on one plant, they may be on every plant in that greenhouse or garden center. Consider shopping elsewhere.

Designing Beds and Borders

Once you know what you want from your perennial landscape, you're ready to start planning the layout. Two of the most common ways to group perennial plantings are beds and borders.

Perennial borders are long planting areas that create a visual edge to a lawn or other part of the landscape. They are usually sited so they're viewed from a distance.

While they may stretch along a driveway, walkway, fence, or the edge of woods, they don't really have to "border" anything; borders may merely create the illusion of a boundary to a "room" within the landscape.

Perennial borders are sometimes just that—only perennials. But more and more gardeners are enjoying the benefits of mixing their perennials with other plants, including shrubs, small trees, hardy bulbs, annuals, and ornamental grasses. These plants complement perennials by adding extra height, texture, and color to the border. Shrubs, trees, grasses, and bulbs also add year-round interest, with early spring flowers, attractive fall colors, and showy fruits or foliage that may last well into winter.

Shapes and Sizes

Borders are often rectangular, but you can also design them with gentle curves for a more informal look. Because they're usually seen from one side, borders generally have a distinct front and back, with taller plants located to the rear.

There's no limit to how long a border can be. Long borders need a shortcut of a couple of stepping stones so you can get to the other side without having to walk around either end.

The width of the border will take some thought—4 to 5 feet (1.2 to 1.5 m) is

Create an elegant effect by combining silvery artemisia and lamb's-ears with blue-leaved pinks (*Dianthus* spp.).

Dahlias

enough room to include a good mix of plant heights. Long borders deeper than 5 or 6 feet (1.5 or 1.8 m) are a challenge to maintain because it's hard to reach more than 2 or 3 feet (60 to 90 cm) in from either side to weed, trim, or dig.

If you want a border more than 3 feet (90 cm) wide in front of a hedge or wall, leave space behind it for a grassy or mulched access path so you can get to all

parts of your border. If you plan to make your border longer than about 15 feet (4.5 m), make the access path as wide as your garden cart or wheelbarrow so you can easily haul in manure or compost and cart out trimmings.

Perennial Beds

Beds are often located closer to the house than borders, perhaps along the foundation or edging a patio. If you're going to put a bed where you'll see it all the time, choose your plants carefully for all-season interest. High-visibility beds will also need either some extra work or carefully chosen, low-maintenance plants to look their best all the time.

DIFFERENT WAYS TO BUY PERENNIALS

Container-grown perennials may cost more but give instant effect.

Field-dug plants usually adapt quickly to a new site.

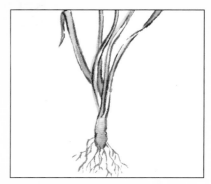

Bareroot plants take a bit of care but are often less expensive.

The Shape of Beds

Perennial beds come in many shapes and sizes. Choose a shape and style (formal or informal) that matches or balances nearby features. The front can curve even if the side up against the house is straight. Keep the bed narrow enough to allow you to reach all the plants from outside the bed, or place stepping stones in it for easy access.

Island Beds

Beds surrounded by lawn are called islands; often these are oval or kidney shaped. They are a great way to add color and height to new property while you're waiting for the trees and shrubs to mature. Island beds are also useful for replacing the grass under trees, reducing the need for trimming and making mowing easier.

Like perennial borders, island beds are usually designed to be seen from a distance. As islands are often viewed from all sides, the design needs to look attractive all around, like a table centerpiece. Since there's no "back," put tallest plants toward the middle and surround them with lower plants.

Bed and Border Planning Pointers

Perennial borders and beds can be designed to feature one big seasonal show or to showcase long, overlapping seasons of bloom. If you have room for several different beds or borders, it can be fun to arrange each one with a different bloom season. That way you will always have at least one bed that is loaded with lovely flowers.

In small gardens or in plantings that you see every day, it's worth planning for long bloom times, attractive foliage, and year-round interest. Here are some planning tips you can try.

- Include some spring, summer, and fall-flowering perennials in each planting area.

Persian onion (*Allium aflatunense*) and golden-chain tree (*Laburnum* x *watereri*) form a splendid spring spectacle.

BELOW TOP: Healthy plants have strong, evenly colored leaves. Check leaf undersides to make sure no pests are lurking.
BOTTOM: Before you buy, look at the leaves. Off-color leaves may indicate nutrient deficiencies.

- Look for perennials that have great-looking foliage all season, such as hostas, artemisias, lady's-mantle (*Alchemilla* spp.), and amsonias (*Amsonia* spp.).
- Pick long-blooming species and cultivars, like wild bleeding heart (*Dicentra eximia*) and 'Moonbeam' coreopsis (*Coreopsis verticillata* 'Moonbeam'); these can bloom for eight weeks or longer.
- Include a few perennials with good-looking evergreen foliage for interest during the colder months. Bergenias (*Bergenia* spp.) and some alumroots (including *Heuchera americana* 'Dale's Strain' and 'Garnet') often turn a lovely reddish color in the cool temperatures of fall and winter.

Creating Great Plant Combinations

Great-looking gardens are basically sequences of many individual plant combinations. The best aren't just based on flower color and season of bloom; they consider the quality, color, and texture of each plant's leaves as well. Good combinations also feature different plant heights and forms: short, medium or tall; mat-like, spiky, or rounded. Equally important is overall texture—whether a plant is fine and delicate looking, like baby's-breath (*Gypsophila* spp.), or coarse and dramatic, like peonies and ligularias (*Ligularia* spp.).

As you decide which plants to grow and how you want to group them, keep these different factors in mind. A little thought at the planning stage can turn a collection of different perennials into a harmonious, pleasing landscape.

Companions for Perennials

Perennials blend wonderfully with many other kinds of plants, including trees, shrubs, groundcovers, vines, annuals, and ornamental grasses. Mixing these other plants with your perennials is a great way to provide excitement when the perennials aren't blooming.

To get the most out of your yard, search for plants that have multiseason interest. Many grasses, for instance, have attractive leaves in spring and summer, showy flower heads and seed heads in fall, and golden winter foliage. Among the shrubs, consider those like shadblow serviceberry (*Amelanchier canadensis*). Its cherrylike blossoms are one of spring's earliest flowers, and the dark summer berries attract birds into your garden.

Plant spring bulbs with bushy perennials that can hide the ripening foliage and fill in when bulbs go dormant.

a landscape that is truly attractive all through the year.

All-season interest starts with flower displays that spread beyond one season. Foliage and plant form are other features you can use to keep your garden looking beautiful as flowers come and go. From spring through fall, many perennials have leaves in attractive colors—like the maroon leaves of 'Palace Purple' heuchera (*Heuchera* 'Palace Purple')— or interesting shapes, such as the starry leaves of blood-red cranesbill (*Geranium sanguineum*). Unusual plant forms—such as the spiky leaves and flowers of yuccas, blackberry lily (*Belamcanda chinensis*), and spike gayfeather (*Liatris spicata*)— add drama, especially next to mounds such as cushion spurge (*Euphorbia epithymoides*). Use different types of foliage and forms to add contrast, or repeat similar leaves and shapes to unify a planting scheme.

You can depend on asters to produce loads of colorful blooms in late summer and fall.

Contrasts and Complements

Well-planned gardens balance contrast and similarity. Contrasting colors, sizes, or other design elements are bold and stimulating. Use contrast to draw attention to a particular location and to add a lively feel. Overusing contrast— too many different textures or too many strong colors—can give your garden a jumbled, chaotic look.

Similarity—the absence of contrasts— increases the sense of harmony. Use subtle variations of closely related colors and gradual height transitions to create soothing garden designs. Too much similarity risks being uninteresting, so add a touch of contrast—a few perennials of different height, color, or texture— for balance.

Repetition acts as a bridge between similarity and contrast. Repeating similar elements will unify even the boldest designs. Exact, evenly spaced repetitions of particular plants or combinations create a formal look. Combine different plants with similar flower colors or leaf shapes to give an informal garden a cohesive but casual look.

Orchestrating All-Season Interest

You see your yard every day of the year, so make sure it's worth looking at. A good selection of spring-, summer- and fall-blooming perennials, plus a few plants with evergreen leaves for winter interest, will give you

Your Spring Landscape

After a long, dreary winter, few things are more welcome than colorful spring flowers. In spring, Lenten rose (*Helleborus orientalis*) and crocuses bloom before most of the garden shrubs off winter. Plant early bulbs where you'll see them from windows or as you enter the house so you can enjoy their bright colors when it's cold outside. Many wildflowers and shade-loving perennials bloom as trees leaf out, so spring is a good season to draw attention to areas that will be shady and green later on.

Supplement early-blooming perennials with the lovely early flowers of shrubs and trees such as forsythias, azaleas, magnolias, dogwoods, flowering cherries, and crab apples.

A Wealth of Summer Color

As spring turns into summer, many old-fashioned perennials—including peonies, irises, and columbines (*Aquilegia* spp.)—reach their peak, making it an easy time to feature flowers. Supplement these with early summer shrubs and vines such as rhododendrons, roses, clematis, wisteria, and honeysuckle (*Lonicera* spp.).

As summer progresses, daisy-like perennials and annuals—including coreopsis and blanket flower—take center stage. Good-looking foliage keeps up appearances where early perennials have finished blooming. Silver leaves make dramatic partners for hot- or cool-hued flowers; yellow, purple, or variegated foliage also attracts attention. Flowering shrubs which are at their best in July and August include abelia (*Abelia* x *grandiflora*), butterfly bush (*Buddleia davidii*), and hydrangeas. Sourwood (*Oxydendrum arboreum*) and Japanese pagoda tree

(*Sophora japonica*) are large trees that bloom prolifically in late summer, as does the large trumpet creeper vine (*Campsis* spp.).

Combinations for Fall

Asters, boltonia, and Joe-Pye weeds (*Eupatorium* spp.) keep blooming after fall frosts nip most annuals. As flowers fade, foliage brightens—and not just on trees or shrubs such as burning bush (*Euonymus alata*). Leaves of peonies and common sundrops (*Oenothera tetragona*) turn beautiful shades of red, amsonias (*Amsonia* spp.) and balloon

Campanula in raised bed

ABOVE: Plants that have variegated leaves—such as hostas (left) and some kinds of lemon balm (right)—provide all-season interest.

flower (*Platycodon grandiflorus*) leaves turn bright yellow, and many ornamental grasses bleach to gold. White baneberry (*Actea pachypoda*) and Jack-in-the-pulpit (*Arisaema triphyllum*) are perennials with dramatic berries that may last into fall.

Perennials for Winter Interest

After the leaves drop, attention turns to evergreen plants and those with interesting seedpods or fruits. Perennials with showy winter seedpods include blue false indigo (*Baptisia australis*), coneflowers (*Rudbeckia* and *Echinacea* spp.), blackberry lily (*Belamcanda chinensis*), and astilbes (*Astilbe* spp.).

Many crab apples and shrubs such as viburnums, cotoneasters, and deciduous and evergreen hollies (*Ilex* spp.) display fruits well into winter. Ornamental grasses remain attractive for months; cut them to the ground when they look tattered to make way for spring's new growth.

Lenten roses (*Helleborus orientalis*) are usually sold as small plants, but they make large clumps in a few years.

Month by Month in the Perennial Garden

This calendar is based on Zone 6, where the frost-free growing season is approximately late April to mid-October. If your garden is in a different zone, it's easy to adapt this calendar to fit your region. Not sure which zone you're in? Check out the USDA Plant Hardiness Zone Map on page 310.

In warmer climates (Zones 7 to 9), spring comes sooner, so do your March to May chores a month or two earlier (the warmer the climate, the sooner you can start); wait until frost for fall cleanup. In Zone 10 (you lucky gardeners), ignore the fall cleanup and mulching information; keep weeding, watering, and watching for pests throughout the year.

In colder zones and at high elevations (where the frost-free season is more like late May or early June to late August or early September), this calendar will be about a month ahead of you for much of the year. Wait a month to do your March to May chores, finish the September chores in August, and start your fall garden cleanup after the first frost.

January
- Take stock of seeds and stored summer bulbs; toss out any that aren't sound.
- Order summer bulbs and plants from mail-order catalogs soon to avoid the rush.

February
- Inventory the garden to list cleanup chores for next month.

March
- Clean up stray leaves, winter debris, and anything left undone last fall. Cut back ornamental grasses.

Perennials That Grow Best Lean and Light

If you think more nutrients are always better, think again. Many perennials, including coreopsis (*Coreopsis* spp.), yarrows, and common thrift (*Armeria maritima*), are sun-loving and drought-tolerant. They grow best where soils are not lush. If you overfeed them, they become soft and succulent—too tender to stand upright without staking. On disease-susceptible plants like garden phlox (*Phlox paniculata*), this soft, succulent tissue is more prone to mildews and other diseases. Rich soil also gives an extra boost to plants that spread by rhizomes or stolons, like bee balm (*Monarda didyma*). These creeping stems will run all over the place instead of staying in more controlled clumps. Excess fertility will also make silver- and gray-leaved perennials such as artemisias and lavenders fade to a dull green color.

Delphiniums

- When the forsythias begin to flower, pull some of the winter mulch off of your perennial beds so the soil can warm up.
- Turn last year's compost pile so it will be ready to spread when the ground warms up.
- Take soil tests.

April
- Finish garden cleanup; pull any weeds.
- Add nutrients recommended by your soil test results.
- Start scouting for pests.

- As you enjoy your spring bulbs, jot down some notes to remind you what you want to add in the fall for next year, and where you want to put them.
- Top-dress bulb plantings with compost. Remove spent flowers, but leave the foliage until it dies back.
- Side-dress clumps of emerging perennials with compost or manure.
- Divide summer- and fall-blooming perennials when the new shoots are about 3 inches (7.5 cm) tall.

May
- Plant bareroot perennials and container-grown plants as you get them.
- Divide and replant spring-blooming perennials and bulbs after they flower.
- Replace and replenish mulch.
- Pinch back leggy perennials.
- Pull or dig weed seedlings as soon as you spot them.
- Plant tender perennials and tender bulbs (including dahlias and gladioli) outside once danger of frost has passed.
- Plant annuals to hide dying foliage of hardy bulbs.

June
- Stake perennials that need support.
- Remove spent blossoms to prevent unwanted self-seeding.
- Watch the weather and water if rainfall is scarce. Wait until the top inch or two of soil is dry; then water thoroughly. Container plantings may need daily watering during hot spells.

July
- This is your chance to relax and enjoy the garden. Just keep watering.
- Order spring bulbs now.
- Cut flowers for indoor arrangements in the morning, before the heat of the day.
- Remove spent flowers.

August
- Keep up watering, deadheading, weeding, and pest patrol.
- Cut leafy herbs for drying.

September

- Divide any perennials that have finished flowering.
- Start new beds. Plant a cover crop to protect the soil over winter. Or dig in chopped leaves and garden wastes; they will have decomposed by spring.

October

- Cover tender plants at night when frost is expected.
- Dig and store tender bulbs when their foliage withers.
- Pull annuals after frost and toss them in the compost pile.
- Rake leaves for the compost pile or till them into new beds. Chop leaves with the lawn mower for good winter mulch (but don't mulch yet).
- Plant spring bulbs.
- Water perennial beds (as well as new shrub and bulb plantings) thoroughly before they go dormant to help them survive the winter.

November

- Mow wildflower meadows.
- Drain and store hoses; shut off and drain outdoor water taps.
- Clean your gardening tools.
- After the ground freezes, add a thick layer of mulch.

December

- Make a wish list of garden supplies for holiday presents.
- Catch up on gardening reading.

Low-Maintenance Perennials and Bulbs

If you really want to avoid labor, shun tall or floppy plants—like hybrid delphinium (*Delphinium* x *elatum*) and baby's-breath (*Gypsophila paniculata*)—that need staking. Steer clear of tender perennials, such as canna (*Canna* x *generalis*) and dahlia (*Dahlia* spp.), that you have to dig up and store

Sun-loving coreopsis (*Coreopsis verticillata*) is one of the brightest and most easy-care plants you can have in your garden.

Sun-Loving Perennials

The secret to an easy-care garden in the sun is to pick plants that need lots of light and aren't fussy about their soil. It's even easier if they also don't need much water or fertilizer (like the perennials listed below):

Armeria maritima (thrift)
Coreopsis spp. (coreopsis)
Echinacea purpurea (purple coneflower)
Hemerocallis spp. (daylily)
Rudbeckia spp. (coneflowers)
Sedum spectabile (showy stonecrop)

Shade-Loving Perennials

If your site gets some direct sun for part of the day, or light shade all day, you can still grow a variety of perennials. A few of the best and most reliable are listed below:

Aquilegia spp. (columbines)
Astilbe spp. (astilbes)
Cimicifuga spp. (bugbanes)
Dicentra spp. (bleeding hearts)
Hosta spp. (hostas)
Pulmonaria spp. (lungworts)

over the winter. Unless you want to cover a large area, avoid those that spread, like lamb's-ears (*Stachys byzantina*) and goutweed (*Aegopodium podagraria*). Pass up those that die out after a few years, like many perennial asters (*Aster* spp.). And don't plant those that are susceptible to a serious pest in your area, unless you can get a specially resistant cultivar.

What's left? A lot, starting with dependable spring bulbs like crocuses and daffodils; irises, if iris borer isn't a severe problem in your area; daylilies (there are thousands to choose from); and hostas, for shady areas. Try short cultivars of balloon flower (*Platycodon grandiflorus*) and bellflowers (*Campanula* spp.). Choose coreopsis (*Corepsis* spp.) and other native wildflowers, especially in a natural garden. Don't forget old-time favorites like bleeding heart (*Dicentra* spp.). Ornamental grasses like fountain grass (*Pennisetum alopecuroides*) and blue fescue (*Festuca cinerea*) are great for their foliage and interesting seed heads.

The list goes on. For more ideas, look at neighbors' gardens that bloom even though you know no one bothers with them. Before you plant any perennial, research its growth requirements to be sure it suits your conditions.

Helenium

Annuals and Biennials

Annual flowers come in a palette of colors to suit every gardener's fancy. Some also offer handsome foliage. Others are treasured for their fragrance, their nostalgic associations, or their charm as cut flowers. It's hard to imagine a garden that wouldn't benefit from the addition of a few more annuals.

Annuals for Beds and Borders

Flower beds are traditionally one of the most popular ways to display annuals. Some gardeners like to showcase their annual flowers in separate beds; others enjoy mixing annuals with bulbs, perennials, herbs, ornamental grasses, and other plants. Either way, the possibilities for creating exciting plantings are virtually endless.

Annuals Alone

Setting aside separate beds for annual flowers is an easy way to go. Since you start with an empty area each year, spring soil preparation is a snap—you simply clean up any debris left in the bed, scatter some compost over the top to add nutrients and organic matter, and dig or till to loosen the top layer of soil.

When you are planning and planting annual flower beds, you need to decide if you want a formal look or an informal look. The style you choose will determine how many different annuals you'll plant and how you'll arrange them.

Formal Gardens

Formal flower beds tend to have a simple, geometric shape—such as a square, rectangle, or circle—and a limited number of different plants. The simplest may contain a mass of just one annual, such as marigolds or geraniums. For a little more variety, you could combine two or three different annuals, planted in straight rows or patterns.

Sweet peas, one of the prettiest and most delightfully fragrant annuals, needs rich soil, lots of sun and moisture, and a support to climb.

Many annuals, including cornflowers (*Centaurea cyanus*), will self-sow for an informal, cottage-garden look.

If you grow different annuals together, pick those with varying heights. Select one that's low and spreading—such as sweet alyssum (*Lobularia maritima*) or edging lobelia (*Lobelia erinus*)—for the outer edge. The plants for the inside of the bed should be taller, usually no more than about 2 feet (60 cm). If the bed is in a spot where you can see it from all sides, you might want to include a taller "focal point" annual, such as castor bean (*Ricinus communis*) or love-lies-bleeding (*Amaranthus caudatus*), as a dramatic accent in the center of the garden.

The key to success with a formal bed is uniformity: You want the plants to be evenly spaced and evenly developed. If you're growing a bed of just one kind of annual—all marigolds, let's say—you could sow seed over the prepared bed, thin the seedlings to an even spacing, and expect fairly uniform results. In most cases, though, you'll get the best results by starting with transplants. All of the plants will be at the same stage, so they'll start blooming at the same time, and you can set them out at the proper spacing to get a nice, even look, with no bare patches.

TOP: If you like the casual look of a cottage garden, sow a mixture of plants that are adapted to your conditions.

MIDDLE: Create beautiful season scenes by combining annuals with bulbs that bloom at the same time of the year.

BOTTOM: Try a colorful planting of low-growing annuals as a groundcover around new tree and shrub plantings.

Informal Gardens

If you enjoy a more casual-looking garden, an informal planting may be more your style. Informal gardens can be any shape you like; they often have a flowing outline that curves around the base of shrubs or other structures. Informal plantings usually include at least three or four different annuals. As with formal plantings, the plants you choose for informal beds should have varying heights for visual interest. But you aren't limited to planting informal beds in masses or rows. You can set plants out in whatever drifts or groupings look good to you.

Starting an informal flower bed from transplants is a good idea if you have specific plant groupings in mind. Placing transplants just where you want them gives you the most control over which colors and plant heights are next to each other. If you plan to plant different annuals in separate drifts, you could also start from seed sown directly in the garden. Or, if you want a really casual, meadow-like effect, you could mix all the seeds together and scatter them over the soil.

Annuals with Other Plants

Although they look wonderful by themselves, annuals also have a lot to offer in groupings with other plants. In borders predominantly planted with perennials, bulbs, and shrubs, you can use annuals as a formal or informal edging, suggesting a flowering necklace around the border. While the other plants come in and out of bloom, the annual edging adds consistent color through most of the season. Repeating the same annual edging in different flower beds and borders is an excellent way to link the separate areas and give the garden a planned, finished look. Change the annuals every year if you like.

Of course, you can also add annuals to the inside of borders as well. While the compact, uniform annuals that are excellent for formal bedding can look stiff and awkward next to perennials, many other annuals have a looser, more graceful habit. In fact, annuals and biennials such as larkspur (*Consolida ambigua*), foxgloves (*Digitalis purpurea*), and Canterbury bells (*Campanula medium*) are so charming when mixed with perennials that they are often considered traditional parts of a perennial border. Tall annuals and biennials such as cosmos, cleome, hollyhocks, and mulleins (*Verbascum* spp.) are ideal for adding height to the back of a mixed border. And shorter, airy annuals blend easily into border edgings; try plants like pot marigolds (*Calendula officinalis*), annual candytuft (*Iberis umbellata*), and annual baby's-breath (*Gypsophila elegans*) with low-growing perennials and bulbs.

Besides making a great garden accent, globe amaranth (*Gomphrena globosa*) dries well for flower arrangements.

Morning glory

Annuals as Fillers

When you start any new garden, one of the hardest parts of the process is waiting for plants to fill in. This is especially true with perennial and shrub beds, since these plants can take three or four years to really get established and look like anything. New groundcover plantings can appear pretty sparse for the first few years, too. While you need to allow ample space for these plants to fill in as they mature, the bare soil in between is boring and empty, and it provides an open invitation for weeds to get started.

Planted in groups, compact zinnias make a colorful, season-long filler in flower beds and borders.

Foxgloves (*Digitalis purpurea*) will provide a temporary and very attractive "fence" to screen your garden from the outside world.

While mulch can suppress weeds, it doesn't add much excitement to a new planting. That's where filler annuals come in handy. A few seed packets of quick-growing annuals can provide welcome color and excitement for minimal cost. Sweet alyssum (*Lobularia maritima*), flowering tobacco (*Nicotiana alata*), and cornflower (*Centaurea cyanus*) are a few great filler annuals that can quickly cover the soil and deprive weed seeds of the light they need to grow. Many annuals may also self-sow to provide cover in succeeding years, gradually yielding space to expanding perennials.

Fillers for Flower Beds

If you're looking for annuals to fill in around new perennial plantings, choose those with a similar range of heights and colors as the perennials will have. Select a few short or trailing annuals for the front of the border, a few medium-sized plants for the middle of the border, and a few tall annuals for the back. While you could sow annual seed directly into the ground around the perennials, it's often easier to start with annual transplants.

Some good filler annuals, such as cleome (*Cleome hasslerana*) and cornflower, will drop seed and come back year after year. If your annuals do reseed, thin the seedlings where they're not wanted to allow the expanding perennials room to develop.

Fillers for Groundcovers

Low-growing annuals such as sweet alyssum, rose moss (*Portulaca grandiflora*), and baby-blue-eyes (*Nemophila menziesii*) can be excellent fillers for young groundcover plantings. Stick with one kind of annual for a uniform effect. In this case, it's just as easy to scatter seed around the groundcover plants, although you could also set out annual transplants in the available spaces instead. While many low-growing annuals will self-sow, you may want to scatter some fresh annual seed over the planting for the first few springs until the groundcover fills in.

Fillers for Foundation Plantings

New foundation plantings also benefit from annuals the first few years as they develop. Shrubs and groundcovers may take over their allotted space in a few years, but a carpet of annuals is most welcome in the meantime. A few market packs of your favorite annuals will be easy to plant, and the resulting flowers and foliage will provide infinitely more interest than a dull covering of bark chips.

Annuals for Screens

While the word "annual" commonly brings to mind compact, small plants like petunias and marigolds, there are a number of fast-growing annuals that can reach amazing heights of 6 feet (180 cm) or more in a single season. There are also annual vines, the twining stems of which quickly cover trellises for welcome shade and privacy. With these great plants to choose from, why spend another season staring at your neighbors' yards—or your neighbors, for that matter? Screen them off with fast-growing annuals while you're waiting for your trees and shrubs to grow.

Aleca rose and hollyhocks

Tall Annuals

Grow tall annuals in your yard to block or cover unattractive features, such as dog runs, alleys, or clothesline poles. Or plant a row or mass of tall annuals to create a "neighbor-friendly" temporary fence that delineates your property line, and at the same time, gives you privacy and an attractive view. Tall annuals can also be used to separate different areas of your

Nasturtiums

New gardens may look rather bare the first year or two. Annuals can cover the soil until perennials get established.

Black-eyed Susan vine climbs quickly to cover fences or trellises with bright blooms from summer into fall.

garden. Some top-notch tall annuals include castor bean (*Ricinus communis*), summer cypress (*Kochia scoparia*), hollyhocks (*Alcea rosea*), sunflowers (*Helianthus annuus*), and Mexican sunflower (*Tithonia rotundifolia*).

Annual Vines

A leafy curtain of annual vines is an ideal way to ensure privacy on a porch or patio without appearing to be unneighborly. Flowering vines also add a quaint, old-fashioned touch to the most ordinary support. A cloak of morning glories can convert a ho-hum garden shed into a charming and colorful garden feature, while a mass of scarlet runner beans will accent an arch or liven up a lamppost.

Most annual vines cover territory in a hurry. You can easily train them to climb a wooden or wire trellis, chain-link fences, lattice work, or even strong twine. Tall wooden or bamboo stakes also make effective supports. While annual vines are usually lighter than woody vines (such as

wisteria or trumpet creeper), they can put on a lot of growth in one season, so supply a sturdy support. Unlike clinging vines such as ivy, annual vines climb mostly with tendrils or twining stems, so don't expect them to scamper up a bare wall without assistance.

Morning glories (*Ipomoea tricolor*) have long been loved for their heart-shaped leaves and beautiful, trumpet-shaped flowers. The closely related moonflower (*Ipomoea alba*) is another popular vine; it offers large, white, heavily fragrant flowers that open in the evening. Besides being covered with clusters of colorful blooms, scarlet runner bean (*Phaseolus coccineus*) has the added bonus of edible beans. Other popular annual vines include cup-and-saucer vine (*Cobaea scandens*), hyacinth bean (*Dolichos lablab*), and black-eyed Susan vine (*Thunbergia alata*).

Annuals for Herb Gardens

Besides adding colorful flowers and handsome foliage to your garden, some annuals can even add flavor to your food! Annual herbs are easy to grow, and they'll produce generous quantities of tasty leaves or seeds to spice up your favorite dishes.

Cosmos

As with other annuals, annual herbs are quite useful for filling the gaps around new perennial plantings. If you have a formal herb garden with traditional perennial herbs, such as sage, thyme, and mint, scatter seed of annual herbs among the young plants. Or use the annual herbs throughout your yard as you would any other filler annual, and you'll have flower beds that are productive as well as beautiful. Pick herbs throughout the growing season from the outside of the clump, as evenly as you can, to keep them looking good. Pick off flower heads as they appear unless you want self-sown seeds.

Picking Annuals for Containers

As with any kind of garden, the first step to planning successful container plantings is choosing plants that have similar growth needs. If you have a shady area, impatiens, monkey flower (*Mimulus* x *hybridus*), and other shade-lovers are your

Create a colorful and practical planting by mixing herbs with annual flowers, such as pot marigold (*Calendula officinalis*).

best bets. Sunny spots can support a wider range of colorful annuals, including treasure flower (*Gazania rigens*), mealy-cup sage (*Salvia farinacea*), and narrow-leaved zinnia (*Zinnia angustifolia*).

When planning a container garden—whether it is a pot, hanging basket, window box, or planter—you also need to consider the ultimate height of the annuals you select. As a general guideline, try to choose annuals that are the same height or smaller than the height of the container; otherwise, the planting may look top-heavy.

Single-annual containers can be pleasing, but mixed plantings of three or four different annuals are even more exciting. While the exact plants you pick to grow together is up to you, there are some basic guidelines you can follow to create a successful container planting.

Asters, cosmos and dahlias

Shade-Loving Annuals

If your site gets some direct sun for part of the day, or light shade all day, you can still grow a variety of annuals. A few of the best are listed below:

Begonia Semperflorens-Cultorum hybrid (wax begonia)
Celosia cristata (cockscomb)
Impatiens wallerana (impatiens)
Lobelia erinus (edging lobelia)
Nicotiana alata (flowering tobacco)

First, select a "star" plant. Base your container planting around one centerpiece plant—perhaps a bushy marguerite daisy (*Chrysanthemum frutescens*), a free-flowering tuberous begonia, or a bold ornamental cabbage. Then choose a "supporting cast" to complement the star plant and fill out the container. Try one or two with bold leaves or an upright habit—such as coleus or dusty miller—and one or two that sprawl or trail—such as edging lobelia (*Lobelia erinus*) or creeping zinnia (*Sanvitalia procumbens*).

Sun-Loving Annuals

The secret to an easy-care garden in the sun is to pick plants that need lots of light and aren't fussy about their soil. Here are a few of the best easy-care annuals for sun:

Ageratum houstonianum (ageratum)

Antirrhinum majus (common snapdragon)

Calendula officinalis (pot marigold)

Centaurea cyanus (cornflower)

Helianthus annuus (common sunflower)

Lobularia maritima (sweet alyssum)

Nicotiana alata (flowering tobacco)

Verbena x *hybrida* (garden verbena)

Zinnia elegans (common zinnia)

Start Your Own Annuals

For an "instant" effect, you can buy and plant annuals that are already blooming. If you're not in a real hurry, however, you can start your own plants from seed. Growing your own annuals is also a good way to save money, especially if you need a lot of plants.

Some kinds of annuals, such as marigolds, mature quickly, so you can sow them directly into outdoor pots. Other annuals that are easy from direct-sown seed include sweet alyssum (*Lobularia maritima*), nasturtiums (*Tropaeolum majus*), morning glories (*Ipomoea* spp.), and zinnias. Sweet alyssum is cold-tolerant, so you can plant the seed in early spring; for the rest, wait until after the danger of frost has passed.

Other annuals have very tiny seeds or take a little longer before they start flowering, so they are best started indoors under lights. Check the instructions on the seed packets, and start the seeds the recommended number of weeks before your last expected spring frost so they'll start flowering shortly after you move them outside.

Zinnias are colorful and easy to grow, but tall cultivars will need staking. Choose compact cultivars for less work.

Bulbs

Beautiful and versatile, bulbs belong in every landscape. Many popular bulbs—including daffodils, crocus, hyacinths, and tulips—are traditionally associated with spring gardens. But with a little planning, you can have bulbs in bloom in your garden from late winter through midfall. And to fill the few months that bulbs aren't blooming outdoors, you can bring some kinds indoors and enjoy their colorful flowers all winter long.

Bulbs for Spring

Many gardeners have a special affection for spring-flowering bulbs. These early-blooming beauties signal the return of life to the garden after the rigors of a long, cold winter, adding welcome color and fragrance to any planting.

Bulbs from around the world have found a home in American gardens, despite our wide diversity of climate conditions. Most of the best-beloved bulbs—including daffodils and crocus—have earned their popularity because of their ability to adapt to a wide variety of growing conditions. Not all bulbs thrive in all parts of the country, but there are at least a few beautiful spring bulbs for virtually every area.

Create a pretty spring picture by pairing snowdrops (*Galanthus* spp.) with Italian arum (*Arum italicum*).

Create a sea of spring color by planting some crocus in your lawn. Wait to mow until the crocus leaves have yellowed.

Tulips

How Spring Bulbs Grow

Spring-flowering bulbs are best adapted to temperate areas where they can take advantage of a particular weather "window." These bulbs send up shoots early in the season—sometimes before winter has finally relinquished its icy grasp. Melting snow and ample spring rain provide a good supply of moisture as the bulbs send up their buds, hoping to attract the first bees and other insects to ensure pollination. Even though the ground is still cool, the lengthening rays of sunshine provide enough warmth to promote bloom. As summer approaches the days get longer and the bulbs set seed and ripen their foliage, preparing to end this part of their life cycle.

By the time summer's heat arrives—often accompanied by a drop in rainfall—the bulbs are plump and moist and packed with stored nutrients. Their leaves wither away, their seed drops, and the bulbs become dormant for the summer.

As fall returns, it brings cooler temperatures and increased rainfall—conditions that encourage the bulbs to start growing again. The still-warm ground provides great conditions for root growth, while increasingly colder temperatures generally discourage the bulbs from making much topgrowth. As spring arrives once again, the warm sun triggers the bounty of blossoms that we anticipate so eagerly.

Early Bulbs

In much of the nation, the first flowering bulbs often jump the gun and bloom in late winter. These little treasures are called "minor" bulbs because of their small stature compared to taller tulips, daffodils, and hyacinths. But even though they're small in size, they're big on charm, and welcome due to their early appearance.

Grape hyacinths may produce some leaves in fall, but spring is the time to enjoy their blooms.

The beautifully shaped blooms and spiky foliage of reticulated irises may appear even before the last of the snow has melted.

Examples of early bulbs are snowdrops (*Galanthus nivalis*), spring snowflakes (*Leucojum vernum*), winter aconite (*Eranthis hyemalis*), snow crocus (*Crocus chrysanthus*), Dutch crocus (*C. vernus*), and grape hyacinth (*Muscari armeniacum*).

Showy Spring Standbys

The early-spring show of minor bulbs sets the stage for the most spectacular spring-flowering favorites, including daffodils, hyacinths, tulips, and crown imperials.

Let's face it—spring just wouldn't be spring without daffodils. Sometimes referred to as jonquils, daffodils belong to the genus Narcissus. With hundreds of species and perhaps thousands of hybrids and cultivars, the variations on the standard yellow, large-cupped daffodil are almost endless. Some types are best suited for mild Southern gardens, while others prefer cooler climates. There's a perfect daffodil for nearly every spot in a garden. As a plus, most daffodils have a pleasant light scent, and many have distinct, powerful fragrances.

Of course, when you're thinking about fragrant spring bulbs, you can't forget the heady scent of hybrid hyacinths (*Hyacinthus orientalis*). The impressive flower spikes, packed with many small blooms, usually grow 6 to 10 inches (15 to 25 cm) tall.

Along with daffodils and hyacinths, tulips are a spring-garden standby. Blooming in white and nearly every shade of red, pink, orange, yellow, and purple, hybrid tulips are only lacking true blue in the color department. By choosing a range of cultivars with different bloom times and leaf patterns, you can enjoy tulips throughout the entire spring season.

Bulbs for Summer

Don't think the bulb season is over when the last spring blossom fades! The tulips may be just a memory, but there are many more beautiful blossoms ahead, like lilies and ornamental onions.

Ornamental Onions

While onions, garlic, and leeks are staples of the vegetable garden,

ornamental onions are a mainstay of the early-summer flower garden. The most impressive of the ornamental onions is the giant onion (*Allium giganteum*). Its strong flower stems—up to 4 feet (1.2 m) tall—are topped with grapefruit-sized globes of tightly packed purple flowers in early summer. Their dried seed heads make beautiful fall and winter flower arrangements. Persian onion (*A. aflatunense*) is slightly smaller but also quite showy, with softball-sized clusters of lavender-purple flowers on 3-foot (90-cm) tall stems. Other popular early-summer ornamental onions include star of Persia (*A. christophii*), drumstick chives (*A. sphaerocephalum*), and lily leek.

Daffodils

Some Like It Cool

Winter chilling is an important step in the life of most spring-blooming bulbs. If you live in a warm climate, where winter temperatures generally stay above freezing, you may find that some spring bulbs bloom poorly or don't bloom at all in the years after planting. Hybrid tulips commonly have this problem; some daffodils and crocus also grow poorly without a chilling period.

To have a great show of blooms each year, look for species and cultivars that don't need much chilling. (Ask your local nursery, neighbors or your Cooperative Extension Service to recommend the bulbs that grow best in your area.) You can also look for "precooled" bulbs, or give new bulbs an artificial cold period by storing them in the vegetable drawer of your refrigerator for six to eight weeks before planting them in early- to mid-winter.

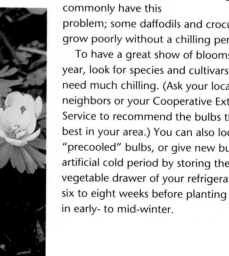

Winter aconites add bright spring color to borders and woodlands.

Lovely Lilies

Lilies are the stars of the mid- to late-summer garden. True lilies (*Lilium* spp. and hybrids) grow from a bulb and have straight stems with many short leaves. Hybrid lilies are divided into several broad groups. The three main groups are the Asiatic hybrids, trumpet lilies, and oriental hybrids. Asiatic hybrids are the first to bloom, flowering from late May into July in most parts of the country. They are noted for their large, beautifully colored and shaped flowers; most are not fragrant. July and August belong to the trumpet lilies (also known as *Aurelian* hybrids). They come in a more limited color range (mainly white, yellow, pink, and apricot), but their huge, horn-shaped blooms bear a sweet perfume. Fragrance is also a feature of the oriental hybrids, which bloom from midsummer into fall (depending on the cultivar).

Great Gladioli

Gladioli are flower-garden favorites with spikes of satin-textured blooms in an almost infinite variety of colors—from pastel pink, white, and yellow to rich purple, orange, and magenta. Breeders have also created many bicolor types, with various degrees of petal ruffling and feathering. If you plant at two-week intervals from midspring to midsummer, you can enjoy blooms throughout the growing season.

Bulbs for Fall

The end of summer doesn't spell the end of the bulb season. The fall show continues with holdovers from summer, such as dahlias, cannas, tuberous begonias, and some oriental lilies. These are complemented by bulbs that wait until the return of cold weather to bloom, including lilies, crocus, and cyclamen.

The charm of fall-blooming bulbs is the grace and freshness they add to the late-season garden. They are wonderful companions for fall-flowering perennials, including asters, mums, and Japanese anemone (*Anemone* x *hybrida*). For extra interest, plant low-growing groundcovers, such as sedums, creeping veronicas (*Veronica* spp.), creeping Jenny (*Lysimachia nummularia*), and thyme, directly over the bulbs. As the bulbs bloom, the groundcover provides a leafy backdrop that is far more pleasing than bare soil.

Bulbs for Indoor Bloom

There's nothing more heartwarming to a gardener (or anyone, for that matter) than a pot of flowering bulbs on the windowsill in the depths of winter. Happily, it's relatively easy to convince most spring bulbs to rush the season a bit. The process is called "forcing," although there's not much force involved. You simply provide a condensed version of the winter the bulbs would otherwise get when growing in the ground outdoors.

Choosing Bulbs for Indoor Bloom

Most spring bulbs can be forced, but some perform better in pots than others. Spring-blooming crocus, Siberian squill (*Scilla sibirica*), glory-of-the-snow (*Chionodoxa luciliae*), and reticulated iris (*Iris reticulata*) are very easy to chill and bring into bloom. A few tulips that perform especially well in pots include pale orange 'Apricot Beauty', plum purple 'Atilla', and some of the small, rock garden species (such as the yellow-and-white *Tulipa tarda* and the yellow or bronze-pink *T. batalinii*).

Daffodils are also gratifyingly easy to force. Although the large, yellow, trumpet daffodils are traditional favorites both in the garden and in pots, many gardeners also enjoy smaller, free-flowering cultivars such as 'Pipit', 'Hawera', and 'Tete-a-tete'. Hyacinths, too, usually perform very well in pots; a few that are especially good include pale pink 'Lady Derby', darker pink 'Pink Pearl', and deep blue 'Blue Jacket'.

Preparing Bulbs for Forcing

The best time to plant bulbs for forcing is in late fall and early winter. Set the bulbs shoulder to shoulder in clay or plastic pots in ordinary, well-drained potting soil. This kind of crowding produces wonderful displays. The "nose" of the bulb should just peek above the soil surface. Label the pot with the name of the bulb and the date, water it thoroughly, and stash it in its winter quarters for chilling.

To get a good show, you can plant bulbs close together in the pot; it's okay if the bulbs touch.

Different tulip cultivars bloom at different times, so you can enjoy them all through the spring.

ABOVE: Combine fall bulbs with groundcovers, such as leadwort (*Ceratostigma plumbaginoides*), to help support the blooms and keep them clean. BELOW: Naked ladies (*Amaryllis belladonna*) and *Nerine bowdenii* ripen their leaves in spring but don't bloom until fall.

Giving Bulbs a Chance to Chill

Your bulbs need a cool, dark place while they're producing roots. The ideal temperatures for forcing bulbs are between 33° and 45°F (1° and 7°C). Protect the bulbs with a heavy layer of straw, newspapers, or even old blankets to keep

them from getting too cold. If you don't have another place to chill your bulbs, you can try the mound technique. Simply set the bulb pots on the ground outdoors (perhaps in a corner of the vegetable garden), cover them with several inches of perlite or potting soil, and top the whole thing with a thick insulating layer of straw or wood chips. Keep in mind, though, that this pile will provide an inviting home for local mice and other rodents, and it's a messy job to dig your bulbs out of a snow-covered pile in the middle of winter.

Bringing Bulbs into Bloom

No matter where you chill your bulbs, check on them every few weeks to see if they need more water. At the same time, look for signs of growth. Your bulbs will signal they're ready to grow in two ways: Tiny white roots will be visible in the drainage holes of the pot, and new shoots will appear at the tops of the bulbs. Crocus and reticulated iris may be ready in as little as eight weeks, while larger bulbs can take twelve weeks or more.

When the shoots are an inch or two (2.5 to 5 cm) tall, bring them inside to a cool, bright window. Fertilize lightly each time you water, and turn the pots regularly to keep the shoots from stretching unevenly toward the light. Keep pots away from radiators, and other heat sources; bulbs like it cool.

Bulbs for Naturalizing

Wouldn't you love to find flowers that you could plant once and enjoy forever, without lots of yearly fussing? If this is your gardening style, you'll love the idea of "naturalized" bulbs.

Naturalizing means planting bulbs in random, natural-looking drifts under trees,

Showy crocus look wonderful naturalized in grassy areas for fall bloom.

in woodlands, or in grassy areas. It's easy to do, and the results look better and better every year as the bulbs multiply to produce even more blooms.

Deciding Where to Plant

Naturalized bulbs are often best in low-maintenance areas, where you can enjoy the blooms but not be bothered by the sight of the ripening leaves. Very early bulbs, such as spring crocus, are sometimes naturalized in lawns to provide color. You may have to put off the first spring mowing for a week or two to let the bulb foliage turn yellow, but after that you can mow as usual. Fall-blooming bulbs can also look good in grassy areas, but you'll have to stop mowing in late summer, as soon as you see the flower buds.

Thick grass may be too competitive for some bulbs, but a sparse lawn—especially under deciduous trees—is just the right environment to help bulbs take hold. The bulbs get plenty of spring sun and moisture before the trees leaf out, and the flowers add cheerful spring and/or fall color to otherwise drab areas. If you have many trees, you can combine sweeps of naturalized bulbs with shade-loving annuals, perennials, and shrubs to create a charming woodland garden with four-season interest.

Create a carpet of bloom by naturalizing snowdrops, winter aconite (*Eranthis hyemalis*), *Cyclamen coum*, and other small spring bulbs under deciduous trees.

Best Bulbs for Naturalizing

Small bulbs tend to be best for naturalizing: They bloom dependably, and they're easy to plant. Best of all, they're usually relatively inexpensive, so you can buy hundreds to make a good show. Daffodil bulbs tend to be large, but even they are often sold in bargain mixtures for naturalizing. Listed below are some of the bulbs that adapt well to naturalizing across much of the country.

Lily leek (*Allium moly*)
Grecian windflower (*Anemone blanda*)
Showy autumn crocus (*Colchicum speciosum*)
Crocus (*Crocus* spp.)
Common snowdrops (*Galanthus nivalis*)
Spanish bluebells (*Hyacinthoides hispanicus*)
Summer snowflake (*Leucojum aestivum*)
Grape hyacinth (*Muscari armeniacum*)
Daffodils (*Narcissus* hybrids)
Siberian squill (*Scilla sibirica*)

Iris

Grape hyacinths (*Muscari* spp.) and tulips make a stunning display when mass-planted. They are both excellent cut flowers too.

Planting Naturalized Bulbs

The key to successful naturalizing is planting bulbs in random-looking arrangements rather than in straight rows or patterns. It's usually best to place them randomly over the planting area by hand until the arrangement looks right to you. Don't just toss out handfuls of bulbs from a standing position; the bulbs may get bruised or damaged as they fall and be prone to pest and disease problems. If you do want to use this super-random method, use potatoes and plant the bulbs where the potatoes fall.

Many gardeners find that a narrow trowel is the easiest tool to use for planting small bulbs. You simply insert the trowel into the ground at an angle, lift up a flap of sod, tuck the bulb into the soil, and replace the flap. Or you can plant bulbs in groups by lifting up larger sections of sod, loosening the exposed soil, pressing the bulbs into the soil, and replacing the sod. (This technique works best with small bulbs such as crocus.) If you have lots of bulbs to plant, you may want to try using an auger attachment that connects to a power drill to dig many holes quickly and easily. (These attachments are usually sold in garden centers.)

Buying Healthy Bulbs

A key part of growing bulbs successfully is starting with healthy plants. By being a smart shopper, you can get the best bulbs for your garden at the best possible price.

Knowing What to Look For

With bulbs, as with most things, you get what you pay for. High-quality, full-sized bulbs command top dollar, based on the amount of time and labor it takes to produce them, but you can rely on them for spectacular results.

A higher price, however, doesn't always mean that one tulip or daffodil cultivar is better than another. New cultivars tend to be much more expensive than older ones that have been around awhile. New cultivars are fun to try, but the old standbys that have proven to be good performers through the years are usually both economical and dependable.

A top-quality bulb is firm to the touch (not mushy or squishy) and free of large blemishes or scars. Some bulbs, such as tulips and hyacinths, may have a trace of blue mold on them. A few small mold spots will not harm the bulb, but a noticeable layer may indicate that the bulb was stored improperly before being offered for sale.

Look for bulbs that show little or no root or shoot growth except for a pale growth bud at the top. (Lilies are an exception, since they often have fleshy roots attached.) It's wise to shop early in the season so you can get the bulbs before they dry out from sitting in a store.

Handling Bulbs When You Get Them Home

If you can't plant right away, store your bulbs in a cool, dark, and relatively dry place. Keep them in the paper or mesh bags they came in. A refrigerator can be handy for storing spring bulbs but is too cold for summer bulbs, such as gladioli or dahlias. Keep summer bulbs in a cool spot until you're ready to start them indoors or plant them outdoors.

Planting Bulbs

The great thing about most bulbs is that they can adapt to a wide range of growing conditions. But if you really want your bulbs to thrive, it's worth putting some thought into giving them the best conditions possible. Take a little time to prepare a good growing site and plant your bulbs properly. Then you can stand back and enjoy the bounty of beautiful flowers in the years to come.

Hardy cyclamen make an unusual groundcover under trees and shrubs. You'll enjoy both the leaves and the flowers.

Getting the Soil Ready

Many bulbs can grow for years in the same place, so it's worth putting some effort into preparing an ideal planting site. Bulbs tend to thrive in soil that's on the loamy or sandy side, since good drainage is critical for most bulbs. If your soil isn't naturally loamy, you can improve its drainage and fertility by adding some organic matter before you plant your bulbs. Spread a 1- to 3-inch (2.5 to 7.5 cm) layer of compost or chopped leaves over the planting area, then work it into the top 10 to 12 inches (25 to 30 cm) of soil. (When you're only planting small bulbs, such as crocus and grape hyacinths, you can get away with loosening just the top 4 to 6 inches [10 to 15 cm] of soil.) Or, if you're digging individual holes, work a handful of organic matter into the soil at the base of each hole, and add another handful to the soil you use to refill the hole. As it breaks down, the organic matter will release a steady supply of nutrients for good growth.

Planting Bulbs in Beds and Borders

Once you've loosened the soil, planting is easy—just dig the hole to the proper depth, pop in the bulb, and cover it with soil. The proper depth will vary, depending on what bulbs you're growing. A general rule of thumb is that the hole should be dug to a depth that is three to four times the height of the bulb. For example, a crocus corm that measures 1 inch (2.5 cm) high should be planted 3 to 4 inches (7.5 to 10 cm) deep; a 2-inch (5-cm) high tulip bulb needs a hole 6 to 8 inches (15 to 20 cm) deep. If your soil is on the sandy side, plant the bulb or corm a bit deeper.

Set the bulb in the hole with the pointed growth bud facing upward. If you can't tell which side should be up—as often happens with small bulbs such as Grecian windflowers (*Anemone blanda*)—set the bulb on its side or just drop it in the hole and hope for the best. Most bulbs have a strong will to grow, and they'll find a way to send up their shoots.

Space the bulbs so each has ample room to grow. As a general rule, you should leave 5 to 6 inches (12.5 to 15 cm) between large bulbs and 1 to 3 inches (2.5 to 7.5 cm) between small bulbs. Once you've got the spacing the way you want it, carefully replace the soil around the

Buy generous quantities of bulbs and plant them in drifts or large clumps to create a dramatic display in the garden.

bulbs to refill the hole. Firm the soil by patting it with your hand or the back of a rake, then water thoroughly.

Caring for Bulbs

Hardy bulbs—including daffodils, crocus, and other dependable favorites—are about as close to "no work" as you can get. You just plant them once, and they come back year after year. Many will even multiply over time to produce large sweeps of blooms without any help from you. But as with any other garden plants, a little extra care can help your bulbs grow and look better.

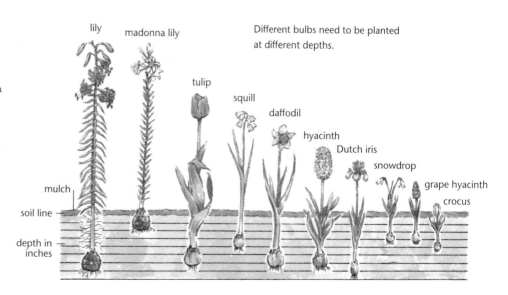

Different bulbs need to be planted at different depths.

Watering for Good Growth

Watering is most important when your bulbs are actively growing. This means fall and spring for fall- or spring-blooming bulbs and spring through summer for summer-blooming bulbs. During these times, most bulbs can survive a moderate drought without watering, but they may not bloom well the following year.

The daisy-like blooms of Grecian windflowers are a welcome sight in spring. They will thrive in well-mulched well-drained soil.

Mulching

Mulching your bulbs is one of the best ways to keep them healthy. Mulch will help to hold moisture in the soil and minimize rapid temperature changes, providing ideal rooting conditions. It shades the soil and helps to keep bulbs cool, protecting the shoots of bulbs from being lured out of the ground too early in spring. Mulch also benefits summer-flowering bulbs, such as lilies, which dislike hot, dry soil.

Mulch your bulbs after planting in fall or spring. Apply a 1- to 2-inch (2.5- to 5-cm) layer of mulch over the soil. Avoid putting on more than that, or your bulbs may have trouble poking their

Mulch and stake dahlias to keep them growing strong and healthy.

shoots up through the mulch. To protect hardy bulbs (such as daffodils and crocus), add more mulch each fall to keep it at the right depth.

Fertilizing

Most bulbs will get along just fine without a lot of extra fertilizer. Working compost or other organic matter into the soil at planting time and using it as a mulch will provide much of the nutrient supply your bulbs need.

For top-notch growth, you can also sprinkle commercial organic fertilizer over the soil, following the package directions. Use a mix blended especially for bulbs, if you can find one; otherwise, a general garden fertilizer is acceptable. Fertilize both spring-blooming and fall-flowering bulbs in spring. Summer-flowering bulbs usually grow best with several small applications of fertilizer in early- to mid-summer.

Handling Tender Bulbs

It's easy to fall for the lure of daffodils, crocus, and other cold-hardy bulbs—you just plant them once and enjoy them for years. Tender bulbs, on the other hand, tend to need more work, since you may have to dig or lift them for winter storage indoors. Exactly what counts as a tender bulb? Well, it depends on what climate you live in, but the bulbs that usually come to mind are those that are from tropical and subtropical climates. These include dahlias, tuberous begonias, gladioli, cannas, and caladiums. Some tender bulbs can take more cold than others. Cannas, for instance, may survive winters in areas as cold as Zone 7. But others, including tuberous begonias and caladiums, can survive over winter only in frost-free areas.

Lifting Tender Bulbs for Storage

Digging tender bulbs for indoor storage is just another part of routine fall-garden cleanup. When the bulb foliage turns yellow or brown, that's a good sign that the bulb is ready for storage. If the leaves stay green or if you don't have time to dig the

bulbs when they are first ready, you can wait until just after the first frost. The cold temperatures will cause the leaves to turn black, but the bulbs are protected by the soil and should survive a light frost just fine. Don't wait any longer, though—get out and start digging, or your bulbs may be damaged by the increasingly cold temperatures.

Actually digging the bulbs is simple. First, cut any tall stems back to about 6 inches (15 cm), so you can clearly see the base of the stem. Then carefully loosen the soil all the way around the plant. Use a trowel or hand fork to work around small bulbs and those growing in pots. (You can also turn whole pots over to dump out the soil and the bulbs at the same time.) A shovel or spading fork works better for big clumps, like dahlias and cannas.

Once the soil is loose, you can lift the bulb easily. Shake off as much soil as you can from the bulbs, label them, and set them on newspaper in a cool, shady place, such as a garage, potting shed, or porch. Dust any cuts on the bulbs or tubers with sulfur, and leave them to dry for several days. Keep the bulbs out of the hot sun and away from areas where squirrels, mice, and other animals can get at them.

Storing Tender Bulbs

Once your bulbs have dried for a few days, you can store them. Some gardeners keep their bulbs in mesh bags (like the kind onions come in) or paper bags with a few holes punched in them for better air circulation. Others prefer to store bulbs in boxes of slightly damp wood shavings or peat moss to keep the bulbs from drying out too much over winter. The storage spot should be dark to prevent the bulbs from sprouting and on the cool side—ideally about 50° to 60°F (10° to 16°C). During the storage period, check your bulbs every three to four weeks. Throw away any that are rotting. Sprinkle water on those that are starting to look shriveled. When spring arrives, plant them as you would new bulbs.

Propagating Bulbs

Once you've had fun growing a few bulbs, it's hard to resist the urge to grow more and more.

Dividing for Multiplying

Division is the fastest and easiest way to propagate nearly all bulbs, corms, tubers, tuberous roots, and rhizomes. Besides being quite simple, division has another advantage: All the new plants will be identical to the parent bulb, so you can easily increase your favorite colors and flower forms.

Dividing Bulbs and Corms Some bulbs, such as tulips and daffodils, form small "bulblets" near their base. Gladioli and other corms produce similar off-sets called "cormels." With good care, both bulblets and cormels can grow to full flowering size in as little as a year or two.

To divide spring bulbs, lift the clump with a spade or digging fork after the foliage has died back in late spring. To divide gladiolus corms, lift them in late summer or fall, as the foliage turns yellow. Separate the bulblets or cormlets by gently pulling them away from the mother bulb or corm. Plant the bulblets or cormlets in a nursery bed or a corner of the vegetable garden, where they can grow undisturbed for a few years. Water and fertilize them regularly. When the bulbs reach flowering size, move them to their final spot in the garden.

Dividing Tubers and Tuberous Roots

Division is also an effective way to increase tuberous plants, such as dahlias and tuberous begonias. The best time to divide is in spring, just after you bring these tender plants out of winter storage. Use a sharp knife to cut begonia tubers into two or three pieces, each with at least one growth bud. On dahlias, cut tuberous roots apart at the stem end, so each root has at least one bud.

Plant each new piece in a pot and set it under grow lights or in a greenhouse. Keep the temperature between 65° and 75°F (18° and 24°C). Water as needed so the potting soil stays evenly moist, but not wet. (Don't fertilize newly cut bulbs—wait until they're growing in soil.) In a few weeks, you should have healthy new plants that are ready for transplanting into outdoor gardens and containers.

Dividing Rhizomes Cannas and bearded irises are the two common examples of plants that grow from rhizomes. Use a sharp knife, a spade (if the clump is really big), or your hands to pull or cut apart the rhizomes. Discard any old, woody pieces from the center of the original clump.

Divide canna clumps into pieces about 6 inches (15 cm) square, making sure that each has at least one growth bud. The best time to divide cannas is in spring, right before you plant them in pots or outdoors in the garden. Bearded irises, on the other hand, prefer to be divided just after they flower. Separate them into pieces with at least one "fan" of leaves on each. Trim the foliage back by at least half, and replant the irises into soil that you've enriched with compost, leaf mold, or well rotted manure.

Plant daffodils with early rhododendrons for a delightful spring display.

Growing Bulbs from Seed

If you're really patient, you can also grow your bulbs from seed. When they bloom, the seedlings may not look like the parent plant, which can be fun if you like surprises but disappointing if you wanted the exact color of the original.

Gather seed in summer or fall, after your bulbs flower. Check the developing seedpods every few days, then collect the

Buy new dahlia roots each year, or dig your favorites in fall and store them indoors for winter.

seeds as the seedpods begin to open. Sow the seed in well-drained seed-starting mix in pots or trays. Cover it with a thin layer of mix, and set the containers in a cool, shaded place outdoors. Water as needed to keep the soil evenly moist.

When seedlings appear, move the containers to a sunny place. Keep watering until the seedlings die down. (Seedlings will go dormant for part of the year, just like their garden-grown parents.) Water sparingly until new growth appears again; then keep them evenly moist. Depending on the species you're dealing with, your baby bulbs may reach flowering size in as little as one year, although they're more likely to take three to five years.

Bluebells (*Hyacinthoides* spp.) can reseed prolifically to produce large patches. Give them a site where they can spread, or mow off the seedpods to prevent reseeding.

Trees, Shrubs, and Vines

ABOVE: This magnificent white cherry, *Prunus* 'Tai Haku', is one of the finest flowering cherry trees in cultivation.

(15 to 19.5 m), and a large tree matures at 75 to 100 feet (22.5 to 30 m) or taller. Growing conditions, climate, competition with grass and other plants, mechanical or animal damage, and pollution can prevent a tree from reaching its mature height.

These versatile plants frame views, develop patterns for your landscape, and unify your design. To get the most out of the trees you select, consider the following features and what they can add to your design.

Beauty Trees serve as backdrops for other plants or garden features and as focal points, like large, living sculptures. You can use them to screen unwanted views and give you privacy. Your trees establish the walls and ceilings for your outdoor rooms. You can use them to soften the architecture of your house or to call attention to it.

Climate Control By shading your house, trees keep things cool, reducing energy bills. (Don't plant evergreen trees for summer shade, though; they'll block the sun in winter, preventing passive solar heating of your house.) You can use trees as a windbreak, to intercept and buffer prevailing winds. If winter winds are your bane, needle-leaved evergreens are the best choice for a windbreak. If you live near a seacoast, choose salt-tolerant species to soften the sea winds.

Livability Trees absorb noise and reduce glare, and they purify the air you breathe. Patios or play areas become more usable during hot summers when shaded by trees. Many trees have edible fruits that can feed your family or attract wildlife.

Consider Form and Function
When you select trees for your yard, use your landscape plan to help you decide what size and shape of tree to select and how each tree will function in the landscape. The arrangement of the branches gives each species of tree a distinctively shaped crown.

Using Trees in the Landscape
The biggest investment in your landscape—in both time and money—is the selection, purchase, and planting of trees. Trees dominate the landscape and have a psychological benefit, too, by making you feel rested and peaceful.

Landscaping with Trees
By horticultural definition, trees are woody plants with one main stem or trunk, although some, such as river birch (*Betula nigra*) and smoke tree (*Cotinus coggygria*), are often grown in multitrunked clumps. Trees generally have a mature height ranging from 15 to 100 feet (4.5 to 30 m) or more. A small tree is defined as one that generally doesn't exceed 25 to 35 feet (7.5 to 10.5 m) in mature height. A medium-sized tree matures at 50 to 65 feet

Most needle-leaved evergreens, like pines and spruces, tend to have more symmetrical or rigid shapes than deciduous trees, such as oaks or maples. Needle-leaved evergreens often display the familiar conical or pyramidal "Christmas tree" look. Deciduous trees and broad-leaved evergreens come in many shapes, including round, vase-shaped, and columnar.

Trees are often classified according to their intended use—as specimens, shade trees, or street trees. Choose your landscape trees according to their function. For an upright, narrow screen, for example, you might select either a tree with a columnar shape or a pyramidal needle-leaved evergreen.

Casual plantings, with a mixture of trees, shrubs, and wildflowers, can produce a charming effect.

Trees that have attractive bark, like this river birch (*Betula nigra*), can provide year-round interest.

If you're looking for a large tree to add shade to your yard, consider planting a sugar maple (*Acer saccharum*). It will thrive on a sunny site with evenly moist (but not waterlogged) soil that is slightly acid.

Specimen Trees

Specimen trees are showy in some way. They may put on an eye-catching display of flowers in spring, like a flowering crab apple, or blaze with autumn color, like the red maple 'October Glory' (*Acer rubrum* 'October Glory'). Or they may have unusually colored leaves, such as purple smoke tree (*Cotinus coggygria* 'Royal Purple'), or bright berries, such as those on the American mountain ash (*Sorbus americana*).

Specimen trees are valuable as focal points in a winter landscape. Fruits that hang on the branches after the leaves drop, such as the fruits of crab apples, are eye-catching. Trees with attractive winter silhouettes, such as flowering dogwoods, also make good specimen trees.

Select a specimen tree which has multiseasonal interest. A saucer magnolia (*Magnolia* x *soulangiana*) is very showy for a couple of weeks during the spring when in flower, but it fades into the background the rest of the year. A kousa dogwood (*Cornus kousa*) on the other hand, bears showy flowers in spring, raspberry-like red fruits in fall, and has attractive peeling bark in winter.

Shade Trees

Shade trees may have showy features, but it's their cooling effect that's most important. A tree with a round or vase shape is ideal for use as a shade tree. Decide the location of a new shade tree with care: Make sure the shadow of the tree will shade the area you intend it to.

If you want filtered shade or want to be able to grow grass under your tree, use a tree with small, fine leaves, such as a thornless honey locust (*Gleditsia triacanthos* var. *inermis*), not one with a dense canopy of large, overlapping leaves, such as a Norway maple (*Acer platanoides*).

Street Trees

Street trees are tough species that withstand the difficult growing conditions along the street. They're tolerant of heat and pollution, grow well in poor soils, and can stand drought. Their roots must grow in very limited spaces, and their crowns must fit under overhead utility lines. Street trees have to be neat: Look for trees that don't have messy fruit, falling branches or twigs, or large leaves that can block storm sewers.

In spite of these demands, a number of attractive and adaptable trees are available for roadside planting. Among small trees, consider trident maple

Maple tree

Trees come in a wide range of shapes and sizes. Keep these differences in mind when planning your landscape.

Consider Growth Rates

Trees grow at different rates, ranging from less than 1 foot (30 cm) per year to several feet (about 1 m) per year. Species with a slow-to-medium growth rate, like oaks, generally require less maintenance than fast-growing ones. Fast-growing trees, such as poplars and willows, are often short-lived, surviving only 20 to 30 years, and they also generally have weak wood, which is more susceptible to damage from wind, storms, and pests.

(*Acer buergerianum*), thornless cockspur hawthorn (*Crataegus crus-galli* var. *inermis*), or golden-rain tree (*Koelreuteria paniculata*). Suitable medium to large trees include thornless honey locust (*Gleditsia triacanthos* var. *inermis*), Japanese pagoda tree (*Sophora japonica*), and silver linden (*Tilia tomentosa*).

Using Shrubs in the Landscape

Shrubs are hardworking plants in any landscape. They can be used to add a touch of greenery at the foundation of the house, make a thick screen between neighbors, add seasonal color from flowers or fruit, or outline the garden's "rooms."

Types of Shrubs

Shrubs are woody plants with multiple stems, ranging from a few inches tall to approximately 15 feet (4.5 m) at maturity. Occasionally an individual shrub is trained to a single treelike stem, called a standard. And large shrubs are sometimes "limbed up," by removing the lower branches, into small trees.

Like trees, shrubs can be deciduous, evergreen, or semi-evergreen. If all leaves drop each fall, with new leaves each spring through summer, the shrub is deciduous. Deciduous shrubs, including such favorites as roses (*Rosa* spp.) and spireas (*Spiraea* spp.), often have attractive flowers. For heavy flower

production, plant them in full sun. Evergreen shrubs have leaves year-round, though you will notice that each year some of the oldest leaves drop off and are replaced by new leaves. Shrubs with wide, often thick, leaves, such as rhododendrons (*Rhododendron* spp.), and camellias (*Camellia* spp.). are called broad-leaved evergreens. Shrubs with thin, narrow leaves, such as junipers (*Juniperus* spp.) and dwarf mugo pines (*Pinus mugo* var. *mugo*), are classified as needle-leaved evergreens. Semi-evergreen shrubs means

FAR LEFT: You may choose to highlight the unusual branching structure of a tree you already have. LEFT: Lindens (*Tilia* spp.) can be tough, adaptable street trees. Their yellow fall color is a bonus.

they hold some of their leaves well into winter. Glossy abelia (*Abelia* x *grandiflora*), for example, is evergreen in the South becoming semi-evergreen the farther north it is planted.

Some shrub genera include both deciduous and evergreen species. Hollies (*Ilex* spp.) are a good example. When the deciduous hollies, possum haw (*I. decidua*) and winterberry (*I. verticillata*), drop their leaves in the fall, large clusters of bright red berries are revealed. Their berry display is generally much showier than that of many of the evergreen hollies, such as Chinese holly (*I. cornuta*) and English holly (*I. aquifolium*), whose berries are often hidden by their leaves. Other shrub genera with both deciduous and evergreen species include viburnums (*Viburnum* spp.), rhododendrons and azaleas (*Rhododendron* spp.), and barberries (*Berberis* spp.).

Hydrangea

Choosing and Using Shrubs

One of the most creative and ornamental ways to use shrubs in a landscape is in mixed plantings. Try combining deciduous and evergreen species, interplanting shrubs that bloom at different seasons, or adding flowering shrubs to a perennial border to create year-round interest.

If you need to block the noise of traffic year-round, plant evergreen shrubs, such as yews (*Taxus* spp.), hollies (*Ilex* spp.), or, in warm regions, camellias (*Camellia* spp.). If you want shrubs to provide privacy only

You can choose from a variety of shrub shapes.

Troublesome Trees

While no tree is perfect, some species tend to be much more of a bother than others. These troublemakers may be weak-wooded (drop lots of branches that you have to pick up), produce massive quantities of annoying fruits or seeds, or just have a combination of unattractive features. Below is a list of some common nuisance trees, along with their bad habits:

Acer platanoides (Norway maple): shallow-rooted, reseeds prolifically

Ailanthus altissima (tree-of-heaven): reseeds prolifically, odiferous male flowers

Albizia julibrissin (mimosa): pest- and disease-prone, messy seedpods

Morus spp. (mulberries): messy fruit, pest- and disease-prone

Populus spp. (poplars): weak-wooded, invasive roots, pest- and disease-prone

Salix spp. (willows): pest- and disease-prone, weak-wooded

Ulmus pumila (Siberian elm): weak-wooded, pest-prone

for summertime barbecues, deciduous shrubs would make a fine choice.

Specimens Shrubs make excellent specimen plants. Use them to call out a special feature in your yard such as the beginning of a path or the end of a border or patio. For specimens, look for shrubs

that are attractive for as many months as possible. Many viburnums, for example, have attractive spring flowers, summer fruit, and good fall color.

Backdrops and "Walls" You can use shrubs to mark the garden rooms or the parts of your landscape—to screen a quiet sitting area from an area designed for active play, or to wall utility areas off for trash or storage. You can also use shrubs as a backdrop for plantings of flowers. But if you use shrubs in this manner, look for ones that will complement but not compete with your flowers. Choose green shrubs like boxwoods or junipers, for example, and avoid those with showy blossoms of their own.

Screens and Hedges Shrubs are the perfect choice for hedges and screens, to block unattractive views or the sights and sounds of nearby neighbors and traffic. To calculate how many shrubs you need to buy for an effective hedge or screen, determine the mature spread of the species you've selected. Figure on spacing the shrubs closer together than their mature spread so that they'll form an unbroken line. For example, if a particular shrub has a mature spread of 5 feet (1.5 m), plan to space the plants 3 to 4 feet (0.9 to 1.2 m) apart, depending upon how large they are when you buy them and how quickly you want a solid screen or hedge. Divide the total hedge length by the spacing you select to determine the number of shrubs to buy.

Groundcovers Shrubs are an excellent substitute for grass in areas where lawns don't grow well, where mowing is difficult, or where you want less maintenance. Planted in a well-mulched bed, low-growing junipers (*Juniperus horizontalis* and *J. procumbens* 'Nana') or rockspray cotoneaster (*Cotoneaster horizontalis*) will form a low-maintenance cover on a steep hill. Where soil erosion is a problem, use shrubs with creeping underground stolons, such as red-osier dogwood (*Cornus sericea*), or shrubs with arching stems that root when they touch the ground, such as winter jasmine (*Jasminum nudiflorum*).

Seasonal Attractions In your landscape, shrubs can be utilitarian, but they can also be a focal point. Look for shrubs with multiseasonal interest—especially for use

BELOW TOP: A border of carefully chosen shrubs can provide an attractive, low-maintenance option to flower beds.
CENTRE: Flowering shrubs, like this weigela, are often most attractive when allowed to grow in a natural arching form.
BOTTOM: Many flowering shrubs, such as camellias (*Camellia* spp.), can provide a dramatic show during their bloom season.

as accents or specimens. Oak-leaved hydrangea (*Hydrangea quercifolia*), for instance, has interesting oak-leaf-shaped leaves that turn purple in fall. Its showy clusters of off-white flowers dry on the plant and persist well into the winter. The peeling bark provides additional winter interest. The fruit on shrubs such as pyracanthas (*Pyracantha* spp.) and viburnums (*Viburnum* spp.) provide food for birds, while the plants serve as protective cover. Fruiting shrubs are also excellent for attracting wildlife.

Size Up Your Selections

If you want your shrubs to stay short, regular pruning will keep them in bounds. But a better approach is to choose shrubs that mature at the height you need. There are dwarf or miniature cultivars of many popular shrubs, including 'Bronxensis' forsythia, which matures at 2 feet (60 cm) in height. Dwarf cultivars of many trees—especially spruces (*Picea* spp.) and arborvitae (*Thuja* spp.)—are also commonly used as shrubs. Look for plants with names like 'Prostrata', 'Nana', 'Compacta', 'Densa', and 'Pumila', but don't stop there. Be sure to verify mature height before you buy; compact forms of some trees and large shrubs may still be much larger than you want at maturity.

Investigate Potential Pest Problems

Consider how attractive the tree or shrub may be to pests. In general, vigorous plants attract fewer pests and withstand those that do find them. But if you can choose species and cultivars that are naturally more problem-resistant, you're several steps ahead of the game. A plant's susceptibility to insects and diseases can vary depending on where you live, so check with your Cooperative Extension Service to learn which pests are common in your area.

A final word about pests: Planting a tree or shrub that's prone to a particular

If you like a formal look in your garden, you may choose to include tightly sheared shrubs as accents.

problem need not doom you to more work. Many insects and diseases look bad but don't really threaten the life of the plant. Lilacs, for example, often get powdery mildew, which is basically harmless and sometimes barely noticeable.

Easy-Care Foundation Plantings

That small strip of soil that surrounds the bottom of the house may be the most misunderstood area in the landscape. All too often it's relegated to a boring hodgepodge of badly pruned evergreens, but it doesn't have to be that way. The two secrets to an interesting, attractive, and low-maintenance foundation planting are a simple design and well-chosen plants.

Designing a Foundation Planting

Start with a design so you can "see" how the plants will fit together before you buy and install them. At some point, your design should be on paper, drawn to scale. You may want to draw the plan first, then try to visualize how it will look in real life. Or you may find it easier to experiment with different layouts right on the site, and then record your best effort.

To help visualize the design, lay a rope along the ground to define a possible outline for the planting. Stick in upside-down brooms or tall stakes to represent

Some shrubs, like barberries (*Berberis* spp.), offer both flowers and showy fruit for multiseason interest.

Make sure each tree and shrub has enough room to develop without crowding—you'll minimize diseases and pruning.

Foundation plantings don't have to be boring! Try a lively mixture of shrubs, trees, flowers, and groundcovers.

small trees; inverted bushel baskets or buckets could stand for shrubs. As you decide where things should go, keep in mind that you'll be planting them out at least 1 foot (30 cm) beyond the drip line to protect them from rain falling off the roof. (Cover the unplanted area along the drip line with a layer of gravel or a row of flat rocks or pavement blocks to prevent erosion.) When you are pleased with the broom-and-basket layout, translate that design to paper.

Picking the Right Plants

Once you have a pleasing design, you can select plants to fit it. The most important step to making your planting low maintenance is choosing plants that won't

Large shrubs like lilacs can be "limbed up" (by removing the lower branches) to look like small trees.

get too big or too wide. That may mean selecting dwarf shrub species or cultivars that won't grow up to block your windows. It may also mean planting far enough from the house for the plants to spread out. The second most important thing is choosing plants that are well adapted to the site conditions: the soil (especially its drainage) and the amount of light (including the light and heat that bounce off the house wall).

Foundation plantings have traditionally contained mostly evergreen conifers, such as yew and juniper, or broad-leaved evergreens, like azaleas and boxwood. Evergreens do add color and hide the foundation all year, but deciduous shrubs have their place, too. Many species—including dwarf fothergilla (*Fothergilla gardenii*) and Japanese kerria (*Kerria japonica*)—offer multiseason interest with flowers, fall color, or attractive stems. Also look for dwarf or slow-growing cultivars that will stay low without regular pruning. A few interesting choices include maroon 'Crimson Pygmy' barberry (*Berberis thunbergii* 'Crimson

Pygmy'), white-flowered dwarf slender deutzia (*Deutzia gracilis* 'Nikko'), and dwarf cranberry bush virnum (*Viburnum opulus* 'Nanum').

Though there are many wonderful plants to choose from, limit your design to a few different species—not only will it look better, but you'll have fewer types of plants to care for. If you choose interesting species, you don't have to worry that the lack of diversity will be monotonous. Look for plants with attractive textures, or growth habits, or with interesting fruit, flowers, or bark. And don't forget groundcovers, which unify the planting and help link it with the house and the lawn beyond. Some also offer seasonal flowers, fruits, or fall color.

Caring for Trees and Shrubs

One of the greatest things about trees and shrubs is that they don't need much maintenance. You need to do a few simple things to care for them while they're young and even fewer simple things once they mature.

Special Care for New Plants

Water your new plants regularly (once a week if you don't get any rain) for the first two years, until they can form enough roots to search out water on their own. To encourage a good root system, water deeply, slowly, and in an area wider than the end of the branches farthest from the trunk.

To make it easier to mow under trees and shrubs and to protect them from lawn-mower damage, leave a big grassless zone at the base. If you don't plant flowers or groundcovers under the trees, you can prevent weeds by putting down a weed barrier (like landscape fabric) or a 2- to 3-inch (5- to 7.5- cm) layer of mulch. (Leave a mulch-free zone several inches wide around the trunk to discourage rot.)

Maintaining Established Plants

Once your trees and shrubs are in and growing, they'll mostly take care of themselves. Unless you have a prolonged drought, established plantings should be able to scavenge the water they need from deep in the soil. Topping off organic mulches as they break down helps keep the soil moist and discourages weeds.

Fertilizing Trees and shrubs don't really need regular fertilizer applications since they can send roots long distances in search of needed nutrients. But for really good growth, spread a 1-inch (2.5-cm) layer of compost around each plant in spring. As it breaks down, the compost will slowly release a balanced dose of plant nutrients; it will also add organic matter to keep soil conditions ideal for good root growth. If you've used an organic mulch, pull it back from the base of the plant, apply the compost, and replace the mulch. If you've used a landscape fabric, you'll have to remove it to put down the compost. Don't fertilize after midsummer in the North or early fall in the South; otherwise, the plants may produce succulent new growth that will be damaged by early fall frosts.

Pruning Pruning is perhaps the least understood and most poorly done aspect of tree and shrub maintenance. Why? Because people use it to reduce the size of plants they shouldn't have planted where they did in the first place. In truth, the real purpose of pruning is to remove wood that's damaged, dead, or growing in the wrong place or direction.

Big-leaved hydrangea (*Hydrangea macrophylla*) thrive in compost-rich moist soil.

The time of year you prune flowering shrubs is not a concern when you prune selectively, because you're only removing a few branches.

For your own safety, and for the plants' ultimate health, it's smart to leave pruning on large trees to professionals. As with small trees and shrubs, the only reason to prune large trees is to remove dead or damaged wood. Don't let anyone talk you into having your tree topped (a technique that shears the whole crown of the tree back to large stubs). Besides ruining the natural form and beauty of the tree, topping creates large wounds and crowded masses of succulent twigs that are easy targets for disease organisms.

Rounded hedges have a slightly more casual look; tightly trimmed hedges provide a geometric, formal effect.

Using Vines in the Landscape

Vines are often used simply for the beautiful flowers and foliage they bring to the garden. But vines have functional uses as well: They are fast-growing and quickly lend an established look to the landscape. They can also soften or hide the harsh architectural lines of buildings, create or define garden spaces, provide privacy, screen unsightly views or noise, cover up ugly masonry, and break up the monotony of long fences and walls.

Types of Vines

While all vines twine or climb, keep in mind that there are three basic types of vines: annuals, herbaceous perennials, and woody perennials. Most vines are fast growers, although some of the woody perennials may take a year or two to become established.

Annual vines, such as common morning glory (*Ipomoea purpurea*), climb a lamppost or trellis in a hurry, making a good show in a single season. You'll need to replant annual vines each year, although some will self-sow. Some vines grown as annuals in the North, including black-eyed Susan vine (*Thunbergia alata*), are perennial in warm climates.

Herbaceous perennial vines, such as crimson starglory (*Mina lobata*), die back every winter and regrow in spring.

Hardy woody vines include such familiar species as clematis (*Clematis* spp.), honeysuckles (*Lonicera* spp.), and wisteria (*Wisteria* spp.). Most hardy woody vines are deciduous, dropping their leaves each fall but leaving a woody stem from which new leaves, flowers, and fruits grow the following year. Others, including English ivy (*Hedera helix*), are evergreen.

Choosing and Using Vines

You can find a vine for any type of soil—fertile or poor, wet or dry—and any exposure from full sun to deep shade. Just as with trees and shrubs, the best course is to match the plant to your site rather than trying to alter your conditions to suit the plant. Most vines are adaptable plants and accept a wide range of growing conditions. A few vines require special conditions. Clematis, for example, need sun for good flower production but do best with cool roots, so plant them in full sun but shade their roots with a groundcover, low-growing perennials, or an organic mulch.

Climbing vines will soften the look of a raw new fence or quickly screen an unsightly view. A hot, sunny porch becomes much more inviting when a trellised vine adds dappled shade. Vines trained on upright supports can fit in spaces too small for most trees and shrubs. They can be used as a vertical accent in flower or herb gardens or to mark the corners of an outdoor living area. Many vines also do well in containers on a deck or patio, or in a courtyard garden.

Deciduous vines growing on the south and west sides of your house will shade the walls in summer, reducing your home's energy needs. Where banks are steep or grass is difficult to grow, evergreen vines make excellent groundcovers. Some vines, such as grapes and Chinese gooseberry (*Actinidia chinensis*), provide edible fruit for you or for wildlife.

How Vines Climb

Vines either trail along the ground or climb appropriate supports. If you want your vines to climb, you'll need to know how they do it. Then you can choose an appropriate support for the vine you have in mind.

Some vines, such as passionflowers (*Passiflora* spp.) and sweet peas (*Lathyrus* spp.), climb by means of tendrils that grasp any objects they touch. These vines soon blanket a trellis or pergola, with little training from you. Vines that climb with tendrils need supports that are thin enough for their tendrils to grasp. Thick columns, for example, are no good. Some tendrils will coil around supports themselves, while others will loop around supports, then twine around themselves.

Wisteria

A mixture of vines can be quite striking. Shown here is a combination of clematis, grapes, and yellow-leaved hops.

Other vines, such as wisterias, climb by twining their entire stems around supports. Twining vines need no encouragement to wrap themselves around a pole or porch post. These vines wrap themselves around slender supports, like wires, railings, or other vines, as well as around large objects like columns and tree trunks.

English ivy (*Hedera helix*), wintercreeper euonymus (*Euonymus fortunei*), and climbing hydrangea (*Hydrangea anomala* var. *petiolaris*) use adhesive aerial rootlets along their stems to cling to wood, brick, stone, or other materials. Virginia creeper and Boston ivy (*Parthenocissus quinquefolia* and *P. tricuspidata*) bear tendrils that end in adhesive disks, which attach themselves to surfaces.

A few plants, like climbing roses, are often classified as vines even though they have no natural way to attach to a support. To help this type of vine climb, either weave its stems back and forth through a fence, trellis, or arbor, or tie them to the support.

Climbing Supports for Vines

If you want your vines to grow upright, begin training them on supports as soon as you plant them. Use a structure big enough to support the mature plant, and put it in place before you plant the vine.

Buy or build freestanding supports that are constructed of sturdy, durable materials. Wood is a traditional and attractive choice for fan-shaped trellises, lattice panels, graceful arbors, or other supports. For longevity and durability, choose cedar or another naturally rot-resistant wood, or keep the support structure painted. Wire fencing framed with two-by-fours is a low-cost option that will give a vine years of sturdy support. Use galvanized or plastic-coated fencing to prevent rust. Copper or aluminum wire and tubing can also be fashioned into rustproof supports.

Training Vines

Use string to guide young vines to the structure you want them to climb. Fasten one end of the string to the support and tie the other end around a rock or a stick. Place the rock at the base of the plant, or poke the stick into the ground nearby, avoiding the vine's rootball. Use string or soft fabric strips to tie vines to their supports until they begin to twine.

Vine Growers Beware

Because of their vigorous nature, some vines can become a gardener's headache. To avoid common problems such as rampant growth, insufficient support, and structural damage, do some research and pick your plants carefully.

Lawns, Grasses, and Groundcovers

A lush, velvety green lawn can be a great addition to your home, but it can also become an obsession that dominates your summer weekends and empties your pocketbook. Compared to gardeners around the world, Americans are particularly hung up on keeping impeccable lawns. Taking into account the cost of mowers, trimmers, waterers, aerators, dethatchers, spreaders, grass seed and plants, fertilizer, lime, weed killers, pest controls, and labor, Americans spend more money on lawns each year than the gross national product of many countries.

Fortunately, you can have a healthy, attractive lawn without going through lots of money or devoting weekends to tedious work. Understanding the conditions your property has to offer and deciding what you want from your yard will help you plan and maintain an easy-care lawn that you can enjoy.

A key part of planning is selecting the right grasses for your site. Lawn grasses—or turf grasses, as they are technically called—are extremely sensitive to their environment. Your climate, light and shade conditions, and soil type all affect which grasses will thrive there and which will need a great deal of maintenance to survive. Starting a new lawn is like planting a garden—you

Small lawns are usually easy to care for, but tiny spaces with many curves and narrow paths are very difficult to mow.

You don't need to sacrifice all of your free time to have a great-looking lawn. Limit your lawn to areas where you really need grass, then use low-maintenance techniques to make the work easy.

need to prepare the soil well, plant at the right time, and care for the area properly to get the grass off to a healthy start. And you need to maintain it to keep it looking lush.

Planning an Easy-Care Lawn

Here's a handy checklist of things you'll want to consider when planning a lawn.

- Start small. The old adage "Admire large gardens but plant a small one" applies equally well to lawns. Even the smallest lawn takes a certain amount of time to keep it mowed, fed, and reasonably weed-free. If your time or energy is limited, it makes sense to plant lawn grass only on the amount of land you can easily maintain.

- Plant grass where it will grow best. Lawn grasses thrive with lots of sun, ample moisture, and fertile soil. In shady spots and areas with wet, dry, or infertile soil, it will take extra effort to keep the grass looking even halfway decent. Groundcovers and ornamental grasses are great choices for spots that are too shady, dry, or wet for lawn grasses to grow well.

- Keep your lawn on the level. Smooth, level sites make for easiest mowing. Lawns on a gentle slope are fine, but steep grades can make mowing exhausting and hazardous. Sturdy groundcovers like daylilies (*Hemerocallis* spp.) and creeping juniper (*Juniperus horizontalis*) are well suited for holding slopes without much maintenance. Mowing is also difficult around exposed tree roots and in rocky or rough areas; go for groundcovers here, too.

- Plan for pathways. Constant foot traffic can wear out even the most durable grasses, so install gravel or paved paths where you want people to walk. Also make pathways between garden areas wide enough to push a mower through; otherwise, you'll have to lift the mower to get it through without damaging the plants on either side of the path.

- Keep clutter to a minimum. Anything in the middle of the lawn demands more time and effort for careful mowing and additional trimming. If possible, keep swings, benches, birdbaths, and other features around the outside of the lawn area.

- Cluster plants for easy care. Group trees and shrubs into planting beds with groundcovers beneath them. That way, you'll avoid having to mow and trim around individual plants.

- Avoid fancy curves and tight angles. Keep lawn edges straight or gently rounded, avoiding sharp curves and narrow spots that are difficult to trim.
- Plan for easy edge maintenance. Installing edging strips along fences, flower beds, and walkways will eliminate almost all of those boring trimming chores.

Choosing the Right Grass

Out of the thousands of grass species that grow all over the world, only a dozen or so are well suited for lawn use. The best produce narrow, rich green or blue-green leaves, grow in low dense mats, and have deep, sturdy roots that support vigorous growth. If you want to create a beautiful, low-care lawn, you need to spend the time to find out which grass (or grasses) will thrive in your particular climate and site conditions. Check your neighbor's lawns and ask at your local nursery.

Consider Your Climate

Lawn grasses are described as either cool season or warm season, depending on their temperature requirements. The cool-season grasses grow best in the North, in temperatures from 60° to 75°F (15° to 24°C). That's why a lawn of bluegrass (which prefers cool climates) seldom grows well in the heat of a Florida summer. Likewise, if you live in the North, don't expect great success with the zoysia grass you admired on a trip to Atlanta: Zoysia and other warm-season grasses thrive when temperatures are between 80° and 95°F (27° and 36°C).

Think about Your Site Conditions

Most turf grasses thrive in bright, sunny areas with balanced, well-drained but evenly moist soil. If your site can't provide these ideal conditions, rethink your plans to have a lawn in that spot. Grasses that struggle along in too much shade tend to be weak and spindly, and seeds sown in soggy spots are likely to rot before they even sprout.

If you really want to have a lawn in less-than-ideal conditions, you'll have to tailor your grass choices to match the available sunlight, soil, and moisture. Here are some of the most common challenges to lawn growing, along with suggestions of the most appropriate cool- and warm-season grasses.

Drought-Prone Areas In hot-summer areas, try bermuda grass or buffalo grass. Cool-season tall fescue and wheat grass are better in more temperate zones.

Shady Sites No grass thrives in deep shade, but a few types grow well in spots that get only a few hours of direct light or a full day of bright but filtered light. If you really

A plastic or metal edging strip isn't very noticeable, and it will reduce the amount of trimming you need to do.

Cool-Season Grasses

Annual ryegrass
Bent grass
Bluegrass
Perennial ryegrass
Red Fescue
Tall Fescue

Warm-Season Grasses

Bahia grass
Blue grammagrass
Bermuda grass
Buffalo grass
Centipede grass
St. Augustine grass
Zoysia grass

want to grow a lawn under trees, try Chewings fescue or 'Pennlawn' red fescue in Northern areas. Tall fescue will take some shade in cool Southern gardens; St. Augustine grass grows well throughout the South.

Very Acid or Alkaline Soil If your soil has a pH that's very high (alkaline) or low (acid), you'll get the best results if you choose a lawn grass that is adapted to that condition. Cool-season Canada bluegrass, Chewings fescue, and hard fescue can adapt well to acid soil. In alkaline areas, try cool-season perennial ryegrass or wheat grass or warm-season bermuda grass.

Salty Soil Salt, carried by coastal winds or runoff from melting snow on roads and sidewalks can damage or kill tender lawn grasses. No lawn grass is completely salt-proof, but cool-season fescues and warm-season St. Augustine grass are quite tolerant.

High-Traffic Areas If you need a grass that can stand up to heavy use, consider cool-season perennial ryegrass or tall fescue or warm-season bahia grass, bermuda grass, or zoysia grass.

Starting a New Lawn

A newly graded and tilled lawn, like a freshly dug flower bed, is filled with potential. You are free to create a space that is environmentally sound, beautiful, and easy to maintain.

Seed, Sod, or Sprigs?

You have three main options for starting a new lawn: sowing seed, laying sod, or planting plugs or sprigs. The one you'll choose depends on how much you're willing to spend and how fast you want to get the lawn started.

Seed-Grown Lawns Seed is the least expensive way to establish a lawn, making it the method of choice for many homeowners. Seed is also the only way to start many of the desirable new turf grass cultivars. On the down side, it can take several months before a new seed-grown lawn is ready for regular use, giving weeds a chance to spring up. Seeds are also prone to being eaten by birds or washed away by rain, especially on sloping sites.

Starting with Sod Sod is basically just strips of turf that have been cut from one area to be installed in another, creating an instant lawn. A landscaper or turf farm operator will deliver precisely the amount of lawn you need, ready to lay out on your yard like carpet.

A sod lawn is more expensive than seeds, and you may not be able to get precisely the grasses you want. However, sod does have its advantages. In addition to having a lawn you can use quickly, it eliminates the work of seeding and enduring several weeks of the dust and mud that bare earth can produce. You can install sod at times of the year that seed won't germinate.

Plugs and Sprigs If you're starting a lawn of zoysia grass, bermuda grass, centipede grass, or St. Augustine grass and can't face the expense of sod, plugs or sprigs are a good choice for you.

Plugs are like small strips or cubes of sod, usually grown in trays of 12 or 24 plugs. The number of plugs you'll need for a given area depends on the size of the plugs, the size of the area, and how fast you want the grass to fill in.

Sprigs are individual grass plants or runners that have been dug from the soil and pulled apart. They are usually sold in pieces by the bushel, which amounts to 1 square yard (1 sq m) of sod. Most lawns need 4 or 5 bushels per 1,000 square feet (93 sq m).

When to Plant

The best time to plant a new lawn depends on which type of grass you are growing and how you plan to start it. If people are likely to walk on your newly-planted lawn, fence it off temporarily with string or rope.

When to Sow Seed Plant seed of warm-season grasses in late spring or early summer. The best temperatures for germination are between 70° and 90°F (21° and 33°C). If you sow seed after midsummer, the warm-season grasses may struggle to survive the winter.

From late August to mid-September, when the temperature is between 60° and 85°F (15° and 30°C), is the best time to seed a new lawn with cool-season turf grasses. The seeds sprout and grow much better during cooler weather, when weed growth slows and fall rains keep the seedlings moist. In Northern climates, early- to mid-spring planting can also be successful if you keep the seedlings watered until they are well established. However, spring plantings are more prone to weeds, and summer heat can damage the roots of tender plants, leading to sparse growth.

Plan on four weeks from the time you plant until the grass looks like a lawn, and at least three months of growth before you can use it heavily.

When to Lay Sod or Plant Sprigs or Plugs You can install sod, sprigs, and plugs pretty much any time they are available, as long as you keep them well watered for several weeks after planting. The best time, however, is when the grass is actively growing.

FAR LEFT: By choosing the right grass for your growing conditions you will lessen the work of maintaining your lawn.

LEFT: If you want an instant effect and can afford the extra expense, consider starting your new lawn with sod.

Early summer is ideal for warm-season grasses, spring or fall for cool-season types. Never try to install sod, plugs, or sprigs when the ground is frozen.

Preparing the Site

No matter how you plan to plant your lawn, good soil preparation is the key to getting it off to a healthy start.

Check the Soil Depth First, dig down to determine the depth of the topsoil in the lawn area, especially if you have a new home site. If the darker topsoil layer measures less than 4 inches (10 cm) deep over the lighter subsoil, spread enough new soil to reach that depth.

Take a Soil Test The best insurance you can get for a healthy lawn is taking a soil test before you plant. Once you know the pH and nutrient content of your soil, you'll know what—if any—fertilizers and amendments you need to add. You can buy a simple home test kit at your local garden center, or have your soil tested by a lab. Lab tests (done by a private lab or your state Cooperative Extension Service) are usually more accurate and provide detailed reports of the results.

Follow the instructions on the package for collecting a sample. If you're getting your soil tested at a lab, be sure to ask for recommendations for organic fertilizers and amendments. Allow at least six weeks to get your results. A soil test means you can prevent soil problems instead of having to fix them.

Add Needed Amendments Unless your soil is high in nutrients and organic matter, you'll probably need to amend the soil to provide good growing conditions for the new lawn. To add organic matter, spread a 1-inch (2.5 cm) layer of organic material (aged manure or compost) over the area. Also add a natural fertilizer, such as a 4-3-3 blend of nitrogen, phosphorus, and potassium, following the directions on the package. Till in the material to a depth of about 6 inches (15 cm).

If a soil test showed that the pH is below 6.5, add enough garden lime (not hydrated lime or quicklime) to raise the pH to that level. Ten pounds of garden lime per 100 square feet (4.5 kg per 9.3 sq m) raises the pH of most soils about one point. Scatter the lime over the soil, or use a spreader for more even coverage. Till the lime into the soil. (If possible, allow a bit of time— about a week, or ideally one heavy rain—between fertilizer and lime applications to minimize any reaction between them.)

Smooth the Soil Before planting, level the tilled earth to eliminate bumps and depressions. You can smooth out a small lawn with a metal garden rake, but a commercial grading rake that you rent is much easier and more effective for large areas. Be sure that the lawn slopes away from buildings so hard rains or melting snows won't drain into your basement. Also have it slope downward slightly toward a road or driveway, so water won't accumulate on the grass.

After getting the slope you want, rake the area to smooth it and to remove any rocks and weed roots. Soak the ground thoroughly if it doesn't rain, and let it settle for three or four days or more before planting. When the soil has settled, resmooth it, if necessary, before planting.

Planting Grass Seed On a day that's not breezy, you can fling grass seed off the tips of your fingers and get fairly even coverage in a small area. In most cases, though, you'll get better results with either a two-wheeled, drop-type seeder or a rotary broadcast seeder that throws out the seeds over a wide area. Both are often available for rent at hardware or garden-supply stores. The drop type is better for precise seeding, especially if you are

Once you know the basics of good lawn care— including proper mowing, watering, and aerating—you can create and maintain a beautiful, healthy lawn without relying on synthetic chemicals.

working near gardens or other areas where you don't want seed to fall. Overlap the strips slightly to ensure good coverage. The wheel tracks left by the spreader will mark where you have been already.

Rake the seeds lightly into the topsoil, about ¼ inch (6 mm) deep, so that most of them are no longer visible on the surface. They must have good contact with the soil for germination, so it is helpful—but not essential—to firm the surface and eliminate air pockets by going over the site once with a light lawn roller.

If it doesn't rain, water the soil daily to keep it moist (but not wet) until the seeds have sprouted and started growing.

Scattering fertilizer by hand is probably the best option for small areas, but it can give spotty results if you don't spread the material evenly.

Different grass species germinate at different speeds—from less than a week to as long as 30 days—so if you're planting a mixture, keep in mind that they won't all sprout at once.

Establishing Sod Install the sod as soon as it arrives, if at all possible; otherwise keep it damp and shaded until you're ready for it. Ask your supplier for instructions on handling and laying the sod strips. After installation, press the sod into the soil by tamping with the back of a rake or by rolling with a light roller; then water it thoroughly.

Planting Plugs and Sprigs Plant plugs or sprigs 6 to 12 inches (15 to 30 cm) apart in each direction in thoroughly tilled soil. (The exact spacing will vary on the type of grass you're growing; ask your supplier for the recommended spacing for the kind you purchase.) An easy method to keep the spacing right is to mark straight, shallow furrows across the lawn about 12 inches (30 cm) apart, then set the sprigs or plugs in these furrows from 6 to 8 inches (15 to 20 cm) apart. Roll the surface lightly, and water it well.

After Planting Whether you have seeded the lawn, installed sod, or planted plugs or sprigs, never let it dry out until the grass is well rooted (generally after three to four weeks). If the weather is mild and not windy, a good rule of thumb is to water every two or three days for three weeks. In hot, dry weather, your new lawn may need water several times a day to keep the soil moist and allow good growth.

Don't walk on the lawn any more than necessary until the grasses are growing vigorously, and hold off on mowing until they are at least 3 to 4 inches (15 to 20 cm) tall. Set the mower about 3 inches (7.5 cm) high for the first few mowings; then reduce it to the optimum height for the grass you are growing. (This can vary between 1 and 4 inches [1.5 and 10 cm] depending on the site.)

Renovating an Existing Lawn
Lawns often begin to look worn out as the years go by, either from neglect or because they weren't given a good start at planting time. If your lawn needs help, you must decide whether to install a completely new lawn or simply give your existing lawn a facelift. You should strongly consider starting over if:
- The ground under the lawn is so rough and bumpy that it is hard to mow.
- It has large bare spots or worn compacted areas.
- More than 50 percent of the surface of the lawn is covered with weeds.

In such cases, the best prescription is to remove the existing turf and weeds and replant with easy-care grasses that thrive in your climate. Strip off the existing grass with a spade or a rented sod-cutting machine; pile the removed turf in an out-of-the-way spot to decompose. Then follow the instructions above for starting a new lawn.

If at least half of the area is grass, if the surface is fairly level, and if the weeds aren't overpowering, improving the lawn is an easier and better alternative. The area will be less disturbed, so you'll have less dust and mud, and you can continue to use most of the lawn as you recondition the threadbare areas. Patching up a lawn is also cheaper than starting from scratch.

Begin with Spot Treatments Renovating a ragged lawn will take a little time, but it can be worth the effort. Mending the worn and torn spots is the first step in lawn renovation. If foot traffic has worn paths in the grass, build gravel, stone, brick, or paved paths where you want people to walk; if necessary, plant shrubs or install low fences to discourage shortcuts. Sometimes snowplows or traffic disturb the perimeter of the lawn; repair the edges with a shovel and some new topsoil. If vigorous grasses have crept over the sidewalk or into the garden or street, some judicious edging may be necessary.

If you enjoy growing flowers and dislike lawn care, consider turning some of the lawn into flower beds.

In late summer or early fall, fill in any cavities and depressions in the lawn with sifted topsoil and level off the humps. Loosen trampled, compacted areas by digging or tilling. Till or spade up any bare spots and areas of the lawn where weeds dominate (dig out the weeds by hand as thoroughly as possible first). Firm the soil with a roller, sprinkle organic lawn fertilizer over the area (following the application directions on the bag), and rake it in lightly.

Now it's time to sow the seed. You'll find grass seed mixtures formulated especially to fill in bare spots; try to find a mix that will match the rest of your turf grass. Scatter the seed over the area and rake it into the soil, leaving it smooth.

To spruce up areas where the grass is thin, use a technique called overseeding: Rake the area thoroughly to loosen the soil surface, scatter seed over the existing grass, and rake again lightly. Spread a thin layer of sifted topsoil over the seed.

Keep newly seeded lawn areas watered until the grass is established. After a few weeks, if any spots of new grass aren't growing well, sprinkle a liquid fertilizer such as liquid seaweed or fish emulsion over them. The grasses on newly seeded plots are fragile for most of their first season, so avoid walking on them any more than necessary.

TOP: Most grasses are surprisingly problem-free. Animals such as mice and rabbits are probably the most serious pests.
BOTTOM: Upright arching grasses such as variegated Japanese silver (*Miscanthus sinensis*) are ideal for flower borders.

Set the mower at 3 inches (7.5 cm) for the first two or three mowings; the taller grass will be more vigorous and shade out weed seeds. After that, move the blade to the optimum height setting for the kind of grass you are mowing.

Revitalize the Whole Lawn Once you've spot-treated problem areas, let them grow for a few months until they match the rest of the lawn. The following spring is the time to give the whole lawn a thorough reconditioning.

The soil in old or worn-out lawns is often compacted and will benefit from aeration. Use an aerator over all but the newly planted areas to encourage grasses to thrive and compete better with weeds.

Worn-out lawns are likely to lack humus, too, so spread a thin layer of aged manure or compost over the entire surface. Add a nutrient boost by applying a complete organic fertilizer at the rate prescribed on the bag. If a soil test shows that the pH is too low (acidic) or too high (alkaline), wait until a rain has washed in the fertilizer, then apply lime to raise the pH or sulfur to lower it. (Your soil test results will tell you how much of either material to apply.) The little extra care and attention you spend on renovating your lawn will pay off, and the result will be lush, green, and attractive.

Landscaping with Ornamental Grasses

Ornamental grasses is a loosely defined term that describes any grasslike plants that are attractive enough for planting in a landscape. This group includes the bamboos, rushes, and sedges; they grow in a diverse array of sizes, textures, and colors. Whether you need drifts of plants in a dry, sunny border, a groundcover for a shady nook, a rock garden specimen, or a container plant for a roof garden, you'll find a suitable ornamental grass for the spot. These adaptable, easy-care plants serve all kinds of landscape functions, from screening unpleasant views to providing four-season interest in the flower garden.

Pampas grass

Consider the Spread

Some people are wary of planting ornamental grasses, fearful that—like quack grass—they will overtake the property. "Give them an inch, and they'll take a yard," wary homeowners think. But that reputation is deserved only by a few particularly fast-spreading species, such as blue lyme grass (*Elymus arenarius* 'Glaucus'). Clump-forming grasses are less likely to be invasive than those that expand by rhizomes or stolons. Some, however—including pampas grass (*Cortaderia selloana*), fountain grasses (*Pennisetum* spp.) and, to a lesser extent, northern sea oats (*Chasmanthium latifolium*)— can spread by reseeding.

Before you choose a grass, always check whether it is a clump-former or a runner, and whether it tends to reseed. Since some plants are rank spreaders in certain climates but well behaved in others, find out how the grass has performed for other gardeners in your area, if you're concerned about a plant's potential invasiveness. Keep fast-creeping grasses confined by paved paths, metal or plastic edging strips, or other solid barriers.

Divided grass

Grasses for Challenging Sites

Ornamental grasses are great replacements for more traditional shrubs and groundcovers on difficult sites. Drought-tolerant types stop erosion on steep, dry slopes. Short species line pathways nicely, serve as neat edgings in front of gardens or shrubs, or act as substitutes for lawn grasses. Many do well in wet places; some even grow in water. Salt-tolerant species—such as switch grass (*Panicum virgatum*) and dune grass (*Elymus arenarius*)—thrive at the seashore or on a roadside, where salt spray or salt-laden runoff from winter roads would destroy turf grass or evergreen shrubs.

Grasses as Screens and Hedges

Tall ornamental grasses—those that grow 4 feet (1.2 m) or more—can provide a welcome change of texture and color from more rigid shrubs and trees. In large yards, big grasses like pampas grass (*Cortaderia selloana*) and eulalia grasses (*Miscanthus* spp.) provide spectacular backgrounds for shorter grasses, shrubs, and flowering plants.

Tall-growing grasses also make excellent quick screens to provide privacy, eliminate unpleasant views, and cut down on street noise. Such screens can divide a larger area into separate "rooms" and also protect more delicate plants from being buffeted by wind storms.

Most grasses become fully established for screening purposes within two to three years—far more quickly than a standard hedge. This makes them ideal for new gardens where you need fast-growing plants to get an almost immediate effect. Grasses can also fill space while slower-maturing shrubs are getting started. And, unlike hedges, oranamental grasses need no maintenance. Once they're planted they need little but an annual cutting back.

Begonia

Made for the Shade

Many leafy and flowering groundcovers adapt well to life in less-than-ideal light. If you have a spot that gets plenty of filtered light but no direct sun, try some of the species listed below. Low-growing ferns are also naturals for shady sites.

Aegopodium podagraria 'Variegata' (variegated bishop's weed)
Ajuga reptans (ajuga)
Asarum europaeum (European ginger)
Astilbe chinensis var. *pumila* (Chinese astilbe)
Euonymus fortunei (wintercreeper)
Galium odoratum (sweet woodruff)
Hedera helix (English ivy)
Hosta hybrids (hostas)
Lamium maculatum (spotted lamium)
Liriope spicata (creeping lilyturf)
Pachysandra procumbens (Allegheny pachysandra)
Pachysandra terminalis (Japanese pachysandra)
Saxifraga stolonifera (strawberry geranium)
Tiarella cordifolia (Allegheny foamflower)
Tolmeia menziesii (piggyback plant)
Vancouveria hexandra (American barrenwort)
Vinca minor (common periwinkle)
Waldsteinia fragarioides (barren strawberry)

Common periwrinkle

ABOVE: If you enjoy fragrant flowers, consider the sweet violet as a groundcover for a cool, moist, shady spot.
BELOW: Common periwinkle is a fast-spreading groundcover that will cope very well in the shade. Its lavender-blue flowers appear in early spring.

Landscaping with Groundcovers

The term "groundcover" is most often used to describe low, spreading plants—usually those that grow less than 2 feet (60 cm) tall. That still includes a wide range of plants, from spreading grasses and sedges to creeping perennials and suckering shrubs. You'll find no end to the ways you can use these versatile plants in your yard. They'll help you reduce your lawn space or even replace a lawn to save money, work, and energy. In a dry, sunny climate, drought-tolerant species such as succulents are indispensable for creating a water-saving landscape; in damp areas, water-loving plants are just as handy to absorb water. Some groundcovers attractively blanket steep banks to stop erosion and cover rough or rocky areas that are difficult to mow. Shade-lovers border woodland paths or cover low-light areas beneath tees and between buildings. Flat, creeping types fill in the gaps between paving stones and tumble attractively between the crevices in garden walls and steps. Even with the most common groundcovers you can create pleasant, appealing plantings to beautify a garden setting or deal with a difficult site.

Choosing Groundcovers for Garden Challenges

Well-chosen groundcovers are among the most versatile and easy-care garden plants you can grow. Unlike lawn grasses, groundcovers don't need much regular maintenance: Just plant them, weed or mulch a few times for the first year or two, water them, and then let the plants do the work.

Groundcovers for Shady Sites Shady plantings are natural choices for woodlands and forests, but they are, of course, not limited to those spots. Sunlight is also scarce on the north side of buildings, between buildings, beneath lawn trees, and behind tall hedges, fences, or garden walls. It is difficult to grow many flowering plants and evergreens in these spots, but shade-loving groundcovers are ideal there. Many of them will spread quickly and provide lush cover throughout the year. Japanese pachysandra (*Pachysandra terminalis*) and common periwinkle (*Vinca minor*) tolerate shade especially well, as do ferns and many less common foliage plants, and even some wildflowers.

Super Groundcovers for Slopes

Fast-spreading groundcovers are excellent choices for slopes that are too steep or rocky to mow. Set plants out a little closer than normal for quick cover, and mulch between them to protect the soil until they fill in.

Achillea tomentosa (woolly yarrow)
Ajuga reptans (ajuga)
Coronilla varia (crown vetch)
Cotoneaster horizontalis (rockspray cotoneaster)
Euonymus fortunei (wintercreeper)
Hedera helix (English ivy)
Hemerocallis fulva (tawny daylily)
Hypericum calycinum (St.-John's-wort)
Juniperus horizontalis (creeping juniper)
Pachysandra terminalis (Japanese pachysandra)
Parthenocissus quinquefolia (Virginia creeper) *Potentilla fruticosa* (shrubby cinquefoil)
Rosa rugosa (rugosa rose)
Stephanandra incisa (lace shrub)
Vinca minor (common periwinkle)

Groundcovers to Cope with Slopes Sloping sites are another common landscaping challenge. Grassy slopes can be downright difficult, and even dangerous, to mow. Or perhaps you have an ugly, rocky slope where even grass won't grow. Besides being maintenance headaches, slopes are also prime targets for soil erosion. The runoff from heavy rains can easily carry topsoil down a bare slope, depositing the dirt on paths and paving at the bottom. That makes more work for you, as you have to clean up the debris after each rain.

If your property has a troublesome slope, groundcovers are a good solution.

English ivy is a dependable, easy-to-grow groundcover that is ideal for protecting the soil on shaded slopes.

To stabilize the soil, you need species that transplant easily and spread quickly. Drought tolerance is a plus, especially on hot, sunny sites; slopes tend to be dry, since water runs off instead of soaking in. Fortunately, there are some beautiful flowering plants—such as moss pinks (*Phlox subulata*), two-row sedum (*Sedum spurium*), and showy sundrops (*Oenothera speciosa*)—that are well adapted to life on dry, rocky slopes.

Lily-of-the-valley

Groundcovers for Moist Soils Wet spots can be a real landscaping hassle. They may be just moist enough that you can't get the mower in to trim until midsummer; or they're so wet that grass won't grow there at all. Instead of struggling with the site, just plant species that like "wet feet." Certain ferns, Japanese primroses (*Primula japonica*), and creeping Jenny (*Lysimachia nummularia*) are a few of the groundcovers that thrive in soggy soil. Lily-of-the-valley likes moist soil too. Combine them with moisture-loving perennials and shrubs such as turtleheads (*Chelone* spp.), blue flag (*Iris versicolor*), winterberry holly (*Ilex verticillata*), and summersweet for interesting effects.

The Indoor Garden

Most common houseplants are truly easy to grow if you understand their basic needs for light, water, and fertilizer. Even the blackest thumb can grow a drought-tolerant jade plant or ponytail palm. But why settle for the most common, easiest plants when there's a wonderful world of colorful flowers, sparkling variegated leaves, dramatic cacti, and exotic orchids waiting for you to explore? Whatever time and skills you have and whatever the conditions in your home, there are dozens of beautiful houseplants you can grow!

Houseplants can be so much more than just a spot of greenery on a windowsill. Use them to fill your home with sweet scents, such as those of orange blossoms and jasmine. Brighten up the dull days of winter with the brilliant flowers of amaryllis and long-lasting orchids. Grow lush tropical plants to decorate the living room, and raise tasty herbs for the kitchen. Create a gift for a friend or a special feature for your own houseplant collection by planting a terrarium or training a fragrant rosemary plant on a circular topiary frame. With a little imagination, you'll find many wonderful ways to brighten your life with houseplants.

Buying the Best Plants

If you're out shopping, and you see a houseplant you like, and the price is right, you're probably going to bring it home. It may not be the best way to get the

Agaue cactus

perfect plant to match the conditions in your home, but most of the time it works out just fine.

If, on the other hand, you want a plant that will thrive in a particular location, you need to be more careful to choose just the right one. A little advance planning is especially helpful if you intend to buy a large (and therefore more expensive) plant.

Flowering houseplants generally need high light levels, so make sure you have a bright spot for them.

Estimate the Light

Your first step in buying the right plant is to consider how much light is available in the location you've chosen. Unless you're planning to place the plant directly in front of a large south, east, or west window, you should avoid buying houseplants that need bright light or direct sun. Instead, stick with those that need only medium light. Flowering plants will require more light than plants grown just for their attractive foliage, so if you've bought indoor plants for their flowers, it's especially important to be sure the plant gets enough light. If you have to place a plant well away from the windows, try to select a plant that can tolerate low light levels.

Do a Little Research

Once you've estimated the light levels available in the location you've chosen, make a list of plants suitable for your chosen location. Now that you know what you're looking for, you can shop around a little. Prices can vary a lot, especially for large plants, so it's worth investigating several sources; check out the garden centers, florists, and grocery stores in your area. Talk to the employees and find someone who can help you make a good plant selection.

When you've decided exactly which kind of plant you're going to buy and where you're going to buy it, look over all the plants of that type that the seller offers. Some plants will have a nicer overall shape than others; look for those that you find most appealing. Once you decide which plant you want, inspect it closely for any signs of insect or disease problems before you take it home.

Consider Flowering Habits

If you're buying a flowering plant for your home, there are some extra factors to consider. First of all, be aware that many flowering houseplants are grown under special controlled conditions in commercial greenhouses and are not likely to rebloom for you next year unless you have a greenhouse or can give them special care. Some, such as Persian violet (*Exacum affine*), are actually annuals that won't live more than a year or so, even with the best care.

Even though they can be relatively short-lived, flowering plants are still a good choice for brightening up indoor spaces. Live flowering plants will last at least two to three times longer than cut flowers, and some—including florist's cyclamen (*Cyclamen persicum*), orchids, and African violets—will bloom nonstop

LEFT: The stunning flowers of florist's cyclamen certainly brighten dull winter days, but it can be tricky to get plants to bloom again next year. RIGHT: The blooms of potted spring bulbs and primroses will last longest if you keep them in a cool spot. Placing the pots in groups will help to keep the humidity level adequate.

Place Plants Properly

Matching your plants to the best available windows is important, but placing each plant so it's right up near the glass is probably even more important than having the right window. The intensity of light drops off very rapidly as it enters the room, so a plant even a few feet from the window will get only half as much light as it would if it is right next to the window.

If your windowsills are too narrow to hold plants, consider adding a shelf to make the sill wider, or place a table in front of the window so you can set plants on it. Keep the windows clean and remove any sheer curtains that might cut down the light intensity.

Move Plants to Manage Light Levels

There may be times when you want to put a plant in a spot that you know doesn't provide enough light for it. For example, say you buy a spectacular flowering azalea and you really want to keep it on the dining room table where everyone can enjoy it. You can usually get away with this for a week or so; then move the plant back into brighter light in a window. Most plants won't suffer much from such a procedure. Obviously, the lower the plant's light needs, the longer it can tolerate a dim location.

Another way to keep plants thriving in low light locations is to rotate two plants between the dark location and a bright window every few weeks or so. That way you get to enjoy a plant right where you want it all the time, and the two plants will get enough light to thrive. This is how shopping malls and offices keep their

for many months. So go ahead and bring flowering plants home to enjoy; just don't feel like it's your fault if they don't bloom again next year. When choosing a flowering houseplant, always try to pick one that has lots of buds, with just a few already open. That way you'll get the maximum bloom time as the unopened flower buds bloom over the next weeks.

Cyclamen

Find the Right Spot

South-facing windows let in the most light, and most houseplants will flourish there. Although east and west exposures don't provide as many hours of bright light as south windows, many bright-light lovers (and all plants that need medium light) will grow well in most east- or west-facing windows. Save north-facing windows for low-light plants, especially foliage plants.

There are several things besides direction that affect the amount of light coming in a window. A very large east-facing window might actually be brighter than a small, south-facing one. Shade from trees may make a west-facing window more like a northern one.

Fortunately, most houseplants are adaptable. Your plants should do fine, as long as you do your best to match the right plant to the right window.

If you feel more comfortable with a little more precision, you can buy an inexpensive light meter, which will measure the actual amount of light at any given spot. These meters usually measure light in units known as "foot-candles" and come with a chart that tells you how many foot-candles various plants require.

To give all of your plants ample light, you may want to rotate them so each has a chance to be near the window.

Flower production takes lots of energy, so blooming plants generally need all the light they can get.

plants looking so good: The plants are moved back to a greenhouse periodically to recuperate, then they go back to the mall.

By the way, placing a plant close to an incandescent light bulb doesn't help much, but there are other types of lights that work very well for growing houseplants if your window space is limited.

Is Your Plant Getting the Right Light?

If your plant isn't getting the right light, it may show symptoms that tell you it needs a new location. Sometimes, you may notice that plants growing in bright windows develop a yellowy tinge or white or brown patches on the leaves that get the most sun. This may be a signal that the plant is getting too much light. This doesn't happen often with houseplants, but it could be a problem if you put a low-light plant like a Chinese evergreen (*Aglaeonema* spp.) directly in a south-facing window. If these symptoms occur, move the plant farther away from the window a bit or move it to a less-bright window.

Geranium

The opposite problem—plants not getting enough light—is far more common. A plant trying to grow where there's not enough light will gradually become leggy and spindly, and its lower leaves may turn yellow and drop. Or the plant may just sit, not putting out any new growth at all. If you notice a plant is not growing, or if there's new growth but it looks weak and spindly, try moving the plant to a brighter location.

Some plants, such as weeping fig (*Ficus benjamina*), may drop a lot of their leaves when you first bring them home. This is because they were probably grown outside in very bright light. When you move them to the much dimmer interior of your home, they simply don't need as many leaves because there isn't as much light, so they drop them. Don't be alarmed by this. Keep the plant in the brightest location you have, water it moderately, and wait for it to adjust to its new surroundings. It should stop dropping leaves after a few weeks.

If a plant continues to drop leaves or to grow very poorly, move it to a brighter location. Too often when houseplants grow poorly, people give them more water or fertilizer thinking that will solve the problem. Some plants do drop leaves when their soil gets too dry, but if the real cause is low light levels, extra water or fertilizer is the last thing that will help.

Watering Wisely

Next to getting the light levels right, watering is probably the most important aspect of houseplant care. You can't just water this plant once a week and that one twice a week; there are too many different factors that will affect how much water a plant needs. If you understand what those factors are and how they increase or decrease your plants' water requirements, then you'll know what to expect and be better able to give each plant the right amount of water for healthy growth.

The major factors that will affect how much water a certain plant needs include:

• The plant's particular moisture preference. Some plants need dry conditions (as succulents and cacti do) and some need constantly moist soil (as many ferns prefer). Most houseplants fall in the middle and need a steady supply of moisture with the soil surface drying out between waterings.

• The container the plant is growing in. Plants in clay pots will dry out faster than those in plastic pots. Large plants growing in small pots will also need water more frequently. (That's one of the reasons plants either need to be divided or repotted into larger pots as they grow.)

• The soil the plant is growing in. Soil containing ample compost or peat moss will absorb and hold more moisture than mixes containing lots of sand.

• The amount of light the plant gets. Plants growing in bright light will need more water than those placed in dimmer areas.

• The weather conditions. Plants will use much more water during bright, warm, summer periods when they are actively growing than in the winter, when temperatures are cooler and the daylight hours are much shorter. They also need very little water during sustained periods of cloudy weather.

Considering all these varying factors that affect how fast the soil dries, it's easy to see why it's so important to check each plant's soil before you water.

When to Water

Your first clue about when to water should be the soil surface, which usually turns a lighter color when it's dry. If it's dark colored and damp, do not water.

If the surface is dry, you can use your finger to check the soil an inch or two below the surface. If you still feel moisture, wait a day or two and test again. When that top layer feels dry, it's generally the right time to water.

Another way to check soil moisture is to lift the pot. You can tell immediately if the plant feels really light and thus needs water or if it feels relatively heavy, in which case you should wait a few more days before you water. This technique works especially well for small- to medium-sized plants in light plastic pots.

Some pots are just too big to lift, and the soil near the surface may dry out while there's still plenty of moisture deeper in the soil. Always check for moisture several inches deep in large pots; if you go only by whether the soil surface is dry, you could easily overwater. When in doubt, always underwater rather than risk giving too much water and thereby destroying the roots.

How to Water

Once you're sure a plant needs watering, you should water it thoroughly so that a little water runs out into the saucer under it. When you apply more water than the soil can absorb, the excess flows out the bottom into the saucer. This flow of water through the soil, similar to what happens in the garden when it rains, serves an important function in container plants. As the water runs down through the soil, it pushes out used air and allows fresh air to move into the spaces between soil particles. (Plant roots need both water and air to thrive. That's why it's so important to have a loose, well-drained potting soil and to make sure you always water thoroughly.)

By the way, always use pots with drainage holes, and always put saucers under them. Without drainage holes, it's

Clay pots tend to dry out quickly, so pay special attention to watering plants in them.

Standard fuchsia

too easy to overwater and make the soil soggy. (The excess water trapped in a pot without drainage holes could cause the roots to rot and the plant to die.) And if you don't have a saucer under the plant, you'll be tempted to underwater to avoid water running out the bottom and making a mess.

Occasionally when you water, you may notice that the water seems to be running rapidly through the soil and out the bottom without being absorbed by the soil. When this happens, you've let the soil get too dry. When potting soil dries out, it shrinks away from the sides of the pot, leaving space where water can just run right through. To water a dried-out pot, you need to set the entire pot in a bowl or sink full of water up to the pot's rim and let the soil slowly absorb the water. After the soil is thoroughly rewetted, let the pot drain, then return it to its saucer.

Watering for Vacations

If you'll be away for more than a few days, there are several techniques you can use to get extra water to your plants. If you're only going to miss one of your usual watering days, you can water the plants thoroughly and add some extra water to

the saucers. (While you shouldn't make a habit of leaving water standing in the saucers, it's okay to do it occasionally as a way to give plants some extra water while you're gone.)

If you're going to be gone for more than just a few days, you can set your plants up to be wick-watered. To do this, use a strip of nylon pantyhose, a rolled-up paper towel, or some other absorbent material for the wick. Insert one end of the wick into the bottom of the pot, making sure it makes good contact with the potting mix, then run the other end into a container of water. Recycled margarine tubs with lids work well for small plants; just cut a hole in the lid, fill the tub with water, run the wick down through the hole, and set the plant on top of the reservoir. Capillary action will draw water up along the wick and into the pot.

Humidity and Temperature

Although humidity levels and temperature levels are not as critical for good growth as light intensity or proper watering, they can have a marked effect on the health and vigor of your plants.

Handling Humidity

Almost all houseplants will grow better if you can give them higher humidity levels than those found in the average home. Indoor air is usually much drier than outdoor air, especially during the winter when heating systems drive away moisture. Summer air-conditioning also creates dry indoor air.

In general, plants with thin, delicate leaves tend to be more sensitive to low humidity, while plants like Chinese evergreen, with their thick, waxy leaves, can tolerate typical home humidity levels. There are some plants on the market, such as bird's nest fern (*Platycerium bifurcatum*), that look great at the store (because they just came from a greenhouse) but usually grow poorly in most homes unless you provide extra humidity. Always check the label and avoid buying a plant that needs extra humidity, unless you like it so much that you are willing to give it extra care.

You can buy an inexpensive humidity gauge (at hardware stores) to monitor the water vapor in the air. Most plants thrive in humidity levels very similar to what humans like—around 40 to 60 percent humidity. It's more likely, however, that the humidity in your house is below this.

A wick-watering setup is a handy way to water plants while you're away.

In winter, in fact, the humidity level may be as low as only 10 or 20 percent (which is as dry as a desert!).

Symptoms of low humidity include brown leaf tips and edges and leaf curling. Here are some ways to increase humidity levels.

Grouping Plants One way to increase humidity is to cluster your houseplants. This happens naturally when you place plants in groups near windows. As the leaves release water vapor, the extra moisture creates a more humid microclimate for the plants. Using clay pots instead of plastic also helps a little because water vapor evaporates from the sides of the clay pots.

Misting Some people like to mist their plants directly to increase humidity, and this does help a little. However, as soon as the mist evaporates, the humidity level will drop. Misting plants so heavily that water stands on the leaves is not good, either, since that can lead to disease problems. If you decide to mist, do it during daytime hours and do it lightly.

Pebble Trays A better choice than misting is to grow your houseplants on

Signs of Overwatering and Underwatering

Overwatering is just as bad for your plants as underwatering—maybe even worse. When plants are too dry, their leaves will droop, so at least you have a clue that they need to be watered (although it's best to water just before leaves start to droop). When plants are kept too wet, you may see the same symptom—drooping leaves—but it will be because the roots are rotted and the plant can no longer get the food and water it needs from the soil. If this happens, your plant may or may not recover; your only hope is to reduce watering, and cross your fingers.

Clustering several plants together will help to raise the humidity level around the leaves.

trays containing pebbles and water. You can use any kind of saucers or shallow trays to hold the water—plastic cafeteria-type trays work well; even baking sheets are fine. Set the plants on a 1- to 2-inch (2.5- to 5-cm) layer of pebbles or gravel. Add enough water to bring the water level just below the top of the pebbles. (You don't want the bottom of the pots to be sitting in water.)

Moisture will evaporate steadily from the trays and rise to increase humidity around the plants' leaves. This is a very effective way to raise the humidity levels in a certain area, and humidity-loving plants like ferns will definitely benefit if you grow them over these water-filled trays.

Humidifiers If you happen to have a room humidifier or an automatic humidifier installed in your heating or air-conditioning system, you'll be able to raise the humidity in the whole growing area.

Combine spring bulbs with other early-blooming plants that need the same temperatures to grow.

Providing the Right Temperature

Most common houseplants prefer typical home temperatures of around 65°F (18°C) during the day and 55° to 60°F (12° to 15°C) at night. However, some do need cooler temperatures during part of the year. Certain flowering plants, such as azaleas and camellias (*Camellia japonica*), won't bloom well unless you can give them a period of cooler temperatures.

Fertilizing for Healthy Growth

If you want your houseplants to thrive, you have to give them food as well as water. The best organic fertilizers for houseplants are the same ones that work well outside—things like bloodmeal, bonemeal, and fish and seaweed products. You can also use household "wastes" such as wood ashes and coffee grounds. But the first item on your fertilizer list should always be compost, the organic gardener's secret for success.

Compost is especially good for container plants because it releases nutrients slowly over a long period of time, just the way plants growing in the wild receive their nutrients. Compost will never burn roots or cause major salt buildup like synthetic chemical fertilizers. Plus, compost doesn't just feed your plants—it prevents disease and improves the structure of the soil, so air and water reach the roots better. Ample compost also helps the soil retain moisture, so you won't have to water as often. If that's not enough, compost contains the major plant nutrients—nitrogen, phosphorus, and potassium—plus minor nutrients and trace elements, which are not provided by chemical fertilizers.

If you aren't already making your own compost, consider starting. It's easy, and there's just nothing better for making plants grow well. And if you can't make your own compost, check with your local government—many communities are now composting yard wastes and offer the compost free to anyone who wants it.

A Simple Program for Feeding Houseplants

Use compost whenever you pot up a new plant or repot old ones, adding up to one part compost for every three or four parts potting soil.

Each spring thereafter, take your plants to a sink or bathtub and water them heavily with warm water until water runs steadily out the bottom for a few minutes. This leaches out any harmful salts, which can build up over time. It's a good idea to do this once a year, but you should also do it any time you notice a crusty deposit in the saucers or around the pot rims. Rinse the leaves thoroughly, too, to remove dust.

After you've completed the spring leaching treatment, add a ½- to 1-inch (12- to 25-mm) layer of fresh compost to all of the pots. (If there's not room in the pot, just wash away some of the soil with a hose.) Mix a small amount of a balanced organic fertilizer into the compost before you apply it to the pots. That should feed most plants well into midsummer. (Check the fertilizer packages for guidelines on how much to apply.)

Most houseplants will be getting much more light during the summer than in the winter, so a couple of months after the spring compost/fertilizer treatment, begin feeding them about once a month with a half-strength liquid fish fertilizer. The fish fertilizer contains plenty of nitrogen, the nutrient most likely to be in short supply. Keep feeding the plants until growth slows in fall. Always remember that too much fertilizer can be just as bad as too little. Go easy when you fertilize plants in dim locations, and don't fertilize at all during the short days of winter unless you have a plant that continues to grow actively then.

Hibiscus

Potting and Repotting

Your houseplants will eventually need to be repotted, either because they grow too big for their pots or because they need to be moved into fresh potting mix.

Generally, you should repot your plants about once every year or two in the spring or summer, when plants are actively growing. If they get too big for their pot, they can become "root-bound," which means they have grown so many roots that there's not enough soil left to support further growth. Most (but not all) plants shouldn't be allowed to become root-bound. You can check to see how crowded the roots are becoming by lifting the plant and tapping the pot until it slips loose. Lift out the plant to examine the root ball. If you see lots of soil with some roots, all is well. But if you see mostly roots and little soil, it's time to repot.

How to Repot a Houseplant

You have a choice when you repot—you can move the plant to a larger pot size, or you can keep the plant in the same pot. If you want the plant to grow bigger and don't mind going to a larger container, choose a new pot that's only 1 to 2 inches (2.5 to 5 cm) in diameter larger for small- to medium-sized plants or 4 to 6 inches (10 to 15 cm) larger for bigger plants. (If you move a small plant into a very big

Repotting a Houseplant

Choose a new container that is slightly larger than the old one. Add a layer of potting mix.

Carefully turn the plant over onto one hand, and use the other hand to pull off the old pot.

Settle the plant at the same level in the new pot, and fill in around the sides with mix.

pot, you run a risk that the excess soil around the plant's roots will stay too wet and cause the roots to rot.)

When you're moving a plant to a larger pot, add some potting mix to the bottom—enough so that the soil level will be an inch or so below the pot rim when you set in the plant to allow room for watering. Then remove the plant from the pot it's growing in. Holding the base of the pot in one hand, lift the plant slightly and tap around the rim with your other hand to loosen the pot. Carefully lift the plant out and set it on the soil in the new pot. Then add potting mix around the edges, using a trowel or stick to gently settle the soil around the root ball.

If you'd prefer to keep the same pot, remove the plant and shake away as much of the old soil from the roots as you can. If the plant's root ball is so dense and tangled that the soil won't shake loose, use a large knife to slice away an inch or two of the root ball on all sides and the bottom. Add fresh soil to the bottom of the pot, then set the root-trimmed plant back in and add fresh soil in the space you created around the sides. This root pruning allows you to keep the plant to a manageable size. If the plant itself can be pruned, trim it back a bit to bring the top into better balance with the reduced roots.

If you're repotting a very large plant, you may want to ask someone to help you. Removing the plant will be easier if you lay the container on its side, then carefully pull out the plant.

Potting Soils

You can use any commercial potting soil for most houseplants, but your plants will grow much better if you add some compost and slow-release organic fertilizers before you plant. There are a few plants that prefer special soil mixes. Cacti and succulents, for instance, appreciate extra sand for drainage, while African violets (*Saintpaulia* spp.) thrive with extra peat moss for acidity and moisture retention. Orchids generally prefer a very loose, bark-based mix.

Grooming and Pruning

It's natural for houseplants to lose some of their older leaves as they grow. Shrubby plants such as weeping fig (*Ficus benjamina*) may also shed leaves when they're moved to a new location, sometimes leaving a tangle of bare twigs in the center of the plant. If you spend a few minutes now and then trimming off these yellowing leaves or dead twigs, your plants will look much better.

Many houseplants don't require pruning beyond this regular grooming. If all of the leaves grow out from a single center or crown of the plant and there are no stems or branches (as on African violets [*Saintpaulia* hybrids] and florist's cyclamen [*Cyclamen persicum*]), then you can't (and don't need to) prune the plant. Trailing or vining plants (such as wandering Jew [*Zebrina pendula*] and passionflowers [*Passiflora* spp.]), on the other hand, benefit from pruning. Pinch or snip off unwanted leaves and stems with your fingers or scissors; use pruning shears or loppers to remove woodier stems cleanly.

There are three basic reasons to prune your houseplants, as follows.

Pruning for Shape Regular trimming improves a plant's appearance by eliminating any long, awkward stems or branches that grow out of proportion to the rest of the plant. Don't hesitate about this—cutting back gangly branches will help, not harm, the plant.

Pruning to Promote New Growth Pruning is also very helpful to trailing plants, such as Swedish ivy (*Plectranthus australis*). Cutting back the growing tips causes the plant to put out more shoots and become bushier. Always make your pruning cuts right above a side branch or leaf node (the spot where a leaf joins the stem). In many cases, the plant will produce two new stems from the cut point, leading to bushier growth.

Pruning for Size Control The third way in which pruning is helpful is in keeping plants a manageable size. If a bushy plant, such as a hibiscus or a citrus tree, has become larger than you want it to be, you can prune it back really hard, cutting off as much as a third of the leaves and stems. In this way, you keep the top in balance with the roots without having to move the plant to a larger pot.

Inside Out and Outside In

Just like people, many houseplants appreciate a vacation. Moving your plants outdoors for the summer is a great way to keep them healthy and happy. When you bring them back in for the winter, you can also dig and pot up rosemary, geraniums, and other flowers and herbs for indoor enjoyment. To help your plants through these transitions between house and garden, try the tips here.

Moving Indoor Plants Outside

Many indoor plants benefit from spending a summer outside. Flowering plants, which require bright light, will especially appreciate some time outdoors. If your plants have aphids, scales, or other pests, moving them outdoors can give beneficial insects a chance to attack the unwanted insects, solving your pest problems. If you have a large number of plants growing indoors, you may want to move the bright-light-lovers outside for the summer and shift some medium-light plants to the brighter spots vacated by the light-lovers.

Before you move plants outside, wait until the weather is warm and settled. Also, you must introduce indoor plants to outside sunlight gradually. If you don't, their leaves can show brown or white scorched spots—the plant equivalent of sunburn.

To give your houseplants time to adjust, always place them in full shade when you first move them outside. After a few weeks in the shade, you can move the kinds that enjoy brighter light out from the shade to partial or full-sun locations.

Plants growing in the brighter, airier conditions of the great outdoors will grow much faster than they do indoors, so they'll need more water and fertilizer than normal. In the heat of summer they may need daily watering.

Bringing Outdoor Plants Indoors

Many plants typically grown outside can also be enjoyed inside. "Tender perennials" will keep on growing if you protect them from freezing temperatures by moving them indoors for the winter months.

Kumquat tree

Miniature roses bloom on new wood, so they need regular trimming of the old growth to promote new flowers.

Geraniums are dependable favorites for outdoor containers, but they also make great indoor plants.

Geraniums (*Pelargonium* spp.) are a perfect example. You can enjoy their colorful flowers or pleasant scents in the garden all summer, then bring them indoors in fall and keep them in a bright window. Other great plants for indoor growing include rosemary (*Rosmarinus officinalis*), wax begonias (*Begonia semperflorens-cultorum* hybrids), and coleus (*Coleus* x *hybridus*), just to name a few. You can even bring hot pepper plants inside to hold them over for the next year.

To move plants indoors, you can dig them up and set them in a pot. Usually you'll want to trim them back pretty hard to bring the top growth into balance with the now much smaller root ball. After they're potted up and trimmed, keep them well watered, and let them stay outside for a few weeks in part shade. This transition period will help them recover from the shock of being transplanted, so they can grow back nice and bushy. Be sure to bring any cold-tender plants inside as soon as frost is predicted.

If you'd rather have smaller plants (which fit better on windowsills), you can take root cuttings from many garden plants in summer or early fall. Cut off 3- or 4-inch (7.5- to 10-cm) long shoot tips, and remove all but two or three of the top leaves. Insert the bottom 2 to 3 inches (5 to 7.5 cm) of each cutting into a small pot of moist sand, vermiculite, or potting soil, and cover the cuttings with a clear plastic bag to keep the humidity high. Place them in a warm, medium-bright location until they root and begin growing, then remove the plastic and move them to your brightest south windows for the winter. You can move the plants back out to the garden in spring, after all danger of frost has passed.

When you bring any outdoor plants inside, there's always a chance you may bring in some pest problems as well. Once those pests are inside, they can spread to your other plants quickly, since there are no natural enemies in the house to keep them in balance.

To minimize the chance of problems, inspect your plants carefully before you bring them in. Certain garden plants are very susceptible to aphids when grown indoors. Hot peppers are a good example. If you find that aphids keep coming back even when you have sprayed the plant several times, it may be best just to enjoy that particular plant outdoors each summer and not try to keep it indoors.

Or, if it's a plant you really love, you can order specific beneficial insects from mail-order suppliers and release them on the plants to munch on the aphids or other troublemakers.

The Productive Garden

*Home-grown fruit, vegetables, and herbs are not only
more delicious and nutritious than store-bought, but there's a sense
of satisfaction unlike any other in picking your own produce.
You've planted it, watered it, nurtured it, and now you can eat it.*

The Herb Garden

There are so many wonderful herbs that it can be hard to decide which ones to grow. Some herbs, like oregano and peppermint, are used in cooking or for tea; others, like lavender and sage, are ideal for potpourris and other fragrant crafts. Some herbs, like bee balm, thyme, and yarrow, are attractive in their own right as ornamentals, even if you never plan to harvest them for any purpose. Many herbs fall into more than one of these categories.

How you plan to use your herbs will affect how you'll grow them and how much attention they'll need from you. If you're just growing herbs to use fresh in cooking, you don't need much space for an herb garden, since one or two plants of each kind you like should be enough. You'll be most likely to use your culinary herbs if you plant them close to the house. If you're only growing one or two types, try growing them in large pots on the deck or patio. You'll need more space to grow quantities of herbs if you plan to harvest them for drying and crafting.

Grown in the right conditions, herbs such as chives will reward you with flowers as well as edible leaves.

Growing Your Herbs

Most herbs prefer full sun, although some (like sweet woodruff, chervil, lemon balm, and many mints) will grow in partial shade. Many herbs tolerate rocky, thin soils, but they will be more productive in average, well-drained soil. You may choose to plant your herbs in a separate garden, but they also look great mixed into flower beds and vegetable gardens.

You can grow many herbs—including such favorites as dill, sage, marjoram, and basil—from seed sown directly in the garden. Other herbs are easier to grow from transplants than seeds; these include rosemary, lavender, peppermint, and tarragon, among others.

When planning your herb garden, don't forget to take into consideration your climate, topography, and soil conditions. Ask your neighbors what grows well in their garden—and what doesn't!

Herb Garden Style

Regardless of the size, shape, or location of your garden, its style is a reflection of your own tastes. At one extreme are the formal herb gardens with their angular knots and pruned hedges, and at the other are random groupings of whatever suits the season. The number of possible herb-garden styles is limited only by your imagination and creativity. You can plan one or more theme gardens to concentrate on a particular aspect.

As you choose herb plants, consider how they are going to look when grouped together.

Garden Shape

The simplest gardens to set out and manage are square or rectangular. If you must take advantage of every square inch of space, it makes sense that you will follow the general outline of your property, and land is most often sold in boxlike shapes. Laying out your herb garden with square or rectangular beds may be not only the most practical way, but can give the garden a formal look that appeals to many gardeners.

Of course, squares and rectangles aren't the only shapes. You may choose to lay your garden beds following the curve of a hill, stream, fence, or stone wall, or design

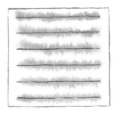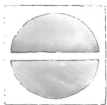

These diagrams show four practical approaches to designing an herb garden. Avoid circles and curves if space is limited.

them to accent the shape of a building. If you want to be especially creative, garden within unusual boundaries like circles or ovals. You can make a garden in the shape of a spiral with one continuous bed beginning in the center and spiraling out in circles. A book or magazine on garden landscaping will offer you examples to follow in shaping your garden beds.

If you choose to garden in several small patches, position plants that need daily attention or frequent picking close to the house. If space is limited, take advantage of borders along paths and fences. At the least, you can dress your windows outdoors with boxes of luscious herbs close at hand.

Garden Design

Whatever design you choose, try it out on paper first. If you're planting in beds, keep them under 5 feet (1.5 m) wide, not more than twice the distance you are able to reach from the side. You'll want to avoid walking on beds as you work. Make garden paths 4 to 5 feet (1.2 to 1.5 m) wide. Once you've located your paths, beds, or rows, begin selecting and

Working with the natural landscape, simple terracing is used to create a level herb garden on a slope.

arranging your plants. Prepare a list of the plants you want to grow, along with their growth habits, size at maturity, and special soil, space, or environmental requirements. Remember that single plants tend to become lost in the crowd; it's more effective to plant in clumps. It's generally best to plant the tallest herbs at the back, the shortest in the front.

Keep the following in mind when you plan the design of your herb garden:

• Use your site's limitations to your advantage. If you're confined to gardening in the shade, use the opportunity to grow as many shade-loving herbs as possible. Include angelica, chervil, lemon balm, and sweet cicely. In wet areas, select from the wide assortment of plants in the mint family. You'll find herbs to fill just about every niche in your garden.

• Divide a large garden, or create several small gardens, by grouping herbs that serve particular purposes. Medicinal, dye, fragrance, and culinary gardens are some examples.

• Select herbs that flower at the same time or share the same color. Lavender and blue themes especially are easy to create with herbs. Or focus on foliage, and plant blue-green or silvery herbs mixed with darker greens for contrast.

• It's a good idea to group the perennials together since they tend to have similar requirements and this will help you avoid mistakes. If you're planning to grow invasive perennials like mint among other herbs, plant them in buried containers like clay drainage pipes or bottomless large pots that are at least 1 foot (25 cm) deep.

Ideally, the well-organized garden will include culinary herbs which are positioned as close as possible to the kitchen.

Helpful Hints for Easy Herbs

Before you decide which herbs you want to grow, check out their maintenance considerations below.

Basil: For best leaf production, pick off flower heads as they form (every few days). May also need extra water.

Chives: Easy to grow, but can reseed prolifically if you don't clip off spent flowers.

Dill: Let a few plants self-sow the first year, and you'll probably never need to replant. Pull seedlings from where they're not wanted or remove flowers, if you don't want seedlings.

Mints: Most tend to spread rapidly unless contained. Plant in bottomless pots sunk in the soil to 1 inch (2.5 cm) below the rim. Or grow as container plants.

Parsley: Seeds are slow to germinate and seedlings can get swamped by weeds. Often easiest to start from transplants.

Rosemary: In cold climates, treat as an annual and buy new plants each year.

Sage: Start from transplants; easy to grow.

Thyme: Won't compete well with weeds, so keep weeded until plants get established.

Chives are popular for their mild onion-flavored leaves and flowers. Remove spent blooms.

Cool-Climate Herbs The following herbs are adapted to cool climates, with winter temperatures commonly dropping below 10°F (−5°C). Nearly all these herbs can be grown readily in moderate climates, but in subtropical and tropical climates many of them will not thrive: angelica, anise, anise hyssop, arnica, barberry, bearberry, bee balm, betony, birch, borage, burdock, caraway, catmint, chamomile (Roman), chervil, chicory, chives, clary, comfrey, costmary, dandelion, dill, dock, elecampane, garlic, goldenrod, hop, horseradish, horsetail, hyssop, lady's bedstraw, lemon balm, lovage, marsh mallow, mugwort, mustard, nasturtium, nettle, New Jersey tea, plantain, red clover, roses, saffron, sassafras, savory (winter), soapwort, sorrel, sweet cicely, sweet woodruff, tansy, tarragon (French), valerian, vervain, wormwood, yarrow.

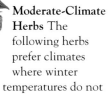

Borage

Moderate-Climate Herbs The following herbs prefer climates where winter temperatures do not fall below 10°F (−5°C) and summers are warm and dry with cool nights: agrimony, basil, bay (sweet), calendula, *casacara sagrada*, coriander, eucalyptus, fennel, fenugreek, feverfew, geranium (scented), germander, horehound, lavender (English), lemon verbena, madder, marjoram, mint, oregano, orris, parsley (curled), passionflower, pennyroyal, rosemary, rue, safflower, sage, santolina, southernwood, thyme (garden), violet, witch hazel.

Warm-Climate Herbs The following herbs grow best in tropical or subtropical climates,

THE HERB GARDEN 145

The key to having a beautiful and productive herb garden is using herbs that are adapted to your climate.

but some can be grown in cold climates in summer or as houseplants: aloe, cayenne pepper, coffee, ginger, lemongrass, and Madagascar periwinkle.

Shade-Tolerant Herbs The following herbs will tolerate shade (although dill, fennel, rosemary, and scented geraniums really prefer full sun): agrimony, angelica, bay, bergamot, betony, catmint, chamomile, chervil, comfrey, coriander, costmary, feverfew, germander, ginger, horsetail, hyssop, lemon balm, lovage, Madagascar periwinkle, mint, parsley, pennyroyal, pipsissewa, plantain, sweet cicely, sweet woodruff, tansy, tarragon, thyme, valerian, violet, wormwood.

Harvesting

One of the first rules to learn about growing herbs is to harvest them early in the morning. The best picking time is just after the morning dew has dried, but before the sun has had a chance to warm them. The reason is that essential oils, those mysterious components that give herbs their flavor and fragrance, are most

intense early in the morning, and lose their quality when exposed to heat.

There's nothing wrong with morning dew, but wet leaves require a longer drying period before you can store them. For the same reason, refrain from harvesting on rainy days. A cool, dry, sunny morning is best. You need not be so fussy if you plan to use fresh herbs immediately. You may pick and use these whenever you need them.

Your herbs will produce more foliage if you pinch off the flower heads as they develop. But if you're growing the herb for seed (like dill or caraway), leave the flower head and harvest the seed after it turns brown.

The intended use of your herbs, maturity of the plant, and climate all influence the time of harvesting. Cold-climate gardeners will have fewer chances to harvest; they're happy to get their herbs up and growing before the frosts return. Gardeners in warmer climates have the advantage of a longer growing season, and the chance to harvest more often.

A small herb garden can provide plenty of material for cooking, crafts, or drying.

Perennials Avoid heavy harvests of perennial herbs during the first year of growth to allow them to establish themselves in their new surroundings and to encourage root growth.

You may want to trim them lightly to promote bushiness.

Once they're established, you can harvest up to two-thirds of the foliage of a hardy perennial at one time in the spring and again in summer. In colder climates, take only a third of the growth in the fall and stop cutting 40 to 60 days before you expect the first frost. During winter, perennials will subsist mainly on foods they've stored in their roots. Plenty of foliage and lots of autumn sun will let perennials manufacture and store adequate food for winter and the following spring's new growth. If food reserves are low, they're less likely to make it through a stressful winter. In warmer climates, plants will suffer little winter stress and the plants' dormant period may be relatively short. In these areas gardeners can harvest lightly right into the late fall.

Lavender

Annuals and Biennials Since annuals are limited to one season of growth, your only concern in cold climates is harvesting as much as you can before the killing autumn frosts. The same is true if you are growing biennial herbs, like parsley, for their foliage. During the growing season, harvest annuals and biennials for foliage so that at least 4 to 5 inches (10 to 12.5 cm) of growth remains. A good general rule is to harvest no more than the top half of the plant at one cutting. Most annuals and biennials may be harvested several times each season.

Before the first frosts, you can cut annual plants to the ground, or pull them for drying. If you are growing biennial plants, like caraway, for their seeds, avoid harvesting the foliage the first year. The more energy the plants can make and store, the more seeds they can set the following year.

Parsley

Coriander

How to Harvest Use sharp scissors or a garden knife when harvesting your herbs. If you're collecting leaves, cut the whole stem before stripping away the foliage. With small-leaved perennials, like rosemary and thyme, save only the leaves and discard the stems—or use them for potpourris. When harvesting herbs that spread from a central growing point, like parsley and sorrel, harvest the outer stems or leaves first. If you're collecting leaves or flowers from bushy plants, do so from the top of the plant; new growth will come from below.

Of course, you can harvest foliage and flowers from both perennials and annuals continuously if you're just snipping a few leaves and blooms here and there to collect the ingredients for a recipe.

Herbs retain their best qualities if they're left unwashed until it's time to use them. Some growers advise sprinkling the plants the day before harvesting to wash away the dust. If your plants are surrounded by a mulch that limits their contact with soil, you may not have to wash them. If they are gritty with soil, however, you can swish them through cold water and pat them dry, or hang them in shade to drip.

If you plan to dry your herbs, bunching them as you collect them saves handling

When harvesting herbs during the growing season, pick from the outside to retain their attractive shape.

time later. Collect enough stems to make a 1 inch (2.5 cm) thick bundle, then wrap a rubber band over the cut ends. When harvesting annuals in autumn, simply pull and hang the whole plant, after first cutting away the roots and soil.

Drying Herbs
Some growers claim that dried, summer-grown herbs have better flavor than herbs grown indoors in winter. If you enjoy cooking with herbs, you may want to try preserving some of the summer garden's bounty for use in winter recipes. Most herbs dry easily, and under the proper conditions they will retain their characteristic aroma and flavor.

Hanging herbs to dry in mixed bunches makes a very attractive kitchen decoration.

Where to Dry Herbs The best place for drying herbs is somewhere dry and dark, with good ventilation. Depending on what the weather is like, you may find it necessary to speed the process with fans, dehumidifiers, or an air conditioner. The best weather conditions for air drying are low humidity and soft breezes.

Dried herbs store best in cool, dark places. If you like the look of the bunches, it's fine to hang some around your home for decoration. But store the herbs you plan to use for cooking in airtight jars.

Drying screens and bunches can be placed in a dry attic, around the hot-water heater, on top of the refrigerator, or in a gas oven with a pilot light. Barns make excellent drying sheds as long as they are shady and well ventilated. In summer some gardeners dry their herbs on small screens placed inside the car. Cover the herbs with paper toweling and park the car in light shade.

If the weather hasn't cooperated and the drying process seems painfully slow, you can speed the action in your oven. Just place your herbs on baking sheets and set the oven temperature at its lowest setting. Monitor progress until leaves are crispy dry.

Drying in Bunches Long-stemmed herbs like lavender, mint, and yarrow are easy to dry in bunches. Select only the highest-quality foliage and blossoms, removing

Bunches of herbs hanging from a beam add a touch of summer to the kitchen.

any dead or wilted leaves. Make bunches about 1 in (2.5 cm) in diameter for quick drying; the number of stems in each bunch will naturally vary. You can tie the bunches with string, leaving a loop for hanging, but small rubber bands are easier to use.

For very simple storage, hang your herb bunches from clothes hangers. First, wrap each bunch with a rubber band. Then take one loop under the bottom of the hanger. Bring it over the wire and the top of the stems to secure the bunch.

Wire Clothes Hangers Hold the bunched stems along one side of the horizontal wire of the hanger, then pull a loop of the rubber band down and then up over the wire. Pull the band over the stems and release it. Hanging one full hanger in one spot is easier than hanging separate bunches all over the place. Each herb species or cultivar gets its own hanger, making organization easy. You can label each bunch or each hanger. When you're ready to use the herbs, simply pull the bunch down to release it.

Hang your herbs where you have plenty of space, and where you can leave them undisturbed until they're dry. If your house has exposed ceiling rafters, arrange wooden dowels along them and hang the herbs from the dowels. Single bunches may be hung from conveniently placed hooks or nails. When the bunches are crispy dry, remove the leaves from the stems. Dried herbs will gather dust if left too long.

Dry long-stemmed herbs in paper bags. Punch a hole in the bottom of the bag, secure the stems, and hang to dry. Cut flaps in the bag to increase air circulation.
To dry seeds, place seed heads inside a paper bag, stems up. After two weeks, the seeds will collect at the bottom of the bag.

Brown Bag Method If dust is a problem, place the bunches inside paper bags, lantern style. Punch a hole in the base of the bag, pull the stems through this hole, and fasten them with string or a rubber band. Cut flaps in the side of the bag and hang in a cool, dry place. After one week, look inside a few bags to make sure the herbs are drying and free of mold. They may take up to two weeks to become crisp and crumbly. (Seeds can be dried by placing seed heads, with stems up, in an unpunched paper bag.) When the herbs are dry, remove the stems and spread the leaves on a baking sheet. Place in an oven, set at about 100°F (40°C), for several minutes to complete the drying.

Drying on Screens Herbs with short stems and small leaves, like thyme, are difficult to bunch. The best drying method is simply to snip off the foliage with scissors and spread it on a screen in a single layer. You can dry large-leaved herbs on screens, but first strip the foliage from the stems. Hold the stems upside down in one hand while running the other hand down the stem. Loose herb blossoms and flower petals can also be dried on screens. Stir the herbs once a day on the screens for even drying.

You can construct your own screens with scrap lumber and window screening, then set them on bricks or wooden blocks so that air circulates freely. If the herbs are small and fine, spread a paper towel or sheet of paper on the screen first. Your herbs should be dry in seven to ten days.

Drying in the Oven Oven-drying is the best method, since the herbs dry quickly and retain their aromatic oils. In a conventional oven, spread herbs one layer deep on paper toweling set on baking sheets, and set the temperature at 80° to 100°F (25 to 38°C). If you smell the herbs immediately, lower the temperature to avoid losing essential oils. Stir once every half hour. Drying should be complete in three to six hours. Herbs with fleshy leaves will take longer than those with tiny or thin leaves, so it is wise not to mix different leaf types in one batch. Remove the herbs when they are crispy dry, and before they turn brown.

Food dehydrators are good for drying herbs, too. Follow the same instructions as for regular oven-drying.

You can also dry herbs in a microwave oven. Sandwich the herbs between sheets of microwave-safe paper towels. Put a cup of water in the microwave while drying the herbs. Leave the herbs in the oven for about one minute on a low setting. Remove them and check for dryness. If they're still moist, repeat the process for a few seconds. Watch the herbs carefully during drying, and stop the process if any sparks appear.

Drying Herb Seeds Many of the herbs you'll grow are used for their seeds. If you're collecting coriander, dill, caraway, or other herb seeds for the kitchen, snip off the seed heads when they've turned brown. You'll have to blanch them in order to destroy the seemingly invisible insect pests that can hide inside. Gather the seeds in muslin and dip them in boiling water, or place the seeds in a sieve and pour boiling water over them. Spread them on paper or a fine-mesh screen to dry in the sun.

If you plan to sow the seeds you've saved, skip the blanching. Dry them in the sun for several days before transferring them to a cool, dry location.

Preserving and Storing Herbs

When your herbs have dried thoroughly, strip the leaves from their stems or remove them from the drying screens. Discard stems or save them to add to potpourris. If you're saving herbs for culinary use, crush them, or push them through a coarse strainer. Leaves and blossoms saved for tea can be left whole. Crumble dried roots to sizes that will fit their use.

Store dried herb foliage, blossoms, roots, or seeds in airtight containers away from bright light. Tins or canning jars with rubber seals work best. Or pack the dried materials into resealable plastic bags, squeezing out the air before you seal them. Label your containers, since all dried herbs tend to look the same.

It's fine to dry your herbs on top of the refrigerator, but don't store them there. Ideally, dried herbs should be kept cool and dry. If you like the look of herb bunches and arrangements hanging about the kitchen, make them especially decorative with added ribbons or lace and decorative jars, and use them as ornaments, but keep culinary herbs in airtight containers.

If your herbs were grown, harvested, dried, and stored properly, they will remain green and fragrant for a long time. If you're in doubt, just crush a few leaves

Braided garlic bulbs are a good way to store them, and they look decorative in the kitchen.

and sniff—scentless, brown herbs will have little flavor. Toss them in your compost pile.

Freezing Herbs If you have more freezer space than cupboard space, you may want to freeze your herbs instead of drying them. Chervil, dill, fennel, marjoram, mint, parsley, and tarragon freeze very well. Herb growers report mixed results with coriander and chives—it seems they freeze very well or very poorly! You'll have to experiment, and keep records of what works best for you.

Harvest the herbs at their peak and wash them gently but thoroughly, then pat dry. You can chop the herbs by hand, of course, but the simplest method is to chop them in the food processor until the pieces are the right size to add to soups or other recipes. Pack them in freezer bags, squeezing out the air until you have a flat layer of herbs, and seal. Be sure to label the bags, since most frozen herbs look alike in the middle of winter. When you're ready to use them, simply break off a corner, or as much as you need, and return the bag to the freezer.

Some herb savers purée fresh herbs with water or oil. They pour the purée into ice-cube trays and, when the cubes are solid, move them to labeled freezer

bags. Herb cubes are easy to use—just toss them into soups or stews. Basil retains the best quality when frozen in an olive oil purée. It's easy to prepare winter pesto—mix in the cheese, pine nuts, and garlic as the basil thaws.

Salting Herbs Salting is an old method of culinary herb preservation, and it works especially well with basil, chives, garlic, marjoram, oregano, rosemary, savory, tarragon, and thyme. Cooking with herb salt will add flavor to your meals and encourage you to reduce actual salt use. Harvest the herbs at their peak and wash and dry thoroughly. Then pack alternate layers of fresh leaves and salt in a glass jar. Make the first and last layers of salt thicker than the middle layers, which should be quite thin and just cover the herbs. Store the tightly sealed jar on a cool, dry shelf in the kitchen. Pick out the salted herbs for use in stews and sauces. Use the remaining flavored salt for salad dressings, roast meat, or wherever the flavor of herbs is needed.

Herb Salt for the Table

1 cup (8 oz/250 g) non-iodized sea salt or kosher salt, 1 cup (1½ oz/45 g) packed fresh herbs, washed, dried, and minced, or 2 tablespoons dried herbs.

Grind the salt and herbs together in a blender, or finely crumble the herbs by hand and mix them into the salt. Place the mixture in a shaker, and use it to add flavor to your meals. You can make different mixtures to accompany vegetables or meat.

Medicinal Herbs

Compared with the precision of modern diagnosis and prescription medicine, herbal remedies can seem out of place and rather old-fashioned. Wild and homegrown herbal preparations were once the only medications used, but they've been largely replaced by synthetic drugs today.

Modern physicians argue that synthetic medicines are superior since they are free of impurities, are of known strength and

The equipment in this herbal apothecary is beautiful as well as functional. But all you really need to prepare simple herbal remedies is a few basic materials, including measuring spoons and clean containers.

effects, and are more stable. Herbal practitioners claim that when used properly, herbal remedies have an important role even today. In many countries, herbal remedies remain the only readily available treatment. And, of course, many of today's medicines are derived from naturally occurring plants.

Quick Guide to Medicinal Herbs

Use the following as a quick reference to some of the more common and beneficial medicinal herbs and their soothing and healing properties.

Aloe Apply the fresh transparent gel from the leaves externally to scalds and sunburn, blisters, scrapes, and acne to promote healing and prevent infection.

Arnica Make a tincture from the flower heads and apply as a compress to soothe sore muscles and sprains. Do not take this herb internally.

Barberry Prepare a decoction from the roots and take 1 cup (8 fl oz/250 ml) daily before a meal for its laxative properties.

Calendula Make a compress from the flowers and apply to stings, bruises, scrapes, and burns.

Catmint Make an infusion from the flowers and leaves and drink 1 cup (8 fl oz/250 ml) for a calming effect.

Chamomile Make an infusion from the flowers and drink 1 cup (8 fl oz/250 ml) two to three times daily to relieve cramps and upset stomachs, and to aid digestion.

Comfrey Make a compress or poultice from the leaves and apply to bruises and sprains. Or make an ointment to treat burns and abrasions.

Dandelion Make an infusion from the leaves or a decoction from the roots. Drink 1 cup (8 fl oz/250 ml) up to three times daily as a diuretic and laxative.

Eucalyptus Make an infusion from the leaves and inhale the vapors as a decongestant and to relieve other cold and flu symptoms.

Fennel Make an infusion from the seeds or leaves and drink 1 cup (8 fl oz/250 ml) up to three times daily to soothe an upset stomach and to relieve flatulence.

Garlic Use raw cloves to prepare antibiotic and antiseptic infusions, syrups, and plasters. (If you ingest raw garlic, chew a sprig of parsley afterward to freshen breath.)

Hops Make an infusion from the fresh "cones" and drink 1 cup (8 fl oz/250 ml) up to three times daily to calm nerves and settle an upset stomach.

Horehound Make an infusion from the leaves and drink 1 cup (8 fl oz/250 ml) up to three times daily as an expectorant. Make a syrup from the leaves and take ½ to 1 teaspoon up to three times daily for coughs, colds, sore throats, and bronchitis.

Hyssop Make an infusion from the leaves and drink up to 2 cups (16 fl oz/500 ml) per day as a cold and flu remedy. Add honey to disguise hyssop's bitter taste.

Marsh Mallow Make a decoction from the roots and drink 1 cup (8 fl oz/250 ml) up to three times daily to soothe sore throats.

Parsley Make an infusion from the leaves or seeds and drink 1 cup (8 fl oz/250 ml) two to three times daily as a diuretic.

Passionflower Make an infusion from the leaves and drink 1 cup (8 fl oz/250 ml) up to three times daily to relieve nervous tension, and aid digestion.

Peppermint Make an infusion from the leaves and drink 1 cup (8 fl oz/250 ml) up to three times daily as a decongestant, or for an upset stomach.

Rose Make an infusion from the hips and drink 1 cup (8 fl oz/250 ml) up to three times daily to treat cold and flu symptoms.

Rosemary Make an infusion from the leaves and flowers and drink up to 3 cups (24 fl oz/750 ml) daily as an antiseptic, or for stomach upsets.

Sage Make an infusion from the leaves and drink as needed, up to 3 cups (24 fl oz/750 ml) daily, for cold symptoms and stomach upsets, and to aid digestion.

Thyme Make an infusion from the leaves and stems and drink up to 3 cups (24 fl oz/750 ml) daily for colds and flu.

Valerian Make an infusion from the roots and drink about ½ cup (4 fl oz/125 ml) once or twice daily to calm the nerves and relieve insomnia, headaches, and menstrual discomfort.

Witch Hazel Make a decoction from the leaves or the bark and use it as a compress for aching joints, sore muscles, cuts, bruises, and insect bites.

Yarrow Make an infusion from the flowers and leaves and drink 1 cup (8 fl oz/250 ml) up to three times daily for indigestion and menstrual cramps.

Herbal Remedy Precautions

Use all herbal remedies cautiously, avoiding large doses of any herb. Stop using herbal treatments if you notice any side effects, no matter how minor, such as headaches, dizziness, or an upset stomach.

The Vegetable Garden

Anyone who has eaten really fresh produce knows that a garden that produces food is worth the effort. The trick is to be realistic about what and how much you can grow. You may require only a small vegetable garden near the kitchen that will meet your day-to-day demands for organically grown vegetables. Or you may decide to dedicate a substantial area of your yard to vegetable growing so that you'll have enough produce to freeze or store for later consumption.

The best strategy is to start small. Choose a few of the vegetables that you like best, and plant a limited quantity of each. (Maybe only one each of large plants like zucchini or cucumbers, two or three each of tomatoes and peppers, and six to eight plants each of smaller crops like lettuce and beans.) In following years, adjust the amounts based on how much you used this year.

To a large extent, your climate will determine which vegetables you can grow well. Various aspects of climate, such as average high and low temperatures, frost-free periods, and rainfall, can influence your choice of crops. Special areas in your garden may offer slightly different conditions than the open garden, for instance, warm, sheltered nooks can give heat-loving crops an extra boost, and lightly shaded spots can prolong the season for heat-intolerant crops. An awareness of these different microclimates will help you choose the best sites for the crops you want to grow.

Topography, exposure, and soil are other factors to consider when planning your garden, Hilltops, slopes, and valleys all have their unique advantages and disadvantages for gardening. The amount of sunlight a site receives will determine which vegetables you can grow there, so you'll need to keep that in mind as you choose a site for your garden. The quality of the soil is another critical factor to consider for successful garden planning. Healthy soil will yield healthy plants.

Once you've considered all of these factors, you'll want to put your new knowledge to work in planning your best vegetable garden ever. After you know where you want to put your garden, you need to decide how big to make it, depending on the time you have to care for it and the amount of produce you plan to use. Other factors to keep in mind are the style of gardening you plan to use (such as rows or raised beds), the specific crops you want to grow, and how much of each crop you're going to plant.

As you start planning your vegetable garden, you'll begin to appreciate the value of maintaining a good system of garden records. You'll want to keep track of all the things you learn about your particular site, the decisions you make about what and how much to grow, and also the performance of your garden over each season. These sorts of garden records are invaluable reference tools for planning future gardens, and will lead you on to even greater success in growing healthy and flavorful vegetables.

Pumpkins and squash "curing" in the sun.

This vegetable garden is sheltered by a natural windbreak. A combination of tall trees on the outside, and smaller trees and shrubs on the inside, provides a wall of protection and keeps wind damage to a minimum.

Site Selection

The first decision to make is where to locate your vegetable garden. You may want to reassign a section of your existing flower garden, or perhaps create a whole new garden devoted entirely to vegetables. Consider the site carefully, because selecting a good location now can prevent many problems later.

Let your garden site influence your selection of plants. Maybe you will have to choose vegetables that prefer shade, or species that can cope with high moisture levels for most of the year. If you have a range of possible sites, choose the one that most closely matches the requirements of your favorite crops.

Light

Most vegetable plants need six to twelve hours of sunlight each day. Pick a site well away from shade trees and buildings that cast the garden in shade for more than half the day. If you have a city garden nestled between tall buildings, you may be limited to shade-tolerant vegetables.

Gardens located to the south or west of houses or slopes will receive the most light. With such a favorable position, you can start planting as much as two weeks earlier, since the soil warms faster.

Moisture

Since most vegetables need at least 1 inch (25 mm) of water each week, be prepared to water during dry periods. Make sure you can reach the site with a garden hose or irrigation pipe, or be prepared to carry water to the site by hand. Avoid gardening in low areas that are apt to be flooded, as well as on high areas with excessive drainage.

Soil

You'll have the best success if you start with a suitable soil. Avoid heavy clays and loose sands, or amend them with plenty of organic materials (like compost) before you start. Have the soil tested before you begin; adjust pH and nutrient levels the season before, if possible.

Avoid areas that have had heavy foot or vehicle traffic, because this activity compacts the soil and damages its structure. Testing your soil for pollutants is an unnecessary expense unless you suspect the presence of certain contaminants. Urban soils may be polluted by dump sites, industrial waste, motor vehicle exhaust, leaded paint, and chemical insecticides. If you do plan to grow vegetables in a city garden, contact your soil-testing laboratory to see if it tests for toxic materials, and learn how to collect the samples required for investigative testing.

Topography

Slopes and contours influence the way that you arrange your vegetable plants. Your goal is to minimize the loss of soil through erosion and maximize water retention. If you have to plant on a slope, place your rows or beds across the slope. If your rows of vegetables are arranged running up and down the slope, water will run down the slope instead of penetrating

Make sure you have paths between beds for easy access. Herbs are ideal to plant along the edges.

the soil to reach plant roots, and will also carry the precious topsoil away with it.

You'll also want to avoid gardening in low-lying areas, where poor air circulation and boggy conditions make your plants more susceptible to disease.

Obstacles and Access

Locate your garden in a place that's easily accessible, both to you and to vehicles that will deliver materials you may need later, like soil or compost. Paths should be wide enough for a wheelbarrow or cart. As you choose a site, investigate for hidden obstacles like tree roots, shallow boulders, septic systems, and utility lines, and avoid these problem areas.

Time

When planning your garden, think about how much time you will have available to spend in it. The amount of work your garden requires will depend on size and will vary with climate and seasons. Don't build a garden that is too big for you to look after. The work will be faster and easier if you have modern equipment, such as a reliable rotary tiller, than if you're using "elbow grease," a shovel, and heavy garden gloves. To save time and energy, you may want to spread the heavy work, like digging new beds or making paths, over several years.

Finances

If necessary, you can spread the cost of making your garden over several years. Although equipment such as rotary tillers can lighten the workload, it's not necessary to buy expensive equipment at the outset. Start small and enlarge your garden and your equipment collection over time. Your garden plan may include elaborate designs, but you don't need to accomplish everything in one season. If your soil is poor and dry, concentrate on the soil first, and reclaim and improve a new section each season. When vegetable production is steady and you're satisfied with the site, you can concentrate on other aspects, like planting flowers and herbs to make your vegetable garden look more attractive, or enlarging your workspace with structures like cold frames or a toolshed.

Special Requirements

Look for a site that fits your individual needs. If your mobility is limited, make sure your garden is easy to reach—for example, just outside the back door. If you're in a wheelchair, you can have a

Container gardening is an effective way of utilizing space in your garden. It also has a decorative effect.

Rows are easy to plan and plant, but they may need more frequent weeding and watering due to the exposed soil.

smooth, cement path built and then sculpt a waist-high garden from a slope, or build up a terrace that you can reach easily from a chair. Chair-side gardening is easy if you grow vegetables in tall, recycled garbage cans spruced up with some paint and filled with potting soil.

Picking a Planting Pattern

Once you've chosen the best site, think about how you want to arrange your plantings. Parallel rows are easy to plan and plant, but they're not necessarily easy to maintain. Since lots of soil is exposed, you'll probably need to weed and water more often, unless you mulch early and heavily, and replenish the mulch twice a year or as often as necessary.

In a small garden, planting in beds is a much more efficient use of garden space. Since plants are closer together, you'll do less weeding and get higher yields from small areas. The beds do take some time to make the first year, but in following years, you can concentrate your soil-improvement efforts there instead of working up the whole garden area.

Garden Records

Once you have chosen a site, style, and size for your garden, it's a good idea to draw your plan on paper before you go out and start digging.

Use graph paper marked to the appropriate scale (1 square foot [900 sq cm] per square works well). Mark the outline of your garden first, then add permanent features like trees and paths.

Next, make a list of vegetables you want to grow and then arrange them on your graph paper in rows or beds. Keep in mind their planting and harvest dates, size at maturity, and any special growth requirements they might have.

As the season progresses, keep track of planting dates, pest problems, fertilizer rates, and harvests. Some gardeners make notes in a diary or on a calendar. You can create your own tables of garden data using column headings like planting date, harvest date, yield, and quality. As well as monitoring your vegetable garden's day-to-day progress, your garden records will also help you plan for greater success with the next harvest. For example, by keeping a note of planting dates and harvest, you can record how well different cultivars perform in your garden, or when space will become available for replanting. Update your map and other records with each new gardening season.

Choosing Your Crops

Deciding what you'll grow is one of the most fun parts of garden planning. The best way to start is to list the vegetables you like to eat already. Then if lack of time or garden space must limit what you grow, you will have to make some choices. If you just can't live without fresh sweet corn, for instance, you may decide to devote all your available time and space for one short but glorious harvest. If you'd rather grow a variety of vegetables but still have a minimum of work, concentrate on crops that will bear over a long season. Pole beans, peppers, carrots, cucumbers, summer squash, and tomatoes can yield produce over a period of weeks or months from a single planting. As a bonus, these all produce slowly but steadily, so you won't have to be out harvesting every day, and you won't be swamped by an excess of produce at one time.

A well-organized vegetable garden can be an attractive and functional part of even the smallest yard.

Before selecting cultivars, you need to think about how much you want your plants to yield, which cultivars will be best suited to your garden, how much time you're prepared to spend dealing with pests, and what qualities are important to you in your vegetables.

When you go to buy your vegetable seeds and plants, you'll often have a choice between several different cultivars of the same crop. Cultivars can vary widely in characteristics like heat tolerance, size, and disease resistance. If your garden is in a particularly cool or hot area, it's smart to select cultivars adapted to those extremes. Check for frost resistance, hardiness, and the number of days to maturity. Pick one or several cultivars that fit your planting schedule,

Herbs are excellent companions for vegetables. Cabbage pests are repelled by mint, while basil repels tomato hornworms.

especially if you plan to make successive sowings or use season extenders. Whenever possible, use cultivars that have a good local reputation. Check at your local nursery and ask your vegetable-growing neighbors. If a cultivar of string bean has done well for your neighbor's family over several years, chances are it will do just as well for you.

Bean seeds require warm soil to germinate and are an ideal crop for a warm-weather garden. Pole beans take more time to mature than bush beans but bear their crops over a longer period.

Yield If you have a large family to feed, you might prefer a cultivar that has a high yield. You might choose a less productive cultivar if some other factor, like flavor or pest tolerance, has greater priority.

Pest Resistance Choose insect- and disease-resistant cultivars whenever possible. These are plants that have been bred specifically for their pest resistance. Older cultivars that were selected before the widespread use of synthetic pesticides may also offer some pest resistance.

Other Considerations Most gardeners want high yields, but there are also other factors that you'll want to keep in mind when selecting which vegetables and cultivars you want to grow. Flavor, for example, is a top priority with many growers. If you're going to the trouble of growing your own vegetables, you want

them to taste better than their store-bought cousins. Heirloom cultivars in particular are known for their "true" flavors, although many new cultivars also offer good flavor.

Another thing you might want to consider is the ease of harvest. Harvesting can quickly turn from a pleasure to a chore if your crops are difficult to pick. Vegetables like snap beans are easier to pick if the pods are clustered at the top of the plant, instead of at the bottom. If you have sensitive skin, prickly vines and leaves may cause a rash, so look for "hairless" or "spineless" cultivars of squash, okra, and other vegetables. If you have trouble bending over, you may want to choose vining cultivars that you can train up a fence or wall, putting the harvest within arm's reach.

Keep in mind that the ripening and harvesting period for each vegetable varies. Commercial growers find it easier to harvest cultivars that ripen all at once, but a home gardener may prefer to spread out the harvest with a cultivar that ripens over a period of several weeks. You'll also want to consider how much time you are willing to contribute to harvesting. Some crops, like corn and snap beans, require daily harvesting to get produce at the peak of quality, so unless you have time to do this, avoid these plants. Others, like

Before planting a high yield garden, take into account how much produce you will actually use, to avoid waste.

lettuce, onions, and carrots, mature more slowly, so there are several days to wait between harvests.

Post-harvest preparations, like washing, peeling, or slicing can be simple or complex. Some cultivars are easier to use than others. Cylindrical-shaped beets and carrots, for example, are easier to slice than round ones. Nutritional quality can vary, depending on the cultivar. Some new cultivars claim higher nutritional value than others. Certain carrot cultivars, for example, have more beta carotene than others.

Storage quality is important if you don't use vegetables immediately. Onion cultivars differ in holding quality when stored during winter. And most vegetables vary in freezing, canning, and dehydrating quality. Always check this information on the seed pack or with your nursery.

Deciding between Seeds and Transplants

Many vegetables, including cucumbers, corn, lettuce, radishes, carrots, and beans, are easy to grow from seed sown directly in the garden. Others, though—like tomatoes and peppers—germinate poorly in the soil or grow too slowly if you direct-sow the seed. These crops need to be set out as transplants. When deciding which crops to grow, you must decide whether to buy the transplants or start the seed yourself.

It's far easier to let a commercial grower raise the transplants from seed—all you have to do is pick them out at the garden center and pay for them. One disadvantage of buying transplants is that you spend slightly more per plant than if you grew your own. Another is that you have fewer cultivars to choose from. Of the hundreds of tomato cultivars on the market, for example, you may find only half a dozen offered for sale as transplants.

If you desperately want to try cultivars that you can't find at the garden center, grow your own from seed. But if you really want to keep the fuss and muss to a minimum, it's worth the slight extra initial cost to buy transplants.

While parsley can take the cold, beans and marigolds grow best in midseason, when the weather is warm and settled.

Starting a Schedule

Once you decide what to grow, make a planting schedule for the upcoming season. Jot down the planting dates for your chosen crops on a calendar or in a special gardening notebook. The schedule will remind you when to shop for seeds or transplants, so you can buy the things you need at the right time.

How early you can start planting depends on the frost tolerance of the crops you've chosen. (If you're not sure of the average date of the last frost in your area, ask gardening neighbors or your local Cooperative Extension Service.)

- 4 to 6 weeks before last frost date: very hardy vegetables such as pea (seeds), onion (sets), and spinach (seeds).
- 2 to 4 weeks before last frost date: hardy vegetables such as carrot (seeds) and celery (transplants).
- Last frost date: tender vegetables like tomato (transplants) and beans (seeds).
- 2 to 3 weeks after last frost date: very tender vegetables like cucumber (seeds or transplants) and green pepper (transplants).

How Much to Plant

Experience is the best tool when it's time to decide how much to plant. After only one season of gardening, you can decide to grow more or less than last year. Yield, however, can go up or down seasonally,

When young plants are well established, they may need to be thinned to avoid overcrowding. Pull them out carefully, or snip them off at soil level.

depending, for example, on local weather and pest outbreaks. That's why many gardeners plant more than they need if they have the space to do it.

You might know roughly the amount of tomatoes or onions you'd like your garden to produce, but not how many plants to grow. Some seed catalogs offer a wealth of information when it comes to production estimates, and others don't provide any. Use the informative catalogs as a guideline, and thank them with your business. If you buy packs of seed in local stores, look to the planting information on the back for an idea of yield and when to expect it.

Planting Checklist

- How much produce will you use fresh, canned, frozen, and dried? Even gardeners without families tend large gardens if they're growing for the whole year. A garden planted for fresh use is a pretty small affair. Use your seed source as a guide for how much yield to expect, and figure accordingly.
- When do you want to harvest the crop? Like the preceding question, this depends on how you plan to use it. For example, 1 pound (0.5 kg) of bean seeds will give you a lot of beans at one time, or smaller quantities if you stagger the planting dates throughout the season. Instead of 1 pound of one cultivar, you

could select smaller amounts of several cultivars with various maturity times for a longer harvest period.

- How much growing space do you have? You can stretch your growing space with raised beds, trellises, succession planting, containers, and other techniques. Check your vegetable seed source for the most specific plant spacing recommendations.
- How much storage space do you have? If you are growing crops like potatoes and onions for winter storage, try to avoid planting more than you'll have room to keep properly.

Hints for Better Harvests

Here are some tips for getting the highest or longest-lasting yield for the least amount of work.

Beans To get a steady supply of bush beans, instead of massive quantities that have to be picked all at once, plant successive crops at seven- to ten-day intervals. Or try pole beans—they grow tall, so you have to set up a tripod of stakes for them to twine around, but they'll produce for a long season from a single planting. And you don't have to stoop to pick them!

Broccoli For a longer harvest, look for cultivars like 'Packman' and 'Goliath' that will produce smaller side shoots after you harvest the main head.

Carrots Sow more thickly than usual, and harvest some of the thinnings for eating each week.

Corn Plant successive crops every seven to ten days for a more even yield.

Cucumbers Choose bush cultivars to get a high yield from a small space.

Lettuce If summer heat stops spring sowings early, try late-summer plantings for harvesting well into fall.

Peas Like lettuce, peas may stop producing when summer's heat starts. Late-summer plantings will extend the season.

Corn

Peppers If your peppers stop producing in midsummer, don't pull them out—they'll often set more fruit when slightly cooler weather comes.

Squash Like cucumbers, squash are available in bush cultivars that offer high yields from limited growing space.

Tomatoes Some gardeners carefully stake and prune their tomatoes, but you don't have to. It's all right to let the plants grow on the ground. They'll take up more space and you'll have to wash the tomatoes, but they're much less work. Or set up cages around the young plants, and let the cages support the stems.

Garden Care through the Year

Vegetables do require more work than almost any other landscape plant, but they will also reward you with quantities of tasty produce. Follow the simple care calendar below, and your crops will thrive with a minimum of fuss.

Winter

This is the time to decide what you want to grow and how much you are going to plant. As you search through seed catalogs, look for compact, high-yielding vegetable cultivars that will provide a bountiful harvest in a small space. Also consider cultivars that are insect- or disease-resistant, so you'll have fewer pest problems to cope with. Order your seeds now, and save yourself a trip to the garden center later on. This is also a good time to plan the planting schedule so you'll put your crops in at the right time for best growth.

Spring

The weather's getting warmer, the spring bulbs are in full bloom, and you've got the itch to get your vegetable garden going. Start with the soil. The first time you prepare your garden you'll need to till or dig the whole thing to remove the grass and weeds, loosen the soil, work in organic matter, and remove buried rocks. By doing a good job the first year, future

planting will be easy: instead of tilling the entire garden, you can just dig a row for seeds and a hole for each transplant.

Keep your soil in good shape by not working it when it's too wet or too dry. To check soil moisture, take a handful of the soil and squeeze it into a ball. If the soil won't make a ball, it's probably too dry. Water the area thoroughly, and wait a day or two before digging. If the soil does stick together, tap the ball with a finger. If the ball falls apart, it's safe to work the soil. If the soil stays in a lump, it's too wet. Wait a few days, and try the test again.

Planting For direct-sown seed, loosen the soil in the area you're going to plant, rake it, and firm it gently. Sprinkle the seed evenly over the bed, or plant in straight rows. Keep the seedbed evenly moist until the seeds sprout.

For transplants, loosen the soil in an area slightly bigger than the transplant's root ball. Set the plant in the hole and fill in around the roots with soil. Keep transplants well watered until they start showing new growth.

To help your plants be as vigorous as possible and to make working among them easier, be sure to space them properly. The seed packet or plant tag gives the correct spacing distance. If you sow seeds too thickly, they'll come up crowded and you'll have to thin them out by pulling out the smaller seedlings and leaving the strongest ones.

Mulching will boost garden productivity by enriching the soil (during decomposition) with plant nutrients, thereby encouraging earthworms and friendly bacteria.

It's best to lay soaker hoses (dew hoses) with the holes facing down, between long rows of plants.

Summer

As your vegetables mature in the warm summer weather, a little extra attention can keep yields high and routine maintenance minimal.

Mulching When applying loose organic mulches, like compost or straw, wait until direct-sown seedlings are about 6 inches (15 cm) tall or your transplants are in the ground. Lay down a 1- to 3-inch (2.5- to 7.5-cm) layer of mulch. Keep organic mulches about 1 inch (2.5 cm) away from plant stems to discourage rot.

Black plastic mulch is commonly used in vegetable gardens to smother weeds and retain soil moisture, but it won't add any nutrients or organic matter to the soil.

Watering Mulches save water, but not enough for you to forget about watering. A general rule of thumb is that most crops need 1 inch (25 mm) of water a week, from rain or irrigation. But what really matters is how moist the soil is. If it hasn't rained for a few days, dig down 2 to 3 inches (5 to 7.5 cm) into the soil. If the soil feels moist, wait a few days and check again. If the soil is dry, it's time to water.

Water slowly and deeply to encourage deep roots that don't get stressed easily during hot, dry weather. With a sprinkler, this could take several hours. Soaker hoses, which ooze water evenly along their length, are easy to install, and they save water by delivering it right to the soil. For the ultimate easy maintenance, install an automatic drip irrigation system.

Weeding Pull or dig up the weeds that make it through the mulch, preferably while they're tiny. If for some reason a weed grows to adult size, be sure to yank it before it sets seed so you don't have to contend with its more numerous offspring next year.

Fertilizing If you've done a good job preparing the soil and working in ample amounts of organic matter, the layer of compost or aged manure you put down each year is enough to replenish the nutrients your vegetables remove from the soil.

Some gardeners like to give their vegetables an additional boost around midsummer. You can apply a liquid fertilizer such as fish emulsion or seaweed by either pouring it on the soil or spraying it on the leaves. You can also scratch a balanced dry organic fertilizer into the soil around the plant (pull back the mulch first, apply the fertilizer, then replace the mulch) and water the soil deeply to evenly distribute the fertilizer.

Flowering cabbage provides good fall color in the vegetable or flower garden.

Fall

As the lower temperatures of fall arrive, many vegetables that took a break during the summer heat will put on new growth or set more fruit. Late summer plantings of crops like peas and lettuce can yield well into the fall season, when the cool weather makes picking a pleasure rather than a chore.

Lettuce

Fall Cleanup Once your crops are done for the season, spend a few minutes putting the garden to bed so it will be ready for spring planting next season. In addition to making the garden look tidier during the winter, picking up dead plants and dropped vegetables eliminates hiding places for insect eggs and disease pathogens. (Add seed- and disease-free materials to your compost pile; bury seedy or diseased plants or dispose of them with your household trash.) While you're at it, pull up and clean off any metal or wooden stakes and stick them in the garage so they don't rust or rot. Finally, wash all your tools and wipe a light coating of oil on them before storing.

Beets

Carrots

Cool-Weather Crops
Arugula, beet, broccoli, brussels sprouts, cabbage, cauliflower, chicory, Chinese cabbage, collard, corn salad, escarole, kale, kohlrabi, lettuce, mustard, onion, pea, radish, spinach, turnip.

Warm-Weather Crops
Cantaloupe, carrot, corn, cucumber, eggplant, lima bean, okra, parsnip, peanut, pepper, potato, pumpkin,

Peas

rutabaga, snap bean, summer squash, sweet potato, Swiss chard, tomato, watermelon, winter squash.

Vegetables Tolerating Dappled Sunlight

Although most vegetables need a full day of sun for good growth, there are a few that can tolerate partial shade. Choose crops that fit your conditions from the list provided below:
arugula, cabbage, corn salad, endive, horseradish, lettuce, pea, radish, rhubarb, spinach, Swiss chard.

Vegetables Requiring Full Sun

If you want to grow a wide range of vegetables, you need to site your garden in the sunniest spot possible. Listed below are some commonly grown vegetables that need full sun:
artichoke, asparagus, bean, beet, broccoli, brussels sprouts, carrot, cauliflower, celeriac, celery, corn, cucumber, eggplant, kale, kohlrabi, leek, melon, mustard, okra, onion, parsnip, peanut, pepper, potato, pumpkin, rutabaga, shallot, summer squash, sweet potato, sunflower, tomato, turnip, watermelon, winter squash.

Acid Tolerance

Vegetable crops vary in their tolerance to acid soil conditions. Match the crops below with the conditions you have available, or amend your soil with lime to raise the pH for the vegetables you want to grow.

Slightly Tolerant (pH 6.0 to 6.8)

Asparagus, beet, broccoli, cabbage, cauliflower, celery, Chinese cabbage, cress, leek, lettuce, okra, onion, parsnip, salsify, spinach, Swiss chard, watercress.

Moderately Tolerant (pH 5.5 to 6.8)

Lima bean, brussels sprouts, carrot, collard, corn, cucumber, eggplant, garlic, horseradish, kale, kohlrabi, mustard, pea, pepper, pumpkin, radish, rutabaga, squash, tomato, turnip.

Very Tolerant (pH 5.0 to 6.8)

Chicory, dandelion, endive, fennel, potato, shallot, sorrel, sweet potato.

Crop Rotation

You're already practicing simple crop rotation if you avoid planting the same vegetable in the same place each year. Most organic gardeners practice crop rotation for several important reasons. By rotating crops, you'll prevent the build-up of pests that might result if the same crop were grown continuously. You'll also make better use of soil nutrients, since different crops remove nutrients from the soil at different rates.

There are several steps you can take to get the full benefits of crop rotation.
1. On paper, divide your crops into different categories according to their growth habits or families. You might, for example, separate them into root crops, leafy crops, and fruiting crops. Or you might group them according to their respective families, such as *Gramineae* for corn, *Cruciferae* for cabbage and its relatives, *Leguminosae* for peas and beans, and *Solanaceae* for tomatoes and potatoes.
2. Draw a map of your garden, and divide the growing space into the same

Plot A   Plot B   Plot C   Plot D

With raised beds, organizing crop rotations is simple. Each year, move your crop over to the next bed in the sequence. Set one bed aside for perennial vegetables, like asparagus and rhubarb.

Fast-growing lettuce and slower-growing cabbage-family crops make a good combination for interplanting.

number of areas as you have categories of crops. If you are just using root, leafy, and fruiting crops, you'd divide your garden into three areas.
3. Plant one type of vegetable, or a group of vegetables, in each area of the garden. Record on your map where each is growing.
4. Next year, move each crop or grouping to a different area.

Interplanting

You'll get twice the harvest variety if you interplant your vegetables. Interplanting means planting two (or more) kinds of vegetables *at the same time, in the same space*. Mixing vegetables enhances pest prevention, since many insect pests can't locate their favorite plants when scents and sights are mixed. More foliage means a greater variety of hiding and feeding places for beneficial insects that help control pests. You'll save gardening space, too.

To interplant in your garden, determine the length of your growing season, then choose several early- and late-crop combinations to fit. The first vegetable should mature quickly, like radishes or lettuce. It should be easy to harvest, without damaging the remaining crop. (For example, potatoes aren't a good first crop if digging will destroy the interplanted crop.) Or you

Interplant carrots and onions. The carrots will be harvested before the onions have had time to reach maturity.

could plant a traditionally long-season crop like leeks and harvest it at an early, tender stage. The second vegetable should be slow-growing, like melons, for a harvest scheduled later in the season.

The best crops for interplanting are unrelated and have complementary nutritional needs. You can plant both crops at once, or spread planting dates apart as necessary. Fulfill space requirements of the late-maturing vegetable first (since it will be there all season), then fill in extra space with the quick crop. Plant both vegetables at a lesser density, since moisture and nutrient demands on the soil are greater. If necessary, supplement the second crop with liquid fertilizer or a midsummer application of compost.

Suggestions for early vegetables are: amaranth, arugula, baby beets, carrots, cress, garden peas, leeks, lettuce, mustard greens, oriental greens, radicchio, radish, scallions, spinach, summer squash, and turnip.

Suggestions for late vegetables are: beets, brussels sprouts, cabbage, carrots, cauliflower, eggplant, leeks, lima beans, okra, onions, peppers, pumpkins, snap beans, sweet corn, sweet potato, Swiss chard, tomatoes, and winter squash.

Succession Planting

Like interplanting, succession planting means harvesting two crops from the same space in one season. But unlike interplanting, in succession planting you don't plant the second crop until after you've harvested the first. In this way you fully utilize your vegetable garden, and keep your supply of fresh vegetables coming all through the growing season. Determine the length of your growing season by counting the number of days between the average date of the last spring frost and the average date of the first fall frost. Then select two vegetables whose combined days to maturity fit that limit. Plant seeds or transplants of the first crop in early spring, then harvest it and replant with the second crop in midsummer. Between crops, prepare the soil as needed but avoid tilling. By midsummer, most weed seeds have germinated, and tillage will only bring more seeds to the surface. You can add compost before the second planting, or after planting, as a mulch.

Timing is the challenge, since the first and second plantings don't overlap. Each crop must get off to a quick start and finish. Good choices for quick crops to grow in spring and fall are: arugula, beets, carrot, collards, chicory, endive, kohlrabi, mustard greens, radish, shallots, spinach, and Swiss chard.

Successive sowings of crops like bush beans will ensure a continuous harvest. As one planting finishes bearing, the next is ready to harvest.

Successive Sowing

Another way to ensure a continuous harvest is to make successive plantings. Sow the same carrot cultivar, for example, at several locations at 10- to 14-day intervals until the last harvest approaches the season's end. Lettuce, carrots, snap beans, and radicchio are good candidates for successive sowings.

Or reap successive harvests by planting several cultivars of the same vegetable, with a range of maturity dates, on the same date at the beginning of the season. For example, choose sweet corn cultivars that mature on a range of dates from 65 to 90 days. Familiarity with the cultivars will help in making your selections, and seed catalogs are the best reference to consult. You can make comparative charts and lists of cultivars once current seed catalogs begin arriving in early winter.

Raised Beds

Raised beds are the ultimate in outdoor, custom-built plant containers. They require an initial investment of energy, but you'll save both time and labor later.

Raised beds are more productive than rows for several reasons. Since traffic is restricted to paths, soil in dug beds remains loose and friable. Building a bed gives you the chance to correct both physical and chemical soil imperfections. If your soil drains poorly or lacks certain nutrients, this is an excellent time to make the necessary changes. Since the soil

Leave enough room for yourself and your equipment between beds. Gravel is a popular surface for paths.

environment is ideal, you can plant closer than usual and harvest more. And, since plants are closer, the soil stays shaded and cool so weeds are less likely to develop, and less soil moisture is lost to evaporation. Since beds are discrete units, they're easier to manage when it's time to plan crop rotations. You can build beds wherever you like, in partial shade or full sun, depending on the site and your plants.

Bed Size Make your beds narrow enough so you can reach one half from either side. Four feet (1.2 m) is a good width for most people. If you find bending and reaching difficult, make them narrower. Beds can be as long, short, straight, or curved as you like. When building them on uneven ground, make them perpendicular to the slope to prevent soil erosion.

Leave 4 to 5 feet (1.2 to 1.5 m) between beds as paths, or as much room as necessary for yourself and your equipment. Paths can be paved, mulched, or planted. If you plant grass, make sure the paths are wide enough to accommodate your lawn mower.

Digging There are at least two ways to form your beds: by simply incorporating lots of organic matter into the soil, or by double-digging. Before you start either method, decide where to locate beds and paths, and mark off the boundaries with flags or stakes and string. After digging, rake the tops smooth and allow the soil to settle for several weeks before planting.

If you're satisfied with your soil, the simplest method is to simply dig in plenty of organic matter like compost, rotted manure, or shredded leaves and straw. It's almost impossible to add too much organic matter. Using a shovel, work the top 6 inches (15 cm) of soil. Work one strip at a time, moving backward so you're always standing on undug ground. As you

Double-digging your soil and adding plenty of compost will produce a thriving and productive vegetable garden.

work, add other amendments (like lime or rock phosphate) as needed. When finished, you'll have a mound of soil.

If your soil is heavy and compacted or poorly drained, consider investing some more time and labor to double dig your raised bed. Double-digging will help to loosen up the soil and improve drainage. (For instructions, see page 51.)

Framing Raised beds can be left as mounds of soil, or you can add permanent sides. A frame allows you to build deeper beds, helps to prevent the soil from washing away, and defines the bed border. If the frame is sturdy and wide enough, you can stand or sit on it while you garden. Simply place the material you are using around the edge of the bed, and

press it firmly into the soil. Wood, bricks, cement blocks, flat rocks, old construction timbers, and railroad ties are all good materials for frames.

Solving Drainage Problems If your soil drains poorly, you can correct the problem by growing your crops in raised beds. Double-digging alone might solve your drainage problem. Or build a bed frame and import topsoil and organic matter to fill it, without mixing the native soil. If you're forced to garden in a low spot where water forms puddles, build a framed raised bed and put a layer of crushed stone in the bottom. Or, place a length of drainage pipe in the bottom, before filling with improved soil.

Training Methods

Training vegetable plants to grow vertically, instead of horizontally, saves space and makes cultivating and harvesting easier. Staking improves plant health, since better air circulation promotes drying and lessens the chance of disease. Since fruits aren't in contact with soil, they're less likely to succumb to soilborne pathogens. Staked plants are more attractive, and leave you more room for special techniques like interplanting and companion planting.

Timber framing is used for raised beds as well as vertical trellising.

You can purchase stakes made of wood, metal, plastic, or bamboo in a variety of heights to fit the needs of the vegetable. Sturdiness is more important than appearance, since vegetable plants take up lots of space and become heavy with fruit as the season progresses.

No matter what method you use, put your support system in place before you plant. Vines like peas and beans will attach themselves by wrapping tendrils or twining stems around the support. Plants like tomatoes or peppers need some help: Tie them loosely to the support, using scraps of soft cloth or cotton rope.

Universal Plant Cages

You can make long-lasting, univer cages from concrete reinforcing wire for supporting tall plants like tomatoes and peppers, as well as vines like cucumbers, pole beans, and peas. Buy the wire at building-supply stores in rolls 100 feet (30 m) long and 6 feet (2 m) high. mesh is large—each square measure 5¼ x 6 inches (13 x 15 cm), big enc for reaching through to harvest most vegetables.

You'll need bolt cutters and a pair of pliers. Cut off an 8-foot (2.4-m) section for each cage, making your cut through the middle of the sixteenth row of squares. Wrap the wire around to form a cylinder, using the cut ends of wire as fasteners. To use the cage for tomatoes or peppers, stand the cylinder upright. You can cut away the horizontal wire on the bottom, leaving 5-inch (13-cm) prongs to insert into the soil as anchors. For added strength in windy climates, drive a 4-foot (1.2-m) stake into the soil 12 inches (30 cm) deep next to the cage and another on the opposite side. Use twine or wire to fasten the cage to the stakes. Place one plant in the center of each cage. As the plants grow, they'll fill the cage with foliage as they push themselves upward.

You can also grow vining crops like cucumbers or gourds with the cage upright, or turn the cage on its side and

Successive sowings of fast growers like lettuce, planted several weeks apart, can extend the harvest into summer.

Squash and spinach are vegetables than can be harvested and eaten before they reach maturity.

secure it with several stakes. Plant inside the cage; the vines will loop around and form a horizontal tube. This works well for heavier crops like melons.

Harvesting and Storing

How you pick and store your harvest influences vegetable quality and flavor.

When to Pick Harvest vegetables early, often, and at their peak tenderness and flavor. Quality declines with time, so you'll sacrifice flavor, texture, and storage quality the longer you neglect to pick. Frequent harvests prolong the productive lifespan of most vegetable plants—the more you pick, the more the plant produces, since harvesting delays or prevents the production of seed. After producing seed, many vegetables stop producing or die.

Mark the expected date of maturity for your crops on your garden calendar, and begin inspecting vegetables for ripeness at least one week before this date. In your garden, vegetables may mature earlier or later than expected due to the influence of climate or pests. For example, unseasonably warm weather can hasten a harvest; or pests may weaken plants and delay ripening.

Pick vegetables in the early morning while they're still cool, but after the dew has dried. Flavor and nutrition are at their peak when you pick, so aim for using vegetables soon after harvest.

If you're growing "baby" vegetables, plan on picking every day for the best quality and production. You can pick baby leeks and onions when they're the size of a pencil. Baby squash should have even color—you'll know that you've picked too early if the flavor is bitter. Select baby carrots that have good color and flavor. Many carrot cultivars grown for their large roots aren't suitable to pick early since they don't develop that deep, orange color until later. You can choose vegetable cultivars bred especially for immature production; they'll offer the best quality at an early age.

Handling Brush away the soil clinging to roots or leaves, but don't wash vegetables before storing: Adding moisture just seems to invite spoilage. Pull away bruised or damaged parts before you store and add them to the compost pile.

Most vegetables grown for long-term storage should be "cured" before they're tucked away. The best way to cure garlic and onions is by hanging them in braids or mesh bags, in a dry and airy place out of direct sun—barn or attic rafters are ideal. Leave them to dry for several weeks. You can cut away their tops, but leave several inches of stem.

When you cut pumpkins and winter squash from the vine, leave several inches of stem. Leave them in the field for two weeks after picking to toughen their skins. If freezing weather arrives early, bring them indoors and keep them at about 70°F (21°C) for the same period. Potatoes will store best if they're held at 50° to 60°F (10° to 15°C) and high relative humidity for 10 to 14 days before storing.

Storing When it's time to store, sort your harvest into two groups: vegetables that require moisture, and those that have to be kept dry.

In cool climates, you can leave crops like carrots, leeks, and turnips in the ground over winter (in warm climates, vegetables left in the ground will attract insect pests). Cover with at least 6 inches (15 cm) of mulch; in severe climates, cover the row with bales of straw. Push aside the covering to harvest the roots. Or place harvested vegetables in a single layer sandwiched between 6-inch (15-cm) layers of mulch. Build several layers, then top with 2 feet (60 cm) of mulch and cover with a plastic tarp. Other options for winter storage include empty growing (cold) frames and root cellars. The ideal spot is cold and dark but not freezing

Onions

Storing Fresh Vegetables

Refrigerate and use within several days to one week: artichokes, asparagus, beans, broccoli, collards, eggplant, endive, kale, lettuce, mushrooms, mustard greens, okra, peas, radishes, spinach, sweet corn, Swiss chard.

Refrigerate and store up to 12 weeks: beets, brussels sprouts, cauliflower, celery, leeks, melons, onions (green), peppers, radicchio, summer squash.

Keep cool and damp up to 18 weeks (32° to 40°F [0° to 4°C] and 90 percent relative humidity): cabbage, carrots, kohlrabi, parsnips, potatoes, rutabagas, turnips.

Keep cool and dry up to 7 months (32° to 40°F [0° to 4°C] and 65 to 70 percent relative humidity): garlic, onions (except green).

Keep warm and dry up to two to three months (50° to 55°F [10° to 12°C] and 50 to 70 percent relative humidity): pumpkins, winter squash.

Vegetables for Containers

You can grow some common garden vegetables, like potatoes, in containers. You can also grow dwarf cultivars of larger-sized vegetables in pots and barrels. Some newly introduced cultivars of tomato, cucumber, pepper, and squash are ideal for growing in containers—they save space *and* produce heavily.

Be sure to choose containers with holes in the bottom for adequate drainage. The size of container you select depends on what vegetable you plan to grow. Small pots are fine for hanging baskets of ornamentals, but may not provide the best environment for heavy-producing vegetable plants. You can recycle wastebaskets, garbage cans, and even heavy plastic bags as container gardens. Looking for some ideas of crops to start with in containers? Here are some surefire favorites.

Tomatoes Tomatoes come in all sizes, from giant vining types that may grow to 6 feet (1.8 m) or more (they're called "indeterminate" types) to tiny, compact, cherry tomato cultivars that are perfect for growing in hanging baskets.

Peppers Hot and sweet peppers are excellent plants to grow in containers. Because they are perennials, you can cut them back at the end of each season, move them inside for the winter, and then move them back outside again next spring.

Lettuce Lettuce is easy to grow in containers and looks as great as it tastes. Try a packet of a "cutting mix," which contains several kinds of lettuce, along with other spicy salad greens such as mustard, mizuna, and arugula. With these cutting mixes, you just plant the seed rather thickly, then cut handfuls with scissors as the lettuce grows.

Create a Container Salad Garden A container garden can be perfect for one-stop salad harvesting. Plant your salad greens in a container or window box outside the kitchen, and add some chives and basil. Hang a basket of cherry tomatoes above the pot or box, and you'll have salads literally at your fingertips!

Lettuce and spinach do best in cooler temperatures, so start some in early spring. Plant again in late summer, and you'll enjoy months of delicious salads. If your greens are still going strong when hard frosts arrive, just move them inside— they'll continue to grow nicely in a bright south window.

Fruits, Berries, and Nuts

Cover arbors, trellises, and other structures with carefully trained fruiting trees or fruit-bearing vines for beauty and productiveness.

There's nothing quite like the taste of just-picked, sun-warmed, homegrown fruit. And it's even better when you know that the fruit has been grown organically, so you're free to enjoy it right off the plant without worrying about residues from synthetic pesticides. But what's best of all is harvesting these juicy, flavor-packed fruits right from your own yard.

It's surprising that fruiting plants have been neglected so long for landscape use. After all, most of them have at least two outstanding features: attractive flowers and edible fruits. Many have other special features as well, such as showy fall color or interesting bark. Compare that to a traditional but limited-interest ornamental, such as a forsythia or a lilac, and you too may wonder why you never thought of growing fruiting plants instead.

Deciding What to Grow

Even before you start planning your fruit planting, you probably have at least a mental wish list of what you want to grow. Go through it crop by crop to see if the plant in question will fit your growing conditions. Consider each crop's sun, moisture, and temperature requirements, as well as its size and maintenance needs. You may also want to refer to mail-order fruit catalogs to find out all the special features and needs of specific cultivars.

Fine-Tune Your Crop Choices

If space is a limitation, you may need to drop some crops. Don't forget that some fruits and nuts require (or benefit from) cross-pollination for good production, so you'll need to allow room for at least two plants of those.

Pollination Planning Pointers It's a basic principle of botany: To produce a fruit, a flower needs to be pollinated. From there, though, it gets a little trickier. You see, sometimes the flowers on a particular plant can be fertilized by pollen from the same plant, so you can have just one plant and still get a good crop. Peaches, nectarines, tart cherries, strawberries, some plums, and some citrus crops fall into this group.

Other fruit and nut trees need pollen from another plant or cultivar of the same crop. Examples of plants that need (or at least benefit from) cross-pollination include sweet cherries, pears, pecans, walnuts, most apples, and some plums and apricots.

Because different cultivars can bloom at different times, you can't just buy two trees and assume they'll pollinate each other. Mail-order catalogs that sell fruit trees will suggest pollinators for the crops that need them; follow these guidelines when you buy to get the best results.

Planning for Season-Long Harvests

If you're planning to stock a roadside stand or do plenty of preserving, you might prefer to choose crops that all ripen about the same time. Otherwise, it makes sense to spread out your harvests through the growing season. As you're working on your list of crops to grow, check the prospective harvest times of all the crops you've chosen to see if they are fairly well spread out. (The actual harvest time can vary each year, depending on the weather, but the spread of time between the peak for each crop should remain fairly consistent.) If the harvest times aren't evenly distributed through summer and fall, try some or all of the approaches outlined below to get the longest possible picking season.

Most sweet cherries need cross-pollination, so make sure you have enough space to grow at least two trees.

Oranges, peaches, and several other fruits have cultivars that ripen at different times, extending your harvest.

Make a Mixed-Fruit Garden Some home gardeners prefer to grow a few each of several different kinds of fruit, so they have prime produce to pick and enjoy at any time during the growing season. Choosing one or two crops for each season from the following list will help you make sure you have all your harvesting times covered.

- Late spring (in warm climates): Citrus fruit and apricots
- Early summer: Apricots, sweet cherries, early blueberries, and June-bearing strawberries
- Midsummer: Early apples, early peaches, midseason blueberries, blackberries, summer-bearing raspberries, day-neutral strawberries, and gooseberries
- Late summer: Grapes, late blueberries, elderberries, hardy kiwi, filberts, ever-bearing strawberries, midseason apples, midseason peaches, and plums
- Fall: Late apples, late peaches, fall-bearing and ever-bearing raspberries, cranberries, persimmons, chestnuts, walnuts, and pecans

Pick Different Cultivars Even if you only concentrate on one or two crops, you can still have a longer harvest season by choosing different cultivars that mature at different times. For instance, you could start out the strawberry season with June-bearing cultivars, continue picking all summer with day-neutral cultivars, and keep on harvesting into fall with ever-bearing strawberries. The same technique works to spread the raspberry season: Plant summer-bearing types for midsummer picking, then get another sweep of berries in fall with ever-bearing and fall-bearing raspberries.

Any time you have to plant two or more compatible cultivars of a particular fruit for pollination, look for those that flower at the same time but mature at different times. With apples, for instance, you could choose the cultivars 'Liberty' and 'Prima'. They will bloom in time to cross-pollinate each other, but 'Prima' ripens near the

If you have a short growing season, look for early-ripening cultivars.

end of August while 'Liberty' ripens at around the end of September.

Choose Your Harvest Carefully By keeping an eye on natural variations in ripening times, you can sometimes extend the harvest time for a particular crop by a month or more. When you're picking apples, for instance, take the early-ripening ones on the sunny outer portions of the tree first, followed a couple weeks later by the inner apples. Pick some ripe rabbiteye blueberries or grapefruits when they first become sweet, then let the others linger on the plant a little longer. If you want an extended harvest of currants, for instance, grow black currants (which ripen over several weeks) instead of simultaneously ripening white and red currants.

Select Different Planting Sites If you're determined to grow two crops that ripen at the same time but are afraid you'll be swamped with produce, you can try to alter their timing a little. Plant one on a south-facing slope or in front of a south-facing wall to speed up its flowering and fruiting times. To delay flowering and fruiting on the other plant, site it on a

north-facing slope or beside a north-facing wall, and leave mulch on the soil in spring to keep the roots cooler longer. Remember that if you're growing a crop that needs cross-pollination, you'll have to plant compatible companions in each area.

Options for Edible Landscaping

The options for including edibles in your yard are as extensive as your imagination. Here are some suggestions for ways you can add these beautiful and productive plants to your landscape plans.

Shade Trees If you're starting a new landscape or renovating an old one, consider growing an edible plant as a shade tree. Walnuts, hickories, chestnuts, and other full-sized fruit and nut trees provide height and shade just like a maple or oak tree, but they produce a useful crop as well.

Flowering Trees Short fruit trees, such as peaches, semidwarf apples, almonds, and sour cherries, make excellent small trees as handsome as any dogwood or crab apple. Use them alone as special

Training fruit trees and vines to grow along walls will give you a harvest from a previously useless space.

specimens, or include them as accents in a large foundation planting, mixed border, or shrub bed. For even more excitement, try an extra-showy type like weeping 'Santa Rosa' plums, double-flowered 'Double Delight' and 'Double Jewel' peach trees, or curly stemmed 'Flying Dragon' citrus trees.

Shrubs and Hedges Instead of a boring evergreen hedge or another single-season flowering shrub, why not add some fruiting shrubs to your landscape? Fruit- and nut-bearing bushes, such as European filberts, Manchurian bush apricots, elderberries, currants, and highbush blueberries, form large shrubs substantial enough to edge the boundary of your property, mass into an informal hedge, or naturalize. Prickly shrubs such as raspberries, blackberries, citrons, and gooseberries make a barrier that neighborhood children, dogs, and deer won't be quick to push through.

Flower Borders and Foundation Plantings Low-growing fruit bushes, such as compact half-high blueberries, make great shrubs for foundation plantings or mixed flower borders. Creeping fruit-bearing plants—including lowbush blueberries and strawberries—fit easily in the foreground of a flower or shrub border. They also make interesting groundcovers, just as long as they get their fair share of sunshine and a little help from you to beat the weeds.

Walls, Fences, and Trellises Vining fruits such as grapes and kiwis can cover arbors or trellises, shading sitting areas, highlighting special views, or screening off utility areas. Espaliered trees (those trained to grow flat against a wall or trellis) can form a living fence that's both unique and productive.

Containers Decks, patios, and even balconies can be fruitful when you grow suitable edibles in containers. Dwarf citrus, apple, and peach trees are all good candidates for container culture. Strawberries also look super cascading out of hanging baskets or strawberry pots.

Factors to Consider

With so many exciting edible plants to choose from, it can be tempting to start filling your yard with them right away. But there are factors you need to consider in order to have success with fruits and berries. Before you start digging holes and buying plants to fill them, review the points below, and keep them in mind as you plan and plant your new landscape.

Think About Maintenance Just like any other landscape plant, fruiting plants need care to keep them healthy and productive. While some have lower maintenance needs than others, all will require some of your time. If you don't have a lot of time to devote to yard care, stick with some of the less complicated crops, such as strawberries, blueberries, gooseberries, currants, blackberries, and raspberries.

Choose Adapted Crops It's possible to grow just about any fruiting plant in any climate, but it isn't always easy. To have healthy, high-yielding plants, it's best to stick with crops and cultivars that are naturally well adapted to the growing conditions in your area. These conditions include the amount of sunlight, the

Carefully trained espaliered fruit trees can produce a unique and effective fence that's both beautiful and productive.

fertility and drainage of the soil, the amount and distribution of rainfall, and the high and low yearly temperatures. Talk with your local Cooperative Extension Service, fruit tree nurseries, and nearby gardening organizations or publications to find out which fruits do well in your area and which don't.

Allow Ample Space Fruiting plants come in a range of sizes, from tall trees to compact container plants, so there's at least one kind for any size garden. Before you buy, however, make sure you have enough space to allow each plant to grow up and out without crowding. You'll also need to consider whether you have to grow more than one plant of each kind for cross-pollination. Sweet cherries, apples, pears, blueberries, and most nuts, for example, need at least one other plant with compatible pollen, so you need to have enough space for at least two plants.

Pick a Good Planting Place Put fruiting plants where they can grow easily, without a lot of competition from other woody plants and turf when they are young. It's also best to keep them away from the road, so they won't be doused by

Cherry trees flower and set fruit early in the season, so avoid low-lying areas that are prone to late spring frost.

Grapevines grow quickly and can be quite heavy, so make sure you can provide a sturdy structure for them to climb.

exhaust fumes. If you grow fruiting plants that need spraying, put them where the spray won't drift to other crops, garden furniture, or house siding.

Consider Plant Habits As you're deciding where to put a particular plant, also think about the kind of fruit it produces and how the fruit falls. Tall hickory trees, for example, let large nuts drop fast, which could be very unpleasant if you're lounging on the patio below. The hulls of black walnuts contain a black dye that

Ripe apricots are so soft that they don't ship well. The way to enjoy them at their peak is to grow your own.

can discolor pavement and garden furniture (as well as your hands). Cherries and mulberries can stain clothes and walkways. Soft fruits can be slippery if they drop on a walk or driveway. Fallen fruit can attract yellow jackets, so keep fruit trees away from children's play areas. Rodents may also feed on dropped fruit, so you'll need to be diligent about cleanup with plants next to the house.

Ripe peaches and nectarines are quite soft, so handle them gently to avoid bruising the tender flesh.

Harvesting and Storing Fruit

There's nothing like the thrill of picking and eating fresh, homegrown fruit that's still warm from the sun. Get the reward you deserve from your fruiting plants by picking produce at just the right time and storing the surplus to maintain the flavor as long as possible.

Picking Pointers Pick fruit in the cool of the morning—just after the dew dries— and store it in a cold place right away. Harvest perishable fruit, such as berries and cherries, every day or two as new fruit ripens. Discard any rotten fruit you find so it won't infect the rest. You can harvest less perishable fruit, such as apples and pears, once or twice a week.

Gather fruit gently to avoid damaging it; cuts and bruises can greatly reduce storage time. When harvesting large fruit, put one hand beneath the fruit to support it. With the other hand, gently work the

Pointers for an Easy-Care Edible Landscape

Don't wait until your fruit trees are delivered to your doorstep to decide what to do with them. An attractive landscape requires planning in advance, starting with careful plant and site selection. Here are a few points to consider as you choose the crops you want to grow and decide where you're going to put them.

• Pick problem-resistant plants. For easiest maintenance, look for cultivars that are naturally resistant to the pests and diseases that are common in your area. (Local fruit growers and your Cooperative Extension Service can tell you which problems to watch out for; catalog descriptions will list the problems a particular cultivar can resist or tolerate.)

• Plan for plant size. Think carefully about how large a tree you can handle. Trees over 6 feet (1.8 m) high will require you to climb on a ladder to harvest or prune; that will slow you down and be more strenuous (and dangerous).

• Consider the water supply. When picking a planting spot, try to find one near a water supply that you can tap into without much trouble. Otherwise, you may be spending lots of time hauling buckets of water or lugging long hoses around. If dry spells are common in your area, you may want to install permanent irrigation systems before you plant. This can save you hours of labor and provide super results.

stem free from the plant. Place the fruit in a soft bag or a bucket, preferably one you can suspend from your shoulder or belt. Empty the bag or bucket frequently when collecting soft fruits, such as peaches and raspberries, so the weight won't damage fruit on the bottom of the container. You can gather dropped fruit from the ground if it's not bruised, but use it immediately.

As you pick, make sure you keep your safety in mind. Get a sturdy, no-tip ladder if you need to climb up into fruit or nut trees. Or, better yet, check garden-supply catalogs for a long-handled fruit picker—basically a small wire basket with curved "fingers" that pull off the fruit and let it drop into the basket. The long handle lets you pick from the safety of the ground.

Wear leather gloves when harvesting from thorny-stemmed plants, such as raspberries.

Apples get sweeter as they mature on the tree, so you can spread out your harvest over a few weeks.

Storing Your Bounty

Most fruit, nut, and berry plants will produce more fruit than you'll be able to eat right away. If you store the produce properly, you can enjoy it over a long period without letting any go to waste.

If you grow grapefruit or persimmons, you can leave them on the plant for weeks

Clues to Fruit Ripeness

It's important to know how to tell when fruit is ripe, so you can harvest it at its prime. Most fruit is ready when the skin changes to its ripe color and the fruit becomes soft, sweet, and easy to pluck from the plant. There are a few exceptions, however, listed below.

- **Apples:** Pick when the fruit is firm but fully colored and the seeds are brown. Take one apple and try it for flavor and seed color before picking them all. Leave the stem on for storage.
- **Blueberries:** Let the berries turn blue, then wait a few days—or for rabbiteye blueberries, a week or two—until the fruit is sweet and comes off easily.
- **Cherries:** Harvest cherries when they're fully colored. Sweet cherries should taste sweet and juicy. Pick tart cherries when they're still firm for cooking, or let them soften on the tree for fresh eating. If rain threatens when cherries are nearly ripe, pick them all to prevent cracking.
- **Citrus:** No matter what the skin color is, evaluate fruit flavor and harvest when it's sweet enough to your taste.
- **Gooseberries:** Berries will remain firm even when ripe, so go by the color to judge picking time.
- **Grapes:** Pick when the fruit turns to its ripe color and is flavorful but still firm.
- **Nuts:** Collect nuts once they've fallen to the ground.
- **Pears:** Pick European pears slightly underripe, when the pores on the fruit surface change from white to brown. The pear will be rounded with waxy skin and brown seeds. Let it finish ripening at room temperature. Allow Asian pears to ripen on the tree until they are sweet but still crisp.

Victoria plums

in cool weather, harvesting as you need them. Most other fruits require cold storage. The ideal is 32°F (0°C) and 90 percent relative humidity. Under these conditions, late apples and pears will store for months, especially if you wrap them in

oiled paper or newspaper or nestle them in shredded paper.

You can make a special fruit storage area in a cold, damp root cellar. Or keep fruit in a second refrigerator with the temperature set low and an open pan of water in it to raise the humidity.

Perishable berries and soft fruit (such as peaches, cherries, and plums) will only last for a few days in cold storage. An ordinary refrigerator is fine for keeping them. Eat them up as soon as possible and freeze, can, or make preserves out of the extra. Wash berries just before use, not before refrigeration.

After harvesting nuts, keep them dry and cool. Stomp on or thrash the nuts to remove the hulls, husks, or burs. Dry all nuts except chestnuts until the shells are crackling dry. Pop chestnuts and any other hulled nuts into the freezer. Store dry nuts at about 70 percent humidity and 35° to 40°F (2° to 4°C); in warmer temperatures they are likely to become rancid.

Fruits for Small Gardens

Fruiting plants can pack a lot of pizzazz into small gardens, letting you make the most of limited space. But you'll need to choose pint-sized plants that won't overwhelm your yard or require extensive pruning to stay small. Fortunately, you can choose from a wide array of compact edibles that let you grow two or three plants in the space you'd otherwise devote to one full-sized tree. Adding a few more fruit crops in containers will further expand your planting options.

Fruit-bearing bushes and groundcovers are natural choices for spots where space is limited. Fruit trees are also an option, since they come in an assortment of sizes.

Super-Easy Alpine Strawberries

Alpine strawberries (*Fragaria vesca*) are an excellent choice for low-maintenance gardens. Even if these tidy little plants never produced fruit, they'd be worth growing for their tiny white flowers, lush green leaves, and compact habit. But as a bonus, you get tiny and flavor-packed berries all season long. These plants don't produce runners, so they are great as edgings for flower or vegetable gardens, and they will produce for several years. Look for alpine strawberry plants at your local garden center, or start your own plants from seed.

Currants grow on bushy plants that are useful for hedges and shrub borders. The fruit is beautiful too.

The smallest are normal trees grafted on dwarfing rootstocks or natural dwarfs growing on their own roots.

Grafted Dwarf Trees When fruit trees are grafted, the top of the graft is called the scion, and the bottom part of the graft is called the rootstock. The scion grows into the trunk and branches and produces the fruit. The rootstock forms the base of the tree and the roots.

Fruit trees are sometimes grafted onto particular rootstocks to take advantage of the rootstocks' special characteristics, such as dwarfing. Dwarfing rootstocks can keep a normally full-sized tree from growing out of your reach, which is convenient when tending the tree and nearly essential in a small garden. Although the plant is dwarf, the fruit is full-sized. Compared with full-sized trees of the same cultivar, dwarfs bear fewer fruit per tree, but you can plant more dwarf trees in a given space and end up with a larger harvest.

Many dwarfing rootstocks have been developed for apples. These different rootstocks are best for different soil conditions and climates; some are even resistant to common soilborne diseases. If none of the dozens of dwarfing apple rootstocks is perfect for your situation, you can buy a tree grafted on more vigorous roots with a dwarfing interstem (a short piece of trunk from a compact tree) that will keep its height down.

Dwarfing rootstocks are not as well developed for other fruit trees. Most pears can be dwarfed with reasonable success by grafting them onto quince rootstocks. Cherries will grow a little smaller if grafted on roots of *Prunus mahaleb*. Plums can grow on over 50 other species of plant roots, including some good dwarfing forms. Peaches and nectarines also have a wide variety of root compatibility. To date, there are no truly dwarfing rootstocks for apricots, sweet cherries, or nut trees. But work is continuing on dwarfing rootstocks, so keep an eye on the nursery catalogs for new developments.

Pears

While dwarfing rootstocks are very useful, they are not without drawbacks. They do, for instance, tend to shorten the life span of peach and nectarine trees. Most dwarfing apple roots are brittle, so you'll need to stake dwarf apple trees to keep them from falling over when laden with fruit or tossed in a strong wind. 'Bartlett' pears tend to bond weakly with quince roots, so the resulting trees may break off at the graft. And 'Anjou' pears grafted onto *Pyrus betulifolia* roots will develop dark, corky spots inside the fruit. Differences caused by rootstocks are less common in cherry, peach, and nut trees than in apple, pear, and plum types.

When growers mix up tree parts in an attempt to build a better plant, they can end up with some unexpected results. The same rootstock, for instance, can produce very different-sized trees when grafted to scions of different cultivars. Reputable nurseries should be able to tell you what characteristics to expect from the different grafts they sell.

Apple tree

Genetic Dwarf Trees You can avoid rootstocks entirely by planting genetic dwarfs, which grow on their own roots. These plants naturally stay small and bushy, and they grow well in containers. Unfortunately, genetic dwarfs often lack good fruit flavor and disease resistance.

But now that they have the size down, fruit breeders are working on developing great flavor, so keep an eye out for improved types in new nursery catalogs.

Use dwarf and semidwarf fruit trees in place of small flowering trees for seasonal interest.

Great Fruits and Nuts for Small Gardens

Even if your growing space is limited, your choices aren't! Here are some suggestions for compact fruiting plants that can enhance any small yard.

- **Trees:** Dwarf and spur forms of apples, dwarf peaches and nectarines, dwarf pears, dwarf plums, sour cherries, Nanking cherries, compact citrus, dwarf almonds, and dwarf figs
- **Shrubs:** Blueberries, elderberries, blackberries, raspberries, currants, and gooseberries
- **Perennials:** Strawberries

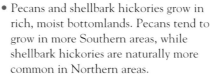

Peaches

Nut-Bearing Plants

Nut trees are attractive and productive additions to any landscape. You'll enjoy the beautiful pink flowers on almonds and the creamy-colored flower clusters on chestnuts. For great fall foliage color, try hazelnuts, which change to burgundy before the leaves drop. As a bonus, you'll get a crop of tasty nuts from any of these easy-care plants.

As with any crop, the key to success with nut growing depends on choosing the right plants for your site and needs. First, decide what role you want the plant to play in your landscape. For a tall, regal shade tree, consider plants such as chestnuts, hickories, oaks, pecans, and walnuts. If space is limited, smaller plants are probably more in line with your needs. Almonds make good small ornamental trees, while bushy hazelnuts look great in shrub borders or as informal hedges.

Almonds

Once you have an idea of the kind of plant you want, take a look at your growing conditions—especially the soil.

Hazelnuts

- Pecans and shellbark hickories grow in rich, moist bottomlands. Pecans tend to grow in more Southern areas, while shellbark hickories are naturally more common in Northern areas.
- Shagbark hickories thrive on slightly higher land that's better drained.
- Black and English walnuts grow in deep, rich but well-drained soil. They will thrive on slight slopes or in sandy soil along rivers.
- Chestnuts are native to sandy mountainsides with acidic soil; good drainage is critical.

It's also important to choose a spot with good air circulation and lots of sunlight. Before finalizing your choice, make sure you have enough room for the plants to reach their mature size. Pecans, for instance, can reach 150 feet (45 m) tall and 50 feet (15 m) across.

You'll actually need twice this space, however, since pecans and most other nut-bearing plants require a second compatible tree for pollination. Also keep in mind that big trees can drop their nuts quickly, so keep them away from patios, walkways, children's playing areas, and other places where the falling nuts could be a problem.

Most nut trees have long taproots, which make them hard to handle in the nursery and hard to get going when planted out. It's best to start with a young field-grown plant that's been specially handled several times to develop a bushy set of roots.

Put the young plant in a broad, deep hole with loose soil. Then keep the planting site moist until the tree begins growing strongly.

Walnuts have deep roots, so it's easy to plant under them. However, they also release a substance that is harmful to some plants.

Strawberries are super for containers. Try them in pots or hanging baskets, or grow them in special "strawberry jars."

Easy Edibles for Containers

Containers are a great way to grow fruit crops without putting a lot of work into a full-scale garden. You can have a steady supply of fresh produce right outside your door, within easy reach for a finishing touch to any meal. Mix some flowers in with your edibles, and you can have a container garden that's pretty as well as productive.

Mixed berries

Choose Compact Crops

Standard selections of some fruits can get too big for successful container culture. Fortunately, plant breeders have worked with many crops to develop compact cultivars specifically suited for container growing. Read the descriptions in your favorite seed and nursery catalogs to find cultivars that are recommended for container growing.

Consider the Container

You'll get better yields if you use a good-sized container—one that can hold at least 2 gallons (9 L) of potting mix. If you're more interested in good production than how beautiful your containers are, 5-gallon (23 L) plastic buckets make excellent inexpensive and effective

containers. (You may be able to find some used buckets you can recycle from a restaurant or delicatessen. Be sure to drill plenty of drainage holes in the bottom.)

Fruits for Containers

Strawberries You can buy strawberry plants from your local garden center in the spring and pop them into pots and planters for luscious, full-sized fruit. Or you might want to try the super-flavorful alpine types like 'Mignonette', which can be grown from seed. Their great taste more than makes up for the smaller size of the berries. Strawberries look good in almost any container or hanging basket. There are even special planters called strawberry barrels, with holes all around the sides so you can cover the barrel with berry plants.

Blueberries Another top container choice is blueberries. They're small shrubs that grow only a few feet high, so they don't need a lot of pruning. Even if you have room for them in the garden, you may choose to grow your blueberries in containers; it's easier to meet the plants' need for acid soil by blending a special container growing mix. Use a soil mix that's at least one-quarter to one-half acidic peat moss and never add any lime, and you'll have blueberries before you know it.

Citrus How about your very own lemons, limes, and oranges? Citrus trees can't tolerate frost, but they grow nicely in containers, especially if you buy plants that have been grafted onto a special dwarfing rootstock to keep them small.

Containers allow you to grow fruit in areas that you normally can't plant, such as patios and sunny decks.

The plants need plenty of sun and fertilizer in the summer. Bring them inside in the winter (except in very mild climates, where they can stay outside year-round), and place them next to a very bright south-facing window. Not only will they give you fruit but the flowers are also wonderfully fragrant.

Dwarf Fruit Trees You can enjoy harvesting full-sized apples, peaches, and cherries from container-sized dwarf fruit trees. Provide rooting room by choosing a container at least 30 inches (75 cm) wide and deep. In cold climates (Zone 5 or colder), move the pots to an unheated garage during the coldest part of the winter. In warmer zones, potted fruit trees can stay outside through the winter. Some fruits—including apples and peaches—need a certain amount of cold to set fruit properly, so if you live in Zone 8 or warmer, make sure you buy "low-chill" cultivars, developed especially to grow well in your climate.

Trees in containers can be heavy; the containers will be easier to move if you set them on a wheeled platform.

Encyclopedia of Popular Garden Plants

Plants are arranged alphabetically by their botanical names, with their most often-used common name displayed prominently. Each plant is illustrated with a color photograph to make identification easy. Here you'll find plant descriptions, cultivation tips, and a guide to the right climate zone.

Acanthus mollis
ACANTHACEAE

BEAR'S-BREECH

Bear's-breech is a robust plant with lustrous evergreen leaves, 1–2 feet (30–60 cm) long and edged with jagged teeth. It grows from a stout crown with thick, fleshy roots.

Flower color Unusual 1-inch (2.5-cm) flowers with three white petals and overarching purple hoods carried in tall spikes.

Flowering time Late spring or summer; flowers open sequentially up the spike.

Height and spread 2½–4 feet (75–120 cm) tall; 3 feet (90 cm) wide. Spreads to form broad clumps.

Temperature requirements Zones 8–10. Sensitive to winter frost and humidity.

Position Evenly moist, humus-rich soil. Full sun to partial shade.

Cultivation Mulch after the ground freezes in winter and remove mulch gradually in spring to protect plants from heaving. Keep moist; dry soil will reduce the size of the leaves.

Propagation Divide plants in spring when they first emerge or take root cuttings in spring or late fall. Roots left in the ground when plants are divided will form new shoots.

Pest and disease prevention Bait slugs with pans of beer set flush with the surface of the soil.

Landscape use Use bear's-breeches as foundation plantings or as bold accents in formal and informal gardens.

Achillea filipendulina
COMPOSITAE

FERN-LEAVED YARROW

Fern-leaved yarrow bears flat-topped heads of tiny flowers on dozens of tall, leafy stems. This aromatic herb grows from fibrous roots and has deeply incised, ferny, olive green leaves.

Flower color Dozens of tightly packed golden yellow flowers cluster in heads 4–5 inches (10–12.5 cm) across.

Flowering time Summer. Flowers last for several weeks; rebloom if deadheaded.

Height and spread 3–4 feet (90–120 cm) tall; 3 feet (90 cm) wide.

Temperature requirements Zones 3–9. Thrives in moderate summer humidity.

Position Average, dry to moist, well-drained soil. Full sun to light shade.

Cultivation Plants spread rapidly and need frequent division. Lift and divide clumps every three years to keep vigorous.

Propagation Take tip cuttings in spring or early summer. Divide in early spring or fall. Replant healthy divisions into soil enriched with organic matter.

Pest and disease prevention Plants develop powdery mildew, a cottony white coating on the leaves, especially in areas with warm humid nights. Rot causes stems to blacken and topple over. Remove and destroy all affected parts and dust plants with sulfur.

Landscape use Plant at the front or middle of formal perennial borders or with grasses in wildflower meadows. Use them in cutting gardens or on dry, sunny banks.

Alstroemeria aurantiaca
AMARYLLIDACEAE

PERUVIAN LILY

Peruvian lilies have tall, leafy stems crowned by open clusters of flaring, saucer-shaped flowers. The gray-green leaves are narrow and pointed. Plants grow from thick, fibrous roots.

Flower color Showy orange or yellow flowers with brownish purple flares on the upper petals.

Flowering time Throughout summer.

Height and spread 2–3 feet (60–90 cm) tall; 2 feet (60 cm) wide.

Temperature requirements Zones 7–10.

Position Evenly moist but well-drained, humus-rich soil. Full sun to partial shade; protect from strong winds.

Cultivation Plant dormant roots in early spring or fall. Growth begins early in the season, and plants may be damaged by late frost. Mulch with organic matter in fall to avoid frost heaving. Achieves best performance after the third year.

Propagation Divide clumps in early spring or fall. Take care not to damage the brittle roots. Sow fresh seed indoors after 4–6 weeks of cold (35°–40°F [4°–5°C]), moist stratification. To stratify, mix seed with damp peat moss or seed-starting medium in a plastic bag and close with a twist-tie. Place the bag in the refrigerator for the appropriate time period, then sow the mixture as you would other seed.

Pest and disease prevention No serious pests or diseases.

Landscape use Plant in beds and borders.

Anemone x *hybrida*
RANUNCULACEAE

JAPANESE ANEMONE

Japanese anemone produces clouds of flowers on slender stems. The deeply divided, hairy leaves are mostly basal. Stem leaves have fewer dissections. Plants grow from thick, tuberous roots.

Flower color Ranges from white to pink and rose; single or double blooms.
Flowering time Late summer and fall.
Height and spread 3–5 feet (90–150 cm) tall; 2–3 feet (60–90 cm) wide.
Temperature requirements Zones 5–8.
Position Humus-rich, evenly moist soil. Full sun to light shade. Protect from hot afternoon sun in warmer zones.
Cultivation Spreads by creeping underground stems to form broad clumps once established. Thin overgrown clumps in spring if bloom wanes. Replant into soil that has been enriched with organic matter. Mulch plants in colder zones.
Propagation Take root cuttings after plants go dormant in fall. Sow fresh seed outdoors in summer or fall. Divide in early spring.
Pest and disease prevention No serious pests or diseases.
Landscape use Group with other late-season perennials and ornamental grasses. Combine with shrubs or ferns in moist, open shade.
Cultivars 'Honorine Jobert' bears pure white single blooms. 'Margarete' has deep pink semidouble flowers. 'Max Vogel' has large pink single flowers.

Aquilegia x *hybrida*
RANUNCULACEAE

HYBRID COLUMBINE

Hybrid columbines are graceful plants with curious nodding flowers. Each flower has five spurred petals surrounded by five petal-like sepals. Plants grow from a thick taproot.

Flower color Single- or bi-colored variable flowers. Yellow, red, blue, purple, pink, and white are common. The spurs may be ½–4 inches (12–100 mm) long.
Flowering time Spring and early summer.
Height and spread 2–3 feet (60–90 cm) tall; 1–2 feet (30–60 cm) wide.
Temperature requirements Zones 3–9. Tolerate heat and cold.
Position Light, average to humus-rich, well-drained soil. Full sun to partial shade.
Cultivation They generally live two to four years, rewarding the gardener with a month or more of bloom. Self-sowing.
Propagation Sow seed outdoors in spring or summer. Sow indoors in winter after dry storing them in a refrigerator for four to six weeks.
Pest and disease prevention Leafminers create pale tunnels and blotches in the leaves. Remove and destroy damaged foliage. In severe cases spray weekly with insecticidal soap. Borers cause the plant to collapse dramatically. Remove and destroy all portions of affected plants.
Landscape use They look best in groups or drifts. Plant with spring and early-summer perennials, tulips, and daffodils. Combine with wildflowers in light shade.

Armeria maritima
PLUMBAGINACEAE

THRIFT

Thrift forms dense tufts of grasslike, gray-green evergreen leaves. The taller bloom stalks arise from the centers of the tightly packed rosettes.

Flower color Small pink flowers crowded into rounded 1-inch (2.5-cm) heads.
Flowering time Late spring and summer.
Height and spread 10–14 inches (25–35 cm) tall; 8–10 inches (20–25 cm) wide.
Temperature requirements Zones 4–8.
Position Average to humus-rich, moist but well-drained soil. Full sun. Prefers cool nights and low humidity.
Cultivation Drought-tolerant once established; will grow in rock crevices where water is scarce. Tolerates air- and soilborne salt; perfect for seaside gardens.
Propagation Divide clumps in early spring or fall. Sow seed indoors in winter on a warm (70°F [21°C]) seedbed.
Pest and disease prevention No serious pests or diseases.
Landscape use Plant in rock and wall gardens or along paths.
Other common names Sea pink.
Cultivars 'Alba' has white flowers on 5-inch (12.5-cm) stems. 'Dusseldorf Pride' has wine red flowers on 6–8-inch (15–20 cm) stems. 'Robusta' has 3-inch (7.5-cm) pink flower heads on 12–15-inch (30–37.5-cm) stems. 'Vindictive' is only 6 inches (15 cm) tall with bright rose pink flowers.

Aruncus dioicus
ROSACEAE

GOAT'S BEARD

Goat's beards are showy shrub-like perennials with large three-lobed leaves and airy plumes of flowers. Male and female flowers are borne on separate plants.

Flower color Creamy white flowers with small petals.
Flowering time Late spring and early summer.
Height and spread 3–6 feet (90–180 cm) tall; 3–5 feet (90–150 cm) wide.
Temperature requirements Zones 3–7; avoid areas with hot nights.
Position Moist, humus-rich soil. Full sun (in cooler zones) to partial shade.
Cultivation Plant 4–5 feet (1.2–1.5 m) apart to allow for the plants' impressive mature size. The tough rootstocks are difficult to move once established. Divide plants only if necessary to revitalize the clumps. Lift in early spring and replant strong, healthy divisions into soil that has been enriched with organic matter.
Propagation Sow seed in summer outdoors or inside on a warm (70°F [21°C]) seedbed.
Pest and disease prevention No serious pests or diseases.
Landscape use Use with ferns, wildflowers, and hostas in a lightly shaded woodland garden or as an accent with flowering shrubs. Combines well with other perennials in beds and borders.

Aster novae-angliae
COMPOSITAE

NEW ENGLAND ASTER

New England aster is a tall, stately plant with hairy stems and clasping, lance-shaped leaves. Most selections are best planted at the back of the perennial border.

Flower color Lavender to purple 1½–2-inch (3.5–5-cm) flowers with bright yellow centers. Flowers may vary in color from white to pink and rose.
Flowering time Late summer through fall.
Height and spread 3–6 feet (90–180 cm) tall; 3 feet (90 cm) wide. Matures into broad clumps.
Temperature requirements Zones 3–8.
Position Moist, humus-rich soil. Full sun to light shade.
Cultivation Clumps become quite large with age. Divide every three to four years in spring. Plants may need staking.
Propagation Take 4–6-inch (10–15-cm) stem cuttings in late spring or early summer. Divide in early spring or fall.
Pest and disease prevention Powdery mildew turns leaves dull gray. Thin stems to promote air circulation. Dust affected plants with sulfur.
Landscape use Plant with fall perennials like sunflowers (*Helianthus* spp.), Japanese anemone (*Anemone* x *hybrida*), and ornamental grasses.
Cultivars 'Alma Potschke' has dark salmon-pink flowers on 2–4-foot (60–120-cm) plants. 'Purple Dome' is a dwarf selection with royal purple flowers.

Astilbe x arendsii
SAXIFRAGACEAE

ASTILBE

Astilbes have showy flower clusters and ferny, dissected leaves with shiny broad leaflets. The emerging spring shoots are often tinged with red.

Flower color Upright, often-plumed flower clusters bear tightly packed, fuzzy blooms in shades of red, pink, rose, lilac, cream, and white.
Flowering time Spring and early summer.
Height and spread 2–4 feet (60–120 cm) tall; 2–3 feet (60–90 cm) wide. Leafy clumps spread steadily outward.
Temperature requirements Zones 3–9.
Position Moist, slightly acid, humus-rich soil. Full to partial shade; tolerates more sun in cool-summer areas.
Cultivation Benefits from an annual application of balanced organic fertilizer. Top-dress with compost or lift and replant the clumps if crowns rise above the soil. Divide clumps every three to four years and replant into soil enriched with organic matter. Keep plants well watered.
Propagation Propagate the true species by sowing fresh seed outdoors in summer or early fall. Propagate cultivars by spring or fall division only.
Pest and disease prevention Spider mites may be a problem in warm areas. Spray with insecticidal soap as necessary. Control root rot with good drainage and good air circulation.
Landscape use Plant at stream- or pondside and in borders.

Aurinia saxatilis
CRUCIFERAE

BASKET-OF-GOLD

Basket-of-gold produces mounds of 6-inch (15-cm) oblong gray-green leaves from a thick crown. Hairy leaves and deep roots help the plant endure dry soil and warm temperatures.

Flower color Brilliant yellow flowers have four rounded petals and are carried in upright, branched clusters.
Flowering time Early spring.
Height and spread 10–12 inches (25–30 cm) tall; 12 inches (30 cm) wide.
Temperature requirements Zones 3–7. Tolerates hot, dry conditions.
Position Average, well-drained, loamy or sandy soil. Full sun. Avoid excessively hot and humid climates.
Cultivation Clumps spread by creeping stems and may flop after flowering. Cut stems back by two thirds after flowering to encourage compact growth.
Propagation Divide in fall. Take stem cuttings in spring or fall. Sow seed in fall.
Pest and disease prevention Heavy moist soils and high humidity will encourage root rot. Plant in well-drained soils only.
Landscape use Basket-of-gold lends color to rock walls, rock gardens, and walkways. Combine with rock cresses (*Aubrieta* spp.) and pinks (*Dianthus* spp.).
Cultivars 'Citrinum' has clear lemon yellow flowers. 'Compactum' forms tight clumps only 8 inches (20 cm) tall. 'Sunny Border Apricot' has peach-colored flowers.

Boltonia asteroides
COMPOSITAE

BOLTONIA

Boltonias are tall, late-season perennials with masses of flowers smothering the gray-green willowlike foliage. The mounded plants are lovely in foliage; the flowers are a bonus.

Flower color A profusion of 1-inch (2.5-cm) white daisies with bright yellow centers is carried in open clusters.
Flowering time Late summer through fall.
Height and spread 4–6 feet (1.2–1.8 m) tall; 4 feet (1.2 m) wide.
Temperature requirements Zones 3–9.
Position Moist, humus-rich soil. Full sun to light shade. Dry soil produces much smaller plants.
Cultivation These easy-to-grow plants form sturdy, dense stems that will seldom need staking.
Propagation Divide oversized clumps in spring. Take cuttings in early summer. Seed collected from cultivars will produce seedlings unlike the parent plants and in most cases inferior to them.
Pest and disease prevention No serious pests or diseases.
Landscape use Combine with fall-blooming perennials like asters, Japanese anemones (*Anemone* x *hybrida*), goldenrods (*Solidago* spp.), Joe-Pye weeds (*Eupatorium* spp.), and ornamental grasses.
Cultivars 'Pink Beauty' sports soft-pink flowers in open clusters. Cool summers produce brighter colors. 'Snowbank' is a compact selection with white flowers.

Campanula carpatica
CAMPANULACEAE

CARPATHIAN HAREBELL

Adaptable Carpathian harebell spreads to form tidy mounds of dark green leaves topped with cup-shaped, blue-purple flowers. Mulch to keep the roots cool in warm climates.

Flower color Clumps of lively blue-purple or white flowers.
Flowering time Early summer.
Height and spread 9 inches (22.5 cm); slightly wider spread.
Temperature requirements Zones 3-8.
Position Well-drained, moist, fertile soil. Full sun; light shade in hotter sites.
Cultivation Mulch with compost during summer. Water in drought.
Propagation Short-lived unless you divide and renew every couple of years. Deadhead for an extended bloom period or leave a few flowers on so the plant can self-sow.
Pest and disease prevention Trap slugs and snails in saucers of beer set shallowly in the ground near the plants.
Landscape use Set in clumps or rows in front of a flower or shrub border. Or use plants individually in a rock garden or beside a stone patio.
Cultivars 'Alba' has pure white flowers.

Catananche caerulea
COMPOSITAE

CUPID'S DART

Cupid's dart produces tufts of narrow, woolly leaves from a fibrous rootstock. The straw-like flowers look great in the summer garden and dry easily for flower arrangements.

Flower color Blue 2-inch (5-cm) flowers resemble asters but lack the bold yellow center. Carried singly on wiry stems.
Flowering time Summer.
Height and spread 18–24 inches (45–60 cm) tall; 10–12 inches (25–30 cm) wide.
Temperature requirements Zones 4–9. Heat-tolerant.
Position Light, well-drained, humus-rich soil. Full sun. Good drainage is imperative for healthy growth.
Cultivation Plants may be short-lived, especially in heavy soil. Divide plants every year to promote longevity.
Propagation Divide in fall. Take 2–3-inch (5–7.5-cm) root cuttings in fall or winter. Sow seed indoors in early spring. Plants will bloom the first year.
Pest and disease prevention No serious pests or diseases.
Landscape use Use in mass plantings in rock gardens or at the front of a dry, sunny perennial garden. Combine with yarrows and sundrops (*Oenothera* spp.).
Cultivars 'Blue Giant' is a stout cultivar with dark blue flowers. 'Major' has lavender-blue flowers on 3-foot (90-cm) stems.

Chrysanthemum x superbum
COMPOSITAE

SHASTA DAISY

Shasta daisies are showy, summer-blooming plants with dense clusters of shiny 10-inch (25-cm), deep green, toothed leaves and short, creeping, fibrous-rooted stems.

Flower color Bright white 3-inch (7.5-cm) daisies with large, bright yellow centers are carried on stout, leafy stems.
Flowering time Throughout summer.
Height and spread 1–3 feet (30–90 cm) tall; 2 feet (60 cm) wide.
Temperature requirements Zones 3–10. Extremely cold- and heat-tolerant. Exact zones vary by cultivar.
Position Average to rich, well-drained soil. Full sun. Tolerates seaside conditions but not waterlogged soil.
Cultivation Shasta daisies are easy-care perennials. Deadhead plants to promote continued bloom. Plants grow quickly but may be short-lived especially in warmer zones. Divide and replant clumps in organically enriched soil every three to four years to keep them vigorous.
Propagation Remove offsets from the main clump or divide in spring.
Pest and disease prevention No serious pests or diseases.
Landscape use Combine with summer-blooming perennials like daylilies, irises, and poppies. In a seaside garden, plant them with blanket flowers (*Gaillardia* spp.) and coreopsis.
Other names *Leucanthemum x superbum*.

Coreopsis verticillata
COMPOSITAE

THREAD-LEAVED COREOPSIS

Thread-leaved coreopsis is an airy, rounded plant with threadlike, three-lobed leaves and masses of bright yellow summer flowers. Plants grow from a fibrous-rooted crown.

Flower color The 1–2-inch (2.5–5-cm) starry flowers are butter to golden yellow.
Flowering time Throughout summer.
Height and spread 1–3 feet (30–90 cm) tall; 2–3 feet (60–90 cm) wide.
Temperature requirements Zones 3–9.
Position Average to rich, moist but well-drained soil. Full sun or light shade; drought-tolerant once established.
Cultivation Thread-leaved coreopsis is an easy-care perennial that demands little attention once established. Plants eventually die out at the center. Divide old clumps and replant in enriched soil.
Propagation Divide in spring or fall. Take stem cuttings in early summer.
Pest and disease prevention No serious pests or diseases.
Landscape use Perfect for the front of the border with cranesbills (*Geranium* spp.), yarrows, daylilies, and coneflowers (*Rudbeckia* and *Echinacea* spp.). Combine them with ornamental grasses or use a mass planting with shrubs.
Cultivars 'Golden Showers' grows 2 feet (60 cm) tall with golden yellow flowers. 'Moonbeam' is a spreading plant with pale yellow flowers. 'Zagreb' is a compact selection similar to 'Golden Showers'.

Delphinium x *elatum hybrids*
RANUNCULACEAE

HYBRID DELPHINIUM

Hybrid delphiniums are stately border plants with dense flower clusters atop tall stems with deeply cut, palmately lobed leaves. Plants grow from stout crowns with thick, fleshy roots.

Flower color White through all shades of true blue to lavender and purple.
Flowering time Late spring through summer. Plants may rebloom in fall.
Height and spread 4½–6 feet (1.35–1.8 cm) tall; 2–3 feet (60–90 cm) wide.
Temperature requirements Zones 4–7.
Position Evenly moist but well-drained, fertile, humus-rich soil. Full sun.
Cultivation Often short-lived in warm climates. Delphiniums benefit from an annual spring top-dressing of organic fertilizer. Set out new plants in spring, thin the clumps to three to five stems as they emerge. To encourage plants to rebloom, cut off old flowering stems above the foliage below the flower spike. Divide overgrown plants.
Propagation Divide in spring. Sow fresh seed in summer or fall. Take cuttings in spring from the new shoots; use the stems removed from thinning for propagation.
Pest and disease prevention Powdery mildew may cause white blotches on the leaves. Dust affected parts with sulfur.
Landscape use Plant at the rear of borders where their showy spires will tower over other summer-blooming perennials.

Dianthus plumarius
CARYOPHYLLACEAE

COTTAGE PINKS

Cottage pinks are popular, sweet-scented plants for the garden or for cutting. The broad, mounded plants produce dense clusters of 3-inch (7.5-cm), blue-green, grasslike leaves.

Flower color Fragrant white or pink flowers are borne in clusters on wiry stems.
Flowering time Early to midsummer.
Height and spread 1½–2 feet (45–60 cm) tall; 1 foot (30 cm) wide.
Temperature requirements Zones 3–9. Tolerates extreme heat and cold.
Position Average, well-drained, sandy, or loamy soil. Full sun. The soil should be neutral or only slightly acid for best growth. Plants tolerate alkaline soil.
Cultivation Plants may be short-lived, especially in warmer zones. Divide clumps every two to three years.
Propagation Layer or take stem cuttings from the foliage rosettes in summer. Strip leaves from the lower third of a 2–3-inch (5–7.5-cm) cutting. Place cutting in a medium of one part vermiculite and two parts sand or perlite to allow excellent drainage and air circulation.
Pest and disease prevention Rust causes yellow blotches on the upper surface of the leaves and raised orange spots on the lower surface. To discourage rust, thin clumps for better air circulation and dust with sulfur.
Landscape use Plant at the front of borders or use them as an edging along paths. Grow them in sunny rock gardens.

Dicentra spectabilis
FUMARIACEAE

COMMON BLEEDING HEART

Common bleeding hearts are beloved, old-fashioned perennials with strings of hearts held above deeply divided blue-green foliage. Plants grow from thick, fleshy roots.

Flower color Bright pink heart-shaped flowers consist of two reflexed lobes with a central column that resembles a dangling drop of blood.
Flowering time Early spring to early summer.
Height and spread 1–2½ feet (30–75 cm) tall; 2–3 feet (60–90 cm) wide.
Temperature requirements Zones 2–9. Extremely tolerant of heat and cold. Mulch in winter in colder zones.
Position Evenly moist, humus-rich soil. Partial shade; full sun in cooler zones.
Cultivation They will bloom for four to six weeks in spring. In warm climates or if soil is dry, plants will go dormant after blooming. Top-dress with well-rotted manure in early spring to maintain soil fertility. If plants lose vigor, lift and divide.
Propagation Divide clumps in fall. Sow fresh seed in summer. Take root cuttings in late summer.
Pest and disease prevention No serious pests or diseases.
Landscape use Plant common bleeding hearts with spring bulbs, primroses, and wildflowers for a striking spring display. In warm zones combine them with hostas to fill the void left by the declining foliage.

Digitalis x *mertonensis*
SCROPHULARIACEAE

STRAWBERRY FOXGLOVE

The popular strawberry foxglove has fuzzy, broad, lance-shaped leaves. Rosettes of foliage form at the base of the flowering stems and persist over winter.

Flower color The 2–3-inch (5–7.5-cm) tubular flowers are flushed with pink, rose, or purple on the outside and heavily spotted with dark purple or brown on the inside. Some selections are pure white.
Flowering time Plants flower throughout summer and often rebloom.
Height and spread 3–4 feet (90–120 cm) tall; 1 foot (30 cm) wide.
Temperature requirements Zones 3–8.
Position Moist but well-drained, humus-rich soil. Full sun to partial shade.
Cultivation Strawberry foxgloves are easy-care perennials that bloom tirelessly with little care. Divide overgrown clumps and replant into soil that has been enriched with organic matter. Remove spent bloom stalks to promote rebloom. Leave one stalk to self-sow.
Propagation Divide in spring or fall. Sow fresh seed outdoors in fall. Seedlings emerge the next spring and will bloom the second year.
Pest and disease prevention No serious pests or diseases.
Landscape use Plant at the middle or rear of perennial gardens. In informal and cottage gardens combine them with ferns and ornamental grasses. Use mass plantings along a wall or fence.

Doronicum orientale
COMPOSITAE

LEOPARD'S BANE

Leopard's bane is a brightly colored spring daisy with deep green, triangular leaves in open clusters from a fibrous-rooted crown.

Flower color Dozens of 1–2-inch (2.5–5-cm) bright yellow single daisies are borne on slender, leafless stems.
Flowering time Spring and early summer.
Height and spread 1–2 feet (30–60 cm) tall; 1 foot (30 cm) wide.
Temperature requirements Zones 3–8.
Position Moist, humus-rich soil. Full sun to shade. Soil must not dry out while plant is actively growing.
Cultivation Leopard's banes emerge early in spring and may be damaged by late frosts. Plants go dormant after flowering in warmer zones. In colder zones, the foliage remains all season, so moist soil is imperative. Mulch will help keep the soil cool. Divide clumps every two to three years to keep them vigorous.
Propagation Divide in spring or fall. Sow seed indoors in late winter or early spring.
Pest and disease prevention No serious pests or diseases.
Landscape use Combine with clustered bellflower (*Campanula glomerata*), Virginia bluebells (*Mertensia virginica*), spring bulbs, and wildflowers. Plant foliage plants such as hostas to fill the voids when plants go dormant.
Cultivars 'Magnificum' has showy 2-inch (5-cm) flowers.

Echinacea purpurea
COMPOSITAE

PURPLE CONEFLOWER

Purple coneflowers are showy summer daisies with sparse, 6-inch (15-cm) oval or broadly lance-shaped leaves on stout, hairy stems. Plants grow from thick, deep taproots.

Flower color Red-violet to rose pink flowers have broad, drooping rays (petal-like structures) surrounding raised, bristly cones.
Flowering time Mid- to late summer.
Height and spread 2–4 feet (60–120 cm) tall; 1–2 feet (30–60 cm) wide.
Temperature requirements Zones 3–8. Extremely heat-tolerant.
Position Average to humus-rich, moist but well-drained soil. Full sun. Drought-tolerant once established.
Cultivation Plants increase from basal buds to form broad, long-lived clumps. Division is seldom necessary and is not recommended.
Propagation Sow seed outdoors in fall or indoors after stratification. To stratify, mix seed with moist peat moss or seed-starting medium in a plastic bag. Close the bag with a twist-tie and place it in the refrigerator for four to six weeks. Sow the mixture as you would normal seed. Take root cuttings in fall.
Pest and disease prevention No serious pests or diseases.
Landscape use Plant in formal perennial gardens or meadow and prairie gardens.

Erigeron speciosus
COMPOSITAE

DAISY FLEABANE

Daisy fleabane forms leafy clumps of hairy, 6-inch (15-cm) lance-shaped leaves that spring from fibrous-rooted crowns. The colorful flowers bloom in summer.

Flower color The pretty 1½-inch (3.5 cm) aster-like flowers have white, pink, rose, or purple rays which surround bright yellow centers.

Flowering time Early to midsummer; occasional rebloom.

Height and spread 1½–2½ feet (45–75 cm) tall; 1–2 feet (30–60 cm) wide.

Temperature requirements Zones 2–9. Tolerant of heat and cold.

Position Moist but well-drained, average to humus-rich soil. Full sun to light shade.

Cultivation Fleabanes are long-lived perennials that benefit from division every two to three years.

Propagation Divide in fall. Take cuttings in spring before the flower buds form. Sow seed outdoors in fall or indoors in spring.

Pest and disease prevention No serious pests or diseases.

Landscape use Plant at the front of beds and borders with summer-blooming perennials like cranesbills (*Geranium* spp.), cinquefoils (*Potentilla* spp.), evening primroses (*Oenothera* spp.), and phlox. Daisy fleabanes make long-lasting and delightful cut flowers.

Filipendula rubra
ROSACEAE

QUEEN-OF-THE-PRAIRIE

Queen-of-the-prairie is a towering perennial with huge flower heads on stout, leafy stalks. The showy 1-foot (30-cm) leaves are deeply lobed and starlike. Plants grow from creeping stems.

Flower color Small five-petaled pink flowers are crowded into large heads that resemble cotton candy.

Flowering time Late spring and early summer.

Height and spread 4–6 feet (1.2–1.8 cm) tall; 2–4 feet (60–120 cm) wide.

Temperature requirements Zones 3–9.

Position Evenly moist, humus-rich soil. Full sun to light shade. Plants will not tolerate prolonged dryness.

Cultivation Established clumps make an arresting display when in bloom. If leaves become tattered after bloom, cut plants to the ground; new leaves will emerge. Plants spread quickly in moist soil. Divide every three to four years to keep them from overtaking their neighbors.

Propagation Division is the best method. Lift clumps in spring or fall, or dig crowns from the edge of the clump. Sow seed indoors in spring.

Pest and disease prevention No serious pests or diseases.

Landscape use Plant queen-of-the-prairie at the rear of borders with shrub roses, irises, daylilies, and phlox. Use them at the side of ponds with ferns and ornamental grasses.

Gaillardia x grandiflora
COMPOSITAE

BLANKET FLOWER

The showy hybrid blanket flower blooms throughout the summer on loose stems with hairy, lobed leaves. Plants grow from fibrous-rooted crowns and may be short-lived.

Flower color Ragged yellow-and-orange daisy-like flowers have single or double rows of toothed petal-like rays surrounding a raised yellow center.

Flowering time Throughout summer.

Height and spread 2–3 feet (60–90 cm) tall; 2 feet (60 cm) wide.

Temperature requirements Zones 4–9.

Position Average to poor, well-drained soil. Full sun. Rich, moist soil causes plants to overgrow and flop.

Cultivation Blanket flowers are drought-tolerant and thrive in seaside conditions. Divide every two to three years.

Propagation Divide in early spring. Sow seed outdoors in fall or indoors in spring after stratification. To stratify, mix seed with moist peat moss or seed-starting medium in a plastic bag. Close the bag with a twist-tie and place it in the refrigerator for four to six weeks. Then sow the mixture as you would normal seed. Seedlings often bloom the first year.

Pest and disease prevention No serious pests or diseases.

Landscape use Choose blanket flowers for rock gardens, seaside gardens, or borders.

Gaura lindheimeri
Onagraceae

White gaura

White gaura is a shrubby perennial with airy flower clusters on wiry stems and small, hairy leaves. This dependable, long-blooming plant grows from a thick, deep taproot.

Flower color Unusual white flowers are tinged with pink. They have four triangular petals, long curled stamens (male reproductive structures), and dance in slender spikes above the foliage.

Flowering time Throughout summer.

Height and spread 3–4 feet (90–120 cm) tall; 3 feet (90 cm) wide.

Temperature requirements Zones 5–9. Extremely heat-tolerant.

Position Moist, well-drained, average to rich soil. Full sun.

Cultivation White gaura is an easy-care perennial that thrives for years with little attention. Plants bloom nonstop all summer despite high heat and humidity. Remove old bloom stalks to make way for the new ones.

Propagation Sow seed outdoors in spring or fall. Self-sown seedlings are likely.

Pest and disease prevention No serious pests or diseases.

Landscape use White gaura is a lovely addition to formal and informal gardens alike. The flower clusters look like a swirl of dancing butterflies. Combine them with low-mounding perennials like verbenas (*Verbena* spp.), cranesbills (*Geranium* spp.), and sedums.

Helenium autumnale
Compositae

Common sneezeweed

Common sneezeweed is a showy, late-season perennial with tall, leafy stems that spring from a fibrous-rooted crown. The hairy, lance-shaped leaves are edged with a few large teeth.

Flower color The 2-inch (5-cm), golden yellow daisy-like flowers have broad, petal-like rays.

Flowering time Late summer and fall.

Height and spread 3–5 feet (90–150 cm) tall; 2–3 feet (60–90 cm) wide.

Temperature requirements Zones 3–8.

Position Evenly moist, humus-rich soil. Full sun or light shade. Tolerates wet soil.

Cultivation Either stake it or pinch the stem tips in early summer to promote compact growth. Divide the clumps every three to four years to keep them vigorous.

Propagation Divide in spring or fall. Take stem cuttings in early summer. Sow seed outdoors in spring or fall.

Pest and disease prevention No serious pests or diseases.

Landscape use Common sneezeweeds offer late-season color. Combine them with asters, goldenrods (*Solidago* spp.), and garden phlox (*Phlox paniculata*).

Other common names Helen's flower.

Cultivars 'Butterpat' has bright yellow flowers on 3–4-foot (90–120-cm) stems. 'Crimson Beauty' has mahogany flowers. 'Riverton Beauty' has golden yellow flowers with bronze-red centers.

Hemerocallis hybrids
Liliaceae

Daylily

Daylily hybrids are among the most popular perennials. Although each flower lasts only one day, a profusion of new buds keeps the plants in bloom for a month or more.

Flower color Daylily flowers vary in color and form. The majority of the wild species are orange or yellow with wide petals and narrow, petal-like sepals. Modern hybrids come in many colors.

Flowering time Spring through summer.

Height and spread 1–5 feet (30–150 cm) tall; 2–3 feet (60–90 cm) wide.

Temperature requirements Zones 3–9.

Position Evenly moist, average to humus-rich soil. Full sun to light shade.

Cultivation Plant container-grown or bareroot plants in spring or fall. Place the crowns just below the soil surface. Plants take a year to become established and then spread quickly to form dense clumps.

Propagation Divide hybrids in fall or spring. Seed-grown plants will be variable and are often inferior to the parent plant.

Pest and disease prevention Aphids and thrips may attack the foliage and flower buds. Wash off aphids with a stream of water or spray them with insecticidal soap. Thrips make small white lines in the foliage and may deform flower buds if damage is severe. Spray with insecticidal soap or a botanical insecticide.

Landscape use Perfect for mass plantings in beds and borders.

Hosta hybrids
LILIACEAE

HOSTA

Hostas are indispensable foliage plants for shaded gardens. Their thick, pleated or puckered leaves grow from stout crowns with thick fleshy roots.

Flower color Lavender, purple, or white flowers are carried in slender spikes.
Flowering time Summer or fall depending on hybrid and origin.
Height and spread 6 inches–3 feet (15–90 cm) tall; 6 inches–5 feet (15–150 cm) wide.
Temperature requirements Zones 3–8. Some selections are hardy to Zone 2.
Position Evenly moist, humus-rich soil. Light to full shade. Adaptable to both dry and wet soil conditions. Filtered sun encourages the best leaf color in the gold- and blue-leaved forms. All hostas need protection from hot afternoon sun, especially in warm zones.
Cultivation Hostas take several years to reach mature form and size; allow ample room when planting. New shoots are slow to emerge in spring, so take care not to damage them during spring cleanup.
Propagation Divide in late summer.
Pest and disease prevention Set shallow pans of beer flush with the soil surface to drown slugs and snails.
Landscape use Use the smaller cultivars to edge beds or as groundcover under shrubs and trees. Choose giants for creating drama in a mixed planting or alone as an accent.

Iris sibirica
IRIDICEAE

SIBERIAN IRIS

Siberian irises produce graceful early-summer flowers in a wide range of colors. Plants form tight fans of narrow swordlike leaves from slow-creeping rhizomes.

Flower color Flowers range in color from pure white, cream, and yellow to all shades of blue, violet, and purple. Some cultivars come close to true red.
Flowering time Early summer; some cultivars rebloom.
Height and spread 1–3 feet (30–90 cm) tall; 1–2 feet (30–60 cm) wide.
Temperature requirements Zones 3–9. Heat- and cold-tolerant.
Position Evenly moist, humus-rich soil. Full sun to partial shade. Plant bareroot iris in fall and container-grown plants in spring, summer, and fall.
Cultivation Siberian irises thrive for many years without division. If bloom begins to wane, divide and replant.
Propagation Divide plants in late summer. Seed collected from cultivars will be variable and often inferior to the parent plant. Sow fresh seed of the species outdoors in summer or fall.
Pest and disease prevention Susceptible to iris borer. Smash the grubs between your fingers while they are in the leaves. Dig up affected plants and cut off affected portions of the rhizome.
Landscape use Plant with perennials, ornamental grasses, and ferns.

Lobelia cardinalis
CAMPANULACEAE

CARDINAL FLOWER

Cardinal flowers have fiery colored flower spikes on leafy stems and grow from a fibrous-rooted crown. The lance-shaped leaves may be fresh green or red-bronze.

Flower color Brilliant scarlet tubular flowers have three lower and two upper petals that look like delicate birds in flight.
Flowering time Late summer to fall.
Height and spread 2–4 feet (60–120 cm) tall; 1–2 feet (30–60 cm) wide.
Temperature requirements Zones 2–9.
Position Evenly moist, humus-rich soil. Full sun to partial shade.
Cultivation Cardinal flowers are shallow-rooted and subject to frost heaving. Where winters are cold, mulch plants to protect the crowns. In warmer zones winter mulch may rot the crowns. Replant in spring if frost has lifted them. Plants may be short-lived, but self-sown seedlings are numerous.
Propagation Divide in late fall or spring. Sow seed uncovered outdoors in fall or spring, or indoors in late winter. Seedlings grow quickly and will bloom the first year from seed.
Pest and disease prevention No serious pests or diseases.
Landscape use Cardinal flowers need even moisture so they are commonly used around pools, along streams, or in informal plantings. Combine them with irises, hostas, ligularias (*Ligularia* spp.), and ferns.

Lupinus polyphyllus
LEGUMINOSAE

WASHINGTON LUPINE

Washington lupine has conical flower spikes on stout stems with large palmately divided leaves. Plants grow from thick roots. Lupines add a dramatic vertical accent to borders.

Flower color The ¼-inch (18-mm), blue-purple or yellow pealike flowers are crowded into 1–2-foot (30–60-cm) spikes.
Flowering time Spring and summer.
Height and spread 3–5 feet (90–150 cm) tall; 2–3 feet (60–90 cm) wide.
Temperature requirements Zones 3–7. Sensitive to high summer temperatures.
Position Moist but well-drained, acid, humus-rich soil. Full sun to light shade.
Cultivation They are heavy feeders. Top-dress in spring with organic fertilizer. Protect plants from hot, dry winds.
Propagation Remove sideshoots from around the clump in fall. Sow seed outdoors in fall or inside in winter. Before sowing indoors, soak seed overnight and then stratify. To stratify, mix seed with moist peat moss or seed-starting medium in a plastic bag. Close the bag with a twist-tie and place it in the refrigerator for four to six weeks. Then sow the mixture as you would normal seed.
Pest and disease prevention No serious pests or diseases.
Landscape use Plant with border perennials like columbines (*Aquilegia* spp.), cranesbills (*Geranium* spp.), bellflowers (*Campanula* spp.), irises, and peonies.

Lychnis chalcedonica
CARYOPHYLLACEAE

MALTESE CROSS

Maltese cross is an old-fashioned perennial with brilliant flower clusters atop tall stems with opposite, oval leaves. Plants grow from fibrous-rooted crowns.

Flower color Brilliant scarlet flowers are held in compact, domed, terminal clusters.
Flowering time Midsummer.
Height and spread 2–3 feet (60–90 cm) tall; 1–1½ feet (30–45 cm) wide.
Temperature requirements Zones 4–8.
Position Average to humus-rich, moist but well-drained soil. Needs full sun to light shade.
Cultivation Maltese cross spreads quickly to form tight clumps. Divide every two to three years to keep it strong and healthy.
Propagation Divide in spring or fall. Sow seed outdoors in fall.
Pest and disease prevention No serious pests or diseases.
Landscape use Use the strong-colored flowers of Maltese cross to create excitement in a subdued scheme of blues and pale yellows. Perfect for hot color combinations with coneflowers (*Rudbeckia* spp.), blanket flowers (*Gaillardia* spp.), and sundrops (*Oenothera* spp.).

Monarda didyma
LABIATAE

BEE BALM

Bee balm is a lovely perennial with bright flowers on sturdy stems that grow from fast-creeping runners. The pointed oval leaves give Earl Grey tea its distinctive aroma and flavor.

Flower color Tight heads of tubular red flowers are surrounded by a whorl of colored leafy bracts (modified leaves).
Flowering time Summer.
Height and spread 2–4 feet (60–120 cm) tall; 2–3 feet (60–90 cm) wide.
Temperature requirements Zones 4–8.
Position Evenly moist, humus-rich soil. Full sun to partial shade. If plants dry out, the lower foliage will be shed.
Cultivation Plants spread quickly; divide every two to three years.
Propagation Divide in spring or fall. Sow seed indoors or outdoors in spring.
Pest and disease prevention Powdery mildew causes white blotches on the foliage and may cover the entire plant. Thin the stems for good air circulation. Cut affected plants to the ground.
Landscape use Plant in formal or informal gardens. Bee balm's lovely flowers add brilliant color to the summer garden and are favored by hummingbirds.
Other common names Bergamot, oswego tea.
Cultivars 'Blue Stocking' has violet flowers. 'Cambridge Scarlet' has brilliant scarlet flowers. 'Croftway Pink' is soft pink. 'Mahogany' has ruby red flowers.

Oenothera macrocarpon
ONAGRACEAE

OZARK SUNDROPS

Ozark sundrops are showy perennials with yellow flowers and narrow pale green leaves on sprawling stems. Plants grow from a deep taproot and spread by creeping stems.

Flower color Bright lemon yellow flowers are saucer-shaped and 3–4 inches (7.5–10 cm) wide.

Flowering time Late spring and early summer, sporadically through the season.

Height and spread 6–12 inches (15–30 cm) tall; 12–36 inches (30–90 cm) wide.

Temperature requirements Zones 4–8.

Position Average to humus-rich, well-drained soil. Full sun. Established plants are extremely drought- and heat-tolerant.

Cultivation Plants form large clumps with age so space at least 30 inches (75 cm) apart. Stems root as they spread.

Propagation Divide rosettes in early spring. Take stem cuttings in early summer. Sow seed outdoors in fall or indoors in early spring.

Pest and disease prevention No serious pests or diseases.

Cultivars 'Greencourt Lemon' has 2-inch (5-cm) soft, sulfur yellow flowers.

Landscape use Use ozark sundrops at the front of borders with phlox, cranesbills (*Geranium* spp.), catmints (*Nepeta* spp.), yarrows, and other early-season perennials. Performs well in rock gardens and looks lovely in meadow plantings.

Paeonia lactiflora
RANUNCULACEAE

COMMON GARDEN PEONY

Common garden peonies are shrub-like, with sturdy stalks clothed in compound, shiny green leaves. Plants grow from thick, fleshy roots and may live 100 years or more.

Flower color Ranges in color from white, cream, and yellow to pink, rose, burgundy, and scarlet. Flowers may be single, semidouble, or double.

Flowering time Common garden peonies are classified by their bloom time; early May (April in the South) blooming; mid-May blooming; and late May (early June in the North) blooming.

Height and spread 1½–3 feet (45–90 cm) tall; 3–4 feet (90–120 cm) wide.

Temperature requirements Zones 2–8.

Position Moist, humus-rich soil. Full sun to light shade. Good drainage is important.

Cultivation Plant container-grown peonies in spring or fall. Plant bareroot plants in September and October. Mulch new plants to protect from frost heaving. Taller selections and those with double flowers may need staking to keep their faces out of the mud. Lift plants in fall, divide the roots leaving at least one eye (bud) per division, and replant.

Propagation Divide in fall.

Pest and disease prevention Spray or dust foliage with an organically acceptable fungicide to discourage Botrytis.

Landscape use Combine with early spring bulbs like snowdrops and squills.

Papaver orientale
PAPAVERACEAE

ORIENTAL POPPY

Oriental poppies are prized for their colorful, crêpe-paper-like flowers. Plants produce rosettes of coarse, hairy, lobed foliage from a thick taproot. They often go dormant after flowering.

Flower color The 3–4-inch (7.5–10-cm) flowers have crinkled scarlet-red petals with black spots at their base. They surround the seedpod.

Flowering time Early summer.

Height and spread 2–3 feet (60–90 cm) tall; 2-feet (60–90 cm) wide.

Temperature requirements Zones 2–7.

Position Average to rich, well-drained, humus-rich soil. Full sun to light shade. Established plants are long-lived.

Cultivation In warm zones plants go dormant after flowering, leaving a bare spot. In fall new foliage rosettes emerge. Divide overgrown plants at this time.

Propagation Divide in fall. Take root cuttings in late summer, fall, or winter.

Pest and disease prevention No serious pests or diseases.

Landscape use Plant showy oriental poppies with border perennials and ornamental grasses. Combine them with bushy plants like catmints (*Nepeta* spp.) or asters which will fill the gap left by the declining foliage.

Cultivars 'Bonfire' has brilliant red flowers. 'Helen Elizabeth' has pale salmon-pink flowers without spots. 'Snow Queen' is pure white with large black spots.

Penstemon barbatus
SCROPHULARIACEAE

COMMON BEARDTONGUE

Common beardtongue is a showy plant with erect flower spikes clothed in shiny, broadly lance-shaped leaves. Flowering stems and basal foliage rosettes grow from fibrous-rooted crowns.

Flower color The 1–1½-inch (2.5–3.5 cm) irregular tubular pink flowers have two upper and three lower lips.
Flowering time Late spring to early summer.
Height and spread 1½–3 feet (45–90 cm) tall; 1–2 feet (30–60 cm) wide.
Temperature requirements Zones 3–8.
Position Average to humus-rich, well-drained soil. Full sun to light shade. Good drainage is essential for success.
Cultivation Plants form dense clumps with maturity and benefit from division every four to six years. More frequent division is required in rich soil.
Propagation Divide in spring. Sow seed outdoors in fall or indoors in winter after stratification. To stratify, mix seed with moist peat moss or seed-starting medium in a plastic bag. Close the bag with a twist-tie and place it in the refrigerator for four to six weeks. Then sow the mixture as you would normal seed. Seedlings may bloom the first year.
Pest and disease prevention No serious pests or diseases.
Landscape use Plant in formal borders, informal gardens, and rock gardens.

Phlox paniculata
POLEMONIACEAE

GARDEN PHLOX

Garden phlox is a popular summer-blooming perennial with domed clusters of fragrant, richly colored flowers atop stiff, leafy stems. Plants grow from fibrous-rooted crowns.

Flower color Varies from magenta to pink and white. Hybrids have a wide color range, including purples, reds, and oranges. There are also bicolored and "eyed" forms.
Flowering time Mid- to late summer.
Height and spread 3–4 feet (90–120 cm) tall; 2–4 feet (60–120 cm) wide.
Temperature requirements Zones 3–8. Cold hardiness varies with cultivars.
Position Moist but well-drained, humus-rich soil. Full sun to light shade.
Cultivation Divide clumps every three to four years to keep them vigorous.
Propagation Divide in spring. Take stem cuttings in late spring or early summer. Take root cuttings in the fall.
Pest and disease prevention Powdery mildew is the bane of phlox growers. It causes white patches on the leaves or, in bad cases, turns entire leaves white. To avoid problems, thin the stems before plants bloom to increase air circulation. Select resistant cultivars, especially hybrids with *P. maculata*.
Landscape use Garden phlox are beautiful and versatile garden perennials. Combine with summer daisies, bee balms (*Monarda* spp.), daylilies, asters, goldenrods (*Solidago* spp.), and ornamental grasses.

Platycodon grandiflorus
CAMPANULACEAE

BALLOON FLOWER

Balloon flowers are showy summer-blooming plants with saucer-shaped flowers on succulent stems clothed in toothed, triangular leaves. Plants grow from thick, fleshy roots.

Flower color The rich blue flowers have five-pointed petals that open from inflated buds that resemble balloons.
Flowering time Summer.
Height and spread 2–3 feet (60–90 cm) tall; 1–2 feet (30-60 cm) wide.
Temperature requirements Zones 3–8.
Position Well-drained, average to humus-rich soil. Full sun to light shade. Established plants are drought-tolerant.
Cultivation New shoots are slow to emerge in spring. Take care not to damage them by mistake. Remove spent flowers to encourage more bloom. Established clumps seldom need division.
Propagation Lift and divide clumps in spring or early fall; dig deeply to avoid root damage. Take basal cuttings of nonflowering shoots in summer, preferably with a piece of root attached. Sow seed outdoors in fall. Self-sown seedlings occur.
Pest and disease prevention No serious pests or diseases.
Landscape use Plant balloon flower with summer perennials like yellow yarrows (*Achillea* spp.), sages (*Salvia* spp.), bee balms (*Monarda* spp.), and phlox.

Primula x *polyantha*
PRIMULACEAE

POLYANTHUS PRIMROSE

Polyanthus primroses are hybrids with large, showy flowers in a rainbow of colors. The broad, crinkled leaves rise directly from stout crowns with thick, fibrous roots.

Flower color Flat, five-petaled flowers vary in color from white, cream, and yellow to pink, rose, red, and purple. Many bicolored and eyed forms are available.
Flowering time Spring and early summer.
Height and spread 8–12 inches (20–30 cm) tall; 12 inches (30 cm) wide.
Temperature requirements Zones 3–8.
Position Evenly moist, humus-rich soil. Light to partial shade. Plants can tolerate dryness in the summer if they go dormant.
Cultivation In cooler zones mulch plants to avoid frost heaving and crown damage. Divide overgrown clumps after flowering and replant into soil that has been enriched with organic matter.
Propagation Divide in fall to increase your stock. Easy to grow from fresh seed sown outdoors or indoors in early spring.
Pest and disease prevention No serious pests or diseases.
Landscape use Plant drifts of primroses with spring bulbs like daffodils, tulips, and Spanish bluebells (*Hyacinthoides hispanicus*). Combine them with early-blooming perennials like hellebores (*Helleborus* spp.), lungworts (*Pulmonaria* spp.), forget-me-nots (*Myosotis* spp.), and cranesbills (*Geranium* spp.).

Pulsatilla vulgaris
RANUNCULACEAE

PASQUE FLOWER

Pasque flowers are early-blooming perennials with cupped flowers over rosettes of deeply incised, lobed leaves clothed in soft hairs. Plants grow from deep, fibrous roots.

Flower color The purple flowers have five starry petals surrounding a central ring of fuzzy orange-yellow stamens (male reproductive structures). The flowers are followed by clusters of fuzzy seeds.
Flowering time Early to midspring.
Height and spread 6–12 inches (15–30 cm) tall; 10–12 inches (25–30 cm) wide.
Temperature requirements Zones 3–8.
Position Average to humus-rich, well-drained soil. Full sun to light shade. Does not tolerate soggy soil.
Cultivation Pasque flowers begin blooming in spring and continue for several weeks. After seed is set, plants go dormant unless conditions are cool. Seldom needs division.
Propagation Divide clumps after flowering or in fall. Sow seed outdoors in fall or spring. Self-sown seedlings appear.
Pest and disease prevention No serious pests or diseases.
Landscape use Perfect for rock gardens with bulbs, rock cresses (*Arabis* spp.), basket-of-gold (*Aurinia saxatilis*), perennial candytuft (*Iberis sempervirens*), and columbines (*Aquilegia* spp.).

Rodgersia pinnata
SAXIFRAGACEAE

RODGERSIA

Rodgersias are bold perennials with pinkish red flowers and large, pinnately compound leaves. These moisture-loving plants grow from stout, fibrous-rooted crowns.

Flower color The small rose red flowers are carried in 1–2-foot (30–60-cm) plume-like clusters.
Flowering time Late spring and early summer.
Height and spread 3–4 feet (90–120 cm) tall; 4 feet (1.2 m) wide.
Temperature requirements Zones 4–7.
Position Constantly moist, humus-rich soil. Partial to full shade. Protect from hot afternoon sun in warm zones.
Cultivation Rodgersias form huge clumps from large crowns that can remain in place for years. Be sure to provide at least 3–4 feet (90–120 cm) for each plant.
Propagation Divide plants in fall or spring. Sow seed outdoors in fall or indoors in spring.
Pest and disease prevention No serious pests or diseases.
Landscape use Plant rodgersias in bog and water gardens or along streams. Combine them with hostas, irises, astilbes, ferns, ligularias (*Ligularia* spp.), and primroses.
Other common names Rodger's flower.

Rudbeckia fulgida
COMPOSITAE

ORANGE CONEFLOWER

Orange coneflowers are summer daisies with oval to broadly lance-shaped, rough, hairy foliage on stiff stems. Plants grow from fibrous-rooted crowns.

Flower color The daisy-like flowers have yellow-orange rays (petal-like structures) and raised dark brown centers.
Flowering time Mid- to late summer.
Height and spread 1½–3 feet (45–90 cm) tall; 2–4 feet (60–120 cm) wide.
Temperature requirements Zones 3–9. Extremely heat-tolerant.
Position Average, moist but well-drained soil. Full sun to light shade. Good drainage is important.
Cultivation Orange coneflowers are tough, long-lived perennials. They spread outward to form large clumps. The edges of the clumps are the most vigorous. Divide every two to four years and replant into soil enriched with organic matter.
Propagation Divide in spring or fall. Sow seed outdoors in fall or spring, or indoors in late winter.
Pest and disease prevention No serious pests or diseases.
Landscape use Plant orange coneflowers with other daisies, sedums, phlox, bee balms (*Monarda* spp.), chrysanthemums, and ornamental grasses.
Other common names Black-eyed Susan.

Salvia x *superba*
LABIATAE

VIOLET SAGE

Violet sage is covered with colorful flower spikes in summer. The bushy, well-branched plants have aromatic triangular leaves. They grow from a fibrous-rooted crown.

Flower color The violet-blue flowers are carried in narrow spikes. Below each flower is a leaf-like bract.
Flowering time Early to midsummer. Plants often rebloom.
Height and spread 1½–3½ feet (45–105 cm) tall; 2–3 feet (60–90 cm) wide.
Temperature requirements Zones 4–7.
Position Average to humus-rich, moist but well-drained soil. Full sun to light shade. Drought-tolerant once established.
Cultivation After flowering wanes, shear back flowering stems to promote fresh growth and renewed bloom. Plants seldom need division.
Propagation Divide in spring or fall. Take cuttings in late spring or early summer; remove the flower buds.
Pest and disease prevention No serious pests or diseases.
Landscape use Plant violet sages in borders or rock gardens with early summer perennials such as yarrows, lamb's-ears (*Stachys byzantina*), daylilies, coreopsis (*Coreopsis* spp.), and ornamental grasses.

Sanguinaria canadensis
PAPAVERACEAE

BLOODROOT

Bloodroot is a bright, spring wildflower with a single, deeply cut, seven-lobed leaf that emerges wrapped around the single flower bud. Plants grow from a thick, creeping rhizome.

Flower color The snow-white flowers have 8–11 narrow petals surrounding a cluster of yellow-orange stamens (male reproductive structures). Flowers last only a few days.
Flowering time Early to midspring.
Height and spread 4–6 inches (10–15 cm) tall; 6–8 inches (15–20 cm) wide.
Temperature requirements Zones 3–9.
Position Moist, humus-rich soil. Light to full shade. Spring sun is important but summer shade is necessary. During prolonged dry spells, plants go dormant with no ill effect.
Cultivation Bloodroot foliage remains attractive all summer when ample moisture is available. Plants form dense clumps that can be divided.
Propagation Divide in late summer. Sow fresh seed outdoors in summer. Self-sown seedlings often appear.
Pest and disease prevention No serious pests or diseases.
Landscape use Plant bloodroot in woodland gardens with spring bulbs, wildflowers, hostas, and ferns. Use them as a groundcover under shrubs.

Sedum spectabile
CRASSULACEAE

SHOWY STONECROP

Showy stonecrops are late summer perennials with clusters of pink flowers atop thick stems clothed in broad gray-green leaves. Plants grow from fibrous-rooted crowns.

Flower color Small bright pink flowers are borne in 4–6-inch (10–15-cm) domed clusters. The pale green buds are attractive in summer and the brown seed heads hold their shape all winter.
Flowering time Mid- to late summer.
Height and spread 1–2 feet (30–60 cm) tall; 2 feet (60 cm) wide.
Temperature requirements Zones 3–9. Plants are heat-tolerant.
Position Average to humus-rich, well-drained soil. Full sun. Extremely drought-tolerant.
Cultivation Clumps get quite full with age and may fall open. To counteract this, divide overgrown plants.
Propagation Divide anytime from spring to midsummer. Take cuttings of nonflowering shoots in summer. Sow seed in spring or fall.
Pest and disease prevention No serious pests or diseases.
Landscape use Plant in formal borders, informal gardens, and rock gardens. Combine with yarrows, purple coneflowers (*Echinacea* spp.), cranesbills(*Geranium* spp.), coreopsis (*Coreopsis* spp.), and ornamental grasses.

Stokesia laevis
COMPOSITAE

STOKE'S ASTER

Stoke's aster is attractive in foliage and flower. The broad, lance-shaped leaves are deep green with a white midvein. The leaves form a rosette from a crown with thick, fibrous roots.

Flower color The 2–3-inch (5–7.5-cm) daisy-like flowers have ragged blue rays and fuzzy white centers.
Flowering time Summer.
Height and spread 1–2 feet (30–60 cm) tall; 2 feet (60 cm) wide.
Temperature requirements Zones 5–9.
Position Average to humus-rich, moist but well-drained soil. Full sun to light shade. Established plants tolerate dry soil.
Cultivation Plants can grow undisturbed for many years. Divide in spring or fall.
Propagation Divide in early spring. Sow seed outdoors in fall or indoors in winter after stratification. To stratify, mix seed with moist peat moss or seed-starting medium in a plastic bag. Close the bag with a twist-tie and place it in the refrigerator for four to six weeks. Then sow the mixture as you would normal seed.
Pest and disease prevention No serious pests or diseases.
Landscape use Combine with verbenas (*Verbena* spp.), phlox, goldenrods (*Solidago* spp.), columbines (*Aquilegia* spp.), and ornamental grasses.
Cultivars 'Alba' has white flowers. 'Blue Danube' has lavender-blue flowers. 'Klaus Jelitto' has deep blue flowers.

Thalictrum aquilegifolium
RANUNCULACEAE

COLUMBINE MEADOW RUE

Columbine meadow rue has billowy plumes crowning erect stalks clothed in intricately divided leaves that resemble those of columbines. Plants grow from fibrous-rooted crowns.

Flower color The ½-inch (1 cm) lavender or white flowers consist of many fuzzy stamens (male reproductive structures) in dense, branched clusters.
Flowering time Late spring and early summer.
Height and spread 2–3 feet (60–90 cm) tall; 1–2 feet (30–60 cm) wide.
Temperature requirements Zones 5–8.
Position Evenly moist, humus-rich soil. Full sun or partial shade. Plants tolerate wet soil.
Cultivation Clumps spread slowly and seldom outgrow their position. Can be divided if necessary.
Propagation Divide in spring or fall. Sow seed outdoors in fall or indoors in early spring.
Pest and disease prevention No serious pests or diseases.
Landscape use Plant columbine meadow rue in formal or informal gardens. It performs well at pondsides or along streams with irises, hostas, hibiscus (*Hibiscus* spp.), daylilies, and ferns.
Cultivars 'Album' has white flowers. 'Atropurpureum' has violet flowers. 'Thundercloud' has deep purple flowers.

Alcea rosea
MALVACEAE

HOLLYHOCK

Hollyhocks are perennials usually grown as annuals or biennials. Cut down the flower stalks after the blooms fade, or leave a few to set seed and self-sow.

Description Hollyhocks form large clumps of rounded leaves and thick bloom stalks. Plump flower buds produce bowl-shaped, single or double blooms up to 5 inches (12.5 cm) wide from midsummer until fall in white or shades of red, pink, and yellow.

Height and spread Height 3–6 feet (90–180 cm); spread about 2 feet (60 cm).

Best site Needs full sun; average, well-drained soil.

Growing guidelines For bloom the same year, sow seed indoors eight weeks before your last frost date. Sow ¼ inch (6 mm) deep in individual pots. After risk of frost has passed, set plants out 18–24 inches (45–60 cm) apart. For earlier bloom the following year, sow outdoors in large pots or in a nursery bed in spring or early summer. Move the young plants to their garden position in fall. Stake hollyhocks growing in exposed sites to keep stems upright. Hollyhocks are prone to rust, a fungal disease that produces orange spots on leaves. If rust shows up in your garden, pull plants out after bloom.

Landscape uses Use the tall spires of hollyhocks as accents in a flower border, with shrubs, or along a wall or fence.

Antirrhinum majus
SCROPHULARIACEAE

SNAPDRAGON

A mass planting of snapdragons makes an eye-catching landscape accent. Pinch the stem tips of dwarf types once after transplanting to promote branching and bushiness.

Description These tender perennials are usually grown as hardy or half-hardy annuals. The plants may be low and mound-forming or tall and spiky. The slender stems carry narrow, bright green leaves and are topped with spikes of tubular flowers. The velvety flowers bloom through summer in nearly every color but true blue; some have two colors in one flower.

Height and spread Height ranges from 1 foot (30 cm) to 4 feet (1.2 m). Spread ranges from 8–18 inches (20–45 cm).

Best site Full sun to light shade; average, well-drained soil with compost added.

Growing guidelines Buy transplants in spring, or start your own by planting seed indoors six to eight weeks before your last frost date. Sow seed directly into prepared garden soil after the last frost date. Water during dry spells. Snapdragons are prone to rust, a fungal disease that shows up as brownish spots on leaves. The best prevention is to grow them as annuals.

Landscape uses Use the low-growing cultivars in masses or as edging plants for annual beds. Tall-stemmed snapdragons are a must in the cutting garden for fresh arrangements, and in cottage gardens.

Begonia Semperflorens-Cultorum hybrid
BEGONIACEAE

WAX BEGONIA

Wax begonias require little or no care during the season. Pull them out after frost, or cut them back by one-third after frost and pot them up for indoor bloom in winter.

Description These tender perennials are grown as tender annuals. The succulent stems bear shiny, rounded, green or reddish brown leaves. The mounded plants are covered with single or double, 1½-inch (37-mm) flowers in red, pink, or white from June until frost.

Height and spread Height and spread 6–8 inches (15–20 cm).

Best site Partial shade to sun; evenly moist soil with added organic matter. Morning sun and afternoon shade is ideal in hot-summer areas. Brown-leaved types tend to be more sun- and heat-tolerant.

Growing guidelines Wax begonias are easiest to grow from purchased transplants in spring. If you want to try raising them yourself, sow the dustlike seed at least twelve weeks before your last frost date. Don't cover the seed; just press it lightly into the soil and place the pot in a plastic bag until seedlings appear. Set transplants out 6–8 inches (15–20 cm) apart after the last frost date, when temperatures stay above 50°F (10°C) at night.

Landscape uses Wax begonias are ideal as edging plants for flower beds. They also look great in pots, window boxes, and hanging baskets.

Brachyscome iberidifolia
COMPOSITAE

SWAN RIVER DAISY

If Swan River daisy plants get floppy after the first flush of bloom, shear them back by half and water well to promote compact growth and more flowers until frost arrives.

Description This half-hardy annual forms bushy mounds of thin stems and lacy, finely cut leaves. From midsummer until frost, plants bear many 1-inch (2.5-cm), rounded, daisy-like flowers in shades of blue, purple, pink, and white. The delicately scented blooms may have a black or yellow center.

Height and spread Height to 12 inches (30 cm); spread to 18 inches (45 cm).

Best site Full sun; average, well-drained soil with added organic matter.

Growing guidelines For earliest bloom, buy flowering plants and set them out after your last frost date. You can also start Swan River daisy from seed planted indoors or outdoors. Sow indoors six to eight weeks before your last frost date. Scatter the seed over the surface, lightly press it into the soil, and enclose the pot in a plastic bag until seedlings appear. Set plants out after the last frost date, or sow directly into the garden in late spring. Space plants 6–8 inches (15–20 cm) apart to form a solid, even carpet of flowers.

Landscape uses Swan River daisy makes an unusual edging for beds and borders. Its trailing habit is ideal for window boxes and hanging baskets.

Callistephus chinensis
COMPOSITAE

CHINA ASTER

China asters bloom from late summer to frost in white, cream, pink, red, purple, or blue. To minimize disease problems, plant them in a different spot each year.

Description This tender annual is grown for its showy blooms. The stems carry toothed, green leaves and are topped with daisy-like or puffy, single or double flowers up to 5 inches (12.5 cm) wide.

Height and spread Height 12–24 inches (30–60 cm); spread 12–18 inches (30–45 cm).

Best site Full sun; average, well-drained soil with added organic matter.

Growing guidelines For late-summer bloom, buy transplants in spring or sow seed indoors, ⅛ inch (3 mm) deep, six weeks before your last frost date. Set plants out 12 weeks after the last frost date, when the weather is warm. For fall bloom, sow seed directly into the garden after the last frost date. Pinch off stem tips once in early summer to promote branching. Stake tall cultivars. Control aphids with soap sprays to prevent the spread of aster yellows, which causes yellowed, stunted growth; destroy infected plants. Aster wilt is a soilborne disease that causes plants to droop; destroy infected plants.

Landscape uses Grow in masses or mix with other plants in beds, borders, and planters for late-season color. Grow a few in the cutting garden, too.

Catharanthus roseus
APOCYNACEAE

MADAGASCAR PERIWINKLE

In most areas, Madagascar periwinkle blooms from early summer until frost; it can flower nearly any time of the year in frost-free climates. Try it in pots and planters.

Other common names Rosy periwinkle, vinca.

Description A tender perennial commonly grown as a tender annual, Madagascar periwinkle forms compact, bushy clumps of glossy, dark green leaves with white central veins. Stems are topped with flat, five-petaled, white, rose, or pink flowers up to 2 inches (5 cm) wide.

Height and spread Height and spread usually 12–18 inches (30–45 cm); larger in frost-free areas.

Best site Full sun; average, well-drained soil. Tolerates heat, pollution, and drought.

Growing guidelines For best results, buy transplants in spring; it grows slowly from seed. If you want to try raising your own, sow seed ¼ inch (6 mm) deep indoors 10–12 weeks before your last frost date. Keep pots in an especially warm place (75–80°F [24–27°C]) until seedlings appear; then move pots to regular room temperature. Set transplants out 12 weeks after the last frost date, when the soil is warm. Pinch off stem tips in early summer for compact growth and more flowers.

Landscape uses This is a beautiful, easy-care annual for edging flower beds, borders, and walkways.

Centaurea cyanus
COMPOSITAE

CORNFLOWER

Stick brushy prunings into the ground around young cornflower plants to support the stems as they grow. Pinching off spent blooms can prolong the flowering season.

Other common names Bachelor's buttons.

Description This is a dependable, easy-care, hardy annual. The bushy plants have narrow, lance-shaped, silvery green leaves and thin stems topped with fluffy flower heads. The 1–2-inch (2.5–5-cm) flowers bloom through the summer in white or shades of blue, purple, pink, or red.

Height and spread Height 12–30 inches (30–75 cm); spread to 12 inches (30 cm).

Best site Full sun, but tolerates partial shade; average, well-drained soil.

Growing guidelines Grows easily from seed sown directly into the garden in early fall (in mild-winter areas) or early spring. Plant seed ⅛ inch (3 mm) deep. To extend the flowering season from an early-spring planting, sow again every two to four weeks until midsummer. Other ways to establish cornflowers include buying transplants in spring or starting the seed indoors about eight weeks before your last frost date. Set plants outdoors about two weeks before the last frost date. Cornflowers will self-sow if you leave a few flowers to set seed.

Landscape uses Cornflowers are charming in meadow gardens and flower beds. They are also excellent cut flowers.

Cheiranthus cheiri
CRUCIFERAE

WALLFLOWER

The fragrant blooms of wallflowers are normally orange or yellow, but they also bloom in shades of red, pink, or creamy white. The flowers are ideal for spring arrangements.

Description This perennial is commonly grown as a half-hardy annual or biennial. The bushy clumps of slender green leaves are topped with clusters of 1-inch (2.5-cm) wide four-petaled flowers from midspring to early summer.

Height and spread Height 12–24 inches (30–60 cm); spread to 12 inches (30 cm).

Best site Full sun to partial shade; average to moist, well-drained soil, ideally with a neutral to slightly alkaline pH.

Growing guidelines Sow outdoors in early spring or indoors about eight weeks before your last frost date. Plant seed ¼ inch (6 mm) deep. Set plants out 8–12 inches (20–30 cm) apart around the last frost date. In frost-free areas, grow wallflowers as biennials. Sow seed in pots or in a nursery bed in early summer; move plants to their flowering position in early fall. Water during dry spells to keep the soil evenly moist. Pull out and compost plants when they have finished blooming.

Landscape uses Grow in masses or in flower beds for spots of early color. One classic combination is orange wallflowers underplanted with blue forget-me-nots (*Myosotis sylvatica*). Wallflowers also combine beautifully with tulips.

Cleome hasslerana
CAPPARACEAE

CLEOME

Cleome is a must for butterfly-attracting gardens; it's also popular with bees. Plant it in large groupings to show off the spidery white, pink, or rosy lavender flowers.

Other common names Spider flower.

Description Cleome is a fast-growing half-hardy annual. Its tall, sturdy stems and palmlike leaves are slightly sticky and have a musky (some say skunk-like) odor. Small spines form on the stems and on the undersides of the leaves. From midsummer until midfall, the stems are topped with globes of four-petaled flowers. Long stamens protrude from the flowers, giving them a spidery look. The blooms are followed by long, narrow seedpods.

Height and spread Height 3–4 feet (90–120 cm); spread 18 inches (45 cm).

Best site Full sun to light shade; average, well-drained soil with added compost.

Growing guidelines Easy to grow from seed sown directly in the garden in mid- to late-spring. For earlier bloom, buy transplants or start your own by sowing seed indoors about four weeks before your last frost date. Lightly press the seed into the surface, then enclose the pot in a plastic bag until seedlings appear. Set plants out around the last frost date.

Landscape uses Try cleome in the back of flower beds and borders. Its pretty, delicate blooms look particularly nice in cottage gardens.

Coleus x hybridus
LABIATAE

COLEUS

Keep favorite coleus plants from year to year by taking cuttings in summer; they'll root quickly in water. Pot up the cuttings for winter; then put them outdoors in spring.

Description These tender perennials are grown as bushy, tender annuals. Their sturdy, square stems carry showy, patterned leaves with scalloped or ruffled edges. Each leaf can have several different colors, with zones, edges, or splashes in shades of red, pink, orange, yellow, and cream.
Height and spread Height 6–24 inches (15–60 cm); spread 8–12 inches (20–30 cm).
Best site Partial shade; average to moist, well-drained soil with added well-rotted organic matter.
Growing guidelines Buy transplants in spring, or start your own by sowing seed indoors eight to ten weeks before your last frost date. Don't cover the seed; just press it lightly into the soil and enclose the pot in a plastic bag until seedlings appear. Set plants out 8–12 inches (20–30 cm) apart after the last frost. Water during dry spells. Pinch off the spikes of the pale blue flowers to promote more leafy growth.
Landscape uses Coleus are great for adding all-season color to beds, borders, and container plantings. Groups of mixed leaf patterns can look too busy when combined with flowering plants, so grow them alone in masses.

Coreopsis tinctoria
COMPOSITAE

CALLIOPSIS

Calliopsis grows easily from direct-sown seed and needs little fussing. Shearing the plants back by one-third in mid- to late-summer can prolong the bloom season.

Description Calliopsis is a colorful, fast-growing, hardy annual. Its wiry stems carry narrow, green leaves and 1–2-inch (2.5–5-cm)-wide, single or double, daisy-like flowers. The flowers are usually golden yellow with maroon centers but may also be all yellow or all orange. Plants can bloom from midsummer until frost.
Height and spread Height 24–36 inches (30–90 cm), depending on the cultivar; spread to 12 inches (30 cm).
Best site Full sun; average, well-drained soil. Adapts well to poor soil.
Growing guidelines Grows quickly from seed sown directly into the garden in early- to mid-spring. You can also sow seed ⅛ inch (3 mm) deep indoors about six weeks before your last frost date. Set plants out around the last frost date. Space transplants or thin seedlings to stand about 8 inches (20 cm) apart. Push twiggy brush into the soil around young plants of tall-growing cultivars to support the stems as they grow.
Landscape uses Depend on calliopsis for adding fast, easy-care color to beds and borders. It also looks wonderful in meadow gardens. Grow some in the cutting garden for fresh arrangements.

Cosmos bipinnatus
COMPOSITAE

COSMOS

Use fast-growing cosmos to fill spaces left by early-blooming annuals and perennials. Pinch off spent flowers to encourage more bloom; leave a few to self-sow.

Description These popular half-hardy annuals are grown for their colorful blooms. The bushy plants bear many finely cut, green leaves. In late summer and fall, the stems are topped with white, pink, or rosy red flowers. The single or semidouble, daisy-like blooms can grow up to 4 inches (10 cm) across.
Height and spread Height 3–4 feet (90–120 cm); spread to 18 inches (45 cm).
Best site Full sun is best, although plants can take partial shade; average to moist, well-drained soil.
Growing guidelines For earliest blooms, buy transplants in spring or start seed indoors three to four weeks before your last frost date. Plant seed ¼ inch (6 mm) deep. Set plants out 12 weeks after the last frost date. You can also sow seed directly into the garden around the last frost date. Pinch off stem tips in early summer to promote branching and more flowers. Stake individual stems as needed, or just let the plants sprawl; they'll send up more flowering stems.
Landscape uses Cosmos adds height and color to flower beds, borders, and meadows. They look great in cottage gardens. Grow a few in the cutting garden for arrangements.

Dianthus barbatus
CARYOPHYLLACEAE

SWEET WILLIAM

Sweet Williams may rebloom the following year if you shear them back after flowering, but you'll generally get a better show by starting new plants each year.

Description This short-lived perennial is grown as a hardy biennial or annual. It forms clumps of narrow, lance-shaped, green leaves and the stems are topped with dense, slightly rounded clusters of five-petaled flowers in early- to midsummer. Each fragrant bloom is ¼–½ inch (6–12 mm) wide. Red, pink, and white are the most common colors; some flowers have eyes, or zones of contrasting colors.
Height and spread Height 12–18 inches (30–45 cm); spread 8–12 inches (20–30 cm).
Best site Full sun to partial shade; average, well-drained soil.
Growing guidelines For earliest bloom, grow as a biennial Sow seed outdoors in pots or in a nursery bed in summer, then move plants to their garden position in fall. For bloom the same year, sow seed indoors (just barely cover it) about eight weeks before your last frost date. Set plants out two to three weeks before the last frost date. Space transplants 8–10 inches (20–25 cm) apart. Sweet William will self-sow if you leave a few flowers to form seeds.
Landscape uses Sweet William looks super as an early-summer filler for beds and borders. It is ideal for fresh arrangements.

Eschscholzia californica
PAPAVERACEAE

CALIFORNIA POPPY

The cup-shaped flowers of California poppy open during sunny days but close in cloudy weather and at night. Pinch off developing seedpods to prolong the bloom season.

Description This tender perennial is usually grown as a hardy annual. Plants form loose clumps of deeply cut, blue-green leaves. The thin stems are topped with pointed buds that unfurl into single, semidouble, or double flowers up to 3 inches (7.5 cm) across in early summer through early fall. The silky-looking petals are usually orange or yellow, but they can also bloom in white, pink, or red.
Height and spread Height 12–18 inches (30–45 cm); spread 6–12 inches (15–30 cm).
Best site Full sun; average to sandy, well-drained soil.
Growing guidelines They transplant poorly, so it's usually not worth starting seed indoors. Plants will grow quickly from seed sown directly into the garden in very early spring (or even in fall in frost-free areas). Scatter the seed over the soil surface and rake it in lightly. Thin seedlings to stand 6 inches (15 cm) apart. If blooms are sparse by midsummer, cut plants back by about one-third to encourage a new flush of flowers. Plants usually self-sow in mild-winter areas.
Landscape uses Grow as fillers for flower beds and borders and in meadow gardens.

Gypsophila elegans
CARYOPHYLLACEAE

ANNUAL BABY'S-BREATH

Sowing seed of annual baby's-breath every two to three weeks from early to late spring can extend the bloom season well into summer. Pull out plants that have finished flowering.

Description This hardy annual is grown for its airy sprays of dainty flowers. Plants form loose clumps of slender stems with pairs of narrow, gray-green leaves. Loose clusters of many five-petaled flowers bloom atop the stems for up to two months in spring and early summer. The ¼–½-inch (6–12-mm) wide flowers are usually white or light pink; some cultivars have deeper pink flowers.
Height and spread Height 18–24 inches (45–60 cm); spread 6–12 inches (15–30 cm).
Best site Full sun (afternoon shade in hot areas); average, well-drained soil.
Growing guidelines Plant seed directly into the garden where you want plants to grow; cover it with ⅛ inch (3 mm) of soil. Sow seed in early spring (or in fall in mild-winter areas). Thin seedlings to stand 6 inches (15 cm) apart. Push twiggy brush into the soil around young plants to support the stems as they grow.
Landscape uses Makes a nice filler for flower beds and borders. It looks especially charming in masses with other cool-loving annuals, such as rocket larkspur (*Consolida ambigua*) and sweet peas (*Lathyrus odoratus*).

Helianthus annuus
COMPOSITAE

COMMON SUNFLOWER

Common sunflowers are much-loved hardy annuals grown for their large, showy blooms (and often for their tasty seeds as well). Tall cultivars will usually need staking.

Description This easy-to-grow plant produces large, sturdy stalks with coarse, heart-shaped leaves. From midsummer through midfall, the stems are topped with flat, daisy-like flower heads to 12 inches (30 cm) wide or more. The flower heads normally have a purple-brown center, with bright yellow, bronze, mahogany red, or orange petals.
Height and spread Height 2–8 feet (60–240 cm) or more; spread 12–18 inches (30–45 cm).
Best site Thrives in full sun; needs average, well-drained soil.
Growing guidelines Common sunflowers grow so quickly that it's easiest to sow seed directly into the garden after your last frost date. Plant seed ½ inch (12 mm) deep. Thin seedlings to stand 12 inches (30 cm) apart. Unless you're growing plants for the edible seeds, remove spent flowers to prolong the bloom season.
Landscape uses Sunflowers tend to drop their leaves along the bottom half of their stem, so place them in the middle or back of the border where other plants will hide their bare ankles. Small-flowered types are excellent as cut flowers. Plant seed-producing types in the vegetable garden.

Helichrysum bracteatum
COMPOSITAE

STRAWFLOWER

Cutting strawflowers for fresh arrangements or drying will promote branching and prolong the bloom season. The flowers dry quickly when hung upside down in a dark, airy place.

Description This half-hardy annual is grown for its colorful, long-lasting blooms. The bushy plants have long, narrow, green leaves and daisy-like flower heads with stiff, papery, petal-like bracts. The flower heads bloom from midsummer until frost in white, pink, rose, red, orange, or yellow. Fully open flower heads are 1–2 inches (2.5–5 cm) wide and have yellow centers.
Height and spread Height 24–48 inches (60–120 cm); spread to 12 inches (30 cm).
Best site Needs full sun; average, well-drained soil.
Growing guidelines For earliest blooms, buy transplants or start your own by sowing seed indoors six to eight weeks before your last frost date. Just press the seed lightly into the surface and enclose the pot in a plastic bag until seedlings appear. Set plants out two weeks after the last frost date, or sow seed directly into the garden after the last frost date.
Landscape uses Strawflowers add long-lasting color to flower beds and borders. Grow an ample supply in the cutting garden for drying, as well. Harvest flowers when they are about one-quarter open; they'll open more as they dry.

Iberis umbellata
CRUCIFERAE

ANNUAL CANDYTUFT

Annual candytuft needs little care and tends to self-sow. In hot-summer areas, pull out plants after bloom and replace them with summer- to fall-blooming annuals.

Other common names Globe candytuft.
Description This dependable, hardy annual forms mounds of narrow, green leaves on many-branched stems. The mounds are covered with dense, slightly rounded flower clusters approximately 2 inches (5 cm) across from late spring through midsummer. Each cluster contains many ¼–½-inch (6–12-mm) wide, four-petaled blooms. Flowers may be white, pink, pinkish purple, rose, or red.
Height and spread Height 8–12 inches (20–30 cm); spread 8–10 inches (20–25 cm).
Best site Full sun to partial shade; average, well-drained soil.
Growing guidelines For the earliest flowers, sow seed indoors six to eight weeks before your last frost date. Plant seed ¼ inch (6 mm) deep. Set plants out around the last frost date. Annual candytuft also grows easily from seed sown directly into the garden. Make the first sowing in early- to mid-spring, sowing again every three to four weeks. Thin seedlings or space plants to stand 6–8 inches (15–20 cm) apart.
Landscape uses Annual candytuft makes a colorful edging or filler for flower beds and borders.

Impatiens wallerana
BALSAMINACEAE

IMPATIENS

A mixed planting of impatiens makes a colorful annual groundcover under trees and shrubs. For good growth, they need moist soil; mulch them and water during dry spells.

Other common names Busy Lizzie, patient Lucy, patience, sultana.

Description Plants form neat, shrubby mounds of well-branched, succulent stems; the lance-shaped, green or bronze-brown leaves have slightly scalloped edges. The plants are covered with flat, spurred flowers up to 2 inches (5 cm) wide from late spring until frost. The single or double blooms may be white, pink, red, orange, or lavender; some have an eye, or swirls of contrasting colors.

Height and spread Height 6–24 inches (15–60 cm); similar spread.

Best site Shade; average to moist, well-drained soil with added organic matter.

Growing guidelines Buy transplants in spring or sow seed indoors eight to ten weeks before your last frost date. Don't cover the seed; just press it lightly into the soil surface. Enclose the pot in a plastic bag and keep it in a warm place until seedlings appear. Young seedlings tend to grow slowly. Set transplants out about two weeks after your last frost date.

Landscape uses Impatiens are the stars of shady gardens. Mix them with other annuals and perennials in beds and borders, or grow them alone in masses under trees.

Lathyrus odoratus
LEGUMINOSAE

SWEET PEA

Dozens of sweet pea cultivars are available in a range of heights and colors. Many modern cultivars aren't very fragrant; check catalog descriptions to find scented types.

Description These old-fashioned hardy annuals are grown for their charming flowers. Plants produce leafy vines that climb by tendrils. Dainty, pealike flowers to 2 inches (5 cm) long bloom on long, slender flower stems from midspring into summer. Flower colors are usually white or bright or pastel shades of pink, red, or purple. The flowers often have crimped or ruffled petals.

Height and spread Height usually 4–6 feet (1.2–1.8 m); spread 6–12 inches (15–30 cm).

Best site Full sun (or afternoon shade in hot-summer areas); loose, evenly moist soil enriched with organic matter.

Growing guidelines Before planting, set up some sort of string or netting trellis for the vines to climb. Start seed indoors six to eight weeks before your last frost date. Soak seed in warm water overnight, then plant ½ inch (12 mm) deep in peat pots. Set plants out in midspring, after danger of frost, or sow seed directly into the garden in early spring.

Landscape uses Train sweet peas to climb a tripod of stakes as an early-season accent for beds, borders, and cottage gardens. Include them in the cutting garden.

Limonium sinuatum
PLUMBAGINACEAE

ANNUAL STATICE

Annual statice is a natural for fresh or dried arrangements. To dry it, pick stems when the clusters are about three-quarters open; hang them in a dark, airy place.

Description This biennial or tender perennial is usually grown as a half-hardy annual. Plants form low rosettes of wavy-edged, green leaves that send up sturdy, winged stems in summer. The loosely branched stems are topped with flattened clusters of ¼-inch (6-mm) wide, white flowers, each surrounded by a papery, tubular calyx—the colorful part of the flower head. Annual statice comes in many colors, including white, pink, peach, red, orange, yellow, purple, and blue.

Height and spread Height 12–24 inches (30–60 cm); spread to 12 inches (30 cm).

Best site Needs full sun; average, well-drained soil.

Growing guidelines Buy transplants in spring, or sow seed indoors six to eight weeks before your last frost date. Plant the seed ¼ inch (3 mm) deep. Move seedlings to individual pots when they have two or three sets of leaves. Plant them in the garden around the last frost date, or sow seed directly into the garden after the last frost date. Space transplants or thin seedlings to stand 8–10 inches (20–25 cm) apart. Established plants need little care.

Landscape uses An attractive filler for flower beds and borders.

Lobelia erinus
CAMPANULACEAE

EDGING LOBELIA

If you grow edging lobelia from seed or buy seedlings in trays, transplant them in clumps (rather than separating them into individual plants) to avoid damaging the stems.

Description This tender perennial is usually grown as a half-hardy annual. Plants form trailing or mounding clumps of slender stems with small, narrow, green leaves. Plants are covered with ½–¼-inch (12–18-mm) wide flowers from late spring until frost. The five-petaled flowers bloom in white and shades of blue, purple, and pinkish red.

Height and spread Height 6–8 inches (15–20 cm); spread 6–10 inches (15–25 cm).

Best site Full sun to partial shade (especially in hot-summer areas); average, well-drained soil with added compost.

Growing guidelines Buy transplants in spring, or start your own by sowing seed indoors eight to ten weeks before your last frost date. Don't cover the seed; just press it lightly into the soil and enclose the pot in a plastic bag until seedlings appear. Set plants out 6–8 inches (15–20 cm) apart after the last frost date. Water during dry spells. Shear plants back by half after each flush of bloom and fertilize for rebloom.

Landscape uses Looks great along the front of beds and borders or as a filler among taller plants. Cascading types make attractive fillers for container gardens.

Lobularia maritima
CRUCIFERAE

SWEET ALYSSUM

Sweet alyssum may stop blooming during summer heat but will start again when cool weather returns. Shear off spent flowers and water thoroughly to promote new growth.

Description Sweet alyssum is a tender perennial grown as a hardy annual. Plants form low mounds of many-branched stems and narrow, green leaves. Domed clusters of many ¼-inch (6-mm) blooms cover plants in summer and fall. The sweetly scented, four-petaled flowers bloom in white and shades of pink and purple. Sweet alyssum is also listed in seed catalogs as *Alyssum maritimum*.

Height and spread Height 4–8 inches (10–20 cm); spread 10–12 inches (25–30 cm).

Best site Full sun to partial shade (especially in hot-summer areas); average, well-drained soil.

Growing guidelines Buy transplants in spring, or sow seed indoors six to eight weeks before your last frost date. Just barely cover the seed with soil. Set plants out around the last frost date. It also grows easily from seed sown directly into the garden in mid- to late-spring. Space transplants or thin seedlings to stand 6 inches (15 cm) apart.

Landscape uses Grow as an edging or filler in flower beds and borders or as a groundcover under roses and shrubs. It also grows well in container gardens.

Malcomia maritima
CRUCIFERAE

VIRGINIA STOCK

Virginia stock can bloom in as little as four weeks from seed sown directly into the garden. Sow every three to four weeks through midsummer to have flowers from summer until frost.

Description The upright, branching stems of this fast-growing hardy annual carry small, pointed, grayish green leaves. Flat, four-petaled, lightly fragrant flowers bloom in loose clusters atop the stems. The purple, pink, or white flowers are ¼–½ inch (6–12 mm) wide.

Height and spread Height 6–8 inches (15–20 cm); spread to 4 inches (10 cm).

Best site Full sun to partial shade (in hot-summer areas); average, well-drained soil.

Growing guidelines Grows best from seed sown directly in the garden. For the longest bloom season, sow at three to four week intervals from early spring through midsummer. (In mild-winter areas, you can sow in fall for even earlier spring bloom.) Rake the seedbed to cover the seed lightly, then keep the soil moist until seedlings appear. Thin seedlings to stand 3–4 inches (7.5–10 cm) apart. Plants will often self-sow freely.

Landscape uses Virginia stock makes a nice filler or edging annual for flower beds and borders. The flowers are very popular with bees.

Matthiola incana
CRUCIFERAE

COMMON STOCK

The fragrant, single or double flowers of common stock bloom in white and shades of pink, red, yellow, and purple. They are wonderful in the garden or in arrangements.

Description This biennial or short-lived perennial is usually grown as a hardy annual. The fast-growing, bushy plants have upright stems and lance-shaped, grayish leaves. The stems are topped with spikes of four-petaled, 1-inch (2.5-cm) wide flowers in summer.

Height and spread Height 12–24 inches (30–60 cm); spread to 12 inches (30 cm).

Best site Full sun; average, well-drained soil with added organic matter.

Growing guidelines Grows easily from seed sown directly into the garden. Make the first sowing about one month before your last frost date. To extend the bloom season, make another sowing in late spring or early summer. (In mild-winter areas, you can also sow in late summer for winter and early-spring bloom.) Scatter seed on the soil surface, then rake lightly to just cover the seed. Keep the seedbed moist until seedlings appear. Thin seedlings to stand 6–8 inches (15–20 cm) apart. Mulch plants to keep the roots cool and moist. Water during dry spells.

Landscape uses Use as a filler in beds and borders near your house or outdoor sitting areas, where you can enjoy the sweet fragrance.

Myosotis sylvatica
BORAGINACEAE

FORGET-ME-NOT

Forget-me-not blooms are often sky blue with white or yellow centers, but they can also be pink or white. They are ideal companions for spring bulbs and other early annuals.

Description These short-lived perennials are usually grown as hardy biennials or annuals. Plants form dense clumps of narrow, lance-shaped, hairy leaves. Sprays of many ⅓-inch (8-mm) wide flowers bloom over the leaves from midspring through early summer.

Height and spread Height usually 12–18 inches (30–45 cm); spread 8–10 inches (20–25 cm).

Best site Partial shade; average to moist, well-drained soil with added compost.

Growing guidelines To grow forget-me-nots as biennials, sow seed outdoors in pots or in a nursery bed in spring or summer. Plant seed ⅛ inch (3 mm) deep. Move plants to the garden in early fall. For bloom the same year, buy plants in early spring, or start seed indoors four to six weeks before your last frost date. Set plants out 12 weeks before the last frost date. Space plants or thin seedlings to stand 6 inches (15 cm) apart. Water during dry spells. Shearing off spent flowers often promotes rebloom. Plants often self-sow freely.

Landscape uses Forget-me-nots are invaluable for spring color in shady gardens. Try them as an early-season groundcover under shrubs.

Nemesia strumosa
SCROPHULARIACEAE

NEMESIA

Nemesia usually stops flowering in warm weather, but plants may recover and rebloom if you cut them back by half, water thoroughly, and give them a dose of fertilizer.

Description Nemesia is a tender, cool-weather annual grown for its beautiful flowers. Plants form clumps of branched stems with pairs of narrow, slightly toothed, green leaves. Clusters of trumpet-shaped, lipped flowers bloom atop the stems in summer. The 1-inch (2.5-cm) wide flowers bloom in a range of colors, including white, pink, red, orange, yellow, lilac, and even light blue.

Height and spread Height 12–24 inches (30–60 cm); spread 6–8 inches (15–20 cm).

Best site Full sun to partial shade (especially in warm- and hot-summer areas); evenly moist, well-drained soil with added organic matter. Nemesia needs a long, cool growing season; it does not tolerate heat or humidity.

Growing guidelines Start seed indoors six to eight weeks before your last frost date. (In mild-winter areas, you can also sow in fall for winter bloom.) Sow seed ⅛ inch (3 mm) deep. Set plants out 4–6 inches (10–15 cm) apart after the last frost date.

Landscape uses Nemesia makes an attractive edging for flower beds and borders. It is also showy when planted in masses for early-summer color. Try a few in containers and window boxes.

Nicotiana alata
SOLANACEAE

FLOWERING TOBACCO

Hybrids and red-flowered types of flowering tobacco often have little or no scent, but old-fashioned, white-flowered types tend to be quite fragrant, especially at night.

Description This tender perennial is usually grown as a half-hardy annual. Plants form lush rosettes of broad, oval to pointed, green leaves and many-branched stems; both the stems and leaves are sticky and hairy. Trumpet-shaped flowers to 2 inches (5 cm) across bloom atop the stems from midsummer until frost. Flowers come in a range of colors, including white, pink, purple, and red.

Height and spread Height 18–36 inches (45–90 cm); spread to 12 inches (30 cm).

Best site Full sun to partial shade; average to moist, well-drained soil with added organic matter.

Growing guidelines Buy transplants in spring, or start seed indoors six to eight weeks before your last frost date. Don't cover the fine seed; just press it into the soil and enclose the pot in a plastic bag until seedlings appear. Set seedlings out 10–12 inches (25–30 cm) apart after the last frost date. Water during dry spells. Cut out spent stems to prolong the bloom season. Plants may self-sow.

Landscape uses Excellent as a filler or accent in beds and borders. Grow some in the cutting garden and plant fragrant types around outdoor sitting areas.

Nigella damascena
RANUNCULACEAE

LOVE-IN-A-MIST

Sowing every three to four weeks from early spring to early summer can extend the bloom season of love-in-a-mist through the summer and possibly into fall.

Other common names Fennel flower, devil-in-the-bush.

Description A fast-growing, hardy annual that forms bushy mounds of slender stems and threadlike, bright green leaves. Single or double, 1–2-inch (2.5–5-cm) wide flowers are nestled into the leaves at the tops of the stems. The blue, pink, or white flowers are followed by swollen, striped seedpods with short, pointed horns.

Height and spread Height 18–24 inches (45–60 cm); spread 6–8 inches (15–20 cm).

Best site Full sun to partial shade; average, well-drained soil.

Growing guidelines For the earliest flowers, start seed indoors six to eight weeks before your last frost date. Sow seed (just barely cover it with soil) in peat pots. Move plants to the garden after the last frost date. In most cases, though, you'll get better results by sowing directly into the garden, starting in early spring. Space transplants or thin seedlings to stand 6 inches (15 cm) apart. Established plants are care-free. Plants may self-sow.

Landscape uses Grow as a filler in beds, borders, and cottage gardens. It's also a natural for the cutting garden. Leave some plants to mature into the puffy seedpods.

Papaver nudicaule
PAPAVERACEAE

ICELAND POPPY

Removing spent flower stems can prolong Iceland poppy's bloom season. As summer approaches and new growth slows, leave a few flowers to mature so plants can self-sow.

Description This short-lived perennial is usually grown as a hardy biennial or annual. Plants form compact rosettes of hairy, deeply cut, gray-green leaves. Long, slender, leafless stems are topped with plump, hairy, nodding buds that open to bowl-shaped, four-petaled flowers. The 2–4-inch (2.5–5-cm) wide, lightly fragrant flowers have crinkled petals. They bloom mainly in early- to mid-summer in a range of vibrant colors, including white, pink, red, orange, and yellow.

Height and spread Height 12–18 inches (30–45 cm); spread 4–6 inches (10–15 cm).

Best site Full sun; average, well-drained to dry soil. Grows poorly in hot weather.

Growing guidelines Easiest to grow from seed sown directly into the garden. Plant in late fall or very early spring for summer bloom. (In hot-summer areas, sow this cool-loving plant in late summer to early fall for spring bloom.) Scatter the fine seed over the soil and rake it in lightly. Thin seedlings to about 6 inches (15 cm) apart.

Landscape uses Plant Iceland poppies for early color in beds and borders; follow them with summer-blooming annuals. Grow some in the cutting garden, too, for fresh cut flowers.

Pelargonium x hortorum
GERANIACEAE

ZONAL GERANIUM

Colorful and dependable, zonal geraniums are a mainstay of summer flower gardens. You can also bring them indoors in the fall and enjoy their flowers through the winter.

Description The sturdy, branched stems carry hairy, rounded, bright to dark green leaves with scalloped margins. The pungent leaves are often marked with dark green or brown, curved bands (zones). Plants produce thin but sturdy stems topped with rounded clusters of many 2-inch (5-cm) wide flowers. The single or double flowers bloom from late spring until frost in white or shades of pink, red, salmon, and bicolors.
Height and spread Height 12–24 inches (30–60 cm); spread 12–18 inches (30–45 cm).
Best site Full sun to partial shade; average, well-drained soil.
Growing guidelines If you just need a few geraniums or if you want special kinds (such as those with double flowers or fancy leaves), start with a few purchased plants in spring. During the summer, pinch off spent flower stems to promote rebloom. To save special plants for next year, dig them up in fall, move them into pots, and grow them on a sunny windowsill. Take 4-inch (10-cm) long cuttings from the shoot tips in spring.
Landscape uses Grow them alone in masses, or tuck them into beds and borders.

Petunia x hybrida
SOLANACEAE

PETUNIA

Petunias are tender perennials usually grown as half-hardy annuals. They may self-sow, but the seedlings seldom resemble the parent plants.

Description Plants form clumps of upright or trailing stems with oval, green leaves. Funnel-shaped, single or double flowers bloom from early summer until frost in nearly every color of the rainbow; some have stripes, streaks, or bands of contrasting colors.
Height and spread Height 6–10 inches (15–25 cm); spread to 12 inches (30 cm).
Best site Full sun (can take light shade); average to moist, well-drained soil.
Growing guidelines Petunias are among the most popular annuals, and many types are sold as transplants each spring. You can also grow your own from seed, although the fine, dustlike seed can be hard to handle. If you want to try, sow the seed indoors eight to ten weeks before your last frost date. Don't cover the seed; just press it lightly into the soil and enclose the pot in a plastic bag until seedlings appear. Move plants to the garden 12 weeks after the last frost date; space them 8–12 inches (20–30 cm) apart. Water during dry spells.
Landscape uses Petunias—especially the multiflora and floribunda types—are favorites for flower beds and borders, planted alone in masses or mixed with other plants. They are particularly good for filling in gaps in the garden.

Phlox drummondii
POLEMONIACEAE

ANNUAL PHLOX

Annual phlox is a hardy annual grown for its colorful flowers. If plants stop blooming, cut them back by half and water thoroughly; they should resprout and rebloom in fall.

Description Plants form bushy clumps of narrow, lance-shaped, green leaves. From midsummer to fall, the leafy stems are topped with clusters of flat, five-petaled flowers, each ½–1 inch (12–25 mm) across. The flowers bloom in a wide range of colors, including white, pink, red, pale yellow, blue, and purple; some have a contrasting eye.
Height and spread Height 6–18 inches (15–45 cm), depending on the cultivar; spread 6–8 inches (15–20 cm).
Best site Needs full sun; average, well-drained soil.
Growing guidelines For the earliest flowers, buy transplants in spring, or start seed indoors six to eight weeks before the last frost date. Sow seed ⅛ inch (3 mm) deep in individual pots. Set plants out around the last frost date. You can also sow seed directly into the garden around the last frost date. Set plants or thin seedlings to stand 6 inches (15 cm) apart. Pinching off spent flowers and watering during dry spells can prolong the bloom season.
Landscape uses An excellent filler for flower beds and borders. Try the compact cultivars in container gardens. Tall cultivars are excellent cut flowers.

Portulaca grandiflora
PORTULACACEAE

ROSE MOSS

Rose moss comes in many vibrant colors, including white, pink, red, orange, yellow, and magenta. The flowers tend to close by afternoon and stay closed on cloudy days.

Description A low-growing, tender annual, rose moss forms creeping mats of fleshy, many-branched stems with small, thick, almost needle-like leaves. Single or double, 1-inch (2.5-cm) wide flowers bloom from early summer through fall.

Height and spread Height to 6 inches (15 cm); spread 6–8 inches (15–20 cm).

Best site Full sun; average, well-drained to dry soil.

Growing guidelines For earliest bloom, buy transplants in spring, or sow seed indoors six to eight weeks before your last frost date. For easy transplanting later, sow the seed in cell packs or small pots. Do not cover the seed; just press it lightly into the soil and enclose the containers in a plastic bag until seedlings appear. Set plants out 12 weeks after the last frost date, when the soil is warm; space them about 6 inches (15 cm) apart. You can also sow the fine seed directly into the garden after the last frost date; keep the soil moist until seedlings appear. Thin seedlings only if they're crowded. Plants may self-sow.

Landscape uses Makes a great groundcover for dry, rocky slopes. It also looks charming as an edging for sunny beds and borders.

Salvia splendens
LABIATAE

SCARLET SAGE

Compact cultivars of scarlet sage tend to flower mostly in summer; taller types generally start blooming in midsummer and last until frost. Pinch off faded spikes.

Description This tender perennial is grown as a half-hardy annual. Plants form clumps of upright stems with oval, deep green leaves that have pointed tips and slightly toothed edges. The stems are topped with thick, showy spikes of colorful, petallike bracts and 1½-inch (37-mm) long tubular flowers. The flowers are most often red, but they are also available in white, pink, salmon, and purple.

Height and spread Height 12–24 inches (30–60 cm); spread to 12 inches (30 cm).

Best site Needs full sun; average, well-drained soil.

Growing guidelines Widely sold as transplants in spring. If you really want to grow your own, sow indoors eight to ten weeks before your last frost date. Don't cover the seed; just press it lightly into the soil and enclose the pot in a plastic bag until seedlings appear. Set plants out after the last frost date; space them 8–12 inches (20–30 cm) apart. Fertilize several times during the summer.

Landscape uses If you enjoy mixing bright colors, grow scarlet sage as an edging or filler for flower beds and borders. For a somewhat more restrained effect, surround scarlet sage with leafy green herbs.

Senecio cineraria
COMPOSITAE

DUSTY MILLER

Dusty miller can live through mild winters, but second-year plants tend to be more open. Where uniformity is important (as in an edging), start with new plants each year.

Description This tender perennial is usually grown as a half-hardy annual. Plants form shrubby mounds of deeply lobed leaves that are covered with matted, white hairs. The plants may produce clusters of daisy-like yellow flowers in summer, but these are usually removed so they won't detract from the silvery foliage. Dusty miller is also listed in seed catalogs as *Cineraria maritima*.

Height and spread Height 8–24 inches (20–60 cm); spread to 12 inches (30 cm).

Best site Needs full sun; average, well-drained soil.

Growing guidelines Buy transplants in spring. They grow slowly from seed, but if you want to raise your own, sow seed indoors eight to ten weeks before your last frost date. Don't cover the seed; just press it lightly into the soil and enclose the pot in a plastic bag until seedlings appear. Set plants out after the last frost date; space them 8 inches (20 cm) apart. Pinch out stem tips in early summer for bushy growth.

Landscape uses Dusty miller's silvery foliage is invaluable as an edging or accent for flower beds, borders, and all kinds of container plantings. The silvery leaves and stems also dry well.

Tagetes hybrids
COMPOSITAE

MARIGOLDS

Marigolds can add bright color to any sunny spot. Mix them with other annuals and perennials, or grow them alone in masses. Tall-stemmed types may need staking.

Description These popular half-hardy annuals are grown for their bright, 2–4-inch (5–10-cm) wide summer flowers and bushy mounds of lacy, green leaves. African or American marigolds (*T. erecta*) tend to be large plants, with 18–36-inch (45–90-cm) stems and large, usually double, yellow or orange flowers. French marigolds (*T. patula*) tend to be much daintier, with many smaller, single or double flowers in yellow, orange, or red on 12-inch (30-cm) tall plants.
Height and spread Height 6–36 inches (15–90 cm); spread 6–18 inches (15–45 cm).
Best site Full sun; average, well-drained soil. Light afternoon shade can help prolong bloom in hot-summer areas, especially for creamy-flowered cultivars.
Growing guidelines For earliest bloom (especially for tall-growing types), start seed indoors four to six weeks before your last frost date. Plant seed ⅛–¼ inch (3–6 mm) deep. Set plants out after your last frost date. You can also sow seed of small, early-blooming types directly into the garden after the last frost date.
Landscape uses Grow as summer fillers or edgings for flower beds and borders.

Tithonia rotundifolia
COMPOSITAE

MEXICAN SUNFLOWER

Mexican sunflowers are popular with bees and butterflies, and they make good cut flowers. Pinch off spent blooms to extend the flowering season.

Other common names Torch flower.
Description Mexican sunflower is a half-hardy annual with colorful blooms. Plants produce tall, sturdy, hairy stems with velvety, lobed or broadly oval, pointed, dark green leaves. During summer, the shrubby clumps are accented with many 3-inch (7.5-cm) wide, glowing orange, daisy-like flowers.
Height and spread Height 4–6 feet (1.2–1.8 m); spread 18–24 inches (45–60 cm).
Best site Full sun; average, well-drained soil with added organic matter.
Growing guidelines For earliest flowers, start seed indoors six to eight weeks before your last frost date. Sow seed ¼ inch (6 mm) deep in individual pots (two or three seeds per pot); thin to leave one seedling per pot. Set plants out after the last frost date. Mexican sunflowers also grow quickly and easily from seed sown directly into the garden about two weeks after the last frost date. Set plants or thin seedlings to stand 18 inches (45 cm) apart. Water during dry spells. Plants growing in exposed sites may need staking.
Landscape uses Makes an attractive flowering screen or hedge. It also looks great as a tall accent or background plant.

Torenia fournieri
SCROPHULARIACEAE

WISHBONE FLOWER

Wishbone flowers are usually purplish blue with a yellow throat; they may also be white or pink. The mouth of each bloom has two short, curved stamens that resemble a wishbone.

Other common names Bluewings.
Description This tender, shade-loving annual forms clumps of upright, many-branched stems with oval, pointed to narrow, toothed, green leaves that take on reddish purple tints in fall. The stems are topped with trumpet-shaped, lipped blooms to 1 inch (2.5 cm) long from early summer through fall.
Height and spread Height to 12 inches (30 cm); spread 6–8 inches (15–20 cm).
Best site Partial shade; moist, well-drained soil. Plants can take more sun in cool Northern gardens.
Growing guidelines Sow seed indoors eight to ten weeks before your last frost date. Don't cover the seed; just press it lightly into the soil. Enclose the pot in a plastic bag, and set it in a warm, dark place. When seedlings appear (in about one week), remove the bag and set the pot in a bright place. Set plants out after the last frost date; space them 6 inches (15 cm) apart. Water during dry spells. If plants start to flop, shear them back by about half to promote branching.
Landscape uses Use as an edging or filler for shady beds and borders. It also looks good in containers and window boxes.

Tropaeolum majus
TROPAEOLACEAE

GARDEN NASTURTIUM

Garden nasturtiums are half-hardy annuals with brightly colored flowers. Bushy types are great as edgings or fillers for beds and borders. Nasturtiums may self-sow.

Description Plants grow either as a climbing or trailing vine or as a bushy mound. The plants bear showy, fragrant, five-petaled blooms to 2 inches (5 cm) wide from early summer through fall. Garden nasturtiums bloom in a range of colors, including cream, rose, red, orange, and yellow.

Height and spread Height of vining types to about 8 feet (2.4 m), bush types to about 12 inches (30 cm); spread 6–12 inches (15–30 cm).

Best site Full sun; average, well-drained to dry soil.

Growing guidelines If you're growing vining types, put up some kind of support before planting. For an extra-early start, sow seed indoors four to six weeks before your last frost date. Soak the seed overnight before planting; then sow it ¼–½ inch (6–12 mm) deep in peat pots. Set plants out after the last frost date. They will also grow easily from seed sown directly into the garden 12 weeks before your last frost date. Watch for aphids; use a strong spray of water to wash them off.

Landscape uses Use climbing types to quickly cover trellises; grow the compact types in containers or as edgings or fillers.

Viola x wittrockiana
VIOLACEAE

PANSY

To keep pansies happy, mulch the soil around them and water during dry spells to keep the roots moist. Pinching off spent flowers can prolong bloom; leave a few to self-sow.

Description These short-lived perennials are usually grown as hardy annuals or biennials. Plants form tidy clumps of oval to narrow, green leaves with rounded teeth. Flat, five-petaled flowers bloom just above the clumps, mainly in spring but also sometimes in fall. The 2–5-inch (5–12.5-cm) wide flowers bloom in a range of colors, including white, pink, red, orange, yellow, purple, blue, and near black; many have contrasting faces.

Height and spread Height 6–8 inches (15–20 cm); spread 8–12 inches (20–30 cm).

Best site Full sun to partial shade; moist, well-drained soil.

Growing guidelines For bloom the same year, buy plants in early spring or start seed indoors eight to ten weeks before your last frost date. Sow seed ⅛ inch (3 mm) deep. Set the pot in a refrigerator for 12 weeks, then move it to a bright place. Set seedlings out 12 weeks before your last frost date. To grow pansies as biennials for earlier spring bloom, sow the seed outdoors in a nursery bed in late spring; move plants to the garden in midfall.

Landscape uses Use them as fillers or as an edging. They are also cute in containers.

Zinnia elegans
COMPOSITAE

COMMON ZINNIA

Common zinnias are excellent for replacing early-blooming annuals and filling in gaps left by dormant spring-flowering bulbs and perennials. They are also great cut flowers.

Description Plants produce stiff, sturdy stems with pairs of oval to pointed, green leaves. The stems are topped with blooms from midsummer until frost in nearly every color of the rainbow (except true blue). Common zinnias come in a range of flower forms, from 1–6 inches (2.5–15 cm) across. The petals of the single or double blooms may be quilled (curled), ruffled, or flat.

Height and spread Height 6–36 inches (15–90 cm), depending on the cultivar; spread usually 12–24 inches (30–60 cm).

Best site Full sun; average, well-drained soil with added organic matter.

Growing guidelines Buy transplants in spring, or sow seed indoors three to four weeks before your last frost date. Plant seed ¼–½ inch (6–12 mm) deep in peat pots (two or three seeds per pot). Thin seedlings to one per pot. Set plants out after the last frost date. Common zinnias also grow quickly from seed sown directly into the garden one to two weeks after the last frost date, when the soil is warm. Mulch plants to keep the roots moist. Tall cultivars may need staking.

Landscape uses Grow them alone in masses, or mix them with other plants in flower beds, borders, and cottage gardens.

Allium giganteum
LILIACEAE

GIANT ONION

The large bulbs of giant onion produce showy flower heads in early summer. Plant perennials or summer-blooming annuals at the base to fill in when the bulbs go dormant.

Description Wide, flat, sprawling, blue-green leaves emerge in mid- to late-spring; they have an oniony odor when bruised. A tall, slender stem rises from the center of the leaves in late spring. By early- to mid-summer, the stem is topped with a 6-inch (15-cm) globe that's densely packed with many small, reddish purple flowers. The leaves will turn yellow and die back to the ground by midsummer.
Height and spread Height of leaves usually 6–12 inches (15–30 cm); flower stems grow to 5 feet (1.5 m). Spread to about 12 inches (30 cm).
Best site and climate Full sun, but tolerates light shade; average, well-drained soil. Zones 5–8.
Growing guidelines Plant bulbs in early- to mid-fall or in early spring. Set them in individual holes or larger planting areas dug 8 inches (20 cm) deep. In Zones 5 and 6, protect bulbs over winter with a loose mulch; remove in spring. Cut down spent flower stems, unless you want to collect seed or use the dried seed head for arrangements. Leave established bulbs undisturbed in the garden.
Landscape uses A showstopping accent for the back of flower beds and borders.

Anemone blanda
RANUNCULACEAE

GRECIAN WINDFLOWER

Grecian windflowers bloom in mid- to late-spring in most areas; in warm Southern gardens, they may appear in late winter or early spring. They thrive in sun or light shade.

Description Grecian windflowers grow from knobbly tubers to produce carpets of deeply lobed, toothed, green leaves. Daisy-like blue, pink, or white spring flowers to 2 inches (5 cm) across bloom just above the ferny leaves.
Height and spread Height of leaves and flowers to 6 inches (15 cm); spread 4–6 inches (10–15 cm).
Best site and climate Full sun to partial shade (ideally under deciduous trees and shrubs); average to moist, well-drained soil. Zones 5–8.
Growing guidelines Buy and plant the tubers in late spring through early fall. Soak them overnight before planting, and set them in individual holes or larger planting areas dug about 2 inches (5 cm) deep. It can be hard to tell which side is up. If you can see a shallow depression on one side, plant with that side up; otherwise, plant the tubers on their sides or just drop them into the hole. Space the tubers 4–6 inches (10–15 cm) apart. Grecian windflowers propagate themselves by spreading and self-sowing.
Landscape uses Naturalize masses of them under trees for sheets of spring color. They combine well with daffodils.

Begonia Tuberhybrida hybrids
BEGONIACEAE

HYBRID TUBEROUS BEGONIAS

Hybrid tuberous begonias bloom in a wide range of colors, except for blues and purples; many are edged or shaded with other colors. Pinch off spent flowers to keep plants tidy.

Description Hybrid tuberous begonias grow from flattened, circular, light brown tubers. These tubers produce fleshy, upright or trailing stems with pointed oval to heart-shaped, hairy, toothed, green leaves. The bushy plants produce an abundance of gorgeous single or double flowers up to 4 inches (10 cm) across from summer through fall.
Height and spread Height to 18 inches (45 cm); spread 12–18 inches (30–45 cm).
Best site and climate Partial shade; evenly moist but well-drained soil with added organic matter. Hardy in Zone 10; elsewhere, grown as annuals or stored indoors in winter.
Growing guidelines Buy thick tubers that are 1½–2 inches (37–50 mm) across. Start them growing indoors about four weeks before your last frost date. Give developing plants plenty of bright light, and keep the soil evenly moist. Set plants out when night temperatures stay above 50°F (10°C). Water and mulch to keep the soil evenly moist. Fertilize several times during the season.
Landscape uses Plants are beautiful in shaded beds and borders and in containers and hanging baskets.

Caladium x hortulanum
ARACEAE

CALADIUM

Caladiums are grown for their showy leaves; pinch off any of the small, hooded flowers that appear in summer. These shade-loving plants thrive in heat and humidity.

Description Caladiums grow from tubers. They produce bushy clumps of long-stalked and usually heart-shaped leaves from late spring until frost. The lush leaves are shaded and veined with combinations of green, white, pink, and red.

Height and spread Height 12–24 inches (30–60 cm); spread to 24 inches (30 cm).

Best site and climate Partial shade; moist but well-drained soil with added organic matter. Hardy in Zone 10; elsewhere, grown as annuals or stored indoors for winter.

Growing guidelines Start the tubers indoors in early spring. Set them with the knobby side up in pots of moist potting mix, and cover them with 2 inches (5 cm) more of mix. Keep them in a warm, bright spot and keep the soil evenly moist. Move plants out to the garden when night temperatures stay above 60°F (16°C); space them about 12 inches (30 cm) apart. Mulch and water as needed to keep the soil moist until late summer. When the leaves die, dig up the tubers and store them in a warm place.

Landscape uses Caladiums provide summer color in shady beds and borders, especially in warm- and hot-summer areas.

Camassia quamash
LILIACEAE

COMMON CAMASS

In full sun, steady soil moisture is critical for success with common camass; in lightly shaded spots, the bulbs can withstand drier conditions.

Other common names Quamash, wild hyacinth.

Description In spring, common camass produces grassy clumps of long, narrow, gray-green leaves. By late spring, these clumps send up leafless stems topped with dense, spiky flower clusters. These spikes are made up of many 1–2-inch (2.5–5-cm) wide, starry flowers in white, or pale to deep blue. The leaves die in mid- to late-summer. Common camass is also sold as *C. esculenta*.

Height and spread Height 24–30 inches (60–75 cm); spread to 12 inches (30 cm).

Best site and climate Full sun to partial shade; moist but not waterlogged soil. Zones 4–8.

Growing guidelines The bulbs usually aren't available for sale at garden centers, so you'll probably have to buy them from a mail-order source. Plant the bulbs as soon as they arrive in fall. Set them in individual holes or in larger planting areas dug about 4 inches (10 cm) deep. Space the bulbs 8–10 inches (20–25 cm) apart. Cut down faded flower stems after bloom.

Landscape uses A natural choice for planting in low spots or along streams and ponds. It also grows well with moisture-loving shrubs and perennials.

Canna x generalis
CANNACEAE

CANNA

Cannas are drought-tolerant, but they grow even better with mulch and watering during dry spells. Pinch off spent flowers to prolong bloom.

Description Cannas grow from thick rhizomes. They produce tall, sturdy stems with large, oval, green or reddish purple leaves from spring until frost. The stems are topped with showy clusters of broad-petaled flowers up to 5 inches (12.5 cm) across from mid- through late-summer. The flowers bloom in shades of pink, red, orange, and yellow, as well as bicolors.

Height and spread Height 2–6 feet (60–180 cm) or more; spread 12–24 inches (30–60 cm).

Best site and climate Full sun to partial shade; average to moist, well-drained soil with added organic matter. Usually hardy in Zones 7–10; elsewhere, grown as annuals or stored indoors in winter.

Growing guidelines For the earliest show, start rhizomes indoors in pots about one month before your last frost date. Set out started plants two to three weeks after the last frost date. Or plant rhizomes directly into the garden around that time, setting them 3–4 inches (7.5–10 cm) deep and 12–18 inches (30–45 cm) apart.

Landscape uses Grow them alone in masses, or plant them with annuals and perennials in beds and borders. Cannas also grow well in containers.

Colchicum speciosum
LILIACEAE

SHOWY AUTUMN CROCUS

Showy autumn crocus grows from large, plump corms. Once established, each corm will produce showy clumps of rosy pink flowers in late summer to early fall.

Description Wide, flat, glossy green leaves emerge in late fall or early spring, elongate through spring, then turn yellow and die to the ground in early summer. Rosy pink, 4-inch (10-cm) wide, goblet-shaped, stemless flowers rise directly from the ground in late summer to early fall.

Height and spread Height of leaves to about 8 inches (20 cm); flowers 4–6 inches (10–15 cm) tall. Spread to about 6 inches (15 cm).

Best site and climate Full sun to partial shade; average, well-drained soil. Zones 4–9.

Growing guidelines Plant corms in mid- to late- summer, as soon as they are available; they may begin to bloom even before you plant them if you delay. Set the corms in individual holes or in larger planting areas dug about 4 inches (10 cm) deep. Space bulbs 6 inches (15 cm) apart. Divide just after the leaves die down only if needed for propagation.

Landscape uses Showy autumn crocus is beautiful but a little tricky to site effectively. It's usually best coming up through low groundcovers or under shrubs, where the coarse spring leaves won't detract from or smother other flowers.

Crocus vernus
IRIDACEAE

DUTCH CROCUS

Dutch crocus are one of the earliest spring flowers, a welcome sight after a long, cold winter. After bloom, the leaves continue to elongate until they ripen and die back to the ground in early summer.

Description Dutch crocus grow from small corms. They appear in late winter to early spring, with leaves and flowers at the same time. The grasslike leaves are thin and green with a white center stripe. Goblet-shaped, stemless flowers up to 3 inches (7.5 cm) across bloom just above the leaves. The flowers are white, lavender, purple, or yellow; they may be striped with contrasting colors.

Height and spread Height of leaves to 8 inches (20 cm); flowers usually to 4 inches (10 cm) tall. Spread 1–3 inches (2.5–7.5 cm).

Best site and climate Full sun to partial shade (under deciduous trees and shrubs); average, well-drained soil. Zones 3–8.

Growing guidelines Plant the corms in fall. Set them pointed side up in individual holes or larger planting areas dug 2–4 inches (5–10 cm) deep. Space the corms 2 inches (5 cm) apart. Dutch crocus usually return year after year and spread to form showy clumps. Interplanting crocus corms with daffodil bulbs (which are toxic if eaten) may help discourage mice.

Landscape uses Include them in beds and borders for early color. Grow them in containers for outdoor spring bloom.

Cyclamen hederifolium
PRIMULACEAE

HARDY CYCLAMEN

Hardy cyclamen grow well under shrubs and trees— even in dry summer shade-—and are attractive through most of the year. Top-dress with a thin layer of compost in late summer.

Description Hardy cyclamen grow from smooth tubers. They bloom in early fall, with leafless flower stalks topped with pink or white flowers. The 1-inch (2.5-cm) long, nodding flowers have upward-pointing petals. Handsome, heart-shaped, silver-marked, green leaves emerge shortly after the blooms finish. The leaves die back by midsummer but return again by midfall.

Height and spread Height and spread of flowers and foliage 4–6 inches (10–15 cm).

Best site and climate Partial shade; average, well-drained soil. Zones 5–9.

Growing guidelines Many commercial cyclamen sources sell wild-collected tubers. Avoid supporting this irresponsible practice Buy nursery-propagated tubers or start your own from seed. Soak the seed overnight, then sow it ¼ inch (6 mm) deep in a pot. Enclose the pot in a plastic bag, then set it in a dark place. Set plants into the garden in spring or summer. Or plant dormant tubers shallowly in summer, making sure the smooth, unmarked side is on the bottom.

Landscape uses Hardy cyclamen look good in shady spots with ferns and hellebores (*Helleborus* spp.).

Dahlia hybrids
COMPOSITAE

DAHLIAS

Pinch off stem tips in early summer to promote bushy growth and more (but smaller) flowers. Or, to get the largest flowers, pinch off sideshoots to leave one or two main stems.

Description Some types, known as bedding dahlias, form compact, bushy plants; others produce the tall, large-flowered border favorites. Both types have upright stems with divided, green (or sometimes purple-tinted) leaves. Dahlias bloom from midsummer through fall, with flowers 1–8 inches (2.5–20 cm) across. They come in almost every color but true blue—even in near black and bicolors.
Height and spread Height varies from 1 foot (30 cm) for bedding types to 5 feet (1.5 m) for border types. Spread to 1 foot (30 cm) for bedding types and 4 feet (1.2 m) for border types.
Best site and climate Full sun; average, well-drained soil. Hardy in Zones 9 and 10; elsewhere, grow as annuals.
Growing guidelines Start bedding types from seed sown indoors six to eight weeks before your last frost date. In Northern areas, start tuberous roots indoors two to three weeks before your last frost date; set started plants out one to two weeks after the last frost date. Elsewhere, plant the roots directly into the garden around the last frost date.
Landscape uses Plant in beds and borders and in the cutting garden.

Fritillaria imperalis
LILIACEAE

CROWN IMPERIAL

Crown imperials may take a few seasons to get established and bloom well; mature clumps can live for many years. All parts of the plant have a musky (some say skunk-like) odor.

Description Crown imperial grows from a large, fleshy bulb. Sturdy shoots of green stems and glossy green leaves emerge in early spring and elongate for several weeks. By mid- to late-spring, the tall stems are topped with a tuft of green leaves and hanging, bell-shaped, yellow, orange, or red flowers about 2 inches (5 cm) long. Soon after bloom, the leaves and stems turn yellow; they die back to the ground by midsummer.
Height and spread Height 24–48 inches (60–120 cm); spread to 12 inches (30 cm).
Best site and climate Full spring sun; average to sandy, well-drained soil. Zones 5–9.
Growing guidelines Plant the bulbs in late summer or early fall. Dig a large hole for each bulb or prepare a large planting area; make either about 8 inches (20 cm) deep. Loosen the soil at the base of the hole to promote good drainage. When you set the bulb in the hole, tilt it slightly to one side to discourage water from collecting in the depression at the top of the bulb.
Landscape uses Crown imperial make striking spring accents for beds and borders.

Fritillaria meleagris
LILIACEAE

CHECKERED LILY

The pretty nodding flowers of checkered lilies add a charming touch to spring gardens. Naturalize them in wild areas, or plant them in clumps in beds and borders.

Other common names Guinea-hen flower, snake's-head lily.
Description Checkered lily grows from small bulbs. Slender, arching stems with narrow, gray-green leaves rise in early spring. By midspring, broad, nodding, bell-like blooms dangle from the ends of the nodding stems. The 1–2-inch (2.5–5-cm) long flowers range in color from white to deep purple; many are marked with a checkered pattern. Checkered lilies die back to the ground by midsummer.
Height and spread Height to 12 inches (30 cm); spread 2–4 inches (5–10 cm).
Best site and climate Partial shade; average, well-drained soil. Zones 3–8.
Growing guidelines Plant in early fall. Dig the holes or planting areas 2–3 inches (5–7.5 cm) deep. Space bulbs 4–6 inches (10–15 cm) apart. Leave established clumps undisturbed to form large sweeps of spring color.
Landscape uses Checkered lilies look lovely when naturalized in masses in woodland or meadow gardens. Or grow them in beds and borders under deciduous trees; these small bulbs combine beautifully with ferns and hellebores (*Helleborus* spp.).

Galanthus nivalis
AMARYLLIDACEAE

COMMON SNOWDROP

Common snowdrops are among the earliest flowers to bloom in the spring garden. Established bulbs are trouble-free; they will spread and reseed freely.

Description Common snowdrops grow from small bulbs. Each bulb produces two or three flat, narrow, green leaves and an upright to arching green flower stem in midwinter through early spring. Dainty, nodding flowers to 1 inch (2.5 cm) long bloom at the tips of the stems in late winter or early spring. The single or double flowers are white; each of the shorter, inner petals has a green tip. Plants die back to the ground by early summer.

Height and spread Height of flowers and foliage to 6 inches (15 cm); spread 2–3 inches (5–7.5 cm).

Best site and climate Full sun to partial shade; average to moist, well-drained soil with added organic matter. Zones 3–9.

Growing guidelines Plant bulbs in fall. Set them in individual holes or larger planting areas dug 3–4 inches (7.5–10 cm) deep. Space each bulb 3–4 inches (7.5–10 cm) apart.

Landscape uses Grow clumps of common snowdrop in the garden with other early flowers, such as snow crocus and Christmas rose (*Helleborus niger*). Or naturalize them in lawns, groundcovers, and low-maintenance areas or under deciduous trees and shrubs. (In lawns, you'll have to wait until the leaves have died before mowing.)

Gladiolus x hortulanus
IRIDACEAE

GLADIOLUS

Gladioli bloom in nearly every color but true blue; many have spots or splashes of contrasting colors. For cut flowers, pick them just as the bottom bud begins to open.

Description Gladioli grow from flattened corms. They produce tall fans of flat, sword-shaped, green leaves. A slender flower stem rises from the center of each fan in summer to early fall (depending on the planting time). The flower stem is topped with a many-budded spike that blooms from the bottom up. The buds produce open, funnel-shaped flowers up to 4 inches (10 cm) across. The leaves usually turn yellow several weeks after bloom.

Height and spread Height 2–5 feet (60–150 cm); spread 6–12 inches (15–30 cm).

Best site and climate Full sun; average, well-drained soil. Usually hardy in Zones 8–10; elsewhere, grow as annuals.

Growing guidelines Start planting the corms outdoors after the last frost date in spring. Set them in individual holes or larger planting areas dug 4–6 inches (10–25 cm) deep. To extend the bloom season, plant more corms every two weeks until midsummer. Tall-flowering types benefit from staking. In cold areas, dig the corms before or just after the first frost, and store them indoors in a frost-free area.

Landscape uses Plant in the middle and back of beds and borders.

Hyacinthoides hispanica
LILIACEAE

SPANISH BLUEBELLS

Established patches of Spanish bluebells increase quickly, often to the point of becoming invasive. Removing spent flower stalks will minimize reseeding; mow unwanted plants.

Description Spanish bluebells grow from small bulbs. In spring, the plants form clumps of sprawling, strap-shaped, green leaves. Upright, leafless flower stems topped with spikes of many bell-shaped blooms appear in late spring. The ¼-inch (18-mm) wide flowers bloom in white, pink, or shades of purple-blue. Plants go dormant by midsummer. Spanish bluebells are still sold under a variety of former names, including *Scilla campanulata*, *Scilla hispanica*, and *Endymion hispanicus*.

Height and spread Height of flowers 12–18 inches (30–45 cm); leaves usually to 8 inches (20 cm) tall. Spread 4–6 inches (10–15 cm).

Best site and climate Full sun to partial shade; average, well-drained soil with added organic matter. Zones 4–8.

Growing guidelines Plant the bulbs in fall. Set them in individual holes or larger planting areas dug 3–4 inches (7.5–10 cm) deep. Space each bulb 4–6 inches (10–25 cm) apart.

Landscape uses Include clumps in beds and borders, combine them with groundcovers, or naturalize them in woodlands and low-maintenance areas.

Hyacinthus orientalis
LILIACEAE

HYACINTH

After the first year, hyacinth bloom spikes tend to become smaller; in some cases, they may not flower at all. Plant new bulbs every year or two to ensure a good display.

Description Hyacinths grow from plump bulbs. Sturdy shoots with wide, strap-shaped, green leaves and upright flower stalks emerge in early spring. By midspring, each stalk is topped with a dense spike of starry, 1-inch (2.5-cm) wide, powerfully fragrant flowers. The single or double flowers bloom in a wide range of colors, including white, pink, red, orange, yellow, blue, and purple. Hyacinths go dormant in early summer.
Height and spread Height 8–12 inches (20–30 cm); spread to 4 inches (15 cm).
Best site and climate Full sun; average, well-drained soil with added organic matter. Zones 4–8.
Growing guidelines Plant bulbs in midfall. Set them in individual holes or larger planting areas dug 5–6 inches (12.5–15 cm) deep. Space the bulbs 6–10 inches (15–20 cm) apart. Double-flowered types may need staking. Remove spent flower stalks. Dig up and divide crowded clumps as the leaves yellow.
Landscape uses Hyacinths contribute cheerful spring color to flower beds and borders. Combine them with primroses and pansies for extra excitement. They also grow well in containers.

Iris reticulata
IRIDACEAE

RETICULATED IRIS

Reticulated irises return year after year to grace your garden with their delicate spring flowers. Tuck them into beds, borders, and rock gardens; they look great in pots, too.

Description Reticulated irises grow from small bulbs. The dainty blue, purple, or white, early spring flowers have three upright petals (known as standards) and three outward-arching petals (known as falls). The falls have gold and/or white markings. The grasslike, dark green leaves are short at bloom time but elongate after the flowers fade; they ripen and die back to the ground by early summer.
Height and spread Height of flowers 4–6 inches (10–15 cm); leaves to 12 inches (30 cm). Spread to 2 inches (5 cm).
Best site and climate Full sun; average, well-drained soil. Zones 5–9.
Growing guidelines Plant the bulbs in fall. Set them in individual holes or larger planting areas dug 3–4 inches (7.5–10 cm) deep. For propagation, lift and divide clumps after the leaves turn yellow.
Landscape uses The delicate, lightly fragrant blooms are beautiful in spring beds and borders. For extra color, combine them with Grecian windflowers (*Anemone blanda*) and early crocus. Reticulated irises also grow well in pots for spring bloom outdoors or winter forcing indoors.

Leucojum aestivum
AMARYLLIDACEAE

SUMMER SNOWFLAKE

Despite their name, summer snowflakes actually bloom in spring. Plant the small bulbs in groups; over time, they'll form large clumps.

Other common names Giant snowflake.
Description Clumps of strap-shaped, green leaves emerge in early spring. In mid- to late-spring, plants produce slender, green flowering stems tipped with loose clusters of nodding, bell-shaped, ¼-inch (18-mm) wide flowers. The white flowers have a green spot near the tip of each petal. After bloom, the leaves turn yellow and die back to the ground by midsummer.
Height and spread Height of foliage and flowers to 18 inches (30 cm); spread to 6 inches (15 cm).
Best site and climate Full sun to partial shade; moist but well-drained soil with added organic matter. Zones 4–9.
Growing guidelines In early fall, set bulbs in individual holes or larger planting areas dug 4 inches (10 cm) deep. Space them about 6 inches (15 cm) apart. For propagation, divide in early fall.
Landscape uses Grow summer snowflakes with tulips and daffodils in flower beds and borders. Interplant with summer- and fall-blooming annuals that will fill in when the bulbs go dormant. They also look great naturalized in moist meadows and woodlands.

Lilium hybrids
LILIACEAE

LILIES

Lilies are excellent as cut flowers; pick them when the first one or two buds open. You may want to remove the orange anthers to keep them from dropping pollen on furniture.

Description Lilies grow from scaly bulbs. They produce upright, unbranched stems with narrow to lance-shaped, green leaves in spring through early summer. By early to late summer (depending on the hybrid), the long, plump flower buds open to showy, flat or funnel-shaped flowers. After bloom, the leaves and stems usually stay green until late summer or early fall.
Height and spread Height 2–5 feet (60–150 cm), depending on the hybrid; spread usually 6–12 inches (15–30 cm).
Best site and climate Full sun to partial shade; average, well-drained soil. Usually Zones 4–8.
Growing guidelines Plant bulbs in fall or early spring. Dig individual holes or larger planting areas 6–8 inches (15–20 cm) deep. Pinch off spent flowers where they join the stem. Cut stems to the ground when the leaves turn yellow; divide clumps at the same time if needed for propagation.
Landscape uses Lilies add height and color to any flower bed or border. They're also elegant mixed into foundation plantings, grouped with shrubs, or naturalized in woodlands. Combine them with mounding annuals, perennials, or groundcovers that can shade the soil.

Lycoris squamigera
AMARYLLIDACEAE

MAGIC LILY

Magic lily bulbs produce leaves in spring and leafless flower stalks in late summer. Some gardeners like to combine them with bushy plants to hide the bare stems.

Description Slender, greenish brown, leafless stems rise from the ground in late summer to early fall. They are topped with loose clusters of funnel-shaped, rosy pink flowers up to 4 inches (10 cm) long. The broad, strap-shaped, green leaves usually begin to emerge several weeks after the blooms fade. The foliage elongates in spring and dies back to the ground in summer, one to two months before new blooms appear.
Height and spread Height of flowers to 24 inches (60 cm); leaves to 12 inches (30 cm). Spread to 6 inches (15 cm).
Best site and climate Full sun to partial shade; average, well-drained soil that's dry in summer. Zones 5–9.
Growing guidelines Plant bulbs in midsummer. Set them in individual holes or larger planting areas dug 4–5 inches (10–12.5 cm) deep. Space bulbs about 8 inches (20 cm) apart. Water during dry spells in fall and spring. Protect the leaves over winter with a loose mulch, such as evergreen branches, pine needles, or straw.
Landscape uses They grow best when naturalized on slopes, among groundcovers, or in low-maintenance areas.

Muscari armeniacum
LILIACEAE

GRAPE HYACINTH

Once planted, grape hyacinths are trouble-free. They naturalize well under trees and shrubs, and they look attractive combined with groundcovers.

Description Grape hyacinths grow from small bulbs. The narrow, grasslike, green leaves appear in fall and elongate through the spring. The clumps are accented by short, leafless stems topped with dense spikes of grapelike blooms in early spring. The individual purple-blue, white-rimmed flowers are only ¼ inch (6 mm) wide. The leaves turn yellow and die back to the ground by early summer.
Height and spread Height of flowers and foliage 6–8 inches (15–20 cm); spread 3–4 inches (7.5–10 cm).
Best site and climate Full sun to partial shade (under deciduous trees and shrubs); average, well-drained soil. Zones 4–8.
Growing guidelines Plant bulbs in early- to mid-fall, as soon as they are available. Set them in individual holes or larger planting areas dug 2–3 inches (5–7.5 cm) deep. Space the bulbs about 4 inches (10 cm) apart. For propagation, divide just after the leaves die back in early summer. Otherwise, leave the bulbs undisturbed to form sweeps of spring color.
Landscape uses Scatter the bulbs liberally throughout flower beds and borders. Mix them with primroses, pansies, daffodils, and tulips for an unforgettable spring show.

Narcissus hybrids
AMARYLLIDACEAE

DAFFODILS

It's hard to imagine a garden without at least a few daffodils for spring color. Grow them in borders, plant them under trees, or naturalize them in low-maintenance areas.

Description Daffodils grow from large, pointed bulbs. Clumps of flat, strap-shaped, green leaves emerge in early spring, along with leafless flower stalks. The sometimes-fragrant flowers appear in early-, mid-, or late-spring. Each flower has a cup or trumpet (technically known as a corona) and an outer ring of petals (known as the perianth). The single or double blooms are most commonly white or yellow but may also have pink, green, or orange markings.
Height and spread Height of foliage and flowers 6–20 inches (15–50 cm), spread usually 4–8 inches (10–20 cm).
Best site and climate Full sun to partial shade; average, well-drained soil with added organic matter. Zones 4–8.
Growing guidelines Plant the bulbs in early- to mid-fall. Set them in individual holes or larger planting areas dug 4–8 inches (10–20 cm) deep. Allow the leaves to turn yellow before cutting them back or pulling them out.
Landscape uses Create unforgettable combinations by grouping daffodils with other early bloomers, including pansies, crocus, Siberian squill (*Scilla sibirica*), grape hyacinths (*Muscari* spp.), and Grecian windflower (*Anemone blanda*).

Scilla sibirica
LILIACEAE

SIBERIAN SQUILL

The deep blue blooms of Siberian squill look marvelous in masses. They also combine beautifully with many other spring-flowering bulbs, annuals, and perennials.

Description Siberian squills grow from small bulbs. They produce narrow, strap-shaped, green leaves and leafless flower stems starting in late winter. By early- to mid-spring, the flower stems are topped with clusters of nodding, starry or bell-shaped blue flowers to ½ inch (12 mm) across. By early summer, the leaves gradually turn yellow and die back.
Height and spread Height of flowers and foliage to 6 inches (15 cm). Spread 2–3 inches (5–7.5 cm).
Best site and climate Full sun to partial shade; average, well-drained soil. Zones 3–8.
Growing guidelines Plant bulbs in early- to mid-fall, as soon as they are available. Set them in individual holes or larger planting areas dug 3–4 inches (7.5–10 cm) deep. Established bulbs are trouble-free. For propagation, divide bulbs after the leaves turn yellow; otherwise, leave them undisturbed to spread into large clumps.
Landscape uses Tuck them into beds and borders with pansies, primroses, and daffodils. They are also excellent for naturalizing in lawns and low-maintenance areas and under trees and shrubs; wait until the bulb leaves have turned yellow to mow.

Tulipa hybrids
LILIACEAE

TULIPS

Hybrid tulips often bloom poorly after the first year. For a great show each year, pull them out after bloom and replace them with summer annuals; plant new tulips in fall.

Description Tulips grow from plump, pointed bulbs. The bulbs produce broad, dusty-green leaves that are sometimes striped with maroon in early- to mid-spring. The slender, upright, usually unbranched flower stems are topped with showy single or double flowers up to 4 inches (10 cm) across. By midsummer, leaves gradually turn yellow and die back to the ground.
Height and spread Height from 6–30 inches (15–90 cm), depending on the cultivar; spread 6–10 inches (15–25 cm).
Best site and climate Full sun to partial shade; average, well-drained soil that's dry in summer. Usually best in Zones 3–8; in Zones 9 and 10, treat hybrid tulips as annuals and plant precooled bulbs each year in late fall or early winter.
Growing guidelines Plant bulbs in mid- to late-fall. Set them in individual holes or larger planting areas dug 4–6 inches (10–15 cm) deep. Pinch off the developing seedpods after flowering, and allow the leaves to yellow before removing them. Or pull them out after bloom.
Landscape uses Tulips are an indispensable part of the spring garden. They are also charming as cut flowers.

Abies homolepis
PINACEAE

NIKKO FIR

Like all firs, Nikko fir is a coniferous evergreen tree that grows best in cool, moist climates. It has a columnar habit and glossy needlelike leaves held in whorls on the branches.

Flower color and season Insignificant green or yellowish flowers in spring, followed by upright tannish cones in summer to winter.
Height and spread To 100 feet (30 m) tall and 30 feet (9 m) wide.
Best climate and size Zones 4–7. Deep, moist, well-drained soil. Full sun to light shade.
Cultivation Best transplanted in spring or winter, balled-and-burlapped. Pruning not necessary.
Propagation Sow seed in fall. Take cuttings in winter. Graft in late winter and early spring.
Pest and disease prevention Heat- and water-stressed plants are more attractive to pests and susceptible to diseases. Mulch regularly with organic matter to keep soil moist. Avoid planting in hot, dry areas.
Common problems Intolerant of city pollution.
Landscape use Specimen tree; screens.
Other species *A. concolor*, white or Colorado fir, has curving, claw-shaped needles that are gray-green or blue-gray. It grows to 100 feet (30 m) tall and 40 feet (12 m) wide. 'Conica' is a dwarf pyramidal form.

Acer spp.
ACERACEAE

MAPLE

A. saccharum, sugar maple, is a handsome shade tree for a large yard. Prized in the landscape for its outstanding fall color, it is also the chief source of maple syrup and sugar.

Flower color and season *A. griseum*: yellow-green flowers; *A. palmatum*: purple flowers; *A. platanoides*: yellow flowers; *A. rubrum*: red flowers; *A. saccharum*: greenish yellow flowers. All bloom in early spring.
Height and spread Height varies from 12 feet (3.6 m) to 100 feet (30 m); spread from 15 feet (4.5 m) to 70 feet (21 m).
Best climate and site Depending on species, Zones 3–9. Partial shade for *A. palmatum*; other species prefer full sun.
Cultivation Transplant bareroot, container-grown or balled-and-burlapped plants in spring. Prune in winter only to initially shape the young tree.
Propagation Sow seed in fall or spring. Take cuttings in late spring or winter. Graft in late winter or early spring.
Pest and disease prevention Avoid damaging the bark with gardening tools such as lawn mowers. Wounds are entry points for pests and diseases.
Common problems Many maple species have shallow, spreading roots that make growing other plants under them difficult.
Landscape use Specimen plant; shade trees. *A. platanoides* and *A. rubrum* make excellent street trees.

Betula papyrifera
BETULACEAE

CANOE BIRCH

Native to northeastern North America, canoe birch is a tall deciduous tree that grows best in cool climates. Its mature trunks and branches are white with distinct black markings.

Flower color and season Tannish green flowers in catkins in early- to mid-spring.
Height and spread To 60 feet (18 m) tall and 30 feet (9 m) wide.
Best climate and site Zones 2–6. Moist, well-drained, deep soil. Full sun to partial shade.
Cultivation Plant in spring. Prune only in late summer or fall, as pruning at other times can cause excessive "bleeding." Pruning is only necessary initially to shape the tree.
Propagation Sow seed in fall. Graft in late winter and early spring.
Pest and disease prevention Drought stress can weaken tree, making them more susceptible to pests and diseases. Plant in evenly moist soil and water during extended drought periods.
Common problems Can be short-lived, especially in hot, dry areas.
Landscape use Specimen tree; group plantings.
Other species *B. nigra*, river birch, is a pyramidal tree with reddish brown exfoliating bark. It is tolerant of swampy conditions. Zones 4–8. *B. pendula*, European white birch, has silvery white bark marked with black. Zones 2–6.

Carpinus betulus
BETULACEAE

EUROPEAN HORNBEAM

European hornbeam is a slow-growing deciduous tree with an upright oval form and serrated green leaves. This easy-care tree tolerates heavy pruning and is often used for hedges.

Flower color and season Yellowish green flowers in catkins in early- to mid-spring.
Height and spread To 60 feet (18 m) tall and 30 feet (9 m) wide.
Best climate and site Zones 5–9. Moist, well-drained soil. Full sun to partial shade.
Cultivation Plant in spring. Prune in winter for hedges.
Propagation Sow seed in fall. Graft in late winter or early spring.
Pest and disease prevention May be subject to scale infestation. Prune and destroy affected parts. Plants in fertile soil with adequate moisture tolerate attacks better than plants that are water-stressed, nutrient-deficient, and overcrowded.
Common problems European hornbeam is difficult to transplant; plant young container-grown plants.
Landscape use Specimen tree; group plantings; hedges.
Other species *C. caroliniana*, American hornbeam, is a small bushy tree that provides excellent red fall foliage. 'Pyramidalis' grows to a pyramidal shape. Zones 2–7.

Cercidiphyllum japonicum
CERCIDIPHYLLACEAE

KATSURA TREE

Katsura tree is a deciduous tree from China and Japan. Its leaves are heart-shaped and mostly opposite; they turn yellow, orange, or red in fall and become sweetly fragrant.

Flower color and season Small reddish flowers without petals in mid- to late-spring.
Height and spread To 60 feet (18 m) tall and 3–50 feet (0.9–15 m) wide.
Best climate and site Zones 4–8. Very moist, well-drained soil. Full sun to light shade.
Cultivation Transplant container-grown or balled-and-burlapped plants in early spring. Prune only to shape when young.
Propagation Sow fresh seed as soon as available. Take cuttings in winter.
Pest and disease prevention Water during prolonged periods of drought to maintain vigor. Healthy plants are less susceptible to pest and diseases.
Common problems Usually trouble-free.
Landscape use Specimen tree; street trees, screens. If it grows to a single trunk, the form is markedly columnar; if multiple trunks form, the result is a wide-spreading tree.

Cercis canadensis
LEGUMINOSAE

EASTERN REDBUD

Eastern redbud is a flat-topped, broadly spreading deciduous tree native to eastern North America. It produces masses of pink flowers in spring; the foliage may turn yellow in fall.

Flower color and season Pink flowers in mid- to late-spring before leaves appear. Blooms are produced profusely at the joints of old wood (even along the trunk).
Height and spread To 30 feet (9 m) tall and 20 feet (6 m) wide.
Best climate and site Zones 4–9. Tolerant of a variety of soil conditions. Full sun to light shade.
Cultivation Difficult to transplant; best moved in winter when young.
Propagation Sow seed immediately upon ripening in late summer or fall.
Pest and disease prevention Keep vigorous by regular watering and feeding. Healthy plants are less susceptible to pests and diseases.
Common problems Sometimes subject to canker and verticillium wilt.
Landscape use Excellent small specimen tree; use alone or in combination with *Cornus florida* as a shade tree.
Other species *C. siliquastrum*, Judas tree, is very similar but is native to the eastern Mediterranean and Asia Minor. It produces purplish rose flowers and yellow fall foliage. Zones 6–9.

Chamaecyparis obtusa
CUPRESSACEAE

HINOKI FALSE CYPRESS

Hinoki false cypress is a slow-growing coniferous evergreen tree with flat sprays of waxy, dark green scalelike foliage. It grows in a broadly pyramidal form.

Flower color and season Inconspicuous flowers in spring; followed by brown cones in fall.
Height and spread To 100 feet (30 m) tall and 40 feet (12 m) wide.
Best climate and site Zones 5–8. Deep, loamy, moisture-retentive soil. Full sun.
Cultivation Transplant container-grown or balled-and-burlapped plants in spring. Prune plants to shape in spring.
Propagation Take cuttings in fall.
Pest and disease prevention Avoid damaging the trunk with lawn mowers or sharp gardening tools; these wounds are common entry points for pests and diseases.
Common problems Plants may be subject to a fungal disease that attacks roots. Dig out and destroy diseased plants. Plant in moist but well-drained soil to help prevent injury.
Landscape use Specimen tree; background trees.
Other species *C. lawsoniana*, Lawson false cypress, is a slender to broadly pyramidal tree with horizontal branches. The scalelike leaves differ widely in color. 'Allumii' is a conical spreading form with blue foliage. 'Aurea' has golden leaves.

Chionanthus virginicus
OLEACEAE

WHITE FRINGE TREE

White fringe tree is a deciduous small tree or large shrub with medium green leaves that turn yellow in fall. The loose clusters of white flowers bloom from late spring into summer.

Flower color and season Slightly fragrant white flowers borne in loose clusters from late spring to early summer; followed by blue grapelike fruit on female plants.
Height and spread To 30 feet (9 m) tall and as wide.
Best climate and site Zones 5–8. Humus-rich, moisture retentive, well-drained soil. Full sun.
Cultivation Transplant balled-and-burlapped or container-grown plants in spring. Prune after flowering only if shaping is required.
Propagation Sow seed in fall; may take two years to germinate. Take semihardwood cuttings in late summer.
Pest and disease prevention No serious pests or diseases.
Common problems Slow-growing.
Landscape use Specimen tree or shrub.
Other species *C. retusus*, Chinese fringe tree, is native to China, Korea, and Japan. It has smaller leaves and grows to 20 feet (6 m) tall with a rounded bushy form.

Cladrastis lutea
LEGUMINOSAE

AMERICAN YELLOWWOOD

Native to the southeastern United States, American yellowwood is a deciduous tree growing to a wide-spreading rounded form. The bark is pale gray and glossy; the leaves are compound.

Flower color and season Bell-shaped slightly fragrant white flowers, marked with yellow, borne in 1-foot (30-cm) long terminal clusters from late spring to early summer; flowers attractive to bees.
Height and spread To 4 feet (12 m) tall and slightly wider.
Best climate and site Zones 3–8. Tolerates a wide range of soil conditions but needs good drainage. Full sun to light shade.
Cultivation Transplant young balled-and-burlapped or container-grown plants in fall or spring. No pruning necessary unless shaping is desired.
Propagation Sow seed in fall. Take root cuttings in winter.
Pest and disease prevention No serious pests or diseases.
Common problems Bleeds profusely if pruned in winter or spring. Prune only in late summer or fall.
Landscape use Specimen tree; woodland plantings.
Cultivars 'Rosea' has light pink flowers.

Cornus spp.
CORNACEAE

DOGWOOD

Cornus florida, flowering dogwood, is often considered to be the finest native North American flowering tree. It produces showy white blooms in spring and red berries in fall.

Flower color and season C. *alternifolia*: small white or yellow flowers late winter to early spring; C. *florida*: inconspicuous yellow flowers with four broad, rounded white bracts in mid- to late-spring; C. *kousa*: similar flowers to C. *florida* from late spring to early summer, but bracts are pointed at the tips; C. *mas*: profuse yellow flowers from late winter to early spring.
Height and spread Height varies from 20 feet (6 m) to 40 feet (12 m); spread from 12 feet (3.6 m) to 40 feet (12 m).
Best climate and site Depending on species, Zones 3–9. Moisture-retentive, humus-rich, well-drained soil. Full sun to partial shade.
Cultivation Young plants transplant best during early spring. Prune trees only if necessary to shape.
Propagation Remove seed from its fleshy covering and sow in fall. Take cuttings in late spring. Graft in early spring.
Pest and disease prevention Plant in evenly moist soil.
Common problems Anthracnose has become a severe problem for C. *florida* in parts of North America.
Landscape use Excellent specimen or lawn tree, used singly or in groups.

Fagus sylvatica
FAGACEAE

EUROPEAN BEECH

European beech is a magnificent long-lived deciduous tree with smooth gray bark. It varies considerably in growth habit and in the form and color of its large leaves.

Flower color and season Inconspicuous greenish flowers in midspring; followed by small triangular nuts.
Height and spread To 100 feet (30 m) tall; spread varies with cultivar.
Best climate and site Zones 4–8. Deep, loamy, moist, humus-rich, well-drained soil.
Cultivation Transplant balled-and-burlapped plants in spring. Prune in summer only when young enough to establish a straight, upright trunk.
Propagation Graft in late winter and early spring. Sow seed in fall.
Pest and disease prevention Avoid overfeeding, which results in succulent growth that is attractive to aphids. Protect the shallow roots from compaction and other forms of soil disturbance.
Common problems Intolerant of poor drainage. The shallow roots and dense shade make it difficult to grow other plants under these trees.
Landscape use Specimen tree; shade trees; hedges.
Cultivars 'Laciniata' has ferny and deeply incised leaves. 'Pendula' has a weeping habit.

Gleditsia triacanthos
LEGUMINOSAE

HONEY LOCUST

Honey locust is a deciduous tree with compound leaves, and trunks and branches armed with sharp thorns. 'Sunburst' is a thornless cultivar with golden yellow young leaves.

Flower color and season Greenish flowers borne in clusters in late spring. The female flowers are followed by long scimitar-shaped brown pods.
Height and spread To 100 feet (30 m) tall and 60 feet (18 m) wide.
Best climate and site Zones 4–8. Moist, loamy, well-drained soil. Full sun.
Cultivation Plant in winter or spring. Prune in fall if necessary.
Propagation Graft in late winter or spring. Sow seed in spring.
Pest and disease prevention Honey locusts are prone to many pests and diseases. Healthy plants are more resistant to pest invasion. Mulch to keep the soil evenly moist. Look for resistant cultivars.
Common problems The thick, sharp thorns can be hazardous; choose thornless cultivars. Self-sown seedlings can be a nuisance; plant male cultivars.
Landscape use Specimen tree; shade trees.
Other species 'Moraine' is a thornless male cultivar that is somewhat resistant to webworm.

Halesia carolina
STYRACACEAE

CAROLINA SILVERBELL

Native to the southeastern United States, Carolina silverbell is a deciduous tree or shrub with elliptical leaves. The delicate bell-shaped white flowers bloom in spring.

Flower color and season Bell-shaped white flowers in clusters of three to five from mid- to late-spring.
Height and spread To 30 feet (9 m) tall and as wide.
Best climate and site Zones 5–8. Moisture-retentive, humus-rich, well-drained soil. Full sun to light shade; shelter from strong winds.
Cultivation Transplant balled-and-burlapped or container-grown plants in spring. Rarely needs pruning.
Propagation Sow seed in fall; may take two years to germinate.
Pest and disease prevention No serious pests or diseases. Keep soil moist with organic mulch.
Common problems Loses leaves very early in the season.
Landscape use Specimen tree, most effective against an evergreen background; woodland planting.
Other common names Snowdrop tree.
Cultivars 'Rosea' has light pink flowers.

Koelreuteria paniculata
SAPINDACEAE

GOLDEN-RAIN TREE

Golden-rain tree is a deciduous tree with compound leaves that turn bright yellow in fall. Its showy yellow summer flowers come at a time when few other trees are blooming.

Flower color and season Rich yellow flowers borne in dense, terminal racemes in midsummer; followed by bladderlike greenish pods.
Height and spread To 50 feet (15 m) tall and 40 feet (12 m) wide.
Best climate and site Zones 5–9. Adapts to a variety of soil conditions; tolerant of heat, drought, and air pollution. Full sun.
Cultivation Transplant container-grown or balled-and-burlapped plants in fall and spring. Pruning is unnecessary except to shape the tree; then prune in winter.
Propagation Sow seed in fall. Take root cuttings in winter.
Pest and disease prevention No serious pests or diseases.
Common problems Will flower poorly, or not at all, in shade.
Landscape use Good specimen tree for midsummer color.
Cultivars 'Apiculata' has finely divided leaves. 'Fastigiata' has a narrow columnar habit. 'September' is late-blooming with exceptionally large flower clusters.
Other species *K. bipinnata* is a similar but late-blooming species. Zones 8–10.

Laburnum x *watereri*
LEGUMINOSAE

GOLDEN-CHAIN TREE

Golden-chain tree is a deciduous tree with trifoliate leaves. L. x watereri *'Vossi', a cultivar of this hybrid, has a denser habit and exceptionally long flower clusters.*

Flower color and season Golden yellow flowers borne in long, pendulous clusters in late spring; followed by 2–3 inch (5–7.5 cm) pods.
Height and spread To 30 feet (9 m) tall and 18 feet (5.4 m) wide.
Best climate and site Zones 5–9. Virtually any well-drained soil. Full sun.
Cultivation Transplant container-grown or balled-and-burlapped plants in spring. Prune after flowering only as necessary to remove unwanted or crowded shoots.
Propagation Sow seed in fall. Graft in spring.
Pest and disease prevention No serious pests or diseases.
Common problems Tends to be short-lived. Remove whatever seedpods you can to counteract this. Seeds are poisonous when ingested.
Landscape use Particularly effective grouped against a background of evergreens; shrub borders.
Other species *L. anagyroides* is a wide-spreading tree with branches close to the ground. It grows to 20 feet (6 m) tall. 'Aureum' has golden yellow leaves. 'Involutum' has curled leaves. 'Pendulum' is a form with weeping branchlets.

Lagerstroemia indica
LYTHRACEAE

CRAPE MYRTLE

Crape myrtle is a summer-blooming deciduous tree with gray peeling bark and privet-like leaves that are bronze in spring, deep green in summer, and yellow, orange, and red in fall.

Flower color and season Curiously crinkled white, pink, red, lavender, or purple flowers in terminal 6–9-inch (15–23-cm) clusters in mid- to late-summer.
Height and spread To 20 feet (6 m) tall and 12 feet (3.6 m) wide.
Best climate and site Zones 7–10. Moist, deep, well-drained soil. Full sun.
Cultivation Transplant container-grown or balled-and-burlapped plants in spring. Prune in early spring, shortening the previous year's shoots to half or one-third of their length.
Propagation Take cuttings in late spring or early summer.
Pest and disease prevention Allow sufficient air circulation between plants to deter mildew.
Common problems Stems may die back to the ground in particularly cold winters; new flowering shoots will grow up from the roots.
Landscape use Specimen tree; shrub borders; screens. Plants often have multiple trunks.
Cultivars 'Catawba' has dark purple flowers and is mildew-resistant. 'Natchez' has white flowers and is mildew-resistant.

Liquidambar styraciflua
HAMAMELIDACEAE

SWEET GUM

Native to the eastern United States, sweet gum is a deciduous tree growing to pyramidal form. It has star-shaped leaves that turn shades of purple, crimson, and orange in fall.

Flower color and season Insignificant yellow-green flowers in downy spikes in late spring; followed by ball-shaped fruit.
Height and spread To 100 feet (30 m) tall and 50 feet (15 m) wide.
Best climate and site Zones 3–8. Moist well-drained soil. Full sun to light shade.
Cultivation Transplant balled-and-burlapped or container-grown plants in spring. Prune in early winter only if necessary to shape young trees or to remove dead wood.
Propagation Sow seed in fall. Take cuttings from semihardwood in summer.
Pest and disease prevention No serious pests or diseases.
Common problems Difficult to transplant and slow to become established. The persistent spiny fruit can be a nuisance.
Landscape use Specimen tree; woodland plantings.
Cultivars 'Pendula' has pendulous branches. 'Variegata' has leaves marked with yellow.

Magnolia spp.
MAGNOLIACEAE

MAGNOLIA

Magnolias are deciduous or evergreen trees and shrubs with simple leaves. M. stellata, star magnolia, is a bushy shrub or small tree with starry white spring flowers.

Flower color and season M. *grandiflora*: fragrant, waxy, creamy white flowers from late spring to midsummer; M. *kobus*: white, six-petaled flowers in midspring; M. x *soulangiana*; saucer-shaped white or rosy purple flowers in early spring; M. *stellata*: white flowers with strap-shaped petals in early spring; M. *virginiana*: fragrant creamy white flowers from late spring to early fall.
Height and spread Height varies from 15 feet (4.5 m) to 90 feet (27 m); spread from 15 feet (4.5 m) to 55 feet (16.5 m).
Best climate and site Depending on species, Zones 5–10. Moist, humus-rich, well-drained soil. Partial shade.
Cultivation Transplant balled-and-burlapped or container-grown plants in spring. No need to prune.
Propagation Layer in spring. Remove seed from its covering and sow in fall. Take cuttings in mid- to late-summer. Graft in winter.
Pest and disease prevention If scales attack, causing yellow leaves, prune out badly infested growth and spray the remaining stems with horticultural oil.
Common problems Late frosts can spoil early-blooming plants.

Malus floribunda
ROSACEAE

CRAB APPLE

Japanese flowering crab apple is a round-headed deciduous tree. It is prized for its profuse display of pink spring flowers, followed by showy yellow-red fruit in fall.

Flower color and season Deep pink flowers in spring; followed by red or yellow fruit.
Height and spread To 20 feet (6 m) tall and slightly wider.
Best climate and site Zones 4–8. Deep, humus-rich, moist, slightly alkaline soil. Full sun.
Cultivation Plant early in spring. Prune soon after flowering.
Propagation Graft in spring. Take softwood cuttings in late spring.
Pest and disease prevention Avoid overfeeding, which results in succulent growth attractive to aphids and other insects. To reduce possibility of rust, keep at least 500 feet (150 m) from eastern red cedar (*Juniperus virginiana*). Prune to keep the center of the plant open to light and air to reduce disease problems. Choose disease-resistant cultivars.
Common problems Many cultivars bloom heavily only in alternate years.
Landscape use Specimen tree; shade trees for small gardens.

Nyssa sylvatica
NYSSACEAE

BLACK TUPELO

Black tupelo is a deciduous tree of pyramidal form. The branches are somewhat pendulous; the leaves are leathery and glossy dark green, turning brilliant orange or scarlet in fall.

Flower color and season Greenish white flowers in late spring; followed in midsummer by small blue fruits on the female trees.
Height and spread To 90 feet (27 m) tall and 45 feet (13.5 m) wide.
Best climate and site Zones 4–8. Moist, humus-rich, well-drained soil. Full sun.
Cultivation Transplant small balled-and-burlapped or container-grown plants in early spring.
Propagation Sow seed when ripe in fall.
Pest and disease prevention Few serious pests or diseases. Mulch with organic matter to keep soil moist and to provide a home for beneficial insects.
Common problems Black tupelo is intolerant of alkaline soil.
Landscape use Specimen tree; woodland plantings; chiefly valued for its fall color.
Other common names Black gum, pepperidge.

Ostrya virginiana
BETULACEAE

AMERICAN HOP HORNBEAM

American hop hornbeam is a slow-growing deciduous tree with alternate simple leaves and graceful horizontal or drooping branches. It ultimately forms a round-headed tree.

Flower color and season Inconspicuous greenish catkins in early spring.
Height and spread To 40 feet (12 m) tall and 30 feet (9 m) wide.
Best climate and site Zones 4–9. Tolerant of a variety of well-drained soils. Full sun to partial shade.
Cultivation Transplant balled-and-burlapped or container-grown plants to permanent position in spring.
Propagation Sow seed when ripe in fall.
Pest and disease prevention No serious pests or diseases.
Common problems Difficult to transplant and slow to establish.
Landscape use Specimen or street tree; chiefly valued where other trees will not grow.
Other common names Ironwood.

Oxydendrum arboreum
ERICACEAE

SOURWOOD

Native to the eastern United States, sourwood is a slow-growing deciduous tree or shrub with oval leaves that turn vivid scarlet in fall. The tree usually grows in pyramidal form.

Flower color and season White flowers borne in pendulous clusters in midsummer.
Height and spread To 50 feet (15 m) tall and 20 feet (6 m) wide.
Best climate and site Zones 5–9. Moist, well-drained, humus-rich, acid soil. Full sun.
Cultivation Transplant balled-and-burlapped or container-grown plants in late winter or early spring. Plant in permanent position as established plants are difficult to move. Sourwood rarely needs pruning.
Propagation Sow seed indoors in spring. Take cuttings in midsummer. Cuttings should be 2–3 inches (5–7.5 cm) long and made of short sideshoots with a thin heel of old wood. Bottom heat promotes rooting.
Pest and disease prevention No serious pests or diseases.
Common problems Flowering and fall color are less dramatic in shade.
Landscape use Specimen tree.
Other common names Sorrel tree.

Parrotia persica
HAMAMELIDACEAE

PERSIAN PARROTIA

A wide-spreading, round-headed deciduous tree, Persian parrotia is often multitrunked with horizontal branching. Leaves turn orange, yellow, and scarlet in fall.

Flower color and season Inconspicuous, petal-less flowers with protruding red stamens from late winter to early spring.
Height and spread To 40 feet (12 m) tall and 45 feet (13.5 m) wide.
Best climate and site Zones 5–10. Tolerant of a variety of well-drained soils. Full sun for best leaf color.
Cultivation Transplant balled-and-burlapped or container-grown plants in early spring.
Propagation Sow seed in fall. Graft in late winter or early spring on witch hazel (*Hamamelis* spp.). Take cuttings in midsummer.
Pest and disease prevention No serious pests or diseases.
Common problems Large trees are difficult to transplant, so they are best moved when small.
Landscape use Specimen tree; of interest for its fall foliage color and for its mottled bark.

Platanus occidentalis
PLATANACEAE

AMERICAN PLANETREE

American planetree, also known as sycamore, is native to eastern North America. This moisture-loving tree has coarse dark green leaves and mottled white bark.

Flower color and season Inconspicuous cream flowers in spring; followed by ball-shaped fruit.
Height and spread To 90 feet (27 m) tall and 65 feet (19.5 m) wide.
Best climate and site Zones 4–8. Adaptable to most well-drained soils, but grows to greatest size in rich, moist soil. Full sun. Tolerates air pollution.
Cultivation Prune in winter if necessary.
Propagation Take hardwood cuttings in winter. Sow seed in spring.
Pest and disease prevention Avoid damaging the bark with sharp gardening tools; such wounds are prime entry sites for diseases. Clean up dropped leaves and twigs to remove overwintering sites for disease spores.
Common problems Drops leaves, twigs, and fruit, which may become unsightly.
Landscape use Specimen tree; street trees. Plant in borders of large properties.
Other common names Plane, buttonwood, sycamore.
Other species *P.* x *acerifolia*, London planetree, has palmately lobed leaves to 10 inches (25 cm) wide and grows in wide-spreading form. 'Bloodgood' and 'Liberty' are very disease-resistant.

Populus deltoides
SALICACEAE

EASTERN COTTONWOOD

Eastern cottonwood is a fast-growing deciduous tree with large leaves. It is planted primarily for its rapid growth and ability to survive where few other trees can.

Flower color and season Inconspicuous greenish catkins from mid- to late-spring.
Height and spread To 90 feet (27 m) tall and 70 feet (21 m) wide.
Best climate and site Zones 2–8. Tolerant of a variety of soil conditions, even poor, dry ones, but prefers deep, moist, well-drained soil.
Cultivation Plant in fall or spring. Prune in summer or fall; bleeds if pruned at other times.
Propagation Sow seed in summer.
Pest and disease prevention Keep soil evenly moist with organic mulch. Healthy plants will resist pests and diseases far better than stressed plants.
Common problems Weak-wooded and short-lived. Questing roots can spread into and clog drains and sewers.
Landscape use Screens and mass plantings.
Other species *P. alba*, white poplar, has whitish bark and white undersides to the leaves. 'Richardii' has yellow upper leaf surfaces. *P. nigra*, 'Italica' Lombardy poplar is a narrow columnar grower to 90 feet (27 m) tall.

Prunus serrulata
ROSACEAE

FLOWERING CHERRY

Japanese flowering cherry is a rounded deciduous tree with an eye-catching display of spring flowers. The new leaves are often reddish brown; they mature to deep green.

Flower color and season Clustered white or pink flowers, single, semidouble, or double in form, in midspring.
Height and spread To 25 feet (7.5 m) tall and nearly as wide.
Best climate and site Zones 5–8. Deep, humus-rich, well-drained, moist soil. Full sun.
Cultivation Transplant container-grown or balled-and-burlapped plants in spring. Prune after flowering.
Propagation Sow seed in fall. Take cuttings in summer or fall. Graft in late winter and early spring.
Pest and disease prevention Avoid overfeeding, which can stimulate succulent growth that is susceptible to pests and diseases. Also avoid planting in poorly drained soil.
Common problems Plants tend to be short-lived.
Landscape use Specimen tree; mass plantings.
Cultivars 'Kwanzan' ('Sekiyama') has bronze foliage and double deep pink flowers. 'Shirotae' ('Mt. Fuji') has semidouble white flowers. 'Ukon' has bronze new foliage and unusual pale yellow flowers.

Pyrus calleryana
ROSACEAE

CALLERY PEAR

Callery pear is a pyramidal to round-headed deciduous tree grown primarily for its spring flower display. Its rounded glossy dark green leaves turn purplish or reddish in fall.

Flower color and season White flowers from early- to mid-spring; followed by roundish green fruit.
Height and spread To 30 feet (9 m) tall and 18 feet (5.4 m) wide.
Best climate and site Zones 5–9. Deep, moist, humus-rich, well-drained soil. Full sun.
Cultivation Transplant container-grown or balled-and-burlapped plants in late winter while they are still dormant. Prune in winter or early spring.
Propagation Sow seed in fall. Graft in late winter and early spring.
Pest and disease prevention Avoid injury with sharp gardening tools; these wounds provide easy access for pests and diseases. Try to buy disease-resistant cultivars for best results.
Common problems Callery pear tends to form narrow branch angles that are prone to splitting.
Landscape use Specimen tree.
Cultivars 'Aristocrat' has darker foliage and better fall color. 'Bradford' is more vigorous and bigger than the species, growing to 50 feet (15 m) tall and 30 feet (9 m) wide.

Quercus spp.
FAGACEAE

OAK

Q. rubra, red oak, is an adaptable, fast-growing tree with dark green leaves that may turn red in fall. Unlike some other species, red oak is not too difficult to transplant.

Flower color and season Inconspicuous greenish catkins in midspring; followed by roundish fruit (acorns).
Height and spread Height from 45 feet (13.5 m) to 100 feet (30 m); spread from 35 feet (10.5 m) to 100 feet (30 m).
Best climate and site Depending on species, Zones 4–9. Tolerant of a variety of soil conditions but thrives in moist, humus-rich, well-drained soil. Full sun.
Cultivation Transplant young balled-and-burlapped plants in fall and spring. Prune in winter only as necessary to shape the tree.
Propagation Graft in late winter and early spring. Sow seed in fall.
Pest and disease prevention Tie burlap bands around main trunks to trap gypsy moth larvae; remove and destroy the caterpillars as they accumulate. Build up soil organic matter content with mulch and correct nutrient imbalances to ensure healthy plants with greater vigor to fight pest invasions.
Common problems Many species difficult to transplant.
Landscape use Specimen tree; shade trees for large properties. *Q. palustris* is an excellent street tree.

Robinia pseudoacacia
LEGUMINOSAE

BLACK LOCUST

A thorny deciduous tree, black locust has an open, upright habit and pinnately compound leaves. The cultivar 'Frisia' has bright yellow foliage all season long.

Flower color and season White or pink pealike flowers borne in long pendulous clusters in early summer; followed by long brown pods.
Height and spread To 75 feet (22.5 m) tall and 45 feet (13.5 m) wide.
Best climate and site Zones 3–8. Tolerant of a variety of soil conditions but prefers slightly alkaline soil. Full sun to partial shade.
Cultivation Plant in winter or early spring. Prune in late summer or fall only if necessary to shape the tree; bleeds if pruned in winter or spring.
Propagation Graft in spring. Sow seed when ripe in fall. Remove rooted suckers from the parent plant in winter.
Pest and disease prevention Mulch with organic matter to keep the soil evenly moist. Healthy, vigorous plants are most resistant to borers and other pests.
Common problems Tends to produce many new shoots (suckers) at the base. Thorns can be hazardous and plant parts may be toxic.
Landscape use Mass plantings for difficult sites, especially where other trees won't thrive.

Sophora japonica
LEGUMINOSAE

JAPANESE PAGODA TREE

Japanese pagoda tree is a deciduous tree from the Orient. It grows to a round-headed form and has alternate, compound leaves. It is one of the last of the large trees to bloom.

Flower color and season Profuse creamy white mildly fragrant flowers in large 12- by 12-inch (30- by 30-cm) pendant terminal clusters in large summer and early fall; followed by brown pods that persist most of the winter.
Height and spread To 65 feet (19.5 m) tall and 40 feet (12 m) wide.
Best climate and site Zones 4–8. Prefers moist, well-drained soil. Full sun to light shade. Widely tolerant of city conditions, heat, and drought.
Cultivation Transplant young balled-and-burlapped or container-grown plants in fall or early spring. Prune in fall only if necessary to shape the tree.
Propagation Sow seed when ripe in fall.
Pest and disease prevention No serious pests or diseases.
Common problems Species tends to grow in a rather loose, open form.
Landscape use Specimen tree; street trees.
Cultivars 'Fastigiata' is an upright grower. 'Pendula' is a densely rounded tree with pendulous branches. 'Regent' is a fast grower with an upright habit and deeper leaf color.

Sorbus aucuparia
ROSACEAE

EUROPEAN MOUNTAIN ASH

European mountain ash is a deciduous tree with compound leaves that turn red in fall. The white spring flowers are followed by clusters of showy orange-red fruit.

Flower color and season Clustered small white flowers in late spring; followed by bright orange-red fruit.

Height and spread To 35 feet (10.5 m) tall and nearly as wide.

Best climate and site Zones 2–7. Tolerant of a variety of well-drained soil conditions. Full sun to partial shade. Grows best in cooler climates.

Cultivation Transplant balled-and-burlapped or container-grown plants in fall or spring.

Propagation Graft in late winter and early spring. Sow seed in spring.

Pest and disease prevention Avoid overfeeding, which can stimulate young succulent growth that is susceptible to rusts and fire blight. Keep soil moist with organic mulch.

Common problems Short-lived in alkaline or dry soil.

Landscape use Specimen tree; shade trees.

Other common names Rowan tree.

Cultivars 'Edulis' bears large fruit, often used for preserves. 'Fastigiata' is a very upright, columnar form. 'Pendula' has pendulous branches. 'Xanthocarpa' has yellow fruit.

Styrax japonicus
STYRACACEAE

JAPANESE SNOWBELL

Japanese snowbell is a showy deciduous tree with a horizontal branching structure. The bell-shaped white flowers bloom profusely on the undersides of the branches.

Flower color and season Pendulous white flowers bloom from late spring to early summer.

Height and spread To 30 feet (9 m) tall and nearly as wide.

Best climate and site Zones 5–9. Moist, humus-rich, well-drained, acid soil. Full sun to light shade. Tolerates city conditions; shelter from strong winds.

Cultivation Transplant container-grown or balled-and-burlapped plants in early spring. Prune in summer only if necessary to shape the plant.

Propagation Take cuttings in summer. Sow seed in summer; may take two years to germinate.

Pest and disease prevention No serious pests or diseases. Keep soil moist by mulching with organic matter.

Common problems Plants grow poorly in dry or alkaline soil.

Landscape use Handsome small trees, ideal as a specimen near a patio; excellent shade trees.

Other species *S. obassia*, fragrant snowbell, bears its flowers in long clusters. It grows to 20 feet (6 m) tall and 15 feet (4.5 m) wide. Zones 6–9.

Thuja occidentalis
CUPRESSACEAE

AMERICAN ARBORVITAE

American arborvitae is a large upright pyramidal evergreen tree with scalelike dark green or golden green leaves borne in flattened fans. The leaves are aromatic when crushed.

Flower color and season Inconspicuous reddish male and yellowish brown female flowers in midspring; followed by small dried capsules.

Height and spread To 60 feet (18 m) tall and 20 feet (6 m) wide.

Best climate and site Zones 2–7. Best where atmospheric moisture is high. Tolerant of a variety of soil conditions but prefers deep, loamy, humus-rich soil. Full sun.

Cultivation Transplant balled-and-burlapped plants preferably in spring. Prune in early spring if necessary.

Propagation Sow seed in fall or spring. Take cuttings in late summer.

Pest and disease prevention Mulch to keep the soil evenly moist. Bagworms may attack, producing soft cone-like cocoons; use a knife to carefully cut the cocoons from the branches.

Common problems Subject to sun scorch when exposed to bright afternoon winter sun and wind.

Landscape use Screens; hedges; foundation plantings; accent plants.

Tilia x europaea
TILIACEAE

EUROPEAN LINDEN

European linden is a tall, fast-growing deciduous tree with heart-shaped leaves. The creamy white summer flowers are exceptionally fragrant and attractive to bees.

Flower color and season Fragrant creamy white flowers in drooping clusters in early summer.

Height and spread To 100 feet (30 m) tall and 60 feet (18 m) wide.

Best climate and site Zones 3–7. Tolerant of a wide variety of soil conditions but thrives in deep, moist humus-rich, well-drained soil. Full sun. Adaptable to city conditions.

Cultivation Plant in winter or early spring. Thin out branches in late summer when overcrowded.

Propagation Graft in late winter and early spring. Sow seed in fall.

Pest and disease prevention Mulch with organic matter to keep soil evenly moist. Healthy plants are more resistant to pests and diseases. Clean up dropped leaves to remove overwintering sites for pests and diseases.

Common problems Leaves can turn brown and become unsightly during summer droughts.

Landscape use Specimen tree; street trees; hedges.

Ulmus parvifolia
ULMACEAE

CHINESE ELM

Chinese elm is a round-topped usually deciduous tree that is semi-evergreen in the warmer portions of its range. Its bark peels off in irregular contrasting patches, giving the trunk an interesting look.

Flower color and season Inconspicuous reddish flowers in fall.

Height and spread To 50 feet (15 m) tall and 40 feet (12 m) wide.

Best climate and site Zones 5–9. Moist, humus-rich, well-drained soil. Full sun.

Cultivation Plant in winter or early spring. Prune in fall.

Propagation Sow seed when ripe. Graft in spring.

Pest and disease prevention Keep soil moist with organic mulch. Maintain vigor by feeding and watering copiously. Vigorous trees are less susceptible to pests and diseases.

Common problems Usually trouble-free.

Landscape use Specimen tree; shade trees; street trees.

Cultivars 'Drake' has more upright branches than the species. 'Sempervirens' has broadly arching or weeping branches with smaller leaves than the species. 'True Green' has small glossy leaves and is usually more evergreen and less hardy than the species.

Zelkova serrata
ULMACEAE

JAPANESE ZELKOVA

Japanese zelkova is a deciduous tree from Japan, closely related to the elms. Its habit is rounded with numerous ascending branches; the leaves turn yellow or russet in fall.

Flower color and season Inconspicuous greenish flowers in early spring.

Height and spread To 90 feet (27 m) tall and nearly as wide.

Best climate and site Zones 5–8. Tolerant of a variety of soil conditions and air pollution. Full sun to light shade.

Cultivation Transplant balled-and-burlapped or container-grown plants in fall or spring. No pruning is necessary except to shape the trees by thinning crowded branches in late summer.

Propagation Sow seed in fall. Take cuttings in summer.

Pest and disease prevention No serious pests or diseases.

Common problems Young plants are subject to frost injury.

Landscape use Specimen tree; street trees; screens.

Cultivars 'Village Green' is a fast-growing, vigorous form that is hardier than the species; its leaves turn a reddish color in fall.

Abelia x *grandiflora*
CAPRIFOLIACEAE

GLOSSY ABELIA

Glossy abelia is a dense, semi-evergreen shrub with dark green opposite leaves that turn bronze or purple in fall. The flowers are lightly fragrant.

Flower color and season Pinkish purple or white tubular flowers borne in loose, terminal clusters in late spring to early summer.
Height and spread To 6 feet (1.8 m) tall and as wide.
Best climate and site Zones 6–10. Deep moist, well-drained, humus-rich soil. Full sun.
Cultivation Plant in spring or winter. Grow in a protected site in the colder portion of its range. Prune in late winter or early spring to remove winter-damaged wood.
Propagation Take softwood cuttings in early summer, hardwood cuttings in fall.
Pest and disease prevention No serious pests or diseases.
Common problems Usually trouble-free.
Landscape use A good specimen tree; or use in informal hedges, foundation plantings, or shrub borders.
Cultivars 'Sherwood' is a compact form only 3 feet (90 cm) tall.

Aesculus parviflora
HIPPOCASTANACEAE

BOTTLEBRUSH BUCKEYE

Bottlebrush buckeye is a deciduous shrub, occasionally growing as a single-trunked small tree. Its compound leaves consist of five to seven leaflets.

Flower color and season Upright panicles of white flowers with pink stamens and red anthers in midsummer; followed by spiny fruit.
Height and spread 10–12 feet (3–3.6 m) tall and nearly as wide.
Best climate and site Zones 4–8. Deep, moist, humus-rich soil. Full sun to light shade.
Cultivation Transplant container-grown or balled-and-burlapped plants in early spring.
Propagation Sow seed in fall. Layer established plants in spring.
Pest and disease prevention Provide good air circulation to avoid fungal diseases such as leaf blotch and canker. Healthy plants are better able to resist pests and diseases.
Common problems Spreads freely by suckers. Japanese beetles may attack leaves. To control, knock beetles into a bucket of soapy water.
Landscape use Specimen shrubs; shrub borders. Especially valued as a midsummer source of color.
Cultivars 'Rogers' is a late-blooming form with very long inflorescences.
Varieties *A. parviflora* var. *serotina* is a late-blooming form with larger flowers.

Aronia arbutifolia
ROSACEAE

RED CHOKEBERRY

Red chokeberry is a vigorous deciduous shrub planted for its spectacular display of brilliant red fruit in fall and winter.

Flower color and season White flowers, sometimes tinged with pink, borne in loose clusters in late spring; followed by conspicuous red fruit.
Height and spread To 8 feet (2.4 m) tall and as wide.
Best climate and site Zones 4–8. Average, well-drained soil. Full sun to light shade. Adapts well to both dry or wet conditions.
Cultivation Plant in spring. Best fruit production in full sun. Red chokeberry seldom requires pruning.
Propagation Take cuttings in early summer. Divide in early spring or fall. Remove seed from its fleshy coating and sow in fall.
Pest and disease prevention Choose a site with good air circulation. Clean up all dropped leaves to remove overwintering sites for disease spores. Prune off canes damaged by borers and seal ends with paraffin wax.
Common problems Plants tend to become leggy. Prune after flowering if necessary to promote a bushier habit. Also produces suckers.
Landscape use Valued for its fall fruit color. Most effective in mass plantings.

Aucuba japonica
CORNACEAE

JAPANESE AUCUBA

Japanese aucuba is a shade-loving evergreen shrub with opposite glossy green leaves. The variegated cultivars are often grown as houseplants.

Flower color and season Small purple flowers in terminal clusters in late winter to early spring; followed by bright scarlet fruit on female plants.

Height and spread To 10 feet (3 m) tall and as wide.

Best climate and site Zones 6–10. Deep, moist, well-drained soil. Tolerates dense shade, air pollution, and competition from tree roots.

Cultivation Plant in winter or spring. Male and female flowers are borne on separate plants. You'll need to buy at least one male plant if you want fruit on the females. Seldom need pruning.

Propagation Take semihardwood cuttings in late spring.

Pest and disease prevention No serious pests or diseases.

Common problems In colder areas subject to leaf browning when exposed to wind or afternoon winter sun.

Landscape use Shrub borders; under trees; foundation plantings; containers.

Cultivars 'Crassifolia' is male with large green leathery leaves. 'Crotonifolia' may be either male or female with large leaves speckled with yellow. 'Variegata' is female with leaves blotched creamy yellow.

Berberis thunbergii
BERBERIDACEAE

JAPANESE BARBERRY

Japanese barberry is a dense, very thorny shrub with small leaves that, while deciduous, often turn red or purple and remain on the plant into winter.

Flower color and season Small yellow flowers in late spring; followed by bright red persistent fruit.

Height and spread To 8 feet (2.4 m) tall and 15 feet (4.5 m) wide.

Best climate and site Zones 4–10. Deep, moist, well-drained soil. Full sun to almost full shade.

Cultivation Plant in spring. Prune if necessary to remove overcrowded shoots after flowering or in winter after fruiting.

Propagation Take cuttings in late spring. Remove seed from its fleshy coating and sow in fall.

Pest and disease prevention No serious pests or diseases.

Common problems Does poorly in excessively wet soils. Spiny stems often trap leaves and other debris within the plant, giving it an untidy appearance.

Landscape use Informal hedges; foundation plantings; shrub border. Readily lends itself to pruning as a formal hedge.

Cultivars 'Aurea' has yellow leaves. 'Crimson Pygmy' is a dwarf form with red-purple foliage. 'Rose Glow' has purple leaves.

Buddleia davidii
LOGANIACEAE

ORANGE-EYE BUTTERFLY BUSH

Orange-eye butterfly bush is a deciduous shrub, native to China, with long, narrow, opposite leaves. It dies back to the roots in cold areas.

Flower color and season White, pink, red, purple, violet, or pale purple flowers borne in upright, terminal spikes in midsummer to early fall.

Height and spread To 15 feet (4.5 m) tall and as wide.

Best climate and site Zones 5–10. Deep, moist, well-drained, humus-rich soil. Full sun.

Cultivation Plant in spring. Cut back severely in late winter or early spring.

Propagation Take cuttings in early summer or early fall. Sow seed in spring or fall.

Pest and disease prevention No serious pests or diseases.

Common problems In the northern portion of its range treat *B. davidii* and its cultivars as herbaceous perennials by cutting the stems to the ground and covering them with mulch.

Landscape use Best used toward the back of flower borders. Also great for shrub borders and informal hedges. Highly attractive to butterflies.

Cultivars 'Black Knight' has deep purple flowers. 'Charming summer' bears light lavender pink flowers. 'Nanho Purple' has red-purple flowers and dwarf, spreading habit. 'Royal Red' bears wine-red flowers.

Buxus sempervirens
BUXACEAE

COMMON BOXWOOD

Common boxwood is a spreading shrub with small, glossy dark green leaves. Its dense branching structure make it popular for use in hedges.

Flower color and season Inconspicuous pale green flowers in early spring.
Height and spread To 20 feet (6 m) tall and slightly wider.
Best climate and site Zones 6–10. Deep, moist, well-drained soil. Full sun to partial shade.
Cultivation Transplant balled-and-burlapped or container-grown plants in spring. Use a compost or bark mulch around the base of the plants. This will help keep the shallow roots cool and moist and reduce the need for cultivation.
Propagation Take cuttings in summer.
Pest and disease prevention Leafminer larvae can burrow inside leaves and produce tan patches. Remove and destroy affected leaves to prevent adult flies from multiplying.
Common problems Leaves often turn brown if exposed to cold, dry winter winds. Spray foliage with an antidessicant in fall to prevent this from occurring. Prune out damaged stems.
Landscape use Informal hedges; foundation planting; screen planting; topiary. Lends itself well to pruning.
Cultivars 'Argentea' has leaves bordered with white. 'Aureo-variegata' has leaves variegated with yellow.

Calycanthus floridus
CALYCANTHACEAE

CAROLINA ALLSPICE

Deciduous Carolina allspice bears reddish or yellow flowers and glossy green leaves that turn bronze or purple in fall. Native to southeastern United States.

Flower color and season Very fragrant, strap-shaped reddish purple petals, tinged with brown, in early summer.
Height and spread 6–8 feet (1.8–2.4 m) tall and nearly as wide.
Best climate and site Zones 4–9. Humus-rich, well-drained but moisture-retentive soil. Full sun to light shade. Tends to be much shorter when grown in full sun.
Cultivation Plant in spring. Prune after flowering is finished.
Propagation Take cuttings in early summer. Layer in fall. Sow seed in fall. Remove rooted suckers in spring.
Pest and disease prevention No serious pests or diseases.
Common problems Fragrance varies among plants; smell before you buy.
Landscape use Shrub borders; plant near outdoor living areas for fragrance.
Other common names Carolina sweet shrub, common sweet shrub, pineapple shrub, strawberry shrub.
Cultivars 'Athens' is yellow-flowered.

Camellia japonica
THEACEAE

COMMON CAMELLIA

Common camellia is an evergreen shrub or tree with deep green glossy leaves. It is commonly planted in warm climates for its colorful flowers.

Flower color and season Single, semidouble, or fully double flowers in shades of white, pink, or red in late winter to early spring.
Height and spread 20–25 feet (6–7.5 m) tall and nearly as wide.
Best climate and site Zones 7–10 or in slightly colder areas if protected from winter sun and winds. Peaty, lime-free, humus-rich soil. Partial shade.
Cultivation Transplant container-grown or balled-and-burlapped plants in winter or early spring. Apply adequate water to keep soil evenly moist during summer and winter. Mulch to keep roots cool and moist and to prevent weed problems.
Propagation Take cuttings of current season's growth in late summer.
Pest and disease prevention Flower blight can cause brown spots on petals. Avoid problems by buying only bareroot plants; also pick off and destroy any flower buds before planting. If the disease strikes, remove and destroy all infected buds and flowers, and apply a fresh layer of mulch around the base of the plant.
Common problems Flower buds can be damaged by untimely frosts.
Landscape use Specimen shrub; shrub borders; informal hedges.

Caryopteris x *clandonensis*
VERBENACEAE

BLUEBEARD

Bluebeard is a deciduous subshrub of hybrid origin with blue flowers and dull green leaves. In cold areas it dies back to the roots each winter.

Flower color and season Blue flowers borne in dense spikes in mid- to late-summer.

Height and spread To 4 feet (1.2 m) tall and as wide.

Best climate and site Zones 5–9. Moist, well-drained, loamy soil. Full sun and a sheltered position, such as near a sunny wall, in colder zones.

Cultivation Plant in late winter or spring. Cut back nearly to the ground in late winter since the flowers grow on new wood.

Propagation Take cuttings in early summer. Divide in spring.

Pest and disease prevention No serious pests or diseases.

Common problems Usually trouble-free.

Landscape use Informal hedges; shrub borders; perennial borders.

Cultivars 'Dark Knight' is a compact grower with darker foliage and deep blue flowers. 'Ferndown' has dark blue flowers. 'Heavenly Blue' has light blue flowers.

Chaenomeles speciosa
ROSACEAE

FLOWERING QUINCE

Native to China, flowering quince is a spreading deciduous shrub with spiny branches. Its oval, alternate leaves are deep green above, paler below.

Flower color and season Clusters of showy red flowers; followed by pear-shaped yellow-green fruit. Flowers bloom in late winter (in warm or protected areas) or in late spring to early summer. Sometimes will rebloom lightly in fall.

Height and spread To 10 feet (3 m) tall and 20 feet (6 m) wide.

Best climate and site Zones 4–10. Deep, moist, humus-rich, well-drained soil. Full sun.

Cultivation Plant in fall or spring. Regular renewal pruning will promote more lavish bloom.

Propagation Take cuttings in late summer. Layer in spring.

Pest and disease prevention Subject to scales and aphids. Avoid overfeeding which causes succulent growth that attracts pests. To control scales, prune and destroy infested parts; spray remaining stems with horticultural oil. Control aphids by spraying with insecticidal soap.

Common problems Leaves can turn yellow when plants are grown in an alkaline soil.

Landscape use Shrub borders; specimen shrubs; informal hedges.

Clethra alnifolia
CLETHRACEAE

SUMMER-SWEET

Native to the southeastern United States, summer-sweet is a deciduous shrub valued primarily for its fragrant flower spikes.

Flower color and season White, very fragrant flowers borne in long, narrow upright clusters in mid- to late-summer. The leaves turn bright yellow or orange in fall.

Height and spread 5–8 feet (1.5–2.4 m) tall and as wide.

Best climate and site Zones 5–9. Well-drained, loamy soil. Full sun.

Cultivation Plant in spring. Prune in late winter.

Propagation Take cuttings in midsummer. Sow seed in late fall.

Pest and disease prevention No serious pests or diseases.

Common problems Sometimes slow to become established.

Landscape use Hedges; shrub borders.

Cultivars 'Rosea' has deep pink buds opening to soft-pink flowers.

Other species *C. acuminata*, cinnamon clethra, has nodding flower clusters and cinnamon brown bark. Zones 5–9.

Corylopsis spicata
HAMAMELIDACEAE

SPIKE WINTER HAZEL

Spike winter hazel is a compact deciduous shrub of particular interest for its early flowering period. Fragrant yellow flowers bloom before leaves emerge.

Flower color and season Drooping clusters of fragrant yellow flowers in late winter to early spring.
Height and spread To 6 feet (1.8 m) tall and slightly wider.
Best climate and site Zones 5–9. Moist, well-drained, slightly acid soil. Full sun to partial shade.
Cultivation Transplant container-grown or balled-and-burlapped plants in fall or spring.
Propagation Take softwood cuttings in summer. Leave the cuttings undisturbed until growth begins the following spring; then transplant to a nursery bed or individual containers. Layer in fall.
Pest and disease prevention No serious pests or diseases.
Common problems Flower buds can be injured by late spring frosts.
Landscape use Woodland plantings; shrub borders. Best displayed against a background of evergreens.
Other species *C. glabrescens*, fragrant winter hazel, blooms in early- to mid-spring. It grows to 15 feet (4.5 m) tall and 10 feet (3 m) wide. Zones 5–9.

Cotoneaster horizontalis
ROSACEAE

ROCKSPRAY COTONEASTER

Rockspray cotoneaster is a spreading deciduous shrub with bright red fruit and dark green leaves that turn red in fall and persist well into winter.

Flower color and season Pink flowers in mid- to late-spring; followed by bright coral red fruit.
Height and spread To 3 feet (90 cm) tall and 6 feet (1.8 m) wide.
Best climate and site Zones 4–9. Moist, deep, well-drained soil. Full sun.
Cultivation Transplant container-grown plants in fall or early spring.
Propagation Take cuttings in early summer. Sow seed in spring. Layer in fall.
Pest and disease prevention Take care not to damage the plant with sharp garden tools; these wounds are common entry points for pests and diseases such as fire blight and borers. Lace bugs and spider mites can cause yellow or white speckling on leaves. Spray leaves, especially the undersides, with insecticidal soap.
Common problems Because of rather sparse root systems, plants are often slow to establish. Mulch with organic matter to keep the soil evenly moist, especially while the shrubs are young.
Landscape use Mostly used in rock gardens or as groundcovers.
Cultivars 'Little Gem' is a dwarf, mound-shaped form. 'Variegatus' has leaves edged with white, turning pink in fall.

Daphne cneorum
THYMELEACEAE

ROSE DAPHNE

Rose daphne is a low-growing evergreen shrub with narrow, strap-shaped leaves and exceptionally fragrant spring flowers.

Flower color and season Dense terminal heads of fragrant pink flowers in late spring, sometimes repeating in fall.
Height and spread To 1 foot (30 cm) tall and 3 feet (90 cm) wide.
Best climate and site Zones 4–9. Moist, well-drained, neutral or slightly alkaline soil. Full sun with protection from winter winds.
Cultivation Transplant container-grown plants in early fall or early spring.
Propagation Layer in fall. Take cuttings in late summer.
Pest and disease prevention Few serious pests or diseases. Rose daphne does not like strong fertilizers. A leafy mulch applied in early spring will supply adequate nutrients.
Common problems Plants are often slow to establish.
Landscape use Foundation shrubs; front of shrub borders.
Cultivars 'Alba' has white flowers. 'Eximia' is larger in leaf and flower.
Other species *D. odora*, winter daphne, has purple-and-white flowers and dark green oval leaves. 'Alba' has white flowers. 'Aureo-Marginata' is hardier than the species, with yellow-edged leaves. Zones 7–10.

Deutzia gracilis
SAXIFRAGACEAE

SLENDER DEUTZIA

Slender deutzia is a deciduous shrub with long, lance-shaped leaves and clusters of white blooms in spring. Deutzias look lovely in shrub borders.

Flower color and season Clusters of white flowers in late spring.
Height and spread To 6 feet (1.8 m) tall and nearly as wide.
Best climate and site Zones 4–9. Deep, moist, well-drained soil. Full sun.
Cultivation Plant in spring. After flowering, thin out drastically by cutting away weak and old wood, but leave the young shoots alone as these will bear the best blooms.
Propagation Sow seed in fall. Take softwood cuttings in summer.
Pest and disease prevention Few serious pests or diseases.
Common problems Lack of pruning will result in few flowers.
Landscape use Specimen shrub; flowering shrub borders.
Cultivars 'Aurea' has yellow leaves. The leaves of 'Marmorata' are spotted with yellow.
Other species *D. scabra*, fuzzy deutzia, has oval or heart-shaped leaves and brown peeling bark. Its white early-summer flowers are often tinged with pink. 'Candidissima' bears double white flowers. Zones 5–9.

Enkianthus campanulatus
ERICACEAE

REDVEIN ENKIANTHUS

Native to Japan, redvein enkianthus is a tall deciduous shrub with oval, whorled leaves clustered at the ends of the branchlets.

Flower color and season Drooping clusters of creamy yellow flowers, lightly tinged with red, in late spring. Leaves turn brilliant scarlet in fall.
Height and spread To 12 feet (3.6 m) tall and not as wide.
Best climate and site Zones 4–8. Deep, moist humus-rich, well-drained, acid soil. Full sun to dense shade.
Cultivation Plant in spring. Expose to western sun for best fall color. No pruning is necessary.
Propagation Take cuttings in late spring. Sow seed in early spring. Layer in fall.
Pest and disease prevention No serious pests or diseases.
Common problems Will not flourish in dry or alkaline soils. Mulch with compost to keep the soil evenly moist.
Landscape use Foundation plantings; shrub borders; woodland plantings.
Cultivars 'Albiflorus' has pure white flowers; 'Red Bells' has red flowers.

Erica cinerea
ERICACEAE

TWISTED HEATH

Twisted heath is an evergreen shrub with small bell-shaped flowers and tiny needlelike leaves on stiff, much-divided branches.

Flower color and season White, pinkish red, or purplish flowers in early to late summer.
Height and spread To 18 inches (45 cm) tall and 4 feet (1.2 m) wide.
Best climate and site Zones 5–7. Acid, moist, peaty soil, preferably low in fertility. Full sun to light shade. Best where nights are cool and moist.
Cultivation Plant in fall or spring. Prune lightly after flowering. Do not fertilize. Shelter plant from sweeping winds, and keep watered during dry periods.
Propagation Sow seed or take cuttings in spring. Layer in summer.
Pest and disease prevention No serious pests or diseases.
Common problems Will not flourish where summers are extremely hot and winters extremely cold. Intolerant of drought; mulch to keep the soil evenly moist. High soil fertility can cause loose, open growth.
Landscape use Looks at its best used in masses as groundcovers.
Other species *E. carnea*, spring heath, has white, pinkish red, or purplish flowers in winter to midspring.

Euonymus alata
CELASTRACEAE

BURNING BUSH

Native to China and Japan, burning bush is a deciduous shrub with dark green leaves that turn rich rosy scarlet in fall.

Flower color and season Inconspicuous green white flowers in mid- to late-spring; followed by purplish fruit.
Height and spread 10–15 feet (3–4.5 m) tall and nearly as wide.
Best climate and site Zones 3–9. Virtually any well-drained soil. Full sun to partial shade.
Cultivation Transplant balled-and-burlapped or container-grown plants in fall or spring. Prune in winter if you want to shape the plant; otherwise it seldom requires pruning.
Propagation Take cuttings during the growing season. Remove seed from its fleshy coating and sow in fall.
Pest and disease prevention Prune and destroy parts infested by scales, which cause leaves to yellow and drop.
Common problems Not tolerant of very wet or very dry soil.
Landscape use Specimen shrub; shrub borders; informal hedges.
Other common names Winged euonymus.
Cultivars 'Compacta' is a low-growing, dense plant.

Forsythia x *imtermedia*
OLEACEAE

BORDER FORSYTHIA

Border forsythia is a deciduous shrub with clusters of yellow flowers that bloom in spring before the leaves emerge. The foliage may turn purple in fall.

Flower color and season Bright yellow flowers in early- to mid-spring.
Height and spread To 8 feet (2.4 m) tall and nearly as wide.
Best climate and site Zones 5–9. Deep, moist, well-drained soil; tolerates lime and air pollution. Full sun.
Cultivation Plant in spring. Remove older weak-growing or dead wood after flowering. The bushes will then have the whole summer to produce fresh growth on which next year's flowers will be borne.
Propagation Take softwood cuttings in summer or hardwood cuttings in late fall. Layer in fall. Remove suckers in fall.
Pest and disease prevention No serious pests or diseases.
Common problems In severe climates, late frosts can damage flowers.
Landscape use Specimen shrub; informal hedges. Plant in masses against an evergreen background.
Cultivars 'Lynwood' has yellow flowers as long entire stems. 'Spring Glory' bears pale yellow flowers.
Other species *F. suspensa*, weeping forsythia, is a rambling shrub with yellow spring flowers, arching branches, and three-lobed leaves. It grows to 10 feet (3 m) tall. Zones 5–9.

Fothergilla gardenii
HAMAMELIDACEAE

DWARF FOTHERGILLA

Dwarf forthergilla is a low-growing deciduous shrub with fragrant white flowers in spring and dramatic yellow or orange fall color.

Flower color and season Fragrant white flowers borne in spikes in mid- to late-spring.
Height and spread To 3 feet (90 cm) tall and as wide.
Best climate and site Zones 5–9. Deep, moist, humus-rich, well-drained soil. Full sun to partial shade.
Cultivation Transplant container-grown or balled-and-burlapped plants in late winter or early spring.
Propagation Sow seed in summer. Take cuttings in summer and leave rooted cuttings undisturbed until the following year. Layer in fall.
Pest and disease prevention No serious pests or diseases.
Common problems Will not thrive in wet or alkaline soils.
Landscape use Useful in shrub borders or as woodland plantings.
Cultivars 'Blue Mist' has frosty blue foliage that turns yellow and red in fall.
Other species *F. major* is a larger pyramidal or rounded plant, growing to 9 feet (2.7 m) tall and as wide. Zones 5–9.

Fuchsia x hybrida
ONAGRACEAE

COMMON FUCHSIA

Largely derived from South American species, common fuchsias are alternate-leaved deciduous shrubs of upright or spreading habit.

Flower color and season Pendant flowers, usually with contrasting corollas, in combinations too numerous to name. Possible colors include white, yellow, pink, red, and purple. Bloom in early summer to fall. Leaves are often tinged with purple.
Height and spread To 6 feet (1.8 m) tall and as wide.
Best climate and site Zones 9–10. Deep, moist, humus-rich, well-drained soil. Partial shade.
Cultivation Plant in winter or spring. Prune in early spring. Do not allow to dry out, particularly when grown in baskets.
Propagation Take cuttings in fall and early winter.
Pest and disease prevention Sprinkle foliage with water during hot, dry weather to discourage spider mites. If they become a problem, spray the undersides of the leaves with insecticidal soap.
Common problems May die to the ground in winter, but will bloom on new wood produced in spring.
Landscape use Where hardy, shrub borders and informal hedges. Upright types can be trained to standard form. Widely used as hanging basket plants.

Gardenia jasminoides
RUBIACEAE

COMMON GARDENIA

Native to China, common gardenia is an evergreen shrub with very glossy leathery leaves. Its creamy white, waxy summer flowers are intensely fragrant.

Flower color and season Very fragrant single, semidouble, or double white flowers in early- to mid-summer.
Height and spread To 6 feet (1.8 m) tall and as wide.
Best climate and site Zones 8–10. Peaty, humus-rich, moisture-retentive, acid soil. Partial shade; protect from hot afternoon sun.
Cultivation Transplant in spring. Cut untidy plants well back in early spring.
Propagation Take cuttings in summer.
Pest and disease prevention Avoid damaging plants with gardening tools; these wounds are common entry points for pests and diseases such as mealybugs and stem canker. If affected by mealybugs, aphids, or whiteflies, spray with insecticidal soap.
Common problems Sensitive to dry soil; mulch to help retain moisture.
Landscape use Where hardy, foundation shrubs or specimen plants; elsewhere, a greenhouse plant. Gardenias also grow well in containers.
Other common names Cape jasmine.
Cultivars 'Mystery' is a bushy plant with large, double flowers. 'Radicans' is low-growing and has small flowers.

Hamamelis mollis
HAMAMELIDACEAE

CHINESE WITCH HAZEL

Chinese witch hazel is a deciduous shrub or tree with heart-shaped leaves and zigzag branches that are downy when young.

Flower color and season Fragrant yellow flowers with strap-shaped petals in winter.
Height and spread To 25 feet (7.5 m) tall and nearly as wide.
Best climate and site Zones 5–9. Light, moist, well-drained, humus-rich soil. Full sun.
Cultivation Transplant container-grown or balled-and-burlapped plants in fall or spring. For best habit train to single stem by removing low-growing side branches.
Propagation Layer in late summer. Graft in spring. Sow seed outdoors in summer; may take up to two years to germinate.
Pest and disease prevention No serious pests or diseases.
Common problems Intolerant of dry soil.
Landscape use Specimen plant; shrub borders; woodland plantings; city gardens.
Other species *H.* x *intermedia* is of hybrid origin and has variously colored fragrant spring flowers. 'Arnold Promise' is free-flowering, with yellow flowers and good reddish fall color. 'Feuerzauber' has copper red flowers' Zones 5–9.
H. virginiana, common witch hazel, is a fall-blooming shrub to 10 feet (3 m) tall. Zones 5–9.

Hibiscus syriacus
MALVACEAE

ROSE-OF-SHARON

Rose-of-Sharon is a late-blooming deciduous shrub with upright branches and a bush habit. It has showy hibiscus-like single or double flowers.

Flower color and season 2 ½–4-inch (6–10-cm) trumpet-shaped flowers in white, pink, red, lavender, or purple in late summer to early fall.
Height and spread To 15 feet (4.5 m) tall and 10 feet (3 m) wide.
Best climate and site Zones 5–9. Deep, moist, well-drained soil. Full sun.
Cultivation Plant in spring or fall. Prune in winter by removing at least two-thirds of the previous season's growth.
Propagation Take cuttings during summer. Layer in spring. Graft in late winter and early spring.
Pest and disease prevention If aphids or whiteflies attack leaves, spray with insecticidal soap. Control Japanese beetles by knocking them into a bucket of soapy water.
Common problems Lack of pruning will result in small flowers. Young, vigorous plants can be winter-killed. Protect from wind and do not fertilize after midsummer. Self-sown seedlings can be a problem; choose cultivars such as 'Diana' and 'Helene' that set little if any seed.
Landscape use Use as a specimen plant or in shrub borders.
Cultivars 'Blue Bird' has blue flowers. 'Diana' has pure white flowers.

Hydrangea spp.
HYDRANGEACEAE

HYDRANGEA

Hydrangeas are deciduous shrubs with opposite, broad leaves and showy summer flowers which are blue or pink, depending on soil pH.

Flower color and season *H. macrophylla* has blue or pink flowers (blue in acid soils, pink in alkaline) borne in large, flat clusters up to 10 inches (25 cm) across in midsummer. *H. paniculata* has white flowers in immense pyramidal clusters in midsummer to early fall. *H. quercifolia* has white flowers borne in erect, pyramidal clusters in early to late summer. Flower clusters contain both fertile and sterile flowers; the latter are more showy.
Height and spread Height varies according to cultivar to 20 feet (6 m); spread to 10 feet (3 m).
Best climate and site Zones 4–9, depending on cultivar. Deep, moist, well-drained soil. Partial shade; protect from hot afternoon sun.
Cultivation Plant during fall or spring. Keep well watered during summer. Prune after flowering for more compact growth.
Propagation Propagate by cuttings, layering or seed, depending on cultivar.
Pest and disease prevention No serious pests or diseases. Mulch with organic matter to keep the soil evenly moist.
Common problems Buds or stems may be damaged in cold-winter areas.
Landscape use Best as a specimen shrub, or use in shrub borders.

Ilex spp.
AQUIFOLIACEAE

HOLLY

The brilliant red berries of I. verticillata, winterberry, are a natural choice for brightening up the winter garden. This deciduous holly loves moist, acid soil.

Flower color and season Inconspicuous white flowers in late spring to early summer; followed by red or occasionally yellow fruit on female plants.
Height and spread Height varies according to cultivar to 60 feet (18 m) with a similar spread.
Best climate and site Zones 5–8. Deep, moist well-drained soil. Full sun to light shade.
Cultivation Transplant container-grown or balled-and-burlapped plants in fall or spring. Hollies are dioecious, which means that the male and female flowers are borne on separate plants. You'll need at least one male for every five female plants of the same species to get berries on the females. Prune in late spring if necessary. Mulch to keep soil moist.
Propagation Layer in summer. Take cuttings of evergreen types anytime, deciduous types in midsummer. Remove seed from fleshy covering and sow in fall; may take 18 months to germinate.
Pest and disease prevention Leafminers are a major problem. Remove and destroy affected leaves.
Common problems Leaves may turn yellow due to lack of nitrogen; fertilize regularly to keep plants green.

Itea virginica
SAXIFRAGACEAE

VIRGINIA SWEETSPIRE

A summer-blooming deciduous shrub native to the eastern United States. Its alternate leaves are narrowly oval, turning brilliant red in fall.

Flower color and season Creamy white fragrant flowers borne in dense, narrow terminal clusters in early summer.
Height and spread To 5 feet (1.5 m) tall but not as wide.
Best climate and site Zones 5–9. Deep, humus-rich, constantly moist soil. Full sun to partial shade.
Cultivation Plant in spring. Rarely requires pruning.
Propagation Take cuttings in early summer. Divide or remove rooted suckers in spring.
Pest and disease prevention No serious pests or diseases. Avoid growing in dry, alkaline soil.
Common problems Does not do well in dry soil.
Landscape use Woodland plantings; shrub borders. Valued for its fragrance and fall color.
Cultivars 'Henry's Garnet' has reddish purple fall color and long flower clusters.

Juniperus spp.
CUPRESSACEAE

JUNIPER

Junipers are evergreen shrubs or trees. Their leaves are needlelike when young, becoming flat and scalelike when mature.

Flower color and season Inconspicuous spring flowers, yellow on the male, greenish on the female; followed by small blue fruit on the female.
Height and spread Height varies according to cultivar to 60 feet (18 m); spread to 10 feet (3 m).
Best climate and site Zones 3–8, depending on cultivar. Widely tolerant of different soil conditions—even dry. Full sun to light shade.
Cultivation Transplant container-grown or balled-and-burlapped plants in late winter or spring. No pruning is necessary.
Propagation Take cuttings in late summer, fall, or winter. Layer low-growing types in summer. Remove seed from its fleshy covering and sow in fall.
Pest and disease prevention Handpick and destroy bagworms, which spin silken bags that are studded with needles and resemble pine cones. Plant as groundcover to encourage predators of mites, or spray leaves with insecticidal soap. Prune and destroy infected parts.
Common problems Several species are alternate hosts to cedar-apple rust. Avoid planting junipers near apple trees.
Landscape use Specimen shrub; foundation plants; groundcovers.

Kalmia latifolia
ERICACEAE

MOUNTAIN LAUREL

Native to the eastern United States, mountain laurel is a robust evergreen shrub with alternate glossy green leaves.

Flower color and season White, pink, or rose flowers in terminal clusters in late spring to early summer.
Height and spread To 20 feet (6 m) tall and as wide.
Best climate and site Zones 4–7. Moisture-retentive, humus-rich, peaty soil. Full sun to partial shade.
Cultivation Transplant container-grown or balled-and-burlapped plants in spring or fall. Mulch to keep shallow roots cool and to control weeds. No pruning.
Propagation Layer in fall. Sow seed in early spring. Cuttings in late summer.
Pest and disease prevention Avoid damaging plants with sharp gardening tools; these wounds are common entry points for pests such as borers. Lace bugs can cause yellow speckling on leaves; spray foliage (especially the undersides of the leaves) with insecticidal soap.
Common problems Grows poorly in dry or alkaline soil.
Landscape use Foundation shrubs; shrub borders; woodland plantings.
Cultivars 'Bullseye' bears white flowers banded with red. 'Elf' is a very dwarf form with pink buds that open to near white flowers. 'Ostbo Red' has red buds that open to light pink flowers.

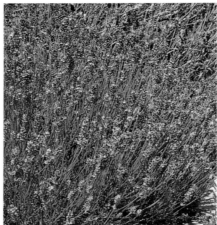

Kerria japonica
ROSACEAE

JAPANESE KERRIA

Japanese kerria is a bushy deciduous shrub with slender green branches that hold their color year-round. Yellow spring flowers.

Flower color and season Golden yellow five-petaled flowers in mid- to late-spring.
Height and spread To 6 feet (1.8 m) tall and as wide.
Best climate and site Zones 4–8. Deep, moist, humus-rich, well-drained soil. Full sun to partial shade.
Cultivation Plant in early spring. Thin out old stems after flowering. Mulch with compost or aged manure after pruning.
Propagation Take cuttings in summer or fall. Divide clumps in fall.
Pest and disease prevention No serious pests or diseases.
Common problems Slow to establish.
Landscape use Use as a specimen shrub or in shrub borders.
Cultivars 'Pleniflora' has ball-shaped double flowers. 'Variegata' has single flowers with leaves that are deeply margined in white.

Lavandula angustifolia
LABIATAE

LAVENDER

Lavender is a rounded shrub beloved for its herbal and ornamental qualities. It has fragrant gray-green leaves with spikes of purple-blue flowers.

Flower color and season The ½-inch (1-cm) purple-blue flowers are carried in tight, narrow clusters in summer.
Height and spread 2–3 feet (60–90 cm) tall; similar spread.
Best climate and site Zones 5–8. Average to humus-rich, well-drained soil. Full sun to light shade. Neutral or slightly alkaline soil is best. Lavender is extremely drought-tolerant.
Cultivation Prune out any dead wood and reshape the shrubs in spring. Shear plants every few years to encourage fresh new growth and to promote bloom.
Propagation Layer or take tip cuttings in summer. Place cuttings in a well-drained medium; transplant them as soon as they root to avoid rot.
Pest and disease prevention No serious pests or diseases.
Common problems Shoots may be partially killed in winter.
Landscape use Plant lavender in ornamental and herb gardens. Use as an edging plant or to configure knot gardens. In borders combine them with other plants that need excellent drainage such as yarrow and sundrops (*Oenothera* spp.).

Mahonia aquifolium
BERBERIDACEAE

OREGON GRAPE

Oregon grape is a broad-leaved evergreen shrub with prominent yellow flower clusters which give way to showy blue fruit that resembles grapes.

Flower color and season Clustered bright yellow flowers in late spring to early summer; followed by grape-like blue fruit.
Height and spread To 3 feet (90 cm) tall and as wide.
Best climate and site Zones 5–9. Deep, moist, well-drained soil. Full sun to light shade.
Cultivation Transplant container-grown or balled-and-burlapped plants in spring. After flowering cut a few of the oldest stems to the ground each year for more compact growth.
Propagation Take cuttings in late winter. Sow seed in late spring. Divide in fall.
Pest and disease prevention Alternate host to black stem rust; avoid planting where wheat is a major commercial crop.
Common problems In colder zones the leaves may be damaged if exposed to winter winds and afternoon sun.
Landscape use Specimen shrub; foundation plantings; shrub borders.
Other common names Holly grape.
Other species *M. bealei*, leather-leaved mahonia, has leathery blue-green leaves and very fragrant flowers. It grows to 6 feet (1.8 m) tall and as wide. Zones 6–9.

Myrica pensylvanica
MYRICACEAE

BAYBERRY

Bayberry is a deciduous or semi-evergreen shrub with fragrant leaves. The wax-coated fruits are sometimes used in candle making.

Flower color and season Insignificant greenish catkins in late spring; followed by clustered waxy white fruit.

Height and spread To 9 feet (2.7 m) tall and as wide.

Best climate and site Zones 2–7. Adapts to a wide range of soil conditions. Good tolerance to seaside conditions. Full sun to partial shade.

Cultivation Transplant container-grown or balled-and-burlapped plants in spring. Prune lightly anytime to encourage compact growth; rejuvenate older plants by pruning heavily every couple of years.

Propagation Take cuttings in late spring. Layer in fall. Soak seed in hot water or rub it against a rough surface to remove the waxy coating, sow in fall.

Pest and disease prevention No serious pests or diseases.

Common problems Leaves can become chlorotic (turn yellow) when grown in alkaline soils.

Landscape use Shrub borders; hedges, woodland plantings.

Other species *M. cerifera*, wax myrtle, is an evergreen native to the southeastern United States and grows as a tall shrub or tree. Zones 6–9.

Nandina domestica
BERBERIDACEAE

HEAVENLY BAMBOO

Heavenly bamboo is an evergreen shrub with glossy green alternate, compound leaves that turn rich red in fall. Young foliage is often tinged with pink.

Flower color and season White flowers are borne in large clusters in midsummer; followed by clustered red fruit that persists nearly all winter.

Height and spread To 10 feet (3 m) tall and 6 feet (1.8 m) wide.

Best climate and site Zones 6–10. Deep, moisture-retentive, well-drained soil. Full sun to dense shade.

Cultivation Transplant container-grown or balled-and-burlapped plants in late winter or spring. Cut a few of the oldest stems to the ground each spring to encourage new growth.

Propagation Take cuttings in summer. Remove seed from its fleshy covering and sow in fall.

Pest and disease prevention No serious pests or diseases.

Common problems Plants may be damaged by low winter temperatures, especially in the colder areas.

Landscape use Use as foundation plantings or hedges.

Cultivars 'Alba' is white-fruited. 'Compacta' is a dwarf form. 'Harbour Dwarf' is a dwarf form with foliage that is tipped pink or bronze in spring and that turns orange or bronzy red in winter. 'Royal Princess' has delicate foliage.

Nerium oleander
APOCYNACEAE

OLEANDER

Native to the Mediterranean coast, oleander is a vigorous evergreen shrub with narrow, leathery dark green leaves.

Flower color and season Single or double flowers in various shades of white, yellow, pink, red, and purple sometimes measuring up to 3 inches (7.5 cm) across, in midspring to late summer.

Height and spread To 20 feet (6 m) tall and 10 feet (3 m) wide.

Best climate and site Zones 7–10. Widely tolerant of heat, drought, and seaside conditions. Full sun.

Cultivation Plant in spring. Prune lightly after flowering to maintain thick bushy growth. Prune by half to rejuvenate old plants in winter.

Propagation Take cuttings anytime in growing season.

Pest and disease prevention Subject to scales, which turn plants yellow. Prune off infested plant parts.

Common problems All parts of the plant are toxic if eaten.

Landscape use Informal hedges; screen plantings; shrub borders; street plantings; container plantings.

Cultivars 'Calypso' bears single cherry red flowers. 'Isle of Capri' has single light yellow flowers. 'Mrs. Reoding' has double salmon-pink flowers. 'Sister Agnes' has single white flowers.

Osmanthus fragrans
OLEACEAE

FRAGRANT OLIVE

Native to Asia, fragrant olive is an evergreen shrub with holly-like dark green opposite leaves. Clusters of sweetly scented white flowers start in spring.

Flower color and season Very fragrant, small white tubular flowers in drooping clusters in early spring to early summer; followed by blue-black berries.
Height and spread To 20 feet (6 m) tall and as wide.
Best climate and site Zones 8–10. Deep, moist, well-drained soil. Full sun to light shade.
Cultivation Plant in winter, fall, or spring. Cut back after flowering to maintain desired height and form.
Propagation Take cuttings in late summer. Layer in spring or summer.
Pest and disease prevention No serious pests or diseases.
Common problems Very frost-sensitive.
Landscape use Informal hedges; foundation plantings; shrub borders container plantings.
Other common names Sweet olive.
Forms *O. fragrans* f. *aurantiacus* has orange flowers.

Paeonia suffruticosa
PAEONIACEAE

TREE PEONY

Unlike the more familiar garden peony, tree peony does not die back to the roots each winter. Instead, it forms a magnificent dense, deciduous shrub.

Flower color and season Very large single or double flowers in white, pink, red, lavender, or yellow in mid- to late-spring.
Height and spread To 5 feet (1.5 m) tall and slightly wider.
Best climate and site Zones 5–8. Deep, moist, humus-rich, well-drained soil. Full sun to partial shade.
Cultivation Plant in spring or fall. Keep soil evenly moist in summer. Benefits from organic mulch. Do not cut back when foliage dies in winter, as you would an herbaceous peony. Just prune off any winter-damaged wood in spring.
Propagation Layer in spring. Graft onto the roots of herbaceous peonies in late summer.
Pest and disease prevention No serious pests or diseases.
Common problems Leaves and flowers can be damaged by late spring frosts.
Landscape use A magnificent specimen shrub—truly a garden gem.
Cultivars 'Age of Gold' bears golden yellow double flowers. 'Godaishu' has pure white semidouble flowers. 'Hana Kisoi' has deep shell pink semidouble flowers. 'Kamada Nishiki' has raspberry red double flowers. '

Philadelphus coronarius
SAXIFRAGACEAE

SWEET MOCK ORANGE

Native to southern Europe, sweet mock orange is a deciduous shrub with opposite leaves. The single or double white flowers are usually very fragrant.

Flower color and season Single or occasionally double white flowers, usually highly fragrant, in late spring.
Height and spread To 8 feet (2.4 m) tall but not as wide.
Best climate and site Zones 4–9. Tolerant of many soil conditions, even dry soil. Full sun to partial shade.
Cultivation Plant in spring. Prune leggy plants immediately after flowering. Cut back by one-third and cut out old canes.
Propagation Take cuttings in summer. Remove a few rooted stems in spring or fall.
Pest and disease prevention No serious pests or diseases.
Common problems Provides little interest when not in flower.
Landscape use Shrub borders.
Cultivars 'Belle Etoile' bears single flowers over 2 inches (5 cm) in diameter. 'Boule d' Argent' has double flowers that are 2 inches (5 cm) in diameter. 'Minnesota Snowflake' has double flowers that are 2 inches (5 cm) in diameter; it is exceptionally vigorous and winter-hardy. 'Virginal' bears double flowers that are 2 inches (5 cm) in diameter.

Pieris japonica
ERICACEAE

JAPANESE PIERIS

Japanese pieris is an evergreen shrub with dark green leaves that are often bronze or reddish when young. Flower buds are conspicuous all winter.

Flower color and season Fragrant white flowers in midspring.

Height and spread To 8 feet (2.4 m) tall and as wide.

Best climate and site Zones 4–9. Moist, humus-rich, well-drained, acid soil. Full sun to light shade.

Cultivation Transplant container-grown or balled-and-burlapped plants in spring. Prune after flowering.

Propagation Layer in spring or summer. Take cuttings in summer. Sow seed in fall or early spring.

Pest and disease prevention Lace bugs frequently attack, causing yellow leaves. To control, spray leaves (especially the undersides) with insecticidal soap.

Common problems Cannot tolerate poorly drained soil.

Landscape use Specimen shrub; shrub borders; foundation plantings.

Cultivars 'Dorothy Wycoff' is a compact grower with deep red buds that open to pink. 'Red Mill' is exceptionally hardy. 'Valley Valentine' bears very long-lasting deep pink flowers. 'Variegata' has white-edged leaves. 'White Cascade' has pure white flowers.

Potentilla fruticosa
ROSACEAE

SHRUBBY CINQUEFOIL

Shrubby cinquefoil is a compact deciduous shrub. The flowers are usually yellow, but also come in red, pink, orange, or white.

Flower color and season Yellow five-petaled flowers in early summer to early fall.

Height and spread To 4 feet (1.2 m) tall and as wide.

Best climate and site Zones 2–8. Tolerant of many soil conditions including alkaline soil. Full sun to very light shade.

Cultivation Transplant in spring. Prune during winter for a thicker habit. Cut all stems back by one-third or remove a few of the oldest stems at ground level.

Propagation Take cuttings in summer. Sow seed in fall.

Pest and disease prevention No serious pests or diseases.

Common problems Will not thrive in dense shade.

Landscape use Informal hedges; shrub borders; edgings.

Cultivars 'Coronation Triumph' is a vigorous form with soft green foliage and many bright yellow flowers. 'Katherine Dykes' has pale yellow flowers and silvery green foliage. 'Mount Everest' has large white flowers. 'Tangerine' has orange flowers (when grown in light shade).

Pyracantha coccinea
ROSACEAE

SCARLET FIRETHORN

Scarlet firethorn is grown for its masses of orange-red berries that last through fall. Evergreen in warm areas, deciduous in colder regions.

Flower color and season White flowers in flat clusters from late spring to early summer; followed by persistent fruit that is typically red but occasionally orange or even yellow.

Height and spread To 15 feet (4.5 m) tall and as wide.

Best climate and site Zones 6–9. Deep, moist, humus-rich, well-drained soil. Full sun to light shade.

Cultivation Transplant container-grown or balled-and-burlapped plants in spring. Prune anytime to remove suckers or excessively long shoots.

Propagation Take cuttings in summer. Sow seed in fall or late winter.

Pest and disease prevention Avoid overfertilizing, which can promote succulent growth that is subject to fire blight. Plant disease-resistant cultivars.

Common problems Leaves may be damaged by cold winter temperatures.

Landscape use Specimen shrub; foundation plantings; espalier; hedges.

Cultivars 'Aurea' has yellow fruit. 'Lalandei', somewhat hardier than the species, is an upright grower to 12 feet (3.6 m) tall with orange-red fruit; it is resistant to scab and fire blight.

Rhododendron spp. and hybrids
ERICACEAE

RHODODENDRON

The genus Rhododendron is generally divided into smaller-leaved, deciduous types called azaleas, and larger-leaved evergreen rhododendrons.

Flower color and season White, pink, red, lavender, orange, rosy purple, or yellow flowers in early spring to midsummer, varying with cultivar.
Height and spread Height varies according to cultivar to 20 feet (6 m); similar spread.
Best climate and site Zones 4–9, varying with cultivar. Moist, acid soil. Light shade.
Cultivation Transplant container-grown or balled-and-burlapped plants in spring. Prune after flowering to control size.
Propagation Take cuttings in midsummer. Layer in summer. Sow seed indoors in late winter.
Pest and disease prevention Avoid planting in poorly drained soil. Mulch with compost or aged manure to keep the shallow roots cool and moist.
Common problems Very sensitive to salinity and high pH.
Landscape use Foundation plantings; specimen shrub; massed plantings; container plantings.
Other common names Azalea.
Species *R. arborescens*, sweet azalea; *R. calendulaceum*, flame azalea; *R. carolinianum*, Carolina rhododendron; *R. catawbiense*, Catawba rhododendron.

Rosa hybrids
ROSACEAE

ROSE

Floribunda roses, such as the red-flowered 'Europeana', bear large clusters of flowers on vigorous plants.

Flower color and season White, pink, orange, yellow, red, lavender, or multicolored single or double flowers, often fragrant, from late spring to late summer, depending on cultivar.
Height and spread Depends on type and cultivar.
Best climate and site Zones 4–10, varying with cultivar. Deep, moist, well-drained, humus-rich soil. Full sun.
Cultivation Transplant bareroot plants in fall or winter or container-grown plants in fall or spring. Fertilize regularly in spring and again in summer to ensure many blooms. Prune hybrid tea and floribunda roses in early spring, and climbers and species roses after flowering.
Propagation Take softwood cuttings in summer, hardwood cuttings in winter. Layer in spring or fall. Remove seed from its fleshy covering and sow in spring or fall. Bud-graft hybrids in spring.
Pest and disease prevention Choose a site with full sun and good air circulation. Plant disease-resistant species and cultivars. Avoid wetting foliage.
Common problems Hardiness varies greatly among species and cultivars. Some plants may be damaged or killed by cold winter temperatures.

Spiraea thunbergii
ROSACEAE

THUNBERG SPIREA

Thunberg spirea is a small twiggy deciduous shrub that produces masses of small white flowers in spring before the leaves appear.

Flower color and season Clusters of small white flowers in midspring.
Height and spread To 5 feet (1.5 m) tall and as wide or slightly wider.
Best climate and site Zones 4–8. Tolerates a wide range of soil conditions. Full sun to partial shade.
Cultivation Plant in spring. Prune back after flowering.
Propagation Sow fresh seed in summer. Take cuttings in midsummer. Divide in spring or fall.
Pest and disease prevention Avoid overfeeding, which promotes succulent growth that is attractive to aphids. If these pests become a problem, spray with insecticidal soap.
Common problems Will not thrive in poorly drained soils.
Landscape use Informal low hedges; shrub borders; specimen shrub.
Other species *S. japonica*, Japanese spirea, produces small pink flowers in flat clusters in late spring to early summer. 'Atro-sanguinea' has deep red flowers. 'Ruberrima' has deep pink flowers. 'Shirobana' has white, pink, and red flowers borne simultaneously. Zones 5–9.

Syringa vulgaris
OLEACEAE

COMMON LILAC

Common lilac is a deciduous shrub with heart-shaped leaves. The species bears lavender purple spring flowers.

Flower color and season Very fragrant lavender flowers in long clusters in mid- to late-spring.
Height and spread To 20 feet (6 m) tall and 12 feet (3.6 m) wide.
Best climate and site Zones 3–7. Neutral or alkaline, humus-rich, well-drained soil. Full sun to light shade.
Cultivation Plant in fall or spring. Prune after flowering to prevent seed formation. Cut some of the oldest stems to the ground each year.
Propagation Take cuttings in fall. Layer in spring or summer.
Pest and disease prevention Thoroughly clean up dropped leaves to remove overwintering sites for disease spores. Select sites with good air circulation.
Common problems Lilacs are sometimes grafted onto privet (*Ligustrum* spp.) rootstocks, which produce suckers. Prune off suckers as they appear.
Landscape use Specimen shrub; shrub borders; screens or hedges.
Cultivars 'Lavender Lady' bears lavender flowers and blooms reliably in areas too warm for other lilacs. 'Miss Ellen Willmott' bears double white flowers. 'President Lincoln' has single blue flowers. 'Sensation' has wine red flowers.

Viburnum carlessi
CAPRIFOLIACEAE

FRAGRANT VIBURNUM

Fragrant viburnum is a deciduous shrub with dark green leaves that turn purplish-red in fall. The pink flower buds open to sweetly scented white flowers.

Flower color and season Very fragrant white flowers tinged with pink in midspring; followed by blue-black fruit.
Height and spread To 5 feet (1.5 m) tall and nearly as wide.
Best climate and site Zones 4–9. Virtually any well-drained soil. Full sun to light shade.
Cultivation Plant in fall or spring. If necessary, prune after flowering to shape the plant.
Propagation Take cuttings in summer. Sow seed when ripe. Layer in fall.
Pest and disease prevention Avoid overfeeding, which encourages succulent growth attractive to aphids. If aphids attack, spray with insecticidal soap. Clean up dropped leaves to remove overwintering sites for mildew spores.
Common problems Avoid poorly drained soils.
Landscape use Specimen shrub; shrub borders; screens or hedges.
Other species *V. opulus*, European cranberrybush viburnum, has clusters of white flowers in midspring, yellowish to purplish red fall color, and red fruit that persists into winter. Zones 3–8.

Weigela florida
CAPRIFOLIACEAE

OLD-FASHIONED WEIGELA

Old-fashioned weigela is an opposite-leaved free-flowering deciduous shrub native to Korea and northern China. It has pink spring flowers.

Flower color and season Funnel-shaped, rosy pink flowers in late spring.
Height and spread To 8 feet (2.4 m) tall and nearly as wide.
Best climate and site Zones 4–8. Cool, deep, moist, humus-rich, well-drained soil. Full sun to light shade.
Cultivation Transplant bareroot or container-grown plants in spring or fall. Prune back severely after flowering.
Propagation Take cuttings in summer.
Pest and disease prevention No serious pests or diseases.
Common problems Old canes produce few flowers.
Landscape use Use in shrub borders and mass plantings.
Cultivars 'Bristol Ruby' has ruby red flowers. 'Bristol Snowflake' has white flowers tinged with pink. 'Candida' has pure white flowers. 'Eva Supreme' is very dwarf with deep red flowers. 'Foliis Purpureis' is a dwarf form with purplish foliage. 'Variegata' has leaves edged with page yellow.
Varieties The variety *venusta*, with its purplish pink flowers, is hardier than the species.

Actinidia kolomikta
ACTINIDIACEAE

HARDY KIWI

Hardy kiwi is a twining deciduous vine with heart-shaped leaves. The foliage is purple at first and later becomes variegated with pink and white, especially on male plants.

Flower color and season Fragrant white or green flowers in late spring and early summer; followed by edible green fruit on female plants.

Height and spread To 20 feet (6 m) with support.

Best climate and site Zones 4–10. Moist, well-drained soil. Full sun to partial shade. Alkaline soil produces best leaf and flower color.

Cultivation Plant in early spring. Prune in winter if necessary. Male and female flowers are borne on separate plants. You'll need to buy one male for every three to four female plants to get fruit on the females.

Propagation Layer in spring. Take cuttings in midsummer.

Pest and disease prevention Keep soil moist in hot weather. No serious pests or diseases.

Common problems Will not survive severe drought.

Landscape use Excellent foliage vines to use on wire supports.

Other common names Cape gooseberry, kolomikta vine.

Ampelopsis brevipedunculata
VITACEAE

PORCELAIN AMPELOPSIS

A deciduous vine native to Asia, porcelain ampelopsis bears three- or occasionally five-lobed leaves and distinctly hairy young shoots. It is a vigorous grower, climbing by tendrils.

Flower color and season Clusters of small white flowers in late spring; followed by clustered fruits of amethyst-blue in fall.

Height and spread To 20 feet (6 m) with support.

Best climate and site Zones 4–9. Humus-rich, moist, well-drained soil. Full sun to partial shade.

Cultivation Plant in winter or spring. Grows quickly. Cut to ground in late winter to produce new fruiting growth.

Propagation Take cuttings in midsummer.

Pest and disease prevention Avoid planting in poorly drained soil.

Common problems Japanese beetles may attack and skeletonize the leaves. Shake beetles from plants into a bucket of soapy water in early morning. Deter with an organically acceptable insecticide.

Landscape use Chiefly valued for its striking fruit. Grow on fences, arbors, or trellises.

Cultivars 'Elegans' has foliage handsomely variegated with white and pink. Less hardy than the species. Zones 5–9.

Aristolochia elegans
ARISTOLOCHIACEAE

CALICO DUTCHMAN'S PIPE

Calico Dutchman's pipe is a twining evergreen vine with heart-shaped alternate leaves. The speckled flowers are curiously twisted and resemble a curved smoking pipe.

Flower color and season 3-inch (7.5-cm) purple-and-yellow scentless flowers in late spring and early summer.

Height and spread 10–15 feet (3.5–5 m) with support.

Best climate and site Zones 9–11. Rich moisture-retentive but well-drained soil. Full sun to partial shade.

Cultivation Transplant container-grown plants in spring. Cut back in winter to control size.

Propagation Take stem cuttings in early summer or root cuttings in late winter. Sow seed in spring.

Pest and disease prevention Avoid poorly drained soil.

Common problems Occasionally susceptible to spider mites, which cause yellow curled leaves with fine webs on undersides. Deter with an organically acceptable insecticide, such as insecticidal soap.

Landscape use Grow on fences or trellises; excellent for screening.

Bougainvillea glabra
NYCTAGINACEAE

LESSER BOUGAINVILLEA

Native to Brazil, lesser bougainvillea is a spiny alternate-leaved vine that occasionally grows into a loose shrub. The small summer flowers are surrounded by showy bracts.

Flower color and season Inconspicuous flowers surrounded by brilliantly colored bracts of red, yellow, purple, white, or magenta all summer.

Height and spread 20–30 feet (6–9 m) with support.

Best climate and site Zone 10. Well-drained, humus-rich soil. Full sun.

Cultivation Plant in spring. Cut back severely after flowering to maintain desired shape and size. Mulch freely in spring with aged cow manure or compost.

Propagation Take cuttings during active growth.

Pest and disease prevention Avoid damaging with pruning tools; these wounds are common entry points for pests and diseases.

Common problems Vigorously growing plants often produce ferocious thorns; avoid planting in areas where children play or where passersby will come in contact with the thorns.

Landscape use Where hardy, excellent to cover trellises and porches or to hang over walls and banks. Elsewhere, a lovely hanging basket plant.

Other common names Paper flower.

Campsis radicans
BIGNONIACEAE

TRUMPET VINE

Trumpet vine is a summer-blooming deciduous climber that supports itself by means of rootlike holdfasts. Its leaves are pinnately compound, with 7–11 leaflets.

Flower color and season Orange or red flowers, borne in pendulous, terminal clusters of 2-inch (5-cm) wide, trumpet-shaped blooms in early to late summer.

Height and spread 30–40 feet (9–12 m) with support.

Best climate and site Zones 4–9. Virtually any well-drained soil. Full sun.

Cultivation Plant in early spring. Prune in spring to restrain growth. Often needs additional support because of its weight.

Propagation Take cuttings in spring to summer; layer in fall to spring; sow seed in spring.

Pest and disease prevention Enrich soil with organic matter to promote healthy growth. No serious pests or diseases.

Common problems *C. radicans* can become invasive as it tends to spread by underground runners. Remove unwanted shoots at soil level.

Landscape use Excellent flowering vines for fences, walls, and trellises or to climb up trees.

Cultivars 'Fiava' bears yellow flowers.

Other species *C. grandiflora*, Chinese trumpet creeper, native to China, is somewhat less rampant. Its leaves consist of seven to nine leaflets. Zones 7–11.

Clematis spp. and hybrids
RANUNCULACEAE

CLEMATIS

Clematis are usually deciduous vines with opposite, compound leaves that climb by twining. C. montana 'Rubens' has fragrant lavender-pink flowers in early summer.

Flower color and season White, pink, red, blue, lavender, or purple blooms, in early summer to midfall—varying according to cultivar.

Height and spread 8–24 feet (2.4–7.2 m) with support, varying with species or cultivar.

Best climate and site Zones 5–9. Moisture-retentive, humus-rich soil. Full sun at the tops, partial shade at the roots.

Cultivation Plant during spring or fall. Prune after flowering to remove dead wood and to shape the plant. Many clematis tend to die back during winter in the colder parts of their range. Mulch around the root of the climber to keep it cool. Water regularly during hot weather.

Propagation Take cuttings in spring or early summer. Layer in spring.

Pest and disease prevention When planting, set the crown 2–3 inches (5–7.5 cm) below the soil surface to encourage strong, healthy growth.

Common problems Clematis borer may be a problem. Prune off damaged canes and seal ends with paraffin.

Landscape use Outstanding flowering vines to grow on arbors, trellises, or even to intertwine with climbing roses.

Clerodendrum thomsoniae
VERBENACEAE

BLEEDING GLORYBOWER

Native to West Africa, bleeding glorybower is a twining evergreen vine with opposite 5-inch (12.5-cm) leaves. The showy red-and-white flowers bloom from summer into fall.

Flower color and season Clusters of flowers with red petals, striking white calyces, and long, curving, protruding stamens in summer and fall.

Height and spread To 10 feet (3 m) with support.

Best climate and site Zones 9–10. Rich, loamy, moisture-retentive soil. Partial shade.

Cultivation Plant in spring. Prune lightly after flowering if needed to control growth. Never allow to dry out.

Propagation Sow seed in spring. Take cuttings in spring and summer.

Pest and disease prevention Avoid overwatering during winter when plant is not growing as quickly. Mulch with organic matter to keep soil evenly moist during spring and summer.

Common problems Drought-sensitive.

Landscape use Where hardy, grow on a fence or trellis. Elsewhere, a fine hanging-basket plant.

Other common names Bag flower, bleeding heart vine, glory tree, tropical bleeding heart.

Gelsemium sempervirens
LOGANIACEAE

YELLOW JESSAMINE

Native to the southeastern United States, yellow jessamine is a twining vine with glossy opposite leaves; it is evergreen in the warmer portions of its range.

Flower color and season Funnel-shaped, fragrant yellow flowers borne in axillary clusters in early- to mid-spring.

Height and spread To 20 feet (6 m) with support.

Best climate and site Zones 7–10. Virtually any well-drained soil. Full sun to light shade.

Cultivation Transplant container-grown plants in spring. If necessary, prune after flowering to control growth.

Propagation Take cuttings in summer. Sow seed in spring.

Pest and disease prevention Avoid waterlogged sites. No serious pests or disease problems.

Common problems Flowers, leaves, and roots are poisonous when eaten. Keep children and animals away from plants.

Landscape use Excellent flowering vine for woodland plantings or as a groundcover for banks. Plant on a fence, trellis, or arch as a screen.

Other common names Carolina jasmine, evening trumpet flower, woodbine.

Cultivars 'Price of Augusta' ('Plena') is a vigorous and free-flowering double form.

Hedera helix
ARALIACEAE

ENGLISH IVY

English ivy is a vigorous evergreen vine native throughout Europe. It climbs by means of rootlike holdfasts. Leaves are lobed, except on mature, fruiting stems.

Flower color and season Cream-colored flowers on mature plants in fall; followed by inconspicuous black fruit.

Height and spread 30–40 feet (9–12 m) with support.

Best climate and site Zones 5–10. Virtually any well-drained soil. Full sun to partial shade.

Cultivation Plant in spring or fall. In colder zones shield from winter sun. Cut back in late winter to promote growth.

Propagation Take cuttings or layer in spring or summer.

Pest and disease prevention Choose a site with good air circulation and thoroughly clean up all dropped leaves to remove attractive overwintering sites for disease spores.

Common problems In colder areas leaves tend to turn brown if exposed to winter afternoon sun. Subject to attack by scales, mealybugs, and red spider mites; deter with organically acceptable insecticides. Bacterial leaf spot may also be a problem; destroy infected plants.

Landscape use Excellent foliage vines to climb walls and trees or to use as a groundcover.

Humulus lupulus
CANNABACEAE

HOP

Hops are hardy, deciduous twining vines with large, three- to five-lobed leaves. The female plants are the source of hops used in the commercial brewing industry.

Flower color and season Insignificant greenish flowers in late spring; followed, on female plants, by green cone-like pods.
Height and spread To 30 feet (9 m) with support.
Best climate and site Zones 3–8. Virtually any well-drained soil. Full sun to light shade. Best where nights are cool and moist.
Cultivation Plant in spring. Prune to the ground after frost.
Propagation Take cuttings in spring.
Pest and disease prevention No serious pests or diseases.
Common problems Can be invasive.
Landscape use A fast-growing cover or screen vine for a trellis, arch, or pergola.
Cultivars 'Aureus' has attractive golden yellow leaves.

Hydrangea anomala subsp. petiolaris
HYDRANGEACEAE

CLIMBING HYDRANGEA

Climbing hydrangea is a deciduous vine with rounded, glossy dark green leaves, white summer flowers, and peeling brown bark. It climbs by means of rootlike holdfasts.

Flower color and season White flattened clusters with large, sterile flowers on the outside of the clusters and small fertile ones in the center; blooms in early summer.
Height and spread To 60 feet (18 m) with support.
Best climate and site Zones 4–9. Virtually any moisture-retentive soil. Full sun to nearly full shade.
Cultivation Transplant container-grown plants in spring. Prune only if necessary to maintain shape.
Propagation Cuttings will root if taken in early summer.
Pest and disease prevention Mulch with organic matter to keep the soil evenly moist. No serious pests or diseases.
Common problems Often very slow to grow until established.
Landscape use A superb flowering vine for walls or to climb on trees or over boulders.

Ipomoea purpurea
CONVOLVULACEAE

COMMON MORNING GLORY

Common morning glory is a twining vine that is grown in many gardens for its colorful flowers. Although perennial in the warmest zones, it is most commonly used as an annual.

Flower color and season White, pink, red, blue, or variegated, varying with the species and cultivar; summer to early fall.
Height and spread To 15 feet (5 m) with support.
Best climate and site Zone 10; grow it as an annual in colder regions. Rather dry, moderately fertile soil. Full sun.
Cultivation Plant in spring. Water freely during spring and summer and less at other times. Thin out or cut back congested growth of perennials in spring.
Propagation Sow seed in spring. Take cuttings in summer.
Pest and disease prevention Avoid overfeeding, which promotes succulent growth that is attractive to pests.
Common problems Seedlings slow to develop. Excessive fertility and moisture can promote vegetative growth at the expense of flowers.
Landscape use Use on a trellis or fence or grow in containers.
Other species *I. alba*, moonflower, is also sold as *Calonyction aculeatum*. It bears oval or three-lobed leaves and fragrant white flowers that open at night. *I. nil* bears large flowers in a range of colors.

Jasminum officinale
OLEACEAE

COMMON WHITE JASMINE

Native to the Near East and China, common white jasmine is a vigorous semi-evergreen vine or loose shrub with compound leaves. The white flowers are delightfully fragrant.

Flower color and season Very fragrant white flowers which bloom in late spring to late summer.
Height and spread 30 feet (9 m) with support.
Best climate and site Zones 8–10. Moist, humus-rich, well-drained soil. Full sun to light shade.
Cultivation Plant during spring. Prune after flowering to keep vigorous growth under control.
Propagation Take cuttings during active growth in spring or fall.
Pest and disease prevention Keep soil evenly moist in summer to avoid stressing the plant. No serious pests or diseases.
Common problems Needs protection, such as a warm wall, in all but the warmest zones.
Landscape use Where hardy, excellent for growing on trellises or arbors.
Other common names Poet's jessamine.
Varieties *J. officinale* var. *grandiflorum* bears larger flowers, up to 1¼ inches (4.3 cm) across.

Lonicera periclymenum
CAPRIFOLIACEAE

WOODBINE HONEYSUCKLE

Woodbine honeysuckle is a scrambling shrub or vine with oval, deciduous leaves. The fragrant late-spring to late-summer flowers are followed by small red berries.

Flower color and season Fragrant flowers in varying proportions of yellow, white, and red which bloom in late spring to late summer.
Height and spread To 30 feet (9 m) with support.
Best climate and site Zones 4–9. Moist, humus-rich, well-drained soil. Full sun to partial shade.
Cultivation Plant in spring. Prune back after flowering to keep vigorous growth under control.
Propagation Cuttings will root if taken in early spring.
Pest and disease prevention Mulch with organic matter to keep soil moist.
Common problems Subject to scales which suck the plant sap, weakening plants and causing them to turn yellow. Prune and destroy infested parts; spray remaining stems with organically acceptable insecticide such as horticultural oil.
Landscape use Well suited for clambering over bushes and fences.

Mandevilla suaveolens (syn. M. laxa)
APOCYNACEAE

CHILEAN JASMINE

Chilean jasmine is a fast-growing, twining semi-evergreen vine with narrow heart-shaped leaves. Clusters of fragrant white flowers grace the plant in summer.

Flower color and season Very fragrant white to pinkish trumpet-shaped flowers borne in clusters in late spring to midsummer.
Height and spread To 20 feet (6 m) with support.
Best climate and site Zones 9–10. Any well-drained, humus-rich soil. Full sun to light shade.
Cultivation Plant in spring. Water freely when in full growth; sparingly at other times. Thin out and cut back in early spring.
Propagation Take cuttings or sow seed in spring.
Pest and disease prevention No serious pests or diseases when grown outdoors. As a greenhouse plant, whiteflies and spider mites may cause trouble. Spray with insecticidal soap to deter pests.
Common problems Sensitive to frost.
Landscape use Where hardy, an excellent plant for growing on a pillar. Elsewhere, a lovely greenhouse or hanging-basket plant.

Mina lobata (syn. Quamoclit lobata)
CONVOLVULACEAE

CRIMSON STARGLORY

Crimson starglory is a vigorous, twining herbaceous vine with alternate three-lobed leaves. Clusters of reddish flower buds fade to orange and yellow as the flowers open.

Flower color and season Long-stalked clusters of fiery scarlet buds and creamy yellow-and-orange flowers all summer.
Height To 20 feet (6 m) with support.
Best climate and site Zones 8–10; in colder regions, treat as an annual. Light, well-drained soil. Full sun to light shade.
Cultivation Plant in spring. Mulch with organic matter to keep soil evenly moist.
Propagation Start seed indoors in pots about five weeks before planting outside.
Pest and disease prevention No significant pest or disease problems.
Common problems Will not thrive in poorly drained soil or in dense shade.
Landscape use Use on a trellis or fence.

Parthenocissus quinquefolia
VITACEAE

VIRGINIA CREEPER

Virginia creeper is a native plant that grows as either a clinging vine or a groundcover. The deciduous leaves turn bright red before dropping in fall.

Flower color and season Shiny, green leaves with five leaflets turn shades of brilliant scarlet and red in fall. Birds enjoy the black fruits that come in clusters, like grapes.
Height To 60 feet (18 m) with support.
Best climate and site Zones 3–9. Most soil types; salt-tolerant. Sun to partial shade.
Cultivation Set plants 2–6 feet (60–180 cm) apart in spring or fall. Prune anytime to control growth.
Propagation Take hardwood cuttings in early spring, or layer stems anytime.
Pest and disease prevention No significant pest or disease problems.
Common problems Plantings easily become invasive. Grow where the spread isn't a problem, or cut back heavily in late fall if necessary.
Landscape use Use to cover a wall, fence, tree trunk, or pergola.
Other common names Woodbine.
Cultivars 'Engelmannii' has smaller leaflets than the species and a more compact growth habit.

Parthenocissus tricuspidata
VITACEAE

BOSTON IVY

Boston ivy is a deciduous vine that climbs by means of rootlike holdfasts. The large, maple-like, three-lobed leaves turn from lustrous green to brilliant scarlet in fall.

Flower color and season Inconspicuous creamy white flowers in late spring; followed by purple fruit.
Height and spread To 60 feet (18 m) with support.
Best climate and site Zones 4–10. Humus-rich, well-drained soil. Full sun to light shade.
Cultivation Transplant container-grown plants in early spring.
Propagation Take softwood cuttings in late summer; hardwood cuttings in early spring.
Pest and disease prevention Avoid overfeeding, which provides succulent growth that is attractive to pests.
Common problems Sometimes slow to become established. Japanese beetles, which skeletonize leaves, may be a major problem. Shake beetles into a bucket of soapy water. Scales, mildew, and leaf spot may also appear. Prune and destroy infested parts.
Landscape use The premier foliage vine to mask a wall.
Other common names Japanese ivy.
Cultivars 'Lowii' has small leaves that are sometimes purple when young. 'Veitchii' bears small purple leaves.

Passiflora caerulea
PASSIFLORACEAE

BLUE PASSIONFLOWER

Blue passionflower is a deciduous summer-flowering vine that climbs by means of tendrils. It dies back to the roots each winter in the colder portions of its range.

Flower color and season Blue or (rarely) white flowers in summer; followed by conspicuous orange fruit.

Height and spread To 12 feet (3.6 m) with support.

Best climate and site Zones 7–10. Well-drained, humus-rich soil. Full sun to light shade.

Cultivation Plant in spring near a warm wall for winter protection.

Propagation Sow seed in spring. Take cuttings in summer.

Pest and disease prevention Mulch with organic matter to keep soil evenly moist. No serious pests or diseases.

Common problems Dies back to the ground annually in all but the warmest portions of its range.

Landscape use Grow on a trellis for the flowers and foliage.

Cultivars 'Constance Elliott' is a white-flowered form.

Other species *P. incarnata*, wild passionflower or maypop, is native to the southeastern United States and has three-lobed leaves. It bears white flowers with blue stamens in summer; followed by edible fruit.

Stephanotis floribunda
ASCLEPIADACEAE

MADAGASCAR JASMINE

Madagascar jasmine is a twining opposite-leaved vine with rather large round to oval glossy green leaves. Its beautiful waxy white summer flowers are highly fragrant.

Flower color and season Narrowly tubular waxy white flowers borne in clusters in midspring to fall.

Height and spread To 12 feet (3.6 m) with support.

Best climate and site Zone 10. Humus-rich, moisture-retentive soil. Full sun to light shade.

Cultivation Plant in spring. Cut back long or crowded stems in fall.

Propagation Take cuttings in summer.

Pest and disease prevention Keep soil moist with organic mulch. Avoid dry or poorly drained soil. Ensure adequate air circulation.

Common problems Subject to scales and mealybugs when grown as a greenhouse plant. Treat plants with insecticidal soap.

Landscape use Where hardy, a compact vine to grow on a trellis. Elsewhere a beautiful greenhouse plant. Also grown for its cut flowers, which are used in bridal bouquets and leis.

Thunbergia alata
ACANTHACEAE

BLACK-EYED SUSAN VINE

Black-eyed Susan vine is a perennial climber that is commonly grown as an annual. The triangular bright green leaves are accented by the colorful summer flowers.

Flower color and season White, yellow, or orange blooms, often with purple-black centers, in midsummer.

Height and spread To 6 feet (1.8 m) with support.

Best climate and site Zone 10; in colder regions, treat as an annual. Moist, humus-rich, well-drained soil. Full sun to partial shade.

Cultivation Plant in spring. Thin crowded stems in early spring. Water during periods of drought.

Propagation Sow seed in spring. Take cuttings in summer.

Pest and disease prevention Avoid dry or poorly drained soil. No serious pests or diseases.

Common problems Very sensitive to frost. Protect with mulch.

Landscape use Use on trellises or fences. Also a good hanging-basket plant.

Other common names Clock vine.

Cultivars The 'Susie' series has white, yellow, or orange flowers, with or without black eyes.

Trachelospermum jasminoides
APOCYNACEAE

STAR JASMINE

Star jasmine is a rapidly growing, evergreen twining vine with glossy green leaves up to 4 inches (10 cm) long. Its fragrant white flowers bloom in late spring to summer.

Flower color and season Very fragrant 1-inch (2.5-cm) white flowers borne in clusters in late spring to early summer.
Height and spread To 20 feet (6 m) with support.
Best climate and site Zones 8–10. Moisture-retentive, humus-rich soil. Sun to partial shade.
Cultivation Plant in spring. Mulch to keep roots cool. Prune after flowering to control vigorous growth.
Propagation Take cuttings in late summer or fall. Sow seed in spring. Layer in summer.
Pest and disease prevention Take care not to damage plant when pruning; these wounds are common entry points for pests and diseases.
Common problems Tends to grow beyond desired bounds. Prune back annually to control.
Landscape use Excellent for screening or for growing on a trellis, up trees, or as a groundcover.
Other common names Chinese jasmine, confederate jasmine.

Vitis coignetiae
VITACEAE

CRIMSON GLORY

Crimson glory climbs by means of tendrils. It is an extremely rapid grower, capable of covering up to 1,000 square feet (300 sq. m) of trellis in one year. It displays red fall color.

Flower color and season Clusters of small inconspicuous cream flowers in late spring, followed by black fruit in fall.
Height and spread To 100 feet (30 m) with support.
Best climate and site Zones 5–9. Well-drained soil of low nutrient content. Full sun.
Cultivation Plant in winter or spring. Prune to desired dimensions in winter. Provide stout wire or trellis support on which to climb.
Propagation Layer in fall. Take cuttings in fall; graft in late winter or early spring. Sow seed in spring.
Pest and disease prevention Take care not to damage plant when pruning. These wounds are common entry points for pests and diseases.
Common problems V. *coignetiae*, as a result of its enormous growth rate, can easily exceed its desired limits. Choose a site carefully to avoid problems. Japanese beetles may skeletonize leaves; shake or brush beetles into a bucket of soapy water.
Landscape use Especially valued for its fall foliage color. An excellent cover for trellises or arbors.

Wisteria floribunda
LEGUMINOSAE

JAPANESE WISTERIA

Japanese wisteria is a deciduous, vigorous twining climber with alternately compound leaves. The vines are covered with long hanging flower clusters in late spring.

Flower color and season Long clusters of slightly fragrant white, pink, lavender, or violet flowers in late spring.
Height and spread To 50 feet (15 m) with support.
Best climate and site Zones 4–10. Moist, well-drained soil preferably with low nitrogen content. Lighter, infertile soil reduces vegetative growth and increases flowering. Grows best in full sun to light shade.
Cultivation Plant in spring. Prune back after flowering.
Propagation Take cuttings in late winter and spring. Layer in fall. Graft in late winter or early spring. Sow seed in fall or spring.
Pest and disease prevention Avoid poorly drained soil. Stress makes plants more prone to pests and diseases.
Common problems Requires stout hardwood or wire support. Plants produced from seed may be slow to bloom. Subject to leaf beetles, scales, crown gall, leaf spot, and mildew. Treat with organically acceptable controls.
Landscape use Fine vines to climb on stout supports like arches or pergolas. May be trained to standard form.

Ajuga reptans
LABIATAE

AJUGA

The short, spinach-like leaves of this excellent, low-growing groundcover spread rapidly to form a solid carpet. There are many colorful cultivars of ajuga to choose from.

Best climate and site Zones 3–8. Thrives in well-drained garden soil. Full sun to partial shade (shade is especially important in hot climates).

Height and spread Height of foliage to 3 inches (7.5 cm); spread unlimited. Flower height to about 6 inches (15 cm).

Description The leaves are usually dark green; cultivars are available with purple, bronze, or variegated foliage. Ajuga is evergreen in warm areas but tends to turn brown by midwinter in cold climates. Spikes of ¼-inch (6-mm) blue or purple flowers bloom in spring or early summer.

Growing guidelines Set plants 12–15 inches (30–37.5 cm) apart during the growing season. They need little maintenance. Don't give them fertilizer, otherwise the lush growth will be prone to fungal disease. Propagate by division any time during the growing season.

Landscape uses Plant ajuga as a flowering groundcover under trees and shrubs and on slopes. It will easily invade lawns, creating a maintenance headache; use an edging strip to avoid the problem. Ajuga can also overwhelm less vigorous plants, so it's not a good choice for edging flower beds or borders.

Alchemilla mollis
ROSACEAE

LADY'S-MANTLE

Lady's-mantle is superb as a carpet beneath trees. It also looks great in borders and rock gardens, but there you'll want to snip off the spent flowers to prevent reseeding.

Best climate and site Zones 3–8. Grows well in light-textured, well-drained, humus-rich, fertile soil. Likes partial shade; tolerates full sun in the North.

Height and spread Height of foliage 9–12 inches (22.5–30 cm); spread to 2 feet (60 cm). Flower height to 15 inches (37.5 cm).

Description Grow lady's-mantle for its attractive mounds of soft, silvery gray, deeply lobed, rounded foliage. The large leaves can grow up to 6 inches (15 cm) wide. Small, greenish yellow, petal-less flowers bloom in airy clusters in late spring and early summer.

Growing guidelines Set plants 20 inches (50 cm) apart in spring. If leaves look tattered by midsummer, cut plants to the ground to get a flush of new growth. Plants self-sow easily and can become weedy; cut off the spent flowers to prevent seed formation, or grow the plants where reseeding isn't a problem. Propagate by division in spring or fall, or by seed in summer.

Landscape uses Plant alone or combined with other vigorous perennials in flower borders. They also make an excellent, long-lasting cut flower.

Arctostaphylos uva-ursi
ERICACEAE

BEARBERRY

Bearberry, also called kinnikinnick, is a native American evergreen with spring flowers and red fall berries. It is one of the best groundcovers for hot, sandy areas.

Best climate and site Zones 2–7, but varies with cultivars. Sandy, dry, acid, poor soil. Full sun.

Height and spread Height 6–12 inches (15–30 cm); spread to 12 feet (3.6 m).

Description Bearberry forms creeping mats of woody stems clothed in shiny green leaves that turn bronze in winter. The stems are tipped with tiny, waxy, bell-shaped, white to light pink flowers in spring and bright red berries in fall.

Growing guidelines Set plants out about 1 foot (30 cm) apart. They can be slow to establish, so be prepared to weed between plants until they fill in. They're difficult to propagate, but you could try layering (covering parts of the creeping stems with soil until roots form); it's best to use nursery-grown transplants.

Landscape uses Bearberry is ideal for erosion control on well-drained slopes; it looks particularly nice with rocks. It is also excellent in seaside gardens; it thrives in sandy soil.

Asarum europaeum
ARISTOLOCHIACEAE

EUROPEAN WILD GINGER

European wild ginger is one of the best evergreen groundcovers for partial shade. The glossy, leathery leaves and thick, creeping roots are aromatic when you walk on them.

Best climate and site Zones 4–8. Moisture-retentive, humus-rich, somewhat acid soil. Partial shade.

Height and spread Height 5–7 inches (12.5–17.5 cm); spread to 1 foot (30 cm).

Description European wild ginger forms spreading colonies of kidney-shaped, evergreen leaves that are up to 3 inches (7.5 cm) wide. In late spring, small, purplish brown flowers bloom beneath the foliage.

Growing guidelines Set plants 8–12 inches (20–30 cm) apart in early spring. Don't plant too deep; set the crowns (where the leaves meet the roots) just at the soil surface. Keep them evenly moist the first season after planting; water established plantings in dry weather. Fertilize lightly in early spring with a light top-dressing of compost or leaf mold. To propagate, divide in spring.

Landscape uses European wild ginger grows quickly into a weed-suppressing clump. Combine it with ferns and shade-loving perennials, such as hostas and crested iris (*Iris cristata*).

Bergenia cordifolia
SAXIFRAGACEAE

HEART-LEAVED BERGENIA

Sometimes called elephant's ears or heartleaf, this evergreen native of Siberia is grown for its thick, handsome leaves. The flower buds may be killed by very cold winters.

Best climate and site Zones 3–8. Humus-rich, well-drained, moist, slightly alkaline soil; but will grow anywhere if kept watered. Partial shade.

Height and spread Height of foliage to 1 foot (30 cm); spread to 2 feet (60 cm). Flower stems to 18 inches (45 cm) tall.

Description The heart-shaped, evergreen foliage turns shades of red-bronze in fall and holds the color well into winter. Clusters of tiny, rose-pink flowers hang on stems that emerge from the base of the plant in mid- to late-spring.

Growing guidelines Set plants 2 feet (60 cm) apart in spring or fall. It's best to choose a location sheltered from wind so the leaves won't get tattered. Mulch lightly before winter, especially in the coldest parts of its range. Use a loose mulch like coarse leaves, and remove it in early spring so the flower stems can emerge. Cut off old, damaged leaves as needed. Trap slugs under cabbage leaves (remove pests daily). Propagate by division in spring, or sow fresh seed in late summer.

Landscape uses Dramatic along paths, under shrubs or trees, in large rock gardens, near ponds, and in containers.

Campanula portenschlagiana
CAMPANULACEAE

DALMATIAN BELLFLOWER

The trailing stems of Dalmatian bellflower creep over the ground or sprawl over stone walls. This pretty plant is also attractive along the front of flower borders or in pots.

Best climate and site Zones 4–8. Well-drained, sandy soil. Full sun; light shade in hot climates.

Height and spread Height 6–8 inches (15–20 cm); spread to 2 feet (60 cm).

Description This low-growing campanula has heart-shaped, toothed leaves. It is covered with large numbers of bell-shaped, lavender-blue, 1-inch (2.5-cm) flowers from late spring to midsummer.

Growing guidelines Set plants 12–18 inches (30–45 cm) apart in spring. Plants are easy to grow and need no special care. Propagate by division in early spring.

Landscape uses Dalmatian bellflower is ideal as a groundcover in rock gardens, on rocky slopes, and in nooks and crannies in stone walls.

Cultivars 'Resholt' has deep violet flowers that are larger than the species. It thrives in partial shade as well as in sunny conditions.

Cephalotaxus harringtonia
'PROSTRATA' CEPHALOTAXACEAE

JAPANESE PLUM YEW

Try Japanese plum yew where you need a large, shrubby groundcover. It's one of the few needle-leaved evergreens that grows very well in shady spots.

Best climate and site Zones 6–9. Average, well-drained soil. Partial shade.
Height and spread Height to 3 feet (90 cm); spread to 12 feet (3.6 m) or sometimes more.
Description This shrubby, shade-tolerant evergreen resembles true yews (*Taxus* spp.) but has larger, flat needles. The dark green color is best in shade—too much sun may cause the needles to turn yellowish. The insignificant flowers bear only the male parts, so the plant does not set seed. Japanese plum yew seems to be deer-resistant.
Growing guidelines Set plants 3 feet (90 cm) or more apart in spring. Japanese plum yew needs practically no maintenance to thrive. Propagate by layering branches (covering them with soil where they touch the ground to encourage rooting).
Landscape uses Japanese plum yew is an excellent evergreen groundcover for shady sites. It's a good substitute for yews where deer are a problem.

Cerastium tomentosum
CARYOPHYLLACEAE

SNOW-IN-SUMMER

Snow-in-summer carpets the ground with mats of woolly gray leaves. It can become invasive in spots it likes, so plant it where it can spread, or surround it with a barrier strip.

Best climate and site Zones 2–10. Dry, well-drained, poor soil—even sand. Needs full sun.
Height and spread Height 6–10 inches (15–25 cm); spread to 3 feet (90 cm) or sometimes more.
Description This fast-growing evergreen with light gray, woolly foliage forms large mats with its creeping stems. Its abundant white flowers with star-shaped petals cover the foliage for several weeks in late spring.
Growing guidelines Set plants 12–18 inches (30–45 cm) apart in spring. Once they are established, cut the stems back after flowering to prevent seeding. Snow-in-summer can become invasive; divide plants every few years as they get out of bounds, or cut them back hard in early spring to control the spread. Propagate by division or seed in spring or fall, or take cuttings in early summer.
Landscape uses Snow-in-summer forms a good groundcover for dry, sunny spots, especially in difficult spots like dry, rocky slopes. Plant it where the spread won't be a problem, or surround the planting with an edging strip.

Clematis integrifolia
RANUNCULACEAE

SOLITARY CLEMATIS

Unlike most other clematis, which grow as vines, solitary clematis forms a sprawling mound that makes an unusual and attractive lavender-blue-flowering groundcover.

Best climate and site Zones 4–9. Light, loamy, alkaline soil. Full sun.
Height and spread Height 2–3 feet (60–90 cm); similar spread.
Description Solitary clematis forms bushy mounds of egg-shaped, deciduous leaves. Bell-shaped, lavender-blue flowers bloom over a long period in midsummer, followed by charming silvery seed heads.
Growing guidelines Set plants out 2–3 feet (60–90 cm) apart in spring or fall. Maintain an organic mulch (such as compost or shredded leaves) to keep the soil cool and moist; otherwise, plants need no special care. Propagate by seed in late summer or cuttings in late spring.
Landscape uses Solitary clematis is not especially showy, but the flowers and seed heads can provide several months of subtle interest. It looks best combined with other plants, as part of a perennial border, or as an accent with other low-growing groundcovers.
Cultivars 'Rosea' has pink flowers.

Convallaria majalis
LILIACEAE

LILY-OF-THE-VALLEY

Established clumps of lily-of-the-valley compete well with weeds and can thrive in the same spot for decades with little or no care. They spread quickly by creeping roots.

Best climate and site Zones 2–8. Moist, well-drained, fertile soil enriched with organic matter. Partial to full shade.
Height and spread Height of foliage 6–8 inches (15–20 cm); spread unlimited. Flower height 8–10 inches (20–25 cm).
Description Lily-of-the-valley is beloved for its fragrant, bell-shaped, waxy, white flowers. Each crown (known as a pip) produces two large, oblong, green leaves and one upright flower spike in late spring. The flowers may be followed by glossy, orange-red berries in summer.
Growing guidelines Set plants 4–6 inches (10–15 cm) apart in late fall or very early spring. The deciduous leaves turn brown in mid- to late-summer, so place them where the unsightly appearance isn't a problem. If desired, you can cut down the brown leaves to tidy up the planting. Lily-of-the-valley benefits from an application of compost or leaf mold each fall if the area isn't fertile. Thin out crowded plantings if they stop blooming well. Propagate by division after flowering or in fall.
Landscape uses Clumps of lily-of-the-valley are ideal groundcovers in shady borders and foundation plantings.

Delosperma cooperi
AIZOACEAE

HARDY ICEPLANT

Long-blooming hardy iceplant offers a colorful show of purple flowers from summer through frost. It looks wonderful cascading down slopes and over stones in rock gardens.

Best climate and site Zones 7–9. Rich, well-drained, dry soil. Full sun.
Height and spread Height 4 inches (10 cm); spread to 12 inches (30 cm).
Description This low-growing South African succulent is becoming increasingly popular in the United States for its small, rosy purple, daisy-like flowers, which bloom from summer until frost over mats of narrow, curving leaves.
Growing guidelines Set plants 12 inches (30 cm) apart in spring. They like dry soil in winter and do best when temperatures don't go below 50°F (10°C). In warm climates, the plants bloom all year but grow mostly in the summer. Established plants need little care. Propagate by seed or cuttings in spring or summer.
Landscape uses Hardy iceplant is a tough, beautiful, long-blooming groundcover for rock gardens, driveways, or sunny banks.
Other species *D. nubigenum* grows to 2 inches (5 cm) tall and 8–10 inches (20–25 cm) wide. This fast-growing, tough plant has bright yellow flowers in late spring and yellow-green leaves that turn red in winter. Zones 5–9.

Epimedium x versicolor
BERBERIDACEAE

PERSIAN EPIMEDIUM

Persian epimedium is a good plant for growing along the edge of woods. Established clumps compete well with tree and shrub roots to get the moisture and nutrients they need.

Best climate and site Zones 5–8. Humus-rich, moist, somewhat acid soil. Light to heavy shade; plants tolerate some sun if they receive enough moisture.
Height and spread Height to 1 foot (30 cm); spread 9–12 inches (22.5–30 cm).
Description Striking, heart-shaped, leathery leaves on wiry stems are purple-red or mottled in early spring and later become green. Clusters of distinctive, hooded, waxy, red-and-yellow flowers that resemble columbines bloom on wiry stems in early- to mid-spring. Persian epimedium is evergreen in the South; leaves in Northern gardens turn brown by midwinter.
Growing guidelines Set plants about 12 inches (30 cm) apart in spring. In early spring, cut all of the leaves to the ground to tidy the planting and to make it easier to see the delicate flowers. To propagate, divide after flowering.
Landscape uses Use Persian epimedium in shady rock gardens and woodland gardens and as an edging along paths. It is also an excellent foundation plant for the north side of a building.

Erica carnea
ERICACEAE

SPRING HEATH

Spring heath grows in low, spreading clumps with evergreen, needlelike leaves and bell-shaped spring flowers. It prefers a sunny site with moist but well-drained, acid soil.

Best climate and site Zones 5–7. Well-drained, sandy, acid soil with plenty of moisture. Full sun.

Height and spread Height to 18 inches (45 cm); spread to 3 feet (90 cm).

Description This small, evergreen shrub forms clumps or woody stems with narrow, needlelike, dark green foliage. Clusters of bell-shaped, red flowers bloom along shoot tips over a long period in early spring.

Growing guidelines Set plants 3 feet (90 cm) or more apart in spring or early fall. Keep the soil mulched, and water as necessary to keep it evenly moist. Clip plants back after blooming to promote compact growth. Propagate by softwood cuttings in early summer, by division in early spring, or layering (covering parts of low-growing stems with soil to promote rooting) anytime.

Landscape uses Spring heath forms an excellent and long-flowering cover for slopes and rock gardens.

Cultivars 'Springwood Pink' has clear pink flowers and bronze foliage in spring. 'Springwood White' has pretty creamy white flowers.

Euonymus fortunei
CELASTRACEAE

WINTERCREEPER

This evergreen produces long vining stems that take root as they travel over the earth. The clinging stems will also climb up trees, walls, and buildings. It prefers sun, but will grow in shade.

Best climate and site Zones 5–9. Well-drained, slightly acid, fertile, humus-rich soil. Sun to partial shade.

Height and spread Height 1–2 feet (30–60 cm); stems spread to about 30 feet (9 m).

Description The oval, waxy, green, 2-inch (5-cm) leaves become deep red in fall when grown in full sun. Inconspicuous white flowers bloom on mature stems in summer, followed by pink fruits in fall.

Growing guidelines Set plants 1 foot (30 cm) or more apart in spring or fall. Trim and shape established plants as needed in early spring. Plants may be susceptible to euonymus scale, especially in warm areas. Spray with organic insecticide such as insecticidal soap, if necessary. Propagate by cuttings in early summer or by layering anytime.

Landscape uses Wintercreeper is useful as a low-growing evergreen for erosion control on banks. It grows relatively slowly in shade, but it is one of the best groundcovers for dry, shady spots.

Galium odoratum
RUBIACEAE

SWEET WOODRUFF

Delicate-looking sweet woodruff is a fast-spreading groundcover for shady gardens. It can crowd out less vigorous plants but combines well with shrubs and trees.

Best climate and site Zones 3–8. Well-drained, moist, humus-rich, somewhat acid soil. Partial to full shade.

Height and spread Height 6–12 inches (15–30 cm); spread to 2 feet (60 cm).

Description Sweet woodruff forms carpets of deciduous, 1-inch (2.5-cm) leaves in whorls on square stems. The leaves have a sweet fragrance when dried. In early spring, loose clusters of small, star-shaped, white flowers appear just above the leaves. Sweet woodruff is also commonly called bedstraw and was formerly known as *Asperula odorata*.

Growing guidelines Set plants 8 inches (20 cm) apart in spring. Trim back established plants in spring to prevent leggy growth, but always leave the foliage closest to the ground intact. Propagate by division in spring or fall.

Landscape uses Sweet woodruff is a charming groundcover for woodland gardens. It is also useful under shrubs, such as rhododendrons. The dried leaves are used in sachets.

Gaultheria procumbens
ERICACEAE

WINTERGREEN

Wintergreen spreads slowly to form handsome carpets of glossy evergreen leaves in spots with moist, humus-rich, acid soil. The leaves are accented by bright red fall fruit.

Best climate and site Zones 3–8. Acid, humus-rich, evenly moist soil. Plant in light shade or in sunny spots that get midday shade.

Height and spread Height 3–4 inches (7.5–10 cm); spread to 1 foot (30 cm).

Description This evergreen native of eastern North America has shiny, oval, 2-inch (5-cm) leathery leaves that become reddish in fall. The leaves are fragrant when crushed. Small, solitary, nodding, urn-shaped, white flowers dangle under the leaves in early summer, and edible, bright red fruits appear in fall. Wintergreen spreads slowly by creeping underground roots.

Growing guidelines Set plants about 1 foot (30 cm) apart in spring. A thick mulch is beneficial in hot climates to keep the roots cool and moist. Propagate by division in spring or fall or by cuttings in summer.

Landscape uses Wintergreen makes a nice year-round cover in naturalized woodland plantings, under trees, and in shady rock gardens.

Geranium macrorrhizum
GERANIACEAE

BIGROOT CRANESBILL

Bigroot cranesbill grows in spreading clumps to form lush mats of aromatic, lobed, green leaves. The foliage turns reddish in fall and may hold its color into early winter.

Best climate and site Zones 3–8. Well-drained, fairly rich, moist soil; tolerates dry soil once established. Sun or light shade. (Plants prefer not to be in hot sunlight all day, particularly in southern regions.)

Height and spread Height 12–18 inches (30–45 cm); spread 2–3 feet (60–90 cm).

Description This slow-spreading, mound-forming perennial is one of many delightful and versatile species of hardy geranium (*Geranium* spp.)—not to be confused with *Pelargonium* spp., the common houseplant geranium. Bigroot cranesbill bears 1-inch (2.5-cm) pink or reddish purple flowers in early summer. The spreading clumps of aromatic, lobed, green leaves stay attractive throughout the season and turn reddish in fall.

Growing guidelines Set plants about 2 feet (60 cm) apart in early spring. They need little maintenance, but divide them whenever they become too large and stop blooming well. Propagate by division in spring or fall.

Landscape uses Grow bigroot cranesbill in border plantings, rock gardens, and wild gardens and on slopes. It can even take dry shade.

Hedera helix
ARALIACEAE

ENGLISH IVY

English ivy is available in a range of leaf colors and patterns. The plain green ivies tend to be most cold-tolerant, but many of the variegated ones are surprisingly hardy.

Best climate and site Zones 5–9. Prefers moist, well-drained, rich soil; tolerates poor, dry soil. Partial to full shade.

Height and spread Height to 6 inches (15 cm); forms a mat that spreads limitlessly.

Description This handsome evergreen vine has lobed, green leaves that are 2–5 inches (5–12.5 cm) long on woody stems. The stems creep over the ground, sending down roots as they travel. When they meet an upright surface, they climb with clinging rootlets. These upright stems mature to produce unlobed leaves, green flowers, and black berries.

Growing guidelines Set plants about 2 feet (60 cm) apart in spring or fall. Prune as needed to control and direct the growth. Propagate by cuttings in early spring to early summer and by layering (covering parts of the creeping stems to promote rooting) anytime.

Landscape uses English ivy is a dependable, fast-spreading groundcover. Use it on slopes for erosion control. It's also attractive as a groundcover beneath deciduous trees. English ivy can quickly become invasive in spots it enjoys, creating a maintenance nightmare.

Helianthemum nummularium
CISTACEAE

SUN ROSE

Sun rose, also called rock rose, is a low-growing shrub with small green or gray-green leaves. It blooms for many weeks, although each flower only lasts for one day.

Best climate and site Zones 6–8. Well-drained, sandy, neutral to slightly alkaline soil. Full sun.
Height and spread Height 8–18 inches (20–45 cm); spread to 3 feet (90 cm).
Description This low-growing woody shrub forms spreading mounds of narrow, hairy, evergreen leaves. Clusters of yellow, pink, or white blooms that resemble single roses begin blooming just above the foliage in late spring or early summer.
Growing guidelines Set plants 2 feet (60 cm) apart in spring or fall. This shrub needs little or no care. Prune back by one-third to one-half after flowering stops if you wish to stimulate a second bloom. Protect plants with a light winter mulch in the coldest parts of their range; you may also need to trim them back in early spring to remove winter-damaged tips. Propagate by cuttings in summer.
Landscape uses Sun rose is a good choice as a drought-tolerant cover for dry, hot, troublesome areas. It is also a fine addition to rock gardens and borders.

Houttuynia cordata
'VARIEGATA' SAURURACEAE

VARIEGATED HOUTTUYNIA

Variegated houttuynia is a fast-spreading groundcover that thrives in moist soil. The showy green, red, and yellow leaves are accented by white flowers in summer.

Best climate and site Zones 5–9. Damp, rich soil; will grow in standing water. Partial to full shade.
Height and spread Height 15–18 inches (37.5–45 cm); spread 18 inches (45 cm).
Description Variegated houttuynia forms creeping clumps of 2–3-inch (5–7.5-cm) long, green leaves variegated with reds and yellows; the leaves turn purplish in fall. Some people describe the crushed leaves as citrus-scented; others call them foul-smelling. Small white flowers surrounded with white, petallike bracts in summer resemble tiny dogwood blossoms. Plants are deciduous in cold climates and evergreen in warm areas. The species was named after Dutch horticulturist Martin Houttuyn; the name is pronounced "how-tyne-nia."
Growing guidelines Set plants 12 inches (30 cm) apart in spring. In ideal (boggy) areas, houttuynia can become invasive. Propagate by division in spring or fall or take cuttings in summer.
Landscape uses Variegated houttuynia is useful for stabilizing banks along ponds and streams. Or try it as a groundcover for moist woodlands. Just make sure you're prepared to deal with the spread.

Juniperus horizontalis
CUPRESSACEAE

CREEPING JUNIPER

Plant creeping junipers for erosion control on slopes or for an evergreen accent in rock gardens and foundation plantings. They prefer full sun and well-drained soil.

Best climate and site Zones 3–9. Prefers well-drained, sandy soil, but tolerates any soil, even clay. Full sun.
Height and spread Height varies with cultivar, from 6–18 inches (15–45 cm); spread also variable to 8 feet (2.4 m).
Description Creeping junipers are low-growing, evergreen shrubs with spreading branches carrying scaly or needlelike, blue-green leaves. Dark-colored fruits form on short stems in late summer.
Growing guidelines Spacing varies according to size; check the ultimate spread in the catalog description. Set out bareroot plants in spring and potted or balled-and-burlapped plants any time during the growing season. Prune in summer only to control size. Don't just shear off shoot tips; cut unwanted stems back to another stem or to the ground. Phomopsis twig blight may be a problem in wet springs, causing browned shoot tips; remove and destroy diseased branches. Propagate by cuttings or seed in summer.
Landscape uses Junipers are ideal for covering slopes, including steep slopes where other plants won't thrive.

Lamium maculatum
LABIATAE

SPOTTED LAMIUM

Spotted lamium, also known as spotted dead nettle, is a vigorous groundcover for shady gardens. It is a good choice for growing under trees and shrubs.

Best climate and site Zones 3–8. Prefers moist, rich soil; tolerates dry shade. Partial to deep shade.

Height and spread Height 12–14 inches (30–35.5 cm); spread to 2 feet (60 cm) or sometimes more.

Description This vigorous plant grows quickly to form a dense cover of dark green, oval or heart-shaped leaves with a distinctive silvery white mid-rib. Lavender-pink, hooded, 1-inch (2.5-cm) flowers bloom in clusters throughout the summer. Spotted lamium is less invasive than its relative, yellow archangel (*Lamiastrum galeobdolon*), but it is still a fast grower.

Growing guidelines Set plants 12–14 inches (30–35 cm) apart in spring or fall. Cut plants back by about half in midsummer to promote a new flush of leaves. Plants often self-sow. Propagate by division in spring or fall or by cuttings in summer.

Landscape uses Spotted lamium is handsome in wild areas, woodland gardens, and shady rock gardens.

Cultivars 'Alba', white lamium, has white flowers and green leaves with silver centers. 'Aureum' has yellow leaves with a creamy white stripe and pink flowers.

Lysimachia nummularia
PRIMULACEAE

CREEPING JENNY

Creeping Jenny is an attractive groundcover for moist-soil areas where its spread isn't a problem. The yellow-leaved cultivar 'Aurea' is less invasive than the species.

Best climate and site Zones 3–8. Moist, fertile soil. Full sun (in cool climates) to full shade (in warm climates).

Height and spread Height 4–8 inches (10–20 cm); spread to 3 feet (90 cm).

Description This creeping perennial, also known as moneywort, has shiny, round, ¼-inch (18-mm) leaves that resemble coins. The trailing stems bear bright, 1-inch (2.5-cm), yellow flowers throughout the summer. The stems root rapidly as they creep over the soil.

Growing guidelines Set plants 8 inches (20 cm) apart in spring or fall. Creeping Jenny can be very invasive, and it rapidly becomes a weed problem when it spreads into lawn areas. Propagate by division in spring or fall.

Landscape uses Creeping Jenny is a particularly good groundcover around ponds and streams.

Cultivars 'Aurea', golden creeping Jenny, grows 2 inches (5 cm) tall with golden yellow spring foliage that turns lime green in summer. It is a vigorous mat-forming creeper but not as invasive as the species. Zones 4–8.

Mazus reptans
SCROPHULARIACEAE

MAZUS

Mazus forms ground-hugging mats of small leaves topped with tubular, lipped flowers in spring and early summer. It thrives in moist soil in sun or partial shade.

Best climate and site Zones 5–8. Well-drained, moist, rich soil. Full sun to partial shade.

Height and spread Height 1–2 inches (2.5–5 cm); spread 15–18 inches (37.5–45 cm).

Description This creeping plant from the Himalayas sends out roots along its stems to form a carpet of bronzy green, toothed, 1-inch (2.5-cm) leaves. Light blue-violet, ¼-inch (18-mm) flowers have a lower lip spotted in white, greenish yellow, and purple in spring and early summer. Plants are evergreen only in warm climates.

Growing guidelines Set plants 12 inches (30 cm) apart in spring. They can be invasive; surround plantings with edging strips if the spread is a problem. Propagate by division in spring or fall or by cuttings in summer.

Landscape uses Plant mazus in crevices between flagstones on pathways; it mingles happily with creeping thyme and similar low-growing plants. Grow it in rock gardens as a carpet for small bulbs, like crocuses. Mazus competes with grass and will invade lawns.

Cultivars 'Alba' has white flowers.

Oenothera speciosa
ONAGRACEAE

SHOWY SUNDROPS

Showy sundrops spread quickly by underground runners. They bloom in early summer during the day, unlike the many night-blooming species of the Oenothera genus.

Best climate and site Zones 3–8. Well-drained, average soil. Full sun to very light shade.

Height and spread Height to 18 inches (45 cm); spread to 2 feet (60 cm) or more.

Description Showy sundrops produce wiry stems clothed in toothed, green leaves and topped with 2-inch (5-cm), cup-shaped, white flowers that fade to soft pink and turn toward the sun.

Growing guidelines Set plants about 2 feet (60 cm) apart in spring or fall. Showy sundrops can be invasive, especially in moist, fertile soil; plant where the spread isn't a problem, or surround the planting with an edging strip that extends a few inches below the ground. Propagate by division or seed in spring or fall.

Landscape uses Showy sundrops look wonderful massed in low-maintenance areas, such as dry, sunny slopes.

Cultivars 'Rosea' grows to 15 inches (37.5 cm) with clear pink, 3-inch (7.5-cm) blooms.

Ophiopogon japonicus
LILIACEAE

MONDO GRASS

Mondo grass is an excellent, sod-forming, grass-like perennial from the Orient. It is sometimes confused with lilyturf (Muscari spp.), which it closely resembles.

Best climate and site Zones 7–9. Light-textured, well-drained, humus-rich, fertile soil with a pH of 5–7. Full sun to shade; does not tolerate midday sun in hot climates.

Height and spread Height to 8 inches (20 cm); spread unlimited.

Description The dark green, coarse-textured leaves are 15 inches (37.5 cm) long and 1/8 inch (3 mm) wide. Lavender to white, 1/4-inch (6-mm) flowers bloom in summer in short, loose clusters that are often hidden by the leaves. The flowers are followed by blue, pea-sized fruits. Mondo grass spreads by rhizomes (underground runners).

Growing guidelines Set plants about 1 foot (30 cm) apart in spring. If the foliage has deteriorated over the winter, you can cut it down in spring. Slugs can be a problem; trap them under cabbage leaves (remove pests daily) or in pans of beer set flush with the soil surface. Propagate mondo grass by division in spring or early fall.

Landscape uses Mondo grass is an excellent groundcover under trees in the South. It is also a fine choice for seaside planting, and a good edging for borders.

Pachysandra terminalis
BUXACEAE

JAPANESE PACHYSANDRA

Japanese pachysandra is one of the most common evergreen groundcovers for shady spots, especially in the North. Established plantings need very little in the way of maintenance.

Best climate and site Zones 4–8. Fertile, moist, neutral to slightly acid soil. Partial to deep shade.

Height and spread Height 8–10 inches (20–25 cm); spread unlimited.

Description Attractive, shiny, dark green, oval leaves, 1½–4 inches (3.7–10 cm) in diameter, grow at the top of upright stems. The leaves are toothed near the ends. In spring, clusters of fragrant, creamy white flowers bloom at the stem tips. On mature plants, the flowers are sometimes followed by white berries in the fall. Japanese pachysandra spreads rapidly by rhizomes (underground runners) but it can be controlled.

Growing guidelines Set plants 8–12 inches (20–30 cm) apart in spring. Top-dress plantings yearly with compost or organic fertilizer. Prune back or mow every few years in spring. Euonymus scale can be a problem; cut down and destroy infested plants that have pear-shaped, white-and-gray scales on the leaves. Propagate by division in spring or by cuttings in summer.

Landscape uses Plant under deciduous or evergreen trees or in any shady area. It forms a good covering for slopes or banks.

Phlox stolonifera
POLEMONIACEAE

CREEPING PHLOX

Creeping phlox is available in many colors, making it a versatile plant for mixing with small bulbs and perennials that bloom at the same time.

Best climate and site Zones 2–8. Moist, light, fertile, slightly acid soil. Prefers partial to full shade; will grow in sun.
Height and spread Height of foliage 3–5 inches (7.5–12.5 cm); spread to 18 inches (45 cm). Flower height 6–12 inches (15–30 cm).
Description Creeping phlox is grown for its masses of delicate lavender, pink, blue, or white, 1-inch (2.5-cm) wide flowers that bloom in late spring. Long, creeping, strawberry-like runners clad in small, oval, evergreen leaves root as they touch the earth to form solid mats. This shade-loving groundcover is native to eastern North America.
Growing guidelines Set plants 1–2 feet (30–60 cm) apart in spring. For more compact growth, trim back flowering shoots after blooming. Propagate by division after flowering or by cuttings in late spring to early summer.
Landscape uses Creeping phlox is an ideal groundcover for moist woodland plantings, beneath deciduous trees, in front of shady borders, or along the north and east sides of buildings. For a pretty colour combination, try purple cultivars with bright yellow primroses or pink fringed bleeding heart (*Dicentra eximia*).

Potentilla tridentata
ROSACEAE

THREE-TOOTHED CINQUEFOIL

Three-toothed cinquefoil is an evergreen, mat-forming groundcover with glossy green leaves. It prefers sunny, well-drained sites in cool climates.

Best climate and site Zones 3–7. Well-drained, sandy, slightly acid soil. Full sun.
Height and spread Height to 1 foot (30 cm); spread to 2 feet (60 cm).
Description Each leaf is divided into three leaflets that are three- to five-toothed at their tips. The leaves turn wine red in fall, giving the plant another common name: wine-leaved cinquefoil. Clusters of tiny, ¼-inch (6-mm) white flowers bloom in early summer and intermittently the rest of the season.
Growing guidelines Set plants 1–2 feet (30–60 cm) apart in early spring. Three-toothed cinquefoil spreads fairly rapidly and needs little care. Propagate by removing rooted suckers in early spring or by cuttings in early summer.
Landscape uses Three-toothed cinquefoil is a natural choice for covering dry, rocky slopes.
Cultivars 'Minima' is low-growing, reaching only to 3 inches (7.5 cm) tall.
Other species *P. tabernaemontani*, spring cinquefoil, has five-toothed, evergreen, green leaves and ½-inch (12-mm) bright yellow flowers in late spring. Height to 4 inches (10 cm); spread to 2 feet (60 cm). Zones 4–7.

Pulmonaria saccharata
BORAGINACEAE

BETHLEHEM SAGE

The early-spring flowers of Bethlehem sage combine nicely with daffodils and other bulbs. The foliage looks wonderful with hostas, which enjoy the same growing conditions.

Best climate and site Zones 3–8. Moist, well-drained, humus-rich soil. Partial to full shade; tolerates some sun if the soil is kept moist.
Height and spread Height 8–15 inches (20–37.5 cm); spread 18 inches (45 cm) or more.
Description These easy-to-grow plants form broad clumps of white-mottled, slightly fuzzy leaves. In early spring, cheery, small, tubular flowers bloom in profusion over mounds of foliage. The pink buds open to pink flowers that age to blue.
Growing guidelines Set plants 2 feet (60 cm) apart in spring or fall. Plants may wilt if the soil becomes dry, but they revive quickly when watered; mulch helps to keep the roots moist. Propagate by division after flowering or in fall.
Landscape uses The clumps of mottled foliage look nice all summer at the front of the border, under trees, or in a shady rock garden.
Cultivars 'Mrs. Moon' has silver-spotted leaves and pink flowers that mature to blue. 'Sissinghurst White' has pure white flowers and silvery mottled foliage.

Sagina subulata
CARYOPHYLLACEAE

PEARLWORT

Pearlwort, also known as Irish moss, is a dainty little evergreen for partial shade. It can withstand some foot traffic and looks great growing between stepping stones.

Best climate and site Zones 5–7. Prefers well-drained, moist, fertile soil; tolerates dry, sandy soil. Partial shade.

Height and spread Height of foliage 1–2 inches (2.5–5 cm); spread to 1 foot (30 cm). Flower height to 5 inches (12.5 cm).

Description This mosslike, perennial, evergreen groundcover forms dense mounds of tiny, ¼-inch (6-mm) leaves. Numerous small, translucent white flowers bloom in midsummer.

Growing guidelines Set plants 1 foot (30 cm) apart in spring. Slugs and snails can be problems; trap them under cabbage leaves (remove pests daily) or in shallow pans of beer set flush with the soil surface. Propagate by division in spring.

Landscape uses Grow pearlwort in lightly shaded rock gardens and between flagstones since it tolerates foot traffic.

Cultivars 'Aurea', commonly called Scotch moss, has yellow-green foliage.

Santolina chamaecyparissus
COMPOSITAE

LAVENDER COTTON

Lavender cotton is a shrubby, aromatic evergreen that's native to areas of the Mediterranean. The dried leaves and stems were once used indoors to repel moths.

Best climate and site Zones 5–9. Dry, poor, well-drained soil, including sand and gravel. Full sun.

Height and spread Height 18–24 inches (45–60 cm); spread to 3 feet (90 cm).

Description Lavender cotton forms bushy clumps of many branches with fine, needlelike, aromatic, silvery gray leaves. Bright gold, ¼-inch (18-mm) flowers bloom in profusion in midsummer. Lavender cotton can tolerate both heat and drought.

Growing guidelines Set plants 2–3 feet (60–90 cm) apart in spring. Cut stems back by half after blooming each year (or before blooming, if you don't like the flowers) to encourage compact growth. Propagate by cuttings in early summer or by division in early spring.

Landscape uses Lavender cotton is ideal for a low-growing hedge or edging and for shrub borders. The gray shade combines well with lavender and low-growing ornamental grasses.

Cultivars 'Nana' is a dwarf form. 'Plumosus' has lacy, silvery gray foliage.

Saponaria ocymoides
CARYOPHYLLACEAE

ROCK SOAPWORT

Rock soapwort produces many bright pink flowers in summer. Cut the stems back by half after flowering to keep plants compact and to promote possible rebloom.

Best climate and site Zones 4–10. Light-textured, average, well-drained soil. Full sun.

Height and spread Height 5–8 inches (12.5–20 cm); spread to 2 feet (60 cm).

Description Rock soapwort is a trailing, mat-forming plant with semi-evergreen leaves less than 1 inch (2.5 cm) long. Its star feature is the clusters of phlox-like, bright pink, five-petaled, ½-inch (12-mm) flowers in early- to mid-summer.

Growing guidelines Set plants about 20 inches (50 cm) apart in spring. Propagate by seed in spring, by division in spring or fall, or by cuttings at the beginning of summer.

Landscape uses Rock soapwort trails beautifully over walls, raised beds, and terraces. It also makes a good groundcover for sunny slopes.

Cultivars 'Alba' has white flowers that are somewhat smaller than the species. 'Rubra Compacta' forms compact mounds of deep pink to red flowers. 'Splendens' has rose-pink flowers.

Saxifraga stolonifera
SAXIFRAGACEAE

STRAWBERRY GERANIUM

Strawberry geranium is commonly sold as a houseplant, but its rounded, silver-marked, green leaves also make a handsome groundcover in Southern gardens.

Best climate and site Zones 6–9. Moist, well-drained, slightly acid soil. Partial shade; thrives in morning sun and afternoon shade.

Height and spread Height of foliage to 6 inches (15 cm); spread to 18 inches (45 cm). Flower stalks to 1 foot (30 cm).

Description Strawberry geranium is an excellent evergreen groundcover for the South. It is also called strawberry begonia and mother-of-thousands, as it spreads by runners (like strawberries). The hairy, rounded, dark green leaves are 4 inches (10 cm) wide, have scalloped edges, and are beautifully veined with silver. White flowers bloom on spikes in early summer. This species is also listed as S. *sarmentosa*.

Growing guidelines Plant 12–18 inches (30–45 cm) apart in early spring. To propagate, dig up the small plantlets that form on runners and transplant in spring.

Landscape uses Strawberry geranium is a handsome and unusual groundcover for shady rock gardens or borders. Grow it under trees and shrubs as well.

Sedum spurium
CRASSULACEAE

TWO-ROW STONECROP

Two-row stonecrop is a tough, durable spreader for dry soil. Its mats of fleshy green leaves are topped with clusters of pink flowers in midsummer.

Best climate and site Zones 3–8. Well-drained, sandy, average to poor soil. Light to partial shade.

Height and spread Height of foliage to 6 inches (15 cm); spread to 2 feet (60 cm). Flower height to 10 inches (25 cm).

Description This semi-evergreen, creeping succulent quickly forms a carpeting groundcover with dark green, 1-inch (2.5-cm) long leaves that turn reddish in late fall. Flat, 2-inch (5-cm) clusters of pink flowers appear in midsummer. Stems stay reddish throughout the winter.

Growing guidelines Set plants 10 inches (25 cm) apart in spring. After blooming, cut off the spent blooms with shears or a string trimmer. Although it spreads quickly, two-row stonecrop is easy to control because it has shallow roots. Propagate by seed or division in early spring or by cuttings in early summer.

Landscape uses Try two-row stonecrop as a groundcover on dry, lightly shaded, rocky slopes, alone or mixed with other *Sedum* species.

Stachys byzantina
LABIATAE

LAMB'S-EARS

Lamb's-ears has fuzzy leaves that may rot in humid conditions. Plants usually recover and produce new growth when cool weather returns; in the meantime, remove damaged leaves.

Best climate and site Zones 4–8; thrives in Zone 3 with snow cover. Average, well-drained soil; plants tolerate drought once established. Prefers full, hot sun; tolerates light shade.

Height and spread Height of foliage to 8 inches (20 cm); spread to 3 feet (90 cm). Flower stems to 18 inches (45 cm).

Description This charming groundcover is grown mostly for its woolly, soft, silvery white, 4-inch (10-cm) leaves. Fuzzy, square flowering stems bearing lavender flowers bloom in early- to mid-summer. This species is also listed as S. *lanata* or S. *olympica*.

Growing guidelines Set plants 12–16 inches (30–40 cm) apart in spring. Cut back any damaged leaves in spring. Remove flower stems before they bloom, if desired, to keep plantings tidy. Propagate by division any time during the growing season or by seed in spring.

Landscape uses The gray foliage of lamb's-ears is an excellent foil for brightly colored flowers in beds and borders. The leafy clumps form an attractive edging for garden paths.

Tellima grandiflora
SAXIFRAGACEAE

FRINGE CUPS

Fringe cups are ideal for lightly shaded gardens. Their clumps spread slowly but steadily, and they may self-sow in ideal growing conditions.

Best climate and site Zones 5–8. Fertile, well-drained, slightly acid, cool soil. Light shade.

Height and spread Height of foliage to 1 foot (30 cm); spread to 20 inches (50 cm). Flower stems grow to 2 feet (60 cm) tall.

Description Fringe cups form tidy clumps of heart-shaped, scalloped, hairy, cupped leaves that are 4 inches (10 cm) wide. The green leaves turn reddish in fall. Loose clusters of small, bell-shaped, nodding flowers with fringed petals are greenish white when they open in spring and turn reddish. Fringe cups are evergreen in warm climates and deciduous in cool zones.

Growing guidelines Set plants 18–24 inches (45–60 cm) apart in spring. Divide when plants become crowded. Propagate by division in spring.

Landscape uses This slow spreader makes an attractive, dense cover for the rock garden or woodland garden.

Cultivars 'Rubra' has maroon leaves.

Tiarella cordifolia
SAXIFRAGACEAE

ALLEGHENY FOAMFLOWER

Allegheny foamflower tolerates deep shade and dry conditions once established. It looks great as a groundcover beneath deciduous and evergreen trees and as an edging.

Best climate and site Zones 3–8. Well-drained, moist, fertile, slightly acid soil. Light shade.

Height and spread Height of foliage to 6 inches (15 cm); spread to 2 feet (60 cm). Flower stems 9–12 inches (22.5–30 cm) tall.

Description This evergreen native of eastern North American forests forms clumps of heart-shaped, lobed and toothed green leaves. The leaves are up to 4 inches (10 cm) wide and turn bronze to burgundy in fall; they are evergreen in the South. Feathery bottlebrush-like spikes of tiny white flowers bloom in midspring.

Growing guidelines Set plants 2 feet (60 cm) apart in spring. Removing spent flower spikes may extend the blooming season. Propagate by division in spring or fall or sow seed in spring.

Landscape uses Foamflowers are ideal for massed woodland plantings, shady rock gardens, borders, and edgings.

Cultivars 'George Shenk Pink' has foamy, pink flowers in spring. 'Oakleaf' has deeply lobed leaves and airy, deep pink blooms that last for several weeks.

Vancouveria hexandra
BERBERIDACEAE

AMERICAN BARRENWORT

American barrenwort may look delicate, but it's a tough, vigorous perennial that spreads by underground stems. It prefers moist soil but can adapt to dry conditions.

Best climate and site Zones 5–8. Moist, well-drained, fertile soil, rich in leaf mold. Prefers partial shade but will tolerate full shade.

Height and spread Height to 1 foot (30 cm); spread to 2 feet (60 cm) or more.

Description Spreading clumps of wiry stems are topped with thin, heart-shaped, three-lobed, deciduous, green leaves to 1½ inches (3.7 cm) wide. In late spring or early summer, tiny, ½-inch(12-mm) white flowers bloom in drooping clusters just above the leaves.

Growing guidelines Set plants 18–24 inches (45–60 cm) apart in spring. They may be slow getting started but will begin to spread by the second growing season. Mulch to keep plants moist and cool in summer. If the soil is sandy, feed plants once a year with compost or leaf mold. To propagate, divide in spring.

Landscape uses American barrenwort makes an attractive groundcover beneath trees, in shady rock gardens, and in wild gardens. It's also a nice edging for shady beds of hostas.

Veronica prostrata
SCROPHULARIACEAE

ROCK SPEEDWELL

The spreading foliage mats of rock speedwell are accented by spikes of blue flowers in late spring. This plant is a perfect choice for sunny slopes and rock gardens.

Best climate and site Zones 4–8. Well-drained, moist, average garden soil. Prefers full sun; tolerates partial shade.

Height and spread Height 8–10 inches (20–25 cm); spread to 18 inches (45 cm) or more.

Description Spikes of deep blue flowers bloom on upright stems in late spring above creeping mats of 1½-inch (3.7-cm) green leaves. Rock speedwell is also known as Hungarian speedwell or harebell speedwell.

Growing guidelines Set plants at least 2 feet (60 cm) apart in spring or fall. If needed, surround plantings with an edging strip to keep them in bounds. Propagate by division in spring or fall, by stem cuttings in summer, or by seed in spring.

Landscape uses Rock speedwell is a charming groundcover in rock gardens and on rocky slopes.

Cultivars 'Alba' has white flowers that bloom over a long season. 'Mrs. Holt' has rose-pink flowers.

Viola odorata
VIOLACEAE

SWEET VIOLET

Sweet violet, also called English violet, is the common violet used by florists. It spreads by runners that take root and produce new plants.

Best climate and site Zones 6–8. Well-drained, moist, fertile, cool soil. Full sun to partial shade; tolerates full shade in hot climates.

Height and spread Height 5–8 inches (12.5–20 cm); spread to 2 feet (60 cm).

Description Fragrant, five-petaled, deep violet blooms come up in early spring from clumps of heart-shaped leaves that are 3 inches (7.5 cm) long.

Growing guidelines Set plants 12 inches (30 cm) apart in spring. Start a new patch when older plants become overgrown and weak. Spider mites may be a problem, causing yellowed or browned leaves; spray cold water over the plants, or use a slurry made from buttermilk, wheat flour, and water.

Landscape uses Sweet violet makes a fragrant groundcover in wild gardens and rock gardens and under trees and shrubs.

Cultivars 'Royal Robe' has purple flowers with a white eye on long, 8-inch (20-cm) stems. 'White Czar' has white flowers veined with deep purple on 6-inch (15-cm) stems. Other cultivars come in shades of blue, pink, purple, and white.

Waldsteinia fragarioides
ROSACEAE

BARREN STRAWBERRY

Barren strawberry has shiny, evergreen leaves that take on a purplish color in cold weather. It grows well in partial shade but will take sun if the soil is kept moist.

Best climate and site Zones 5–8. Well-drained, fertile soil. Prefers partial shade, but will tolerate sunny spots if kept moist.

Height and spread Height to 6 inches (15 cm); spread unlimited.

Description This evergreen plant is native to eastern North America. It spreads by creeping roots to form a thick, flat carpet of shiny, strawberry-like foliage that turns purplish in fall. Clusters of five-petaled, ½-inch (12-mm) wide, yellow flowers appear on 6–8-inch (15–20-cm) stems in late spring, followed by inedible, dry, hairy fruits.

Growing guidelines Set plants about 2 feet (60 cm) apart in spring. Keep watered in dry periods and divide when overcrowded. Propagate by division in early spring or fall or by seed in spring.

Landscape uses Grow barren strawberry in rock gardens, on banks and rocky ledges, or cascading over walls.

Other species *W. ternata* grows 6–8 inches (15–20 cm) tall with glossy, green, evergreen leaves and clusters of yellow, strawberry-like flowers in spring. Zones 4–9.

Agrostis tenuis
GRAMINEAE

BENT GRASS, COLONIAL

Think carefully before sowing bent grass in a home lawn. Pure bent grass turf demands lots of maintenance to look respectable, and it's prone to drought and diseases.

Best climate and site Zones 3–8. Light-textured, well-drained soil that contains an average amount of humus and nutrients and has a pH of 6–7. Can tolerate acid soil. Full sun, but tolerates light shade.

Characteristics This creeping grass has fine leaves and a pale green color. Bent grass has good salt tolerance and withstands close mowing, but it can't stand heavy foot traffic. It needs regular watering and fertilizing, and it is prone to many pests and diseases. When mixed with other species, bent grass can crowd them out, leading to patchy turf. For this reason, bent grass is sometimes considered a weed in home lawns.

Getting started If you are willing to put the time and effort into putting green-quality turf, sow bent grass seed in the spring at the rate of 2 pounds per 1,000 square feet (900 g per 93 sq m). Seed germinates in 12–26 days.

Mowing height ½–1 inch (6–25 mm).

Special maintenance Needs close mowing as often as twice a week and preferably with a reel-type mower. Frequent watering and frequent light applications of fertilizer are necessary.

Festuca arundinacea
GRAMINEAE

FESCUE, TALL

Thanks to its deep roots, tall fescue is heat-tolerant and among the most drought-resistant of all cool-season grasses. It is also an excellent choice for erosion control.

Best climate and site Zones 2–7. Grows well in most soil types. Can take both full sun or light shade.

Characteristics Sometimes called meadow fescue, tall fescue is a wide-bladed, sharp-edged, clump-forming grass that takes a great deal of wear and tear. It grows so strong that it can crowd out weeds as well as less vigorous, fine-textured turf grasses. Tall fescue is a good choice for play areas, roadsides, and low-maintenance areas. The only place you'd probably want to avoid it is in a highly manicured lawn, where its broader blades and clumping habit would give the turf a coarse look.

Getting started Plant in either spring or fall, sowing 8 pounds per 1,000 square feet (3.2 kg per 93 sq m). Seed germinates in 12–22 days.

Mowing height 2–3 inches (5–7.5 cm).

Special maintenance Tall fescue doesn't need much special care. You may need to overseed bare spots in spring or fall. Mow fairly high so the grass stays vigorous and looks more even.

Festuca rubra var. rubra
GRAMINEAE

FESCUE, CREEPING RED

The soft, fine-textured blades of creeping red fescue are pleasant to walk on, but they can't take heavy wear. This grass isn't a good choice for play areas.

Best climate and site Zones 2–8. Adapts to most soil types, even dry soil. Full sun or light shade.

Characteristics Creeping red fescue spreads slowly by rhizomes, survives in difficult locations, and looks nice when cut high. Its thin, fine blades are deep green, but the base of the plant is red. Creeping red fescue is not rugged enough for heavy foot traffic, but it is one of the best grasses for shady spots in the North. It is often mixed with perennial rye grass to overseed warm-season grasses when they become dormant in fall.

Getting started For an all-fescue lawn, plant at the rate of 4 pounds per 1,000 square feet (1.8 kg per 93 sq m) in spring or early fall. You may also find creeping red fescue mixed with bluegrass or perennial ryegrass; apply according to the rate suggested on the label. Seed germinates in 12–22 days.

Mowing height 2 inches (5 cm).

Special maintenance Fertilize only when growth is poor; creeping red fescue is actually less competitive when it gets lots of fertilizer. It is quite drought-tolerant. Overwatering may encourage fungal diseases, which are also prevalent in hot, humid seasons.

Lolium multiflorum
GRAMINEAE

RYEGRASS, ANNUAL

Annual ryegrass is used mainly for quick cover while perennial grasses are getting established. It grows rapidly, so it needs frequent mowing.

Best climate and site Zones 3–7. Grows on a wide range of soil types. Full sun or light shade.

Characteristics Annual ryegrass is a rather coarse grass with light green leaves. It is rugged enough to stand moderate use, it holds its color well, and it is drought-resistant. It will set seed and die after one season, so it is not meant for permanent lawns. It is used primarily in mixes with perennial grasses as a quick cover to hold the soil until the higher-quality grasses sprout and take hold. However, beware of cheap lawn mixes that are more than 20 percent annual rye. Straight annual rye can be used to overseed warm-season lawns to provide green during winter.

Getting started Plant annual rye in the spring in the North at the rate of 2–3 pounds per 1,000 square feet (0.9–1.35 kg per 93 sq m) for an all-rye lawn. If sowing a mix, follow the rate suggested on the label. In the South, overseed existing warm-season lawns in fall at 3–5 pounds per 1,000 square feet (1.35–2.25 kg per 93 sq m). Seed germinates in 7–12 days.

Mowing height 2 inches (5 cm).

Special maintenance Annual rye is disease- and insect-resistant.

Lolium perenne
GRAMINEAE

RYEGRASS, PERENNIAL

Perennial ryegrass is one of the most popular cool-season lawn grasses. It looks great alone or mixed with bluegrass, and it's relatively pest- and disease-resistant.

Best climate and site Zones 3–7. Grows on a wide range of soil types. Full sun but tolerates light shade.

Characteristics Perennial ryegrass sprouts quickly for a fast lawn effect. It is tolerant of foot traffic and is more insect- and disease-resistant than other lawn grasses, especially when it's enhanced with endophytes (fungi that live within the grass plants and discourage insect pest feeding). Perennial ryegrass is one of the most popular choices for home lawns.

Getting started Plant either in spring or late summer in the North. For an all-perennial-ryegrass lawn, plant 2–3 pounds per 1,000 per square feet (0.9–1.35 kg per 93 sq m). For a finer-quality lawn, choose a perennial ryegrass/bluegrass mix; seed at the rate suggested on the package. If oversowing an existing warm-season lawn, sow in fall at 3–5 pounds per 1,000 square feet (1.35–2.25 kg per 93 sq m). Perennial ryegrass seed germinates in 7–12 days.

Mowing height Cut at 3 inches (7.5 cm) for the first three mowings of the season and 2 inches (5 cm) for later mowings.

Special maintenance Perennial ryegrass needs little fertilizer once it's established.

Poa pratensis
GRAMINEAE

BLUEGRASS

Fine-bladed bluegrass forms a beautiful smooth turf in full sun. To keep it in peak condition, you need to fertilize it every year and water it regularly in dry weather.

Best climate and site Zones 4–7. Light-textured, well-drained soil that contains an average amount of organic matter and nutrients and has a pH of 6.5–7. Full sun.

Characteristics Bluegrass is one of the highest-quality, fine-bladed grasses for Northern lawns that receive plenty of sunlight and moisture. Its narrow, upright-growing, blue-green blades have a smooth look when mown. Bluegrass can't tolerate a lot of traffic, so don't plant it alone for a heavily used lawn.

Getting started Plant blends of several compatible bluegrass cultivars at 1½–2 pounds per 1,000 square feet (675–900 g per 93 sq m). Seed germinates in 12–30 days. For a more rugged lawn, use a mix of bluegrass, perennial rye, and fescues, especially those that are endophyte-enhanced. Bluegrass is one of the most popular grasses grown on sod farms; bluegrass sod is often available in blends and mixtures.

Mowing height Mow species at 2–2½ inches (5–6 cm). Some cultivars tolerate lower mowing.

Special maintenance Frequent watering during dry periods and an annual light feeding in late summer or early fall.

Bouteloua gracilis
GRAMINEAE

GRAMMAGRASS, BLUE

Blue grammagrass is tough and usually trouble-free. It's a good choice for low-maintenance lawn and unmowed areas; the summer flowers and seed heads are quite attractive.

Best climate and site Zones 3–10. Good in dry soil. Full sun or light shade.
Characteristics Blue grammagrass grows in dense clusters, with narrow, blue-green leaves. Although it is a warm-season grass and is frequently included in mixes for lawns in the Southwest, blue grammagrass also has good cold tolerance. It can take foot traffic and is drought-resistant, although it will go dormant and turn brown during prolonged dry spells. Blue grammagrass is good for either low-maintenance lawn areas or for unmowed meadows, where it grows 10–24 inches (25–60 cm) high. It is even grown as an ornamental flowering grass throughout North America. It is often called mosquito grass because of the unique shape of the flowers, which resemble mosquito larvae.
Getting started Sow 1–1½ pounds of seed per 1,000 square feet (450–675 g per 93 sq m) in spring.
Mowing height 1½–2 inches (37–50 mm).
Special maintenance Blue grammagrass grows slowly, so it needs little care and infrequent mowing. Most insects and diseases don't bother it.

Buchloe dactyloides
GRAMINEAE

BUFFALO GRASS

If you live in a hot, dry climate and really want to have a lawn, consider growing buffalo grass. It seldom needs fertilizing or watering, and it resists pests and diseases.

Best climate and site Zones 3–9. Tolerates any soil, but prefers an alkaline pH. Full sun.
Characteristics This clump-forming, native prairie grass is one of the best choices for dry, hot climates because it tolerates drought. Its fine-textured, blue-green blades make a dense, gray-green lawn, and it can stand being mown at a low height. Its ultimate height is only 4–6 inches (10–15 cm) if unmowed, and it grows well and looks nice on roadsides, even when unmowed and neglected. It is often used for erosion control. Buffalo grass tolerates cold, heat, and foot traffic, and seldom needs fertilizer.
Getting started Plant 5 pounds per 1,000 square feet (2.25 kg per 93 sq m) in late summer or early fall. Seed can germinate in as little as 20–30 days, although it may take up to 2 years to fill in. For faster results, look for buffalo grass plugs (plant them 12 inches [30 cm] apart) or sod.
Mowing height 1½–2 inches (37–50 mm).
Special maintenance This slow-growing, grass may need mowing only once a month. It also needs very little water.

Cynodon dactylon
GRAMINEAE

BERMUDA GRASS

Bermuda grass is a vigorous, fast-spreading turf grass. It can also creep into flower beds and over paving, so contain it with barrier strips and trim the edges often.

Best climate and site Zones 7–9. Prefers light-textured, well-drained, fertile soil. Full sun.
Characteristics Bermuda grass is a vigorous, spreading Southern grass with a medium to fine texture. It spreads by both stolons (aboveground runners) and rhizomes (underground runners). Bermuda grass tolerates heat and drought well because of its deep roots. It is disease-resistant and tolerant of salt and foot traffic. Bermuda grass turns brown after the first frost and stays brown until spring. Scatter some cool-season grass seed, such as ryegrass or fescue, over the lawn in the fall if you want a green lawn all winter.
Getting started Plant seed in either spring or early fall at the rate of 1–2 pounds per 1,000 square feet (450–900 g per 93 sq m). Seed germinates in 7–25 days. Cultivars are usually available as plugs or sprigs; plant them 4–12 inches (10–30 cm) apart.
Mowing height Mow species at 1½–2 inches (37–50 mm). Mow cultivars at ¼–1 inch (6–25 mm).
Special maintenance Bermuda grass grows best when lightly fertilized twice a year with a complete lawn fertilizer.

Eremochloa ophiuroides
GRAMINEAE

CENTIPEDE GRASS

Although its pale green color and coarse texture keep it from being recommended for a first-class lawn, centipede grass does form a dense, vigorous, low-maintenance turf.

Best climate and site Zones 7–9. Grows well in a wide range of soil types, even those that are moderately acid. Full sun to light shade.

Characteristics Centipede grass is insect-resistant and needs only infrequent feeding, but it can stand only light use. It spreads by stolons (aboveground runners).

Getting started Plant seed at the rate of ½ pound per 1,000 square feet (225 g per 93 sq m) in late summer. Seed germinates in 15–20 days. Or plant sprigs or plugs 6–12 inches (15–30 cm) apart in well-prepared soil. Sod may also be available; plant it in late spring or early summer.

Mowing height 1½–2 inches (37–50 mm). Needs mowing only once every two to three weeks and usually grows to 4 inches (10 cm) if unmowed.

Special maintenance Although it requires little maintenance, centipede grass isn't extremely drought-tolerant, so you may need to water deeply once every few weeks during hot, dry spells. It can also turn yellow if iron is lacking in the soil. Prevent this by making sure the soil is adequately supplied with organic matter. Remember that the grass's normal color is yellow-green.

Stenotaphrum secundatum
GRAMINEAE

ST. AUGUSTINE GRASS

St. Augustine grass is one of the best turf grasses for shady Southern gardens. It doesn't tolerate heavy wear but usually recovers well from damage.

Best climate and site Zones 8–9. Prefers moist, sandy soil, but grows in a range of soil conditions as long as it has enough moisture. Full sun to light shade (takes full shade once established).

Characteristics The coarse, thick blades of St. Augustine grass grow quickly into a dense, attractive turf in spots where finer grasses grow poorly. It is remarkably resistant to salt spray and wind and is good along Southern coastal areas. However, St. Augustine grass needs frequent watering in hot areas, and it is susceptible to chinch bugs and diseases such as brown patch, dollar spot rust, and St. Augustine grass decline (SAD) virus.

Getting started Seed is not available. In spring or early summer, plant either plugs or sprigs 6–12 inches (15–30 cm) apart in prepared soil or lay sod.

Mowing height 2–3 inches (5–7.5 cm). Use a sharp mower blade to get a clean cut; otherwise, leaf tips may turn brown.

Special maintenance St. Augustine grass spreads by aboveground runners (stolons), which can lead to a buildup of thatch. Help control this problem by raking the lawn occasionally and by mowing the grass high. Fertilize lightly once or twice during the growing season.

Zoysia japonica
GRAMINEAE

ZOYSIA GRASS

Zoysia is tough and drought-resistant, making it a good choice for most Southern lawns. Yearly fertilization will help to keep its deep green color.

Best climate and site Zones 6–9. Light-textured, well-drained soil that contains an average amount of humus and nutrients and has a pH of 5.5–6.5. Full sun to light shade.

Characteristics Zoysia is among the best lawn grasses for most of the South. It is drought-resistant and, once established, produces a rich, thick turf that competes beautifully with weeds and other grasses. It spreads by both stolons (aboveground runners) and rhizomes (underground runners). A slow grower, it needs less frequent mowing than most other warm-season grasses. And because it is deep-rooted, it doesn't need frequent watering either. It is resistant to pests and tolerates foot traffic well.

Getting started Zoysia seed is sometimes available; sow 4–5 pounds per 1,000 square feet (1.8–2.5 kg per 93 sq m). Most zoysia cultivars are available only as sod, sprigs, or plugs. Lay sod or plant sprigs or plugs 6–12 inches (15–30 cm) apart in spring or early summer. It may take two years for sprigs or plugs to fill in completely.

Mowing height 1–2 inches (2.5–5 cm).

Special maintenance Feed lightly once a year, and remove thatch as needed.

Andropogon glomeratus
GRAMINEAE

BUSHY BLUESTEM

Grow bushy bluestem for its showy flower plumes and purplish fall color. Steady soil moisture is important for the best growth, especially in hot, sunny sites.

Type of plant Warm-season, clumping perennial grass.
Best climate and site Zones 5–10. Moist, fertile soil. Prefers full sun; tolerates light shade.
Height and spread Height 1–2 feet (30–60 cm); similar spread. Flowering stems grow 2–3 feet (60–90 cm) tall.
Description Bushy bluestem is grown for its dense clusters of fluffy, cotton-like flowers above clumps of attractive green foliage in late summer. In late fall the seed heads become orange, and the leaves turn purplish.
Growing guidelines Set plants 24–30 inches (60–75 cm) apart in spring. Cut them back to about 6 inches (15 cm) by late winter. Propagate by seed or division in spring.
Landscape uses Bushy bluestem grows best near streams and in wetlands. It will grow in containers if you keep the soil moist. It looks equally wonderful as a specimen plant or in masses. Use the flowers or seed heads in arrangements. Be aware that bushy bluestem reseeds readily in moist areas and can become invasive under those conditions.

Briza media
GRAMINEAE

QUAKING GRASS

The flowers of quaking grass tremble in the slightest breeze, adding movement to flower borders and rock gardens. Cut plants back in midsummer to promote new leaves.

Type of plant Cool-season, clumping perennial grass.
Best climate and site Zones 4–10. Grows well in a wide range of soil types, but prefers moist, humus-rich soil. Full sun; tolerates light shade.
Height and spread Height 1–2 feet (30–60 cm); clumps to about 1 foot (30 cm) wide. Flowers bloom on 2–3-foot (60–90-cm) tall stems.
Description Quaking grass is an easy-to-grow plant. The tiny, showy, heart-shaped, bright green florets shake in the breeze in late spring, giving the grass its name. They turn purple, then golden yellow in summer. The leaves are green in spring but turn straw-colored by summer.
Growing guidelines Set plants 1–2 feet (30–60 cm) apart in spring or fall. Don't fertilize. Cut back the old flower heads and unsightly old foliage to a few inches above the crown in midsummer to encourage fresh leaves to grow from the base. Cut back again in late fall. Propagate by division in spring or fall, or sow seed in spring.
Landscape uses Quaking grass is good for edgings, rock gardens, and flower borders, or as a groundcover.

Calamagrostis x acutiflora 'Stricta'
GRAMINEAE

FEATHER REED GRASS

One of the most spectacular grasses, feather reed grass has an upright habit and stiff, narrow leaves that are evergreen in warm climates and deciduous in cold regions.

Type of plant Cool-season, clumping perennial grass.
Best climate and site Zones 5–9. May not bloom well in hot climates. Tolerates most soil types, but prefers it moist and humus-rich. Full sun or light shade.
Height and spread Height 18–24 inches (45–60 cm); spread to about 2 feet (60 cm). Flowering stems may rise to 6 feet (1.8 m) tall.
Description Flowers appear in late spring or early summer on tall, erect spikes and consist of 1-foot (30-cm) long, pinkish green clusters that later become beige. Seed clusters form in July and last well into winter.
Growing guidelines Set plants 2–3 feet (60–90 cm) apart in spring or fall (spring is best in Northern areas). Cut back by late winter. Divide plants in spring in cool climates and in spring or fall in warmer ones.
Landscape uses Feather reed grass is an excellent tall accent plant. Its rich, golden, late-summer colors make spectacular screens or masses in backgrounds. Its flowering stems sway in the slightest breeze, adding movement to the garden.

Cortaderia selloana
GRAMINEAE

PAMPAS GRASS

Pampas grass is one of the showiest and most popular ornamental grasses where it is hardy. Wear long sleeves, long pants, and gloves when working around the sharp leaves.

Type of plant Warm-season, clumping perennial grass.
Best climate and site Zones 8–10. Fertile, well-drained soil. Prefers full sun; takes light shade.
Height and spread Height 5–12 feet (1.5–3.6 m); spread to 12 feet (3.6 m). Flowering stems may be 8–15 feet (2.4–4.5 m) tall.
Description Plants form neat clumps of sharp-edged leaves that are usually deciduous in fall. Spectacular, plume-like, 1–3-foot (30–90-cm) flower heads, either white or pink, rise on tall spikes in midsummer and last until late fall.
Growing guidelines Set plants 5–8 feet (1.5–2.4 m) apart in spring in a spot where each can reach its huge, full beauty without being crowded. They tolerate dry soil but do better with adequate moisture. Cut back the foliage every year or two in early spring. Propagate plants by division in spring. Look for cultivars of *C. selloana*, or buy the species from a reputable nursery to be sure you're getting the right plant.
Landscape uses Dramatic tall screens or backgrounds and elegant specimens. The plumes are wonderful as cut flowers.

Festuca cinerea
GRAMINEAE

BLUE FESCUE

The leaf color of blue fescue can range from dark green to bright blue, depending on the cultivar. Most plants will produce spiky clumps of blue-gray foliage.

Type of plant Cool-season, clumping perennial grass.
Best climate and site Zones 4–9. Moist, well-drained soil. Full sun; light shade in hot climates. Plants are drought-resistant but grow poorly in hot, humid conditions.
Height and spread Height 8–12 inches (20–30 cm); clumps spread to 2 feet (60 cm).
Description Blue fescue is noted for its rounded mounds of beautiful silver-blue, spiky, evergreen foliage. The gray-green flowers are not especially noteworthy. Blue fescue is also sold as *F. glauca*, *F. ovina*, and *F. ovina* 'Glauca'.
Growing guidelines Set plants 1–2 feet (30–60 cm) apart in spring or fall. Cut back in early spring or fall to promote tidy, new growth. Individual plants are short-lived; divide and replant every two to three years. Blue fescue may self-sow readily, and the seedlings may range in color from blue to green; clipping off the flower spikes can prevent reseeding. Start species plants from seed or division and cultivars by division in early spring.
Landscape uses Accent plants for borders and rock gardens. Also container plants, groundcovers, and seaside plants.

Hakonechloa macra 'Aureola'
GRAMINEAE

VARIEGATED HAKONE GRASS

Variegated hakone grass forms slow-spreading clumps of elegant, bamboo-like leaves. The yellow-striped foliage takes on pink or reddish tints in fall.

Type of plant Warm-season, slow-spreading perennial grass.
Best climate and site Zones 6–9. Moist, well-drained, fertile soil. Light shade.
Height and spread Height 18–24 inches (45–60 cm); spread to 2 feet (60 cm), sometimes more.
Description Variegated hakone grass is a well-behaved, low-growing, arching, deciduous grass. Its star feature is its soft, bright yellow, bamboo-like leaves that are striped with green in summer and reddish in fall. Clumps get larger with age but are not invasive. Inconspicuous flowers bloom in late summer.
Growing guidelines Set plants 2 feet (60 cm) or more apart in spring or early fall. Keep them out of full sun, and water during dry spells to keep the soil evenly moist at all times. Propagate by division in spring.
Landscape uses This handsome grass is lovely either as a single specimen plant or massed in a shady spot. It is good for edgings, in containers, and as groundcover under trees. It is a favorite for oriental gardens because of its bamboo-like appearance.

Imperata cylindrica 'Red Baron'
GRAMINEAE

'RED BARON' BLOOD GRASS

If possible, site 'Red Baron' blood grass where the morning or late afternoon sun can shine through it; backlighting can really make the red color glow.

Type of plant Warm-season, slow-spreading perennial grass.
Best climate and site Zones 6–9. Fertile, moist, well-drained soil. Full sun; partial shade in hot climates.
Height and spread Height 12–18 inches (30–45 cm); spread to 2 feet (60 cm).
Description This Japanese grass has spectacular foliage, especially in spring and fall. It starts green with red tips in spring but gradually becomes more red; by summer's end, it is deep blood red. The leaves turn copper in late fall, and the color endures throughout winter. Unlike the species, the cultivar 'Red Baron' does not flower, so it does not set seed and is not invasive.
Growing guidelines Set plants 1–2 feet (30–60 cm) apart in spring or early fall. Red color is best in full sun, except in hot climates, where plants need partial shade during the heat of the day. Blood grass tolerates drought, but watering during dry spells will prevent leaf tips from turning brown. Propagate in spring by division.
Landscape uses Blood grass is dramatic as a mass planting. It also adds a colorful touch to flower borders or containers. Blood grass makes a unique background for a low border.

Koeleria glauca
GRAMINEAE

LARGE BLUE HAIRGRASS

Large blue hairgrass is a short-lived perennial that tends to die out in the center as it ages. Divide and replant clumps every two or three years to keep them vigorous.

Type of plant Cool-season, clumping perennial grass.
Best climate and site Zones 6–9; can survive in colder areas with dependable winter snow cover. Well-drained, somewhat alkaline soil with average fertility. Full sun.
Height and spread Height 6–12 inches (15–30 cm) for leaves; similar spread. Flowering stems to 18 inches (45 cm) tall.
Description The narrow, flat, blue-green leaves grow upright in tight clumps. Striking blue-green flower clusters rise above the foliage in late spring; they later change to a buff color.
Growing guidelines Set plants 1 foot (30 cm) apart in spring or early fall. Cut back leaves and flower stems in midsummer to encourage new growth. Propagate by seed in spring or division in spring or fall.
Landscape uses Single specimens are good accent plants in the front of borders. In groups they make effective edgings and good companion plants for low-growing evergreens. Large blue hairgrass is also an interesting pot plant for a terrace or deck. The cut flowers look beautiful and dramatic in arrangements.

Miscanthus sinensis
GRAMINEAE

JAPANESE SILVER GRASS

Japanese silver grass, also commonly called eulalia grass, is one of the best large ornamental grasses. It is especially attractive near streams and ponds.

Type of plant Warm-season, clumping perennial grass.
Best climate and site Zones 5–9. Light, moist, humus-rich soil. Full sun.
Height and spread Height 3–5 feet (90–150 cm) for foliage; spread to 3 feet (90 cm) or more. Flowering stems can grow 6–10 feet (1.8–3 m) tall.
Description Large clumps of long, pointed, sharp-edged leaves show a silvery color in early summer; later they turn beautiful fall reds, yellows, rusts, and browns. Tall, decorative flower plumes in hues from silver to reddish purple bloom above the foliage from midsummer through early fall.
Growing guidelines Set plants 2–4 feet (60–120 cm) apart in spring. Provide light shade and extra water in hot climates. Stake the tall, floppy kinds if necessary, and divide in spring when the plant clumps begin to die in the center. Most cultivars are pest-resistant, but some are susceptible to mealybugs and rust. Propagate the species by seed or division, and cultivars by spring division only.
Landscape uses Large cultivars are excellent for screens, hedges, and background plantings; choose compact cultivars for flower beds and borders.

Pennisetum alopecuroides
GRAMINEAE

FOUNTAIN GRASS

Fountain grass is one of the most beautiful and adaptable of all ornamental grasses. The showy seed heads cascade, like a fountain, over mounds of glossy green leaves.

Type of plant Warm-season, clumping perennial grass.
Best climate and site Zones 5–9. Prefers fertile, moist, well-drained soil but adapts well to other soil types. Full sun; tolerates light shade.
Height and spread Height of foliage to 3 feet (90 cm); similar spread. Flowering stems grow to 4 feet (1.2 m) tall.
Description Fountain grass blooms in midsummer, with creamy white to pinkish flowers in 4–10-inch (10–25-cm) long clusters shaped like little foxtails. The seed heads later turn reddish brown and remain until fall.
Growing guidelines Set plants 2–3 feet (60–90 cm) apart in spring. Keep them watered in dry weather for best growth. Cut off seed heads in fall to keep them from spreading their seeds throughout the garden. Cut back dead leaves by early spring. Propagate the species by division or seed and propagate cultivars by spring division only.
Landscape uses Fountain grasses are excellent single accent plants in borders or grow them in drifts as a groundcover. They are a good choice for coastal plantings, too, since they tolerate wind.

Schizachyrium scoparium
GRAMINEAE

LITTLE BLUESTEM

Little bluestem is a good groundcover for large areas, for erosion control on dry slopes, and for naturalizing in meadows—wherever its reseeding habit isn't a problem.

Type of plant Warm-season, clumping perennial grass.
Best climate and site Zones 3–10. Any soil that is not soggy. Full sun.
Height and spread Height of foliage to about 1 foot (30 cm); spread to about 1 foot (30 cm). Flowering stems grow to 3 feet (90 cm) tall.
Description This common North American native has light green, somewhat hairy, deciduous leaves. The plant is not especially showy in summer, but the cool temperatures of fall transform its green leaves into shades of copper and bright orange. Spiky flowers in midsummer become attractive seed clusters in fall.
Growing guidelines Plant about 2 feet (60 cm) apart in spring. Cut back dead leaves and stems by early spring. Propagate by seed or divide the clumps in spring.
Landscape uses Little bluestem can make a fine accent plant in the border if you remove the seed heads by late summer to prevent reseeding. The cut flowers and foliage are handsome and dramatic in arrangements.

Stipa gigantea
GRAMINEAE

GIANT FEATHER GRASS

Giant feather grass is especially stunning where its handsome flower plumes are backlit by the morning or late afternoon sun. The seed heads remain showy until fall.

Type of plant Cool-season, clumping perennial grass.
Best climate and site Zones 7–9. Well-drained, fertile soil. Established plants are somewhat drought-tolerant; must have excellent drainage wherever rainfall is heavy. Full sun.
Height and spread Height of foliage to 2 feet (60 cm); clumps spread to 2 feet (60 cm) or more. Flowering stems grow to 5 feet (1.5 m).
Description Giant feather grass forms dramatic clumps of arching, rolled, evergreen leaves. Golden flowers hang from tall stems that rise 2–3 feet (60–90 cm) above the gray-green foliage in late spring.
Growing guidelines Set out plants 2–3 feet (60–90 cm) apart in spring or fall. If needed, cut back the foliage to about 6 inches (15 cm) by early spring. Propagate by early-spring or fall division, which can be difficult with the tight-growing clumps, or by seed, which may take three months or more to germinate.
Landscape uses Looks great in masses as a screen or singly as a dramatic, tall specimen. The cut flowers are captivating in fresh or dried arrangements.

Allium sativum
LILIACEAE

GARLIC

Garlic is one of the most familiar herbs, used to flavor dishes from almost every ethnic group. It is easy to grow from store-bought bulbs.

Best climate and site Zones 5–10. Full sun to partial shade.
Ideal soil conditions Humus-rich, deep, well-drained soil.
Growing guidelines Separate individual cloves from the bulb immediately before planting, then plant in October for harvesting the following summer; space 6 inches (15 cm) apart and 2 inches (5 cm) deep. For largest bulbs, prune away flowering stems that shoot up in early summer; side-dress with compost in early spring; avoid planting after heavy applications of fresh manure.
Growing habit Biennial or perennial; height to 2 feet (60 cm); foliage narrowly strap-shaped.
Flowering time Early summer; small, white to pinkish blooms atop a tall, central stalk.
Pest and disease prevention Avoid wet soil to prevent bulb diseases.
Harvesting and storing Dig bulbs after tops have died down, and before bulb skins begin to decay underground; place in a single layer in a shaded spot to dry, then cut away tops leaving a 2-inch (5-cm) stem; or plait together the tops of freshly dug plants. Hang plaits from the ceiling in a cool, humid, dark place.

Allium schoenoprasum
LILIACEAE

CHIVES

The graceful leaves and blossoms have a mild onion flavor, especially when used fresh. Use the leaves in cooking and toss the flowers in salads.

Best climate and site Zones 3–9. Full sun.
Ideal soil conditions Well-drained soil high in organic matter.
Growing guidelines Sow seed indoors in late winter, covering seed lightly and keeping the soil moist; transplant in clumps in early spring; space 5–8 inches (12–20 cm) apart. Sow outside in spring. Divide older clumps in early spring every three years, and freshen with compost or rotted manure.
Growing habit Height 6–12 inches (15–30 cm); perennial bulb with green, tubular leaves.
Flowering time June; pink or lavender to purple globular flower heads.
Pest and disease prevention Avoid wet, boggy areas that encourage stem and bulb diseases.
Harvesting and storing Use fresh leaf tips all summer once plants are 6 inches (15 cm) tall; leave at least 2 inches (5 cm) remaining. Best used fresh; or chop and dry. Freezes poorly.
Special tips Chives are recommended companion plants for carrots, grapes, roses, and tomatoes.

Aloe barbadensis [A. vera]
LILIACEAE

ALOE

For color and textural contrast, grow several of the more than 300 perennial species of succulent aloe. The y contain a medicinal as well as cosmetic gel.

Best climate and site Zones 9–10. Prefers full sun but tolerates light shade.
Ideal soil conditions Well-drained soil low in organic matter.
Growing guidelines Separate new shoots from established plants. In cool climates, plant in pots and move them indoors in winter. Aloes thrive with little attention. Indoors, avoid overwatering and mix coarse sand with potting soil to facilitate good drainage.
Growing habit Variable height; stemless rosette of spiny, tapered leaves.
Flowering time Rarely flowers in cool climates; drooping, tubular, yellow flowers atop a stalk up to 3 feet (90 cm) tall.
Pest and disease prevention Spray with insecticidal soap to control mealybugs, or purchase biological controls. Control insect pests before bringing indoors.
Harvesting and storing Cut leaves for gel as needed; remove outer leaves first.
Special tips Grow on sunny windowsills in the kitchen and bathroom.
Precautions Unsafe to use internally.
Other common names First-aid herb, healing herb, medicine plant.

Anethum graveolens
UMBELLIFERAE

DILL

Select dill varieties for either seed or foliage (called "dill weed") production. Dill's tall, graceful habit makes it an attractive background in flower beds.

Best climate and site Zones 2–9. Full sun.

Ideal soil conditions Well-drained soil rich in organic matter.

Growing guidelines Sow seed shallowly in rows or in 5-inch (12-cm) bands outdoors in early spring after danger of frost; thin to 8–10 inches (20–25 cm); transplants poorly. Keep seedlings moist; weed diligently until plants shade the soil.

Growing habit Height 2–3 feet (60–90 cm); dill is a hardy annual, resembling fennel.

Flowering time Summer to fall; yellowish flowers in umbels.

Pest and disease prevention Usually free from pests and diseases.

Harvesting and storing Clip fresh leaves at the stem as needed. Freeze whole leaves, or chop first; or dry foliage on nonmetallic screens. Collect flower heads before the seeds mature and fall; hang in paper bags or dry on paper. Store dried foliage and seeds in an airtight container. Fresh leaves can be refrigerated for up to one week.

Special tips Sow seeds at two- or three-week intervals for a continuous leaf harvest through fall.

Anthriscus cerefolium
UMBELLIFERAE

CHERVIL

Chervil grows best when temperatures are cool in spring and autumn. Grow this lacy, delicate-looking plant for medicinal, culinary, and craft uses.

Best climate and site Zones 3–7. Partial shade.

Ideal soil conditions Moist, but well-drained humus-rich garden soil.

Growing guidelines Sow fresh seed shallowly outdoors in early spring or fall; thin to 9–12 inches (23–30 cm); keep seedlings moist. Sow again at two-week intervals until mid-July for continuous harvest. Transplants poorly. Mulch to protect fall-sown seeds. Chervil can seed itself each year if flowers are left to mature in the garden.

Growing habit Annual; height 1–2 feet (30–60 cm); fernlike leaves.

Flowering time Summer; small, white umbrella-like clusters.

Pest and disease prevention Usually free from pests and diseases.

Harvesting and storing Snip leaves continuously after six to eight weeks; best used fresh.

Special tips Loses flavor quickly when heated, so add to recipes at the end.

Other common names Garden chervil.

Armoracia rusticana
CRUCIFERAE

HORSERADISH

Horseradish is the white perennial root of a weedy herb. Folklore claims that horseradish should be planted near potatoes to protect them from disease.

Best climate and site Zones 5–8. Full sun.

Ideal soil conditions Fertile, moist but well-drained soil.

Growing guidelines Plant straight, young roots 8–9 inches (20–22.5 cm) long and ½ inch (1 cm) wide so that crown or growing point is 3–5 inches (7.5–12.5 cm) below the soil surface, and plants are 12–18 inches (30–45 cm) apart. Plant at an angle to the horizontal.

Growing habit Second-year plants grow 2–3 feet (60–90 cm) tall; leaves are stalked and oblong.

Flowering time Midsummer; small, white blossoms do not produce viable seed.

Pest and disease prevention Usually free from pests and diseases.

Harvesting and storing Harvest roots in late October or November, and scrub them before storing in the refrigerator, or pack in dry sand in the cellar for spring planting. Or leave roots in the soil and harvest as required.

Special tips Harvest early for the most tender roots.

Artemisia dracunculus var. *sativa*
COMPOSITAE

TARRAGON, FRENCH

Tarragon's heavy licorice flavor holds well in cooking, making it an extremely useful herb in the kitchen. It's traditionally served with chicken dishes.

Best climate and site Zones 4–8. Full sun to partial shade.
Ideal soil conditions Well-drained garden soil.
Growing guidelines Cannot be grown from seed. Take cuttings from new growth in fall, overwintering the young plants indoors until the following spring. Or divide older plants in spring every three years; space 12–24 inches (30–60 cm) apart. Prune away flower stems each year for most vigorous growth and best flavor. To grow indoors in winter, pot young plants in summer, cutting foliage to just above the soil. Seal pot in a plastic bag and refrigerate to mimic winter. In fall, unwrap and place in a sunny window for winter harvests.
Growing habit Height 2–4 feet (60–120 cm); hardy perennial with long, branched green stems.
Flowering time Remove inconspicuous yellow-green blossoms to encourage growth of foliage.
Pest and disease prevention Generally free from pests and diseases.
Harvesting and storing Clip foliage as needed all summer. Fresh foliage lasts several weeks in the refrigerator wrapped in paper toweling inside a plastic bag.

Borago officinalis
BORAGINACEAE

BORAGE

This green, robust and bristly plant contrasts nicely with dark greens in the garden. The drooping clusters of blossoms attract honeybees.

Best climate and site Zones 3–9. Prefers full sun but tolerates partial shade.
Ideal soil conditions Fairly rich, moist soil with good drainage.
Growing guidelines Sow seed ½ inch (1 cm) deep outdoors after danger of hard frost. Indoors, plant in pots to avoid disturbing the sensitive taproot when transplanting. Control weeds to reduce competition for moisture. To promote blooming, go easy on the nitrogen. Self-sows well. Tall plants may need support.
Growing habit Annual; height 1½–2 feet (45–60 cm), width up to 18 inches (45 cm)with broad, hairy leaves arising from a central stalk.
Flowering time Continuously from midsummer until first frost; star-shaped circles of pink, purple, lavender, or blue, with black centers.
Pest and disease prevention Mulch with light materials like straw to keep foliage off soil and prevent rotting.
Harvesting and storing Harvest foliage anytime and use raw or cooked. Snip blossoms just after they open and candy or toss fresh in a salad.
Precautions Borage may be toxic if eaten in large quantities over a long period of time.

Carum carvi
UMBELLIFERAE

CARAWAY

The seeds of this annual or biennial have been used for 5,000 years for flavoring and for their carminative effect.

Best climate and site Zones 3–7. Full sun to light shade.
Ideal soil conditions Prefers fertile, light garden soil.
Growing guidelines Sow seed shallowly outdoors as early as the soil can be worked, or indoors in pots; thin to 6–12 inches (15–30 cm). Sow seed outdoors for early spring plants. Don't allow seedlings to dry out. A long taproot makes transplanting difficult.
Growing habit Height 1–2 feet (30–60 cm); glossy, fine dissected foliage resembling the carrot plant.
Flowering time Spring and early summer of the second year; white or pink flowers in umbels on stalks.
Pest and disease prevention Watch for pests in dried, stored seeds.
Harvesting and storing Snip tender leaves in spring and use fresh in salads, soups, and stews. After blooming, cut plants when seeds are brown and almost loose, then hang them upside down in paper bags to dry. Collect seeds and dry a few more days in the sun; store in a tightly sealed container.
Special tips Excessive pruning during the first year weakens the plant.

Chamaemelum nobile
COMPOSITAE

CHAMOMILE, ROMAN

Herb gardens of yesterday often included a lush lawn of chamomile that released a sweet, apple-like scent when walked upon. The tea is relaxing after a stressful day.

Best climate and site Zones 3–8. Full sun to partial shade.
Ideal soil conditions Light, moist but well-drained garden soil.
Growing guidelines Sow seed indoors or outdoors; thin to 6 inches (15 cm). Once established, it can self-sow. Divide older plants in early spring. In the first year, clip to prevent flowering and encourage vegetative growth while it becomes established. Chamomile is a poor competitor, so weed often. Established lawns can be mowed like grass.
Growing habit Height 6–9 inches (15–23 cm); low-growing perennial with aromatic lacy foliage.
Flowering time Summer; white daisy-like flowers with yellow centers.
Pest and disease prevention Usually free from pests and diseases.
Harvesting and storing Collect flowers at full bloom and dry on screens or paper. Store in tightly sealed containers.
Other common names Garden chamomile, ground apple, Russian chamomile.

Coriandum sativum
UMBELLIFERAE

CORIANDER

In seed catalogs, select types grown for either seed or foliage production. The seeds become more fragrant with age, and are popular ingredients in the kitchen and in potpourri.

Best climate and site Zones 2–9. Full sun to partial shade.
Ideal soil conditions Moderately rich, well-drained soil.
Growing guidelines Sow seed ½ inch (1 cm) deep outdoors after danger of frost, or in fall; thin to 4 inches (10 cm). Can self-sow. Weed diligently to prevent delicate seedlings from being overcome by more vigorous weeds. To prevent sprawling, avoid feeding with heavy applications of nitrogen.
Growing habit Annual; height 1–3 feet (30–90 cm); graceful, glossy, finely dissected foliage which resembles Queen Anne's lace.
Flowering time Early to late summer, depending on when sown; tiny white flowers in umbels.
Pest and disease prevention Usually free from pests and diseases.
Harvesting and storing Harvest foliage before seeds form and use fresh. Harvest ripe seeds before they shatter, dry them, and store them in airtight containers in the refrigerator.
Other common names Chinese parsley, cilantro.

Cymbopogon citratus
ANNONACEAE

LEMONGRASS

Grassy foliage provides contrast with broad-leaved garden herbs. Use the dried foliage for teas, or add it to potpourri. Only the lower part of the stem is used in cooking.

Best climate and site Zones 9–10. Full sun to partial shade.
Ideal soil conditions Well-drained garden soil enriched with organic matter.
Growing guidelines Propagate by division of older plants. Trim the leaves to several inches before dividing.
Growing habit Tender perennial; height to 6 feet (1.8 m); forms dense clumps of typical grass leaves.
Flowering time Seldom flowers.
Pest and disease prevention Usually free from pests and diseases.
Harvesting and storing Snip fresh foliage as needed. Harvest foliage anytime in summer; dry quickly for best flavor. Use the base of fresh stems, crushed or sliced, in stir-fries and other Asian dishes.
Other common names Fevergrass, West Indian lemon.

Foeniculum vulgare
UMBELLIFERAE

FENNEL

Grow licorice-scented fennel as a tall ornamental in the flower garden, and for its culinary properties in the kitchen. Both leaves and seeds are used.

Best climate and site Zones 6–9. Full sun.

Ideal soil conditions Humus-rich, well-drained soil.

Growing guidelines Sow seed shallowly outdoors in spring or fall and keep moist; thin to 6 inches (15 cm); fennel transplants poorly.

Growing habit Semi-hardy perennial usually grown as an annual; height to 4 feet (1.2 m); leaves are feathery, and a blue-green color.

Flowering time July to October; small yellow flowers in umbels.

Pest and disease prevention Usually free from pests and diseases.

Harvesting and storing Snip leaves before flowers bloom for fresh use; leaves can also be frozen. Collect seeds when dry but before they shatter, and dry them on paper.

Special tips Fennel's delicate flavor is destroyed by heat, so add at the end of the recipe. Try the bronze-colored variety for foliage contrast outdoors, and on the dinner plate as a garnish.

Laurus nobilis
LAURACEAE

BAY, SWEET

Bay leaf garlands represent victory and accomplishment. Use leaves for flavor in stews and soups, and as an aromatic addition to potpourri.

Best climate and site Zones 8–9, but needs a sheltered site in colder areas. Full sun to partial shade.

Ideal soil conditions Well-drained soil, rich in organic matter.

Growing guidelines Take cuttings from fresh green shoots in fall and keep the soil in which you plant them moist, since rooting may take three to nine months. In warm climates, sow seed outdoors; germination may require 6–12 months. Survives light frost in the garden. Grows well in the North in pots if moved indoors for the winter; trim away roots from large, pot-bound plants and add fresh compost to stimulate new growth.

Growing habit Evergreen tree; height up to 60 feet (18 m) but easily kept to any desired size with pruning.

Flowering time Spring; but not very conspicuous, yellowish flowers; rarely flowers in pots.

Pest and disease prevention Watch for signs of scale and wipe them away with alcohol swabs. Dried leaves sprinkled throughout kitchen cupboards are said to repel storage pests.

Harvesting and storing Collect and dry the leaves as needed; store in jars.

Levisticum officinale
UMBELLIFERAE

LOVAGE

If you are unsuccessful growing celery, try this easy and flavorful substitute. The leaves, stems, and seeds are all edible.

Best climate and site Zones 5–8. Prefers full sun but tolerates partial shade.

Ideal soil conditions Fertile, moist, but well-drained soil.

Growing guidelines Sow ripe seed shallowly in late summer or early fall; thin to 2–3 feet (60–90 cm) apart. Prune flowers to encourage vegetative growth. Each spring, mulch with compost or well-rotted manure. Replace plants every four to five years.

Growing habit Perennial; height to 6 feet (1.8 m) or more; hollow, ribbed stems; glossy, dark green leaves.

Flowering time June to July; tiny greenish yellow flowers in umbels.

Pest and disease prevention Mainly trouble-free.

Harvesting and storing Once established, harvest leaves as needed for fresh use. In fall, bunch foliage and stems and hang to dry. Or blanch small bunches before freezing for winter use. Seeds are ripe and ready to harvest when the fruits begin to split open. Dig roots in late fall, wash and slice into ½-inch (1-cm) pieces, and dry before storing.

Melissa officinalis
LABIATAE

LEMON BALM

Lemon balm has a fragrance much like lemon-flavored candy. Both foliage and flowers are attractive in flower beds.

Best climate and site Zones 4–9. Full sun to partial shade.
Ideal soil conditions Any sandy, well-drained soil.
Growing guidelines Sow shallowly in spring, thinning to 18–24 inches (45–60 cm); readily self-sows. Take cuttings or divide older plants in spring or fall. Each fall, cut away old stalks.
Growing habit Perennial; height 1–2 feet (30–60 cm); stems square, branching, with oval, fragrant leaves.
Flowering time June to October; small white tubular blossoms in bunches in the upper leaf axils.
Pest and disease prevention Thin dense plantings for best air circulation to prevent powdery mildew. Rarely bothered by insects.
Harvesting and storing Collect leaves in late summer and dry quickly to prevent them from turning black. Cut the entire plant, leaving about 2 inches (5 cm) of stem. Use leaves fresh in salads and for cooking, or dry them for making tea.
Other common names Sweet balm, bee balm.

Mentha spp.
LABIATAE

MINT

The mints are herbaceous perennials that thrive in moist locations. Fresh and dried foliage provide flavoring for both sweet and savory dishes.

Best climate and site Zones 5–9. Full sun or partial shade.
Ideal soil conditions Prefers moist, well-drained soil.
Growing guidelines Propagate from new plants that spring up along roots, or by cuttings in spring or fall. Allow 12–18 inches (30–45 cm) between plants. Mint is a rampant spreader. To control, plant in bottomless cans 10 inches (25 cm) deep, or in large pots. Top-dress with compost or manure in fall.
Growing habit Height up to 30 inches (75 cm) or more; square stems with smooth lance-like leaves.
Flowering time July to August; tiny purple or pink blossoms in whorled spikes.
Pest and disease prevention Thin crowded clumps for good air circulation to prevent root and foliage diseases. Watch for aphids, which stipple leaves; control them with a strong spray of water.
Harvesting and storing Harvest fresh leaves as needed. Just before blooming, cut the stalks and hang in bunches to dry; store in airtight containers.
Special tips Mints do well when planted where water drips, such as near outdoor taps that are used often in summer.

Ocimum basilicum
LABIATAE

BASIL, SWEET

Sweet basil is one of the most popular herbs in home gardens, mainly due to its strong flavor (with hints of licorice and pepper).

Best climate and site Zones 4–10. Thrives on heat and full sun.
Ideal soil conditions Accepts a wide range of soil textures; likes rich, moist, well-drained soil.
Growing guidelines Sow seed outdoors, after all danger of frost, to a depth of ⅛ inch (3 mm), then thin to 6 inches (15 cm). Or sow indoors in seed trays in warmth, six weeks before last frost, then transplant to small pots before setting outdoors. Mulch with compost to retain soil moisture. Side-dress with compost in midseason to enhance production. Basil is easily damaged by cold temperatures. In fall, cover with plastic to prolong the season and protect from the earliest frosts.
Growing habit Annual; height 1–2 feet (30–60 cm), width 18 inches (45 cm).
Flowering time Continuous, beginning in midsummer; white blooms, carried in leafy terminal spikes.
Pest and disease prevention Plant away from mint to prevent damage from plant bugs.
Harvesting and storing Harvest leaves every week, pinching terminal buds first to encourage branching. Leaves can be used fresh or dried.

Origanum majorana
LABIATAE

MARJORAM, SWEET

Some herb growers find this bushy aromatic plant with lush foliage an easy-to-grow substitute for oregano.

Best climate and site Zones 9–10. Full sun.

Ideal soil conditions Prefers light, well-drained soil.

Growing guidelines Sow seed shallowly indoors in spring; germinates slowly. Set plants out after danger of frost, spacing clumps of several plants 6–12 inches (15–30 cm) apart. Cut back by half just before blooming to maintain vegetative growth. In fall, divide roots and bring indoors in pots to a cool location, replanting outdoors in early spring.

Growing habit Height to 2 feet (60 cm); bushy, tender perennial.

Flowering time August to September; white or pink blossoms.

Pest and disease prevention Usually free from pests and diseases.

Harvesting and storing Cut fresh leaves as needed for cooking; hang small bunches in an airy location to dry, then store in airtight containers.

Other common names Annual marjoram, knotted marjoram.

Origanum vulgare
LABIATAE

OREGANO

Experiment with several types to find the flavor you like most. Sprigs with small, rounded leaves and miniature blossoms make an attractive garnish.

Best climate and site Zones 6–9. Full sun.

Ideal soil conditions Well-drained, average garden soil.

Growing guidelines Sow seed shallowly indoors in winter for best germination; sow outdoors if soil temperature is above 45°F (7°C). Plant in clumps 1 foot (30 cm) apart. Prune regularly for best shape. Since seedlings will not always produce the same flavor as the original plants, take cuttings or divide roots in spring or early fall for best results. Lightly mulch each spring with compost or well-rotted manure.

Growing habit Perennial; height 12–30 inches (30–75 cm); herbaceous and shrubby.

Flowering time July to September; tubular, rose to white blossoms in broad terminal clusters.

Pest and disease prevention Provide good drainage to prevent root diseases. Wash away mites and aphids with water.

Harvesting and storing Snip fresh sprigs as needed all summer; cut whole plant in June and again in late August; hang foliage in bunches to dry.

Other common names Wild marjoram, pot marjoram.

Pelargonium spp.
GERANIACEAE

GERANIUM, SCENTED

Apple-scented geranium has an intense scent and, like the rose-scented geranium, is a source of geranium oil.

Best climate and site Perennial in Zone 10, annual in cooler zones. Full sun.

Ideal soil conditions Rich, loamy, well-drained soil.

Growing guidelines Cuttings root quickly and easily from new growth in spring or late summer. Grows well in pots near a sunny window. Apply a liquid plant food, like fish emulsion or compost tea, but hold back on the nitrogen for the best fragrance. Plants more than one year old tend to get over-large; take new cuttings and discard the old plants. Remove dead foliage regularly.

Growing habit Height up to 3 feet (90 cm), foliage and growth habit vary with species or cultivar; leaves frilly, variegated, ruffled, velvety, or smooth.

Flowering time Three to six months from rooting; sometimes inconspicuous.

Pest and disease prevention Vacuum whiteflies from foliage, or control with weekly sprays of insecticidal soap or a botanical insecticide. Avoid overwatering.

Harvesting and storing Pick leaves throughout the summer and dry them, storing in an airtight container, to use in winter potpourris. Use fresh leaves in jellies and tea, or as an aromatic garnish.

Petroselinum crispum var. *crispum*
UMBELLIFERAE

PARSLEY, CURLED

Kitchen gardens always include parsley, since it is required in so many recipes. The delicate, dark green foliage makes it an excellent plant for borders or growing on windowsills.

Best climate and site Zones 5–9. Full sun to partial shade.

Ideal soil conditions Moderately rich, well-drained soil.

Growing guidelines Sow seed shallowly outdoors in early spring when soil reaches 50°F (10°C), thinning to 8 inches (20 cm) apart; germinates slowly. Or soak seeds overnight in warm water before sowing in peat pots indoors in early spring. Remove all flower stalks that form, and prune away dead leaves. For productive plants, side-dress with compost in midseason. Usually survives the winter, but quickly goes to flower in spring. Plants may be grown in pots to bring indoors for winter harvests.

Growing habit Biennial grown as an annual; height 8–12 inches (20–30 cm); leaves are finely divided, on a long stalk.

Flowering time Early spring of second year; tiny, greenish yellow umbels.

Pest and disease prevention Usually free from pests and diseases.

Harvesting and storing Cut leaf stalks at the base for fresh foliage all summer. Hang in bunches to dry in shade, or freeze whole or chopped.

Pimpinella anisum
UMBELLIFERAE

ANISE

Use these licorice-scented leaves and seeds in salads, especially when combined with apples. The crushed, aromatic seeds enhance the fragrance of homemade potpourris.

Best climate and site Zones 4–9. Full sun.

Ideal soil conditions Poor, light, well-drained soil.

Growing guidelines Sow seed outdoors in spring where plants will stand, then thin to 1 foot (30 cm) apart. Or sow several seeds in pots several months before the last frost in a warm (70°F [21°C]) room. Transplants poorly. Stake or grow in clumps to prevent plants from sprawling.

Growing habit Annual; height up to 2 feet (60 cm); lacy foliage.

Flowering time Summer; dainty white blossoms in umbels.

Pest and disease prevention Anise oil is said to have insect-repellent properties; few pests bother this plant.

Harvesting and storing Seeds are ready to harvest when they fall easily from the head. Dry seeds on paper for several sunny days outdoors, then pasteurize in oven at 100°F (38°C) for 15 minutes and store in airtight containers. Snip foliage as needed.

Special tips Enhances the growth of coriander. Anise was once used as a bait in mousetraps.

Rosmarinus officinalis
LABIATAE

ROSEMARY

Rosemary is a highly scented herb used to season meat, poultry, and fish (particularly when roasted), bread, and desserts. Use both the flowers and leaves for cooking and garnishing.

Best climate and site Zones 7–9. Grown outdoors where temperatures remain above 10°F (-12°C). Full sun to partial shade.

Ideal soil conditions Prefers light, well-drained soil.

Growing guidelines Sow seed shallowly indoors in early spring, then transplant to pots outdoors; plant out in garden for second season, spacing 3 feet (90 cm) apart. Or take cuttings from new growth in fall, or layer the stems in spring. Larger plants may overwinter better outdoors than smaller ones. Potted plants may be brought into a sunny greenhouse for the winter; or keep them at 45°F (7°C) in a sunny garage or enclosed porch, watering infrequently.

Growing habit Height 2–6 feet (60–180 cm); tender perennial with scaly bark and aromatic, needlelike leaves.

Flowering time Spring and summer. Small pale blue to pink tubular flowers in axillary clusters.

Pest and disease prevention Indoors, wipe scale pests from foliage with cotton soaked with rubbing alcohol.

Harvesting and storing Snip fresh foliage as needed all year.

Rumex spp.
POLYGONACEAE

SORREL

In the spring, use sorrel's tender new leaves to make a delicate soup or add them to salads. The older the leaves, the more bitter the taste.

Best climate and site Zones 5–9. Full sun.
Ideal soil conditions Moderately fertile, moist garden soil.
Growing guidelines Sow seed shallowly outdoors in late spring, thinning to 18 inches (45 cm). Or divide older plants in early spring or fall.
Growing habit Hardy perennial; height 30–36 inches (75–90 cm); wavy, green leaves.
Flowering time Midsummer; greenish yellow to red flowers.
Pest and disease prevention Handpick snails from new spring leaves.
Harvesting and storing Harvest the outside leaves regularly to promote new growth. Sorrel leaves are best eaten fresh, but may also be blanched and frozen.
Species French sorrel (*R. scutatus*): Lower-growing perennial; best-tasting flavor. Garden sorrel (*R. acetosa*): Also called sour dock; has a very bitter flavor.

Salvia officinalis
LABIATAE

SAGE

Sage is an easy-to-grow, shrubby perennial with aromatic foliage used most often with poultry. A tea of sage is said to settle the stomach.

Best climate and site Zones 4–8. Full sun to partial shade.
Ideal soil conditions Well-drained garden soil.
Growing guidelines Sow seed shallowly outdoors in late spring or indoors in late winter; plant at 20–24-inch (50–60-cm) intervals. Take cuttings or divide older plants in spring or fall. Remove flowering spikes when young. Grows easily for several years, then begins to decline.
Growing habit Height 1–2 feet (30–60 cm); woody stems have wrinkled gray-green foliage.
Flowering time Spring; tubular purple flowers in whorled spikes.
Pest and disease prevention Plant in a sandy location at the proper spacing for best drainage and air circulation necessary for preventing disease and slug problems. Rarely bothered by other pests.
Harvesting and storing Snip fresh leaves as needed, or bunch them and hang to dry for use during winter months. Refrain from harvesting the first year.

Satureja montana
LABIATAE

SAVORY, WINTER

This aromatic bushy, hardy perennial has a peppery flavor and has been used in cooking for 2,000 years.

Best climate and site Zones 6–9. Full sun.
Ideal soil conditions Prefers poor, well-drained soil.
Growing guidelines Sow seed shallowly outdoors in late spring, thinning to 1 foot (30 cm). Germinates slowly. Take cuttings, or divide older plants in spring or fall.
Growing habit Height 6–12 inches (15–30 cm); branched, woody stems, oblong, needlelike leaves.
Flowering time June; pale purple blossoms in terminal spikes.
Pest and disease prevention Usually free from pests and diseases.
Harvesting and storing Harvest fresh as needed, or cut and dry the foliage just before flowering. Use as a flavoring in a variety of dishes, teas, herb butters, and vinegars.
Other species Summer savory (*S. hortensis*): Annual; prefers light, well-fertilized soil; transplants poorly; height 12–18 inches (30–45 cm); linear, downy leaves; pale lavender or white blossoms; used as an antiflatulent.

Thymus vulgaris
LABIATAE

THYME, GARDEN

Thyme is a favorite of cooks and gardeners, as it grows easily and there is at least one variety to suit every taste and location.

Best climate and site Zones 5–9. Full sun to partial shade.

Ideal soil conditions Prefers sandy, well-drained soil.

Growing guidelines Sow seed shallowly in late winter indoors, keeping the soil at 70°F (21°C) for best germination. Plant outdoors in late spring in clumps, 1 foot (30 cm) apart. You can divide older plants in spring or take cuttings in late summer or fall. In winter, mulch with a light material like straw. Replace plants every three to four years to control woody growth.

Growing habit Height 6–15 inches (15–38 cm); hardy perennial; woody stems; tiny gray-green, aromatic leaves.

Flowering time Midsummer; tubular lilac to pink blossoms in clusters.

Pest and disease prevention Plant in well-drained soil to prevent root and stem diseases.

Harvesting and storing Snip foliage as needed during the summer, or harvest entirely twice per season, leaving at least 3 inches (7.5 cm) of growth. Bunch together and hang to dry, or first strip the leaves and dry on a screen. Foliage freezes well in airtight containers or bags.

Trigonella foenum-graecum
LEGUMINOSAE

FENUGREEK

Fenugreek is a member of the same family as beans and clover. The seeds are used as a substitute for maple flavoring in baked goods.

Best climate and site Zones 6–10. Full sun.

Ideal soil conditions Rich soil.

Growing guidelines When springtime soil temperatures reach 60°F (15°C), sow a thick band of seed outdoors, covering shallowly. Avoid growing in cold, wet soils since seeds are likely to rot before they germinate.

Growing habit Annual; height 1–2 feet (30–60 cm); clover-like stems and leaves.

Flowering time Summer; white flowers that resemble garden pea blossoms.

Pest and disease prevention Handpick snails from new growth.

Harvesting and storing Harvest pods when ripe but before they fall, like garden beans; leave seeds in the sun to dry, then store in an airtight container.

Other common names Bird's foot, Greek hayseed.

Zingiber officinale
ZINGIBERACEAE

GINGER

Fresh ginger has a zing that the powdered spice lacks. Grow your own in pots placed outdoors during the warm season.

Best climate and site Zones 9–10. Partial shade.

Ideal soil conditions Fertile, moist, well-drained garden soil.

Growing guidelines Plant rhizomes in pots in a mix containing peat, sand, and compost; keep indoors or in a greenhouse in winter, moving the pots outdoors in warm summers.

Growing habit Tender perennial; height 2–4 feet (60–120 cm); leaves strap-shaped, 6–12 inches (15–30 cm) long.

Flowering time Rarely flowers under cultivation; in the wild, dense cone-like spikes on a stalk have yellow-green and purple flowers.

Pest and disease prevention Usually free from pests and diseases. For healthy growth, water well during the hot, summer months.

Harvesting and storing Dig plant after one year and remove the leaf stems, cutting away as much root as you need; replant the remaining root. Refrigerate harvested roots wrapped in paper toweling inside a plastic bag for up to one month. Or dry shaved bits of root and store in an airtight container.

Abelmoschus esculentus
MALVACEAE

OKRA (GUMBO)

The essential ingredient in gumbo, okra is also admired for its lovely, hollyhock-like flowers. It loves hot weather.

Best climate and site Zones 5 and warmer. Full sun.
Ideal soil conditions Fertile and well-drained soil; pH 6.5–7.5.
Growing guidelines Sow when frost danger is past and the soil is warm. Prewarming the soil with black plastic mulch will speed germination. In cooler areas, start indoors in individual pots two to four weeks before last frost and set out when the weather is settled. Set out or thin to stand 12–15 inches (30–38 cm) apart. Grows quickly in warm weather and needs both food and water; irrigate in dry spells and give it compost tea or fish emulsion once a month.
Pest and disease prevention Little troubled by pests. Aphids are a sign of water stress.
Common problems In cooler areas, okra will not bear as prolifically as in warm climates. Red-podded cultivars, such as 'Burgundy', are often better producers.
Days to maturity 50–60 frost-free days.
Harvesting and storing Clip or pinch off young pods when they are 1–4 inches (2.5–10 cm) long and still soft. Larger pods will be woody. Harvest daily in warm weather. Freezes well.
Special tips Blossoms are edible.

Allium ampeloprasm, Porrum group
LILIACEAE

LEEK

Leeks are grown for their stout, flavorful white stem. These onion relatives hold well in the ground for late harvest.

Best climate and site Zones 3 and warmer; grow as a winter vegetable in mild areas. Full sun.
Ideal soil conditions Loose, very rich, well-drained soil; pH 6.0–7.5.
Growing guidelines Start indoors up to 12 weeks before last spring frost. Transplant from seed flats to small, individual pots when large enough to handle. Set out after frost, 6 inches (15 cm) apart, in a 6-inch (15-cm) deep trench, covering all but 1 inch or so (2–3 cm) of leaves. Keep well weeded. As leeks grow, fill in the trench gradually or, if planted on level soil, "hill" them by drawing soil up around the stems. This produces a longer white stem. Keep the soil moist, especially early in the season.
Pest and disease prevention To avoid root maggot damage, do not plant where other onion family members have grown the previous year.
Common problems Short, tough stems indicate lack of moisture or fertility or inadequate hilling.
Days to maturity 70–105 days in garden. Young plants take light frost; mature ones, severe frost.
Harvesting and storing Dig or pull when large enough for use.

Allium cepa, Aggregatum group
LILIACEAE

SHALLOT

An onion relative, shallots produce small, firm bulbs that keep like garlic but are much milder in flavor. They are excellent in sauces.

Best climate and site All Zones; may be fall-planted in Zones 6 and warmer. Full sun.
Ideal soil conditions Humus-rich, well-drained soil. Will tolerate all but the most acid soil.
Growing guidelines Shallots do not grow from seed but from bulblets or "sets." Plant two to four weeks before last spring frost, 1 inch (2.5 cm) deep and 4–6 inches (10–15 cm) apart. Keep cultivated or mulch and water regularly to encourage strong early growth. Each set will produce eight to ten shallots.
Pest and disease prevention To avoid root maggots, do not plant where shallots or their relatives, such as onions or leeks, have grown the previous year.
Common problems Dry conditions or poor soil produces scrawny shallots. Work in plenty of compost or well-rotted manure and water regularly.
Days to maturity 120–150 days; or pull earlier to eat as scallions. Will withstand moderate frost.
Harvesting and storing When the tops are nearly dry, pull plants and dry the bulbs in a well-ventilated, sunny area. Store by hanging in a cool, dry place, or clip stems and store bulbs in mesh bags.

Allium spp.
LILIACEAE

ONION

A staple since before the pharaohs, the bulb of the versatile onion provides plenty of good eating in little garden space.

Best climate and site All Zones for scallions or "green onions"; Zones 3 and warmer for bulb onions, choosing cultivars suited to day length. Full sun.

Ideal soil conditions Humus-rich, well-drained soil; pH 6.0–7.5.

Growing guidelines For summer harvest, start indoors three to four months before last spring frost and set out 3–4 inches (8–10 cm) apart a month before last frost. Sow fall storage onions a month before last frost; thin to 3–4 inches (8–10 cm) apart. For quicker crops or in colder areas, grow onions from small bulbs called "sets." Irrigate and fertilize with fish emulsion or compost tea to encourage good early growth.

Pest and disease prevention Rotate plantings of onions and their relatives, such as garlic and leeks.

Common problems Failure to form bulbs usually indicates an unsuitable cultivar.

Days to maturity 60–115 days from transplanting. Scallions from sets may be harvested in as few as 35 days.

Harvesting and storing Pull scallions and onions for fresh use as needed. For storage onions, wait until tops have fallen over; pull the onions two days later, and let them dry in a cool, dry place.

Apium graveolens var. *dulce*
UMBELLIFERAE

CELERY

It requires care and attention to thrive, but if you're willing to supply its needs, celery will do beautifully in the backyard.

Best climate and site Zones 5 and warmer, except where early summer temperatures fall below 55°F (13°C). Fall and winter crop in mild areas. Full sun.

Ideal soil conditions Moisture-retentive, rich soil, with adequate calcium and plenty of well-rotted manure or compost worked in; pH 5.5–7.5.

Growing guidelines Start indoors four to six weeks before last spring frost. Germination and seedling growth are slow. Keep seedlings watered and do not expose to temperatures below 55°F (13°C), which can cause plants to bolt (go to seed). Set plants out when the weather is well settled, 10–12 inches (25–30 cm) apart. Do not allow the soil to dry out; feed plants with fish emulsion or compost tea at least once a month.

Pest and disease prevention Rotate plantings to avoid blight problems. Handpick parsleyworms or celeryworms.

Common problems Excessive heat, inadequate moisture, or lack of fertility will result in tough or stringy celery.

Days to maturity 80–105 days.

Harvesting and storing Cut celery for immediate use just below soil level.

Apium graveolens var. *rapaceum*
UMBELLIFERAE

CELERIAC

In salads, soups, and stews, or as a cooked vegetable, the root of celeriac has all the flavor of celery.

Best climate and site Zones 5 and warmer. Use as a fall and winter crop in mild areas. Full sun.

Ideal soil conditions Rich, moisture-retentive soil with adequate calcium and plenty of well-rotted manure or compost worked in; pH 5.5–7.5.

Growing guidelines Start indoors six to eight weeks before last spring frost and set out 10–12 inches (25–30 cm) apart when the frost threat is past. Keep bed well weeded and watered. Apply compost tea or fish emulsion at least monthly.

Pest and disease prevention Rotate plantings of celeriac and celery to avoid blights to which they are both vulnerable. Handpick celeryworms or parsleyworms.

Common problems Inadequate moisture and fertility produce small, tough, or fibrous celeriac.

Days to maturity 110–120 days; can withstand increasingly severe frost for the last 30–45 days.

Harvesting and storing Harvest the turnip-like root when large enough for your needs. Harvest all plants before the ground freezes; cut stems close to the roots and store like turnips in damp sawdust or sand in a cool place.

Other common names Celery root.

Asparagus officinalis
LILIACEAE

ASPARAGUS

This classic spring vegetable requires well-prepared soil with high fertility. A well-maintained patch may yield for decades.

Best climate and site Zones 3 and warmer, but asparagus grows best in areas where soil freezes in winter. Avoid low-lying areas subject to heavy dew and morning fogs to reduce the possibility of rust. Prefers full sun, but will tolerate some shade.

Ideal soil conditions Fertile, well-drained soil; will tolerate slightly alkaline pH (6.5–6.8) and saline soils.

Growing guidelines Grow from seed started indoors or in an outdoor seedbed; or hasten the first harvest by using year-old crowns. Follow directions on seed packet or from your supplier for planting and cultivation.

Pest and disease prevention Asparagus rust can be a serious problem in damp locations; use rust-resistant cultivars. Burn or hot-compost old asparagus foliage and cultivate the asparagus patch shallowly before applying fall mulch to reduce damage from asparagus beetles.

Common problems Be sure the area is free of perennial weeds before planting.

Days to maturity New hybrid cultivars may be picked sparingly for one to two weeks in the second year.

Harvesting and storing Harvest while tips of spears are still tightly closed.

Beta vulgaris
CHENOPODIACEAE

BEET

Start harvesting beets when they are 1 inch (2.5 cm) in diameter. You can eat both the leaves and roots.

Best climate and site Beets thrive in almost any climate, but where summers are hot (Zones 8 and warmer), grow them as a fall, late winter, and early spring crop. Full sun.

Ideal soil conditions Well-drained, rich, neutral soil, free of stones; pH 6.0–7.5.

Growing guidelines Soak the seeds in tepid water for several hours to encourage germination. Plant 1 inch (2.5 cm) deep and 2–4 inches (5–10 cm) apart, about one month before last spring frost. Firm the seedbed well. Thin the young plants when they are 2–3 inches (5–8 cm) tall. Beets need regular watering to keep them tender and to prevent interior discoloring that results from uneven soil moisture.

Pest and disease prevention Row covers will thwart flea beetles and leaf miners. Discourage the disease leaf spot by not growing beets where they or their relatives, such as spinach and chard, have been grown in the previous year.

Common problems Beets do poorly in hot weather and dry soil.

Days to maturity 55–70 days.

Harvesting and storing Harvest greens as soon as they are large enough for use. When removing tops, leave 1 inch (2.5 cm) of stem to prevent bleeding.

Beta vulgaris var. *cicla*
CHENOPODIACEAE

SWISS CHARD

Vigorous and easy to grow, a single planting of Swiss chard can provide a full season of fresh greens. Use it like spinach.

Best climate and site Zones 3 and warmer; grow as a winter vegetable in mild areas. Full sun or, in warm areas, partial shade.

Ideal soil conditions Not fussy, but prefers rich, well-drained soil; pH 6.0–6.8.

Growing guidelines Sow one to two weeks before last spring frost. Plant ½ inch (12 mm) deep and firm the soil with the back of a hoe. Thin to stand 8–12 inches (20–30 cm) apart, using thinnings in salads or transplanting them to new beds. Cultivate, and water regularly to keep plants growing strongly.

Pest and disease prevention Little troubled by pests. Row covers will deter flea beetles.

Common problems Fairly tolerant, but water stress causes tough stems.

Days to maturity 50–60 days; thinnings may be harvested sooner.

Harvesting and storing Pick large outer leaves by pulling stems from the base with a slight twist. Leave the center to sprout new leaves. Leaves are usually cooked separately from the wide inner rib, which is often steamed and eaten like asparagus. You can freeze leaves in the same way as you would spinach.

Other common names Silverbeet.

Brassica napus, Napobrassica group
CRUCIFERAE

RUTABAGA

A favorite in Scandinavian countries, rutabaga is a rugged garden vegetable that shrugs off cold and adverse conditions.

Best climate and site Zones 3 and warmer; grow as a winter vegetable in mild areas. Full sun.

Ideal soil conditions Fertile, well-drained soil. Will tolerate heavy soil better than most other root vegetables; pH 5.5–6.8.

Growing guidelines Sow 12–14 weeks before first fall frost and thin to stand 4–6 inches (10–15 cm) apart. Cultivate early; the plant's large leaves will quickly grow to shade out weeds.

Pest and disease prevention Rotate rutabaga and other root crops to avoid root maggots. Protect young plants from flea beetles with row covers; larger plants may suffer cosmetic damage that will not affect yield.

Common problems Rutabagas that mature in hot weather may be tough.

Days to maturity 90–110 days. Will withstand severe frost.

Harvesting and storing Pull rutabagas when they are large enough for use. The greens also are edible. Harvest all roots before hard freeze and store in damp sand or sawdust in a cool place.

Other common names Swede, Swede turnip, yellow turnip.

Brassica oleracea, Botrytis group
CRUCIFERAE

BROCCOLI

Virtually unknown in American gardens 50 years ago, broccoli is now a cool-weather favorite. It can be eaten raw or cooked.

Best climate and site Zones 3 and warmer; grow as a winter crop in mild-climate areas. Where springs are cool, grow as a spring and fall crop; otherwise does best in fall. Full sun.

Ideal soil conditions Well-drained soil with plenty of calcium; pH 6.7–7.2.

Growing guidelines Start spring seedlings indoors, about two months before the last spring frost. Set out hardened-off transplants in the garden a month before the last frost. Sow fall crops directly about 90 days before the first fall frost, or transplant about 60 days before frost. Cultivate or mulch and keep the soil evenly moist.

Pest and disease prevention Use cardboard or metal "collars" to deter cutworms. Row covers will thwart flea beetles, cabbageworms, and root maggots.

Common problems In some areas, spring broccoli bolts (goes to seed prematurely) at the onset of hot weather. Choose quick-maturing cultivars and expect spring-grown broccoli heads to be smaller than those grown in fall.

Days to maturity 70–95 days.

Harvesting and storing Harvest broccoli heads when they have reached maximum size but before flower buds turn yellow.

Brassica oleracea, Botrytis group
CRUCIFERAE

CAULIFLOWER

Cauliflowers are heavy feeders that require plenty of water. Blanching is necessary to keep the heads white. Purple cauliflowers are also available.

Best climate and site Zones 3 and warmer. Use as spring and fall crops in cool-spring areas, and as a winter vegetable in mild climates. Full sun.

Ideal soil conditions Rich, well-drained soil with plenty of calcium, and ample amounts of well-rotted manure or compost worked in; pH 6.0–7.0

Growing guidelines Start spring crops indoors and do not set out too early; severe frost may cause the plant to form a "button" instead of a full-sized head. Start fall crops 90–120 days before fall frost; set out when seedlings are four to five weeks old. Keep cauliflower growing steadily with plenty of water and one or more applications of fish emulsion or compost tea. When heads appear, use a clothespin to clip several large leaves together over the head to shade it and keep it white, or remove a large lower leaf and lay it over the developing head.

Pest and disease prevention Control cabbage-worms with row covers or a spray or dust of BT.

Common problems In humid areas, heads may discolor during blanching.

Days to maturity 50–72 days.

Harvesting and storing Cut heads before curds begin to coarsen and separate.

Brassica oleracea, Capitata group
CRUCIFERAE

CABBAGE

Valued for thousands of years because of its hardiness and storage life, cabbage can be grown almost anywhere.

Best climate and site Zones 3 and warmer, with soil-cooling mulch in hotter climates. Use as a winter vegetable in mild areas. Full sun.
Ideal soil conditions Any soil texture, provided it is well drained and fertile; pH 6.0–6.8.
Growing guidelines Grow as a spring and fall crop in most areas, or as a winter crop where temperatures rarely drop below freezing. Avoid plantings that will mature in hot, dry weather. Start spring crops in a cool place indoors six to eight weeks before last spring frost and set out four weeks before the last frost. Give seedlings plenty of light. Cabbage prefers rich soil; add compost or rotted manure before planting and apply fish emulsion or compost tea a month after planting.
Pest and disease prevention Use row covers or BT to control cabbageworms.
Common problems Use a shovel to sever roots on one side of the plant when the head is fully formed. This slows maturity and prevents the cabbage from splitting.
Days to maturity 60–110 days.
Harvesting and storing Harvest early cultivars as needed; harvest storage-type cabbage before hard freeze and store, roots and all, in dry leaves in a cold cellar.

Brassica oleracea, Gemmifera group
CRUCIFERAE

BRUSSELS SPROUTS

Individual brussels sprouts resemble tiny cabbages. They are a late-season treat, when frost has sweetened their flavor.

Best climate and site Zones 4–7, and Zone 8 as a winter vegetable. Generally unsuited to warmer climates. Full sun.
Ideal soil conditions Well-drained and fertile soil, with adequate calcium levels; pH 6.0–6.8.
Growing guidelines Require a long growing season and are best when matured in cool weather. Short-season vegetable gardeners may set out transplants when they sow other spring crops; in other areas, wait until late spring. Space plants about 24 inches (60 cm) apart and keep weeded or mulched. Pinch off top leaves to encourage side growth.
Pest and disease prevention Rotate with non-cabbage-family crops to avoid soilborne fungal and viral diseases. Use row covers to deter flea beetles, cabbageworms, and root maggots, or BT for cabbageworms. Keep well watered and grow in fertile soil to reduce vulnerability to aphids.
Days to maturity 90–120 days. Mature plants withstand heavy frost.
Harvesting and storing Harvest lower sprouts first, anytime until early winter. Complete harvest before ground freezes. Harvested sprouts freeze well.

Brassica rapa, Rapifera group
CRUCIFERAE

TURNIP

Grown both for its tender leaves and for its crisp root, turnip is at its best in cool weather. Baby turnips are especially tender.

Best climate and site All Zones; grow as a winter vegetable in mild climates. Full sun.
Ideal soil conditions Loose, deep, humus-rich soil; pH 5.5–6.8.
Growing guidelines Sow ½ inch (12 mm) deep four to six weeks before last spring frost. Thin to stand 3 inches (7.5 cm) apart; use thinnings as fresh or cooked greens. Water regularly for fast growth in spring, since turnip bolts in hot weather. Sow fall crop eight to ten weeks before first fall frost.
Pest and disease prevention Use row covers to protect from flea beetles. Reduce root maggot damage, especially in spring crops, by not planting where other root crops have grown the previous year.
Common problems Turnips that mature in hot weather may be fibrous or strong-flavored. For spring crops, choose quick-maturing cultivars.
Days to maturity 35–60 days. Turnips will withstand light frost.
Harvesting and storing Pull turnips as needed, as 1-inch (2.5-cm) wide "babies" up to 3–4-inch (8–10-cm) roots. Larger turnips may be woody. Turnips are more tender than other root vegetables and are damaged by hard frost.

Capsicum annuum
SOLANACEAE

PEPPER

Bell peppers are crisp and juicy when green, but sweeter when allowed to ripen to red, yellow, or orange, depending on cultivar.

Best climate and site Zones 4 and warmer. Full sun.

Ideal soil conditions Light, well-drained soil, not overly rich; pH 6.0–7.0.

Growing guidelines Start indoors six to eight weeks before last spring frost. Do not overwater pepper seedlings. Set out 10–15 inches (25–38 cm) apart when the soil has warmed. Cultivate shallowly; do not mulch until the soil is thoroughly warm. Magnesium is critical; in magnesium-poor soils, scatter 1 teaspoon of Epsom salts around the base of each plant. Irrigate in dry spells.

Pest and disease prevention Do not plant where peppers or other nightshade family members, such as tomato and eggplant, have grown for two years. Protect young plants from cutworms with cardboard or foil collars.

Common problems Sunscald can cause dry, sunken patches on the fruit.

Days to maturity 55–80 days from transplanting for green peppers; 15–20 days more for mature peppers.

Harvesting and storing Pick green peppers when large enough for use. Pick mature peppers when 50–75 percent colored; they will finish ripening in one to two days at room temperature.

Cichorium endiva
COMPOSITAE

ENDIVE AND ESCAROLE

In warm areas grow escarole in between tomatoes, where it will appreciate the shade and save space. The leaves of endive and escarole are slightly tangy.

Best climate and site Zones 4 and warmer; grow as a winter vegetable in mild areas. Full sun or partial shade in warm areas.

Ideal soil conditions Fertile, well-drained, and well-limed soil; pH 5.5–7.0.

Growing guidelines In cool-spring areas, start indoors eight weeks before last frost and set out a month before last frost, 10–12 inches (25–30 cm) apart. Cover plants if hard frost threatens. In warmer areas, they're best as fall crops, started in midsummer and set out two months before first fall frost, or even later in mildest areas. May be blanched by inverting a pot or box over the plant, or by tying outer leaves together at the top. In humid areas, blanching by tying may cause inside leaves to rot.

Pest and disease prevention Provide good air circulation to avoid molds. Control slugs with shallow pans of beer set into the soil.

Common problems Water well and provide shade in hot spells to prevent brown, crisp ends on endive leaves.

Days to maturity 80–100 days.

Harvesting and storing Cut the entire head at its base in the morning. Rinse; wrap in a paper towel and then in plastic.

Cucumis sativus
CUCURBITACEAE

CUCUMBER

Prized in salads and pickles, cucumbers are heat-loving plants that can be grown on a trellis or fence to save garden space.

Best climate and site Zones 4 and warmer. Full sun, in a site with good air circulation.

Ideal soil conditions Light soil with well-rotted manure or compost worked in; pH 6.0–7.0.

Growing guidelines Cucumbers dislike cold soil, so wait for three to four weeks after the last frost to direct-seed or transplant them into the garden. Mulch, or keep cultivated until plants begin to vine. Cucumbers need ample food and water; irrigate in dry spells and give them fish emulsion or compost tea once a month. Plant successive crops six weeks apart, where the growing season permits. Grow on a trellis or fence to save space.

Pest and disease prevention Use row covers to protect young plants from cucumber beetles, but remove when plants bloom. Trellising will improve air circulation and reduce mildew.

Common problems Sudden collapse of cucumber plants indicates wilt disease, which is spread by cucumber beetles. Straw mulch may help deter beetles.

Days to maturity 48–70 frost-free days.

Harvesting and storing Pick often, especially during hot spells, to encourage continued fruiting. Pickle excess crop.

Cucurbita pepo var. melopepo
CUCURBITACEAE

SQUASH, SUMMER

Zucchini is best picked when less than 8 inches (20 cm) long. The flowers are also edible, but must be used soon after they're picked.

Best climate and site Zones 3 and warmer. Full sun in a site with good air circulation.

Ideal soil conditions Humus-rich, well-drained, soil; pH 6.0–6.5.

Growing guidelines Sow when all danger of frost is past, or start indoors in individual pots two to three weeks before last frost and transplant carefully to avoid breaking roots. Squash needs ample moisture to keep the fruit coming, and it benefits from compost or manure.

Pest and disease prevention Use row covers to protect young squash plants from cucumber beetles and squash borers; remove covers when the plants bloom. If plants are attacked by mildew, spray foliage thoroughly with a mild baking soda solution (1 teaspoon per quart [liter] of water).

Common problems Fruit that turns black and rots before reaching picking size has not been pollinated. This often happens early, before male blossoms appear, or in cool spells, when pollinating insects are less active.

Days to maturity 42–65 frost-free days.

Harvesting and storing Pick squash small for best flavor. Pick blossoms in early morning, before pollination.

Cucurbita pepo var. pepo
CUCURBITACEAE

PUMPKIN

As familiar a sight in fall as falling leaves, pumpkin makes fine pies and baked dishes, as well as jack-o'-lanterns.

Best climate and site Zones 4 and warmer. Full sun.

Ideal soil conditions Not fussy about texture, but likes a fertile soil; pH 6.0–7.0.

Growing guidelines Sow after last spring frost, two or three seeds to a hill, in hills 4–5 feet (1.2–1.5 m) apart. In short-season areas, start pumpkins indoors in individual pots two to three weeks before last frost. Set out carefully to avoid disturbing the roots. A good shovelful of compost or well-rotted manure in each hill will boost growth. Mulch or cultivate until the plants begin to vine. Pumpkin's broad leaves will shade out most weeds.

Pest and disease prevention Row covers deter cucumber beetles and squash borers, but remove them when plants bloom to allow pollination. Straw mulch also helps deter cucumber beetles. Prevent mildew by providing good air circulation.

Common problems Plants that collapse before setting fruit are probably victims of the squash borer. Those that collapse before fruit ripens may be infected with a wilt disease spread by cucumber beetles.

Days to maturity 100–115 frost-free days.

Harvesting and storing Harvest when they are fully colored and their shell is hard. Store in a dry, cool area.

Cynara scolymus
COMPOSITAE

ARTICHOKE, GLOBE

This plant is grown chiefly for its large, edible flower heads, but suckers also may be blanched and eaten like asparagus.

Best climate and site Mild coastal climates, Zones 8–9; can be grown in Zones 5–7 with special winter care. Full sun and protected exposure.

Ideal soil conditions Rich, well-drained soil; near-neutral pH.

Growing guidelines Start seed indoors in late winter and transplant in late spring, when soil has warmed thoroughly. Can reach 5 feet (1.5 m) or more in height; space seedlings 24 inches (60 cm) apart in the row and allow 3 feet (90 cm) or more between rows. Be generous with compost or manure. Water deeply; mulch well between rows.

Pest and disease prevention Susceptible to crown rot. Well-drained soil is essential. Do not allow mulch to smother the crown.

Common problems In Zones 7 and colder, winter-kill is the chief problem. Cut the plant back in late fall and protect over winter by inverting a basket or box over the crown and mulching deeply.

Days to maturity May produce edible buds the first year but more likely will not yield a harvest until the second year.

Harvesting Cut buds before the scales have begun to open, with 1 inch (2.5 cm) of stem attached.

Daucus carota var. *sativus*
UMBELLIFERAE

CARROT

Carrots were well known to the ancient Greeks, who used their delicate foliage in corsages and floral decorations.

Best climate and site Zones 3 and warmer. Plant quick-maturing carrot cultivars in colder areas. Full sun.
Ideal soil conditions Deep, light soil. Improve clayey soil with organic matter; pH 5.5–6.8.
Growing guidelines Sow the first crop in early spring, after severe frost threats are past. Seed is very small; mix half-and-half with fine sand to help avoid overseeding. Plant a scant ½ inch (12 mm) deep and firm the seedbed gently with the back of a hoe. Keep the soil evenly moist until the carrots are up. Thin to 2–3 inches (5–8 cm) apart. Plant successive crops every few weeks until three months before fall frost. Do not overwater as a continually wet soil can cause root rot.
Pest and disease prevention Use row covers to deter carrot rust flies. Rotate plantings to avoid bacterial diseases.
Common problems Do not use high-nitrogen fertilizer or fresh manure on carrot beds. Splitting may occur when heavy rain follows a dry period.
Days to maturity 50–70 days.
Harvesting and storing Ready to eat as soon as they have developed full color. Pull when the ground is moist to avoid breaking roots, or dig with a garden fork.

Eruca vesicaria subsp. *sativa*
CRUCIFERAE

ARUGULA

The tender leaves of this European garden favorite add a nutty, peppery bite to salads and sandwiches. It is also known as rocket.

Best climate and site All Zones. Full sun as well as half-day sun or partial shade. Avoid hot, dry positions. In mild climates, grow as a winter vegetable.
Ideal soil conditions Not fussy, but prefers fertile, moist soil; pH 6.0–7.0.
Growing guidelines Direct-seed as early as possible in spring. Light frost will not harm the seedlings. Thin to 8 inches (20 cm) apart, using thinnings in salads.
Pest and disease prevention Use spun-bonded row cover to deter flea beetles.
Common problems Sown too late, spring-planted arugula will bolt (go prematurely to seed) in warm weather before reaching harvestable size. In cold climates, sow seed indoors and set out as soon as ground can be worked. A fall crop, direct-seeded or set out as seedlings one to two months before the first fall frost, will stand longer without bolting. Extend the harvest with successive plantings a week apart.
Days to maturity 40 days, although thinnings may be harvested earlier.
Harvesting and storing Pick large leaves from bottom of plant. New leaves will sprout from center crown. Weekly picking should yield 8–12 large leaves per plant. Use fresh; do not freeze.

Foeniculum vulgare var. *azoricum*
UMBELLIFERAE

FENNEL, FLORENCE

Florence fennel is grown chiefly for its enlarged leaf bases, which have the flavor of licorice. The feathery leaves are used as an herb.

Best climate and site Zones 4 and warmer; grow as a winter vegetable in mild areas. Full sun.
Ideal soil conditions Fertile and well-drained soil; pH 6.5–7.0.
Growing guidelines In cool-spring areas, direct-seed spring crop two to four weeks before last frost and thin to stand 8–10 inches (20–25 cm) apart. Transplants poorly, but may need a head start in warmer areas since it bolts quickly in hot weather. Start seedlings in individual pots or peat pots a month before last frost; do not let roots outgrow the pots before setting out. Sow small, successive crops where the season permits; avoid plantings that will mature in hot, dry weather. Fall crops are easier to transplant; set out two months before first frost. Keep well weeded or mulch; water in dry spells.
Pest and disease prevention Handpick celeryworms or parsleyworms, (green caterpillars with black and yellow stripes).
Common problems Florence fennel becomes woody when overmature. Plant small, successive crops to prolong harvest.
Days to maturity 65–90 days.
Harvesting and storing Cut the entire plant below the base of the bulb.

Ipomoea batatas
CONVOLVULACEAE

SWEET POTATO

Sweet potatoes are a warm-weather crop that produces tasty and nutritious tuberous roots. Sweet potatoes are often erroneously called yams.

Best climate and site Zones 5 and warmer. Full sun.

Ideal soil conditions Loose, well-drained soil that is not too rich; pH 5.5–6.5.

Growing guidelines Plant from growing shoots or "slips," which are available by mail or at many garden centers. Plant after frost danger is well past. With a rake, make a ridge of soil 6–10 inches (15–25 cm) high and 6–8 inches (15–20 cm) wide. Plant slips into the ridge about 12 inches (30 cm) apart. Mound soil onto the ridge at least once before the vining plants make further cultivation impossible. Keep newly set slips watered until they begin to grow. After that, irrigate sweet potatoes only in extended dry spells.

Pest and disease prevention Use disease-free slips. Rotate plantings and keep soil organic matter high to reduce nematode damage.

Common problems Deer love the tender leaves and shoots; if they are a problem in your area, you may need to fence off your sweet potatoes.

Days to maturity 90–120 frost-free days.

Harvesting and storing Dig sweet potatoes before frost or as soon as the vines have been killed by a light frost.

Lactuca sativa
COMPOSITAE

LETTUCE

Leaf lettuce is the quickest and easiest-to-grow member of the lettuce clan. It can double as an ornamental garden edging.

Best climate and site All Zones; grow as a winter vegetable in mild areas. Full sun in cool weather, partial shade in warm weather.

Ideal soil conditions Fertile, well-drained soil; pH 6.0–6.8.

Growing guidelines Direct-seed leafy types a month before last frost. Barely cover the seeds and firm the soil with the back of a hoe. Start head-forming types indoors six to eight weeks before last frost and set out 8–10 inches (20–25 cm) apart, one to two weeks before last frost. Leave leaf lettuces unthinned for "baby" salad greens or thin to encourage large-leaved plants. Water frequently.

Pest and disease prevention Rotate crops to avoid soilborne diseases. Control slugs by trapping them in shallow pans of beer set flush with the soil surface.

Common problems Bitter leaves suggest heat and water stress, or simply overmature lettuce. Plant small crops at frequent intervals.

Days to maturity 40–90 days.

Harvesting and storing Harvest as needed for fresh use. Cut unthinned leaf lettuce with scissors 1 inch (2.5 cm) above roots, leaving the plants to resprout for a second harvest.

Lycopersicon esculentum
SOLANACEAE

TOMATO

To minimize the buildup of soilborne pests and diseases, avoid planting tomatoes where related plants grew the previous year.

Best climate and site Zones 3 and warmer. Full sun.

Ideal soil conditions Fertile, deep, well-drained soil; pH 6.0–7.0.

Growing guidelines In long-season areas, tomatoes may be direct-seeded, but they are usually started indoors five to six weeks before last spring frost. Set out 24–36 inches (60–90 cm) apart if plants are to be allowed to sprawl, or as close as 15 inches (38 cm) if they are to be staked or caged. Water tomatoes regularly but do not fertilize until the plant is well established and in full blossom. Then give weak compost tea or fish emulsion.

Pest and disease prevention Protect young plants from cutworms with cardboard or metal collars. Handpick tomato hornworms or use BT.

Common problems Blossom end rot indicates that the plant is not taking up enough calcium from the soil. Dark brown, circular spots on tomato leaves suggest fungal disease or blight. Provide good air circulation and do not disturb plants when they are wet.

Days to maturity 52–90 frost-free days.

Harvesting and storing Pick the fruit when it is evenly colored but still firm. Can, freeze, or dry excess tomatoes.

Nasturtium officinale
CRUCIFERAE

WATERCRESS

At its best in fall and early spring, watercress is a tasty and healthful addition to salads, soups, and sandwiches.

Best climate and site Zones 3 and warmer; grow as a winter vegetable in warmer areas or indoors in pots almost anywhere. Full sun or partial shade.
Ideal soil conditions Wet, humus-rich, well-limed soil, preferably at the edge of a stream or stream-fed pond; pH 6.0–7.0.
Growing guidelines Start indoors four to eight weeks before the last spring frost, or sprinkle seeds as thinly as possible where they are to grow, about a month before the last frost, pressing them into the soil. Watercress can be grown in pots, indoors or out. Set pots in pans of water and change the water daily.
Pest and disease prevention Little troubled by pests and diseases.
Days to maturity 120–150 days. In short-season areas, a newly established watercress bed may not produce a harvest the first year.
Harvesting and storing Harvest leaves as needed, midfall through early spring, including winter where climate permits. Flavor deteriorates during flowering.

Phaseolus vulgaris
LEGUMINOSAE

BEAN (FRESH)

Pole beans are the perfect vegetable for a small garden. They bear over a long period and may be grown on a trellis or fence.

Best climate and site Zones 3 and warmer; cold climates may require a quick-maturing cultivar. Full sun.
Ideal soil conditions Likes humus-rich but not excessively fertile soil; pH 6.0–7.5.
Growing guidelines Sow seed after frost danger is past. Sow bush snap beans about 1 inch (2.5 cm) deep and 3 inches (7.5 cm) apart in single or double rows. Keep well weeded, or mulch. Thorough watering is critical when beans are in flower. Bush snap beans bear heavily but only for a few weeks. To assure a steady supply, make several small plantings three to four weeks apart, ending two months before the first fall frost date.
Pest and disease prevention Mexican bean beetles can be serious pests from midseason onward; row covers help exclude these pests.
Common problems Sown too early in cold, wet soil, bean seeds may rot before germinating. A small planting for early harvest may be worth the risk, but larger plantings for freezing or canning should be delayed until the weather is settled.
Days to maturity 42–55 frost-free days.
Harvesting and storing Pick at any size, but before seeds have begun to swell.

Pisum sativum var. *sativum*
LEGUMINOSAE

PEA

Tall-growing peas will need some type of trellis to support their climbing stems. They look attractive at the back of a flower garden.

Best climate and site Zones 2 and warmer; grow as a spring and fall crop in most Zones, and as a winter vegetable in frost-free climates. Full sun on a site with good air circulation.
Ideal soil conditions Loose, well-drained soil; pH 6.0–7.0.
Growing guidelines Peas do poorly in hot weather, so plant spring crops early to beat the heat unless your springs are long and cool. In Zones 7 and warmer, seed planted in late fall often overwinters and germinates in early spring. In colder Zones, plant four to eight weeks before last spring frost. Sow fall crops 10–12 weeks before first fall frost. Peas do not need supplementary fertilizer, but make sure you provide adequate moisture when they are in bloom.
Pest and disease prevention Rarely troubled by insects.
Common problems Fall plantings in humid areas, even of resistant cultivars, are often plagued by powdery mildew. Spray foliage thoroughly with a baking soda solution (1 teaspoon per quart [liter] of water).
Days to maturity 55–80 days.
Harvesting and storing Pick shelling-type peas when pods are full and plump.

Raphanus sativus
CRUCIFERAE

RADISH

Fast-growing radishes add a crisp, colorful touch to spring salads. Harvest them while they are young and tender.

Best climate and site All Zones; grow as a winter vegetable in mild areas.

Ideal soil conditions Loose, moisture-retentive soil; pH 5.5–6.8.

Growing guidelines Sow spring radishes three to five weeks before last spring frost, ½ inch (12 mm) deep in double or triple rows. Make the rows short and sow small successive crops every two weeks until a month after frost. Sow fall crops starting eight weeks before fall frost and continuing until frost. Keep radishes moist to avoid strong flavor and toughness. Mulch between rows to keep soil moist in hot weather.

Pest and disease prevention Rotate radishes and other root crops to reduce damage from root maggots. Spring crops are more vulnerable than fall crops.

Common problems Spring radishes, especially slender French breakfast types, become woody when overmature.

Days to maturity 21–35 days for spring radishes; 50–60 days for winter radishes. Will withstand moderate frost.

Harvesting and storing Pull spring and fall crops when large enough for use. Pull winter radishes as needed when they reach eating size; harvest all roots before hard freeze. Store in damp sand.

Solanum melongena var. *esculentum*
SOLANACEAE

EGGPLANT

Eggplant thrives in hot weather. It needs ample amounts of water and fertilizer to produce. Also known as aubergine.

Best climate and site Zones 5 and warmer. Full sun.

Ideal soil conditions Light, rich, well-drained, warm soil; pH 5.5–6.8.

Growing guidelines Eggplant likes hot weather, so it does not pay to start the plants too soon or set them out too early. Start eight weeks before the time when night temperatures can be counted on to stay above 50°F (10°C). Night covers may be needed in colder climates. Space the plants 18–24 inches (45–60 cm) apart. Eggplant needs plenty of water and food to produce well. Use fish emulsion or compost tea at least once a month.

Pest and disease prevention Use row covers to deter flea beetles. Handpick Colorado potato beetles; a light dusting of ground limestone often repels this pest.

Common problems Provide adequate soil moisture and calcium to prevent blossom-end rot, which shows up as a soft, brown spot at the blossom end of the fruit.

Days to maturity 50–75 frost-free days.

Harvesting and storing Clip the fruit with some stem attached; harvest often to encourage further fruiting. Standard eggplant cultivars, such as 'Black Beauty', will bear four to ten full-sized fruits, or more if picked small.

Solanum tuberosum
SOLANACEAE

POTATO

Red potatoes are delicious simply boiled or baked in their jackets. They have moist, white flesh. Fingerling potatoes are waxy, ideal in salads.

Best climate and site Zones 3 and warmer. Full sun.

Ideal soil conditions Loose, well-drained, slightly acid soil with plenty of potash; ideal pH 5.2–5.7, but will also do well at pH 5.8–6.5.

Growing guidelines Potatoes are planted from pieces of tuber called "seed potatoes." Each piece should be about the size of an egg and contain one or more "eyes," or dormant buds. Cut seed potatoes to size and let the pieces dry for one day to prevent rotting in the ground. Plant two to four weeks before last spring frost, about a foot (30 cm) apart in a 3-4-inch (8–10-cm) deep trench. Water regularly.

Pest and disease prevention Covering plants with row covers or dusting them with ground limestone helps deter flea beetles and Colorado potato beetles.

Common problems Exposed to light, potato tubers develop green patches that contain the toxic alkaloid solanine. Hill or mulch deeply to prevent sunlight from reaching the tubers.

Days to maturity 55–80 days.

Harvesting and storing When foliage dies back, potatoes are mature; dig as needed. Store in well-ventilated boxes.

Spinacia oleracea
CHENOPODIACEAE

SPINACH

Delicious and healthy fresh or cooked, spinach needs cool weather and plenty of water to make abundant crisp leaves.

Best climate and site All Zones. Full sun or partial shade.

Ideal soil conditions Moist, fertile, well-limed soil; pH 6.0–7.0.

Growing guidelines Sow ½ inch (12 mm) deep, four to six weeks before last spring frost. In very short-season areas, or where hot weather sets in abruptly, start spinach indoors. Set out or thin to 4–6 inches (10–15 cm) apart. Keep weed-free and water regularly. Sow fall crops four to six weeks before first frost, or later for overwintering. Seed fall crops heavily, as spinach germinates poorly in warm soil.

Pest and disease prevention Use row covers to protect from leaf miners and chewing insects.

Common problems Hot weather and lengthening days can cause plants to bolt (go to seed). Use heat-resistant cultivars and sow spring crops early.

Days to maturity 40–53 days, although thinnings may be harvested sooner. Spinach will withstand moderate frost.

Harvesting and storing Pick larger outside leaves or harvest whole plant at its base. Spinach freezes well for use as a cooked vegetable.

Valerianella locusta
VALERIANACEAE

CORN SALAD

Small, tender, green corn salad can be planted in fall to grace spring's earliest salads. It's expensive to buy, but easy to grow.

Best climate and site Zones 2 and warmer. Overwinters in Zones 5 and warmer; grow as a winter vegetable in mild areas. Full sun or partial shade.

Ideal soil conditions Not fussy, but prefers humus-rich soil; pH 6.0–7.0.

Growing guidelines Sow in early spring, two to four weeks before last frost; cover with fine soil and firm with the back of a hoe. Plant thickly in rows or more thinly in wide beds; keep moist. Thin to stand 2 inches (5 cm) apart; use thinnings in salads. Avoid plantings that will mature in hot weather. Plant in fall near first frost date; mulch lightly after hard freeze. Remove mulch in early spring.

Pest and disease prevention Little troubled by pests or diseases.

Common problems In colder areas, mulch more heavily to avoid heaving of plants over winter.

Days to maturity 45–60 days from spring seeding; thinnings can be harvested earlier. Will withstand light frost.

Harvesting and storing Harvest entire rosettes by pinching off at ground level. Some cultivars remain sweet even when in flower; taste to check.

Other common names Fetticus, lamb's lettuce, mache.

Zea mays var. *rugosa*
GRAMINEAE

CORN

Tender and succulent, fresh sweet corn is a classic summer treat from the garden. Store-bought corn can't compare with its taste.

Best climate and site Zones 3 and warmer. Use only short-season cultivars in coldest areas. Full sun. Avoid high-wind areas.

Ideal soil conditions Accepts many soil textures; prefers deep, well-manured soil with high organic content; pH 6.0–6.8.

Growing guidelines Sow after last spring frost, or one to two weeks earlier if soil has first been warmed by covering with black plastic for a week or more in sunny weather. Corn seed germinates poorly in cold, wet soil and may rot. Corn grows rapidly and needs adequate fertility and water. Apply fish emulsion or compost tea after one month and again when the tassels appear. Water is most critical when corn is in tassel.

Pest and disease prevention Help control earworms by dropping mineral oil into the immature ears as soon as you see the pest's sticky frass on the silks (the hairlike fibers).

Common problems Patchy spots on kernels, or ears that are not filled to the tip, indicate inadequate pollination.

Days to maturity 54–94 frost-free days.

Harvesting and storing Harvest when the silks have turned brown and dry and the ear feels full.

Actinidia chinensis
ACTINIDIACEAE

KIWI

Kiwi vines make excellent covering for trellises and arbors. You can enjoy the shade and reach up to pick the fruit easily.

Best climate and site Zones 7–9. Plant in full sun to light shade in average to poor, well-drained soil.

Height and spread Height 4–6 feet (1.2–1.8 m); spread 15 feet (4.5 m).

Growing guidelines With the exception of a few self-fertile cultivars such as 'Issai' and 'Blake', kiwi vines have either male or female flowers. For pollination, plant a male vine within about 40 feet (12 m) of the females—closer if possible. One male will pollinate up to eight female vines. Keep the soil moist up to harvest time, but water less as winter approaches. Mulch well, but fertilize lightly, if at all.

Pruning Before planting, install a sturdy post-and-wire trellis (as you would for grapes). Insert a stake next to the vine at planting time, and cut out all but one stem. Remove any sideshoots from the remaining stem and train it up the stake.

Propagation Propagate using cuttings or by grafting.

Pest and disease control Surround young plants with a circle of wire mesh fencing to prevent cats from chewing or rolling on the leaves and stems.

Harvesting and storage Pick kiwi fruit in fall, when the seeds are black and most of the fruit is still firm. Peel before eating.

Carya pecan
JUGLANDACEAE

PECAN

Established pecans seldom need much pruning; just trim out dead or damaged branches as you spot them. Call an arborist to remove large limbs.

Best climate and site Zones 6–9. Plant in full sun in average to rich, well-drained soil.

Height and spread Height 50–150 feet (15–45 m); spread 35–50 feet (10.5–15 m).

Growing guidelines The male (pollen-providing) and female (nut-producing) flowers on pecan trees usually don't open at the same time. For this reason, you usually need to plant another tree that can provide pollen when the main crop tree is ready. Space trees 35 to 50 feet (10.5 to 15 m) apart. Mulch with compost and irrigate during drought.

Pruning Pecans naturally take on a central-leader shape. Prune as needed to remove branches that are competing with the main trunk.

Propagation Propagate by grafting.

Pest and disease control Diseases such as scab can be a problem in humid areas. Pecan weevils lay their eggs in almost-mature nuts. Rake up and destroy damaged nuts.

Harvesting and storage Grafted trees will begin bearing nuts in four to seven years. Tap limbs with a padded stick or pick up fallen nuts. Remove the husks and dry the nuts for several weeks.

Castanea spp.
FAGACEAE

CHESTNUT

American chestnuts (Castanea dentata) have been destroyed by chestnut blight disease. But you can still grow blight-resistant Chinese chestnuts.

Best climate and site Zones 5–9. Plant in full sun in average to rich, well-drained acid soil.

Height and spread Height 40 feet (12 m) or more; spread 20–40 feet (6–12 m).

Growing guidelines Chestnuts produce more reliable crops if cross-pollinated with another tree. They can be spaced up to 100 feet (30 m) apart, but for best nut production, plant them 40 to 80 feet (12 to 14 m) apart. Mulch to eliminate weeds; apply compost or balanced fertilizer in late spring after the danger of frost has passed.

Pruning Train chestnut trees to a central-leader system. Remove dead or damaged limbs as you spot them, along with any low-hanging branches.

Propagation Propagate by seed.

Pest and disease control Grow resistant chestnut species and cultivars to avoid the deadly chestnut blight disease. Chestnut weevil larvae may feed inside nuts and then enter the soil when nuts fall to the ground.

Harvesting and storage Chestnuts bear in three to five years. In fall, the nuts mature and drop to the ground. Pick them up promptly.

Chaenomeles spp.
ROSACEAE

QUINCE, FLOWERING

Flowering quince fruits are yellowish green. Even when ripe, they are rock hard and astringent, but they make good jellies and jams.

Best climate and site Zones 5–8. Full sun, slightly acid soil. Tolerates dry soil.
Height and spread Height 3–10 feet (90–300 cm); similar spread.
Growing guidelines Plant container-grown shrubs any time the ground isn't frozen, or set out bareroot plants in spring or fall, while they are dormant. Space plants 3 to 10 feet (90 to 300 cm) apart. Flowering quince is self-fruitful, so you need only one plant to get fruit.
Pruning Prune in winter, periodically cutting away the oldest stems at ground level to make room for young stems. For drastic renovation, just lop the whole plant almost to the ground. Flowering quince can also withstand being sheared as a hedge, although you'll lose some of the flowers and fruit.
Propagation Seed germinates readily following two to three months of cool, moist conditions. Propagate cultivars by softwood cuttings, layering, or division.
Pest and disease control Minimize leaf spot problems by planting in full sunlight in a breezy location, and pruning for good air circulation.
Harvesting and storage Fruits ripen late in the season, changing color slightly. Store in the refrigerator.

Citrus spp.
RUTACEAE

CITRUS

Citrus trees seldom need much pruning; just trim out crossing branches and head back long shoots in late winter.

Best climate and site Zones 8–10. Frost will damage the fruit of any citrus plants and sometimes the rest of the tree. Plant in full sun to light shade in average to rich, well-drained soil.
Height and spread Height 10–30 feet (3–9 m); similar spread.
Growing guidelines Citrus trees are nearly all self-fertile, so you need to plant only one to get a good harvest. Space large citrus trees at least 25 feet (7.5 m) apart and dwarf trees 10 feet (3 m) apart. Paint the trunk with white latex paint (diluted with an equal amount of water) to prevent sunburn. Keep the soil moist to prevent early fruit drop. Mulch well, and fertilize as needed.
Pruning Remove damaged or diseased branches and upright-growing sprouts that emerge from the roots. Trim back long branches to shape the plant.
Propagation Propagate by bud grafting.
Pest and disease control Keep an eye out for scale, whiteflies, thrips, and mites. Use beneficial insects, traps, and insecticidal soap for prevention.
Harvesting and storage Most citrus trees produce fruit three or four years after planting. The only way to know if fruit is ripe is to taste it.

Ficus carica
MORACEAE

FIG

Figs are productive and generally easy to grow. They are seldom troubled by pests, except for birds. Net the tree to discourage them.

Best climate and site Zones 8–10. Plant in full sun in average well-drained soil. In cool climates figs can be planted in large containers and moved inside for winter.
Height and spread Height 10–25 feet (3–7.5 m); similar spread.
Growing guidelines Select self-pollinating cultivars. Space large cultivars up to 25 feet (7.5 m) apart; smaller trees can go as close as 5 feet (1.5 m) apart. Mulch with compost as needed.
Pruning Thin out excess growth as needed to control plant size and allow for good light penetrations into the center of the plant. You can also train figs as espaliers to grow on walls.
Propagation Propagate by cutting rooted suckers off the roots or taking hardwood cuttings.
Pest and disease control Place netting over trees to discourage birds, or grow green-fruited cultivars, which are less appealing to birds.
Harvesting and storage Fig trees produce their first crop a year after planting. Ripe figs are soft, with a slightly flexible "neck;" sometimes the skin splits. You can keep figs for a few days in the refrigerator, or cut them into sections and dry them.

Fortunella spp.
RUTACEAE

KUMQUAT

Kumquat fruit looks like a miniature orange—about the size of a cherry and either round or elongated. The skin is edible and sweet.

Best climate and site Zones 9–10. Plant in full sun and well-drained, slightly acid soil. Kumquat tolerates winter weather as cold as 18°F (−7.7°C), but without sufficient heat in summer, the fruits are few and of poor quality.

Height and spread Height 8–15 feet (2.4–4.5 m); spread 6–12 feet (1.8–3.6 m).

Growing guidelines Plant container-grown stock anytime, or set out bareroot plants in spring or fall, while they are dormant. Space plants 6 to 12 feet (1.8 to 3.6 m) apart. Kumquats make beautiful potted plants that also fruit reliably. Provide a cool, sunny room in winter and repot every year.

Pruning No pruning other than to shape the plant and thin out crowded branches.

Propagation Kumquats are usually grafted onto trifoliate orange (*Poncirus trifoliata*), which also dwarfs the tree, or onto sour orange (*Citrus aurantium*) or grapefruit rootstock.

Pest and disease control Few problems, but keep an eye out for scale, mealybugs, mites, and whiteflies.

Harvesting and storage Harvest fruits when they are fully colored. They keep well in the refrigerator.

Fragaria spp.
ROSACEAE

STRAWBERRY

You'll avoid most problems by starting with certified disease-free plants of disease-resistant cultivars. Strawberries are self-fruitful.

Best climate and site Zones 3–10. Plant in full sun in average to rich, well-drained soil.

Height and spread Height 10 inches (25 cm); spread 12–24 inches (30–60 cm).

Growing guidelines Add extra organic matter to the soil before planting to make it rich and moist. Space plants 1 to 2 feet (30 to 60 cm) apart and keep the soil moist until the berries are almost ripe.

Pruning Weed, pinch out unwanted runners and mow along the edge of the beds as needed to keep walkways clear.

Propagation Propagate by transplanting rooted runners.

Pest and disease control Pick ripe fruit frequently to keep gray mold (Botrytis blight) at bay. Remove and destroy damaged flowers and fruits as you spot them. If plants wilt, dig them up and destroy them.

Harvesting and storage Pick the berries when they are fully colored, tender, and sweet. Leave the stem on for better storage. Eat the fruit fresh, refrigerate it for a few days or can or freeze as soon as possible after picking.

Comments For the longest possible harvest, grow some of each type (June-bearers, ever-bearers, and day-neutrals).

Fragaria vesca
ROSACEAE

ALPINE STRAWBERRY

The fruits of alpine strawberries may be small, but they offer a big taste. The compact, runnerless plants make a tidy garden edging.

Best climate and site Zones 3–10. Plant in full sun or partial shade, with well-drained, humus-rich soil.

Height and spread Height to 6 inches (15 cm); spread 6–12 inches (15–30 cm).

Growing guidelines Set out container-grown plants anytime the ground isn't frozen, or plant bareroot stock in spring or fall, while the plants are dormant. Set plants 6 to 12 inches (15 to 30 cm) apart, planting so that the ground level is just below the lowest leaves on the crown. Alpine strawberries are self-fruitful, so you can get a harvest from just one plant.

Pruning None.

Propagation To divide old plants, dig them up and cut off young crown pieces (with attached roots) from the outside of the clump. Throw away the old center part and replant the divisions. To grow from seed, scatter the fine seed on the surface of potting soil in a container. Transplant the seedlings when they are large enough to handle.

Pest and disease control Keep birds at bay with netting, or grow white-fruited cultivars, which birds leave alone.

Harvesting and storage Harvest the fruits when they are soft and aromatic. Eat them fresh; they do not store well.

Malus pumila
ROSACEAE

APPLE

To get high yields from your apples, you'll need to grow at least two compatible cultivars so they can cross-pollinate.

Best climate and site Zones 3–9, but pick a cultivar that's suited to your area. Plant in full sun and well-drained soil.
Height and spread Height 8–30 feet (2.4–9 m); similar spread.
Growing guidelines Plant full-sized apple trees 25 to 30 feet (7.5 to 9 m) apart, semidwarfs 12 to 15 feet (3.6 to 4.5 m) apart, and dwarfs 6 to 8 feet (1.8 to 2.4 m) apart. Provide plenty of moisture and nutrients to keep young trees growing quickly. Mulch with compost in spring, and make sure the soil is moist around mature trees when they're in bloom.
Pruning Apple trees grow best when trained into a pyramidal, central leader form, with one trunk and several sets of branches emerging off it. Start pruning young trees just after spring planting (or in the spring following fall planting). Continue thinning and pruning each year until the trees mature.
Propagation Propagate by grafting.
Pest and disease control Some problems that might occur are apple maggots, codling moths, plum curculios, rust, scab, mildew, and fire blight.
Harvesting and storage Apples will start producing fruit in two to five years, depending on the rootstock.

Malus spp.
ROSACEAE

CRAB APPLE

Some crab apples taste delicious out of hand, while others taste good only when cooked with sweetener into jellies. You can eat the whole fruit.

Best climate and site Zones 3–9. Plant in full sun and well-drained soil.
Height and spread Height 8–25 feet (2.4–7.5 m); similar spread.
Growing guidelines Plant container-grown stock anytime the ground isn't frozen, or set out bareroot plants in spring or fall, while they are dormant. Space plants 8 to 25 feet (2.4 to 7.5 m) apart. The plants need cross-pollination, but the pollinator can be an apple or a crab apple.
Pruning Train young plants to a sturdy framework of wide-angled, well-spaced main limbs. Mature plants need little pruning beyond removing water-sprouts and thinning congested growth.
Propagation Graft or bud cultivars onto seedling apple or crab apple rootstocks. Seed, for seedling rootstocks, germinates readily once it has been kept cool and moist for two to three months.
Pest and disease control Crab apples can have the same pest and disease problems as apples but are usually less troubled by them.
Harvesting and storage Pick fruits when they are fully colored and come off the plant easily. Store in the refrigerator in a plastic bag with a few holes in it.

Morus spp.
MORACEAE

MULBERRY

Mulberry trees produce black, red, or white blackberry-shaped fruits. Flavor ranges from sweet with a refreshing tang to purely sweet.

Best climate and site Zones 5–10. Plant in full sun and average, well-drained soil.
Height and spread Height 15–30 feet (4.5–9 m); spread 10–20 feet (3–6 m).
Growing guidelines Plant container-grown stock anytime the ground isn't frozen, or set out bareroot plants in spring or fall, while they are dormant. Space plants 10 to 30 feet (3 to 9 m) apart. Do not plant mulberries where falling fruits will cause problems with staining. Cultivars selected for fruit production generally do not need cross-pollination.
Pruning No regular pruning is necessary.
Propagation Russian mulberry (M. *alba* 'Tartarica') makes a good rootstock for most other mulberries. Softwood or hardwood cuttings of most species usually root readily. With hardwood cuttings, either split the lower end or take a small "heel" of two-year-old wood along with the one-year-old wood used for the cutting.
Pest and disease control Control scale insects with dormant oil, and handle dieback by cutting off infected portions.
Harvesting and storage To harvest in quantity, spread a clean sheet under the tree and shake the branches. Ripe fruits do not keep well fresh but can be dried.

Prunus amygdalus
ROSACEAE

ALMOND

Most almonds need cross-pollination to set their crop; check catalog descriptions to make sure you get the right companions.

Best climate and site Zones 6–9. Grow in full sun in average to fertile, well-drained soil.

Height and spread Height 15–30 feet (4.5–9 m); similar spread.

Growing guidelines Most almonds require another tree to pollinate them. Plant trees 25 feet (7.5 m) apart and mulch with compost each spring. Water plants regularly when the weather is hot.

Pruning Train almonds into an open-center form, but as you prune each year, do more heading and less thinning than you would for trees such as peaches, to develop a thick network of branches and, consequently, to get more nuts.

Propagation Propagate by grafting.

Pest and disease control Unfortunately, disease resistance is minimal in almonds so they're seldom grown outside a dry climate. Keep mulch away from the trunk to discourage rodent activity. Pick up all fallen nuts and destroy the bad ones to reduce problems with navel orangeworm—white, brown-headed caterpillars that feed on the nut meat.

Harvesting and storage Most almond trees begin to produce nuts in three to four years. Use a padded stick to knock the nuts from the tree.

Prunus avium
ROSACEAE

CHERRY

Sweet cherries tend to need a compatible partner for cross-pollination. Sour cherries are self-fertile, so you can get a harvest from just one tree.

Best climate and site Zones 4–9. Plant in full sun in average to poor, well-drained soil. Cherries prefer arid climates.

Height and spread Height 15–30 feet (4.5–9 m); similar spread.

Growing guidelines Space standard sweet cherry trees 20 to 30 feet (6 to 9m) apart, sour cherries 20 feet (6 m) apart, and dwarf cherries 10 feet (3 m) apart. Mulch with compost in early spring. In cooler climates, plant with a northern exposure away from valleys to protect cherry flowers from frost.

Pruning Train naturally spreading cherry trees to an open-center form; for more upright growing trees, prune to a central leader form. See your nursery for more specific information.

Propagation Propagate by grafting.

Pest and disease control The major problem with cherry trees is birds. Be prepared to net the trees once the fruit starts to ripen to keep the birds away. Try to grow the cultivars that are resistant to the diseases most prevalent in your area.

Harvesting and storage Cherries begin to bear fruit three to seven years after planting. If the weather is dry, let cherries ripen on the trees for best flavor. They should be fairly soft and very sweet.

Prunus armeniaca
ROSACEAE

APRICOT

Ripe apricots are so soft that they don't ship well. The way to enjoy them at their peak is to grow your own.

Best climate and site Zones 5–9. Plant in full sun in average to poor, well-drained soil. Early opening flowers should be sheltered from frost.

Height and spread Height 8–24 feet (2.4–7.2 m); spread 16–24 feet (4.8–7.2 m).

Growing guidelines Many apricots are self-fertile and will produce some fruit if planted alone. But most will produce more abundant yields with a second cultivar for cross-pollination. Plant full-sized trees 25 feet (7.5 m) apart and dwarf trees 12 to 15 feet (3.6 to 4.5 m) apart. Mulch with compost in spring and fertilize as needed.

Pruning Some cultivars will fruit only every other year unless the fruits are thinned out to leave them 2 inches (5 cm) apart. Apricot trees should be pruned using the open-center system where the leader branch is removed and the tree is pruned to an open vase shape.

Propagation Propagate by bud grafting.

Pest and disease control Susceptible to Eutypa dieback, a disease that attacks through pruning cuts. Treat scale, mite, and aphid infestations with oil sprays.

Harvesting and storage Pluck the fruits when they're soft and sweet.

Prunus persica
ROSAECEAE

PEACH AND NECTARINE

Both peaches and nectarines are attractive as fan-shaped espaliers. Growing them on a wall provides extra warmth.

Best climate and site Zones 5–9. Plant in full sun in average to poor, well-drained soil.
Height and spread Height 8–15 feet (2.4–4.5 m); spread 10–20 feet (3–6 m).
Growing guidelines Most peaches and nectarines are self-pollinating, so you can get a full crop from just one tree. Fertilize with compost in early spring and again with a balanced organic fertilizer when the fruit first forms. Spray the leaves with liquid kelp every three to four weeks during the growing season.
Pruning Train peach trees to an open-center form. Thin young trees lightly in summer to remove unneeded branches. When the tree is mature, cut half the older branches back by about half of their total length during the dormant season so they'll resprout productive new wood.
Propagation Propagate by bud grafting.
Pest and disease control If you live in an area that's prone to peach tree diseases, start with disease-resistant cultivars. Otherwise you may have to spray to control diseases.
Harvesting and storage Peach and nectarine trees begin producing fruit two to four years after planting. Harvest when the fruit is well colored and sweet.

Pyrus communis
ROSACEAE

PEAR

Most pears require cross-pollination to set fruit, so you'll need to plant at least one compatible companion to get a good crop.

Best climate and site Zones 4–9. Plant in full sun in average to poor, well-drained soil.
Height and spread Height 8–20 feet (2.4–6 m); similar spread.
Growing guidelines Space full-sized trees 15 to 20 feet (4.5 to 6 m) apart and dwarfs 8 to 12 feet (2.4 to 3.6 m) apart. Water and mulch as necessary to keep the soil moist and prevent damage to foliage and fruit. Mulch with compost in spring.
Pruning Use the central leader system to shape upright-growing European pears. Heavy-bearing trees will need some fruit thinning. In June, remove the smaller fruit, leaving one or two of the best fruit per cluster.
Propagation Propagate by grafting.
Pest and disease control Keep an eye out for pear psyllas, tiny insects that suck sap from tender shoot tips and fruit, and spread diseases. During the growing season, use insecticidal soap or horticultural oil sprays to control psyllas. Select pear cultivars that are resistant to fire blight.
Harvesting and storage Pear trees generally begin to produce fruit three to five years after planting. Pick European pears when they are mature but not ripe.

Prunus domestica
ROSACEAE

PLUM

'Santa Rosa' is a Japanese plum (P. salicina) with large, high-quality fruit. It yields best when planted with other Japanese plums.

Best climate and site Zones 4–10. Plant in full sun in average to rich soil.
Height and spread Height 8–20 feet (2.4–6 m); similar spread.
Growing guidelines Many European plums and damson plums will self-pollinate, so one tree is enough. But if you plant two compatible cultivars they may set more fruit. Space full-sized plum trees 20 to 25 feet (6 to 7.5 m) apart and dwarf trees 8 to 12 feet (2.4 to 3.6 m) apart. Mulch with compost in spring and keep the soil moist through the growing season. Apply a complete fertilizer when the petals fall.
Pruning Train upright-growing cultivars to a central leader. Open-center training works better for more spreading plums, including most Japanese types. Thin the fruit on trees that are overburdened.
Propagation Propagate by bud grafting.
Pest and disease control Plums are susceptible to black knot, a fungus that causes dark swellings on tree limbs. If black knot was a problem the previous year, spray with lime-sulfur when the buds swell, then reapply a week later.
Harvesting and storage Plum trees generally begin to bear three to four years after planting. Pick when soft and sweet.

Ribes spp.
GROSSULARIACEAE

CURRANT AND GOOSEBERRY

The tart berries of currants are excellent for jams or juice. Plant two or more cultivars if possible; cross-pollination will increase yields.

Best climate and site Zones 3–7. Plant in full sun to light shade in average soil.
Height and spread Height 3–7 feet (0.9–2.1 m); similar spread.
Growing guidelines Most currants and gooseberries are self-pollinating, however, if interplanted with two or three other culivars they'll produce higher yields. Space the plants 6 feet (1.8 m) apart and mulch well. Add compost and a potassium-rich fertilizer in early spring. Water regularly in dry weather.
Pruning At planting time, select one branch to be the main trunk and remove all others. Each winter, remove all shoots that are over three years old (or over two years old on black currants); then remove all but six of the remaining shoots.
Propagation By hardwood cuttings.
Pest and disease control Powdery mildew can devastate gooseberries, and sulfur sprays are not always an effective treatment. Buy mildew-resistant cultivars. Mildew resistance is also available in many currant cultivars.
Harvesting and storage For cooking or making jelly, pick currants and gooseberries when they are not quite ripe. For fresh eating, let them ripen on the bush until they taste right to you.

Rubus idaeus
ROSACEAE

RASPBERRY

If birds are beating you to your berries, cover the plants with netting. Roll back the cover as needed to harvest.

Best climate and site Zones 3–9. Plant in full sun in average to poor soil.
Height and spread Height 4–6 feet (1.2–1.8m); spread 2–4 feet (0.6–1.2 m).
Growing guidelines Buy bareroot plants if possible and plant them 2 feet (60 cm) apart in a row. They'll fill in within a year or two. Apply compost and a little balanced organic fertilizer in late winter, if needed, for good growth. Mulch to discourage weeds and keep the soil evenly moist; water during dry spells.
Pruning Cut off all the old canes at ground level when they have finished fruiting. Leave the new current-season canes to produce berries next year.
Propagation Propagate by division or layering, but only if you are sure your plants are healthy.
Pest and disease control Buy only certified disease-free plants. Several fungal diseases may attack raspberries: powdery mildew, anthracnose, and cane blight. If these diseases were a problem the previous year, spray with lime-sulfur when the buds begin to turn green. Remove and destroy any plant that is affected with any other diseases.
Harvesting and storage Harvest berries when they're sweet and ripe.

Rubus spp.
ROSACEAE

BLACKBERRY

Blackerrries are at their best flavor when the fruits turn dark and lose some of their glossiness. Many thornless blackberry cultivars need support.

Best climate and site Zones 5–9. Plant in full sun in average to rich soil.
Height and spread Height 4–7 feet (1.2–2.1 m); spread 3–6 feet (0.9–1.8 m).
Growing guidelines Buy blackberries as bareroot plants, or as tissue-cultured plantlets. They need plenty of space and good air circulation. Plant thorny cultivars 3 to 4 feet (90 to 120 cm) apart and thornless cultivars 4 to 6 feet (1.2 to 1.8 m) apart. Make paths between the rows for good sun exposure and adequate air circulation. Keep the soil evenly moist and mulch with compost in early spring.
Pruning Cut fruit-bearing canes to the ground right after harvest. In early spring, thin to leave seven strong canes per plant. Shorten side branches to about 1 foot (30 cm) long. For maximum yields, train blackberries to a trellis.
Propagation By division or layering.
Pest and disease control Watch for distorted growth, sterile canes, or orange-spotted leaves that drop early. These are all symptoms of incurable viral or orange rust diseases. Remove infected plants.
Harvesting and storage Blackberries are ready when they turn entirely black and get a little dull, soft, and sweet. Eat them right away or freeze them.

Vaccinium spp.
ERICACEAE

BLUEBERRY

Some blueberries need cross-pollination, so make sure you check catalog descriptions to get the appropriate partners.

Best climate and site Zones 3–9. Plant in full sun in average to rich, well-drained soil.

Height and spread Height 2–15 feet (0.6–4.9 m); spread 3–10 feet (0.9–3 m).

Growing guidelines Depending on whether you're growing lowbush, highbush, midhigh, or rabbiteye blueberries, plant them from 2 to 8 feet (0.6 to 2.5 m) apart. Apply a thick layer of mulch to keep the soil evenly moist. Add compost each spring.

Pruning Pinch off all the flowers on a young blueberry bush the first year after planting so the bush will grow strong. The next year you'll have to remove only dead or damaged wood. Let plenty of sun and air penetrate the entire plant.

Propagation Propagate by hardwood or softwood cuttings, or by division, depending on cultivar.

Pest and disease control If stems begin to die back or show unusual cankers or cracks, cut them back to healthy tissues. Use sticky red balls (such as apple maggot traps) to catch blueberry maggots before they can tunnel into ripening berries.

Harvesting and storage Harvest after the berries turn blue. Don't pick underripe berries; they won't ripen.

Vaccinium macrocarpon
ERICACEAE

CRANBERRY

Cranberries grow as low, creeping bushes. Their white flowers are followed by hard, red berries, each about the size of a thumbnail.

Best climate and site Zones 2–6. Cranberries thrive in sun and moist, well-drained, humus-rich soil with a very acid pH (4.0–5.5). The plants do not tolerate dry soil, but they can withstand flooding in cold weather.

Height and spread Height to 1 foot (30 cm); spread unlimited.

Growing guidelines Plant in spring or fall where winters are mild or in spring where winters are severe. Space plants 1 to 2 feet (30 to 60 cm) apart. Mix plenty of acid peat into the soil before planting. Mulch with sawdust or sand; renew the mulch periodically.

Pruning Cut away some of the sprawling stems and some of the upright fruiting stems when they become overcrowded.

Propagation Summer stem cuttings root readily. Where winters are mild, set rooted cuttings outdoors in fall; otherwise, set them out as early as possible in spring.

Pest and disease control No problems.

Harvesting and storage Pick berries in fall, after they are fully colored. Cranberries will keep for two to four months at high humidity and temperatures just above freezing.

Vitis spp.
VITACEAE

GRAPE

Growing clusters tend to ripen unevenly; prevent this by thinning in early summer, when fruits are small and hard.

Best climate and site Zones 4–10. Plant in full sun in average to rich soil.

Height and spread Height 4–6 feet (1.2–1.8 m); spread 8–15 feet (2.4–4.5 m).

Growing guidelines Start with one-year-old plants that are virus-indexed and certified disease-free. Before planting set up a support system for the vines to cling to. After planting, let the grapevine grow untrained for a year to develop a strong set of roots. Pinch off grape flowers during that year. Keep the soil moist and mulch well. Feed with compost in spring.

Pruning Train the vines over wire strung between posts. In late winter, cut the vine back to a stump with two buds. When the buds start growing, leave the stronger shoot and remove the other one.

Propagation Propagate by cuttings, grafting or, for some varieties, layering.

Pest and disease control Black rot causes reddish brown leaf spots and hard, shriveled fruit. Botrytis bunch rot causes a fluffy gray-brown coating on the fruit. Anthracnose infection produces sunken, dark-ringed spots on leaves and fruit. Remove and destroy all infected fruit and leaves.

Harvesting and storage Harvest the clusters by clipping them off the vine.

Anthurium spp.
ARACEAE

FLAMINGO FLOWERS

The lacquered-looking, puckered blooms of flamingo flowers often fool people into thinking they must be artificial. Each flower can last two to three months.

Description This upright, many-stemmed plant can grow to 20 inches (50 cm) tall, with long, graceful, leathery, green leaves. The flowers can be 3–6 inches (7.5–15 cm) long and range in color from deep red to pink, salmon, white, and speckled. Miniature types are available.
Light needs Medium indirect light.
Best temperatures Warm year-round. Ideal conditions are 85°F (29°C) days and 65°F (18°C) nights. To encourage plants to bloom, reduce the nighttime temperature to 60°F (16°C) for six weeks.
Water and humidity needs Provide constant moisture and high humidity while plants are actively growing. Let the soil dry out a bit between waterings in winter, but never allow it to get bone dry.
Growing guidelines Grow in a mix of equal parts potting soil and sphagnum moss. Repot plants in spring if needed. Fertilize with an all-purpose, organic fertilizer twice a month from early spring to early fall; do not fertilize in winter.
Common problems Flamingo flower does not appreciate cold temperatures or hard water. Keep the temperature at least 60°F (16°C).
Propagation Divide in spring or summer, or grow new plants from seed.

Begonia spp.
BEGONIACEAE

FLOWERING BEGONIAS

The thousands of begonia hybrids and species provide a wealth of houseplant choices. Those grown for flowers often have beautiful foliage too.

Other common names Angelwing (cane), Reiger, and wax begonias.
Description Angelwing begonias can grow to 6 feet (1.8 m) tall, with showy flower clusters and relatively narrow, pointed leaves. Reiger begonias offer outstanding huge flowers and medium to dark green leaves on 12–18-inch (30–45-cm) stems. Wax begonias are compact, 6–12-inch (15–30-cm) plants with succulent stems and thick, waxy leaves. The white, pink, or red single or double flowers form in small clusters.
Light needs Medium; protect from hot summer sun.
Best temperatures Average room temperature; prefers at least 60°F (16°C).
Water and humidity needs Let dry slightly between waterings.
Growing guidelines Grow in humus-rich, soil-less mix. Repot in spring as needed. Fertilize lightly twice a month from spring through fall. Pinch off the stem tips every month or so to encourage branching. To reflower, Reiger begonias need a three-month, cool, dry rest period after bloom.
Common problems Lower leaves may drop if plants get too little or too much water; overwatering can also lead to rot.
Propagation By tip cuttings or seed.

Chrysanthemum spp.
COMPOSITAE

CHRYSANTHEMUMS

Potted chrysanthemums provide a magnificent, if brief, show. Plant spring-blooming kinds outdoors for another set of flowers before frost.

Other common names Florist's chrysanthemum.
Description These 15-inch (37.5-cm) tall, bushy plants come in a wide array of flower colors and shapes—often daisy-like, button, or pompon—and may bloom for two to three weeks.
Light needs Medium, indirect light.
Best temperatures Flowers last longest in cool 55°F (13°C) temperatures.
Water and humidity needs Water frequently to keep the soil evenly moist.
Growing guidelines Grow in well-drained, all-purpose mix. Discard the fall-flowering potted mums after bloom. To get a late-season garden display from spring bloomers, cut them back by one-half to two-thirds after bloom and plant them in the ground. Pinch off the shoot tips every two weeks until mid-July, then stop pinching to allow flower buds to form. Plants may or may not live through the winter.
Common problems Aphids may feed on leaves, shoots, and buds, causing distorted growth. Knock them off with a strong spray of water, or spray with insecticidal soap, superior oil, or neem.
Propagation Take tip cuttings in spring.

Clivia miniata
AMARYLLIDACEAE

CLIVIA

Clusters of spectacular, trumpet-shaped blooms and handsome, glossy leaves make this flowering houseplant a favorite of many indoor gardeners. Clivias may take several years to flower.

Description The strap-like, leathery, green leaves of clivia emerge from a bulbous base. Mature plants can reach 2 feet (60 cm) tall and 3 feet (90 cm) wide. Clusters of winter blooms are usually orange-red with yellow interiors.
Light needs Medium to high indirect light is best.
Best temperatures Average room temperature in spring and summer; much cooler in fall and winter.
Water and humidity needs Keep the soil evenly moist in spring and summer; allow it to dry a bit between waterings in fall and winter.
Growing guidelines Start clivias in small clay pots. Use a blend of three parts all-purpose potting mix and one part sand, with a handful or two of bonemeal. Clivias seem to grow best when crowded, so leave them in their pot for about three years before repotting them in late winter. Feed with liquid fertilizer twice a month during spring and summer.
Common problems Mealybugs produce cottony white clusters on leaves. Knock them off with a strong spray of water.
Propagation Divide when you repot them, or remove offsets in late winter.

Cyclamen persicum
PRIMULACEAE

FLORIST'S CYCLAMEN

The butterfly-like blooms of florist's cyclamen flutter gracefully over beautiful silver-marked leaves. The flowers come in pink, red, lavender, and white.

Description Florist's cyclamen forms compact, 12-inch (30-cm) tall clumps of heart-shaped leaves that grow from an underground tuber. The single-stemmed flowers emerge from October to April.
Light needs High indirect light while in bloom; medium light after bloom.
Best temperatures During the day, florist's cyclamen prefers 60°–72°F (16°–22°C); at night, keep temperatures at 40°–60°F (4.5°–16°C).
Water and humidity needs Keep the soil evenly moist while plant is blooming.
Growing guidelines Grow in all-purpose, soil-based mix. Repot crowded plants to a slightly larger container only when nights are above 55°F (13°C). Fertilize twice a month from fall to early spring. Plants need a cool, dry rest period in the summer to rebloom. Put them outdoors in the shade and turn the pots on their side; water occasionally to keep them barely moist until new leaves begin to appear.
Common problems Spider mites and cyclamen mites can cause distorted growth. Discard infested plants.
Propagation Sow seed in September and keep it dark until seedlings appear. Put seedlings in a cool, bright spot for the winter; repot them in May.

Euphorbia pulcherrima
EUPHORBIACEAE

POINSETTIA

This Mexican native now reigns as the quintessential winter holiday plant. Its showy blooms last for months, with petal-like bracts in red, pink, yellow, or cream.

Description These shrubby plants usually grow to about 2 feet (60 cm) tall in containers. The sturdy stems carry broad, green leaves up to 7 inches (17.5 cm) long. In winter, the stems are tipped with tiny flowers surrounded by leafy bracts.
Light needs High light.
Best temperatures Cool conditions, with days not over 70°F (21°C) and nights around 55°F (13°C).
Water and humidity needs Allow to dry between waterings.
Growing guidelines Grow in well-drained, all-purpose mix. If you want it to bloom again, repot it and cut the stems back to 6 inches (15 cm). Water as needed and fertilize weekly from Labor Day to Thanksgiving. Give the plant 14 hours of total darkness at night for eight weeks beginning in mid-September, with temperatures of 75°F (24°C) during the day and 60°F (16°C) at night. Don't fertilize while the plant is flowering.
Common problems Leaves will drop due to low light, drafts, or overwatering.
Propagation Take tip cuttings in late spring and early summer; allow to dry overnight before rooting in moist sand.

Hippeastrum hybrids
AMARYLLIDACEAE

AMARYLLIS

Spectacular and astonishingly easy to bring into bloom, amaryllis makes a perfect winter gift plant. Keep the plant cool when it is in bloom so the flowers last longer.

Description The large bulb of amaryllis sends up a 2-foot (60-cm) tall bloom stalk, along with or slightly before the long strap-like leaves. One to ten trumpet-shaped, single or double flowers bloom atop the stalk for up to a month.

Light needs Medium light when planted; increase to a half-day of sun when the flower stalk is 6 inches (15 cm) tall.

Best temperatures Warm days—70°F (21°C)—and 60°F (16°C) nights.

Water and humidity needs Moisten the soil thoroughly at planting time, then wait until growth starts before watering again. Keep the soil evenly moist while the plant is actively growing.

Growing guidelines Position the bulb in well-drained potting mix so the top quarter is sticking out of the soil. Choose a pot that is 1 inch (2.5 cm) wider than the bulb. Feed monthly while the plant is growing; stop fertilizing and watering when the leaves turn yellow. Allow the bulb to rest for a month, then repot or replace the top inch of potting soil with fresh mix and 1 teaspoon of bonemeal.

Common problems Lots of leaves but no flowers usually means the pot is too large.

Propagation Remove and replant offsets.

Hoya carnosa
ASCLEPIADACEAE

WAX VINE

Wax vine's long stems can climb up trellises or trail around window frames. This milkweed relative produces clusters of very fragrant, starry blooms from May to September.

Other common names Honey plant, porcelain flower.

Description Wax vine has succulent, 3-inch (7.5-cm), silvery green leaves atop trailing vines that climb to 20 feet (6 m). Clusters of small, pinkish, red-centered flowers dangle from the stems in summer.

Light needs High light; avoid direct, midday sun.

Best temperatures Intermediate to warm conditions not below 50°F (10°C).

Water and humidity needs Let the soil dry between waterings. In winter, reduce water drastically, just enough to prevent shriveling. Do not use cold water.

Growing guidelines Grow in a peat-moss-based mix in a pot, or in a hanging basket lined with sphagnum moss. Provide potted plants with a trellis or wire hoop; wind the stems counterclockwise around the support. Fertilize once in spring with an all-purpose fertilizer. Once buds form, avoid moving the vine. Wax vine must be 3 feet (90 cm) long to bloom, so avoid pruning.

Common problems White, cottony growths are signs of mealybugs. Wash them off with a strong spray of water.

Propagation Take cuttings in spring.

Kalanchoe blossfeldiana
CRASSULACEAE

KALANCHOE

This Madagascar native has beautiful glossy foliage and huge clusters of winter flowers held high above the leaves. Remove the stalks when the flowers fade.

Other common names Flaming Katy.

Description Kalanchoe forms clumps of succulent, 3-inch (7.5-cm), deep green leaves. Plants bloom for two to three months with clusters of red, pink, yellow, orange, or white flowers on 12-inch (30-cm) stems.

Light needs High, indirect light.

Best temperatures Provide cool conditions (50°–60°F [10°–16°C]) in fall while buds are forming, then move to average room temperature.

Water and humidity needs Let the soil dry between waterings. Do not overwater.

Growing guidelines Grow kalanchoe in all-purpose potting mix with added sand. Fertilize with fish emulsion once a month from when bloom ends until late summer. Put the plant outdoors for the summer, then give it a cool, drier rest period in fall to encourage bud formation.

Common problems Aphids and mealybugs may feed on leaves and stems. Knock the pests off with a strong spray of water, or spray the plant with insecticidal soap or neem.

Propagation Take stem cuttings in summer, or grow plants from seed.

Various genera
ORCHIDACEAE

ORCHIDS

Some 25,000 species and 100,000 hybrids make this the largest flowering plant group on Earth, with something for every grower.

Description Most orchids are tropical epiphytes (plants that grow on the sides of trees instead of in the ground). Indoor orchids usually bloom in winter.

Light needs Low to high light, depending on the type of orchid.

Best temperatures Cool to warm conditions, depending on the type of orchid. A 10°–15°F (6°–9°C) temperature drop at night is essential, especially in fall, to set buds.

Water and humidity needs Allow pots to dry between waterings; overwatering is deadly. Extra humidity results in better growth and bloom.

Growing guidelines Grow in small pots in a well-drained epiphytic mix of three-quarters fir bark chips to one-quarter perlite. Repot after bloom with fresh mix to maintain good drainage. Fertilize twice a month with a weak solution of fish emulsion, manure tea, or all-purpose fertilizer.

Common problems Aphids, mealybugs, and scale may feed on orchid plants; treat infected parts with insecticidal soap, superior oil, or neem.

Propagation Divide sympodial types, leaving three stems on each. Remove rooted offshoots from monopodial types.

Saintpaulia hybrids
GESNERIACEAE

AFRICAN VIOLETS

The colorful blooms and compact habit of African violets make them the most popular of all flowering houseplants. Grow them on windowsills or under fluorescent lights.

Description African violets have velvety, green or variegated, fleshy leaves. Single or double blooms to 2 inches (5 cm) wide appear just above the leaves on and off year-round. The blooms can be blue, purple, pink, red, white, or green; some are multicolored or marked with a white edge or star.

Light needs Medium to high indirect light is best.

Best temperatures Warm conditions, with a temperature around 65°F (18°C).

Water and humidity needs Allow the soil to dry slightly between waterings. Try to avoid wetting the leaves.

Growing guidelines Grow in soil-based African violet mix in shallow pots, repotting yearly. Fertilize every two weeks in spring and summer with quarter-strength African violet-type fertilizer.

Common problems Wash off aphids and mealybugs with tepid water, or dab them with a cotton swab soaked in witch hazel. A lack of flowers may be caused by not enough light, the temperature being too high, or the soil too dry. Cold water can cause spots on leaves.

Propagation Take leaf cuttings and replant with the stem in a moist medium.

Schlumbergera bridgesii
CACTACEAE

CHRISTMAS CACTUS

The showy flowers and distinctive, segmented, trailing stems make Christmas cactus an attractive choice for hanging baskets. Put plants outdoors for the summer.

Description This shrubby, 12-inch (30-cm) cactus has arching, flat-jointed, thornless green leaves and stems. It blooms abundantly in winter with starry, 3-inch (7.5-cm) flowers. Red is a traditional favorite, although you can also find pink, white, or yellow flowers.

Light needs Medium to high, indirect light suits the plant best.

Best temperatures Average room temperature for most of the year; provide 55°F (13°C) nights in fall to set buds.

Water and humidity needs Keep the soil evenly moist most of the year, but reduce watering in fall until buds form.

Growing guidelines Grow in small pots with a well-drained mixture of soil, sand, peat moss, and compost. Repot with fresh mix in spring. Bring indoors before frost in fall, and set in a cool dark room to promote bud formation.

Common problems Control aphids by knocking them off with a strong spray of water or insecticidal soap. Too much or too little water, or water that is too cold can cause leaves to drop. Leaves may turn yellow if the light is too bright.

Propagation Take tip cuttings at any time of the year.

Sinningia hybrids
GESNERIACEAE

GLOXINIAS

Gloxinias' velvety leaves make a beautiful background for the showy blooms. The plants grow from firm, rounded tubers and thrive in the same conditions as African violets.

Description The trumpet-shaped, wavy-edged flowers range from reds, pinks, and white to purples and blues. They bloom primarily in summer but may flower year-round.

Light needs Medium to high, diffused light. Gloxinias also grow well under fluorescent light.

Best temperatures Warm conditions, around 65°–70°F (18°–21°C); cooler dormancy after bloom.

Water and humidity needs Keep the soil evenly moist and use tepid water. Provide high humidity.

Growing guidelines Pot in African violet mix, positioning tubers with the cupped side up. Repot each year when new growth begins. Fertilize during growth with African violet-type fertilizer. If the leaves start to die down after bloom, give plants a rest period; cut down on watering and reduce temperatures to 50°–60°F (10°–16°C).

Common problems Cold water can stain leaves. If the leaf edges curl under, the plant isn't getting enough light.

Propagation Take leaf cuttings and replant the leaf with its stem in a moist but loose medium.

Streptocarpus
GESNERIACEAE

CAPE PRIMROSE

These African violet relatives boast a long period of colorful bloom; try them in a north window or under fluorescent lights. Pinch off faded flowers before the seedpods form.

Description The compact, hairy-leaved rosettes of cape primrose grow up to 12 inches (30 cm) tall. They freely produce 2-inch (5-cm) wide trumpets of red, pink, blue, or purple blooms atop 6-inch (15-cm) stalks nearly all year.

Light needs Medium, indirect light.

Best temperatures Average indoor conditions, with a slight drop at night.

Water and humidity needs Keep the soil moist but not soggy. After bloom, allow it to dry somewhat between waterings.

Growing guidelines Grow in shallow pots in African violet mix, repotting only when absolutely necessary. Fertilize twice a month with African violet fertilizer, or add bonemeal or aged manure to the growing mix when you repot. Provide a drier rest period after bloom.

Common problems Limp stems and leaves indicate too little light; wilted, yellowed leaves indicate root rot from overwatering; plants may recover if you let the soil dry out between waterings.

Propagation Take leaf cuttings by slicing a leaf into three or four parts crossways and replanting them upright in a moist growing medium. You can also divide plants in spring.

Aglaeonema spp.
ARACEAE

CHINESE EVERGREENS

Chinese evergreen offers gorgeous foliage marked with a mixture of green, pewter, silver, cream, and white; some kinds may even show a bit of pink. Few houseplants adapt as well to a dark corner.

Description These shrubby, many-stemmed plants can reach 3 feet (90 cm) tall. They are notable for their patterned, elliptic foliage, which grows up to 12 inches (30 cm) long and 4 inches (10 cm) wide.

Light needs Low (even dark).

Best temperatures Warm, 65°F (18°C) nights to 85°F (29°C) days.

Water and humidity needs Keep just moist. Use unchlorinated water, allowing tap water to stand overnight before use for best results.

Growing guidelines Pot in a peat-based mix, repotting when the plant looks tired. Fertilize three times a year, or less if in low light. Putting the plant out in the rain will clean leaves.

Common problems Brown leaf edges indicate dry air, bad drainage, or too many minerals or salts from tap water. Leaf variegation fades in too much light. Mealybugs hide at leaf bases. Wash off with a sharp stream of water or drench with insecticidal soap or horticultural oil or neem.

Propagation Take stem cuttings, divide the stalks, or air layer at any time.

Aphelandra squarossa
ACANTHACEAE

ZEBRA PLANT

For dramatic foliage, it's hard to beat the highly striped leaves of zebra plant. It can also produce bright yellow flowers in late summer and fall.

Other common names Saffron spike.
Description Zebra plant produces oval, glossy, green leaves with cream-colored veins. Individual leaves can reach 1 foot (30 cm) long. The shrubby plants grow to 3 feet (90 cm) tall, although compact cultivars are more popular.
Light needs High, indirect light.
Best temperatures Warm conditions, at least 65°F (18°C).
Water and humidity needs Provide abundant water in spring through fall; allow to dry somewhat during winter rest. Provide high humidity.
Growing guidelines Grow zebra plant in all-purpose potting mix, and fertilize twice a month from spring through fall. After flowering, cut the stem back drastically to just above the lowest node (where the lowest pair of leaves join the stem). Pinch out the tips of new growth when it reaches 6 inches (15 cm).
Common problems Spider mites can cause stippling on leaves; raise the humidity and spray the plant with superior oil. Knock mealybugs off with a strong spray of water. It is normal for leaves to fall after the plant blooms.
Propagation Take tip cuttings in late winter to early summer.

Araucaria heterophylla
ARAUCARIACEAE

NORFOLK ISLAND PINE

Norfolk Island pine's graceful habit makes it a winning houseplant. Purchase full, dense plants, since sparse-looking specimens will stay that way when you get them home.

Description This pyramidal, tiered tree has bright green, soft needles. It can grow up to 200 feet (60 m) tall in nature. Fortunately for indoor gardeners, it usually only reaches about 7 feet (2.1 m) tall as a houseplant. The branches have resinous sap.
Light needs High light, with full sun, is best, but plants can live with less.
Best temperatures Ideal conditions are 70°F (21°C) during the day and 50°–55°F (10°–13°C) at night (particularly in winter). Norfolk Island pine can, however, adapt to a range of temperatures from 45°–85°F (7°–29°C).
Water and humidity needs Keep evenly moist at all times.
Growing guidelines Grow Norfolk Island pine in African violet mix. Repot every three years. Fertilize four times a year.
Common problems Needles drop if the air is too hot and dry; move the plant to a cooler spot and increase the humidity. Lower branches fall as the plant ages.
Propagation Buy new plants or start them from seed. Taking cuttings will ruin the shape of your plant.
Comments Use Norfolk Island pine as a small Christmas tree.

Asparagus densiflorus
LILIACEAE

ASPARAGUS FERN

Show off asparagus fern's arching stems by displaying the plant in a hanging basket. The needlelike leaves are actually flattened stems; they are soft when young.

Other common names Emerald feather.
Description This plant has delicate, feathery, arching, green plumes on distinctive spiny stems to 3 feet (90 cm) long. It has tiny, pink flowers, followed by small berries that turn successively from white to green to red to black.
Light needs High, indirect light.
Best temperatures Average to cool conditions (55°–70°F [13°–21°C]).
Water and humidity needs Keep the soil just moist.
Growing guidelines Grow asparagus fern in a humus-rich mix. Fertilize four times a year. Repot whenever the fast-growing roots start creeping out of the pot.
Common problems Yellowed foliage means too much light or a lack of nitrogen; reduce the light slightly and fertilize with fish emulsion. Brittle stems and dropping leaves usually indicate that the plant has outgrown its pot; move the plant to a larger pot with fresh mix.
Propagation Divide large plants by cutting all the stems down to the soil, then slicing the root ball into 4-inch (10-cm) wide wedges; plant the wedges in individual pots. You can also grow asparagus ferns from seed.

Aspidistra elatior
LILIACEAE

CAST-IRON PLANT

Known since the Victorian age, this Chinese native is renowned for its "cast-iron" constitution. It's suitable for even the most black-thumbed gardener.

Other common names Barbershop plant.
Description Usually between 18 and 24 inches (45 and 60 cm) tall, cast-iron plant has an upright growth habit. Its leaves grow to 30 inches (75 cm) long and 4 inches (10 cm) wide. The foliage is generally dark green, although you can occasionally find variegated forms. Small, bell-shaped, purple blooms may form at the base of the plant.
Light needs Tolerates low light, even very dim corners.
Best temperatures Average room temperature during the day; around 50°F (10°C) at night.
Water and humidity needs Keep evenly moist at all times.
Growing guidelines Repot in all-purpose potting mix only every five years. Fertilize once in spring (and again in fall if the plant gets medium light).
Common problems Spider mites occasionally attack the foliage. Control these pests by washing the leaves monthly with plain water or with a solution of insecticidal soap.
Propagation Divide the roots in early spring and replant in fresh mix; plant two or three pieces together in each pot.

Beaucarnea recurvata
AGAVACEAE

PONYTAIL PALM

Native to the deserts of Mexico, ponytail palm has a thick, swollen base that can store up to a year's supply of water. It's a good choice if you tend to forget to water regularly!

Other common names Elephant foot palm.
Description When young, ponytail palm is just a grassy clump of narrow leaves growing from a swollen, enlarged base. As it ages, the base expands, and the plant develops a greenish brown trunk topped with a tuft of thin, leathery, strap-like, green leaves. Mature plants can reach 3 feet (90 cm) tall.
Light needs High or medium light.
Best temperatures Average room temperature but cooler than 75°F (24°C) in winter.
Water and humidity needs Water thoroughly, then allow the soil to dry before you water again.
Growing guidelines Grow ponytail palm in a well-drained cactus mix. Wait several years between repottings. Fertilize annually in early spring.
Common problems Too little sun causes limp, pale leaves; move the plant to a brighter location. Otherwise, ponytail palm is generally easy.
Propagation Separate and repot offsets.
Comments Ponytail palm produces only one flush of growth a year in spring.

Begonia spp.
BEGONIACEAE

FOLIAGE BEGONIAS

Who needs flowers when you can have leaves like these? Actually, some foliage begonias do produce flowers, but the blooms tend to be inconspicuous.

Other common names Painted begonia.
Description Foliage begonias mostly grow from rhizomes (creeping underground stems) to a height of about 16 inches (40 cm). The leaves are often hairy and heart-shaped, with bold or subtle markings in the form of marbling, mottling, spots, or zones. Leaf colors range from green to silver, bronze, purple, red, pink, and black.
Light needs Medium to high, indirect light; protect from direct sun. They also grow well under fluorescent lights.
Best temperatures Warm—75°F (24°C) during the day and at least 60°F (16°C) at night—for most of the year; slightly cooler in winter.
Water and humidity needs Allow the soil to dry between waterings, especially in winter. Provide extra humidity.
Growing guidelines Grow in all-purpose mix in shallow pots. Repot only when the plant outgrows its container. Fertilize monthly from spring to fall, allowing a slight dormancy in winter.
Common problems Leaf drop in winter is normal. If leaf colors fade, move the plant to a brighter spot.
Propagation Take stem or leaf cuttings at any time. Divide rhizomes in spring.

Various genera
BROMELIACEAE

BROMELIADS

Bromeliads include a variety of striking, slow-growing tropical plants. They may take several years to bloom; in the meantime, enjoy their colorful, beautifully marked leaves.

Other common names Air plants, living vase plants.

Description Bromeliads produce rosettes of stiff leaves that range in height from 1 inch (2.5 cm) to 3 feet (90 cm) tall. Flowers may arise from the center of a rosette, with showy spikes of red, yellow, pink, and green.

Light needs High light with some direct sun; protect from midday sun.

Best temperatures At least 60°F (16°C) or warmer.

Water and humidity needs Keep the center cups of vase-shaped types filled with rainwater; refill the cups every week or two. Other types can dry between waterings. Provide extra humidity.

Growing guidelines Plant in clay pots and an epiphytic wood chip mix. Provide liquid fertilizer twice a month in spring and summer and once a month during the rest of the year. Put plants outdoors for the summer.

Common problems Too much light can burn leaves; if you notice white stains (salt or lime buildup) on leaves, flush the cups weekly with rainwater.

Propagation Remove and pot up offsets, or grow plants from seed.

Various genera
CACTACEAE

CACTI

Cacti are generally rugged enough for even black-thumbed gardeners. Their brilliant flowers are often surprisingly large compared to the size of the plant.

Description Cacti have no leaves to speak of, just thickened, water-storing, spiny stems. They come in a wide variety of shapes and sizes.

Light needs High light, with direct sun.

Best temperatures Average room temperature for most of the year; cool conditions—approximately 65°F (18°C) days and 40°F (4.5°C) nights—in winter.

Water and humidity needs In late March and April, water thoroughly and wait until the soil surface feels dry before watering again. Begin decreasing water steadily from May through December; give almost no water in winter.

Growing guidelines Keep cacti potbound in well-drained clay pots of all-purpose mix with added sand. Fertilize once a year in early spring. Put plants outdoors for the summer. Provide a cool, dry winter rest.

Common problems Plants that do not get a winter rest period may produce weak, spindly growth. Overwatering can lead to wilting and root rot.

Propagation Take stem or leaf cuttings, remove and repot offsets, or grow new plants from seed. Any cactus can be grafted to another by placing the cut bottom of one atop a cut tip of another and tying them firmly until they unite.

Chlorophytum comosum
LILIACEAE

SPIDER PLANT

One of the most common plants for a hanging basket, spider plant is beloved for its graceful habit. It produces baby plants at the ends of its long, arching stems.

Other common names Ribbon plant, spider ivy.

Description Spider plant grows from rhizomes (creeping underground stems) to produce arching, narrow, 12–18-inch (30–45-cm) long, green leaves. It also sends out long, pale yellow stems, with small white flowers along their length.

Light needs Medium light; avoid strong, direct sun.

Best temperatures Average room temperature during the day; approximately 50°F (10°C) at night.

Water and humidity needs Allow the soil surface to dry between waterings. Plants can take dry conditions but prefer extra humidity and rainwater.

Growing guidelines Use all-purpose mix in small hanging baskets, leaving 1 inch (2.5 cm) between the rim of the pot and the top of the soil. Fertilize twice a month in spring and summer.

Common problems High temperatures and over-drying can cause brown leaves.

Propagation Divide the parent plant or grow new plants from seed. You can also remove plantlets and set the base of the plantlet in water until roots begin to form, then move it to a pot.

Cissus spp.
VITACEAE

GRAPE IVY

Grape ivies make splendid foliage vines, adapting to low light and dry air without too much fuss. Provide some kind of trellis so vines can climb.

Other common names Kangaroo vine.
Description These tendril-climbing vines can grow to 10 feet (3 m). The fleshy, green leaves grow to 4 inches (10 cm) long; they are sometimes fuzzy underneath. Grape ivy (*C. rhombifolia*), from tropical America, has large, metallic green, lobed leaves and is very easy to grow. Kangaroo vine (*C. antarctica*) is a vigorous grower with shiny, leathery leaves; it hails from Australia. Dwarf grape ivy (*C. striata*), from Chile, is a compact climber with small, five-lobed leaves.
Light needs Medium to high light, but keep the plant out of direct sun.
Best temperatures Warm conditions but cooler than 75°F (24°C).
Water and humidity needs Keep evenly moist, but don't let the plant sit in water. Tolerates low humidity.
Growing guidelines Provide all-purpose mix in very well-drained baskets. Repot as needed. Fertilize twice a month in spring and summer. Pinch sideshoots back frequently to encourage dense growth.
Common problems Grape ivies are generally problem-free.
Propagation Take stem cuttings at any time, or grow new plants from seed.

Dieffenbachia amoena
ARACEAE

DUMBCANE

Bold, fancy leaves are the trademark of this popular plant. It gets the name dumbcane from its irritating sap, which causes swelling and pain of the tongue if eaten.

Other common names Mother-in-law's tongue.
Description The upright stems of dumbcane grow to 6 feet (1.8 m) tall, with elliptical leaves. The green foliage is marked and spotted in various shades of green, cream, and yellow.
Light needs High, indirect light is best, although the plant can adapt to less.
Best temperatures Warm conditions (at least 60°F [16°C]). Keep out of drafts.
Water and humidity needs Allow the soil to dry a bit between waterings. Provide extra humidity.
Growing guidelines Grow dumbcane in all-purpose mix, and keep it potbound. Fertilize lightly with fish emulsion twice a month in warm seasons. Rinse dust off the leaves several times a year.
Common problems Overwatering and lack of light can produce thin stems and widely spaced leaves. To rejuvenate the plant, cut the stem to about 6 inches (15 cm) tall. Control spider mites by raising the humidity and spraying with superior oil. Knock mealybugs off the plant with a strong spray of water.
Propagation Air layer the stems, or take tip or stem cuttings.

Dizygotheca elegantissima
ARALIACEAE

FALSE ARALIA

False aralia sports upright stems clad in lacy leaves. This South Pacific native is a good choice for warm, shaded, humid spots with low to medium light.

Description This elegant, shrubby tree grows to 6 feet (1.8 m) tall, with serrated, fernlike, palmate leaves. The young foliage is coppery bronze, sometimes mottled with cream; the leaves change to dark greenish black as they age.
Light needs Low to medium, indirect light suits the plant best.
Best temperatures Warm conditions; at least 60°F (16°C) in winter.
Water and humidity needs Allow the soil surface to dry between waterings. Provide extra humidity.
Growing guidelines Grow in all-purpose potting mix. Repot every few years as needed. Fertilize twice a month in spring and summer.
Common problems If spider mites cause light-colored stippling on leaves, control the pests by raising the humidity and spraying the plant with superior oil. Leaves may drop as the plant ages or if it is overwatered or moved from place to place. Age, cold, and lack of humidity can cause the plant to get scraggly; take cuttings in spring and summer to make new plants and keep them in a warm, humid location.
Propagation Take stem cuttings in spring and summer.

Dracaena spp.
AGAVACEAE

DRACAENA

Dracaenas are tough, adaptable plants that are easy to find and easy to grow. With age, they produce a thick trunk and lose their bottom leaves.

Description Dracaenas are treelike plants that can grow anywhere from 18 inches (45 cm) to 8 feet (2.4 m) tall. They are noted for their distinctively marked, bold, often swordlike foliage.
Light needs High, indirect light is best, but dracaena tolerates less.
Best temperatures Warm conditions (65°–70°F [18°–21°C]).
Water and humidity needs Keep evenly moist most of the year; allow it to dry somewhat between waterings in winter. Provide extra humidity.
Growing guidelines Grow dracaenas in all-purpose potting mix. Fertilize twice a month in warm seasons.
Common problems Low light causes thin stems and faded leaves. Browned leaf edges indicate the plant is overdry or that there's a salt buildup.
Propagation Take tip or stem cuttings, or air layer the trunk.

Various genera
POLYPODIACEAE

FERNS

Beloved for their gracefully arching, often feathery fronds, ferns are a mainstay for houseplant growers. These flowerless plants grow from rhizomes and reproduce via spores.

Description Ferns are a broad group of plants that includes many different genera including Boston fern, maidenhair ferns, and rabbit's foot fern.
Light needs Medium to high, indirect light suits ferns best.
Best temperatures Average conditions, with day temperatures up to 75°F (24°C) and nights between 55° and 65°F (13° and 18°C).
Water and humidity needs Keep evenly moist; water daily if necessary. Extra humidity is a plus.
Growing guidelines Grow ferns in small pots in light, well-drained, all-purpose mix with added peat moss and perlite. Repot in spring as needed. Fertilize twice a year—in early spring and early summer—with fish emulsion.
Common problems Scales may produce small, irregularly spaced spots on the fronds; scrape them off with your fingernail or with a cotton swab.
Propagation Divide clump-forming ferns, grow new plants from spores, or pin the runners to the soil and repot them when they are rooted.

Ficus spp.
MORACEAE

FIGS

This large group of tropical plants has produced some of our best-known and easiest-to-grow houseplants. All these plants produce a harmless milky sap when cut.

Other common names Ficus, rubber plant.
Description Figs can be trees, shrubs, or woody vines, usually with thick leaves.
Light needs Medium to high light.
Best temperatures Average room temperature; avoid moving plants from high to low light.
Water and humidity needs Allow the soil to dry somewhat between waterings. Keep creeping types evenly damp.
Growing guidelines Grow figs in all-purpose mix that's been enriched with compost. Keep them potbound to prevent overwatering; repot only every three to four years. Feed twice a year, occasionally providing a very dilute vinegar solution. Wipe large-leaved types periodically with a damp sponge. Fresh air is beneficial.
Common problems Spider mites and scale can attack if the air is hot and dry. Treat by spraying with superior oil. Lower leaves may drop due to temperature or light changes, drafts, or too much or too little water.
Propagation Air layer the stems of upright types. Root creeping types from tip cuttings or divide the rooting stems.

Maranta leuconeura
MARANTACEAE

PRAYER PLANT

This showy foliage houseplant has two special features: The unique markings that look as though a rabbit left tracks down the leaves and the way the leaves fold upward at night.

Other common names Rabbit tracks.
Description Prayer plant's branching stems form clumps to 12 inches (30 cm) tall, with 5-inch (12.5-cm) long, oval leaves. The bright green, satiny foliage is very distinctively marked with brownish purple "rabbit tracks" on either side of the midrib. Each leaf has large, rosy pink veins and a red-purple underside.
Light needs Medium, indirect or artificial light.
Best temperatures Warm conditions, between 60° and 70°F (16° and 21°C).
Water and humidity needs Keep the soil evenly moist through most of the year and somewhat drier in winter. Mist often.
Growing guidelines Grow prayer plant in soil-less mix. Repot into fresh mix each year in early spring. Fertilize twice a month from spring to fall; do not fertilize in winter.
Common problems Prayer plant likes fresh air, but cold drafts can lead to poor growth and a gradual decline in health.
Propagation Divide in spring.
Cultivars The variety *kerchoveana* is deep green and chocolate without rosy veins; 'Variegata' indicates it has yellow and pink spots.

Various genera
PALMAE

PALMS

Palms appreciate a summer vacation outdoors; just make sure they're sheltered from direct sun. If you notice the leaf tips have turned brown, you can trim them off with scissors.

Description Indoor palms range in size from 3–15 feet (0.9–4.5 m) tall, with stiff trunks and fanlike or feathery, compound leaves. Popular species include parlour palm, Chamaedoreas palms, and kentia palm.
Light needs Medium, indirect light.
Best temperatures Average room temperature, not below 55°F (13°C).
Water and humidity needs Water abundantly while the plant is in active growth; allow the soil surface to dry just slightly between waterings.
Growing guidelines Grow in a mixture of equal parts all-purpose potting soil and sandy, organic topsoil. Provide fish emulsion from late spring to early fall. Repot as needed in spring or summer. Put plants outdoors for the summer. Wash foliage frequently with a hose or do it in the shower.
Common problems If spider mites attack, raise the humidity and spray with superior oil.
Propagation Grow new palms from seed.

Philodendron spp.
ARACEAE

PHILODENDRON

If you're nervous about growing houseplants, start with philodendrons—they're durable plants that don't take much fussing to stay looking good.

Description Philodendrons produce climbing or bushy growth that can eventually reach 9 feet (2.7 m) tall. Their stems carry thin aerial roots and usually lobed green leaves that can be marked with gold, red, or white. The young leaves are often not as distinctively shaped or colored as the older ones.
Light needs Medium to high, indirect light; bushy types tolerate lower light.
Best temperatures Warm conditions, with nights around 65°–70°F (18°–21°C).
Water and humidity needs Keep the soil just moist.
Growing guidelines Philodendron grows fine in almost any mix; it will even root and grow in water! Repot at any time. Fertilize every three months.
Common problems Direct sun can produce tan patches of sunburn on leaves; move the plant out of the sun to prevent further damage.
Propagation Take tip or stem cuttings from vining types at any time. Grow self-heading (bushy) types from seed, or separate and pot up the offsets.

Raphidophora aurea
ARACEAE

POTHOS

Pothos is a trailing or climbing houseplant that's often confused with philodendron. It's a real survivor that can take some neglect.

Other common names Devil's ivy.
Description This vining plant produces long stems that can climb to 40 feet (12 m) if left unpruned. The stems will trail out of a hanging basket or climb a support, clinging with aerial roots. The leathery, heart-shaped leaves grow to 4 inches (10 cm) long. The foliage and stems are bright green and richly splashed with yellow and/or white.
Light needs High, indirect light is best, although the plant adapts to less.
Best temperatures Average room temperature suits very well.
Water and humidity needs Let the soil dry somewhat between waterings, especially for plants growing in low light. Make sure the soil is not very wet or dry.
Growing guidelines Grow pothos in a soil-based potting mix in hanging baskets or trained on wire wreath forms. Fertilize twice a year, while the plant is producing new growth. Cut the stems back if they get leggy. Wash the leaves occasionally.
Common problems Pothos is generally pest-free. If you notice the leaf and stem markings are fading, move the plant to a brighter spot.
Propagation Take tip cuttings at any time of the year.

Sansevieria trifasciata
AGAVACEAE

SNAKE PLANT

Extraordinarily striped, stiff leaf swords have made snake plants very popular. They often look dreadful when neglected but are very handsome if you give them just a little care.

Description Snake plant's tall, upright, stemless, spear-like leaves can grow to 4 feet (1.2 m) tall. The green foliage is crossbanded in darker green, yellow, white, and/or black. Plants sometimes produce tall sprays of green-white, fragrant flowers.
Light needs High light is best, although plants can tolerate almost any light level.
Best temperatures Average conditions, with 65°F (18°C) nights.
Water and humidity needs Allow the soil surface to dry between waterings in spring to fall. In winter, water only enough to prevent shriveling. Snake plant endures drought well.
Growing guidelines Grow snake plant in cactus or all-purpose mix in a well-drained pot. This slow-growing plant can wait three to four years between repottings. Fertilize infrequently.
Common problems Cold temperatures can cause leaf edges to turn brown.
Propagation Divide plants at any time, or separate and pot up offsets. Propagate green-leaved types by leaf cuttings. (Leaf cuttings from yellow-edged types will root, but the plants they produce will be all green.)

Spathiphyllum hybrids
ARACEAE

PEACE LILY

Peace lily is popular for its graceful, shiny, green leaves, as well as its curious, hooded flower spikes. This tolerant plant adjusts to many conditions and is generally problem-free.

Other common names Spathe flower.
Description Peace lily grows to 2 feet (60 cm) tall, with swordlike, long leaves. The many-stemmed plant blooms occasionally throughout the year, first in white, then turning green. The flowers can last for six weeks.
Light needs Low to medium, indirect light best suits the plant.
Best temperatures Warm to average conditions (around 65°–70°F [18°–21°C]).
Water and humidity needs Keep the soil evenly moist.
Growing guidelines This easy grower thrives in all-purpose potting mix enriched with compost or other organic material. Fertilize twice a month. Repot in early spring as needed. Provide monthly showers to keep the leaves clean.
Common problems Too much light actually inhibits bloom. If you want flowers but none are appearing, try moving your plant to a slightly darker spot. Too much fertilizer or too little water can cause brown leaf tips.
Propagation Remove and repot offsets, or divide the clumps in spring.

USDA Plant Hardiness Zone Map

These maps of the United States, Canada, and Europe are divided into ten zones. Each zone is based on a 10°F (5.6°C) difference in average annual minimum temperature. Some areas are considered too high in elevation for plant cultivation and so are not assigned to any zone. There are also island zones that are warmer or cooler than surrounding areas because of differences in elevation; they have been given a zone different from the surrounding areas. Many large urban areas, for example, are in a warmer zone than the surrounding land. Plants grow best within an optimum range of temperatures. The range may be wide for some species and narrow for others. Plants also differ in their ability to survive frost and in their sun or shade requirements.

The zone ratings indicate conditions where designated plants will grow well and not merely survive. Many plants may survive in zones warmer or colder than their recommended zone range. Remember that other factors, including wind, soil type, soil moisture, humidity, snow, and winter sunshine may have a great effect on growth.

Some nursery plants have been grown in greenhouses and they might not survive in your garden, so it's a waste of money, and a cause of heartache, to buy plants that aren't right for your climate zone.

Average annual minimum temperature °F (°C)

Zone 1		Below -50°F (Below -45°C)
Zone 2		-50° to -40°F (-45° to -40°C)
Zone 3		-40° to -30°F (-40° to -34°C)
Zone 4		-30° to -20°F (-34° to -29°C)
Zone 5		-20° to -10°F (-29° to -23°C)

Zone 6		-10° to 0°F (-23° to -18°C)
Zone 7		0° to 10°F (-18° to -12°C)
Zone 8		10° to 20°F (-12° to -7°C)
Zone 9		20° to 30°F (-7° to -1°C)
Zone 10		30° to 40°F (-1° to 4°C)

Index

Page references in *italics* indicate photos and illustrations

Wood anenome 42
Woodbine honeysuckle 242
Woodland gardens 42
Woolly yarrow 131
Wormwood 40, 144, 145

X

Xeranthemum annuum 39

Y

Yarrow *19*, 39, 42, 100, 130, 144, 146, 149
Yellow cosmos 39
Yellow jessamine 240
Yew 24, 65, 88, 89, 119
Yucca 98

Z

Zea mays var. *rugosa* 289
Zebra plant 303
Zebrina pendula 138
Zelkova serrata 88, 221
Zeranthemum annuum 39
Zingiber officinale 277
Zinnia spp. 25, *104*, 107, *107*

angustifolia 107
elegans 39, 107, 201
Zonal geranium 198
Zoysia grass 125, 263
Zoysia japonica 263
Zucchini 150

Credits and Acknowledgments

l=left, r=right, c=center, t=top, b=bottom, fp=full page

Addington Turf & Horticultural Consultants 263l (Kenneth R. Smith).

Heather Angel 269r, 277r.

Ardea 41cr (Francois Gohier), 292r (John Mason), 277c (A. P. Patterson).

Allan Armitage 174c, 178c.

Auscape 44/45fp (Jerry Harpur).

A-Z Botanical 299c (The Picture Store), 253r, 271c, 275c, 288l, 290r (Malcolm Richards), 163c.

Gillian Beckett 86tc, 188c, 193c, 204r, 250l, 251l, 253l, 255c, 258l, 258c, 258r, 265l, 265c, 265r, 301r, 302c, 303l, 303r, 304r, 306l, 306r, 308l, 308r, 309r.

Geoffrey Burnie 44fp.

John Callahan 61all, 59all, 63tr all, 65all, 71all, 83all, 116c, 120tl, 123r, 172l, 173c, 174r, 175l, 177c, 179l, 180l, 183r, 184l, 187r, 216l, 219c, 233c, 235l, 237l, 237r, 239l, 245r.

Leigh Clapp 2fp, 4fp, 6c, 92fp, 140fp.

Bruce Coleman 81tr (Jane Burton), 117c (Jules Cowan), 237c, 261l (Eric Crichton), 91b (Geoff Dore), 276l (Halle Flygare), 260l (Michael Freeman), 297c (Charlie Ott), 103t, 133tr (Hans Reinhard), 210c (John Shaw), 264l (Sullivan & Rogers), 270r (Michael Viard), 12br (R. Wanscheidt), 118l (Carl Wallace) 75tr.

Michael Dirr 185r, 211l, 214l, 216r, 217c, 218r, 222r, 224c, 233l, 234l, 234c, 242l.

Thomas Eltzroth 17tr, 21bc, 90t, 102br, 107b, 129b, 130t, 153c, 155r, 158c, 169l, 172c, 172r, 173l, 173r, 176c, 176r, 178r, 179r, 180c, 181l, 181c, 181r, 182r, 183l, 184c, 187c, 188l, 188r, 189c, 190l, 191c, 191r, 192l, 192c, 192r, 193l, 194l, 195l, 195c, 196l, 196r, 197l, 198l, 198r, 199l, 199c, 200r, 201l, 201r, 202r, 203r, 204l, 205r, 207r, 213r, 214l, 215l, 215r, 220l, 221c, 222c, 223l, 228c, 230c, 233r, 238c, 240l, 240c, 241l, 243r, 244c, 244r, 245l, 249r, 250c, 250r, 251l, 252l, 252c, 252r, 254l, 254c, 254r, 256r, 257r, 259c, 260c, 260r, 261c, 261r, 262l, 262c, 262r, 263c, 263r, 264r, 267l, 278r, 279r, 291r, 292l, 293r, 295l, 295r, 298l, 298c, 299l, 302r, 305c, 306c, 309l.

Derek Fell 14c, 33tr, 39b, 41cl, 50all, 66t, 104bl, 106tl, 109r, 117l, 120tr, 121bl, 127t, 129c, 133c, 142l, 158r, 159r, 175c, 177l, 178l, 183c, 189r, 208c, 213l, 214c, 223c, 224r, 247l, 264c, 267c, 281l, 295c.

Garden Picture Library 1r, 38c, 103c, 128r, 133tl, 194r (Lynne Brotchie), 120bl (Linda Burgess), 12bl, 53tr, 120cl, 143l, 145l, 146c, 259r (Brian Carter), 84tr (Dennis Davis), 30bl, 68t, 78cl, 87t, 103b, 115c, 164l, 168l, 197c (John Glover), 1l, 163r, 165bl, 165c, 294r (Neil Holmes) 139c (Michael Howes), 82t, 134tl (Lamontagne), 135c, 162r, 166l, 291c (Mayer/Le Scanff), 146l (Clive Nichols), 31b, 105b (Jerry Pavia), 126l (Joanne Pavia) 104br (Gary Rogers), 113r (J .S. Sira), 1c, 124b, 152c, 162l (Brigitte Thomas), 21bl, 21br, 98c, 112r, 128t (Steven Wooster), 25tr, 89t, 147l, 162c, 195r, 198c, 200c, 202l, 203l, 203c, 289l.

Holt Studios International 246c, 253c, 290c, 293l, 294l, 294c, 302l, 307r, 301l, 301c (Nigel Cattlin), 299r, 299r.

Andrew Larson 46tc, 89b, 99cl, 102bl, 106br, 164r.

Robert E. Lyons 212c, 228r.

Stirling Macoboy 211r, 238r, 271l, 210l, 236c.

Cheryl Maddocks 280l, 284l, 284r.

S & O Mathews 15cr, 19tl, 26l, 36b, 73b, 84tc, 94b, 108br, 111tl, 113l, 115br, 132c, 189l, 191l, 194c, 199l, 200l, 202c, 204c, 206r, 209l, 293c.

Clive Nichols 14t, 15br, 16cr, 20bc, 34c, 34b, 35tr, 38t, 40t, 43cb, 47b, 67t, 74tr, 86cr, 96t, 97t, 98br, 99cr, 99bc, 109c, 110br, 111bl, 111tr, 112l, 114bl, 114tl, 115tr, 124t, 125b, 130b, 139r, 160c, 190c, 205c, 206l, 207c, 208r, 108bl.

Jerry Pavia 18cl, 36t, 43ct, 121c, 165tl, 169r, 190r, 193l, 197l, 201c, 205l, 207l, 208l, 209r, 305l.

Joanna Pavia 152l, 108t.

Photos Horticultural 16br, 17c, 19tr, 20bl, 20br, 21tl, 21tr, 23fp, 29bl, 29br, 31tl, 31tr, 33tl, 34t, 43tl, 46cr, 51cl, 51tl, 64t, 71tr, 72t, 74br, 75br, 85bl, 88t, 95t, 101t, 104tr, 20r, 110tr, 117r, 118c, 121tl, 126r, 131t, 136c, 137tl,145b, 153r, 154r, 157r, 167l,168r, 174l, 176l, 177r, 179c, 185l, 185c, 186l, 186c, 187l, 196c, 209c, 210r, 211c, 212r, 215c, 216c, 217l, 217r, 221r, 222c, 225l, 226c, 226r, 227l, 227r, 228l, 230r, 231l, 235r, 236l, 238l, 239c, 240r, 241c, 241r, 242c, 243l, 243c, 244l, 245c, 247c, 255r, 279l, 283r, 290l, 292c, 296c, 296r, 297l, 297r, 303c.

Lee Reich 291l.

G. R. Dick Roberts 10fp, 170fp.

Rodale Stock Images 54b, 142r, 149l, 156l, 268l, 278l, 282c, 285r.

Tony Rodd 218c, 222l, 223r, 224l, 229c, 229r, 231r, 232c, 232r, 234r, 235c, 236r, 239r, 242r, 246l, 268c, 270c, 272l, 272c.

Lorna Rose 143r, 182c.

Susan Roth 220c, 221l, 225c, 225r, 226l, 227c.

Anita Sabarese 229l.

Harry Smith Collection 79tc, 121tr, 153tl, 175r, 230l, 232l, 246r, 247r, 249l, 249c, 251c, 255l, 256l, 256c, 257l, 257c, 259l, 267r, 272r, 296l, 298l, 304l, 304c, 305r, 307l, 307c, 308r, 309c.

John J. Smith 186r, 219r.

David Wallace 46br, 54all , 55all , 57all, 58all, 60cl, 60cr & b, 62cr, 62cl, 62bl, 62br, 62tl, 63ball, 85br, 97c, 97b, 146r, 150r, 151r, 153bl, 156c, 158l, 159c, 180r, 184r, 212l, 213c, 218l, 219l, 231c, 268r, 269l, 269c, 270l, 271c, 271r, 271l, 271r, 273l, 273c, 273r, 275l, 275r, 276c, 276r, 277l, 278c, 279c, 280c, 280r, 281c, 281r, 282l, 282r, 283l, 283c, 284c, 285l, 285c, 286l, 286c, 286r, 287l, 287c, 287r, 288c, 288r, 289c, 289r.

Mel Watson 70t.

Weldon Russell 148c (Carlo Cantini), 154c (David Wallace), 182l.

Weldon Trannies 79tl.

Ron West 81tc.

All illustrations by Barbara Rodanska except the following.
Tony Britt-Lewis, 113, 129, 138; Mike Gorman, 129, 130; Stuart McVicar 310, 311; Edwina Riddell, 12, 14, 32, 69, 73, 83, 87, 90, 96; Jan Smith, 73, 83, 136; Kathie Smith, 90, 143, 147.

With special thanks to Geoff Burnie, horticultural consultant; Sarah Anderson, editorial support; Claire Craig and Janet Healey, proofreading; Sally Beach, Lisa Boehm, Peta Gorman and Michael Hann, scanning; Caroline Colton & Associates, indexing.